Food and Landscape
Proceedings of the Oxford Symposium on Food and Cookery 2017

Food and Landscape

Proceedings of the Oxford Symposium on Food and Cookery 2017

Edited by Mark McWilliams

Prospect Books
2018

First published in Great Britain in 2018 by Prospect Books, 26 Parke Road, London SW13 9NG.

© 2018 as a collection Prospect Books.
© 2018 in individual articles rests with the authors.

The authors assert their moral right to be identified as authors in accordance with the Copyright, Designs & Patents Act 1988. No part of this publication may be reproduced, stored in a retrieval system or transmitted in any form or by any means, electronic, mechanical, photocopying, recording or otherwise, without the prior permission of the copyright holders.

ISBN 978-1-909-248-62-5

Front cover photo credit: © Sharon Hudgins.

Back cover and title page photo credit: © Charity Robey.

Design and typesetting in Gill Sans and Adobe Garamond by Catheryn Kilgarriff and Brendan King.

Printed and bound in Great Britain.

Contents

Foreword
 Mark McWilliams   9

Plenary Papers

A Challenging Landscape: Scotland's Food and Drink Assets
 Catherine Brown   11

Microbial Landscapes
 Joshua Evans   26

The Future Belongs to the Gourmet
 Colin Tudge   36

Exploring Aeroir, or the Atmospheric Taste of Place
 Nicola Twilley   50

Symposium Papers

'Practically only an English grazing farm': The Irish Landscape and English Beef
 Juliana Adelman   57

Eating into the Countryside: The Case of Hamburg
 Volker Carlton Bach   67

Singapore: Landscape of Loss, Cuisine of Comfort
 Lucey Bowen   78

Landscaping Food and Identity: Rice Paddy Art in Japan
 Voltaire Cang   89

Stories of Rice Lake – Stewards, Settlers, and Storytellers
 Nathalie Cooke   99

From Nature's Garden: Reimagining North African Landscapes through Food in Female French Colonial Literature
 Edwige Crucifix   110

Food and Landscape

Coming in to Graze: The Fall and Rise of Hill-Reared Mutton
Jessica Fagin   121

Dining Outdoors in Renaissance Art
Allison Fisher   131

Global Warming and the Changing Global Food Landscape: The Need to Preserve Diversity
Len Fisher   141

The Landscape of Food and Memory: Cuisine and Cultural Identity in the Sephardic Jewish Diaspora
Sara Gardner   148

'Bigger Was Better?' The Interplay of New Technologies, Field Size, and Basic Commodity Production in the Roman Occupation of Britain, c. 100 BCE – 400 CE
Christopher Grocock   158

Maple Moon: Landscapes of the Sugar Maple in a Time of Climate Change
Naomi Guttman   169

Agriculture without Fences
Hilary Heslop   178

Imaginary Landscapes and Virtual *Terroir*
Ben Houge   188

From Kaluga to *Chak-Chak*: Eating Locally Along the Trans-Siberian Tracks
Sharon Hudgins   198

Nice Day in the Driftless
Tom Hunter   212

'A way of seeing which we learn': Food as Resistance
Fozia Ismail   223

The Terraces of Kea: Producing Food for Subsistence Shaped the Cycladic Landscape
Aglaia Kremezi   232

Ghost in the Cane Fields
Michael Krondl   243

Food and Landscape

Pasture and Pastoralism: The Inextricable Links between Food, Culture, and
Landscape in Samburu District, Northern Kenya
Jane Levi and William Rubel   253

Steps Toward an Ecology of the Cookbook: Landscape in the Cookbook and the
Cookbook in Its Landscape
Don Lindgren   260

Terraced Landscapes: Farming and Performing on Balconies
Morna Livingston   272

Cuscuz Paulista: How an African Staple Became the Gastronomical Symbol of São Paulo
Sandra Mian   282

The Contested Origins of the *Presniz* between Myth and Reality
Giulia Nicolini   291

Mapping Food in France under the First Empire
Guillaume Nicoud   300

Moveable *Terroir*: From Liquid Stability to Rock-Solid Ephemerality
Thomas Parker   308

Climbing Butter Mountain: How Food Law Has Affected the British Landscape,
In and Out of the EU
Olivia Potts   318

A Creature of Salty Estuaries and Glacial Till: The History, Remarkable Qualities,
and Incomparable Flavour of the Wild Peconic Bay Scallop
Charity Robey   327

Americans and the Landscape of Wine
Laura Shapiro   337

'*Le mariage entre mets et vins*': On the Geographical and Historical Origins of Pairing
a Food with a Particular Wine in France
Richard Warren Shepro   346

Lines in the Landscape: How the Olive-Line, the Date-line, and the Vine-line
Have Defined Mediterranean Culture
David C. Sutton   359

Food and Landscape

Turkish Tea for Liberty: Changing the Landscape of a Region and the Drinkscape of a Nation through Political Choice
Aylin Öney Tan — 371

Brandenburg-Prussia's Cultivated Natural Food Landscape
Molly Taylor-Poleskey — 379

Minnesota's Hearty Plums: The Story of a Fruit and Its Ties to Rural and Urban Landscapes
Emily S. Tepe — 388

Reading the English Countryside: A Thousand Years of English Agriculture Etched on the Surface of the Land
Malcolm Thick — 398

Tejate, Tejateras, and the Taste of Place: A Sensory Excavation
Amy B. Trubek — 409

Fratelli Ingegnoli: Reshaping the Landscape of Italian Cooking in the Late Nineteenth and Early Twentieth Centuries
Anne Urbancic — 416

Food in the Context of First-Century Galilee: The Mishnah and the So-Called 'Jesus Diet'
Susan Weingarten — 424

Feasting Is the Finest Prayer: Dreams of the Holy Land in the *Pots* of the Ashkenaz
Michael Yashinsky — 435

Contributors — 444

Foreword

One of the most evocative visions of the English landscape's transcendent power comes from William Wordsworth's 'Tintern Abbey'. The poet celebrates nature – 'These waters, rolling from their mountain springs' and 'these steep and lofty cliffs' – and finds human changes to the land receding into primal forms. Carefully built hedgerows are now 'Little lines / Of sportive wood run wild', and scattered cottages have become 'Green to the very door'. What the poet refuses to see, though, are the many displaced workers who haunted the woods around the ruined abbey during the period of the poem's composition. The poet is well aware that his vision transforms reality; as the famous lines go, what we know of the world comes from our senses: 'both what they half create, / And what perceive'. But the poor remain hidden.

Landscape was a way of seeing before it was a physical thing. According to the *OED*, early uses of the word focused on representation, on scenery, on a 'view', even on 'the object of one's gaze' – centuries before it came to mean 'a tract of land with its distinguishing characteristics and features, especially considered as a product of modifying or shaping processes and agents (usually natural)'. That parenthetical qualification seems crucial, for even as a way of seeing 'landscape' emphasizes the natural. Or at least what appears to be natural, since scenery can be just as much about what is not seen, what is rendered invisible, as about what is made visible.

Over three glorious July days in Oxford, symposiasts explored ways to see – and to hear, smell, feel, and taste – landscape. The 2017 theme had proven the most popular in the Symposium's history, leading to record numbers of both paper proposals and new attendees. We gathered at St Catherine's College to hear papers exploring Food and Landscape from all sorts of different perspectives, including, as seems characteristic of the Symposium, some quirky takes on the theme. Many of the authors documented ways food had led humans to reshape the landscape; some tried to capture lost foodways even while quietly hoping for their revival. Others pointed us to new ways of experiencing food and landscape, through sound or even through the taste of the very air.

The spectre haunting us, though, was change on more catastrophic levels. One paper detailed how UK food regulation and production had been shaped by the EU and are threatened by Brexit; another considered how the 'Leave' campaign seemed to accelerate racist erasures of peoples and foodways. Many of our conversations, though, were shaped by even larger fears about the effects of climate change. Symposiasts considered the new reality of sea level rise reshaping our coastlines and pollution recalibrating our tastes. In the Anthropocene, even the most traditional definitions of *terroir* – the famed taste of place – are under threat, as celebrated Champagne houses buy up warming land in the UK and the great Bordeaux chateaux search for alternatives to Merlot, which will no longer thrive when French summers arrive earlier and hotter. In places like Northern Kenya and many others, new weather patterns threaten ways of living developed over centuries. In such context, many Symposium presentations not only demanded careful attention to how humans have affected the landscape but also became calls for action.

Food and Landscape

Deciding what to see is aesthetic, of course, but it is also political. Sweeping claims about the power of food to transcend divisions are all too easy to make – indeed it seems food divides as often as it unites – but at one meal symposiasts could taste the promise of re-seeing a landscape. Over the past few years, it turns out, women from neighbouring towns in Armenia and Turkey – towns separated by just a few miles but much farther by a militarized border dividing people, languages, and experiences of an unimaginably tragic past – have been quietly visiting each other to cook together. And on Saturday night they cooked for us. Where the world saw two nations at war, these women saw a shared landscape with common foodways. It turns out that the power to transform how we see belongs not just to poets but also to cooks, and there just may be tremendous hope in that possibility.

Here I would like to thank the two remarkable women who organized that dinner, Gamze İneceli and İhsan Karayazi, as well as everyone who helped me with this volume, particularly Elisabeth Luard, Ursula Heinzelmann, Cathy Kaufman, and Catheryn Kilgarriff – and, of course, the many symposiasts who made our gathering such a fabulous success.

Mark McWilliams
Editor, Oxford Symposium on Food and Cookery

A Challenging Landscape: Scotland's Food and Drink Assets

The Jane Grigson Memorial Lecture

Catherine Brown

At a time when British food was not highly rated, Jane Grigson saw a way of saving it. She appealed to us to celebrate the good things in our culinary history. As she said in her introduction to *Good Things* in 1971, 'I think food, its quality, its origins, its preparation, is something to be studied and thought about in the same way as any other aspect of human existence.'[1] She was a genius at skilfully blending scholarship with practical advice in her columns and books.

In the 1970s, I was working on a research project at the University of Strathclyde with Professor John Fuller who was, like Jane, concerned that we were not celebrating the good things in our culinary heritage. Since the rise of the grand hotels of Ritz and Escoffier, the system in professional kitchens in the UK was French, but he thought that British traditions, regional and national, deserved a higher status in both professional and domestic kitchens. Though I had never met her, Jane helped set my compass in the right direction at this time. The result of the research was published as *British Cookery*.[2]

Later I did meet her. When she was researching her *Observer's Guide to British Cookery*, she wrote asking if she could include a recipe from my first book.[3] When her book was published in 1984, a copy arrived in the post with an invitation to its launch at The Dorchester Hotel. Aware that I knew no one, she had reserved a place for me at her table, taking care of me in her motherly way. Seating me beside Sophie, her daughter, and Patrick Rance, she later introduced me to Alan and Jane Davidson, Tom Jaine, Anton Mosimann, and others.

The memory remains vivid. Her generosity was abundant. When I joined the Guild of Food Writers I met her again at events and press trips. On one trip we went to Aberdeenshire to investigate the authenticity of Aberdeen Angus beef: from farmer's field to abattoir and butcher's shop. Her questioning was forensic. She lives on in her writings and books, and in the memories of those who valued her friendship. And it is a great pleasure to be celebrating her legacy.

Scotland's Challenging Landscape

Unlike England, which is mostly arable land, Scotland is mostly rough, hilly and mountainous. The area of Scotland with the most challenging landscape includes everything west and north of the Highland Fault Line drawn from the town of Helensburgh on the southwest coast and Stonehaven on the northeast coast: the area known as the Highlands and Islands. Because it has most (85%) of the country's total amount of less favourable arable land, it has a distinctly different system of agriculture.

Today, most of this region is defined as the area of the crofting counties, where most of the farming system is dependent on small-scale food production with arable units and common grazing for livestock on hills, moors, and mountains.[4] Not all of the Highlands and Islands are in the crofting area. The line drawn for this area is everything north and west of a line from the head of Loch Long on the west coast to the town of Forres on the northeast coast. There are over 17,000 crofts, which represent 30% of households on the mainland and 65% of the households on Shetland, the Western Isles, and Skye.[5]

Other important natural landscape and climatic factors influence food and drink production in this area, compared with the rest of Scotland, include an extensive coastline; proximity to rich fishing grounds; a colder, wetter climate; longer hours of summer daylight; longer hours of winter darkness; and long distances from markets creating problems of transport. Also, its early history is distinct from the rest of Scotland. From around the mid-eighth century, a large part of the area was a separate kingdom ruled by the Lord of the Isles, of mixed Celtic and Norse blood. At their height, they wielded sea-power with fleets of galleys. Today, in the Highlands and Western Isles the native language is Gaelic.

Food Culture in Less-Favourable Areas

It is a wild day with torrential rain as we drive out the Applecross peninsula in Wester Ross, just across the sea from Skye. A road linking the crofting communities on the shores of Outer Loch Torridon was only built in the late 1960s. We have come to visit crofters Alistair and Maggie. Both into their seventies, they have lived here all their lives, a boat their only form of transport.

There is a warm, welcoming orange glow from a peat fire in the hearth that has a large black pot hanging over it, cooking slowly. Its contents create enticing aromas which mingle with wafts of pungent peat smoke. Drams of whisky are poured. Maggie puts crowdie cheese, soft bannocks, and crisp oatcakes on the table. Later, Alistair goes over to the pot and takes out a joint of mutton and cuts slices for us all.

His mutton, he tells us, has been preserved in 'the salt' (a barrel of brine in the barn). His hardy, sure-footed, mature Blackface sheep (Blackies) have roamed the rough hillsides and rocky mountains, winter and summer, for years, living on a diet of heather and wild plants. We all get a slice of the mutton which we eat with an oatcake.

Raised in a Glasgow tenement, on under-a-year-old lamb, for me the flavour of this mutton is an exciting taste discovery. Later, Alistair chops up some kail and adds it to the

A Challenging Landscape:

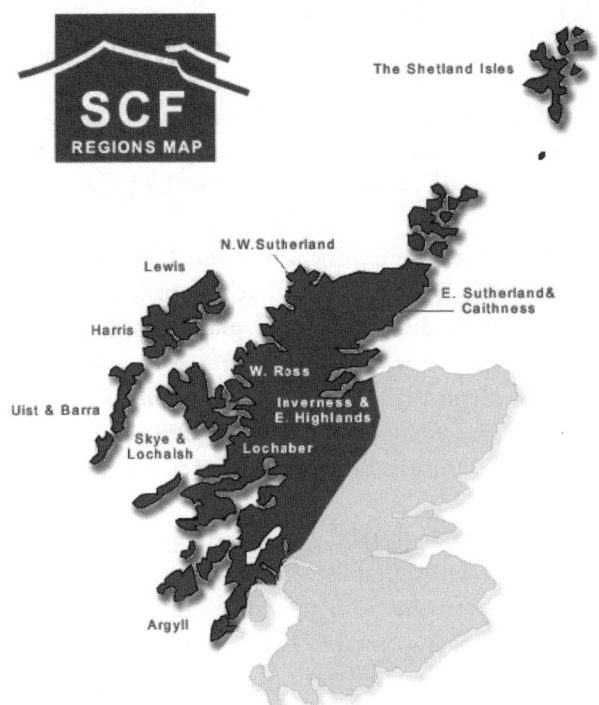

Figure 1. Crofting areas of the Highlands and Islands. Image used by permission of Scotland Crofting Federation.

pot and we get a bowlful of broth, thickened with barley and flavoured with carrots, turnips, and mutton stock. It is the culinary heritage of generations, living by an ingenious system of self-sufficiency, making good things from an inhospitable landscape and difficult climate.

They are dependent for fuel on the dried-out peat which they cut from the peat bog. It burns slowly with a steady glow. Not hot enough to heat an oven or roast a joint of meat, it is perfect to slow-cook the contents of the large black pot, as it simmers gently over the fire throughout the day. The process tenderizes both mature meat and all the less-tender cuts. It is the origin of Scotland's national broth tradition, but also of its stews, stovies, and bag puddings, originally cooked in the broth such as haggis (in a sheep's stomach bag), black puddings, mealie (white) puddings, and clootie dumplings tied up in a cloot (cloth). It has also influenced the baking tradition. A cast iron girdle hanging over the slow burning peat is the origin of the bannocks, oatcakes, pancakes, and girdle scones which Maggie has been baking all her life.

Their generous sharing of food has captured all the essence of the land. When questioned about their self-sufficient lifestyle, they claim to be 'rich in everything, but money'. They buy salt for preserving, but fertilizer for growing crops comes from animal manure and seaweed from the beach. They cut peat for fuel. It's a hard life by today's standards, but they are sustained by these ingredients of the old Scots diet which makes full use of their majestic mountains for breeding hardy animals and their limited arable patches for growing crops. Besides, they are skilled at fishing and foraging, adding to their diet wild berries, herbs, seaweed, fish, and shellfish that has been part of their food culture here since their hunter-gatherer ancestors first settled in coastal caves on this peninsula around 7000 BC, leaving evidence of their eating habits in middens of shellfish and fish bones.[6]

Food and Landscape

The Potential of the Crofters' Land and Food Culture

I was teaching catering at Elgin Technical College in Morayshire, preparing young Scottish students to sit the London City and Guilds 151/152 examinations. Their textbook was *Practical Cookery* by V. Ceserani and R. Kinton. French *haute cuisine* was the norm at the time in the best hotels and restaurants. Scotch Broth and Cullen Skink were the only Scottish recipes in our textbook. Neither were part of the syllabus. But this was Scotland, not France.

My next move was to manage the kitchen at the Loch Torridon Hotel on a deer shooting and salmon fishing estate at the head of Inner Loch Torridon. My aim was to cook Scottish and write menus in English, Scots, and maybe Gaelic. Armed with an 1829 edition of Meg Dod's *The Cook and Housewife's Manual* with its special chapter on Scottish National Dishes, W. Heptinstall's *Gourmet Recipes from a Highland Hotel* (1967), and Janet Murray's *Traditional Recipes from Scotland* (n.d.), I got some useful inspiration. But the book which became my Bible was Florence (Floss) Marian McNeill's *The Scots Kitchen* (1929).

Floss was born on a traditional Orkney croft in 1885. She was the second youngest of twelve children. The family grew their own vegetables, oats, and barley; kept cattle for milk, cheese, and butter; sheep for mutton; and caught as much fish as they could in the summer months. She was one of the first women to have a university education and had been strongly encouraged by her Gaelic-speaking father to preserve her cultural heritage. She says she did not set out to write a 'compendium of cookery', but instead 'to preserve the recipes of our old national dishes, many of which, in this age of standardisation, are in danger of falling into undeserved oblivion'.[7] Her collection from the Shetlands to the Borders includes simple folk recipes, some collected in Orkney and the Hebrides, which had never been published.

Shortly after moving to the Loch Torridon Hotel, I was invited by Alastair Holmes, the gamekeeper, to visit his deer larder. I began by owning-up that I'd never cooked venison, or any other game for that matter. 'Not a problem,' he said. 'My mother will be happy to help.'

Mary Holmes had cooked for most of her life on Highland shooting and fishing estates and was a highly experienced and excellent game cook. She was also a nose-to-tail cook. Nothing wasted. Among her repertoire was Stag's Head Broth, Venison Haggis, and Venison Tripe, known by its colourful Gaelic name: Pocha (bag) Buidhe (yellow). The broth and the haggis were soon on the menu, but I baulked at the tripe. It had a dark brownish, mushroom appearance, totally unlike cow tripe in texture or taste. It was much thinner, more tender, with a pleasingly delicate gamey flavour. Mary insisted I put it on the menu. 'Call it Pocha Buidhe,' she said. 'And if anyone asks, just say it is a Highland Speciality.' So I did, and it sold. Just one curious German guest asked what it was, and she was content with her answer.

Properly handled, there is no finer game to be had in Europe than from these majestic Torridon Highlands. Feeding on rough grasses and heather, shot in its prime and carefully hung, it was this in particular that impressed Continental guests who happily ate it every night.

Excellent Aberdeen Angus beef and Blackface Sheep came from the Dingwall market. There were always plentiful supplies of superb wild salmon and sea trout in season. Creel-caught crabs, lobsters, and langoustines were often on the menu.

I made lifelong friendships with other crofters in the area. These Gaelic-speaking Highlanders were steeped in the traditions of the area. Just a few of the memorable things they shared with me were Mary Macdonald's *croppen heids*; Alice Mackenzie's *tatties 'n' herrin*; Rhoda Mackenzie's *sheep's heid broth*; Peggy Maclean's *clootie dumplings*; and *raw pickled mackerel*, cured in vinegar and brown sugar which old Murdo Matheson kept in a plastic bucket which appeared at ceilidhs (when people gather to socialize) accompanied by malt whisky, tasting of nectar from an unlabelled bottle. The Torridon area has a rich history of illicit distilling.[8] These were the 'old people with long memories' which Floss McNeill loved to meet.

All this lent enthusiasm to the cause, and a new-found confidence in native dishes and local produce at a professional level, letting the excellent quality of the game, fish, and meat speak for itself, uncluttered by rich French saucing. All this food of the landscape needs is a Mary Holmes, cooking, in her tiny stable cottage, a pot of Bawd Bree (Hare Broth) from a well-hung mountain hare. She gives us a wide deep Scottish soup plate with a large 'floury' Scottish potato, making an island in the middle. It is surrounded by a rich, dark brown, velvety liquid and collops of tender hare meat. As the potato disintegrates into the broth, there is the perfect balance of rich hare and bland potato to satisfy all the senses.

While my next move was back to Glasgow to work on the research with Professor Fuller, my family, with no Highland heritage, decided to change lifestyle and have a go at a self-sufficiency on a fertile piece of land in a crofting township on the north side of Loch Torridon. They engineered a road, built a house, planted a fruit orchard, grew vegetables on land that had once been the crofter's potato patch, had a boat and caught fish from the sea loch and brown trout from the hill lochs. Though officially 'incomers', we were welcomed and became a working part of the community, my father a member of the mountain rescue team until he was seventy-five. Four generations on, the land is still in our family.

By the end of the 1980s, however, most of the almost totally self-sufficient crofters that I had made friends with in the 1960s were the last to work the land and sea in the old way. The road round the Applecross peninsula was thirty years too late for them and their children. Many would have dearly loved to have stayed, but were faced with no job opportunities, no houses, and no up-to-date infrastructure. So they left.

The Black Cloud of Depopulation

The Scottish Gaels of the Highlands and Islands held an ancient belief, known in Gaelic as *duthchas*, which lay behind the origins of the clan system.[9] It expresses a sense of being rooted by ancient lineage to a certain area of land, which is communally held by all the people of the clan. Under this early system, a clan chief ensured the general well-being of the clan and provided protection and security of possession for the people living within their lands. He was originally elected by the clan and not chosen by bilineal descent. He had no legal right to evict or take rents and was expected to govern in the best interests of the clan. However, as feudalism was introduced in other parts of the country, the spirit of the old system was not upheld, and clan chiefs began to take rents and sell land.

At the time of the failed 1715 and 1745 Jacobite rebellions, not all clan chiefs in this remote and mostly roadless area supported the Stuart cause. Jacobite loyalties were not confined to the Highlands, but it was no coincidence that the uprisings began and ended in the Highlands.[10] And it was the Highland clans who suffered most after Culloden. Their loyalty to Charles Stuart had brought him so close to success that the victorious Duke of Cumberland considered a wholesale transportation of Jacobites to the colonies.

Instead, he opted for a scorched earth policy of burning, clearing, and pillaging, even in areas that had been loyal. The Highlands remained oppressed by the Hanoverian government's military might as they attempted to break up the clan system.[11] To crush them further, the military confiscated thousands of the clans' hardy black polled Highland cattle, their most valuable assets which they bartered for essential grain, since they did not have enough arable land to fulfil their needs. Less valuable sheep, goats, and horses were also confiscated and sold, mostly in Southern markets.[12]

In the years following, lucrative large-scale commercial sheep farms began to be set up by new landlords, often from England, but also by non-Jacobite clan chiefs. This involved clearing the people from their traditional lands where, under the paternal clan chief, each had an enclosed piece of fertile land for tillage, usually beside their house, and with rights to graze livestock on less fertile land in the glens and mountains. The unique social system of 'crofting' stems from the Highland Clearances. The clanspeople became tenants.

The tradition of a benevolent clan chief who was responsible for his clanspeople's security of tenure no longer operated wherever sheep farming was introduced. Their houses in the glens were destroyed, and they were moved to less favourable land at the coast, where the traditional mix of livestock and crops was not viable. Many took an emigrant ship to America. This was the situation for the dispirited, demoralized, and exhausted generation which had lived through two uprisings and their brutal aftermath. It was the next generation who showed more drive and energy to fight for their rights.

Some acts of defiance were organized, when crofters from several districts came together to drive the hated flocks of landlord's sheep off the land. This was just the start of a period of dissent known as the Crofters' War (1790-1886) which culminated in the Battle of the Braes on Skye in 1882 against landlords who had deprived crofters of the common grazing land they needed to feed their livestock.[13] The crofters made a public protest by refusing to pay their rents until they were given back the land. The landlord, Lord MacDonald, mobilized the law in the form of an Inverness sheriff and fifty policemen, shipped up from Glasgow, to arrest the crofters. But at a strategic location on their route through Skye, they were met by a hundred and fifty crofters who attacked them with sticks and stones.[14] The issue was widely publicized in the media, with journalists visiting the area and reporting in the national press. Public opinion in Scotland favoured the crofters.

As a result of the Braes revolt, the British government set up a Royal Commission to investigate the situation, leading to a radical change. The Napier Commission's work led to the Crofters Act of 1886, which established security of tenure, along with rights to grazing land. A Crofters Commission (CC) was set up with rent-fixing powers.[15] This is seen now as only a partial solution, since it did not include those without a tenant's right to work a croft. These were the landless cotters, squatters, and fishermen who were most vulnerable to transportation. The new law was also too late for all the thousands (the number is unknown) who had already taken a boat to America in the first half of the nineteenth-century, the period of the largest exodus.

During the period of the Crofters' War, another land issue threatened the communities in the Highlands and Islands when Queen Victoria and Prince Albert fell in love with the Balmoral Estate in 1848. They were not into sheep farming. But they did like to hunt and fish. This was an estate amongst spectacular scenery, wild, remote, and private, where they could relax away from the royal pomp of London. Soon the aristocracy, landed gentry, and *nouveau-riche* industrialists were buying up large areas of Highland and Island estates for pleasure. Often, if there was not one there already, they built themselves a castle, as did the royal family.

An Act of Property in 1621 had converted hunting game into an exclusive right of the landowner, taking away the Highlander's right to a share of game and fish from their clan lands.[16] While in the early 1800s there were only six or seven areas actively managed for hunting, just twenty-five years after the royal family's arrival, there were 79. By 1900 there were between 130 and 150, covering 2.5 million acres. By 2002, the extent of the sporting estates, including deer forests and mountains as well as grouse moors, had reached 4.5 million acres.[17]

New owners of sporting estates only employed a few local people for a few months of the year during the season. The rest of the year they became absentee landlords, living a considerable distance away and often unable, or unwilling, to take an interest in the survival or the care of communities on their estate who were paying them rent for their house and land. Not all were bad landlords. Some were interested in supporting the local community, but others were intent on preserving their privacy and keeping their lands wild, barren, and empty of people.

Land Reform on the Political Agenda for the Highlands and Islands

On a clear day in June 1992, the crofters on the Assynt estate in Sutherland were surprised to see some small seaplanes circling the estate. One landed on a sandy beach, and the locals gathered to watch. Out stepped a titled family and an Iranian gentleman who, it transpired, were being given an aerial view of the estate as potential buyers.

Unusual goings-on, but it served as a wake-up call to the crofters who were unaware that the estate was for sale.[18]

By the late twentieth century, large areas of the Highlands and Islands had become a playground for many more than British royalty and their followers. Joining them now is a global super-class who might be sheiks, oligarchs, or self-made millionaires – or they could be completely anonymous landowners who secretly register their investment in a tax haven so tenants must deal with intermediaries.

At the beginning of the twenty-first century, the pattern of private land ownership in Scotland is the most concentrated in the developed world: 432 private landowners account for 50% of all the privately-owned land.[19] Or, put another way, 0.025% of the population owns 67% of the privately-owned rural land.[20] Some might use their estates to hunt and fish. Some see potential profit in agricultural support subsidies, forestry grants, and other taxpayer-financed payments. Some are in it for the lucrative rental charges to be levied on wind farms which only exist by public subsidy. Some are also adept at making arrangements to reduce, or even eliminate, effective taxation of landed wealth.[21] Some treat their estates as playgrounds to entertain their friends. Some may not even visit their estate. But on a badly managed estate, the lives of local communities become so unbearable that their only course of action is a tenants' revolt.

In the early 1990s the community on the small island of Eigg was in revolt. Their dysfunctional landlord, who had owned the estate for almost twenty years, had made their lives a misery. Situated south of Skye, Eigg has a land area of just twelve square miles. In 1991, the islanders (known as Eiggachs) decided on the radical move of setting up a Trust, to fund buying the island from their landlord. They called a well-publicized and well-attended (including their landlord) press conference in an Edinburgh hotel to get some publicity and to invite people to support the Isle of Eigg Trust.

Also attending the event were the worried Assynt crofters. They immediately set up their own fund to buy their land, and in less than a year had raised the asking price (£300,000). Half of the money came from supporters in the UK and the Scottish Diaspora who retain strong links with Scotland, and the remainder from a grant loan from Highland Council. They bought their land in February 1993 to great excitement and rejoicing. A photograph of the late Allan MacRae, the chief mover in the campaign, shows him standing on top of a large rock with the majestic mountain of Suilven in the background. His arms are held high in victory, holding a bottle (probably whisky) in one hand and the other punching the air with a defiant clenched fist. They had become the first crofters to buy back their land.[22]

Meanwhile, the Eiggachs continued to suffer from the actions of their dysfunctional landlord, Keith Schellenberg (AKA Shellie). An eccentric, millionaire playboy, he wafted hot and cold with them. He had bought the estate in 1974 and was fiercely opposed to selling it to the islanders. Despite the island having a reputation as the 'garden of the Hebrides', he had neglected to maintain estate houses, the island's infrastructure, and its land. A housing poverty report in 1988 described 'most of the tenants houses as uninsulated, and therefore severely affected by rising and penetrating damp [.... They] had no proper electricity supply [... and] some had no water supply, so no baths, showers or sinks [...] and no WCs'.[23] Shellie claimed he liked the 'run-down, Hebridean aspect' of the island. While the islanders' health suffered from the appalling state of the houses and the difficulties of eking out a living, he entertained his friends with 'champers and hampers' weekends and costumed Jacobite and Hanoverian mock battles, which did not go down well with the Eiggachs.[24]

A major fund-raising campaign had the support of Highland Council and the Scottish Wildlife Trust. But in 1995, under financial pressure to sell the island, Shellie rejected a bid from the Trust and instead sold to a German, Professor Marlin Eckhart (AKA Maruma). Two years later he was also under financial pressure to sell and the Trust raised the total purchase price of £1.5 million by public donations from Scotland and beyond. Nearing the bid deadline, however, they were still short of £900,000. This shortfall was generously closed by an anonymous female donor from the North of England (rumoured to be Catherine Cookson).[25] Eigg was the first Scottish island to be bought by its tenants. Highlands and Islands Enterprise (HIE) gave the Isle of Eigg Heritage Trust a grant of £17,000 to get started.[26]

The Eiggachs have just celebrated twenty years of independence. During that time they have improved the infrastructure, built their own renewably powered electricity grid (Eiggtricity), repaired and improved old houses and built new ones, and piped water to all establishments. The population has increased from 65 to over 100. Tourism is flourishing. There is a café, bar, and restaurant at the pier – it has its own brewery making artisan craft beers recently on sale in Aldi – and a weekly craft and local produce market with organic eggs and vegetables.[27] Eigg has also been named Britain's most eco-friendly island.[28]

After devolution in 1999, HIE set up the Community Land Unit (CLU) which supports any community exploring the possibilities of ownership. By 2000, 144,000 acres were in community ownership, all made possible by community fund-raising. In January 2000, the Scottish Land Fund (SLF) was set up with lottery funding, and by 2006 420,000 acres of land was in community ownership. As of June 2017, 562,230 acres of Scottish land is community-owned, which amounts to 2.9% of the total land area of Scotland. The Scottish Government have been challenged to aim for another 500,000 acres to be community-owned by 2020.[29]

While progress is being made, many more communities want to take back their land and remove controlling, insensitive, and dysfunctional landlords. Those communities who have succeeded are witness to how improving their living conditions, and their ability to develop the land's potential to produce a local food supply, creates health and prosperity for everyone.

Crofting Empowered: A Long Hard Struggle

The battle for land reform is ongoing, but the crofters' battle for their rights, on the agenda since the demise of the clan system, has attracted illegal protests, murders,

Food and Landscape

Figure 2. Crofting Township of Staffin on the Isle of Skye. Photo: Andy Law (used by permission).

arrests, and prison sentences. Long after the Crofters' War (1790-1886), a high-profile event highlighted a critical situation. In June 1908, a group of ten men, from the islands of Barra and Mingulay, emerged from Waverley station in Edinburgh. Few had travelled in a train before. None had ever been to Edinburgh. But news had already reached the capital of their arrival, and a crowd of around 300 had gathered to cheer them. Their crime: to take land illegally from their absentee landlord, Lady Emily Gordon Cathcart of Berkshire, who had ordered their arrest.[30]

The 'Vatersay Raiders', as they were known, had been existing at minimal subsistence level in overcrowded conditions leading to ill health, malnutrition, and premature death on the islands of Barra and Mingulay. The nearby island of Vatersay had been 'cleared' in 1850 of all indigenous crofters by Colonel John Gordon of Cluny. Also an absentee landlord, he had ordered this action to turn the whole island into a sheep farm, making it more profitable for him than from crofter's rents. But in 1908, the Congested Districts Board (CDB), which had been set up in the 1880s by the Scottish Secretary to regulate crofting land at the same time as the first Crofters Commission, had named Vatersay as having vacant croft land for fifty-eight crofts.

Over several years, the Barra and Mingulay islanders, in their desperate need of more land to grow crops, had appealed to the new owner, Lady Cathcart (Colonel Gordon's daughter-in-law), for this crofting land on Vatersay. But she refused their appeal. She appears to have only once visited the Highlands. She was, however, very active when it came to land management on her several Highland estates. She had inherited other estates and followed the common policy of evicting tenants to increase the value of land for sheep-farming. She had only allowed her tenants on Barra and Mingulay small pieces of land, insufficient for supporting the population, so that island men would be available to work in the fishing industry, which was more profitable for her than crofting.[31] So the desperate 'raiders' set about marking out the vacant crofts on Vatersay, building huts to live in and planting potatoes to keep their families from starvation. It was that, or take a boat to America.[32]

A Challenging Landscape:

The ten 'land raiders' were sentenced to two months imprisonment. They were not the first to be jailed. And neither were they the last. But they were a microcosm of what was going in the Highlands at this time, and their story, well publicized by sympathizers, caught the public's imagination. Large crowds of supporters followed their trial and imprisonment. Within days, petitions were organized for their release. Funds were set up to support them. Lady Cathcart was forced to show mercy. Even the UK Parliament became involved. The House of Lords held a seven-hour debate on how to handle the situation on Vatersay and deal with Lady Cathcart's demands.[33] To resolve the impasse, the government bought the island from her in 1909. The CDB marked-out fifty-eight new crofts in four townships on Vatersay. And the crofters got the land.

The people on the nearby islands of Mingulay, Sandray, and Pabbay were not so lucky. Their population reduced to a point where the community was not viable, and, reluctantly, they left their land. The islands remain uninhabited. Many other Scottish islands on the west coast, which had sustained human life for thousands of years, were completely, and irreversibly, deserted in a very short space of time.[34] Happily for the Vatersay Raiders, this was not the case.

A century on from their arrest, the island's community gathered in 2009 for the launch, by the Scottish Government's Crofting Minister, of a Croft Mark that will identify all produce from Scottish crofts and be managed by the Scottish Crofters Federation (SCF). Surrounding by Vatersay Hall's old photographic reminders of their ancestors, including one of her ten most famous sons, the Crofting Minister, Michael Russell, said, 'The men who raided Vatersay did so because they needed to produce food for their families. In Scotland today, many places have lost that link between the land and what it can produce. That link needs to be restored. This is a role for crofting which could be of huge benefit to Scotland.'[35]

The Croft Mark indicates produce which has come from a croft, or similar small agricultural holding, in the Scottish Highlands and Islands and includes beef, lamb, mutton, pork, eggs, dairy products, honey, preserves, vegetables, soft fruits, knitwear, tweed, and wool. Those who buy these products support the unique heritage and culture of Scottish crofting. They are also helping to preserve some of the nation's most valued landscapes and habitats, particularly including the heather moors and the Hebridean machair, the extensive, fertile grassy plain of wild flower-rich meadows in spring, which borders the many miles of white sandy beaches.

The SCF is the largest association of small-scale food producers in the UK. A directory of producers is listed on their website.[36] Recently, they have petitioned the Scottish Government's Land Reform Group to create 10,000 new crofts by 2020.[37] They argue that crofting is not only the best system to deliver goals for the future of agriculture in the Highlands and Islands, but also to contibute to the sustainability of rural communities. They are also keen to extend the area of the Crofting Counties. In some cases two or three crofts are joined together making them more viable. The

Crofting Commission, the Scottish Government's regulatory body, has a waiting list of people who want to croft.[38]

A New Generation of Crofters

From a young age, Donald McSween (AKA Sweeny) followed his grandfather around as he worked the family croft at Ness, on the Isle of Lewis in the Outer Hebrides. The croft occupies a treeless area of flat land at the coast, where foam-crested Atlantic rollers wash onto white sandy beaches and where people have toiled for centuries under the great arch of sky. They are hard-working folk whose way of life is cooperative, not competitive. On calm, opalescent summer nights sunset merges into dawn, while wild winter nights of lashing rain and gale force winds rattle windows and threaten chimney pots.

Sweeny claims his grandfather inspired him to croft and to love animals. His parents gave him the croft for his twenty-first birthday. Sweeny had been interviewing for BBC Alba, the Gaelic TV channel, when it was suggested that they do a series on how he managed to do part-time work in Stornoway while at the same time working the croft. *An Lot* (*The Croft*) began filming in 2016.

First we meet his small flock of sixty hardy Blackface sheep. These, and his super-intelligent sheepdog Bud, are his favourite animals. But he needs a project that will give him a regular income. Eggs, he decides, are the best idea. He salvages three unwanted porta cabins that he joins together to make a large shed, making space for the egg project. He builds a henhouse for 300 hens. With his student brother, Innes (who claims to hate crofting but still helps out when he is on holiday), he sets off from Lewis to travel to Stirling for the hens. The hens are put into crates, and when they arrive back at Ness the boys happily discover that the hens are none the worse from the journey by road and boat. Bud learns to herd hens.

The demand for *An Lot* eggs regularly outstrips the supply in the Stornoway butchers. There is tedious work to be done with the eggs: collecting, weighing, labelling and then filling boxes. This ends up as mostly mother's work.

Another idea is pigs. He goes for Tamworths and Gloucester Old Spot crosses. He finds them much more wilful than his sheep. The most wilful one is the first to end up in the Stornoway butchers. At the end of the first series, he still needs to keep his part-time work in Stornoway. Innes thinks he is mad. Sweeny replies, 'But I get to live in paradise.'

The second series begins with a new flock of 300 hens to increase the egg production, this time delivered from a supplier in Skye. Egg production from the original flock had reduced, so he offered the hens to anyone who would come and collect them. He has increased his flock of sheep to a hundred. With three female and one male pig, by the end of the series there are twenty piglets. He is excited at the arrival of two very beautiful light golden Highland cows, who are also excited when the local Aberdeen Angus bull visits them.

At the end of the second series he buys eighteen dark brown Hebridean sheep, the native sheep of these islands. They are hardy wee sheep, with handsome heads and rich chocolate brown coats. He has an idea of getting rugs made from their skins. He invites local young people to come and work for a day on the croft. He has increased his income from the croft by diversifying into pigs, cows, and more sheep. But he is still not ready to give up work in Stornoway. 'There is,' he says, 'a gap in the market for wholesome food from animals who have lived a good life, on good fertile lands.' Sweeny can be visited at Air An Lot (Life on a Croft) in Ness.[39]

There is a chance now for Sweeny's generation to reverse the damage that has been done to land in the Highlands and Islands through wars, clearances, emigration, and dominating landowners with no interest in encouraging people to settle in communities and use land for food production. The 2016 Land Reform Scotland Bill has resolved some of the problems.[40] Also, the new Scottish Land Fund has £10m available for community buyouts, another hopeful move. But land which lies derelict because no one knows who owns it, and the land registered in tax havens by unknown companies and individuals, still remain frustrating issues for both the local people, who want to work the land, and the land reform campaigners who carry on the fight.

A Crofter's Celebration

Chef Neil Forbes had the idea of celebrating the crofter's traditions at one of Slow Food Edinburgh's monthly 'Big Table' dinners at his restaurant, Café St Honore.[41] Would I help with the menu? Would I tell the diners the history of the recipes and how I discovered them? Yes, of course I would. But would he be interested in having a go at the crofter's pickled mutton?[42] And what about doing a crofter's *cranachan* with all the ingredients set on the table and everyone getting to mix their own? Yes, he would love to have a go.

So the Blackface legs of organic mutton are carefully salted. And we plan a 'build-your-own *cranachan*'. Bowls of toasted oatmeal, whipped cream, honey, soft fruits, and a measure of whisky are to be shared between four diners. This may be a first in a restaurant. It is certainly unlike a typical chef's *cranachan*, which comes layered decoratively in a wine glass. Slow Food Edinburgh loved it, and the mutton too.

Cranachan derives from a Gaelic noun for a kind of churn. It is also attached to a festive milk-based dish traditionally eaten at harvest-time or Halloween.[43] Children were sent to pick wild brambles from the hedgerows, or blaeberries from the hills and moors. There is unlimited scope for variation.

Cranachan
A bowl of cream, freshly whipped double cream. This might be varied according to taste and availability with some crowdie cheese, added to give a sharp tang. (alternatives: sour cream, fromage frais or crème fraîche).
A bowl of toasted oatmeal, medium or coarse, toast slowly in the oven to give a crunch. Or soak in whisky to soften. Or toast porridge oats in the oven with

brown sugar and butter.⁴⁴

A bowl of fresh soft fruits, either a single fresh fruit, or mixture, foraged in season.

A jar of heather or other honey to sweeten.

A bottle of favourite whisky, Scottish liqueur or any other spirit or liqueur.

Give each person a bowl and spoon (in the old croft house the bowls would have been wooden and the spoons hand-carved horn). Then everyone can create their own *cranachan* nirvana.

Slainte Mhath (Good Health).

Notes

1. Jane Grigson, *Good Things* (London: Michael Joseph, 1971), p. 9.
2. *British Cookery: A Complete Guide to Culinary Practice in the British Isles*, ed. by Lizzie Boyd (London: Croom Helm, 1976).
3. Catherine Brown, *Scottish Regional Recipes* (Glasgow: Molendinar Press, 1981).
4. The Scottish Crofting Federation identifies twelve crofting regions: Shetland Isles, Orkney, East Sutherland and Caithness, Northwest Sutherland, Wester Ross, Lewis, Harris, Skye and Lochalsh, Uist and Barra, Inverness and East Highlands, Lochaber, and Argyll ('The Crofting Counties', *Scottish Crofting Federation* <http://www.crofting.org/index.php/contact_regions_main> [accessed 10 February 2018].
5. Scottish Crofting Federation, 'About Us', *Scottish Crofting Federation* <http://www.crofting.org/aboutus> [accessed 10 February 2018].
6. Applecross History Society, 'Scotland's First Settlers Project', *Applecross Heritage* <http://www.applecrossheritage.org.uk//first_settlers.html> [accessed 10 February 2018]
7. F. Marian McNeill, *The Scots Kitchen: Its Traditions and Recipes*, ed. by Catherine Brown (Glasgow: Blackie, 1929; repr. Edinburgh: Birlinn, 2010), p. xxi.
8. Murdoch MacDonald, *The Battle of the Black Pot: Illicit Distillation in Torridon* (Evanton: Torridon Publishing, 2011), pp. 14-25.
9. T.M. Devine, *The Scottish Nation 1700-2001* (London: Penguin Books, 2006), p. 175.
10. Devine, *The Scottish Nation*, p. 40.
11. Devine, *The Scottish Nation*, p. 45.
12. Devine, *The Scottish Nation*, p. 46.
13. T.M. Devine, *Clanship to Crofters' War: The Social Transformation of the Scottish Highlands* (Manchester: Manchester University Press, 1994), pp. 209-27.
14. James Hunter, *The Last of the Free: A Millennial History of the Highlands and Islands* (Edinburgh: Mainstream, 1999), pp. 308-16.
15. Hunter, p. 320.
16. Andy Wightman, *The Poor Had No Lawyers: Who Owns Scotland* (Edinburgh: Birlinn, 2011), p. 163.
17. Wightman, p. 165.
18. Wightman, pp. 146-47.
19. James Hunter and others, *432:50 – Towards a Comprehensive Landreform Agenda for Scotland: A Briefing paper for the House of Commons Scottish Affairs Committee* 2013, p. 5, 2.1. <https://www.parliament.uk/documents/commons-committiees/scottish-affairs/432-Land-Reform-Paper.pdf> [accessed 10 February 2018]

A Challenging Landscape:

20. Charles Warren, *Managing Scotland's Environment* (Edinburgh: Edinburgh University Press, 2009), pp. 48-49.
21. Hunter and others, p. 5, 2.3, 2.4, 2.5.
22. John MacKenzie, 'The Realisation of the Dream', *Assynt Crofters' Trust*, May 1998 <http://www.theassyntcrofters.co.uk/history> [accessed 10 February 2018].
23. Alastair McIntosh, *Soil and Soul, People Versus Corporate Power* (Edinburgh: Birlinn, 2004), p. 164.
24. Lesley Riddoch, *Blossom: What Scotland Needs to Flourish* (Edinburgh: Luath Press, 2014), p. 149, n. 1.
25. Riddoch, p. 162.
26. 'About Eigg', *Isle of Eigg Heritage Trust* <http://www.isleofeigg.org> [accessed 10 February 2018].
27. 'Food and Drink', *Isle of Eigg Heritage Trust* <http://www.isleofeigg.org/food-drink/> [accessed 10 February 2018].
28. Dixie Wills, 'Eigg, Britain's Most Eco-Friendly Island', *The Guardian*, 29 May 2017 <https://www.theguardian.com/travel/2017/may/29/eigg-island-scotland-cycling-walking-kayaking> [accessed 10 February 2018].
29. Andy Wightman, p. 149-51; 'Estimate of Community Owned Land in Scotland 2017', *Scottish Government*, 8 December 2017 <https://beta.gov.scot/publications/estimate-community-owned-land-scotland-2017/> [accessed 10 February 2018].
30. Ben Buxton, *The Vatersay Raiders* (Edinburgh: Birlinn, 2008; repr. Kindle Edition, 2012), Prologue: 'An Extraordinary Proceeding' [accessed 10 February 2018].
31. Henry Buckton, *The Lost Villages* (London: Tauris, 2008), p. 43.
32. Buckton, pp. 40-48.
33. House of Lords Debate, *Vatersay* (Hansard, 19 May 1909), cc. 1055-80.
34. Buckton, pp. 43-46.
35. Scottish Crofting Federation, 'Scottish Crofting Produce Mark', Scottish Crofting Federation <http://www.crofting.org/scpbrand> [accessed 10 February 2018].
36. Scottish Crofting Enterprise 'Welcome', *Scottish Crofting Enterprise*, 2013 <http://www.scottishcroftingenterprise.co.uk.> [accessed 10 February 2018]
37. Scottish Crofting Federation, 'SCF Call on Land Reform Gurus to Support Creation of New Crofts', *Crofting.org*, 14 January 2013 <https://www.crofting.org/uploads/news/scfnewcrofts.pdf> [accessed 10 February 2018].
38. Crofting Commission, 'Creating a Well Regulated Crofting System that Positively Contributes to the Sustainability of Rural Communities', *Crofting Commission*, 2018 <http://www.crofting.scotland.gov.uk> [accessed 10 February 2018].
39. *An Lot / The Croft*, BBC Alba, Series 1 (June 2017) and Series 2 (January 2018). Donald MacSween, 'About', *Air An Lot,* 2015 <https://www.airanlot.com/about/ > [accessed 10 February 2018].
40. 'Land Reform (Scotland) Act 2016', *Scottish Government* <http://www.gov.scot/Topics/Environment/land-reform/LandReformBill> [accessed 10 February 2018].
41. 'Meet Our Ambassador Chefs: Neil Forbes, Cafe St Honoré', *Eat Scottish*, 12 February 2016 <http://www.eat-scottish.co.uk/2016/02/12/neil-forbes/> [accessed 10 February 2018].
42. Catherine Brown. Scottish Cookery (Edinburgh: Birlinn, 2013), p. 224.
43. McNeill, p. 258; 'Cranachan', *Dictionary of the Scots Language*, Scottish Language Dictionaries <http://www.dsl.ac.uk/entry/snd/sndns1013> [accessed 10 February 2018].
44. 'Buttered Oats: 85g butter; 110g brown sugar; 250g rolled oats. Baking tin 22x33cm. Preheat oven 350F/180C/160Cfan/Gas 4. To make: Melt the butter in a pan with the sugar. When melted add oats. Mix well. Spread out in tin and toast in a moderate oven for about 30-40 minutes till golden brown, turning once. Leave to cool. Store in an airtight jar or tin' (Catherine Brown, *Scottish Cookery*, p. 33).

Microbial Landscapes

Joshua Evans

I remember, as a child, wanting to move through landscapes different from my own. In the park I heaped mounds of wet sand, stuck them with shoots of pine, bored holes and tunnels through them with my fingers, and let my mind wander over these mountains as a bird would, or a moose, or a wandering child, much like me, but smaller. On frigid beaches I shifted rocks and smoothed sand again, making new lagoons for hermit crabs who would, I thought, be glad for shelter. Gliding in my father's canoe I imagined myself a speck, a plankton, swirling in the eddy of his paddle, my world a spinning hyperbolic plane; riding on the ferry (growing up on an island), I played a similar game, much larger this time, in its churning, lurid wake. Peering out the window of my first aeroplane, the game expanded yet again, offering up new mounds of particularly fluffy sand to hike and dance and leap across.

The game was perhaps at its best in the garden. I would stare at a patch of spongy soil for an hour, first following the critters I could see, and gradually the ones I couldn't. Cauliflower offered potential hours of involuted walks across its surfaces, the dew held in its leaves containing whole worlds into which I had been given sole privilege to look. Raspberry canes in the summer were, I learned, best entered from below, their drupes more clearly visible – enormous fruits in a tangled jungle, bumpy planets trembling in a leafy sky.

I imagine you might also have played or play a version of this game.

Most recently I find myself playing it in the kitchen, now with companion species I do not have to conjure.[1] What is it like, I wonder, to be a yeast budding and bubbling in the dough expanding atop the boiler? What is it like to be a bacterial colony inhabiting the sour, slippery walls of my kombucha mother? And what of kōji spores, responding to humid heat on the bumpy landscape of boiled grains, extending mycelia and exploding into a starburst of fruiting bodies, creating a new landscape of fluffy white, new clouds of coconut and guava to dance across with my nose?

Our theme this year is Food and Landscape – a rich one. The breadth of topics, and the various literatures they build on, readily demonstrates how 'landscape' is not a self-evident concept. Sometimes it refers to physical features of the land 'out there', seen from nowhere in particular; other times it refers to perception of one's surroundings from a particular point of view. Sometimes it assumes a 'wild' environment, untouched by human activities; other times it brings human agency in shaping the land to the fore. Sometimes it refers to actual land; other times to representations of land.[2] Yet most often, across these variations in meaning, invoking 'landscape' tends to assume the primacy of the visual, and, even more deeply, the primacy of the human subject to whom the landscape is relevant and revelatory.

I wonder, as another version of this same game, what might happen when we open up the possibility that landscape might make sense not just for humans, at the human scale and with human priorities of moving through and experiencing the world. Microbes, so different from us, are particularly good for thinking with here. With this short paper I hope to offer an account of some things microbes do that make them particularly good at helping us to understand landscape in a more general, 'more-than-human' way – and why perhaps we should.[3]

Drawing from examples of contemporary scientific and culinary research on fermentation, I shall set out to investigate what 'landscape' might mean for microbes, how we can come to know these landscapes, and what we might learn about landscape in general when we explore them in microbial worlds.

What Might 'Landscape' Mean for Microbes?

You and I are on a hill, overlooking a lake. It is evening, in summer. Terraced vines slope down to the water, clusters plumping up but not yet ripe. The air cools; a breeze sweeps up from the far shore. Dry grasses rustle. A tongue of woodsmoke whips briefly into us from somewhere else.

Each grape on each cluster that surrounds us is its own world, neither the same nor unique. There are yeasts, sensing sugars developing, waiting to digest them into alcohol. There are bacteria, wondering whether they will get the chance, with this batch, to convert malic acid to lactic, or even the yeasts' alcohol to acetic. There are fungi, hoping the autumn is humid and long, to let them sprout their fuzzy noble magic, puncturing skins and letting berries shrivel. They may not see the water of the lake, but they would notice – the breeze, diurnal temperatures, would change – if it were not there. Some signals of landscape we share with these critters, yet many are each to their own.

There is a delightful yet powerful concept that lends rigour to this intuition. Jakob von Uexküll was a biologist in the late nineteenth and early twentieth centuries; his work on how non-human organisms sense their environments helped establish the field of biosemiotics. His notion of *umwelt* (literally, 'around-world') describes the world specific to an organism delimited and shaped by its own particular modes of sensory-perception.[4]

You and I are in a sort of shared *umwelt* standing on the hill. The yeasts and bacteria and other fungi have similarly distinct, yet somewhat overlapping *umwelten*, participating in similar environments where the same chemicals and physical forces carry, to a certain extent, shared meanings.

Some parts of these worlds signify more than others. The moon rising mauvely over the hills is beautiful, but it does not, like the grapes hanging there, promise wine. The hints of woodsmoke playing about our noses is calming, beckoning with Maillard smells; a different smoke of wildly singeing grass might alarm us more. Similarly, sugars signify more for some microbes than others, as do alcohols, acids, other molecules that signal ripeness, metabolism, rot. There are priorities, interests, desires at play that structure *umwelten* in different and differential ways. The French philosopher Gilles Deleuze's notion of desire bolsters our ability to understand these interests as different in degree and orientation, though not in kind. This desire is a positive force, not about lack but generativity, a force prior to mind or will that draws agents to one another and to other things in the world.[5] Needs stem from it and not vice versa. This is desire rendered more-than-human.

Figure 1. A window of experiments at Nordic Food Lab (reproduced under a Creative Commons licence).

'Landscape', then, without assuming visual primacy or human appropriateness, might be understood as a space, a section of an *umwelt,* structured by certain desires.

This move also reveals how landscapes are often nested within each other, at different scales and in different orientations and co-produced by many interlocking agencies. Humans planted these vines; different vines grew here and there in different ways, changing the soil, creating niches for other animals and plants and other smaller critters, all the way down; different microbes have contributed to different soils here and there, structuring how different vines and other plants and other critters that live together with them may take root.

This kind of landscape need not only be 'out there'. I have also encountered them inside, in definitively human spaces. At Nordic Food Lab, a non-profit in Copenhagen where I worked that investigates the gastronomic potential of the Nordic region, we would often – though we did not necessarily think about it this way at the time – propose potential landscapes to our microbial collaborators and see which ones co-responded most with their desires.[6]

Once, in the autumn of 2012, a colleague and I began twelve experimental trials of salt-rich, umami-oriented fermented sauces, modelled after soy sauces but containing various configurations

Figure 2. Fermenting 'soy' sauces at Nordic Food Lab (reproduced under a Creative Commons licence).

of grains, legumes, and other flavourful additions like mushrooms, berries, leaves, or wood (Figure 2). We combined these ingredients in a semi-structured way, ensuring that each had similar ratios of starchy, proteinous, and aromatic ingredients, similar levels of salt and moisture, and fermented together on a similar schedule under the same conditions. The results, naturally, varied widely. Some rapidly became inedible; others persisted but did not significantly improve, hovering between the tasty and the rotten; a handful became certainly flavourful; and one in particular blew us away, with its remarkable resemblance to a liquid essence of foie gras. This sauce, being entirely vegan, we named 'faux foie' (Figure 3):

> **Original Faux Foie**
> 500g kōji (grown on quinoa)
> 250g kōji (grown on 4 parts nøgen byg #43 : 1 part sunflower seeds)
> 750g cooked butterbeans
> 30g dry morels
> 500g bean stock
> 1L 20% brine (6.2% salt in total mixture)
> Combine in a sterilized container. Cover the surface of the mixture with plastic wrap, and let ferment at ambient temperature for three months.[7]

We wanted to make more. We tried to replicate the recipe, but it never quite worked in the same way. We had (and still have) yet to fully understand the desires of the microbes that structure the kinds of transformations happening in the pot. Understanding the faux foie as a landscape, a material-semiotic space structured by desires both microbial and human, might help us listen better, notice signs we might otherwise have overlooked. Understanding landscape more broadly might help us pay attention.

How Can We Know These More-Than-Human Landscapes?

At this point, you may very well be thinking, 'What a nice idea, but it is all very wilful.' Naïve, even – or, worse, a simplistic anthropomorphism, whose goal to explore beyond the human is proven disingenuous by implicitly reifying it. Desire and *umwelt* are useful tools for making theoretical incisions here; there are other tools for laying open these cuts more empirically.

When it comes to microbes, rapid developments in DNA sequencing are expanding the empirical possibilities of getting

Figure 3. The 'faux foie' at Nordic Food Lab (reproduced under a Creative Commons licence).

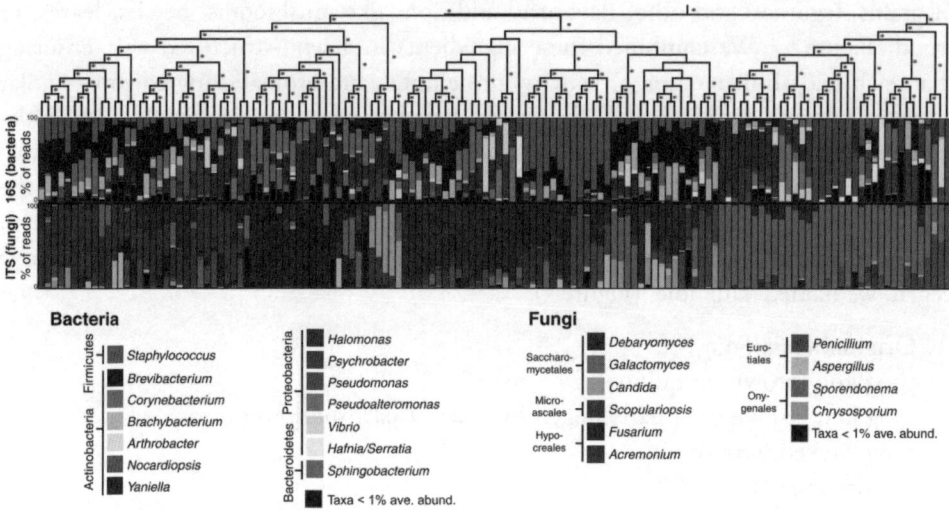

Figure 4. 'Distribution of Abundant Genera across Cheese Rind Communities' (reproduced by permission of Benjamin E. Wolfe).

to know which microbes favour and produce which kinds of landscape. Up until the advent of DNA sequencing, microbiology relied on culturing techniques and microscopy to get to know the microbes living in different environments. The problem with culturing is that only a fraction of microbes can be goaded into growing on plates, requiring different substates and conditions to grow. Sequencing DNA allows the possibility of gaining a fuller picture of the microbial ecology of a sample. It comes with its own methodological challenges, as, for example, we cannot assume that just because there is some DNA in a sample that its corresponding organism was living and metabolizing there (and indeed, samples may be easily contaminated with other things). Nonetheless, these techniques have opened up whole new areas of the field.

The work of microbiologists Rachel Dutton and Ben Wolfe is exemplary here, and set a precedent in the food world for scientists and chefs working together to better understand the complex contributions of microbial ecology to flavour. A few years back Rachel and Ben were working together at Harvard University on the microbial ecology of cheese rinds. They sampled the rinds of more than a hundred cheeses from ten different countries and sequenced all the DNA in the samples – a method known as metagenomics (the genome is the collection of all an organism's genes; the metagenome is the collection of all genomes in a sample).

Their research revealed some fascinating findings, one of which was that the primary factor shaping similarity across cheese rind ecologies was not geographical location, but the treatment, the manipulation of environmental variables such as temperature and humidity, and other practices such as washing and turning used to direct the course of the cheese's ripening.[8] In other words, it was about human craft. The craggy, otherworldly landscapes on the surface of a cheese are shaped by humans and microbes together – and understanding them as emerging through active practices of desire do more to help us understand the resulting cheese and its microbes than does a simpler, narrower notion of 'landscape' as merely a passive, scenic backdrop to the actual activities of interest (Figure 4).

Other researchers have used similar techniques for studying all sorts of more-than-human landscapes that emerge in fermentation. The lab of David Mills at University of California, Davis, specializes in this approach, and has produced a range of fascinating papers investigating the microbiomes of different built spaces of fermentative activity – wineries, breweries, and more. Analyzing this data for both species diversity and relative abundance has allowed Mills and his colleagues to generate 'heat maps' of these spaces, such as that below (Figure 5), that visually depict how different microbes cluster around different areas of the fermentation space.[9]

These maps help us begin to understand how 'landscape' is something that happens and is done not just 'out there', *sotto cielo*, but also within our built spaces, our domus, our hearths, our innermost and most intimate spaces of cultural and culinary transformation. Even the distinction between 'inside' and 'outside' itself, at the microbial scale, starts to make less sense. Wine yeasts, for example, are constantly flowing between the vineyard and the winery, to the extent that it is difficult to tell where they 'originally' come from.[10] For these microbes, 'inside' and 'outside' are less important categories than the nutrients and growth conditions – the desires and landscapes – they pursue, and the human behaviours that help their growth. Across these diverse spaces and practices of fermentation, humans shape microbes and microbes shape humans, body to body, lineage to lineage, in a loopy dance of becoming that is never truly 'done'.[11]

These techniques have more recently been extended to even more quotidian, familiar spaces. Jamie Lorimer, a cultural geographer at Oxford University, has just wrapped up a project in which he and his colleagues investigated what happened when they brought this

Figure 5. 'Mapping microbial contamination sources inside a brewery' (reproduced by permission of Nicholas A. Bokulich).

sequencing technology into people's homes. Designing experiments with them to learn more about their domestic microbiome, Lorimer's team hoped to see in what ways this participatory process might change how people interacted with their home's microbes and how they engaged with these emerging technologies. They visualized their domestic data using similar heat maps as above (Figure 6), and many of the findings were rather surprising.

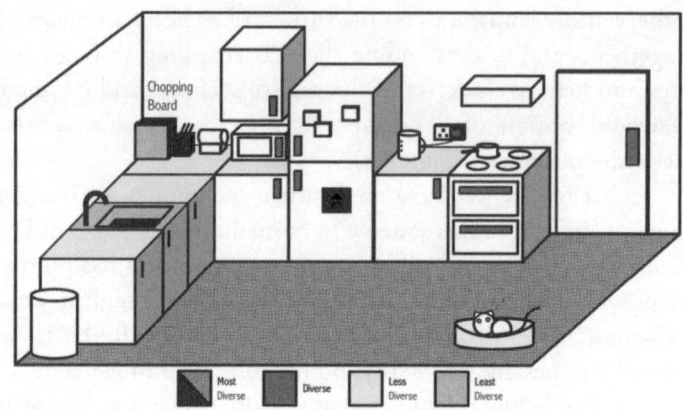

Figure 6. Kitchen heat map from participatory sequencing experiment (reproduced from a forthcoming article with permission from J. Lorimer).

For example, certain locations, like sinks and cutting boards, were much less microbially diverse than participants had expected. Other spaces, like sponges, were shown to be overwhelmingly diverse, and gained participants' newfound antipathy. Yet perhaps the most interesting findings had to do with the experiments' social dimensions: how different spaces and expertises shaped who could know these landscapes and how, how popular understandings of 'species' came to constrain the researchers' ability to communicate more nuanced facets of the ecological data, and how in many cases the methods themselves do not yet allow the desirable degree of certainty.[12]

Rob Dunn, an evolutionary ecologist at the North Carolina State University, has been conducting similar participatory experiments, and on a much larger scale. One of his current projects is about sourdough bread starters, in which his lab has metagenomically sequenced over a thousand starters sent in by bakers from all over the world, to compare them and see what patterns emerge. At the time of writing they have yet to publish their findings, but we can expect that new insights will emerge into how different relationships between microbes and humans structure, and are structured by, different landscapes at different nested scales in the production of fermented foods. One tantalizing preliminary finding was that the hands of some of the professional bakers whose starters they sampled exhibited populations of many of the same microbes living in their starters, compared to non-professional bakers.[13] The microbiomes of human and starter are shaping each other in turn.

In these ways and more, trying to extend our *umwelt* into those of microbes opens up the possibility of thinking about microbial landscapes as being not only composed of microbes, but also composed by and for them. Humans can be – and, when it comes to fermentation, often are – involved, but not as some prime mover.

Microbial Landscapes

What Do We Learn about Landscapes in General when Exploring Them in Microbial Worlds?

A couple of answers to this question have already emerged. I would like to collect them here, and propose a few more.

We have 'seen' how, when we attend to *umwelten* other than our own, landscapes emerge at different scales of space. They also emerge at different scales of time. Compared to humans, most microbes move fast. Through time that is – they reproduce rather quickly, evolve rather quickly, and in many fermented foods, especially more complex ones like miso or traditional kimoto sake brewing, where yeasts, bacteria, and multicellular fungi are all involved, their populations change quite significantly over the course of the fermentation process (Figure 7).

Take kimoto sake brewing, a traditional method of preparing sake involving the cultivation of a highly yeast-and-bacteria-active starter before adding it to a mash of rice saccharified by the kōji fungus, *Aspergillus oryzae*. Certain bacteria and wild yeasts begin the fermentation, but are quickly outpaced by lactic acid bacteria, which consume some of the sugars and produce lactic acid, lowering the pH of the mixture and changing the conditions of growth, allowing certain populations to subside and others to flourish. The yeasts cultivated in the starter then take over, slowly fermenting the sugar to alcohol, while the lactic acid bacteria then subside. Towards the end of the process, the yeast will stop multiplying and metabolizing, as the alcohol, if left unchecked, will eventually become high enough to suppress the yeasts' activity. This landscape in kimoto sake brewing undergoes observable changes as its chemistry and microbiome, its flavours and desires, shape each other in tandem.[14]

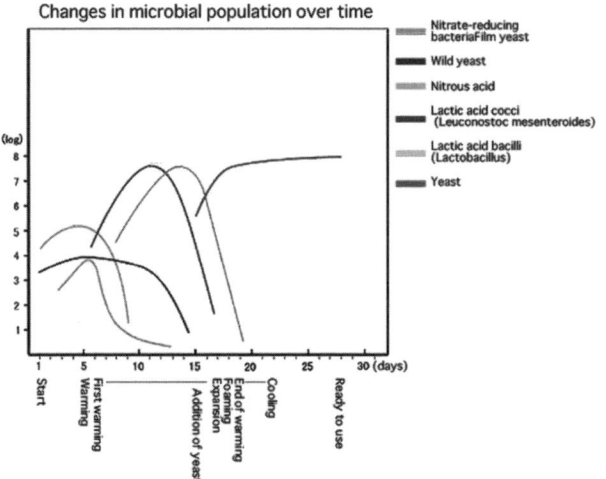

Figure 7. 'Changes in microbial population over time' in kimoto sake brewing (from Daishichi Sake Brewery <http://english.daishichi.com/theme_park/glaph2.html>).

These changes, which are observable to us at our own spatio-temporal scale of experience, suggest that similar changes may be happening in landscapes in *umwelten* of all kinds, including our own. It is often tempting, when struck by a landscape of some kind, to imagine it as timeless, existing unchanged 'since time immemorial'. This understanding of landscape is then often used variously, for example, to empty the landscape of history and human agency, a particularly political move when it concerns indigenous peoples, or to naturalize the landscape as the foundation of certain political projects.[15] Thinking about landscape with microbes reminds us that change is a part of landscapes at all scales, and so the question thus becomes not whether landscapes change, but how.

The work of the Mills lab in particular, as we have seen, dissolves certain distinctions, such as that between 'inside' and 'outside', often invoked in discussions of landscape – a boundary that often serves as a key hinge in longstanding debates in agricultural history, domestication, and nothing less than the histories of human civilizations.[16] Attending to microbes, and the agencies of non-humans in general, reconfigures other deep-seated distinctions, such as that particularly tough walnut: 'found' vs. 'made', 'natural' vs. 'cultural', and all its other guises. Once we concede that landscapes are always more-than-human, multispecies achievements, intersected with and emerging out of entangled *umwelts* all the way down, the question of whether a landscape is 'found' (i.e. 'natural', 'wild', raw, pristine, untouched by human hands) or 'made' (i.e. 'cultural', 'domesticated', realized or sullied by human presence) becomes much less thinkable, and certainly much less interesting, than the question of who made what and how.

Microbes are excellent companions for thinking landscape differently. They help us to see how humans are not necessarily always involved in making landscape, and that when they are, their agency is always involuted with the agencies of many others, living and non-living. This vision of the earth, in which humans are entangled with many other creatures and forces, indivisible from them yet never master of them, is one whose time is come, whose potential and potency in the time of the Anthropocene, when multiple possible futures for life on Earth present themselves with increasing urgency, we must feel as keenly and convivially and deliciously as possible.[17]

Notes

1. D.J. Haraway, *The Companion Species Manifesto: Dogs, People, and Significant Otherness* (Chicago: Prickly Paradigm Press, 2003).
2. J. Dubow, 'Landscape', in *International Encyclopedia of Human Geography*, ed. by Rob Kitchin and Nigel Thrift (Amsterdam: Elsevier, 2009), pp. 124-31.
3. J. Lorimer, 'Multinatural Geographies for the Anthropocene', *Progress in Human Geography*, 36.5 (2012), 593-612 <doi:10.1177/0309132511435352>.
4. Jakob von Uexküll, *A Foray Into the Worlds of Animals and Humans: With a Theory of Meaning* (Minneapolis: University of Minnesota Press, 2010).
5. Gilles Deleuze and Felix Guattari, *A Thousand Plateaus: Capitalism and Schizophrenia* (Minneapolis: University of Minnesota Press, 1987) <doi:10.1017/CCO9780511753657.008>; Jihai Gao, 'Deleuze's Conception of Desire', *Deleuze Studies*, 7.3 (2013), 406-20 <doi:10.3366/dls.2013.0120>.
6. Benedict Reade, Justine de Valicourt, and Josh Evans, 'Fermentation Art and Science at the Nordic Food Lab', in *The Routledge Handbook of Sustainable Food and Gastronomy*, ed. by Philip Sloan, Willy Legrand, and Clare Hindley (London: Routledge, 2015), pp. 228-42 <doi:10.4324/9780203795699>.
7. Josh Evans, 'Faux Foie', *Nordic Food Lab*, 2016 <http://nordicfoodlab.org/blog/2016/3/14/faux-foie> [accessed 15 June 2017].

8. Benjamin E. Wolfe and others, 'Cheese Rind Communities Provide Tractable Systems for in Situ and in Vitro Studies of Microbial Diversity', *Cell*, 158.2 (2014), 422-33 <doi:10.1016/j.cell.2014.05.041>.
9. Nicholas A. Bokulich and others, 'A New Perspective on Microbial Landscapes within Food Production', *Current Opinion in Biotechnology*, 37 (2016), 182-89 <doi:10.1016/j.copbio.2015.12.008>.
10. R. Mortimer and M. Polsinelli, 'On the Origins of Wine Yeast', *Research in Microbiology* 150.3 (1999), 199-204 <doi:10.1016/S0923-2508(99)80036-9>.
11. D.J. Haraway, *When Species Meet* (Minneapolis: University of Minnesota Press, 2008); D.J. Haraway, *Staying with the Trouble: Making Kin in the Chthulucene* (Durham: Duke University Press, 2016).
12. J. Lorimer and others, 'Making the Microbiome Public: Participatory Experiments with DNA Sequencing in Domestic Kitchens' *Transactions of the Institute of British Geographers*, forthcoming 2018.
13. Cynthia Graber and Nicola Twilley, 'Secrets of Sourdough', *Gastropod*, 18 December 2017 <https://gastropod.com/secrets-of-sourdough/> [accessed 20 March 2018].
14. 'The Definitive Kimoto Brewing Compendium', Daishichi Sake Brewey <http://www.daishichi.com/english/theme_park/glaph2.html> [accessed 15 June 2017].
15. Mark David Spence, *Dispossessing the Wilderness: Indian Removal and the Making of the National Parks* (Oxford: Oxford University Press, 1999) <doi:10.1093/acprof:oso/9780195142433.001.0001>; Nancy J. Turner, '"Time to Burn": Traditional Use of Fire to Enhance Resource Production by Aboriginal Peoples in British Columbia', in *Indians, Fire, and the Land in the Pacific Northwest*, ed. by Robert Boyd (Corvallis: Oregon State University Press, 1999), pp. 185-218; Brenda Beckwith, '"The Queen Root of This Clime": Ethnoecological Investigations of Blue Camas and Its Landscapes on Southern Vancouver Island, British Columbia' (unpublished doctoral dissertation, University of Victoria, 2004); D. Deur and N.J. Turner, *Keeping It Living: Traditions of Plant Use and Cultivation on the Northwest Coast of North America* (Seattle: University of Washington Press, 2005); Bill Gammage, *The Biggest Estate on Earth: How Aborigines Made Australia* (Crows Nest, NSW: Allen and Unwin, 2011); Joshua Evans, 'Found Land or Made Land? Indigenous Cultivation and the Politics of Conservation in the Pacific Northwest of North America, 1778–2017' (unpublished master's thesis, University of Cambridge, 2017).
16. I. Hodder, *The Domestication of Europe* (New York: Wiley, 1991); Helen M. Leach, 'Human Domestication Reconsidered', *Current Anthropology* 44.3 (2003), 349-68 <doi:10.1086/368119>; *Where the Wild Things Are Now: Domestication Reconsidered*, ed. by Rebecca Cassidy and Molly Mullin (Oxford: Berg, 2007).
17. On the Anthropocene, the proposed new geologic epoch, justified by human traces in the stratigraphic record, in which humanity has become a planetary force, see: Paul J. Crutzen and Eugene F. Stoermer, 'The Anthropocene', *Global Change Newsletter*, 41 (2000), 17-18 <http://www.igbp.net/publications/globalchangemagazine/globalchangemagazine/globalchangenewslettersno4159.5.5831d9ad1327 5d51c098000309.html> [accessed 15 June 2017]; Lorimer, 'Multinatural Geographies'; D.J. Haraway, 'Anthropocene, Capitalocene, Plantationocene, Chthulucene: Making Kin', *Environmental Humanities* 6 (2015), 159-65; Lorimer, 'The Anthropo-Scene: A Guide for the Perplexed', *Social Studies of Science*, 47.1 (2016), 117-42 <doi:10.1177/0306312716671039>). For further development of this idea, what Kelly Donati calls 'multispecies gastronomy', see her 'The Convivial Table: Imagining Ethical Relations through Multispecies Gastronomy', *The Aristologist* 4 (2014), 127-43 and 'Towards a Multispecies Gastronomy: Stories of More-than-Human Entanglements on Small Farms in Victoria, Australia' (unpublished doctoral dissertation, University of Melbourne, 2016).

The Future Belongs to the Gourmet

Colin Tudge

Shocking though it is and incredible though it may seem, it is an eminently sad and chastening fact that the world's agricultural strategy is based on untruth – misconceptions and/or lies – as anyone can check for themselves by browsing through the stats that are freely available on Google.

Thus we were told in a British government 'Foresight' report of 2011, *The Future of Food and Farming*, that the world will need to produce 50% more food by 2050 just to keep pace with rising numbers and the increasing 'demand' among richer people for higher standards, and, in particular, their 'demand' for more meat. We need, therefore, we're still being told, to focus on production and more production – ever-increasing forever, it seems. Already we have cereals that average ten tonnes or more per hectare (at least three times the yield of a century ago); cows that routinely give 2000 gallons (10,000 litres) per lactation, which is about six times more than a wild, ancestral cow would provide to feed her calf; chickens that reach slaughter weight six weeks from hatching; and so on. After all, the UN tells us that a billion people out of the present seven or so billion are chronically undernourished – and numbers continue to rise – so it stands to reason that we need more food, and urgently. Doesn't it?

The truth, though, is very different. As Professor Hans Herren, President of the Millennium Institute, Washington DC, is forever pointing out, the world already produces enough to feed fourteen billion people – a claim that I will explain later. Thus we already produce enough to feed twice the present population, and since the UN demographers tell us that world numbers should level out at something below ten billion before the end of the century, that is 40% more than we should ever need. As for rising demand, and particularly the alleged 'demand' for meat, that is largely specious. People newly emerging from poverty do tend to eat more meat. But among people who are used to wealth it is chic these days to do without meat altogether. California and Germany are the global epicentres of vegetarianism. In food, as in most other things, social pressure rules – custom, tradition, fashion, the desire for kudos, and to be seen to belong. In human beings, as opposed to lions, there is no strong evidence of innate, irrepressible carnivory.

We are also told that all this extra food we are supposed to need can be supplied only by high technology, including GMOs produced by genetic engineering, and – the *coup-de-grace* – we are further given to understand that only the corporates have the wherewithal to supply the high-tech food that we need. Governments like Britain's have embraced and promulgate this idea, but then governments like Britain's can increasingly be seen as extensions of the corporate boardroom. In truth, most of the world's food is still supplied by small farmers who are not at all beholden to corporates, though they often suffer at their hands. Indeed our best strategy if we really want more food is to support the small farmers who have huge untapped capacity, rather than to throw yet more wealth (in the form of subsidies and tax breaks) at the corporates, who are already hard up against the ecological limits of productivity and rely on methods, including 'factory farms', that damage the biosphere, are often cruel (well beyond the bounds of acceptability), and are in various ways socially undesirable.

Yet agriculture – complemented by true food culture – is the most important thing that human beings do. If farming faltered people would die en masse within days and only a minority would survive much more than a month or so. Farming is the world's biggest industry and by far the biggest employer. It occupies a third of all land on Earth and has already gobbled up most of the world's most fertile land. Thus it sits right at the heart of all the world's affairs, affecting everything else that we do and affected by everything else that we do. The fate of other species depends absolutely on how we to choose to farm. The cause of wildlife conservation is almost dead in the water unless agriculture is wildlife-friendly. Inappropriate farming is at the root, and in some cases is the prime cause, of almost all of the world's current disasters – political, economic, social, and ecological.

Farming, in short, is the thing above all that we absolutely have to get right – yet in practice, in much of the world and perhaps especially among the countries that are seen as the world's trend-setters, it is the thing we are getting the most wrong. And the wrong-headedness comes from the top: from the oligarchy of big governments, corporates, and their chosen academic advisers that dominates our lives. Agriculture cries out for transformation, with all possible urgency. But the powers-that-be seem content with the status quo, and with their own munificence and wisdom.

At first sight, wholesale transformation seems impossible. Over the whole world, at all levels, the food chain 'from farm to fork', as the expression has it, seems to be sewn up. Much if not most of the world's most fertile land is owned or otherwise controlled by a rich few who on the whole have only their own interests at heart – not necessarily because they are bad people but because the idea has got around that universal self-interest is somehow good for the world (which surely is not what Adam Smith, who started this particular hare in the eighteenth century, intended). Increasingly, all the primary components of the food chain from seed to supermarket are controlled by an ever-dwindling shortlist of transnational corporates, supported by the world's most powerful governments, and some at least of the corporates themselves are now as powerful as almost any government and far more powerful than most.

Despite all this there are chinks of hope.

Enlightened Agriculture and the Agrarian Renaissance

All we really need to do to turn things round is to introduce what I am calling Enlightened

Agriculture, also known as Real Farming. Enlightened agriculture is informally but adequately defined as: 'Farming that is expressly designed to provide everyone who is liable to be born onto this Earth with food of the highest quality, nutritionally and gastronomically, without cruelty or injustice, and without wrecking the rest of the world.'

This goal – good food for everyone forever, in a secure and convivial world – is eminently achievable, even at this late hour. To achieve this, though, we have to remove or better still to bypass the oligarchy and take matters into our own hands. The good news is that this is already happening. All over the world many thousands of organizations, many millions of farmers, distributors, cooks, restaurateurs, and people at large are starting to do things differently. If only those people were better coordinated, we would already have a critical mass able to put the world's food supply onto a new footing. Overall, we need nothing less than an Agrarian Renaissance, based on the idea of Enlightened Agriculture, and led by people at large. This, at least in primordial form, is already in train.

Enlightened Agriculture (EA) has three essential components:

- Agroecology
- Food Sovereignty
- Green Economic Democracy

I lay claim to the expression 'Enlightened Agriculture', but its three essential components were dreamed up by others and are now widely accepted – although, of course, since they are rooted in good sense, rather than the simple desire to maximize wealth, they are not mainstream.

The idea behind agroecology is to design individual farms as ecosystems and to treat agriculture as a whole as a positive contributor to the biosphere, insofar as this is possible. In essence, this means that farming should emulate nature. After all, we need agriculture to be productive – though not maximally so, since we already have more than enough. Rather, we need perhaps above all to acknowledge that enough really is enough. We also need farming to be sustainable – we should be able to go on farming the same land for indefinite periods of time without it losing fertility, and preferably it should become more fertile as the years and decades pass. Thirdly, farming has to be resilient. We should be able to continue farming in one form or another however the conditions change – we know that the climate is changing, and climate is all important. Nature does some bad things from our point of view (hurricanes, tsunamis, volcanoes), but much more to the point the biosphere has been impressively productive without interruption for almost four billion years even though the climate and the landscape have changed beyond imagining in that time, from pole-to-pole tropics (almost) to pole-to-pole ice (almost) and back again, several times – proof if ever there was that nature is eminently sustainable and resilient. How does nature achieve this?

By three main tricks, is the answer. First, wild nature above all is diverse. Except in a few special and extreme environments – bogs of *Sphagnum* moss, boreal forest – there are typically thousands of species in any one ecosystem, and there are always thousands in any one ecosystem if we include microbes, which we should, because they are key players in all ecosystems. Among other things, this diversity is perhaps the best possible defence against epidemic. A parasite that takes hold in any one individual animal or plant is likely to find that the creature next to it is of a different type (a different species, or at least a different genotype) and that it just isn't possible simply to hop from one to the other.

Secondly, on the whole, wild ecosystems are low-input. In truth, all natural ecosystems have leaky boundaries. All spread some of their largesse (as well as their pests and parasites) to other ecosystems, and all borrow from other ecosystems. Notably, most terrestrial creatures extract oxygen from the air, and at least half of that oxygen is generated by diatoms and other photosynthesizing organisms that live in the oceans. Some wild ecosystems, as in estuaries or in places where animals congregate, are bombarded with nutrients from the surrounding territory and are extremely nutrient-rich. But most wild ecosystems rely on what the ecosystem itself provides. In most ecosystems, therefore, fertility is middling to low (at least by the standards of industrial farming) – but, as we can see from the general abundance of nature, it is enough for most purposes.

Thirdly, the creatures that share any one ecosystem interact, so the system as a whole is integrated. The individual members of integrated, diverse ecosystems benefit from all kinds of synergies and between them make far better use of the available nutrients than any one species can do alone.

So how do these fundamental ecological principles – diverse, low-input, integrated – translate into farming practice? Diversity and the need for integration obviously lead us to the mixed farm. Different species of livestock and crops all interact as in the traditional English systems where, for example, whey from dairy cows fed the pigs – or the fabulous rice-carp-duck paddy-fields of SE Asia, with horticulture, chickens, and pigs on the higher ground, and water-buffalo to plough, add fertility, give milk, and, eventually, beef. In these traditional systems, each kind of animal or plant is usually genetically diverse – in sharp contrast to modern crops and livestock that are bred to be uniform. Low-input farming generally means organic farming designed to avoid the use of artificial fertilizers, herbicides, or pesticides. Extra fertility is supplied only by manure, various forms of compost, and/or by nitrogen fixation by bacteria in the roots of leguminous plants, like peas or beans, and in some non-leguminous plants like alder, or, in the paddy-fields of Asia, by cyanobacteria within the leaves of the floating ferns known as *Azolla*.

Diverse, organic farms are complex. Complexity is one of their virtues – as in nature. Complex systems need plenty of hands-on farmers and growers – not armies of slaves to do the work of tractors, but craftspeople, with skill, using all available and affordable technologies but not, as now, beholden to machinery and industrial chemistry. Britain right now could do with about eight times as many farmers as it has. A million more for starters would be good. When farms – or enterprises of any kind – are complex and skills-intensive there is little or no advantage in scale-up. Thus the kind of farms that could deliver what we want – ecologically sound, sustainable, resilient, and at least adequately productive – should generally be small to medium-sized.

The expression 'food sovereignty' – the second key component of Enlightened Agriculture – was coined in the 1990s by the world's peasant movement, *La Via Campesina*.

Food and Landscape

The concept of food sovereignty seems complex when formally defined but is essentially straightforward: every society should control its own food supply. This is far easier if the farms are small and mixed and therefore able to supply local markets and thus serve local communities. *La Via Campesina* is represented in Britain in the Landworkers' Alliance.

The third essential ingredient, 'green economic democracy' is a variation on a theme of social democracy. The economy is mixed: some public (government) ownership, some private ownership (but no corporates!), and a great deal of community ownership including ownership by cooperatives – an element that has been far too little emphasized up to now. Overall the economy must be designed to serve the best interests of people at large, while 'green' of course means that we must take due care of the biosphere too. The present economy, the allegedly 'free' market and finance capitalism, is designed by rich people to make rich people richer. Systems that would not make fat cats fatter are deemed to be 'unrealistic'. The present system which does make fat cats fatter is deemed realistic even though it has made a miserable world and threatens to kill us all.

The present approach to agriculture – though promoted by governments like ours, by big industry, and by those sections of academe that have chosen to put their intelligence and expertise behind these powers – is not designed to look after people at large, our fellow creatures, and the fabric of the Earth. As I have often discovered first-hand, leading players among the oligarchy tend to argue, self-righteously, that this utopian dream is merely whimsical, an elitist exercise in nostalgia affordable only by the well-endowed. Instead, they argue, agriculture should be treated as 'a business like any other' (a chilling expression I first heard in the 1970s). Like all businesses in the modern, market-driven economy, farming must compete with all other businesses of all kinds (weapons of war, hairdressing) and strive to be as profitable as possible. So long as oil is available and affordable and the economy is controlled by those with most wealth, it is generally most profitable to replace labour with technology – big machines, industrial chemistry, and biotech, all practiced on the largest possible scale. Polyculture is replaced by monoculture – big machines don't do complexity. Big monocultures in turn require large-scale processing units and an ever-more labyrinthine food chain to turn their produce – cane sugar, rape-oil, soya, maize – into recognizable food. This is said to be 'efficient' since efficiency is measured only in terms of (cash) output per worker, but biologically it is anything but efficient, and socially and ecologically it makes no sense at all. Even though this kind of mega-scale, high-tech farming is not the norm worldwide (most farmers are more traditional, and 70% of the world's farms are one hectare or less) and is novel (its first hints date only to the early nineteenth century), it is commonly called 'conventional' (a very strange and non-historical use of words). In truth, what is now called 'conventional' agriculture should be called 'Neoliberal-Industrial', or NI agriculture. This is the term that I have adopted.

Food as Commodity – or National Self-Reliance?
Monocultures cannot feed local populations, because people cannot live on cane sugar, or soya, or maize, or rapeseed, alone. So long as the world relies on monocultures, therefore,

The Future Belongs to the Gourmet

it must depend absolutely on trade, and, since agriculture in the modern economy is conceived as a global business, the trade must be global too. The farmers who preside over monocultures in poor countries as well as rich must therefore regard their crops not as food for the populace, but as commodities to be traded on the global market; it follows that the requirement is to increase production (a bigger "market share") by the cheapest possible means. As long as oil is available and affordable, the cheapest course is to replace clamorous labour with big machines (the bigger the better), industrial chemistry, and biotech. This 'industrialization' continues until the dispossessed and disenfranchised ex-farmers and farm workers are desperate enough to accept slave wages, whereupon they are hired en masse to do the fiddly jobs that machines find difficult. So it is, as Paul Mason points out in *Postcapitalism* (Allen Lane, 2015), that the big, capital-intensive machines for cleaning cars that were so popular in the 1980s are now giving way to gangs of East Europeans with buckets and sponges. So it is too, as Felicity Lawrence has courageously described in various books and articles, that Britain's farming to a large extent now relies on armies of East Europeans and others of conveniently dubious status to pick fruit and pack vegetables and so on in centralized distribution centres. So it is too that, according to the United Nations, a billion people now live in urban slums – one in seven of us all – and it seems a fair bet that many of them are ex-farmers and farm workers and their families and immediate descendants.

Furthermore, globalized production and commodification makes more and more countries more and more dependent on trade and therefore on the good offices of other countries. Obviously trade is crucially important for providing things that we can't easily produce ourselves and for cementing international relationships. But it is not good at all if it leads countries to abandon ecologically sound, mixed farming to make way for commodity crops, and it is not good if the trading partners are unequal, so that one can bully the other. Then, as indeed has been the norm for the past few hundred years, we finish up with a world of empires and banana republics.

Britain has always been a trading nation with a powerful navy, and since the Thatcher government of the 1980s it has aspired to become the world's exemplar of neoliberalism. Successive British governments, of all parties, have been content to root the economy in whatever is most profitable at the time, thus shifting attention from enterprises that actually produce things – manufacture and farming – to 'service industries', of which the chief by far is banking in all its acceptable and not-so acceptable forms. Farming has been the poor relation for the past two hundred years – ever since we began to import significant quantities of wheat, our principal staple – from the Americas. In general, governments have allowed British farming to sink or swim – except in times of blockade, when they were forced to take it seriously, and in the immediate aftermath: during and after the Napoleonic wars, and then again in and immediately after the First and Second World Wars. So it was that British farmers enjoyed something of a golden age in the 1950s and 1960s, but by the 1970s, with memories fading, we started shifting back to a more money-oriented business model ('a business like any other').

So it is too that Britain now produces only 60% of its own food – confident that as a trading nation and as a one-time world power we will always have enough wealth to import what we don't grow ourselves and enough clout to persuade other people with more sunshine and cheaper labour to grow our food for us. I am reliably informed by a former senior civil servant that Tony Blair's government toyed seriously with the idea that it would be good for Britain to abandon farming altogether – to let it go the way of its mining. I suspect that this didn't happen mainly because too many people in high places, not least in the House of Lords, have interests in the land.

In truth, from a short-term, purely financial point of view it might be advantageous for Britain to give up farming and import what it needs from Spain, or Israel, or the US, or New Zealand, or Brazil, or East Timor, or China – or indeed from whoever could supply us most cheaply. Since elections seem largely to be won by whoever promises short-term economic gain this approach might even help the party that recommended such a course get into power, which for some politicians is all that seems to matter. But from every other point of view – ecological, social, aesthetic, spiritual, and, in the longer term, political and economic – it makes far more sense for every country in the world, including Britain, to adopt the methods and the rationale of agroecology and to seek, as far as possible, to be self-reliant in food.

'Self-reliance' does not mean self-sufficiency. Self-reliance means that a country – every country! – should strive to produce as much of the foods it grows well to ensure that its people can at least get by in times of stress, including times of blockade. Self-sufficiency means that a country produces absolutely everything that it could ever need or want.

Almost all countries could be self-reliant. Only a few, like Monaco or Singapore, with many more people than land to support them, would probably find self-reliance wellnigh impossible. Britain could easily produce enough temperate crops (cereal, pulses, tubers, vegetables, fruit, pasture-fed cattle and sheep and pigs, and poultry fed on leftovers and surpluses) to feed ourselves well, without any imports at all. But we could not reasonably be self-sufficient. We could not sensibly grow enough coffee or oranges, which we certainly find desirable even if they are not exactly essential. Only a few large and otherwise privileged countries in the right latitudes – like the US, Brazil, India, China, Australia, and perhaps New Zealand – could truly be self-sufficient, if they wanted to be.

So, I suggest, a sensible global strategy for food would be for (almost) every country to strive for self-reliance, which most could achieve very comfortably (including most of the poor countries of Africa which periodically crop up on western news channels as disaster areas). Emphatically, though, this would not mean the end of trade. All countries that have agriculture at all should trade in food to some extent for reasons of security (crops may always fail in any one country at any one time), of diplomacy (countries are more likely to form cordial relationships with trading partners), and to fill in the gaps (Britain need not go without coffee just because we can't easily grow it).

It's important, though, that all trade really is fair – fair to the growers and the local wildlife and landscape. Neoliberal thinking, and centuries of imperialist thinking before that, impelled traders and the companies and governments that employed them simply to pay as little as possible for as much as possible, irrespective of the damage to people and places and the biosphere. Among the most foul ads on television is the one in which 'the man from del Monte, he say yes!'. If 'he say yes!', then the family that grows peaches or mandarins or whatever can survive for another year, albeit barely. What happens to the family and the region when the man from del Monte or Tesco or wherever 'say No!' – perhaps for reasons that have nothing to do with the quality of the produce and everything to do with the company's immediate need to balance its own books?

Again, then, on the grandest scale as well as in all matters of detail, 'official' strategy is at odds with what is sensible and morally acceptable. The world as a whole in all contexts needs to be guided by bedrock principles of morality and ecology. But in the global food trade these principles are not simply flouted. They are not even on the agenda.

But can enlightened agriculture – rooted in agroecology – really deliver?

A key issue, of course, is meat: livestock.

Meat

Vegans argue on grounds of nutrition, morality, spirituality, and ecology that we should not eat animals and certainly should not raise them specifically for meat. They point out that we can (very roughly) produce ten times as much protein and energy per hectare by growing cereals than we could by grazing cattle or sheep on the same land, and that we feed about half the cereal that we grow (and more than 90% of the soya) to animals. Since we could eat cereals and soya ourselves this is a terrible waste. Cereal-fed – industrially fed – livestock competes with us. By 2050, if livestock production continues to increase as it is at present, our domestic beasts will be eating enough staple crops to sustain four billion people – roughly equal to the world population of the 1970s when Henry Kissinger persuaded the UN to convene the first ever World Food Conference, in Rome, to discuss what was already seen as a global food crisis. The vegans' arguments are broadly correct – but with some large and important conditional clauses.

In contrast, the industrialists argue that we need to produce loads of meat because people need animal protein and – which to modern neoliberals is the key argument! – because people demand meat and it is the democratic duty of big industry to give people what they want. They claim too that we can produce vast quantities of meat only if we devote large resources to it, including vast quantities of cereals produced with the aid of agrochemistry. This argument too is true as far as it goes – we can't maximize meat production without feeding concentrates sustained by agrochemistry. But for many different reasons including welfare and sustainability, the pressure to maximize meat output is undesirable, not to say insane.

Curiously, although the vegans and the industrialists seem to be on opposite sides, to some extent they agree. They both believe that livestock should not be kept in traditional ways: sheep and cattle fed on natural pasture, and pigs and poultry fed on leftovers and surpluses. Vegans simply argue that we should not be keeping animals at all, while the industrialists argue that the only sensible ('efficient', profitable) way to raise them is on concentrate.

In truth, the moral and metaphysical arguments raised by the vegans are powerful. Most cogently they ask – as we all should ask – do we really have the right to raise and slaughter sentient fellow creatures for our own convenience and pleasure? I think the general answer should be no, but if we want to feed ourselves with least harm to the rest we are more or less forced to keep at least some animals for ecological reasons. In other words, if we want to do least harm to the planet as a whole, then mixed farming, and/or sheep and cattle on pasture, is better than none at all. Livestock farming therefore is not good, morally, but – if done properly! – it is the least bad of our options.

For the ecological case for veganism, which is sometimes presented as the clincher, doesn't stand up to close scrutiny. An all-plant agriculture – just arable and/or horticulture – can always be made more productive and more resilient by the judicious addition of a few appropriate animals: using pigs and poultry to cultivate and manure the ground, to eat weeds and parasites, and to mop up surpluses. Cattle and sheep can and should be raised on land that is too steep or wet or dry or cold to raise crops reliably – on steppe and mountain, in semi-desert and marsh, and in open woodland that is also rich in wildlife (all common domestic animals apart from sheep and goats are mainly forest creatures). When properly managed, such 'extensive' livestock production can be wildlife friendly; not as much, perhaps, as pristine woodland, but if we did things properly then we would have room both for extensive farming and for some pristine woodland. If we kept all our livestock in traditional ways then we would not produce the vast quantities of meat that we do now, but we would certainly produce some.

Here is where we run into a series of serendipities.

Enlightened Agriculture, Sound Nutrition, and Great Cooking

If we practiced enlightened agriculture – led by agroecology – and aspired to self-reliance fuelled by small (usually), mixed, organic farms, we would thereby produce plenty of plants, not much meat, and maximum variety.

These nine words – plenty of plants, not much meat, and maximum variety – more or less summarize the best of nutritional theory of the past sixty years. For whereas in the 1950s and 1960s nutritionists argued that human beings need loads of protein and that only animal protein will do, they began to change their minds in the 1970s and concluded, first, that healthy adults at least need only modest intakes of protein. Indeed in the 1950s and 1960s some nutritionists argued that to be on the safe side total protein intake should be equivalent to 15% of total calorie intake; but in the 1970s some nutritionists were saying that, unless people are growing rapidly or pregnant or otherwise stressed, 5% or even less is probably enough. (I wrote a lot about nutrition in those days and watched this transformation taking place.)

This single insight changes everything. For when nutritionists thought that human beings need a lot of protein – and 'first class' protein at that – it seemed that we had to eat meat. Providing large amounts of nutritionally necessary meat seemed to justify intensive livestock production, based on barley, maize, and 'concentrate' in the form largely of soya. That such an approach could also be enormously profitable reinforced the convenient idea that what is good for business must also be good for the human race (as in 'What's good for General Motors is good for the USA'). But the new assessments in the 1970s suggested that since cereals in general are about 8% protein they contain all the protein needed by a healthy adult. Cereals tend to be low in the essential amino acid lysine, but pulses are rich in lysine, so cereals and pulses together seemed well-nigh perfect – hence dhal and chapatis, frijoles with tortillas, and beans on toast. The combination is universal. Suddenly it seemed that an all-plant diet was perfectly adequate – or at least, that the nutritional role of meat should primarily be to provide micro-nutrients like calcium and zinc, which are low in plants but could be supplied by the laboratory.

It also became clear that it should easily be possible to supply everyone with at least all the macronutrients they need (energy and protein) since we merely had to grow enough cereals and pulses – which we do already. Today the world produces about 2.5 billion tonnes of cereal per year; since one tonne provides enough energy and protein for three people, that's enough macronutrient to feed 7.5 billion people. Cereals, though, provide only about half the world's macronutrient – the rest comes from other kinds of seeds including oilseeds and nuts, tubers, fruits and vegetables, plus meat, dairy, and fish. Overall, then, we produce enough for perhaps 15 billion people. That is twice present numbers (as Hans Herren points out), and since the UN tells us that the human population should level out around 2050 at about 10 billion, it is at least 40% more than we should ever need. In other words, the continuing emphasis on production has nothing to do with need and everything to do with the profit of the people who control the food industry – and governments like ours who think it is their job to support whatever is most profitable. This crass strategy is obviously damaging ecologically and socially – so crass as to be cruel, maybe even wicked.

At the same time as nutritionists were curbing their enthusiasm for animal protein, an American epidemiologist called Ancel Keys was telling the world that the major epidemics of the affluent world – notably, coronary heart disease (CHD) – were largely caused by eating too much fat, particularly the hard, saturated body fats of animals. Later, various cancers including breast cancer were also blamed in large part on animal fat. There has been a huge amount of research on this since then, but in truth, sixty years later, it still isn't clear how fat intake is related to heart disease and cancers, and whether or to what extent its role is causal. All this shows, if nothing else, that with the best will in the world (and many millions of pounds of research money) what look like simply medical-biological problems can be devilishly hard to solve. It also suggests that those who claim to have the answer to our ills – suggesting either that we are still eating far too much fat or, contrariwise, that fat is a red herring – are running ahead of the evidence.

Indeed, in some ways the position doesn't seem to be much clearer than it was in 1976 when Britain's Royal College of Physicians, based on the available evidence, concluded that the best they could offer was 'the balance of probabilities', a legal phrase favoured in civil cases that depend on human judgement. Specifically, the physicians noted that northerners and rich southerners (like Australians) obtain about 40% of their calories from fat, mostly saturated animal fat; the traditional Mediterranean diet was only 20% fat, largely unsaturated, notably in the form of olive oil; while some Asians, often virtually vegan, obtained only about 10% of their calories from fat. But whereas northerners with their fatty diets were suffering a veritable epidemic of coronary heart disease, Neapolitans were almost free of it, and among Asians on traditional diets it was virtually unknown (though the Japanese suffered strokes because they ate too much salt, but that is another story).

So, largely on common-sense grounds, the physicians suggested that northerners should significantly reduce their 40% fat intake – not to the heroically low levels of some Asians or even to those of traditional southern Italians but at least to around 30%. For good measure, too, they said, we English and Scots and Finns and so on (Scots and Finns were the world leaders in CHD) should switch as far as possible from saturated animal fat to unsaturated plant oil. In particular, they emphasized polyunsaturated sunflower oil, although opinion since has shifted somewhat to the monounsaturated olive oil so common on Mediterranean tables.

But that is not the end of the story – for in truth, the story is never ending. All scientific theories no matter how well supported are always ripe for revision (which, some philosophers say, is what makes them scientific). For it now seems that the fat from pasture-fed animals has a far more favourable ratio of unsaturated to saturated fat than that from cereal-fed animals. Indeed, some say, the fat from pasture-fed animals may even be good rather than bad, providing yet another reason for grazing sheep and cattle on non-arable, as agroecologists recommend.

So what do we conclude? In his 2015 *The Diet Myth*, Tim Spector concludes, as the physicians did in the 1970s, that the picture is still uncertain. But he also suggests (as the physicians also did) that on balance it would probably be a good idea to veer towards a Mediterranean-style diet: cut down on total fat, switch as far as possible to sunflower and olive oil, and eat only pasture-fed beef and lamb and free-range chickens and pigs.

There is another giant caveat. For even before Ancel Keys started the fat story, way back in the 1950s, the British nutritionist John Yudkin declared, in *Pure, White and Deadly*, that sugars, not fats, were the prime cause of our troubles. Others extended the idea to include all refined carbohydrates, including starch, the main source of food energy from plants. For various reasons through the 1960s to the 1990s, the fat story began to hold sway, but now it seems that fat is partly vindicated and attention again has switched to sugar. Fructose – 'fruit sugar' – seems to be a major culprit and so therefore is sucrose – table sugar – which is compounded from fructose and glucose. No bona fide nutritionist these days seems to have a good word for sugar except as a modest condiment and – perhaps! – for people who need a quick energy boost. But the food industry continues to use mega-quantities both of sucrose and of fructose, even in ostensibly savoury sauces, and the sugar-beet industry in Europe continues to benefit from subsidies. After all, agricultural strategy must be focused on profit. What should farming have to do with human health?

The Future Belongs to the Gourmet

That is a different government department, with its own Secretary of State.

But while nutritional advice has turned away from sugar, which is refined carbohydrate, it has turned enthusiastically to fibre, which is unrefined carbohydrate (albeit sometimes in modified forms). Before the 1970s fibre was just called 'roughage' and assumed to be inert – good just for scouring the colon, which in turn was largely seen simply to be a conduit, a chute. But fibre for the most part is composed of plant cell walls, and it has long been known that chemically and physically complex plant cell walls have many and various effects on the colon; and the colon in turn is now known to be a complex organ with all kinds of functions, which directly or indirectly affects the whole body (and the state of mind).

Even more to the point, it has become abundantly clear that a prime function of fibre is to provide a substrate for gut microbes – and whereas the bacteria and archaes that live in vast numbers in the gut used to be regarded merely as spivs, hanging round for a free meal and occasionally causing trouble, they are now known to be key players, crucial for sound nutrition and smooth functioning. Indeed they have emerged as the universal intermediaries between our food and us. These days, as Tim Spector describes, good nutrition can be seen as an exercise in microbial ecology – keeping the gut microbes happy. Hence the modern interest in live yoghurts and so on. Hence, too, most bizarrely by the standards of fifty years ago, faecal implants – *soupçons* of poo taken from people who are known to have helpful gut microbes, as opposed to the ones that cause disease – are now seen to be therapeutic.

Finally, there is growing interest in what I have been calling 'cryptonutrients' – a host of different chemical agents present in food in minute quantities whose effects are very hard to measure (and may never be measured exhaustively). Among the few that have been identified are plant sterols, which seem to reduce blood cholesterol. This does not mean that plant sterols necessarily reduce the chances of heart disease, but it does suggest that they should be good rather than bad. Accordingly, plant sterols are now included in some margarines.

It seems to me, though, that the best way to ensure that we take in as wide a variety of cryptonutrients as possible is to eat a diet that is as varied as possible. Thus the last part of the nine-word formula makes perfect sense. We should seek maximum variety.

Still, though, defenders of the status quo object to all these new ideas. They seem to believe that a diet based on 'plenty of plants, not much meat, and maximum variety' would be too austere, too boring for the modern taste. Apart from trendy vegetarians, they note, most people demand more meat: they buy more and more of it when they can. Beijing, once awash with traditional restaurants centred on rice, now bristles with McDonald's burgers and fried chicken, since only now, after centuries of austerity, can the Chinese afford such goodies.

Yet again the truth is at odds with the conventional view. For in truth, the nine-word adage – plenty of plants, not much meat, and maximum variety – perfectly summarizes the basic structure of all the world's greatest cuisines from Italy to Southeast Asia. All are based on lots of locally grown cereal (mainly wheat or rice depending on latitude) supplemented by whatever fruit, nuts, vegetables, and herbs grow locally; in all cases meat (and offal and bones) are used sparingly – as garnish and stock – in large amounts for the occasional feast.

In fact, all we really need to do to feed ourselves well and heathily is to farm sensibly along largely traditional lines – and to re-learn how to cook! Again, this is the complete opposite of what the present power structure urges us to do.

Such a huge turnaround in food lore should lead to a huge turnaround in the economy and in governance, for it should be abundantly clear by now that the neoliberal economy and the thinking behind it are not fit for purpose – and neither is the top-down form of governance, dominated by the oligarchy, that is now the norm. The re-thinking and re-structuring that the world now so obviously needs must be led from the bottom up.

One highly intriguing aspect of all this is seen in science as a whole. Excellent science is of course essential, but it must be the servant of the people and not, as now, the hand-maiden of big-time commerce – and governments like ours that depend on big-time commerce. Science should take its lead from people at large and from groups who have a particular understanding of the things that really matter – including enlightened farmers and cooks. To some extent this is happening, and among other things it has led to a new appreciation of traditional wisdom and even folklore.

So it is that modern nutritional advice veers more and more closely towards folk wisdom.

The Absolute Importance of Traditional Wisdom

In the olden days we were told to eat what grows naturally. Now we know that advice accords perfectly with modern insights into gut microbes and cryptonutrients. Our gut biota and our general physiology have become adapted to the myriad products of nature to which we have been exposed over millions of years of evolution; they are not adapted to laboratory novelties. That it has sometimes been shown that those novelties do not cause cancer or general collywobbles in laboratory rats tells us little about their total effects on human beings.

In wondrous contrast to widespread warnings about germs, our grannies were also wont to tell us to eat a peck of dirt before you die. I confess I have met only two other people apart from myself – a fellow septuagenarian and an octogenarian – who remember this adage. It can of course be taken too far: hygiene still matters, and *E coli* and *Listeria* are always ready to pounce. But that old adage accords well with the advice to nourish and cultivate the gut biota (and indeed to keep the immune system on its toes).

We were also assured that a little of what you fancy does you good. Again this seems perfectly in line with most modern theory, including the advice to eat a diet as varied as possible. These days too zoologists and vets are very impressed by the phenomenon of pica, which prompts animals to seek out particular herbs and minerals that they know, by whatever means, will make them feel better. Thus enlightened zoo-keepers and farmers provide their charges with patches of herbs which, demonstrably, the animals seek out when they are feeling poorly (as revealed, for example, by loose stools or other symptoms). Land animals know when they are short of salt and may walk many miles to the nearest lick, as elephants and Arabian Oryx do; macaws stoke up on kaolin to sequestrate the toxins that perfuse the forest vegetation on which they feed. And so on.

Our elders, though, stressed a little of what you fancy because as Ralph Waldo Emerson advised we should practice moderation in all things, which seems pretty sound in most contexts and certainly in the context of food.

In short, taken all in all, there is perfect correspondence between agroecology, sound nutrition, and the world's greatest cuisines. If we want to be healthy, and really want to keep the world heathy, we have to take food seriously, valuing whatever grows, and has been grown, with tender loving care. In other words, the future belongs to the gourmet. This comes in sharpest contrast to what we have been told from on high, which is that if we want to survive in large numbers then we have to tighten our belts or live on the various kinds of ersatz, like the various kinds of 'textured vegetable protein' – textured, that is, to resemble the fibres of meat. Such putative life-savers can, of course, only be produced by high-tech food companies, and so we are invited once more to give thanks to the corporates for our salvation, and to our governments for so obligingly supporting them with our money.

Given that enlightened farming is skills-intensive, it would of course be a very good thing if about one in ten of the next generation opted to become farmers and growers so we can get the numbers back to where they need to be. But if we don't want to do that, then we should all re-learn the arts and crafts of cooking. This does not necessarily mean emulating the world's most famous chefs. In the history of the world, many millions of people were and still are great cooks, whether working in the tiny kitchens of far-flung cottages or in brass pots on the streets of Mumbai. Raymond Blanc is among the world-renowned chefs who emphasize the absolute importance of traditional cooking, which largely means peasant cooking. He learnt to cook at home, he says. So, surely, did many more. All truly great cooking is rooted in traditional cuisine.

The College for Real Farming and Food Culture

I have been thinking about the ideas in this article for about the past fifty years, and it has become abundantly clear to me that we cannot hope to put the world's food and farming to rights simply by focusing on food and farming. Nothing, in fact, can be put right *ad hoc*. We have to re-think and re-structure everything: the economy that shapes all we do (neoliberalism is particularly inappropriate), the kind of government we need (decidedly not of the top-down, neoliberal kind), and the underlying moral and indeed metaphysical assumptions that shape attitudes and prompt us and our governments to follow one course rather than another. With all this in mind I, my wife Ruth, and a few friends have set up the College for Real Farming and Food Culture in which the aim is to re-think the essential ingredients of life, and to re-think everything in the light of everything else. The College in turn is a project of the Real Farming Trust and so too is the Oxford Real Farming Conference, which began in 2010 and in January 2018 attracted 900 delegates over two days, of whom about half were farmers. Real change is possible.

Exploring *Aeroir*, or the Atmospheric Taste of Place

Nicola Twilley

This all began, as so many great things do, with Harold McGee.[1] Specifically, with a particular turn of phrase in his legendary book, *On Food and Cooking*, in the section dealing with egg foams. Seen through McGee's eyes, egg foams are nothing less than remarkable.

For starters, they're a rare example of physical agitation creating structure, rather than breaking it down. But, more pertinently for my purposes, McGee rather poetically points out that egg whites offer us a way to 'harvest the air' and make it an integral part of meringues and mousses, gin fizzes and soufflés. This is not simply a rhetorical flourish on McGee's part. After all, at the stiff peak stage, he says, an egg foam is approaching ninety per cent air.[2]

My friend and frequent collaborator, Zack Denfeld, read this particular section of McGee's book in 2011, while he was teaching in Bangalore. Denfeld is co-founder of the Center for Genomic Gastronomy, and if you're not already familiar with their work, you have a treat ahead of you when you Google them!

Overall, the air quality in Bangalore is pretty poor – it's not the worst in India, but it's not that great. Still, to Denfeld, it seemed noticeably better in some areas and worse in others. Denfeld read McGee's sentence and wondered whether it might be possible to use meringues to map the city's air quality. He assigned the sophomores he was teaching some homework: Go out to your local street corners or up to your roof, armed with a whisk, a bowl, some egg whites and some sugar, and whip it. Then take it back inside and bake your egg foam into a meringue, and then mail a batch to your local political representative.

Thus was born the smog meringue. As Denfeld wrote at the time, 'The tragedy of the commons never tasted so good!'

The smog meringue was, clearly, a stroke of genius. But it had one really obvious limitation, which was that you couldn't taste meringues from different places side by side very easily. In other words, you couldn't taste a Los Angeles smog meringue alongside a Beijing one, or at least not without some kind of astronomically expensive overnight FedEx situation.

And then I had an idea. I realized that smog scientists probably had a way of recreating smog in the lab to study it, because that's often what scientists do – there are simulated fun-sized volcanoes, lightning storms, and earthquakes in labs all over the world. Some quick Googling led me to the Bourns College of Engineering at the University of California, Riverside, home of the largest smog chambers in America. Riverside is a city immediately to the east of Los Angeles, downwind and up against the hills, so all the Angeleno smog blows in and piles up there.

Back in the 1950s, Arie Haagen-Smit, a flavour chemist based at UC Riverside, decided to study the smog's chemical composition. Before World War II, Haagen-Smit was known for his work on fruit flavours – pineapple, in particular. But, in the 1950s, as the inhabitants of Riverside – mostly farmers, at that time – began to complain about smog damage to their crops, rubber cracking on their car tires, and painful, watering eyes, Haagen-Smit turned his attention to what he came to call 'a super flavor problem – the flavor of Los Angeles'.[3]

Haagen-Smit had noticed that the Angeleno smog did not smell like the sulphurous coal-smoke smogs he remembered from his native Holland. Instead, it had a chlorine-y, bleach-like note. He decided to analyze its flavour chemistry, using the same set-up he used to analyze the volatile aroma molecules of pineapple: a series of freeze out traps that condensed the vapours into a concentrated liquid – an essence, of sorts – that his instruments could break into its constituent chemical parts.

When he performed this analysis on Los Angeles air, the result was a few drops of dark brown, poisonous-smelling liquid. But those few drops allowed him to identify the oxygenated organic molecules that told him that Los Angeles' distinctive smog contained ozone, rather than the sulphur typical of East Coast and European smogs. And that was the clue that allowed him to track down the culprit: partially combusted hydrocarbons from tailpipe emissions, oxidized by the Southern California sunshine.

With that first discovery, this renowned flavour chemist became the 'Father of Smog Science' and the first chair of the California Air Resources Board, which eventually put in place the emissions standards that have attempted to keep air pollution in Los Angeles under control ever since.

To study smog, Haagen-Smit and his colleagues at UC Riverside developed something called a smog chamber. The chamber allows scientists to recreate smog in a controlled environment, so that they can study the reactions that lead to its formation, analyze what happens when you reduce levels of certain chemicals, and so on. The smog forms in deflated Teflon bags, and the mirrored walls and bluish light are designed to simulate what happens in the atmosphere, when the sun's UV light hits all these gases and causes them to react.

In the middle of the bag is a port where researchers can inject the precursor chemicals that will react to form smog. This is an important detail; car exhaust on its own is not smog. Smog is a many-splendoured thing. You take the partially combusted hydrocarbons and nitrogen oxides from cars, you add the emissions from container ships in Long Beach Harbor, you throw in some dust and particulate matter, etc. – and these ingredients all combine and react with each other thanks to the water in the air and the UV light from the sun. The result of those reactions is this toxic mix called smog.

Food and Landscape

What this means is that when you want to recreate smog in the lab, it's actually quite like cooking: you have to reverse engineer a dish to develop your recipe, you have to combine all the ingredients in your vessel, and then you bake it under UV lamps for a certain amount of time, and – hey presto! – you've made smog.

Armed with this information, we decided to build our own smog synthesizer. We fabricated small Perspex chambers for the precursor ingredients, which we inject into a mirrored chamber above using bicycle pumps. We purchased a UV array that we sat on top of the chamber throughout the cooking time. And, of course, we had the meringue-whipping apparatus. Obviously, to whip the meringues we had to be able to reach inside the chamber, so we built gloves into one wall. This ended up being my favourite part of the smog synthesizer, because the only place we could find gloves that were long enough to allow us manoeuvre the whisk was at a sex shop. For the first few years of the smog synthesizer's existence, we had these vampy, above-the-elbow PVC gloves built into the chamber. They've just recently been replaced with real science gloves, because the PVC was cracked and flaking from exposure to the smog. Rubber cracking is a known effect of LA-style smogs, so that actually reassured us that we were indeed cooking up the real deal.

I've already talked about two different smog types: the sulphurous peasouper-style and the ozone-based Angeleno-style. In fact, atmospheric scientists classify smog into a variety of different types, based on the different precursor chemicals and prevailing weather conditions.

Peasouper-style smogs are based on coal-burning fires and power plant emissions and a damp atmosphere – these are the smogs found in 1950s London and today's Beijing. They taste sulphurously eggy and gritty, and they leave your mouth feeling dirty.

Meanwhile, 1960s Los Angeles was characterized by its photochemical smog. You can find that in Mexico City or Buenos Aires today. On the nose, it has a distinctive aroma of cleaning fluids. Another classic type is the Atlanta-style smog, in which anthropogenic precursors mix with emissions from biological sources to form a unique smog. Atlanta has the same levels of nitrogen oxides, sunlight, and hydrocarbons as Los Angeles, historically, but an estimated ten per cent of the city's emissions are in the form of terpenes – volatile chemicals discharged by the region's abundance of pine trees and decaying green matter. As a result, an Atlanta smog is similar in composition to that of Los Angeles, but with the addition of biogenic emissions. The difference is subtle, but, sampled side-by-side, there is a distinctive mulchy note to an Atlanta smog.

Finally, at least among the classical smog types, there's 'ag smog', a distinctive, alkaline smog formed from the amines and ammonia in livestock emissions and manure lagoon off-gassing. This combination is responsible for giving towns in California's Central Valley the worst air quality in America, and it tastes of ammonia with a slightly fishy note.

In the lab, scientists inject the particular gases and particulate matter required for their recipe using nozzles, and then cook them to form a synthetic smog that simulates the average atmosphere of the city they are studying. Unfortunately, Amazon doesn't sell NOx or amines. Fortunately, scientists at UC Riverside helped us come up with make-at-home recipes. We used pine needles and orange peel as a terpene source; we made our own NOx by dissolving copper wire in concentrated nitric acid; and we left a fish out to rot to produce amines. I even hand-harvested particulate matter from my roof deck in Brooklyn, which happens to be conveniently adjacent to one of Robert Moses's famously neighbourhood-destroying freeways, and only a block from one of the most polluted sites in America, the Gowanus Canal.

Imagine our delight when we pumped the precursors into our smog chamber and baked it under UV light, following the scientists' instructions, and were rewarded with our own private smogs! Ecstatic, we beat the smog into our egg whites and sugar. (At this point I should probably say that I don't actually recommend trying this at home; I still owe everyone who lives in my building a huge apology.) The next day, we served our smog meringues – four flavours, incorporating the four different classical smog varieties – as part of the New Museum's annual street festival in New York. The festival organizers had put us next to all the artisanal food vendors, rather than with the other artists. We had hipster Vietnamese sandwiches on one side and savoury popsicles on the other, and we were serving smog meringues in between, which was perfect.

Although this might seem like a fairly frivolous art project, we did have a serious goal. The smog meringue, for us, is a Trojan treat. By transforming the largely unconscious process of breathing to the conscious act of eating, our hope was that we could make people think about a mostly invisible but increasingly serious problem. Outdoor air pollution has grown by eight per cent globally in the past five years, to the point that the World Health Organization now estimates that it is the world's number one preventable cause of death. It kills more people than smoking, more than road accidents – more, even, than wars. Air pollution causes heart disease and lung disease; it's been linked with dementia and Alzheimer's. And, as with so many of these things, there's a huge inequity: the worst air quality is often found in the poorest neighbourhoods and in the developing world.[4]

The problem is that this problem is largely invisible. Yes, on the worst days in Beijing, smog is visible. In fact, smog is the only thing you can see on those days. But most of the time, for most people, air pollution doesn't seem like a problem. We can't see it and we can't taste it and we don't realize it's there. But it is. In the UK, around 40,000 people die prematurely each year from illnesses associated with air pollution. The public health costs have been estimated at £20bn a year.[5] Large parts of London overshot the annual air pollution limit for the whole of 2017 in the first five days of the year.[6]

Our goal in building this smog-synthesizer cart was to create a visceral, thought-provoking interaction with the air all around us. People have to breathe, but eating is a choice, and making that shift is powerful. The most frequently asked question when we serve these meringues has been: 'Is this safe to eat?' Our usual response is, 'Well, is it safe to breathe?'

Meanwhile, when we discuss the flavour notes of a smog meringue, we give people a framework to think about the smell and taste of their city's air – and to wake up to the fact that that taste is due to the ingredients they are putting into it.

Ultimately, the smog meringue is a provocation. We've taken it to the Paris climate talks, to the World Health Organization, and to museums and festivals around the world. (During the Symposium, the cart was in Dublin, at the Science Gallery there, so symposiasts were spared the opportunity to taste smog meringues for themselves.)

Once we started thinking in this way, about the different flavours of air, or what we came to call *aeroir*, we realized the smog meringue was just the tip of the iceberg. Could we taste place in the form of urban atmospheres, too? And would doing that change our relationship with the atmosphere?

Aeroir is a neologism, obviously. I began writing about it in 2015, and haven't yet found an earlier usage. As Tom Parker's symposium paper shows, *terroir*, as a concept, has a long and fascinating history – it's been used to construct identity, to unify, to divide, to denigrate, and to elevate. Most recently, it's been used to talk about how food – first wine, but now cheese, coffee, chocolate, and more – expresses the physical and social environment in which it is grown and produced through its unique flavour profile. Food journalist Greg Atkinson and oyster promoter Jon Rowley coined the term *meroir* in *The Seattle Times* in 2003, to discuss the way in which oysters expressed the varying tastes of the sea.[7] *Aeroir* seemed like the obvious next step.

Now, you might say: *terroir* is the complete environment in which a food is produced, including the climate and weather. Why do we need a separate word for the flavours imparted by the atmosphere?

Of course, we don't. My only defence of *aeroir* is that, thus far, it has acted as a useful framework to open up new ways of thinking. A recent commission from the Headlands Center for the Arts in the Bay Area of California allowed us to begin to explore some of those ideas. We were charged with putting together a multi-course *aeroir* tasting menu, and, as we continued our research, we looked at the notorious Bay Area fog, which is enough of a celebrity in its own right that it has its own Twitter account. By the 1980s, thanks to industrial pollution and car exhaust, San Francisco's fog had become more acidic than acid rain – indeed, on the worst days, it was more acidic than toilet bowl cleaner. So, we began the evening by serving a cabbage soup that changed colour with the addition of a teaspoonful of acidic fog – a lemony foam, – as a way to make the pH of *aeroir* visible.

We also offered welcome cocktails that incorporated condensed atmosphere, in the form of fog-harvested water, and were garnished with lace lichen, an air plant that hangs like a veil from the area's oak trees, absorbing nutrients from the air and fog. Lace lichen is not only the official state lichen of California, it is also used by scientists as an indicator species for air quality, as it changes colour in the presence of atmospheric pollution.

We also looked into dust, and the work that scientists have done to map the atmospheric dust rivers that circumnavigate the globe, spicing the air we breathe with

Exploring *Aeroir*, or the Atmospheric Taste of Place

Saharan sand and scales from insect wings. Our dust bowl course was a metaphorical translation of this idea: we invited diners to smash an edible dust-bowl cracker filled with ingredients such as dried mushroom powder, seeds, cricket fragments, and coconut ash. These dusty fragments landed atop Saharan and Gobi-themed schmears, to be scooped up with shattered bits of cracker.

We also did some microbial mapping, in the form of three wild-fermented sourdoughs that might – although the science is still under investigation – reflect the aerial microbiome of their particular home bakery.

And then I went to Mexico City, where I met with a scientist called Robyn Hudson at the National Autonomous University of Mexico. She has shown that smog radically changes the flavour of food by reducing the sensitivity of both people's sense of smell and that of their trigeminal receptors – oral nerves that sense the tingling heat of chili peppers, wasabi, and menthol.

Dr Hudson's current research focuses on Mexico City's street food vendors – the hundreds of thousands of men, women, and children who sell tamales, tacos, and tortas from the city's busiest intersections, where they are exposed to dangerously high levels of air pollution. Intriguingly, she and her colleagues have already found that these vendors' severely blunted senses can be restored to their original sensitivity after just a few weeks' exposure to clean air. Her research made us wonder: is street food so spicy and boldly flavoured in order to make up for the *aeroir* in which it is served, like a kind of anti-smog seasoning? If so, *aeroir* may well be the missing ingredient that could make tacos taste the same in the restaurant back home as they did on the streets of D.F.

That meal was not the end of our *aeroir* explorations. After all, there are so many ways to think about *aeroir*. There are the tastes it contributes to our food, or the tastes that it takes away. There's also the way that cooking actually creates *aeroir*. Consider cookstoves. Something like three billion people, mostly in the developing world, cook and heat their homes using open fires and simple stoves that burn wood, animal dung, and crop waste. This results in an incredibly high level of particulates inside their homes, which the World Health Organization estimates causes millions of premature deaths each year.[8]

Even in the developed world, cooking and *aeroir* are intertwined. The scientists at UC Riverside told me that the next big focus of their smog research is 'burger smog' – the air pollution caused by particulate emissions from char-broiled hamburger joints. Astonishingly, they have already found that an eighteen-wheeler with a diesel engine would have to drive 143 miles on the freeway to pump out the same mass of particulates as a single charbroiled beef patty.

The ideas shared in this paper are really only a start, to my mind. Might we develop smog flavour wheels? And could you develop a menu of street food pairings for particular atmospheric conditions? How does air contribute to taste and reflect place – and how might our relationship with the atmosphere all around us change, as we create new ways to interact with and experience it? How does thinking about *aeroir* – something that is inherently global and borderless, something microscopic and frequently invisible – offer different insights than the place-based thinking of *terroir*? We've introduced the concept, and we're continuing to play with it – our next project involves shooting a series of *aeroir*-themed cooking shows. Ultimately, however, my hope is that the idea will prove itself useful, not just to us, but to others who can use it to illuminate many more things than we can even imagine.

Notes

1. This paper was written for oral presentation; it has been lightly edited for publication.
2. Harold McGee, *On Food and Cooking: The Science and Lore of the Kitchen* (New York: Scribner, 2004), p. 100.
3. A.J. Haagen-Smit, 'Where We Stand Today in Flavor Research', *Chemistry of Natural Food Flavors: A Symposium Sponsored by the National Academy of Sciences, National Research Council for Quartermaster Food and Container Institute for the Armed Forces, and Pioneering Research Division Quartermaster Research and Engineering Center*, ed. by Jack H. Mitchell, Jr and others (Washington: Quartermaster Food and Container Institute for the Armed Forces, 1957), p. 192 <https://archive.org/stream/chemistryofnaturoo arme/chemistryofnaturoo arme_djvu.txt> [accessed 29 March 2018].
4. 'Ambient (Outdoor) Air Quality and Health', *World Health Organization*, September 2016 <http://www.who.int/mediacentre/factsheets/fs313/en/> [accessed 29 March 2018].
5. 'Every Breath We Take: The Lifelong Impact of Air Pollution', *Royal College of Physicians*, 23 February 2016 <https://www.rcplondon.ac.uk/projects/outputs/every-breath-we-take-lifelong-impact-air-pollution> [accessed 29 March 2018].
6. Damian Carrington, 'London Breaches Annual Air Pollution Limit for 2017 in Just Five Days,' *The Guardian*, 6 January 2017 <https://www.theguardian.com/environment/2017/jan/06/london-breaches-toxic-air-pollution-limit-for-2017-in-just-five-days> [accessed 29 March 2017].
7. Greg Atkinson, 'Treasures of the Tide Flats: On a Beach or at a Bash, Oysters Are Worthy of Celebration', *The Seattle Times*, 14 March 2003 <http://community.seattletimes.nwsource.com/archive/?date=20030314&slug=ptaste16> [accessed 29 March 2017].
8. 'Household Air Pollution and Health', *World Health Organization*, February 2016 <http://www.who.int/mediacentre/factsheets/fs292/en/> [accessed 29 March 2018].

'Practically only an English grazing farm': The Irish Landscape and English Beef

Juliana Adelman

Introduction
During the nineteenth century, more English people began to consume more meat. Even beef, previously reserved for the wealthy and for special occasions, became a regular component of the diet of the working classes.[1] To support increased demand, more food was imported in the form of live animals and (after the advent of refrigeration) dead meat.[2] This paper examines the relationship between the English demand for beef and the Irish landscape that supplied some of that demand. While English meat-eating and Irish grazing have each been studied by historians, the relationship between the two has not attracted as much attention. Recent developments in food studies and in environmental history suggest that we ought to scrutinize how shifting demands for foods have far-reaching impacts upon production systems, environments, and society. Foods have been traded globally for centuries, but the modern era has seen an enormous expansion in this trade. When we think about the meaning of a plate of meat we must ask not just how it was cooked, who ate it and in what company, but also where it came from and how it got to that plate. The effects of what I am eating here and now may be felt very far away in both geography and time.[3] This paper asks what effects the eating of a plate of beef in England during the second half of the nineteenth century might have had for the Irish landscape.

The Irish are still exporting beef to the United Kingdom as well as to the world. Indeed, they are still exporting live animals to some countries. Contemporary debates about the environmental impact of the Irish beef industry have framed the focus for this paper. In what follows I will examine the production of beef cattle for export to England in the period after the Great Famine in Ireland, ignoring the expansion of other livestock exports as well as the industrialization of dairy. This narrow story is worth telling because it encourages us to reflect on how food can shape landscape in the past and present. There is some elision between 'Britain' and 'England' in what follows. This elision reflects that of nineteenth-century writers who tended to refer to England as the force determining Irish fortunes.

The Roast Beef of Old England
The expansion of meat-eating and particularly beef-eating in later nineteenth-century

Britain is well-documented. Richard Perren has estimated that average per-capita meat consumption went from approximately 86.8 pounds per annum in 1831-40 to 126 pounds per annum in 1910-14.[4] Such consumption varied regionally and across classes and may have been as high as 155 pounds per annum in London by 1850 while in Ireland it may have remained as low as 56 pounds per annum into the 1880s.[5] A further indication of expanded meat-eating is its appearance in the workhouse. While meat was generally in scarce supply in the parsimonious and punitive workhouse diet, roast beef for a Christmas treat was increasingly seen as a cultural right of the English poor.[6] To be English was to consume beef, just as to be Irish was to eat potatoes.[7] The Irish origin of this beef did not reduce its Englishness as a foodstuff. A nineteenth-century revision of the traditional song 'The roast beef of old England' drives home the point. Printed in 1853, the new version abandoned the anti-French message of its eighteenth-century predecessor in favour of a straightforward equation of beef-eating with Englishness: 'Since mighty roast beef is an Englishman's food, It accounts for the freedom that runs in his blood, For generous living's the step to all good!'[8]

As English working-class income increased slowly, they could more readily afford meat. Keir Waddington has estimated that even working-class meat consumption may have reached 103 pounds per annum by the end of the nineteenth century. Of the meats available, beef was the most desirable as it suggested an increase in social status.[9] English-produced beef was expensive, so the working-man's beef was often supplied from outside of England. The rising wages and standard of living of industrial England affected the landscapes and economies of places hundreds and even thousands of miles away. In some ways Ireland was the least extreme example of this: in the eyes of the government and of most British citizens Ireland was only a region of the United Kingdom rather than an autonomous country with its own citizens to feed. Transformations of agriculture and transportation networks to produce meat for England were also underway in the United States (particularly the West), South America, Australia and New Zealand.

While the Englishness and prestige of beef-eating does not seem to have been diminished by the origin of the beef, provenance did affect price. Cheaper Irish beef facilitated expanded beef consumption across classes. The reason for the price difference is difficult to determine but there are some hints that Irish cattle were considered inferior and priced accordingly. For example, one writer claimed that fat cattle were damaged in transport and thus the quality of the meat produced from them was diminished. Store cattle, he claimed, retained their value because they could be fattened and sold as English beef.[10] Irish cattle were also accused of carrying disease, a taint that may also have reduced their value. For example, when the government sought to control the spread of foot-and-mouth disease from the 1870s, Irish cattle were targeted. Some blamed Irish cattle for the spreading disease. As the *Irish Times* put it, 'It has been asserted by English journals and by members of English Chambers of Agriculture that Ireland is the grand nursery of all the contagious diseases which have from time to time broken out amongst English cattle.'[11] Similar concerns came to fore with each disease outbreak throughout the latter half of the nineteenth century. In each case, Irish cattle traders felt that they had been discriminated against and lobbied for special allowances to protect the sale of Irish beasts to Britain.[12] The trade also came under increasing critique for its perceived cruelty. Irish cattle had horns and thus were more likely to cause injury to one another while being transported in the crowded holds of ships and railway carriages.[13]

From Field to Fork

Before considering how the Irish landscape changed to accommodate English demand for beef, we should examine the process by which Irish cattle were transformed into English meat. The journey from calf to grazing bovine to roast beef could bring an animal hundreds of miles and through several transfers of ownership. A calf born on a farm spent about the first two months feeding exclusively on its mother's milk, first from the teat and then from a pail. After weaning, the calf was fed a variety of soft solids followed by sliced roots and eventually put out to graze (unless it was sold for veal). After this period of grazing the calf might be sold as a 'store' heifer or bullock, ready for fattening. Store animals were mostly produced west of the River Shannon, whereas fattening took place mostly in the east. In fact the province of Leinster, the most eastern province including county Dublin, dominated fattening because of its superior grasslands and better access to the point of export. Grass-fattened Irish cattle were generally sold between June and January.[14] After eighteen months to two years the animal could be sold as 'fat' but many fattened animals were between three and four years old.[15] After the Famine, some graziers specialized in a very short period of grass fattening, buying beasts only six months before they intended to sell them. The veterinarian's advice to 'buy cattle from a poorer ground than that you have to feed them on' supports a movement of animals from west to east and north to south within the United Kingdom.[16]

Cattle were exported to Britain through many Irish ports, but the vast majority left from Dublin. Some of these were stores, bought in a rural market by an Irish or British middleman and driven directly to the lairs at Dublin's North Wall Quay to await shipment. Once in Britain they would be fattened before being sold, often as British beasts. Most cattle shipped from Dublin were fat and many of these were sold on to British dealers either by salesmasters or at the Dublin market. These beasts were then shipped primarily to Liverpool or Glasgow or Holyhead; there they were either exposed again at markets or sent directly to buyers. In Liverpool many were bought and slaughtered by the city's butchers to supply local demand. Other beasts might be forwarded by rail to dozens of English towns for sale and slaughter or further fattened and rebranded as British beef.[17]

A number of key people controlled different aspects of the cattle trade. Graziers rented (or sometimes owned) large farms of grassland and bought store cattle to fatten. Store cattle were often bought at the Ballinasloe market, a central depot for cattle on their passage from west to east. Salesmasters conducted the trade in the markets, and sometimes brokered export trade, for a commission. Graziers were barred from being salesmasters in the Dublin cattle market, although this may not have been enforced. A grazier might consign beasts to a salesmaster and pay a drover to accompany them on their journey. There were also cattle dealers who would act as middlemen, buying from farmers, at auction, and at markets outside of Dublin. They would then make use of salesmasters, who held the leases on all the pens at the Dublin cattle market, to sell their cattle. Dealers were essentially middlemen.[18] Between them, the people who controlled the trade and the animals they traded in transformed the landscape to suit the needs of livestock growing.

Landscapes of Beef

Many types of landscapes were associated with rising meat consumption in the British Isles during the later nineteenth century. One type was the urban landscape of beef consumption. In the industrial landscapes of the north of England, factory workers and emergent bourgeois factory owners consumed meat in greater and greater quantities. Not only industrial cities, but also centres of administration and trade like London expanded in population and in demand for meat. One of the consequences was the expansion of markets, slaughterhouses, and butcher shops within cities. More meat necessitated more slaughter, and for most cities in England slaughterhouses remained at the back of butcher shops where they continued to pollute the urban landscape.[19] Some cities attempted to rearrange the landscape of meat consumption by centralizing slaughter outside of the city limits to reduce their residents' exposure to rivers of blood and mountains of bone.[20] However they dealt with the slaughter required, the urban landscape was one populated mostly by living humans and dead or doomed cattle. These landscapes of beef consumption were supported by landscapes of production. These landscapes, some argued, were populated by cattle at the expense of humans.

In Ireland there is a suggestive link between rising cattle numbers and declining human population. The annual agricultural statistics show an almost continuous increase in the livestock population while the decennial census attests to the equally continuous decrease in the Irish population. Raymond Crotty has calculated that, from the post-Famine decades to 1911, 'every increase of 1,000 in cattle stocks led to a decrease of 1,215 in the human population'.[21] Whether you see cause and effect between them is a political matter, but the numbers are not in question. These cattle were not increasing for home consumption: they were increasing for export. After 1855 the numbers of cattle exported from Ireland to Britain began to rise steadily from a few hundred thousand up to more than seven hundred thousand by the 1890s.[22] The Dublin Cattle Market became the largest and most important cattle market in the British Isles and vied for a top position in Europe.[23]

A wide variety of Irish people during the nineteenth century believed, like Crotty, that a landscape of beef production was a landscape almost devoid of people. In fact such a relationship had been advocated as early as 1687 by William Petty, who thought that the proper conquest of Ireland should result in its people migrating to England for labour while about 200,000 remained on the island to tend six million cattle.[24] Few in nineteenth-century Ireland would have viewed Petty's plan favourably. In 1865 Francis Jennings, a merchant, published a pamphlet entitled *The Present and Future of Ireland as the Cattle Farm of England and Her Probable Population*. Jennings claimed dramatically that '[t]his country will soon awake to find that it has ceased to be a nation, and is practically only an English grazing farm'.[25] Journalists in newspapers across the political spectrum agreed that the increase in pasture had been all towards the production of meat for English markets. The *Express* equated the threat of the cattle plague in 1865 with the threat of potato blight in 1845 because the country was now dependent on cattle as a single agricultural product. The writer argued that there was still time to stop the Irish landscape from being totally transformed into pasture for English meat and advocated a system of mixed tillage and grazing.[26] The lament for the loss of both population and the tillage landscape entered into poetry, fiction, and song. Even a professor of chemistry entered the fray, writing a lengthy poem entitled 'Christians and Cattle' which included the refrain 'Parents' songs and children's prattle/Now give place to bellowing cattle'. Like the other writers, George Butler Bradshaw was in no doubt that this transformation was down to English demand for beef.[27]

This widespread belief that the landscape of Ireland and Ireland itself had been degraded by the move to grazing continued throughout the century. In 1873 a landholder and local magistrate in county Meath brought his friend on a tour of the district. He described the county as 'one of the most melancholy districts I know' with 'solitude everywhere found'. The cause of this solitude, he claimed, was the conversion of the landscape into 'one vast expanse of pasture land'.[28] As late as 1900 the editor of the *All Ireland Review* called for Irish people to 'wage war upon the grass which now threatens to devour us all'.[29] There was no question in many minds that a landscape suited to grass and cattle was not a landscape suited to people.

There was also no doubt in the minds of most writers as to who was to blame for the creation of this landscape. The *Post* blamed the English newspapers: 'The idea that cattle growing should be the natural and exclusive industry of Ireland has become a sort of fanaticism with the English press.'[30] Nationalists blamed English government policy. For example, the politician John Martin told an audience of National League members that England had formerly used Ireland as her granary but now was 'making Ireland her cattle farm' with the consequence that as emigrants left 'more and more cattle' took their place.[31] The *Nation* blamed English appetites. In a provocative article the newspaper asserted that while the English authorities were unable or unwilling to crack down on the practice of infanticide they were spending enormous sums to curb cattle plague. This suggested an English preference for 'beef versus babies'.[32]

We need not agree that England was conspiring to denude Ireland of people in favour of beef cattle to argue that there was a relationship between English meat-eating and Irish grazing. The press, English and Irish, had often repeated the widely held view that the raising of livestock was both financially rewarding and suited to Ireland's wet climate.[33] There were sound economic reasons for choosing to raise animals rather than crops, particularly on the poor land that dominated the west of the country. The conversion to pasture was embraced by Irish farmers and landlords whose motivation was profit. Raising livestock was increasingly seen by some as the most profitable form of farming. The price of grains had declined in the 1820s and 1830s while the price of livestock increased, and thus economics drove farmers to pasture over tillage. The Great Famine accelerated this trend.[34] As one absentee landlord put it when he went to inspect his properties in Kerry in 1851: 'The great criterion in these times is to watch whether the farmers are increasing their cow & dairy stock. If they are reducing their cattle & ploughing up their lands, depend upon it, they are going to the bad.'[35]

And it wasn't just absentee English landlords supporting a conversion to grazing. Irish Catholic tenant farmers and landowners embraced the benefits of cattle rearing. The reason that the presence of cattle was an indication of improvement was that the price of cattle had increased: the price differential between a calf and a three-year-old animal was about £10. The low cost of feeding the animal for three years insured a tidy profit.[36] Annual profits in the 1850s at Lodge Park in County Kildare, for example, averaged over £400 from the sale of around sixty animals.[37] In the 1860s Woodtown in County Meath made up to £800 annual profit on selling livestock. The profit on each individual beast was around £4.[38] Such profits were most evident in the fattening areas of the country (the east and to a lesser extent the south), although rising store cattle prices also benefitted farmers in the west. The conversion to pasture brought new but uneven prosperity to the Irish landscape and its remaining farmers.[39]

The Longer Term Effects

Whether or not you believe that growing cattle for export also led to high rates of Irish emigration, there is no question that this industry drove landscape change. This landscape change was not evenly distributed. Ireland's most agriculturally productive regions are in the south and east with western regions having poorer quality and thinner soils. As a consequence, cattle tended to travel in one direction and to affect agricultural landscapes in slightly different ways. In the far west (Connacht), grazing of livestock was considered the only use for some lands unable to support crops.[40] Some of these areas had been used to cultivate potatoes before the Famine but as they became depopulated through death and emigration cattle did indeed replace people. Dry cattle numbers grew by 60% in Ireland between 1854 and 1901. Growth in cattle exports tracked the growth in numbers, suggesting that most of the herd was not for home consumption.[41] Leinster dominated this growth, with even County Dublin showing an increase of 31% in cattle numbers.[42] We can modify the polemic of Irish authors in a somewhat surprising way to suggest that the city of Dublin and its surrounding region was perhaps the most affected by the demand for English beef rather than the poor

Western regions that had been most affected by the Famine.

The landscape of Dublin and its rural fringe were particularly affected by the expansion of grazing. Dublin's cattle market and port were the stations through which most of the Irish cattle bound for England passed. Dublin retained the largest share of this market, exporting between 200,000 and 300,000 cattle per year: Leinster and Dublin only increased their hold on the cattle export trade as the century progressed.[43] The cattle market was moved north of Smithfield in 1863 to accommodate the increased number of cattle. The spaces around the new market were soon transformed from fields to housing. Most railway lines led to Dublin, exerting an inexorable pull on livestock from west to east.[44] Steam shipping first enabled livestock export and then grew dependent upon it.[45] Dublin city became a bridge for cattle passing between Irish fields and English butchers.

Irish efforts to supply English demands for beef probably also had environmental impacts that can be extrapolated using contemporary science. In the short term, conversion to grazing might have been beneficial or not necessarily harmful to aspects of the local environment. The hedgerows planted to divide pastures and corral livestock also provide refuges for wildlife. Cattle, in specific environments, can even encourage biodiversity by grazing.[46] A reduced human population and reduced tillage may have made space for other animals and plants. On the negative side, increased manure from increased numbers of animals may have contributed to polluting waterways and thereby damaging aquatic plants and animals. Ultimately, however, these possible environmental benefits could not be sustained as the market for beef in Ireland, England, and further afield expanded in the twentieth and twenty-first centuries.

Conclusions: Towards Food Harvest 2020

Irish cattle were once produced for cheap beef and helped fuel increased demand for meat among the English working classes. These commercial demands drove a shift in agriculture and landscape in Ireland that has continued right up to the present. Nearly a century of political independence from England has done little to change the focus of Irish agriculture on livestock production and on food for export. Of this, the production of beef cattle has remained a key priority for Irish governments of every political stripe as global demand for beef has continued to be strong. The most recent government targets for the agri-food sector are dominated by increasing the value of beef and dairy (although with a greater focus on dairy driven by the elimination of milk quotas).[47]

Whereas once Irish writers decried the landscape of beef, it is now seen as a positive attribute and one that gives value to Irish produce. Irish beef is now marketed as a superior product, and the landscape that shapes it is central to that marketing. Bord Bia has several websites targeting its most important export markets. The website addressing American consumers brags of the 'lush, green grass [that] covers 80% of Ireland's landmass' which contribute to the beef's '*terroir*'. The website's banner includes the phrase 'the flavor shows where the best grass grows'.[48] Similar promotional material targets a British audience on another website.[49] In a change from the nineteenth century, Irish consumers are also being sold a story about the value and quality of Irish beef and encouraged to look for assurance that the beef they buy is genuinely Irish-raised. In a reversal of nineteenth-century trends, British troubles with BSE and foot-and-mouth disease have made Irish beef more desirable. Yet this transition in attitudes has come at a high cost.

We are now very aware of how demand for certain food substances can impact landscapes. We know that our appetite for meat places huge demands on the environment, especially on water supplies. Of all livestock, beef cattle currently have the largest environmental impact. They require much more land and water per unit of meat produced than either pigs or chickens, for example.[50] Environmental history has had much to say about the long-term impact of intensive farming for single crops such as sugar cane and banana.[51] Ireland is now living with the landscape created by demand for meat, and only superficial consideration has been given to what the future of this landscape may look like.

The second half of the nineteenth century saw the intensification of Irish agriculture as a market-driven system dedicated to producing food commodities for export. As many at the time noted, this had profound consequences for the landscape and for the role of people within it. As long as food production remains tied to the export profits of the agri-food sector, the landscape will continue to be shaped by consumer demand rather than by sustainable goals embracing the needs of people, animals, and environment. As environmental science tells us, this continuation will mean water pollution from manure and fertilizers used to increase grass production. Pollution will affect species living in waterways and increase the challenge of supplying clean drinking water to growing urban populations. Hedgerows will be replaced with fences with a resultant loss of habitat. Perhaps most importantly, different types of livestock production will continue to be concentrated in specialized areas of the Irish landscape with the result of concentrating their pollutants.[52] Although no longer 'practically only an English grazing farm', the effects of that nineteenth-century transformation on landscape and on food are still being felt almost two centuries later.

Notes

1. Richard Perren, *The Meat Trade in Britain 1840-1914* (London: Routledge, 1978), p. 3.
2. Perren, p. 123.
3. Matt Garcia, 'Setting the Table: Historians, Popular Writers and Food History', *Journal of American History* (2016), 656-78.
4. Perren, p. 3.
5. Ian MacLachlan, 'A Bloody Offal Nuisance: The Persistence of Private-Slaughterhouses in Nineteenth-Century London', *Urban History*, 34.2 (2007), 227-54.
6. Nadja Durbach, 'Roast Beef, the New Poor Law, and the British Nation, 1834-63', *Journal of British*

Studies 52 (2013), 963-89.
7. Helen O'Connell, '"At our potatoes"': Recipes for Normality in Post-Union Ireland', *Éire Ireland* 48.3&4 (2013), 49-78.
8. 'The Roast Beef of Old England', *The Musical Times and Singing Class Circular*, 5.115 (1853), 297.
9. Keir Waddington, *The Bovine Scourge: Meat, Tuberculosis and Public Health, 1850-1914* (Woodbridge: Boydell and Brewer, 2006), pp. 15-16.
10. Daniel Tallerman, *Railway Abattoirs and Other Papers Relating to Meat Distribution* (London: Simpkin and Marshall, 1891), pp. 11-12.
11. 'The Irish Cattle Trade', *Irish Times*, 2 December 1875.
12. See for example, 'The Irish Cattle Trade' and 'Irish Cattle Export Trade' (*Irish Times*, 9 January 1891).
13. See for example T. W. Moffett, *On Certain Cruelties Practiced in the Cattle Traffic of the United Kingdom* (Belfast: Belfast Society for the Prevention of Cruelty to Animals, 1867); Tallerman.
14. House of Commons Parliamentary Papers, *Select Committee on Trade in Animals* (1866), Evidence of Richard Walsh, p. 278.
15. Matthew M. Milburn, *The Cow: Dairy Husbandry and Cattle-Breeding, Richardson's rural handbooks* (London: W. S. Orr & Co, 1851), pp. 104-06; House of Commons Parliamentary Papers, *Select Committee on Trade in Animals* (1866), Evidence of Samuel Garnett, p. 280.
16. Experienced Veterinarian, *The Cattle Keeper's Guide; or Complete Directory for the Choice and Management of Cattle* (London: Bailey, c. 1820), p. 28. See also Perren, p. 9.
17. David Seth Jones, *Graziers, Land Reform and Political Conflict in Ireland* (Washington, D. C.: Catholic University of America Press), p. 43.
18. Liam Clare, 'The Dublin Cattle Market', *Dublin Historical Record*, 55.2 (2002), 166-80.
19. See for example MacLachlan.
20. See for example *Meat, Modernity and the Rise of the Slaughterhouse*, ed. by Paula Young Lee (Durham: University of New Hampshire Press, 2008).
21. Raymond Crotty, *When Histories Collide: The Development and Impact of Individualistic Capitalism* (Walnut Creek, California: AltaMira Press, 2001), p. 179.
22. Jones, p. 44.
23. Clare.
24. Qtd. in Crotty, p. 169.
25. F. M. Jennings, *The Present and Future of Ireland as the Farm of England and Her Probable Population* (Dublin: Hodges, Smith, 1865).
26. From the *Express*, 3 August 1865 and found in the Larcom Papers, MS 7748, National Library of Ireland.
27. George Butler Bradshaw, *Christians and Cattle, or What Makes Irish paupers? What Banishes Irish Exiles? And What Cuts Off Irish Lives?* (Dublin: Murray, 1868), p. 12.
28. Q., 'Some Results of the Irish exodus', *Irish Monthly*, 1.3 (1873), 117-20 (p. 117).
29. 'The Last Conquest: Perhaps. Grass', *All Ireland Review* 1.38 (1900), 5-6 (p. 6).
30. From the *Post*, 4 August 65 in the Larcom Papers, MS 7748.
31. 'The National League', *Nation*, 9 Sept 1865.
32. 'Beef versus Babies', *Nation*, 11 Nov 1865.
33. R. V. Comerford, 'Ireland 1850-1870: Post-Famine and Mid-Victorian', in *A New History of Ireland V. Ireland Under the Union 1801-70*, ed. by W. E. Vaughn (Oxford: Oxford University Press, 1989), pp. 372-95 (p. 381).
34. Jones, p. 28-35.
35. Diary of Sir John Benn-Walsh, 26 August 1851, reproduced in Melosina Lenox-Conyngham, *Diaries of Ireland, an Anthology 1590-1987* (Dublin: The Lilliput Press, 1998), p. 179.
36. Jones, p. 38.
37. Stock book, Lodge Park, Kildare, MS 23,573, National Library of Ireland.
38. Stock book, Woodtown estate, Meath, MS 19,347, National Library of Ireland.

39. Comerford, pp. 382-83.
40. See Jones, pp. 229-32.
41. Jones, pp. 43-44.
42. See Central Statistics Office, *Farming since the Famine: Irish Farm Statistics, 1847-1996* (Dublin: Stationery Office, 1997).
43. *Thom's Irish Almanac and Official Directory for 1870* (Dublin: Alexander Thom, 1870), p. 858; *Thom's Irish Almanac and Official Directory for 1868* (Dublin: Alexander Thom, 1868), p. 794; *Thom's Irish Almanac and Official Directory for 1872* (Dublin: Alexander Thom, 1872), p. 842; *Thom's Irish Almanac and Official Directory for 1874* (Dublin: Alexander Thom, 1874), p. 857; *Thom's Irish Almanac and Official Directory for 1888* (Dublin: Alexander Thom, 1888),p. 1274; *Thom's Irish Almanac and Official Directory for 1890* (Dublin: Alexander Thom, 189), p. 1274; *Thom's Irish Almanac and Official Directory for 1892* (Dublin: Alexander Thom, 1892), p. 1278.
44. David W. Miller and Leonard J. Hochberg, 'Modernization and Inequality in Pre-Famine Ireland: An Exploratory Spatial Analysis', *Social Science History*, 31.1 (2007), 35-60.
45. Peter Solar, 'Shipping and Economic Development in Nineteenth-Century Ireland', *Economic History Review*, 109.4 (2006), 717-42.
46. Pádraic Fogarty, *Whittled Away: Ireland's Vanishing Nature* (Cork: Collins Press, 2017), p. 258.
47. See Department of Agriculture, Fisheries and Food, Food Harvest 2020: A Vision for Irish Agri-Food and Fisheries, pp. 36-37 <https://www.agriculture.gov.ie/media/migration/foodindustrydevelopment-trademarkets/agri-foodandtheeconomy/foodharvest2020/2020FoodHarvestEng240810.pdf> [accessed 15 May 2017]
48. 'The Flavor Shows where the Best Grass Grows', *Bord Bia: Irish Food Board*, 2017 <www.irishbeefusa.com> [accessed 15 May 2017].
49. 'Irish Beef Encounters', *Bord Bia: Irish Food Board*, 2018 <www.irishbeef.co.uk> [accessed 15 May 2017].
50. M. de Vries and I.J.M. de Boer, 'Comparing Environmental Impacts for Livestock Products: A Review of Life Cycle Assessments', *Livestock Science* 128 (2010), 1-11.
51. See for example Sidney Mintz, *Sweetness and Power: The Place of Sugar in Modern History* (London: Penguin, 1985).
52. See Fogarty, pp. 247-69.

Eating into the Countryside: The Case of Hamburg

Volker Carlton Bach

That politics shapes borders is a familiar fact to anyone who ever read a history book. That political borders can shape cultures and landscapes is at least tacitly assumed.[1] The idea that food played a role in both processes is rarely considered, yet given how central to human existence local food production was, it is obvious that it must have. Part of the reason for this omission is that many culinary historians feel uncomfortable studying the political ramifications of their field, while traditional political historians often focus on events at the level of the nation state. In most cases, food resources were local and regional concerns, not national ones, so most conflicts about them were resolved locally, at a level of history often relegated to folklorists and local amateurs. That is unfortunate. In this essay, I will try to show what the interplay between food, politics, and local landscape could look like and why it can be of interest to 'serious' history.

This essay will look at the growth and development of the territory of Hamburg, a wealthy and powerful city with a history of independence that came to dominate a considerable part of its surrounding countryside and continues to function as a federal city state within modern Germany. This is not the level at which political history is usually studied; most research looks at the macro-scale, the fate and policies of nation states or their predecessors. However, it is the level at which most politics in history took place, and one which historians ignore at their peril. In an age before mass media and mass transit, the activities of a national government – to the extent such a thing existed – were remote from the lives of most people. The affairs of their city, village, district, or tribe, however, had direct bearing on their lives. Disputes could be passionate and violent, especially where no national government stopped local powers from actually going to war with each other. The result, in the case of medieval Germany, was a world where local disputes resulted in conflicts rivalling seventeenth-century warfare in complexity and pointlessness.

The focus of this study is mainly on the period before 1600, when the political boundaries of Hamburg were still in flux and no powerful territorial states had formed in its neighbourhood. Food supply continued to be an important aspect of policy afterwards, but the approaches were much more similar to those of the modern nation state. Here, we look at an age that seems alien to the modern reader, a world where wars were waged and alliances woven across a landscape of places we know only from day trips to the forest or as stops on the commuter railway.

Food and Landscape

A City by Three Rivers

Founded as a city in the ninth century, Hamburg was first built on a low hill overlooking a ford across the river Alster. To its south, the Elbe, already a mighty stream, flowed to the North Sea roughly 100 km further west. On its western flank, the Alster, a small river just barely navigable to the ships of the era, met the Elbe to form the first port. To the east, across a low, swampy area, the Bille, another small but useful river emerging from forested hills, lay nearby. The land around was generally flat, with occasional elevations of a hundred metres or so already designated 'mountains'. It was carved by glaciers during the last ice age that produced its gently sloped hills and deep, dense soils. Except for the occasional boulder deposited by retreating ice sheets, there is almost no rock here, only loess, clay, gravel, and sand. Local farming tradition distinguishes two types of farmland: low-lying *Marsch*, wet, rich, and useful mostly for cattle grazing, and higher *Geest*, easier to drain and suitable for growing bread grain. The cultural differences between these areas have been studied by folklorists and remain visible to this day.

The early history of Hamburg is controversial, but fortunately not very relevant for this study. Though (probably) briefly the seat of an archbishop in the 830s and the final home of an exiled antipope in the 960s, the settlement itself was small and powerless until the twelfth century. While maritime trade featured in its economy from the beginning, it was not until the burghers were able to unite into a single political entity and develop a profitable cooperation with the Baltic port of Lübeck that the city grew in influence.

With greater power and wealth came an expanding population. From a few hundred at its modest start, Hamburg grew to several thousand people by 1200 and more than 10,000 by 1400. In the eighteenth century, it would reach 80,000 and a century later exceed a million. From very early on, the city government faced the problem of ensuring all these people had enough to eat, and its policies proved adequate most of the time, though hunger periodically returned to the city in times of crisis. It has been said that this kind of famine was political, the result of a crisis of government, not of supply, but that is only partly true. No city the size of Hamburg can be self-sufficient in food. The fact that most inhabitants ate on most days was in itself the result of a set of policies that the city's government enforced ruthlessly.

Mills and Bread

The staple food of medieval Hamburg was rye bread, and the first concern of the city was to make sure people had enough of it. Rye was grown locally, and the city was well placed to bring in what it needed over longer distances by river transport. Later on, Hamburg would become a trading hub for grain from Saxony and Bohemia that was exported to Norway and Iceland.

Where the grain to feed the earliest settlement came from is not known. By the time Hamburg became politically significant, we find written evidence of wealthy burghers and canons buying the right to grain rents from local nobility.[2] The lords of nearby villages along the Alster and Bille rivers sold them the right to receive part of the

Eating into the Countryside

Figure 1. The Außenalster, possibly the world's most decorative millpond (Image: Wikimedia commons).

rent their peasants owed. The grain was carried to the city by boat and either stored for personal use or sold in the market. This was not in itself significant for the landscape – villages and grain fields had existed before – but the control that Hamburg's ruling class gained over the surrounding countryside made later developments possible. In a world where government was understood as a personal matter, nobles could sell taxes, tolls, and even jurisdiction. Burghers were happy to buy them, and the city council made a policy of purchasing them from its citizens, establishing a solid hinterland that they could shape as they wished in centuries to come.

The first major impact still visible in the landscape today was made to ensure a steady supply of flour to the city. There had been a seigneurial mill on the Alster owned by the counts of Holstein since at least 1189, and the first dam was built in 1235. When the facilities passed into the hands of the city by 1366, the council decided to add capacity. With the land being flat, the millpond they ended up creating measured 180 hectares. The owners of the flooded land received compensation, and, while the mills have long disappeared, the lake remains a distinctive feature of the city to this day. Some of Hamburg's most expensive real estate lies along its shores.

Even this was not enough to meet the needs of a growing city, and the council also purchased mills on the Eilbek and Osterbek, tributaries of the Alster, in 1310 and another upstream at Fuhlsbüttel in 1350. The lock and dam built there in 1448 created the Ratsmühlenteich, another feature that remains to this day and is maintained carefully, though the water now only powers a generator. Yet even with all these mills, demand often outstripped supply, and a windmill was bought in 1463.

The city spent considerable sums maintaining and servicing the mills. Two councillors were responsible for importing millstones (Bohemian sandstone for grinding meal, Rhenish basalt from Andernach for flour), paying and feeding the staff, supervising repairs, and keeping the accounts. When milling fees produced a profit, it was used to add millstones to the stockpile. The smooth running of the mills was so important that the council barred cargo boats from using the Alster locks when the water level dropped below a certain point in 1548 – a remarkable decision for a city built on trade.

The government's interest in ensuring a supply of bread did not end with milling.

Baking was a strictly controlled profession, and bread prices were fixed by decree. The 1375 ordinances of the bakers' guild stipulate that only members were allowed to bake bread for sale and required them to meet quality standards at a set price.³ Their monopoly was protected by limitations to imported bread, and in 1568 the council forbade the building of new baking ovens in all its lands on pain of fines and the destruction of the newly built oven. This restriction was part of a policy whose impact is still imprinted on the countryside around the city, keeping its villages dedicated to agricultural pursuits and forcing them to look to Hamburg for things as basic as white bread.

Figure 2. *Fuhlsbüttler Schleuse rebuilt in 2014. The old mill is long gone, but the pond and race remain (Image: Wikimedia commons).*

Fisheries and Forestry

The rivers and lakes around Hamburg could supply large quantities of fish, but like all inland fisheries, they were unequal to the demand of urban centres. To provide enough for the market, the city government successfully pursued fishing rights farther afield early. Like the lordship over villages, rights were usually bought from nobles by individual citizens and sold on to the council. Fisheries were significant for the formation of the landscape not so much in what was done as in what wasn't: protecting them often meant not building along certain stretches of river. It also meant supressing fishing industries elsewhere. By the fifteenth century, Hamburg's fishermen had acquired rights to fish along the Alster and far up the Bille as well as on several lesser arms of the Elbe and along all parts that were tidal. Conflicts over such fishing rights with locals could be high-stakes affairs as in 1390, when Hamburg fishermen were imprisoned by local nobleman Johann von Sestersflete, or in 1489, when Stade fishermen drove them off with loaded crossbows.⁴ In this light, the agreement between the fishermen of Hamburg and Grevenhof not to carry arms while fishing seems sensible.⁵

Wood was another scarce and even more vital resource that the burghers sought to control. As early as 1189, they secured the right to harvest wood around their city freely, but the growing community could not long make do. In a world where forests marked high, well-drained lands, cutting them down was tempting. The Lüneburger Heide to the southeast of Hamburg testifies to the fuel needs of Lüneburg's saltworks: an area of sandy soil once densely wooded, but today a scrubland useful for little more than pasturing sheep. The problem was resolved in traditional fashion in the fifteenth century: a military alliance of Hamburg and Lübeck took part of the Sachsenwald, a forest on the north bank of the Elbe upstream from Bergedorf, in 1420, and the two cities cooperated to secure villages along the trade route between them in the following years. Among these, the so-called *Walddörfer* (forest villages) to the northeast of Hamburg were important suppliers of timber that could be floated down the Alster. The council nominated *Waldherren* to manage the forests as absentee landlords and maintained a force of forestry officials to enforce sustainable use. Needless to say the requirements of Hamburg with its insatiable hunger for lumber came first, those of the locals a distant second. That is how the *Walddörfer* became today's leafy suburb and the Sachsenwald – gifted to Bismarck by a grateful nation in 1871 – remains an uninhabited forest of 58 sq km: large enough to function as an unincorporated area and serve as a day trip destination for urbanites.

The Market Gardening Complex

As the Hamburg council gained control of large areas along the Alster, Bille, and Elbe rivers, the city pursued a policy of effectively turning these areas into market gardens. The first step in this direction was improving the land by building dykes and drainage ditches. This was happening all over North Germany at the time: Dutch settlers were invited for their expertise in winning land from the sea and promised secure tenure at low rents in return. Land that had been tidal, waterlogged by periodic flooding and threatened by storm surges, became rich and safe, defended through communal labour to maintain the dykes and locks that protected it. Refusal to work meant loss of all lands, and deliberately damaging dykes or locks was punishable by death. On the whole, this century-long victory is a rarely told heroic tale in German history.

In Hamburg, the earliest evidence for melioration dates to 1188 when the island of Cremon was turned into dry land. By 1250, it had become part of the city proper, and the council tackled bigger projects. The most successful one was the creation of the Marschlande on a series of Elbe islands downstream of the city that it purchased between 1338 and 1395. Dyke-building was a serious enough business for the city to fight a war over it from 1619 to 1620. Dykes in the Vierlande had shifted floodwaters to the less well-protected territories of the dukes of Braunschweig-Lüneburg, and the city was willing to ignore a ruling by the imperial high court and fund a year of warfighting rather than

Figure 3. The upper Bille river running through the Sachsenwald (Image: Wikimedia commons).

remove it. The treaties are long forgotten today, but the dykes still stand, and the landscape created behind them still draws tourists from the city. Its often-picturesque farmhouses are lined up along the inland slope, the fields extending in long strips encompassing the relatively high, dry garden areas and the lower, now drained Marsch. Typically, fruit and vegetables were grown closer to the house, grain further along the strip, and dairy cattle grazed on the lowest-lying, wettest part.

Figure 4. Ochsenwerder, dyke, houses and fields (Image: Wikimedia commons)

The farming culture that emerged in these parts was dominated increasingly by market gardening and dairy farming. Grain was grown to feed the family and sometimes to pay rents in kind, but money income was generated by selling vegetables, fruit, and dairy in the markets of Hamburg. Wealth concentrated by inheritance laws that passed farms undivided to the eldest son created a farming culture with distinctly urban characteristics. As Hamburg acquired more lands to the east through a brief war in 1420, it spread to the Vierlande and Bergedorf, areas administered jointly by Hamburg and Lübeck until the 1860s, but economically more oriented towards Hamburg. Vierländer fruit and vegetable sellers were a traditional presence on its markets, and many farms there still depend on selling their produce directly. The distinctive dress of the peasant women, remarked on by visitors and lovingly preserved in many a home, was created in the eighteenth and nineteenth century not least in order to attract urban customers.[6]

The Vierlande were ultimately eclipsed in importance by the Altes Land, a region south of the Elbe downstream from Hamburg that is today Europe's largest fruit-growing area. This, too, was the creation of Hamburg in a way, though not as deliberately. The city had been trying to gain control over the Elbe since the council obtained (or forged) an imperial privilege granting toll-free navigation to its burghers in 1189. In the process, it eclipsed the neighbouring towns of Stade and Harburg south of the river, the latter's port silting up as a direct result of Hamburg's dyke-building in the Vierlande. The region stayed rural and ultimately concentrated on market-gardening as a source of income, though it did not fully make this transition until the early modern period. In 1612, Hamburg's council briefly banned the import of fruit from there to support its own farmers in the Vierlande and Marschlande. By this time, the region's farmers had already started exporting their fruit on small sailing vessels as far as Britain, though most of it was bound for the markets of Hamburg. In the end, the city's demand proved enough to support both sides, and by the eighteenth century wealthy Hamburg families are recorded making springtime day trips across the river to visit the farmers who supplied

Eating into the Countryside

Figure 5. Vierländer market women posing for a photographer c. 1900 (Image: Wikimedia commons)

them with milk, butter, fruit, and fresh greens. It is still a local tradition to drive or cycle through the area, its fields given over entirely to fruit trees since the great drainage efforts of the late 1800s, when the apples and cherries are in bloom, and many farmers earn extra income by selling fruit, fresh off the tree, directly to passing customers.[7]

If this all sounds rather too nice to be true, it is. The people in the surrounding villages came to a working arrangement with the city, but not in any sense an accommodation between equals. Being governed by Hamburg was not a pleasure. When the city acquired the towns of Krempe and Wilster in 1465, armed revolts followed from 1470 to 1471 and again in 1480. Both were suppressed brutally though the council ultimately had to give up these holdings. In the immediate vicinity to the north of the growing city, several villages were simply dissolved to make room for gardens and pastures for city dwellers.

Butchering and the Livestock Trade

Along with grain, dairy products, and vegetables, meat was needed to feed the city, though in this case the impact on the landscape was less pronounced. Hamburg imported large quantities of beef, and, since oxen could be moved overland over long distances on the hoof, it did so from relatively far afield. We know from surviving wills that many wealthier citizens kept livestock and often exchanged or rented it to each other, recording such debts for their heirs.[8] To keep their cattle, the city acquired and cleared four large areas outside the walls for use as pasture for its citizens in 1256 and 1258. These have long been caught up in urban expansion and only one of them, the Moorweide, still exists as a park today. Papenwärder is now an exclusive neighbourhood on the Alster while the Bürgerweide is a busy thoroughfare, and the Grasbrook, once an idyllic island, is being turned into a trendy new post-industrial living quarter.

The decision to provide these pastures still had a lasting impact on the landscape by making the long-distance ox trade competitive. The *Ossenpadd* (oxpath) from Jutland to the Elbe crossings, today a European long-distance cycling path, saw herds of thousands driven south in its heyday, and the place where it crossed the Hamburg border is still known as *Ochsenzoll* (ox toll). Guilded butchers were banned from buying cattle within the city or from owning it jointly with foreigners, so they often travelled long distances to cattle markets. Oxen from Jutland and Schleswig, driven down the peninsula to be sold, could be fattened again on the municipal pastures before slaughter. This practice led to a gradual decline of cattle raising in the Marsch around Hamburg. Local farmers could not compete with the low costs of Danish landlords who could force serfs to stable oxen over the winter without compensation. Instead, they increasingly opted for more profitable and less vulnerable dairy farming. As a result, Hamburg's famous beef most likely did not come from anywhere near Hamburg. Neither did the concentration on dairy result in a notable cheesemaking tradition. Hard cheeses imported from Central Germany, the Netherlands, and Scandinavia dominated the market, while local dairies mainly provided food for immediate consumption that short transport routes gave them a monopoly on.

Figure 6. Fruit trees in orderly rows right down to the drainage canal. (Image: Wikimedia commons).

Shaping a Territory, Making a Landscape

The fifteenth century saw the end of major changes to Hamburg's territorial boundaries for almost five hundred years. The shape that the city's hinterland had broadly acquired in the course of the Middle Ages held until the 1937 creation of 'Greater Hamburg', when it swallowed up large areas to its south and west including the cities of Harburg and Altona. The motivation for this was purely political and took no account of food resources that, as the postwar years would make painfully clear, were scarce within the city's limits.

The territory of old Hamburg, by contrast, was not an accidental agglomeration of bits and pieces brought about, as feudal inheritances often were, by accident of death. It had a cohesive economic structure evolved to provide for the needs of the city at its core, and one of the guiding concerns was providing food. That the Vierlande, the Walddörfer, or the Alster river's course today look different even from nearby areas can be explained by the policies and developments underlying this dynamic. This is hardly unique; at a lower level, similar events played out everywhere in Europe; in Germany alone, the cities of Lübeck, Cologne, Frankfurt, and especially Nuremberg with its single-minded dedication to forestry offer promising material for similar studies. It is, quite simply, how politics worked for the longest time.

What Cuisine Did It Support?

Finally, it would not be fair to the spirit of the Symposium to end without including some ideas of the cuisine that this landscape supported. Given what we know of the soil and weather, it should come as no surprise that the cuisine is homely and often limited. Like other peripheral cuisines of Europe, though, it has not just redeeming virtues, but unexpected strengths. Cuisine, of course, here refers to what people ate when they had a choice. The everyday diet of the poor – which would have included well over half the

Eating into the Countryside

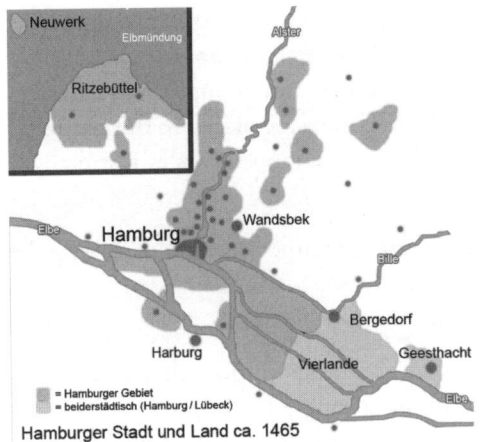

Figure 7. Medieval Hamburg's territory (Image: Wikimedia commons).

Figure 8. Expansion under the law of 1937 (Image: Wikimedia commons).

population – consisted mostly of bread, porridge, and boiled vegetables.

Feast day cooking was heavy on animal protein, something that could be produced or procured locally in good quality. Fish and above all meat were the centrepieces of the festive table; vegetables, though increasingly appreciated, remained side dishes. Butter and milk are often mentioned as cooking ingredients. Surviving recipes, representing the cooking habits of well-off city dwellers, also feature sugar, spirits, spices, and other exotic delights easily found on the markets of Hamburg. How far these things were available in the rural hinterland is uncertain, but the fact that farming households along the lower Elbe prepared pancakes and English-style boiled puddings by the sixteenth century suggests that a measure of culinary sophistication spread outwards.

Fruit, both fresh and dried, plays a central role in Hamburg's cuisine. Summer days with up to eighteen hours of daylight allow berries, apples, plums, and pears to ripen to perfection in the short growing season (at 53°33'N, Hamburg shares its latitude with the Aleutians). Unlike fresh fish, high-end beef, or imported sugar and spices, this was a pleasure available to almost anyone in city and countryside.

A traditional dish eaten in both city and country combined bacon, beans, and pears in a rich stew. Cooking pears are still sold in markets all over Germany, though they are becoming more rare as fewer people know what to do with them. This recipe from a 1975 heritage cookbook reconstructs the basics of an Early Modern recipe that was rarely recorded prior to the twentieth century:

Birnen, Bohnen und Speck
250g streaky smoked bacon, 500g bergamot pears (a hard, tart variety), 500g Turkish peas (a local variety of string bean), 500g new potatoes, salt, pepper, parsley, summer savory

Remove the strings from the beans and boil them in lightly salted water together with the bacon, sliced and well peppered, and the savory. When they are almost soft, the pears are placed on top whole, with their stalks removed, and also cooked until they are soft. Boil the potatoes, peel them, and arrange them along the rim of a pre-warmed shallow serving bowl. The beans are placed in the centre first, then pears and bacon are layered on top. Plenty of chopped parsley is strewn over the whole dish.[9]

The 1879 *Illustrirtes Hamburger Kochbuch* suggests a more refined manner of serving the same variety of green beans:

Beans, Turkish (string beans)
After the strings have been removed, you slice the beans into small segments, wash them in cold water, set them by the fire in strongly boiling water with a little salt and place them on a colander to drain as soon as they are done. Then you prepare a white roux, make a sauce with stock or with cream, cook it with chopped parsley and a good piece of butter, stir in the beans, bring the whole to a boil once more and serve it with a dish of herring.[10]

Though still a humble dish, this reflects a more urban, international style that liberally uses the fresh produce and dairy products the countryside provided. Herring, most likely already salted from fishing grounds in the North Sea, would have come from the city markets.

The pride of Hamburg's culinary art was its prime beef, salted, smoked, and boiled. The poet Matthias Claudius, who lived in the nearby town of Wandsbek, described the dish in fond terms and sometimes purchased a piece jointly with friends to serve to guests.[11] Wealthy citizens bought fattened oxen driven far overland and had them salted by hired butchers, then smoked the meat in their chimneys. Master butchers also sold this meat at a high price. Only choice pieces were good enough. The 1830 *Hamburgisches Koch-Buch* describes the process of cooking it:

Hamburgisches Rauchfleisch
Must be washed with cold water and brushed in lukewarm; then it is set by the fire early in the morning in cold water and let it cook very gently; if it is young meat and not smoked strongly, it will be done in four or five hours; but if it is old, it is best to set it by a gentle fire or in the hot ashes the night before so that it warms up. In either case, you must taste the water once the meat has cooked for an hour to see if it is too salty, and in that case pour it out and pour in fresh, which you must also not fail to do as it boils away since the meat must always be kept covered well with water. It is also good if, once the meat is done, it can stand for an hour or so in its sauce before serving so it stays juicier. Should it not be salty enough, it can be salted. If it is not smoked enough, a piece of saltpetre the size of a pea can be boiled with it and it will turn out nicely red. When serving,

you clean it, take off the black skin and garnish it with parsley.[12]

This was a luxury few villagers ever tasted. The *Illustrirtes Hamburger Kochbuch* suggests serving beef with fruit compote, of which this recipe is an example:

Compote of Gooseberries
The gooseberries are selected carefully, cleaned and washed. Pour boiling water over them and drain them in a colander. Then boil wine in proportion with a good part of sugar, cook the gooseberries in it and thicken it with egg yolks; you may also omit these. Then, the gooseberries are removed, the sauce is boiled down to (the desired) thickness and poured over them (again).[13]

In humbler households, dried (or, in season, fresh) apples, pears, and plums were often added to the cooking liquid of puddings or dumplings and served as a sweet sauce. Unfortunately, though we have many recipes from printed cookbooks, they are all complex and rich. The plain yeast or suet puddings of the common folk are not recorded.

Notes

1. Sometimes infamously, as in the case of Huntingdon's map of global civilizations drawing the boundary between Islam and Western Christianity across the highlands of New Guinea at 141°E latitude.
2. Cf. entries 11, 17, 45, and 53 in *Hamburgisches Urkundenbuch herausgegeben vom Archiv der Hansestadt Hamburg*, Vol. 2: 1300–1399 (Hamburg: Lutcke und Wulff, 1939).
3. Otto Rüdiger, *Die ältesten hamburgischen Zunftrollen und Brüderschaftsstatuten* (Hamburg: Lucas Gräfe, 1874), doc. 5a § 14, 15, 17, 19.
4. Rüdiger, doc. 12a; doc. 12n.
5. Rüdiger, doc. 12e.
6. Wolfgang Kaiser, *Obstland im Norden. Die Geschichte des Obsthandels im Alten Land* (Publikationen der Kulturstiftung Altes Land, Husum, Husumer Druck- und Verlagsgesellschaft, 2009), p. 11
7. Kaiser, p. 21 ff.
8. Hans Dieter Loose, *Hamburger Testamente 1351-1400*. Veröffentlichungen aus dem Staatsarchiv der Freien und Hansestadt Hamburg XI (Hamburg: Hans Christians, 1970), e.g. docs. 6, 31, 34, 50, 78, and 112.
9. Dorothee von Hellermann, *Das Kochbuch aus Hamburg* (Münster: Verlag Wolfgang Hölker, 1975), p. 92.
10. Louise Richter and Sophie Charlotte Hommer, *Illustrirtes Hamburger Kochbuch. Fünfte durchgehends umgearbeitete Auflage* (Hamburg: B.S. Berendsohn, 1879), recipe #645, p. 232.
11. Anette Lüchow, 'Claudius und Klopstock', in *Matthias Claudius: 1740-1815: Leben – Zeit – Werk*, ed. by Jörg-Ulrich Fechner (Tübingen: Niemeyer, 1996), pp. 91-110 (p. 100).
12. *Hamburgisches Koch-Buch oder vollständige Anleitung zum Kochen [...] verfaßt von einigen Hamburgischen Hausfrauen, Achte vermehrt und verbesserte Auflage* (Hamburg: Herold und Wahlstab, 1830), p. 107 ff.
13. Richter and Hommer, recipe #1060, p. 337.

Singapore: Landscape of Loss, Cuisine of Comfort

Lucey Bowen

In Singapore, the connection between landscape and cuisine turns the European notion of *terroir* inside out. Rather than tasting of ingredients produced in a specific place, Singapore's cuisine is the consequence of both the transformation of the landscape over the last two hundred years and the constant stream of immigration to this island city-state. Singapore's Hawker Centre food is its national cuisine, locally cooked from imported foodstuffs. Almost all provisions to feed 5.6 million people enter Singapore through its port or over the causeway from Malaysia.

A Hawker Centre is an open-air complex where cooked food is sold from stalls. 'Hawker' was the English term for the itinerant vendors once common to Singapore's streets. Upwards of fifty vendor-chefs may be housed in a centre, which has plastic-topped tables and stools fixed to the concrete floor. Currently, there are 107 such centres, managed by Singapore's National Environmental Agency.[1]

The food served is an eclectic mix of dishes originating in China, South and South East Asia, reflecting Singapore's history as an entrepôt and crossroads. Singapore has four official languages: Malay, Mandarin, Tamil, and English, and dialects abound. In 2010, 74.1% of the population had Chinese ancestry, 13.4% Malay, 9.2% Indian, and the rest other.[2] Rules and figures don't do justice to the interwoven layers of people, complicated by a thousand years of trade, almost a century and a half of colonial rule, and more than half a century of single party rule.

Singaporeans scoff at numbering the countless dishes offered at hawker centres, but readily discuss their favourite centres and vendors. Dr Leslie Tay, dentist and food writer, lists about forty dishes in his *The End of Char Kway Teow and Other Hawker Mysteries*.[3] Singaporeans will travel to eat at certain stalls, but many choose the centre nearest their residence or workplace.

The Dunman Food Centre is located in the Joo Chiat neighbourhood halfway between the downtown and the airport. I tried it for lunch while visiting some of the historic shophouses there. Many hawker centre dishes involve noodles, and I chose Heng Heng Prawn Mee Soup. The stall is the size of an apartment kitchen, just large enough for two people, with a stove on one side and storage and sink on the other.

I placed my order with the chef-proprietor, a middle-aged Chinese man. He scalded the mee (rice and egg vermicelli) and plopped them into a bowl. His special broth of shrimp heads and pork ribs had simmered since early morning, flavoured with a paste of ground fresh chilli peppers, shallots, and garlic. He ladled this broth over the vermicelli, garnished it with greens, a handful of shrimp and lean pork, and perhaps a quarter of a hard-boiled egg. He set it down on the front counter. The cost for this cooked-to-order dish? Three dollars Singaporean.

With soupspoon and chopsticks, I carried it to one of the communal tables on the covered terrace and dive in. I wondered, is this Chinese food? Something similar can be had in the Fujian region of Southern China, the homeland of Hokkien-speaking immigrants. Singapore's version, with its paste of chillies, scallions, and garlic, reflects the centuries that Hokkien immigrants spent in Malacca and Penang, absorbing Malay culinary practices.

Had it been breakfast I was after, I might have tried nearby Dragon City Claypot Frog Porridge. Here the chef would offer one claypot of steaming rice porridge and another of frog in his homemade kung-pao sauce. At my seat, I would use two soup spoons, one to scoop a spoonful of porridge and the other to ladle a layer of dark sauce and white frog meat on top. Porridge is everywhere in China, but claypot with frog is uniquely Singaporean.

One evening a Singaporean colleague of my husband invited three of us to dinner at Whampoa Makan Place. This merited the twenty-minute drive from the University. On arrival, one of us *choped* (claimed) a table. The others wandered from stall to stall, sniffing and looking. One by one they returned bearing plates of Oyster Omelette, a dish favoured by immigrants from Teochew-speaking area of Southern China; skewers of marinated, barbecued chicken satay with peanut sauce; chicken wings; and *rojak*, a salad found on both sides of the Straits of Malacca. Last was carrot cake, which is neither carrot nor cake, but rather chunks of steamed rice flour and radish stir-fried with thick soy sauce, topped with half a hard-boiled egg and half-inch pieces of chives. For me, *rojak* and carrot cake are emblems of Singapore. Malays, Chinese, and Indians all make *rojak*, Malay for 'mix'. It is a tropical fruit salad, with variations like slices of Chinese cruller, or fish, sauced with peanuts and shrimp paste. Carrot cake is distinctly Chinese in origin, but takes its name from Singapore's English foodways.

At a given Hawker Centre, depending on the time of day, I saw schoolgirls eating breakfast, three-generation-families, business men on lunch break, and retirees. I overheard conversations in Mandarin, English, Teochew or Hokkien dialect, Malay, Tamil, and more. All were eating Singaporean dishes. Some dishes can be traced to South China or the West Coast of India, but Singapore has transformed them.

Hawkers Were Not Always in Government-Regulated Centres

When Singapore separated from Malaysia in 1965, the government turned its attention to 'a public nuisance to be removed from the streets', namely itinerant food hawkers.[4] Until then they had served important needs of the newly independent state. With a low barrier to entry, needing only a small cart with charcoal stove, street hawking provided work for newly arrived immigrants. Men outnumbered women four to one. Housing, and the kitchens that went with it, were in short supply. Hawkers fed labourers close to work.

Yet street hawkers contributed to congestion and pollution. The government's first step was licensing the vendors, and relocating them to side streets and empty parking lots. In 1971, despite resistance from vendors and customers, the hawkers were resettled into stalls with gas, electricity, water, and proper sewer connections at a low rent. Some centres were located in the Central Business District. Others were in or near newly built housing, where they could continue to provide their specialty dishes, cooked to order for each customer, at reasonable prices.

Singaporeans defend Hawker Centre Cuisine. In 2012, the French dining event called *Diner en Blanc* was held in Singapore for the first time. Participants dress all in white and bring elaborate meals and table settings to a secret location. A Singaporean food blogger proposed a menu of favourite dishes from a Hawker Centre. The event's organizers told him the dishes were not in keeping with the event's elegant image. The local reaction was vehement. The blogger observed, 'Singapore local delicacies are the classiest foods ever in our hearts.'[5] Singaporeans discussed a boycott of the event. The organizers were forced to apologize to food-loving Singapore.

France redeemed itself in July 2016, when the authoritative Michelin Guide published its first Singapore edition. Seventeen hawker centre stalls were singled out for the *Bib Gourmand* award, and another received a star. This made the front page and the Arts section of Singapore's *Straits Times* for weeks. Crispy Curry Puffs, those morsels that travelled from India with the British; Indonesian Satay, Hainanese Chicken Rice and Malay, Hokkien and Teochew rice and noodle preparations, all were honoured by Michelin.[6]

The Landscape of Loss

I have shown how this food knits together the cooking styles and techniques that waves of immigrants brought to Singapore. I taste it in the food. Immigrants also brought ideas about how the land should be used. The cultural alterations to the landscape require close looking and research. I was determined to use the knowledge of Asian culture gleaned from my work as a guide at the Asian Art Museum in San Francisco to understand what I was seeing. In the early days of my six-month stay in Singapore, I felt more than I analyzed. Stepping outside the airport doors, I was mugged by tropical humidity. We drove down an eight-lane freeway lined with unfamiliar trees and neck-wrenching skyscrapers. From the twenty-fourth floor of our apartment building, the island city-state resembled Manhattan on the hottest of August days, dense with highways fringed with green. It never cooled off. Not at night, not as the months went by. Almost on the equator, Singapore has no seasons, except rain and more rain. It is green because flowering plants need variation in sunshine to bloom.

Ask a Singaporean about landscape and you'll get a blank stare: 'There isn't any.' By 'landscape' I mean the term as defined by the cultural geographer J.B. Jackson. He argued that landscape is a composition of man-made spaces on the land, not the natural features of the environment. It is land shaped to serve a community. By his definition, tiny Singapore is all landscape.[7]

Singapore: Landscape of Loss, Cuisine of Comfort

The Genius of the Place

S. Dillon Ripley, former director of the Smithsonian Institution who visited Southeast Asia numerous times, observed that in this region, no single element plays a more decisive role than rain. 'Rain', he said, 'is more than rain, it is an erosive torrent.' Singapore is located where monsoons converge. The humidity of a steam bath alternates with rain in solid sheets, blocking the view but bringing no relief from the heat. The temperature averages 27 C (80 F), and annual rainfall is around 2,340 mm (92.1 inches), twice that of Manhattan.[8]

For Singapore's earliest inhabitants, the torrential rains and the thick forest cover meant that only rivers provided access to the interior. Travel up the river and between islands was by boat.[9] Dwellings at the rivers' edges were on stilts. John Stilgoe, one of J.B. Jackson's students, wrote that the margin where sea meets land is to landsmen a dangerous place.[10] For these itinerant sea rovers, called *orang laut* in Malay, it was home – at least a temporary home. They owed allegiance to a succession of maritime regimes that ranged over the archipelago of South East Asia. Subsisting on fish, shellfish, crustaceans, and reptiles, the *orang laut* traded forest products for rice.

In the sixteenth century, maritime traders from Arabia and China spread Islam. Islam was not accompanied to South East Asia by the landscape traditions favoured by the Persian, and later Mughal, sultans. Instead, the earliest palaces and mosques were constructed as Malay houses, of timber, with steeply-pitched, palm-thatched roofs or *atap*, to repel the omnipresent rain. The Malay garden was an orchard, with trees and bushes selected for their fruit, leaves or roots.

British East India's Free Port

When Sir Thomas Raffles arrived in 1819 to establish an outpost of the British East India Company, he found *orang laut* compounds where the rivers met the sea, and, on land, two Malay royal claimants to the rule of Singapore. Between 1819 and 1824, Raffles negotiated the cessation of Singapore to the East India Company. In exchange, the Malay regime, consisting of the *Temenggong* (harbourmaster) and the Sultan, received allowances and properties. Like the Indians of Manhattan, the Malay notion of the ownership of land was quite different than the European concept held by the British East India Company.

Raffles dictated the arrangement of the new settlement of Singapore, and a map was drawn to his specifications.[11] Raffles's plan has all the elements that J.B. Jackson describes as the ideal political landscape: public buildings, roads, water supply, etc. Rectangles and squares, imposed on the land. Parallel to the shore were avenues and a series of *kampongs*, ethnic neighbourhoods, for the Bugis (Indonesian seafarers and traders); a royal claimant, the Sultan of Johor and his followers; Arabs, Europeans, and the Chinese and Indians brought to Singapore by the Company.

Raffles's political ideal of urban planning segregated groups by religion, race, and place of origin. It is characterized by permanence and clear boundaries. Above all is the desire to impose order on the land and its inhabitants. The *Temenggong*, the other aspirant for control of the port, had settled on the southwest shore of the Singapore River. Raffles wanted that land for the numerous Chinese merchants. The *Temenggong* and his followers were made to move west, away from the harbour, to a *kampong* called Telok Blangah.

Kew Gardens botanists like Joseph Banks had begun collecting tropical plants in the service of the British Empire. Raffles followed Banks's tutelage. Raffles's 1824 Botanical Garden did not survive the rapid expansion of his city, but its successor, called the Singapore Botanic Garden (SPG), was founded in 1859. It was part of a web of botanical activities focused on identifying and propagating species of plants useful for extracting the wealth of the tropics. From the Garden, the South American rubber tree became the mainstay of Malaysian plantations.[12]

In 2016, SPG opens to citizens each morning at six. I enter via the Tanglin Gate, north of the Central Business District. The noise of city traffic fades and is replaced by the splash of fountains. I walk past the Victorian bandstand, and see an elevated walkway leading into the six hectare of rain forest preserved in the middle of a garden, in the middle of a city. In spite of bright sun on the rest of the garden, it is dark in there, not colder but more humid. The forest floor is thick with brown leaves. Telephone-pole straight tree trunks are interwoven with liana vines as thick as your wrist. The endless variety of leaf shapes disconcerts me. I am instructed not to stay in the rain forest if there is a thunderstorm. I'm happy to emerge. Maybe I dislike disorder as much as Raffles did.

Raffles' shaping of the landscape was not limited to deciding which plants could produce export crops. The British remodelled the banks of the Singapore River, drained and filled swamps, and reclaimed land with earth from hills in the hinterland. The colonizer intervened in historic and artistic traditions as well. When the Sultan of Johor solicited funds from the East India Company for the rebuilding of his mosque, it was Denis Santry of the British firm of Swan and MacLaren who fashioned for him a mosque in the Saracenic style of Moorish Spain. When the *atap*-roofed Istana of the Sultan fell into disrepair, the Irish architect and mapmaker George Drumond Coleman designed for him the Palladian dwelling now known as Istana Kampong Glam.[13]

When Sir Thomas Raffles arrived, Singapore had the same number of Chinese as Malay. The *Temenggong*, deprived of his income as harbourmaster, had begun leasing river valleys to Chinese immigrants who cleared the jungle and planted pepper and gambier trees, two successful export crops in the mid-nineteenth century. The relentless clearing of the forest cover left the earth exposed to the torrential rains, and the soil was soon exhausted.

In Raffles's Plan for Singapore the section reserved for the Chinese lay to the west of the River. Within the section zones were set aside for Cantonese, Hokkien, and Teochew immigrants. Each group commissioned a temple on the road along the shore. These temples were constructed using the vernacular of mainland Southern Chinese houses, with north-south spatial orientations and walled-and-inner-courtyard ground plans.[14]

I take Singapore Mass Rapid Transit to that road, called Telok Ayer Street, now dwarfed by high-rises in all directions. It is sometimes called the Street of Religious Harmony. Between about 1824 and 1860, more temples were built here, in the heart of the busy port city: Tamil Muslims built Masjid al Abrar; Indian Muslims the Nagore Durgha Shrine. One hundred years later, the Chinese Methodist Church joined the assembly. The National Heritage Board has gazetted these as Heritage buildings.

I purchase incense sticks, light them, and bow three times, letting their fragrant smoke rise to whatever gods there may be. It is midday, and there are more temple attendants than worshippers. My Singaporean friend, Hector, told me that the Government is careful to protect all religious buildings, but does not encourage practices the government regards as superstitious or spontaneous. The major Taoist observances, the Hungry Ghost Festival, the Nine Emperor Gods, and Mazu's Birthday attract large numbers of worshippers. Temples must obtain police permits (free) for processions.

Although the characteristic Singapore shophouse built in nineteenth-century Singapore was a southern Chinese vernacular form, Raffles dictated an additional five-foot-covered walkway on the street side for shelter from rain or sun. British architects imitated the arches of Greece and Rome on this facade, creating something akin to Georgian terrace houses. By 1849, Singapore from the harbour could have been mistaken for a New England village, studded with churches and houses in the Palladian mode. The jungle interior was barely visible.

Planters continued to clear the hinterlands as a succession of export crops were attempted: nutmeg, cotton, sugar, coffee, cinnamon, and pineapple. The British and the towkays, the major Chinese landowners and merchants, shared the same view of Singapore's jungle; a menace, something to be dispensed with, and the land put to profitable use. The disorder of the tropical jungle frightened the Europeans. They were dutifully aghast at a widely circulated lithograph showing a lion attacking the surveying party of architect and mapmaker George Drumgold Coleman, in 1833, as he planned roads in the interior.

Singapore town continued to grow more crowded. The British and wealthy Chinese built villas on its outskirts. Still, the *kampongs* remained. Small pig, poultry, and truck gardens, and even a dairy farm, were attempted on worn-out lands.

The Great Clean Up Begins

In its half century in power, the People's Action Party under Prime Minister Lee Kuan Yew transformed the island on a scale that colonial authorities could never have imagined or accomplished. Civil servants who worked with Lee Kwan Yew thought of him as Singapore's 'Gardener-in-Chief'.[15] The changes he made to Singapore's landscape during his tenure support the title. He spoke of Singapore as 'A Garden City', and 'A City in a Garden'. It is easy to imagine him thinking the whole island was his garden. His job was to make his island a garden and its citizens as productive as those of first world cities. He believed that cleanliness was a characteristic of those cities. This is why he made corralling the street hawkers a priority. The hawkers weren't weeds, but plants in the wrong location, needing to be moved to the right spot.

Garden-making requires shaping space, moulding the earth, irrigating and draining, cultivating, populating, furnishing, naming, and inhabiting.[16] By flattening hills, draining mangrove swamps, and importing sand from all over South East Asia, Singapore expanded.

In 1957 its area was 581 square kilometres. By 2008, its area was 775.5 square kilometres. The Government's Housing and Development Board replaced Chinatown's overcrowded shophouses, the *kampong* villages, and jungle with ten- to twelve-floor apartment buildings. Whole river basins were dammed at their delta to create reservoirs of fresh water. Through recycling and filtration, water reserves grew from four square kilometres to twenty-eight square kilometres. Land was converted to industrial and residential use, reducing agricultural acreage from 25% in 1960 to 2% in 2004. Pig farming was eliminated entirely for the sake of water security.[17]

In the 1970s, even as the human population was transplanted from the city to the former agricultural areas, Lee Kuan Yew inaugurated an extensive 'greening' or tree planting campaign all over the island. New suburban housing was adjusted to match the ethnic balance of the nation as a whole. No more of the casual mixing or ethnic enclaves. Fixtures for Lee Kuan Yew's garden included housing, places for prayer, burial, study, civic rallying points, recreation and importantly, cooked food centres, permanent homes for hawker stalls.

Another daring feat of gardening characterized by the desire for control was begun in 2012. On reclaimed land south of the downtown core, two massive glass houses were constructed, with the opposite function of greenhouses in northern climates. One is temperate, the other, a cool cloud forest with a waterfall cascading down a foliage-covered mountain. Using the trimmings harvested by the National Park Service from Lee's tree planting solved the engineering required to maintain these cool biomes in an equatorial region. This green waste fires a biomass electric generator, exhausted through the Garden's Supertree structures.[18]

The doors at the base of the cloud forest open onto a waterfall cascading from the top of an artificial mountain. It is humid but refreshingly cool to walk here. I circle up around the mountain, greenery planted on all sides. There are species of pine, variegated vines, cascades of flowers, and bursts of cool mist. I walk out above the forest canopy and take an elevator to the top of the waterfall. I like my rainforests cool.

I wonder at the source of Lee Kuan Yew's ideal landscape. Lee's ideas reflect both British and Chinese culture. Both applied engineering to the task of taming the landscape. Think of the role of railroads and waterpower in England's Industrial Revolution. Think of the legendary Emperor Yu who created China's canal system.

For four generations, Lee's family dwelled in the Dutch and British colonies along the Straits of Malacca. Ethnically Hakka, they migrated from Southern China. They married Malay women, and other Straits Chinese, forming the *Peranakan*, or locally born. This elite set themselves aside from the subsequent migration of labourers from China.

Singapore: Landscape of Loss, Cuisine of Comfort

Sometimes called 'the King's Chinese', their languages were English and bazaar Malay.

Lee himself, born in Singapore in 1923, received his education at Raffles Institution, the premier English Language Secondary School. His plans to read law in London were short-circuited by World War II. He was able to travel to England in 1946, but chose rural Cambridge over London. Travel to Cambridge took him near Letchworth, one of Britain's first Garden Cities. His memoirs make clear his affection for the English countryside, his admiration for National Health, and his repulsion for the colonial regime.[19]

Lost Landscapes

Extraordinary feats of mechanical and social engineering brought Singapore, as Lee Kwan Yew said, from 'Third World to First' in less than fifty years. Yet at the turn of the century, its citizens expressed loss and confusion. Rodolphe De Koninck, Julie Drolet and Marc Girard proposed that the erosion of all landmarks at the local level was planned by the government to 'allow for only one level of territorial allegiance: that of the Republic of Singapore'.[20] But having achieved prosperity, citizens questioned the need for more change and feared they had lost their souls. Three Singaporean geographers wrote that, for them, landscape was comprehended through the idiom of loss.[21]

In response, the government formed the National Heritage Board in 1993, 'responsible for telling the Singapore story, sharing the Singaporean experience and imparting the Singapore spirit'.[22] The Board was to focus on the shared heritage of diverse communities for the purpose of education, nation building, and cultural understanding.

Among many other projects, The National Heritage Board supported a series of four gastronomic memoirs from chefs who experienced the loss of the familiar brought about by Singapore's extraordinary transformation.[23] (All four are available in English.) Aziza Ali founded Singapore's first high-end Malay food restaurant. Damian D'Silva is a chef passionate about Singapore's traditional Eurasian cuisine. Devi Sanmugam is known as the Spice Queen of Singapore. *Peranakan* Jocelyn Shu might be called the goddess of mortar and pestle. The four memoirs allow the reader a multi-sensory taste of the childhoods of chefs, acute observers of remembered tastes and smells. To read them is to pick up the threads of Singapore's colonial and post-colonial history from a culinary perspective.

Each born between 1949 and 1956, the four chefs share memories of their childhoods in *kampong* houses, seaside bungalows, and the first HDB estates. Each experienced the growing or gathering of local ingredients, including raising and slaughtering chickens and pigs. Theirs was a multi-sensory world of home kitchens, filled with spices and wood or charcoal smoke; the rhythm of mortar and pestle grinding spices, roots, leaves, grains; the sizzle of frying. Each knew the laborious processes involved in making food for a large family. The scents of the cooking of neighbours encouraged them to try different foods. Through neighbours and schoolmates they experienced the daily life and celebrations of other groups and the foods associated with Deepavali, Hari Raya, and Chinese New Year.

Food and Landscape

A common element in these stories is relocation and displacement. Grandparents and parents moved to Singapore from all over the peninsula and archipelago – Malacca, Java, Tamil Nadu. Once arrived in Singapore, marital strife, financial upheaval, and the work of the Housing Development Board sent each family to a series of lodgings.

I can't imagine what it would be like to lose all trace of where I grew up. I set out one morning to find Number 35 Radin Mas, the childhood home of Aziza Ali. On my way, I pass all that remains of the *Temenggong*'s *kampong* at Telok Blangah: a Mosque, the possession of his descendants in Johor. Aziza Ali wrote about gathering ferns that grew wild behind her house, washing them, and using them to dry fresh laksa noodles. The hill was rented out to a Chinese farmer who provided her family with vegetables. I found the hillside but there were no ferns or farm. *Kampong* houses have been replaced by HDB flats and gated private houses with thick glass windows. I don't suppose today's residents can guess what their neighbours are cooking from the scents that wafted through the tall, open windows of Aziza Ali's Malay-style house.

All the chefs recall the delights of hawker foods when the vendors were mobile. Whether to a one-story wooden house, brick bungalow, or ten-floor HDB unit, a variety of vendors brought food to each neighbourhood. Each chef experienced the relocation of the street vendors to hawker centres with a sense of loss. Chef Damian D'Silva cheered those hawkers who evaded the authorities enforcing relocation.

Will Hawker Centres Share the Fate of Pig Farms?

Daniel Chia, of Slow Food Singapore, identified the challenges to Hawker Centres. The rental costs for stalls are rising, but customers expect low prices. The hawker profession is seen as menial, laborious, and low profit. Young hawkers must amass capital and recognition. Stall rentals are no longer subsidized. Younger customers are more interested in foreign foods, ranging from McDonald's to sushi and even Tex-Mex.[24]

These challenges are being met in a variety of ways. An item from the *Straits Times* told of a start-up enterprise: the Rotimatic, which produces *roti prata* much as tortillas are mass-produced in Mexico. In another story, Indian restaurateurs banded together to share equipment in a common kitchen for the back end of their eateries. Another start-up offered a cell phone application, YiHawker, that allows customers to order from a hawker stall for home delivery at a specified time.

And then there is Hawker Chan of Michelin one-star fame. Backed by a partner, he opened a stand-alone sit-down restaurant on the edge of Chinatown, serving his Hong Kong Soya Sauce Chicken. His prices doubled, but there's air conditioning.

Perhaps Hawker Centres themselves will become the locus of nostalgia for Singaporeans too young to remember street vendors. Thirty-something novelist Cheryl Lu-Lien Tan, author of *Tiger in the Kitchen*, wrote that the one thing that sustained her younger self through the waning hours of the school were Beef Ball Noodles at the food court of Scotts Shopping Centre, the first air-conditioned food court in Singapore. When Scotts was re-developed, the vendor disappeared. Returning to Singapore from New York City, she learned that the stall had re-opened at the newest shopping mall downtown. She corralled two old school friends to go and try them. All agreed that they were mostly as remembered, but just okay. The pleasure was in sharing them with old friends.[25]

Food of Comfort

A curry puff's flaky exterior and spicy interior, steaming porridge, noodles bathed in rich broth, smoky satay drenched with rich peanut sauce: in all of these textures and tastes, Singaporeans can luxuriate in nostalgia for younger selves. Most Singaporeans are no more than two generations removed from the beginning of the profound transformations of the Singapore landscape that began with corralling the street hawkers.

The culinary historians John and Karen Hess observed that it is soil and water that give taste to a *terroir* and its cuisine.[26] We could say that Singapore's cuisine is the product of water everywhere, and not enough earth.

Notes

1. National Environment Agency, 'Hawker Centres and Markets in Singapore', *National Environment Agency*, Singapore Government, 2018 <http://www.nea.gov.sg/public-health/hawker-management/hawker-centres-and-markets-in-singapore> [accessed 29 May 2017].
2. Census of Population 2010, Singapore Department of Statistic, p. 10 <https://www.singstat.gov.sg/docs/default-source/default-document-library/publications/publications_and_papers/cop2010/census_2010_release1/cop2010sr1.pdf> [accessed 10 February 2018]
3. Leslie Tay, *The End of Char Kway Teow and Other Hawker Mysteries* (Singapore: Epigram Books, 2010).
4. Hawkers Inquiry Commission, *Report of the Hawkers Inquiry Commission* (Singapore: Singapore Government, 1950), p. 5.
5. Benson Ang qtd. in Shibani Mahtani, 'Diner en Blanc Cooks Up a Fuss in Singapore', *The Wall Street Journal*, 28 August 2012 <https://blogs.wsj.com/indonesiarealtime/2012/08/28/diner-en-blanc-cooks-up-a-fuss-in-singapore/> [accessed 14 August 2016].
6. Benson Ang, 'Here's What They Queue an Hour for.' *Straits Times*, 23 July 2016.
7. John Brinkerhoff Jackson, The Necessity for Ruins and Other Topics (Amherst: University of Massachusetts Press, 1980), p. 2.
8. Dillon Ripley and the Editors of Life, *The Land and Wildlife of Tropical Asia* (New York: Time-Life Books, 1969), p. 6; Climate of Singapore, Meteorological Service Singapore <http://www.weather.gov.sg/climate-climate-of-singapore/> [accessed 10 February 2018], and US Climate Data, Climate: New York, New York <https://www.usclimatedata.com/climate/new-york/united-states/3202> [accessed 10 February 2018].
9. John Norman Miksic, *Singapore and the Silk Road of the Sea, 1300-1800* (Singapore: NUS Press, 2017), p. 160.
10. John R. Stilgoe. *Alongshore* (New Haven, CT: Yale University Press, 1996), p. 5.
11. Bonny Tan, 'Raffles Town Plan (Jackson Plan)', *Singapore Infopedia*, National Library Board, Singapore Government, 2016 <http://eresources.nlb.gov.sg/infopedia/articles/SIP_658_2005-01-07.html> [accessed 4 March 2017].
12. Daniel R. Headrick, *The Tentacles of Progress: Technology Transfer in the Age of Imperialism, 1850-1940* (Oxford: Oxford University Press, 1988), pp. 243-50.

13. Gretchen Liu, *Singapore: A Pictorial History, 1819-2000* (Singapore: Editions Didier Millet, 1999), p. 214.
14. Kang Ger-Wen, *Decoration and Symbolism in Chinese Architecture: Understanding Singapore's Historic Chinese Buildings* (Singapore: National Heritage Board, 2013), pp. 11-12.
15. Peter Ho, Liu Thai Ker, and Tan Wee Kiat, *A Chance of a Lifetime: Lee Kuan Yew and the Physical Transformation of Singapore* (Singapore: Editions Didier-Millet, 2016), pp. 38-39.
16. Charles W. Moore, William J. Mitchell, and William Turnbull, Jr, *The Poetics of Gardens* (Cambridge, MA: MIT Press, 1988), pp. vi-vii.
17. Rodolphe De Koninck, Julie Drolet, and Marc Girard, *Singapore: An Atlas of Perpetual Terrotorial Transformation* (Singapore: NUS Press, 2008), pp. 14, 16, 40-41.
18. Atelier One, 'Gardens by the Bay', Atelier One Structural Engineers, <http://www.atelierone.com/gardens-by-the-bay/> [accessed 14 August 2016].
19. Lee Kuan Yew, *From Third World to First: The Singapore Story: 1965-2000* (Singapore: Marshall Cavendish, 2015).
20. De Koninck, Drolet, and Girard, p. 1.
21. Elaine Lynn-Ee Ho, Chich Yuan Woon, and Kamilan Ramdas, 'Introduction: Rediscovering Singapore's Changing Landscapes', in *Changing Landscapes in Singapore: Old Tensions, New Discoveries*, ed. by Elaine Lynn-Ee Ho, Chich Yuan Woon, and Kamilan Ramdas (Singapore: NUS Press, 2014), pp. 1-24 (p. xv).
22. National Heritage Board, 'About NHB', *National Heritage Board*, Singapore Government, 2018 < https://www.nhb.gov.sg/who-we-are/about-us> [accessed 15 August 2016].
23. These include Aziza Ali, *Sambal Days, Kampong Cuisine* (Singapore: ATE, 2013); Damian D'Silva, *Rebel with a Cause* (Singapore: ATE, 2012); Devagi Sanmugam with Jocelyn Tully, *Tricks and Treats and Other Childhood Tales* (Singapore: ATE, 2011); and Jocelyn Shu, *Nostalgia is the Most Powerful Seasoning* (Singapore: ATE, 2011).
24. Daniel Chia, 'Singapore's Food Heritage: Eat it, Share it, Save it?', Panel 4: Cuisine: Legacy, Transformation and Transmission, Third Singapore Heritage Science Conference, 26 January 2016.
25. Cheryl Lu-Lien Tan, 'A Remembrance of Beef Ball Noodles Past', *The Atlantic,* 23 March 2010 <https://www.theatlantic.com/health/archive/2010/03/a-remembrance-of-beef-ball-noodles-past/37877/> [accessed 14 August 2016].
26. John and Karen Hess, *The Taste of America* (New York: Grossman, 1977), p. 17.

Landscaping Food and Identity: Rice Paddy Art in Japan

Voltaire Cang

Introduction

Rice paddy art is Japan's way of playing with its food. A recent phenomenon that has gained popularity in many rural areas nationwide, it is the practice of planting different coloured rice stalks and grains in painstakingly meticulous and exact patterns to create giant portraits and other pictures on rice paddy landscapes, usually in whimsical designs that contain references to Japanese traditional and popular culture.

Rice has been the most important food crop in Japan throughout its history and, as in many Asian countries, is considered its 'staple' food. Rice in Japan, however, is 'much more than a staple food, something much closer to the soul of the nation'.[1] Ancient Japanese myth relates the creation and transformation of the Japanese archipelago 'from a wilderness into a land of succulent ears of rice' through the benevolence of the Sun Goddess *Amaterasu*, whose descendants, it is asserted, became Japan's emperors who until today reinforce their legitimacy as sovereigns by officiating at the nation's most important rice rituals.[2] Rice and its by-product, *nihonshu* (or *saké*), are essential offerings and commensal elements in these and other sacred rituals, as they also constitute the main food and drink in the many festivals that dot the Japanese calendar, most of which also originated from rice-planting rituals.[3] Rice is also central to Japanese daily life, as emphasized by the word for 'meal' in the Japanese language: *gohan*, which also means 'cooked rice'. Today, rice remains the only food that Japan grows enough of to sustain itself, and serves as a powerful psychological symbol of its independence and economic self-sufficiency.[4]

It was only in the 1960s, however, after its economic rise and much political manoeuvring over agricultural reforms, that Japan was finally able to produce sufficient quantities of rice to feed itself. Less than a decade after achieving rice self-sufficiency, Japan grew so much rice for domestic consumption that the government had to resort to paying many of its rice farmers to keep their fields idle, not growing rice in a policy named *gentan* (acreage reduction).[5] Japan may grow enough rice to eat today, but it still grows too little of all the other food that it consumes. On a calorie-intake basis (i.e. the volume of food from domestic producers consumed by the population), Japan's food self-sufficiency rate currently stands at 39%. This dismal rate could be alleviated by using its land and agricultural resources to grow other food instead of rice, but nothing substantial has been achieved so far, as the 39-40% rate has remained largely unchanged in the past two decades.[6]

Instead, today an increasing number of traditional rice-growing areas have turned to 'art' rather than food production, transforming rice landscapes through rice paddy art. Within the socio-cultural context of the 'rice nation' that is Japan, it is a curious phenomenon that approaches the anomalous. It is also an economically unsound practice, entailing an inefficient and less productive process that takes away from, instead of contributing to, food self-sufficiency. In the discussion that follows, this paper looks into the historical background of, and current developments in, the phenomenon of rice paddy art, and discusses its roles and implications in Japanese society and food culture today.

The Originator

Rice paddy art originated in 1993 in Inakadate, the smallest municipality in northern Aomori Prefecture. To most Japanese, the name Inakadate (*inaka*=rural hometown; *date/tate*=outpost, dwelling) evokes notions of the rural and bucolic, but also backward, which is not entirely inappropriate for this isolated farming village of 8000 residents, mostly aged and steadily diminishing in number.

As with most successful initiatives, the rice paddy art project began as a fluke. Inakadate's officials had wanted to promote the image of their town as an ancient rice farming community and decided to create a program inviting outsiders and non-farmers to experience farming in their rice fields. Drawing patterns on the rice paddy was an afterthought: as a way 'to make rice-planting into an attractive experience and bring in people from other cities, towns and villages', the program committee decided to add an element of play into their plan and had the rice planted in a specific design to make the participants, especially young children, look forward to later monitoring the process of growth of the rice and perhaps visit a few more times until the harvest.[7]

The earliest design utilized three varieties of rice, each with stalks of a distinctive colour: green, the locally-grown variety, along with yellow and dark purple, both ancient varieties. These were planted to form the distinct, jagged outline of Mt. Iwaki (nicknamed the 'northern Mt. Fuji' that is located west and actually outside of Inakadate) rendered using green rice stalks and the words *Ine bunka no mura, Inakadate* (Rice Culture Village, Inakadate) in Japanese script that appeared in yellow against a dark purple background (Figure 1). This first attempt covered an area of 2500 square meters, a manageable size for the 120 people, including town officials and representatives, who came for the inaugural rice planting event. In the beginning, the project was called *Ine moji* ('Rice words') rather than 'art'.[8]

Ine moji became an annual project thereafter, and the design remained largely unchanged during its first decade. The number of participants in the rice planting

Figure 1.

Landscaping Food and Identity

Figure 2.

and harvesting events did not change significantly, either, and visitor numbers who came to view the 'rice words' were steady in the 200 to 300 range for the first few years, gradually increasing to 1000 by the ninth year. During the growing season, the village set up a temporary viewing space for tourists at the village hall adjacent to the paddy. When the village hall was reconstructed during the project's third year, a permanent viewing deck was built exclusively for the *Ine moji* and attached to the hall.

In 2002, which marked the tenth year of the project, Inakadate decided to widely promote *Ine moji* by way of joining a competition called 'Power of One Thousand' (*Sen nin no chikara*) sponsored by Japan's national public broadcaster, NHK. The competition called for the participation of groups of at least one thousand people who would work together on a particular project to be voted on by television viewers in terms of interest level. Inakadate named their initiative 'Power of One Thousand: Giant Art on the Rice Paddy' (*Sen nin no chikara de tanbo ni kyodai na a-to wo*), officially renaming their project as 'art' and no longer 'rice words'. With NHK's cooperation the village was able to gather participant-volunteers to help plant rice on an expanded 15,000 square meters (1.5 hectares) of rice paddy. The design was based on the original, though now more stylized and complex: Mt. Iwaki would be rendered as a curved mountain range showing rice stalks in the foreground and the moon in the background, with more words added (Figure 2).[9]

The event attracted more than 1000 participants, and was chosen by TV voters as the project with the 'most impact'.[10] This resulted in a flurry of publicity for Inakadate and the now renamed '*tanbo* art', that is, 'rice paddy art'. Since then, the number of participants for the rice-planting event has never fallen below one thousand, reaching a peak of 1800 in 2015, after which the village decided to limit participation to a maximum of 1500 in succeeding years due to insufficient personnel and resources as well as for logistical reasons.

Tourist numbers increased exponentially after the tenth year. After topping 20,000 for the anniversary project event, visitor arrivals exceeded 30,000 in the next year (2003), when the village decided to create a giant portrait for the first time, that of the Mona Lisa. For the first time also, that year computers were used to produce the design as well as the calculations and blueprints for the planting process. Mona Lisa, rendered in dark purple rice stalks, ended up occupying most of the rice paddy landscape. Viewed from the top, she was as perfectly proportioned as in Leonardo da Vinci's masterpiece, but from the perspective of the viewing deck, in the eyes of all visitors, she appeared 'fat', even 'pregnant', with gigantic hands (Figure 3).[11]

The fattened La Gioconda may have attracted more curious crowds to Inakadate. Visitor numbers for the rice paddy art continued to rise as Inakadate also experimented and succeeded with more elaborate designs. In 2013, it was able to create two full-body portraits on the landscape, one of a Japanese courtesan geisha and the other of Marilyn Monroe from *The Seven Year Itch*, both ladies looking neither fat nor pregnant (Figure 4). By 2015, visitors to Inakadate's rice paddy art (depicting a scene from *Gone with the Wind*) reached 340,000, and in 2016 (showing characters from a popular television samurai drama), the number finally breached 400,000.

Figure 3.

The huge and sustained increase in visitors has been a windfall for Inakadate, especially after it started charging 300 yen (slightly more than £2) in entrance fees to the viewing deck, which is the only way to see the rice paddy art. The village has few other income sources, as it does not have any hotels and has a very small number of shops and restaurants. There are, inevitably, several problems resulting from the tourist influx, such as overcrowding during peak season, unmanageable traffic and parking, littering and other environmental concerns, but the rice paddy art project has become an unqualified success for this tiny village, bringing it wide national and international media attention and, more importantly, much income.[12]

The Followers

The success of Inakadate has prompted many agricultural towns and cities in Japan with similarly dwindling incomes and populations to create rice paddy art in their areas in the expectation of gaining the same benefits. These towns and cities recently formed a loose network for the purpose of exchanging information and knowledge on the operations and management of rice paddy art projects, with Inakadate as its de-facto leader. Through Inakadate's initiative, the network has been holding an annual 'National Rice Paddy Art Summit' from 2012, with the participation of representatives from at least twenty rice paddy art areas in Japan found all over the country, from Hokkaido in the north to Minami Kyushu in the south.[13]

One of the most active members of the network is Gyoda City in Saitama, the prefecture that shares a border with Tokyo to its south but shares neither the capital's prosperity nor its prestige. In annual rankings for the level of 'attractiveness' of Japan's 47 prefectures, Saitama always places near the bottom, at 39 out of 47 in 2016, up from 46th place in 2015 and 42nd in 2014. The most attractive three in the same year (2016) were Hokkaido, Kyoto, and Tokyo, which are more or less permanently ensconced at the top of the annual list.[14]

Figure 4.

Gyoda City is on the northern, even quieter end of Saitama Prefecture. It had close to 82,500 residents (about 40% aged 60 and older) in March 2017, representing a steep drop from 85,600 five years ago and its peak of more than 90,500 in the year 2000.[15] Gyoda is known among Japanese history buffs for its ancient burial mounds called *kofun*, the entombment chambers built during Japan's Kofun period (from c. 250 to 538) that have been found to contain the remains of members of the ruling clan and other officials interred with their dress military armour and equipment, jewellery, art objects, and other personal treasures. Gyoda has also been Japan's major manufacturer of *tabi* socks, the two-toed socks usually worn with the kimono by men and women that is experiencing a resurgence among the fashion-conscious in Japan today; Gyoda still makes around half of the all the *tabi* produced in the country.

Burial mounds and *tabi* socks, however, can only do so much to make an outlying city in one of Japan's so-called least appealing prefectures attractive to visitors. In an effort to change its image and bring in tourists, Gyoda has been developing alternative sightseeing areas, such as a sprawling park close to the burial mounds that was transformed into a huge lotus garden for growing the many different varieties of ancient lotus flowers discovered in the city. (The lotus is Gyoda City's symbol flower.) In 2001, it opened the Kodai Hasu Kaikan (Ancient Lotus Hall), an information centre and exhibit area devoted to the study and display of ancient lotus varieties, and equipped it with an observatory, or viewing deck, fifty metres above ground for visitors to have a bird's eye view of the surrounding lotus garden (Figure 5).

Figure 5.

The Kaikan was conveniently located next to several hectares of rice fields, which also happened to be observable from the lotus viewing deck. In the years around the hall's opening, the rice paddy art of Inakadate was already being featured in several domestic and international media outlets, and it did not take long for Gyoda City officials to envision another use for its lotus observatory: plans were soon made for a rice paddy art project.

Gyoda City created its first rice paddy art in 2008 featuring a single lotus flower above the words *Gyoda Hasu* (Gyoda Lotus), using three varieties of rice planted in an area less than 2000 square meters in size (Figure 6). The design was upgraded and more text was added in the second year, while the planting area was also increased to 6000 square meters with four varieties of rice used. In succeeding years, the design has grown even more elaborate, requiring more colours and varieties of rice as the planting space has also been greatly expanded.

Figure 6.

Last year (2016), Gyoda's rice paddy art covered 28,000 square meters (2.8 hectares) and used nine varieties of coloured rice. The design featured characters from one of Japan's most popular role-playing video game series, Dragon Quest, which included the game's mascot, the Slime, with a menacing dragon and a warrior character looming over the words '30th Dragon Quest;' two fully-bloomed lotus flowers, though not officially part of the video game, were added as a reference to Gyoda (Figure 7).

The Dragon Quest design was chosen to commemorate the thirtieth anniversary of the game's release, which is listed in the Guinness World Records as the longest-running Japanese role-playing video game. The allusion to the Guinness listing was, of course, deliberate: it was utilized to draw attention to Gyoda City's own world record achieved by its rice paddy art, the 'world's largest rice field mosaic', also listed in the Guinness World Records and recognized the year before (2015).[16]

Although public transportation access to Gyoda's rice paddy art is inconvenient, it has been attracting a steady stream of visitors who mostly come in their own vehicles or in tourist buses, usually as side trips. On weekends and holidays during the rice paddy art season, the Kaikan's viewing deck receives an average of 2000 visitors, so that entrance (through only one elevator) and viewing times have to be regulated. Last year's Dragon Quest especially attracted visitors of different generations: parents who knew about the game since they had bought it three decades ago for their children, who have in turn bought the game for and now play it with their own children.

Despite Dragon Quest's popularity, Gyoda City was not able to earn as much income from the rice paddy art project as in previous years. In particular, souvenir items such as postcards and other trinkets featuring images from the game could not be sold due to copyright regulations. Nonetheless, the design was a hit with young people. Aside from a sharp increase in school-age visitors who came to view the 2016 project, there was also an unprecedented number who volunteered for the rice planting and harvesting events. On the weekend of the rice-planting activity at the beginning of the project, around 500 people composed mostly of junior and high school students came for the first day, while 1000 volunteers, most under 30 including primary schoolchildren, helped on the second day. About 500 of the volunteers also came back to help with the harvest at the end of the season.[17]

The Rice

The increased participation of young people in its project is particularly gratifying for Gyoda. While it actively promotes its rice paddy art as a tourist attraction, it actually places more emphasis on the project as its way of attracting more people, especially the young, to farm work. After all, the project's official name is 'Rice Paddy Art Rice-Growing Experience Project' (*Tanbo a-to kome zukuri taiken jigyō*). In the city's website that introduces its rice paddy art, there are more images of the rice planting and harvesting processes, many featuring schoolchildren and other young people, than actual images of the rice paddy art.[18]

The website, however, shows only the favourable sides to Gyoda's rice paddy art project. In interviews and correspondence with city officials, it was revealed that some rice farmers who work on the fields used for the paddy art are not entirely pleased with the project. (The land is rented by the city from about sixteen farming households whose fields are part of the 'acreage reduction' policy.) In the first place, rice paddy art is more labour-intensive than regular rice-farming: the complex designs require manual (instead of mechanical or tractor) planting of the rice, while several parts of the paddy that are arranged in curving lines and uneven rows need extra attention and effort for planting, even as these also waste precious growing space.

Different varieties of rice also entail different timings and multiple ways of growing and caring for the plants, as opposed to growing a single variety on the entire plot. And while many volunteers do come to help plant and harvest the rice, almost all of them are new to farm work and inevitably commit mistakes; in the eyes of the farmers, these 'amateurs' are frequently too slow and inefficient in their work. In short, the farmers expend much more energy and time in growing rice for rice paddy art than for the traditional rice paddy, all the while producing much less rice.

The rice grown in Gyoda's rice paddy art may not be sold, since it is produced outside the official and regulated agricultural production channels, where the distribution and sale of farm produce are the purview of the agricultural cooperatives. Not that the rice from Gyoda's rice paddy art, as in every other rice paddy art project elsewhere, would enable anyone to earn significant amounts of income. Much of the rice is unmarketable as it cannot

Figure 7.

be used for food. For example, in Gyoda the frequently planted red-orange (named *Akane-asobi*), yellow (*Kidaikoku*), and pink (*Saikaikan*) rice varieties are 'ornamental' rice mainly grown for use in plant arrangements and decorations. The dark purple (*Murasaki*) rice, which emerges as a dramatic black on the landscape and is one of the most useful, and the most used, rice for paddy art, is an edible variety but it is rarely consumed as is. Purple rice is frequently processed or mixed into other food products, such as noodles and sweets, or used as a colouring agent.[19]

There is some that ends up as white rice and becomes *gohan*. In Gyoda's paddy art, the rice that shows up green on the landscape is a local variety called *Sai-no-kagayaki*, which the city has recently been attempting to develop as a unique 'rice brand' from the area. It has a difficult road ahead: when one performs a Japanese-language internet search and types in the term *Sai-no-kagayaki* in the search box, the first suggestion that follows the name is the word *mazui*, meaning 'bad tasting'.

It is this local variety that is harvested during the public event organized at the end of the rice paddy art season in Gyoda (Figure 8). Some of it is distributed to project volunteers and staff after processing in a small combine set up in the field. The non-edible varieties are harvested separately, earlier or later and without volunteer help. Though these are so-called 'ornamental' varieties, they are not actually processed into or used as decorative items, and some end up as animal fodder. Because of their relative nonutility, however, and also due to distribution and transport expenses, most of the ornamental rice is simply thrown away, burned or disposed of through other means.

Implications

Rice paddy art has dramatically transformed many traditional rice landscapes in Japan's towns and villages, and for some areas, especially Inakadate and to a certain extent, Gyoda, it has improved their reputations and fortunes. Rice paddy art, however, is a very uneconomic practice especially for the economic powerhouse that is Japan. It is also a wasteful use of farmland, particularly in consideration of the country's constantly low rate of food self-sufficiency.

Japan, nonetheless, does not need to grow more rice to feed itself. Not only does it grow enough of it already, Japanese today are eating less and less of this most representative and identity-defining of its traditional foods. In fiscal year 2012, the average annual consumption of rice (as is and as an ingredient in food and drink products) amounted to 57 kilograms per person, which represented less than half the total exactly half a century ago, which was 118 kilograms per person in fiscal year 1962.[20] This dietary transformation has been reflected and evidenced in annual surveys of household (two or more members) spending conducted by Japan's Statistics Bureau, which found that since 2008, Japanese households have been doling out more money for bread than rice, with bread consumption continuing to increase every year while that for rice steadily declines.[21]

Consumption of noodles, mostly made from wheat, is also on the rise. Since more than 90% of the wheat consumed in Japan is imported, these dietary trends are

Figure 8.

worrying, to say the least, to government food policy makers.[22] And yet, the same government's policies continue to coddle its rice farmers, such as through subsidies paid to those who reduce their production acreage, so that 64% of Japan's farmers continue to grow rice instead of other food crops, despite rice representing only 21% of the agricultural output by value in Japan.[23] Although the current (2017) administration is aiming for drastic reforms to these policies, beginning with the abolition of production controls of rice and the attendant subsidies, many of the reforms are as yet unenforced so that their consequences, should there be any of significance, largely remain to be seen.[24]

In the meantime, Japan's aging rate continues to accelerate while its population continues to diminish, a problem that is particularly dire in isolated, traditionally agricultural communities like Inakadate and Gyoda. The situation is more acute for the farming population: the average age of Japan's farmers rose to 65.9 in 2011, while their number dropped to 1.7 million from 2.2 million in the decade from 2004 to 2014.[25] These shifts have resulted in many agricultural lands, mostly rice farms, without enough people to till them, aggravating the situation already worsened by the agricultural policies mentioned.

To improve the situation somewhat, Gyoda, as with all its counterparts in the rice paddy art movement, has been promoting its project as an initiative to introduce children and young people to farming, in the hope of making even a few of them into rice farmers. Although the children do appear to have fun at the rice planting and harvesting events and are clearly eager to see the results of their work, they do actual work on the farm only once (sometimes twice if they come for the harvest) throughout the whole rice paddy art season. Moreover, they work with hundreds of others and are fed by the project organizers in an event that resembles a festival and involves only a small aspect of actual work in the rice farm. After this short and fun experience, it is doubtful that the children go home dreaming of becoming rice farmers in the future; at the very least, their parents would be more than likely aware of the hard work required in the rice farm and would probably not be encouraging their children to pursue the rice farmer's life.

Concluding Thoughts

Rice has been acknowledged as the symbol of the Japanese self, while Japan's rice paddies 'stand for the Japanese nation itself with its quintessential beauty'.[26] Whether or not rice paddy art represents an enhancement of such beauty is a question best left to the viewers of the paddy art. One thing may be said, though: rice paddy art is now transforming Japan's quintessential landscapes in response to the transformation of its basic foodways. As Japan plays with its food, it is also playing with its identity.

Notes

1. Sri Owen, *The Rice Book* (New York: St. Martin's Griffin, 1996), p. 81.
2. Emiko Ohnuki-Tierney, 'Rice as Self: Japanese Identities Through Time', *Education About Asia* 9.3 (2004), p. 5.
3. Naomichi Ishige, *Nihon no shokubunka shi: Kyūsekki jidai kara gendai made* (*History of Japanese Food Culture: From Paleolithic to Contemporary Times*) (Tokyo: Iwanami Shoten, 2015).
4. 'The Problem With Japanese Rice Policy', *Asia Pacific Policy*, 5 February 2015.
5. 'The Problem With Japanese Rice Policy'. *Gentan* is sometimes called the 'set aside' policy.
6. 'Japan's Food Self-Sufficiency Rate Misses Target Again', *The Japan Times*, 2 August 2016 <http://www.japantimes.co.jp/news/2016/08/02/national/japans-food-self-sufficiency-rate-misses-target/#.WSplX8bAPm0> [accessed 25 May 2017].
7. Yukio Kasai, *Tanbo a-to no kiseki* (*The Miracle of Rice Paddy Art*) (Tokyo: Shufu-to-seikatsusha: 2015), p. 33.
8. Kasai, p. 56.
9. Kasai, p. 56.
10. *Inakadate Mura* <http://www.vill.inakadate.lg.jp/_common/themes/inakadate/1000power/html/pow_about.html> [accessed 25 May 2017].
11. Kasai, p. 60. See also Martin Fackler, 'Japanese Village Creates Art From Hues of Rice', *The New York Times*, 25 July 2010 <www.nytimes.com/2010/07/26/world/asia/26japan.html> [accessed 25 May 2017].
12. For example, '*Tanbo a-to de mura zukuri*' ('Making a Village Through Rice Paddy Art'), *National Geographic* (Japan edition), July 2008, pp. 146-52; see also, 'Paddy Art: Farmers Create Colourful Rice Murals in Japan', *Telegraph*, 3 August 2009 <www.telegraph.co.uk/news/worldnews/asia/japan/5965073/Farmers-create-coloured-rice-murals-in-Japan.html> [accessed 25 May 2017].
13. The author participated in the 'National Rice Paddy Art Summit' held in July 2016 in Kagoshima, where he met and spoke to representatives from Inakadate, Gyoda, and other rice paddy art project leaders in Japan. He also visited Gyoda twice and interviewed officials involved in its rice paddy art initiative. The data included in this paper, particularly that concerning Gyoda, is from his visits and interviews unless indicated otherwise.
14. *Regional Brand Survey* (Brand Research Institute, Inc.) <tiiki.jp/news/05_research/survey2016/3301.html> [accessed 25 May 2017].
15. Gyoda City Hall, 'Gyoda City' <https://www.city.gyoda.lg.jp/13/01/11/jinkou/jinnkou_midasi.html> [accessed 25 May 2017 – in Japanese].
16. Yomiuri Shimbun, *Oashisu*, 22 July 2016, p. 37. The Guinness World Records lists the size of Gyoda's rice paddy art field at an official 27,195 square meters. See 'Guinness World Records' <guinnessworldrecords.jp/news/2016/2/largest-ricefield-mosaic> [accessed 25 May 2017].
17. *Tanbo Art in Gyoda* <www.city.gyoda.lg.jp/15/05/10/tanbo27/images/2016tanbo.html> [accessed 25 May 2017].
18. *Tanbo Art in Gyoda*.
19. Tomio Itani, *Aka-mai, shikoku-mai, kaori-mai: Kodai-mai* (*Red, Purple-Black, and Fragrant Rice: Ancient Rice*) (Tokyo: Nobunkyo, 2000).
20. 'Rice Remains Japanese Staple, Despite Popularity Waning', *The Japan Times*, 8 January 2016.
21. *Statistics Japan* (Ministry of Internal Affairs and Communications) <www.stat.go.jp/data/kakei/2.htm> [accessed 25 May 2017 – in Japanese].
22. Nadia Arumugam, 'Waves of Grain: How did Japan Come to Prefer Wheat Over Rice?', *Slate Magazine*, 2 April 2012 <www.slate.com/articles/life/food/2012/04/wheat_in_japan_how_the_nation_learned_to_love_the_american_grain_instead_of_rice_.html> [accessed 25 May 2017].
23. Leo Lewis, 'Japan: End of the Rice Age', *Financial Times*, 22 September 2015.
24. 'A Shift in Rice Production Policy (Editorial)', *The Japan Times*, 1 December 2013; see also Lewis.
25. Justin McCurry, 'Japanese Firm to Open World's First Robot-Run Farm', *The Guardian*, 2 February 2016.
26. Emiko Ohnuki-Tierney, *Rice as Self: Japanese Identities Through Time* (Princeton: Princeton University Press, 1993), p. 98.

Stories of Rice Lake – Stewards, Settlers, and Storytellers

Nathalie Cooke[1]

Rice Lake in the Kawartha Lakes Region of southeastern Ontario, Canada spans no more than three miles across by twenty miles in length, and is twenty-seven feet at its maximum depth. Its size limits its potential as a destination for watersports. However, it has been and continues to be an ideal, albeit contested, site for nurturing a delicious protein-rich food source important to the First Nations and European settlers alike: wild rice. The lake and surrounding area were also the locale for one of Canada's first classics, a settler's guide written by a British emigrant who settled the Rice Lake plains. In her *Female Emigrant's Guide* of 1855, Catharine Parr Traill provided the most detailed description of the backwoods then available; her astute observations and remarkably candid commentary served to manage expectations of female emigrants following in her footsteps. Long recognized in Canada as a significant historical document, Traill's *Guide* is only now being fully recognized as the first authentically Canadian cookbook. It gathered the collective knowledge of her friends and United Empire Loyalist neighbours, and, informed by her hard-won personal experiences, it focused on the foods and food preparation techniques of her region. A new critical edition published in June 2017 brings attention to its important place in Canada's history in the one hundred and fiftieth year of Canadian Confederation.[2] Using Rice Lake, its history, and the practices and cultivation of wild rice as a lens, this study looks over Traill's shoulder to what lies outside her field of vision, within and between the lines that she penned. Indeed, the pages of Traill's *Guide* offer detailed glimpses of the way Upper Canada functioned as what Alison Norman has called a culinary 'contact zone', characterized by the exchange of foods and culinary influences between First Nations and settlers.[3]

My attention was drawn to Rice Lake by Traill's history in the area. However, the history of the region is more complex than Traill's *Guide* conveys. Rich evidence indicates that the Rice Lake Plain had been populated and treasured by Canada's peoples over hundreds of years because of its ideal conditions for nurturing wild rice. Additionally, access to wild rice beds and control over their stewardship has been prized and hotly-contested from the period after European contact and settlement through to the present moment, with access to rice serving as a flash point for negotiations regarding land ownership and sovereignty. Traill's family arrived after much of these negotiations and

Food and Landscape

Figure 1. A 'field' of wild rice on a northern lake. 6 September 2011. Photo: Superior National Forest. Creative Commons License.

conflicts had taken place, leaving a legacy of on-going tension for European settlers. Such settlers were, as Traill describes, in for hard work, threats from fires that ravaged wood structures, Yankee neighbours who 'borrowed' from naïve newcomers, and ague that lurked in damp places. In some cases, Traill provides detailed observations of the Anishinaabeg methods for food harvesting and preparation – for example, gathering wild rice in September or preparing maple syrup during the spring thaw, both of which would have been unfamiliar – and extremely useful – to the British female settlers her *Guide* addressed. In its cultivation, harvest, and preparation, wild rice features prominently in the *Guide* as one example of a local food that needed explaining.

Rice Lake (*Pimadashkodeyong*) gained its name because it was the site of wild rice (*minomiin*) harvesting by the Mississauga Anishinaabeg people.[4] Today Rice Lake, despite diminishment of its historical wild rice bounty as a result of changing water levels due to construction of a nearby canal system, alterations to its shoreline, climate change, and mechanization of harvesting techniques, still provides valuable food supplies. There are two different species of wild rice that grow in southern Ontario and along the Trent-Severn Waterway, which includes Rice Lake, Pigeon Lake, and Mud Lake. Botanical historian Tom Cruickshank explains the two varieties: 'the very tall southern wild rice *Zizania aquatica*, which is at its extreme northern limit here and was never very common in the first place; and the not-quite-as-tall northern wild rice *Zizania palustris*, which was much more abundant and still grows well beyond

Stories of Rice Lake

Rice Lake'.[5] The grains of this so-called rice are actually seeds; the name rice being a legacy of a misnaming by fur traders. Culinary journalist Jennifer Bain sings its praises, reminding us that wild rice is actually the only cereal native to Canada: 'Not only can you store the chewy, nutty rice indefinitely, it's easily digestible, cholesterol-free, low in fat and high in protein and fibre.'[6] Traill knew from bitter experience that when circumstances were grim it would be important to understand how to benefit from such a locally available and rich food source.

A small booklet published by the Ontario Ministry of Northern Affairs asserts that wild rice was probably in the region for more than 2500 years and believed to have been 'first used for human food by the Laurel culture about 1000 years ago'.[7] While this claim is supported by the archaeological record, the latter actually suggests the presence of peoples inhabiting Ontario as much as 10,500 years ago. Specifically, archaeologists have found evidence of the existence of Paleo Indians, the first peoples of Ontario, with an estimated population of between 100 and 200 people living in three site clusters, one located at Rice Lake.[8] The location of communities near waterways seems to have been the result of the trade exchanges such waterways facilitated, and archaeologists have found evidence of mammalian diet. However copper implements found in the burial mounds do provide substantiation that these prehistoric communities had the ability to cook over fire, and it is not out of the question to consider wild rice to be one possible component of their foodways.

Consequently, the arrival of white settlers in 1780 was only one among a series of waves of people travelling to and through the Rice Lake Plains. Unlike the First Peoples, European settlers did not migrate from shoreline to central woodlands on a seasonal schedule, and did not intend to share the land they considered empty. They instead began to expropriate land, and, in the subsequent hundred years after 1780, they dispossessed the First Peoples of the majority of land in southern Ontario, moving them to created reserves of wooded and often non-arable land.[9] Rice Lake itself was finally ceded by the Anishinaabeg to Lord Butler in 1788 in exchange for gifts of 'ammunition, arms and tobacco', which Sir John distributed at the first council in 1784, and which Butler later supplemented in 1788 with 'an extra twenty five guineas to two chiefs' to finalize the agreement'.[10] However, the new settlers were confused about land allocation and about which peoples had which rights to particular parcels of land. In addition to the Rice Lake Treaty No. 20 in 1818, for example, there was a subsequent negotiation in 1819. As Robert Surtees explains: Treaty No. 20 'meant that the government could claim to have purchased all of the land south of the Trent-Severn water system. In actual fact, the land surveyed, and granted to settlers, extended back from Lake Ontario to a depth of only one township. Beyond that, the land was still used and claimed by the Mississaugas of Rice Lake (not from Lake Simcoe), and thus subsequent purchases of the Rideau Tract and the Rice Lake Tract were required in 1819'.[11] Therefore, when the Traills arrived in the backwoods near Rice Lake, they were taking up a long contested and highly problematic 'right' to settle the tract of land assigned to them. Traill's limited perception of the region before the arrival of what she perceived to be legitimate agricultural settlers like herself was that it was largely home to the 'backwoodsman', the 'solitary unchristianized Indian', and animals, that it was a land undeveloped and unpeopled.[12] Those who had come before her, 'those old settlers and their children,' Traill writes, 'have seen the whole face of the country changed. They have seen the forest disappear before the axe of the industrious emigrant; they have seen towns and villages spring up where the bear and the wolf had their lair.'[13]

When Traill and her sister Susanna Moodie settled in the backwoods, the Mississauga Anishinaabeg no longer had stewardship of extensive portions of land; the face of the country had already changed. The first European settlement in Peterborough County was in 1818, and the process by which European settlers could lay claim to a plot of land was remarkably simple.[14] It involved first an oath of allegiance to the crown before an appointed official, next a payment of twenty-five dollars, and finally the affidavit of two witnesses that 'settlement duties' had been performed by way of construction of a house of at least eighteen feet by twenty feet.[15] One of the earliest settlers in Lakefield, near Rice Lake, was Catharine Traill's own brother, Samuel Strickland.

For European settlers like Traill and her relatives, agricultural production could only be understood as farming a particular plot of land by those permanently resident in or nearby it. From the nineteenth-century Eurocentric perspective, it was possible to condone and endorse imposing a particular way of life on the First Peoples. Assumptions involved a distinction between civilized – that is, European – and uncivilized behaviour, which emerges even when the speaker is impressed by the First Peoples. For example, Susanna Moodie can observe of her Chippewa or 'Misasagua' (*sic*) neighbours: 'There never was a people more sensible of kindness, or more grateful for any little act of benevolence exercised towards them. We met them with confidence; our dealings with them were conducted with the strictest integrity; and they became attached to our persons, and in no single instance ever destroyed the good opinion we entertained of them.'[16] In her narrative sketches of life in the backwoods, Moodie offers a number of anecdotes about what she calls 'Indian Life', including numerous instances of her neighbours' generosity and her appreciation of her hospitality to them. Yet even Moodie, who acknowledges her huge debt to these same neighbours whose many gifts of wild foodstuffs were most welcome at times of particular difficulty, nevertheless renders explicit attitudes of her time that distance European settlers from the 'uncivilized' Indigenous Peoples. 'I had heard and read much of savages, and have since seen, during my long residence in the bush, somewhat of uncivilized life,' she writes, before going on to reject the validity of her assumptions by saying, 'but the Indian is one of Nature's gentlemen – he never says or does a rude or vulgar thing.'[17]

There are echoes of Moodie's attitudes in Traill's *Guide*. The 'backwoods' where Traill settled were then the sacred homelands of the Mississauga Anishinaabeg First Nations; however, Traill never identifies these neighbours by name. While Traill's observations of some indigenous food harvesting practices are astute and detailed, she did not always understand the guiding principles behind First Nations' planting and harvesting techniques. In other words, the landscape that seemed so visible to her was actually shaped by a network of associations, claims to particular locales for fishing and hunting, seasonal migration patterns, and sustainable harvesting practices that were largely invisible to her, just as they were unfortunately invisible to other settlers as well. For example, when describing maize or what she and her neighbours called 'Indian corn', Traill notes that it is always planted alongside pumpkin. But she fails to mention beans, the third of the 'three sisters', generally planted with the other two crops. Nor does she discuss the benefits of such combined planting. The First Peoples knew that planting the 'three sisters' together made for efficient use of space and minimal watering and weeding. It also eliminated the need for staking: the beans could climb the corn stalks while providing nitrogen for the soil, while the squash provided cover that inhibited weed growth and encouraged water retention. While Traill noticed the maize, and indeed planted it herself on her farms, she did not understand the significance its cultivation had to the First Peoples, nor the thoughtful and practical sustainability that informed the practice. Likewise, Traill's description of harvesting wild rice shows that she did not understand how carefully the Mississauga Anishinaabeg had nurtured this resource to ensure its continued viability or how much settler society had disrupted their longstanding food practices. Rather than attributing the dwindling supply of wild rice to the impact of new settlement on traditional harvesting practices and places, Traill concluded it was due to the 'Indian' being 'indolent, or possibly, employed in agricultural pursuits or household work'.[18]

Figure 2. Wild Rice in the Fall. September 2011. Photo: Superior National Forest. Creative Commons License.

Poor treatment of the First Peoples is a very dark chapter in Canada's history that afforded European settlers and their descendants remarkable privilege and continues to shape and define social hierarchies. Indeed, Canadians today are wrestling with how to address such inequities in a country wanting to endorse the twin values of diversity and inclusivity. In a damning and alarmingly accurate depiction of white settler society in Canada, Sara Rotz asserts that, even today and despite growing awareness, 'material dominance is maintained through ideological and cultural strategies that shape settlers' perceived relation to two distinctly "othered" groups: Indigenous Peoples and migrant farmers/farm workers'.[19]

By contrast to today's largely unspoken mechanisms of material dominance, note the explicitly paternalistic jargon of this 1884 account, rationalizing the formation of an Indian reserve on Mud (*Chemong*) Lake in the Peterborough area in 1830, just prior to Catharine Parr Traill's arrival:

> Until 1830 these Indians were roaming through the bush; but in that year the New England Company, an English organization which was established to help the poor Indians, received from the Government a grant of 2,000 acres, which form the reserve, and undertook to teach the Indians to follow agricultural pursuits, to educate the children, and to bring all up in the Christian faith. The first agent of the New England Company was Rev. William Scott, who lived in Cobourg. In 1830, on the establishment of the agency, he gathered the Indians together and built a log house for each family.[20]

There is evidence that some First Peoples did choose to adopt European agricultural methods. Fifty years later, by 1883, for example, the thirty families or 180 individuals living on the Mud Lake Reserve of 2000 acres, in addition to baskets, fish, and furs, managed to raise, '550 bushels of wheat, 500 bushels of oats, 50 bushels of peas, 300 bushels of potatoes, and 50 tons of hay'.[21] The hay and likely some of the oats went to feeding domestic animals; for keeping horses within enclosures, in addition to oxen, cows, sheep, and pigs was also a function of the newly-introduced European agricultural practices. But the production of wheat and peas also indicates that by 1883 a nutrition transition had taken place, with the traditional staples of maize and minomiin supplemented by, if not replaced entirely by, wheat and oats.

Similarly, European settlers learned new farming and food sourcing techniques from the First Nations people after their arrival in the region. A group of 297 Irish settlers arrived near Rice Lake in 1820, and by 1826 had produced 1330 pounds of maple sugar and harvested 1042 bushels of 'Indian corn' (maize), in addition to sowing wheat in 195 acres of newly-cleared land and growing what would have been far more familiar to them: turnips and potatoes.[22] One can only imagine how proud these Irish settlers must have been to have triumphed so successfully over the hardships of 'pioneering' in the 'New World'. Even today, as Sarah Rotz notes, 'there is a strong sense of pride in settler endurance, which influences their understanding of colonization.'[23]

Stories of Rice Lake

Those early Irish settlers did not understand the impact their clearing the land had on the peoples who relied on the forests for their food supply. Likewise, Traill did not grasp the importance of the forest to indigenous foodways. She spoke mainly of the forest as 'unreclaimed' and full of 'bodily hardship' for the settler.[24] She saw the forest as an obstacle to a comfortable life. Indigenous Peoples saw the land differently, and their perspectives clashed. Even as early as 1811, when Mississauga spokesman Indun-way-way met with the (ironically-named) British representative, James Givins, he complained about white men cutting timber without consent 'on the borders of the Rice Lakes' and of one Mr Williams who had 'settled on the "Carrying Place from Smith's Creek to the Rice Lake" and was also cutting timber without permission'.[25] Presumably Mr Williams was unaware that his new residence was directly on the route travelled frequently by First Peoples portaging food, supplies, and canoes between lake and creek. Did the settlers consider the detrimental impact of felling trees close to the lake shore, something of which we are acutely aware in the current day? Ironically, but realistically given the circumstances, Indun-way-way concluded his negotiation with Givins by asking that the goods to serve as payment for lands would include hoes as well as spears and axes, suggesting that even in 1811 the Mississauga peoples had begun recognize that they must adapt their agricultural practices.

Before the imposition of European farming methods, what would have been the patterns of food sourcing for the Anishinaabeg? Unlike the Iroquois to the south, who tended to live in villages, the Anishinaabeg were nomadic. During the summer, they camped near waterways where, even such an early history as Charles Pelham Mulvany's 1884 publication explains, 'waters, as yet unpoisoned by the refuse of lumber mills, teemed with fish – the delicious brooktrout of the smaller creeks, the maskinonge, sturgeon, salmon, white fish, eels, and bass of lake and river.'[26] During the winter, when food was scarcer, they moved inland to take advantage of the forest animals. However, after removal of the shoreline trees, the rice supply was further affected in 1838 by rising water levels following the construction of the Hastings dam at the eastern end of Rice Lake, then by the introduction of carp into the lake in 1870, and finally by the construction of the Trent-Severn waterway, which opened in 1920.[27] 'By then,' writes Tom Cruickshank, 'the rice beds were already doomed, although few outside the First Nations seemed to notice.'[28] Of course, wildlife in the area did more than notice. Over time, Cruikshank signalled the significant decline in the population of eels, beavers, ducks, geese, minks, and especially muskrats, as well as a decline in the number of 'muskellunge', a prized fish that likes to spawn on the old rice straw.[29]

However, in recent years, with renewed interest in traditional practices, the rice beds have been rejuvenated. Now aboriginal locals such as James Whetung teach ways to harvest and prepare wild rice.[30] Despite renewed awareness of the need for policies to protect the environment, such as Mud Lake being designated a Class 2 Provincially Significant Wetland, local zoning laws still allow for motorboat use and placement of septic tanks within fifteen metres of the shoreline; to date, the Ontario Ministry of Natural Resources has refused to override these lenient zoning permissions.[31]

*

Currently there are heated debates about the method of harvesting wild rice, the relative merits of painstaking hand gathering, using two sticks to bend the rice stalks over the canoe so the seeds fall away, or harvesting more quickly with machines. As Altiok, Stiles, and Bell note, using the traditional methods, 'much of the rice falls back into the lake to reseed the rice bed for the next year.'[32] Another source of conflict has been the Ontario government's willingness to allow wild rice to be harvested by those outside the Indigenous community. What makes these debates as heated and fierce as they have been over the years? In part, it is because wild rice involves what Altiok and his coauthors have called a 'ghost of taste'. They write:

> We trace the power of political culture through narratives of food authenticity. Central to these narratives of authenticity are what we will term the ghosts of taste: the conjuring of presences in food, which make claims of appropriate social relations [...]. The ghosts of taste are symbolic connections that people make with their food either through labels, commercials, or histories. From these everyday séances come spirited possessions that can shiver the physical sensations of taste, shaping what, and whom, tingles the tongue. The ghosts of taste reveal themselves in the ways we perceive the quality or taste of food. They enliven food with the phantoms of people and environments and can also enliven claims of food as property – as the possessions of particular faces and places.[33]

In this way, wild rice, especially if sourced by traditional means from a particular and sacred locale with a longstanding tradition, enables consumers to experience the 'ghosts of place – the sense of the presence of those who are not physically there'.[34] For some, the traditional practices associated with processing the wild rice continue to the present day. Jennifer Bain explains:

> Traditionally, processing wild rice was a colourful ritual that involved drying green rice in the sun, parching it in a pot over a fire to loosen the chaff from the kernels, and then putting everything into a hole so harvesters wearing moccasins could dance on it to remove the chaff. Finally, everything was put in a blanket and tossed in the air to separate the chaff from the kernels.

One custom for those harvesting the wild rice stand at Mud Lake – which is itself the result of careful and foresighted transplanting of wild rice from Rice Lake over a hundred years ago by Mary Whiteduck, a member of the Algonquin First Nation, and her Mississauga family – is to take some seeds to Harold Perry, 'a Metis of Algonquin ancestry' and a 'fourth generation hereditary steward' of the local rice beds. He keeps the seeds cold until just before the lake freezes, then sows the seeds in places where he knows them to be needed.[35]

Richard McIvor, a processor and packager at Kagiwiosa Manomin plant, an Ojibway cooperative on the Wabigoon Lake First Nations near Dinorwac, has harvested wild rice using both traditional and mechanical means. 'I used to do the dancing on the rice for my grandfather,' reminisced McIvor to Bain, 'but this machine does it all for me now.'[36] By 'this machine', McIvor refers to one that separates husk from kernel, after the rice is cured with lake water and roasted in wood ovens. Efficient mechanized harvesting of wild rice can provide a good source of export revenue. Airboat harvesting, for example, is remarkably efficient, but it is noisy and also depletes all the seeds of a rice stand, whereas the traditional method of harvesting allows for some of the seed to remain to replenish the stand.[37] Of further concern are genetic modifications to wild rice, especially in the States, that allow for greater levels of production of what has come to be known as 'paddy rice'.[38] 'The two are also easy to distinguish by taste,' explains Stiles, 'and the Anishinaabe say that paddy rice is the less flavourful. But paddy rice has been so successful and widely marketed that most people who eat it have never tasted non-paddy wild rice, and are therefore not able to make the comparison themselves.'[39]

If the 'ghosts of taste and place' are one reason why debates over wild rice production and harvesting are so fierce, another reason is the way that wild rice has become a flash point for very different conceptions of land stewardship. For example, the Anishinaabeg believe that wild rice is, by definition, wild and cannot be owned by anyone. Despite their very different notion of land stewardship, rather than ownership, the recent threat of commercial interests has driven them to launch a legal claim. In the late 1970s and early 1980s, the Ardoch Anishinaabeg community confronted the provincial government, both in court and on the ground, over its issuance of commercial licenses for the harvesting of wild rice at Mud Lake. The community asserted such licenses were a violation of their rights under treaty law.[40] Disputes over management of wild rice stands in the area came to a head in the late 1970s with a non-violent protest and confrontation at Mud Lake. By 1981 a democratic organization with equal representation from the Indian, Métis, and Settler groups was formed: the Settlers Wild Rice Association (IMSet).[41] Thirty years later, tensions are still high: in 2015, the harvesting and seeding of wild rice again inspired conflict between cottagers and harvesters on nearby Pigeon Lake. Property owners 'applied for and received a permit to remove "aquatic weeds" along the lakeshore', claiming the rice beds were blocking access to public waterways. They dredged the rice beds until stopped by treaty violation complaints from local First Nations.[42] This clash of values and interests is only a recent instance of different peoples asserting claim to the region around Rice Lake, both because of, and articulated through, access to this important resource and the waterway that hosts it.

Traditions and ceremonies related to wild rice stewardship are notably absent from Traill's *Guide*. At the same time, her inclusion of information about foods and medicines prized by the Anishinaabeg reveals that she was aware of the value of local knowledge.

Indeed, her strong lifelong fascination with botany prepared her for explaining the wild edibles of her new home. Her further detailing of moments of contact and exchange with Anishinaabeg neighbours provides evidence of their honesty, generosity, and fair dealing. Her respect for Anishinaabeg knowledge and code of ethics are at odds with assumptions she shared with other white settlers that their arrival in Canada was the arrival of civilization to the uncivilized world and that the work of settlement was one of which her generation and subsequent generations would be proud.

*

It is surely ironic that 2017, the sesquicentennial of Canada's Confederation, saw the publication of a new edition of her *Female Emigrant's Guide* with an Introduction that points readers to find evidence of indigenous foodways within and between the lines she penned explicitly to describe white settler foodways and that also considers what was lost as well as gained by the process of white settlement. That wild rice continues to be prized and nurtured in its traditional environment attests both to the persistence of this native cereal and to the resolute persistence of the Mississauga Anishinaabeg who continue to steward this important native resource.

Notes

1. My thanks to Fiona Lucas and Shelley Boyd who read an earlier draft of this study and to Mary F. Williamson for providing key insights into the role of wild rice in our nation's foodways and sources providing information about it. Also thanks to research assistants Étienne Gratton, Jacquelyn Sundberg, Nicole Gauvreau, and Hannah Srour.
2. Nathalie Cooke and Fiona Lucas, *Catharine Parr Traill's The Female Emigrant's Guide, Cooking with a Canadian Classic* (Montreal: McGill-Queen's University Press, 2017).
3. Alison Norman, 'Fit for the Table of the Most Fastidious Epicure: Culinary Colonialism in Contact in the Upper Canadian Zone', in *Edible Histories, Cultural Politics: Towards a Canadian Food History*, ed. by Valerie Korinek, Franca Iacovetta, and Marlene Epp (Toronto: University of Toronto Press, 2012), pp. 38-69.
4. Leanne Betasamosake Simpson, 'Land and Reconciliation, Having the Right Conversations', *Electric City*, 5 March 2016 <http://www.electriccitymagazine.ca/2016/01/land-reconciliation/> [accessed 31 May 2017]; Cooke and Lucas, p. xv.
5. Tom Cruickshank, 'Whatever Happened to the Rice on Rice Lake', *Watershed* (2014) <http://www.watershedmagazine.com/index.php/whatever-happened-to-the-rice-in-rice-lake> [accessed 16 May 2017].
6. Jennifer Bain, 'Our Gift to the Gourmet; Wild Rice Is Nutty, Nutritious and Natural. So Why Do We Export Most of It?', *Toronto Star* (2002), D01.
7. 'Manomin Wild Rice Recipes', ed. by Ministry of Northern Development and Mines (Toronto: Queen's Printer for Ontario), p. 3. See also B.G. Trigger, *Natives and Newcomers: Canada's 'Heroic Age' Reconsidered* (Montreal: McGill-Queen's University Press, 1986), p. 79.
8. Hugh Daechsel and others, 'The Archaeology of Ontario: A Summary', *The Ontario Archaeological Society* <http://ontarioarchaeology.on.ca/summary-of-ont-arch> [accessed 17 May 2017].
9. Peter S. Schmalz, *The Ojibwa of Southern Ontario* (Toronto: University of Toronto Press, 1991), p. 120;

10. Robert J. Surtees, 'Indian Land Cessions in Ontario, 1763-1862: The Evolution of a System', (unpublished doctoral dissertation, Carleton University, 1982), p. 90, p. 93.
11. Surtees, p. 113, n. 92.
12. Cooke and Lucas, p. 27.
13. Cooke and Lucas, p. 28.
14. Charles Pelham Mulvany, *History of the County of Peterborough* (Toronto: C. Blackett Robinson, 1884), p. 230.
15. Mulvany, p. 231.
16. Susanna Moodie, *Roughing It in the Bush; or Forest Life in Canada* (Toronto: Maclear & Co., 1871), p. 284.
17. Moodie, chapter XIII, p. 35.
18. Cooke and Lucas, p. xviii.
19. Sarah Rotz, '"They Took Our Beads, It Was a Fair Trade, Get over It": Settler Colonial Logics, Racial Hierarchies and Material Dominance in Canadian Agriculture', *Geoforum* 82 (June 2017), 158-59. 'White settler society' is a phrase signifying oppression that First Nations commentators still use. Many First Nations peoples do not consider themselves Canadian, especially in light of Canada's 150 celebrations in 2017.
20. Mulvany, pp. 369-70.
21. Mulvany, pp. 370-71.
22. Mulvany, p. 405.
23. Rotz, p. 162.
24. Cooke and Lucas, p. 24.
25. Surtees, pp. 178-79.
26. Mulvany, p. 247.
27. Cruickshank.
28. Cruickshank.
29. Known under various names, such as maskinonge and milliganong, the *Esox masquinongy* is commonly called 'muskellunge': see: 'Muskellunge,' *Fisheries and Oceans Canada*, <http://www.dfo-mpo.gc.ca/species-especes/profiles-profils/muskellunge-maskinonge-eng.html> [accessed 17 May 2017].
30. Kelly Jessup, 'Manomin: Wild Rice,' *Peterborough and the Kawarthas,* <http://thekawarthas.ca/manomin-wild-rice/> [accessed 17 May 2017].
31. Peter Cizek, 'Guardians of Manomin: Aboriginal Self-Management of Wild Rice Harvests,' *Alternatives* 19.3 (1993), 29-32.
32. Özlem Altiok, Kaelyn Stiles, and Michael M. Bell, 'The Ghosts of Taste: Food and the Cultural Politics of Identity', *Agriculture and Human Values: Journal of the Agriculture, Food, and Human Values Society* 28.2 (2011), 225-36 (p. 232).
33. Altiok, Stiles, and Bell, p. 226.
34. M. Bell, 'The Ghosts of Place,' *Theory and Society* 26.6 (1997), qtd. in Altiok, Stiles, and Bell, p. 228.
35. Bain.
36. Bain.
37. Cizek.
38. Bain.
39. Stiles, p. 232; Cizek, n. 18.
40. See Susan B. DeLisle, '"Coming out of the Shadows": Asserting Identity and Authority in a Layered Homeland: The 1979-82 Mud Lake Wild Rice Confrontation' (unpublished masters thesis, Queen's University, 2001), pp. 92-139; see also *Perry V. Ontario*, 2 CNLR 167 (1996), cited in Cizek, n. 14.
41. Cizek, n. 14.
42. 'Wild Rice Harvesting Causes Uproar on Pigeon Lake, Ontario', *CBC Radio* <http://www.cbc.ca/radio/asithappens/as-it-happens-tuesday-edition-1.3203220/wild-rice-harvesting-causes-uproar-on-pigeon-lake-ontario-1.3203499> [accessed 12 May 2017].

From Nature's Garden: Reimagining North African Landscapes through Food in Female French Colonial Literature

Edwige Crucifix

Following the bloody repression of the Mokrani revolt in 1871, France officially declared Algeria pacified, proceeding to settle the area and expand French presence to neighbouring Morocco and Tunisia. The ensuing period of French settlement in North Africa also marked a shift in the cultural production showcasing the colonies. In the case of literature, old-fashioned exoticism morphed into what Roland Lebel, a contemporary critic, identified as its more modern version: '*littérature coloniale*', a literary product emanating from French settlers, and, thus it was believed, from the colonies themselves (1931: 86). Because of its geographical origin, colonial literature was perceived as an authentic account of the colonies, developing a realist genre heavily marked by ethnographic pretensions. Although this genre remained largely male-dominated, many women – called to North Africa in order to solidify French settlement since the late nineteenth century – contributed to the production of colonial literature through letters, essays, and reports, as well as fiction.[1]

This form of colonial literature is strikingly self-aware of its female authorship, which is often used as a means to grant its literary legitimacy. Indeed, for many French female writers from the North African colonies, femaleness was a claim to privileged access to the lives and concerns of Maghrebi women, access denied to their male counterparts and displayed through novels typically featuring a North African female protagonist and staged within the boundaries of her household.

Yet, beyond what was often judged to be its overly feminine concerns, this corpus proposes an alternative perspective on colonial cultural processes in North Africa, including in relation to the history of food production and consumption. The novels' domestic focus makes food scenes a conspicuous and omnipresent actor of the stories. The revalorization by these authors of what they perceived to be Maghrebi traditional foods, food-gathering methods, cooking techniques, and consumption practices calls for a different understanding of the connection between land and people. Many of these works construct fantasies of pre-colonial North African landscapes that are distinct from dominant discourses of the time. In this paper, I argue that the relationship between food and nature depicted in this corpus proposes a different way to imagine life in the Maghreb during the colonial period by staging the fantasy of a non-exploitative colonial cohabitation.² Below, I will discuss this imagination of a shared land in the works of Pauline de Noirfontaine, Pierre Coeur, Elissa Rhaïs, Jeanne Faure-Sardet, and Marie Bugéja.

In these novels, food scenes often serve to present nature as a bountiful garden, a depiction that crystallizes the relationship between the region's natural history and its people and provides an alternative cultural narrative to what Diana K. Davis (2007) has identified as the contemporary 'declensionist' discourse justifying the French exploitation of the North African soil. According to this revisionist doctrine, indigenous agricultural practices desertified what was once a verdant region, and only 'modern' French methods could reverse this decline. Though set from a colonial point of view, the works studied here partly reject this discourse and are opposed to certain forms of colonial ideology, namely to rapacious colonial agricultural policies and to colonial alimentary discourses. Thus, the romanticization of North African landscapes found in feminine literature starkly departs from that used by colonial propaganda to increase French emigration. The evocation of Maghrebi landscapes prompted by food scenes in this literature stands in opposition to exploitative logics.

A gender-sensitive approach dedicated to this alternative colonial discourse on food production and consumption reveals the ways in which mundane daily practices, including alimentary practices historically performed by women, shape cultural imaginaries. By uncovering texts that depict food from a feminine and domestic standpoint, these writers move beyond its presentation as a mere exotic narrative detail or as a proof of the superiority of colonial agriculture. A vector for sensuous and communal experiences within the narrative, food scenes propose not only a different way of imagining the North African landscape, but also a different vision of the life of Maghrebi women that gestures towards a different model of colonial cohabitation, albeit an impossible one.

The 'Declensionist' Narrative: Colonial Food Production and Land Exploitation

In the 1880s, following the cooling of expansionist politics in North Africa that began with the French occupation of Algeria in 1830, agricultural exploitation of the land became a priority, supported by a strong institutional and administrative network. Consequently, arable land was freely given to newcomers and confiscated from locals.³ Land possession was seen as the best way to ensure French settlement, and a new class of '*colons agriculteurs*' – an expression borrowed from Joseph Chailley-Bert, president of the *Union Coloniale Française* – was called upon to settle in North Africa and establish an agricultural network capable of feeding the growing colonial population while also benefiting French interests through exportation. In an 1896 essay entitled '*Où en est la politique coloniale de la France?*', Chailley-Bert provides his titular question with the following answer: at the 'age of agriculture'.

Although historical data indicates that pre-colonial North Africa was self-sufficient and even able to export some of its produce (such as Algerian grains, exported since antiquity), French occupation and exploitation of North African land was largely justified by the locals' supposed agricultural ineptitude. As argued by Diana K. Davis in her seminal 2007 *Resurrecting the Granary of Rome*, the first environmental history of the Maghreb, French geographers and historians overwhelmingly embraced a declensionist environmental narrative, recounting the demise from the purported bounty of the Roman empire to what was seen as the contemporary degradation of the land brought about by the 'lazy' locals and their 'primitive techniques' (2007: 2), ignoring their advanced irrigation (permitting the harvest of dates and vegetables in desert areas) and crop rotation practice.

Particularly targeted among these 'primitive techniques' was the traditional practice of semi-controlled burning (*ksir* in Arabic) conducted in certain areas prior to planting cereals. As explained by Davis in the case of Algeria, this technique of land management, used to fertilize the soil but also to repel pests, had evolved in harmony with local ecosystems as it 'was adapted to local precipitation patterns which include dry summers and wet winters' (2007: 28). Based on a four-year harvest cycle, *ksir* demanded little tending to provide farmable land as well as grazing grounds for livestock, a feature suited to the local climate and traditional ways of living.

The correlation between the lifestyle of a people and their environment, theorized by highly influential geographer Paul Vidal de la Blache as *genre de vie*, largely dominated the work of French geographers of the period. As Florence Deprest (2011) stated in a study of French geographical discourses on Algeria, *genre de vie* was considered the best possible human adaptation to natural environments, but that did not prevent state-beholden scientists from twisting the concept around in the case of Algeria in order to serve colonial ideologies and defend French expansion. Blinded by colonial ambitions and cultural biases, French settlers struggled to appreciate Maghrebi farming methods and in fact perceived them as damaging the land, accusing *ksir* and over-grazing – and thus, more generally, nomadic and traditional lifestyles – to be an environmental liability, responsible for the desertification and deforestation of the land.[4]

Backed by carefully selected historico-scientific sources and its paternalist conviction to teaching indigenous populations how to better cultivate their land, France embraced an accusatory stance on traditional farming practices, criminalizing traditional modes of living and establishing wide-reaching agricultural development programs under a humanitarian guise. The agricultural re-education of North African populations was depicted as a colonial duty that would profit settlers.[5] Chailley-Bert writes, in paternalistic prose:

> How can we change this state of affairs? How to bring to our merchants and industrialists the abundant and easy clients that we promised them? The answer, following what was just said, is on everyone's mind: by enriching indigenous

populations first; before all, by showing them how to get more from their land, by showing them new methods, by teaching them how to cultivate or to prepare richer products. (1896: 16)

Some of these 'new techniques' included mechanization along with the introduction of new crops like corn, new types of wheat and fig trees, vines for the cultivation of wine, and potatoes. Exploited by these imported practices, North Africa also became the site of many botanical and agricultural experiments, exemplified by the impressive Algiers *jardin d'essai et d'acclimatation*, built in 1832.

Deprived of their traditional means of subsistence and excluded from the new environmental development of their land, Algerians feared for their survival, additionally endangered by the severe droughts and famine of the 1860s. According to Kjell Halvorsen (1978), the transformations in land tenure and the creation of an export-oriented agriculture (relying primarily on the production of wine, a culturally foreign product to local Muslim populations) through the colonial transformation of agrarian societies, productively disabled this previously self-sufficient region.

The declensionist narrative was not the exclusive prerogative of scientists and colonists but also permeated cultural production, having become a trope propagated through visual arts and colonial literature, including by female writers from North Africa. As early as 1856, Pauline de Noirfontaine, the wife of a colonist traveling through Algeria and sharing her impressions through a compilation of long descriptive letters, subscribes almost exactly to the declensionist narrative identified by Davis: she attributes the development of irrigation in Algeria to the Romans (1856: 310), celebrates the ability of French settlers to 'make the desert bloom', whether for farming purposes or more delicate and civilized ones, like the establishment of Mme de Montauban's '*jardin d'agrément*' (1856: 62). Importantly, Noirfontaine is very critical of traditional lifestyles, depicting the '*Arabes pasteurs*' as lazy and brutish (1856: 192), who stubbornly reject mechanization (1856: 111).

However, in spite of her apparent support of colonization on 'humanitarian' grounds and of her clear disdain for nomadic lifestyle, Noirfontaine also expresses a strong reservation about agricultural colonization. Noting the unpreparedness of French settlers to work the Algerian land, as well as the inhospitable climate and poor colonial management, she is also critical of the fact that some 'utopians' believe it possible to 'model the East on the West' (1856: 207). In her depiction of agricultural colonies, she points to a French misunderstanding of local climates and landscapes and criticizes France's inability to adapt to this different ecosystem, mocking the belief that the 'farmer-soldiers' will transform desert plains into 'the prairies of Normandy or the fields of the Beauce,' when settlers would rather, as she believes, 'do anything else than plant cabbages that won't grow' (1856: 31-32).

Fictional accounts are similarly marked by this tension between colonial loyalties and criticism of French occupation and land management. In one of the earliest novels written by a French woman from North Africa, Mme de Voisins d'Ambre – who wrote under the male pen name of Pierre Cœur – Algeria is simultaneously presented as an arid desert where solitude and boredom drives settlers to gambling, drinking, and sexual violence, and as a 'blessed land for researchers and scientists as well as farmers' (Cœur 1876: 53). More puzzling is the mention of a gastronomical dinner at one character's house in the military camp where the novel unfolds. Dr Schultz has brought with him to this inhospitable land a 'cook-soldier' (reminiscent of Noirfontaine's 'farmer-soldiers') whose Franc-comtois origins and apprenticeship under a famous French chef attest to his culinary talent. Miraculously, in the middle of this supposedly barren land, the cook-soldier serves marvellous a dinner. Although the meal is described as '*exquis*' and the cook as a '*gourmet*' and although the narrator even evokes the august name of Brillat-Savarin, the food is never described. Did the cook manage to concoct a Franc-comtois dinner? Was his expertise enough to transcend the unfamiliarity of local products? And where did these products come from? At first glance, it would seem like the scene is either nothing more than a literary trope, an underhanded way of celebrating French culture or simply a pretext for the verbose and moralizing temperance lesson that follows this episode. However, the mere mention of this luscious gastronomic dinner presupposes some unseen bounty of the land and suggests a different understanding of the surrounding desert landscape through food.

Intimate Geographies: Women and Food in the Colonial Context

Just as the colonial ideology rejected Arab ways of food cultivation, it rejected Arab ways of preparation and consumption. Through the development of nutritional science, foreign foods in general were deemed inferior and even damaging to French – and, therefore, civilized – stomachs (Janes 2014: 75). Colonial propaganda reassured settlers of the year-round availability of French products abroad, and 'exotic' recipes displayed in the period's cookbooks and women's periodicals were adapted to fit within acceptable boundaries. Unsurprisingly, the same sources also systematically presented Arab women as bad cooks and poor homemakers. In Pauline de Noirfontaine's account, it is the lack of proper domestic practices in nomadic tribes – even more than domestic confinement, the usual suspect of colonial feminism – that accounted for their 'secular oppression' (1856: 199). The colonial outlook on traditional North African food practices was as influenced by inappropriate environmental policies as it was by a paternalist outlook on the condition of Arab women. From Pauline de Noirfontaine relating her Algerian travels to later colonial female novelists and essayists like Lucienne Favre, who wrote until the late 1940s, the impression of Arab women was tainted by a maternalist push for assimilation.

Yet, despite this maternalism, female colonial writers treat Maghrebi food ways with a nostalgia and deference not found in colonial propaganda more generally. Maghrebi women in their novels are depicted gathering food, cooking, and eating as part of their daily routines, the prose all the while flirting with the ethnographic tone of much of this period's colonial literature. However, *pittoresque* as they may be, such alimentary depictions depart from colonial discourses that show North African populations as uncivilized. Not just a token revalorization of local food cultures, food scenes in these works also stand as metaphors or metonymies for the North African land that has produced them.

Through food scenes these novels retrospectively travel, via the reminiscences of their protagonists, back to the land where the products originated, resulting in the projected fantasy of pre-colonial landscapes. *Saâda la Marocaine*, the first novel by Jewish Algerian writer Elissa Rhaïs, tells the story of the eponymous Saâda and her family, forced to move from their small Moroccan village to Algeria after the outbreak of WWI that depleted the country of its businesses.[6] Lonely, nostalgic, and hungry – the move having reduced her family to abject urban poverty – Saâda wanders alone to the Arabian market. Bursting with oranges from Blida, cardoons from Médéa, raisins from Bougie, and butter from Cherchell, the market is a microcosm of North Africa, the stalls themselves forming a luscious and colourful landscape (1919: 113-15).

Rather than celebrating the 'glory' of colonial exploitation, the market is a truly indigenous collection, brought together by the labour and love of farmers and merchants coming from all corners of the Maghreb. It is even strongly contrasted with the European market with its 'anemic fruits […] its rotten chickens and its three-days old vegetables offered by white-aproned and heart-mouthed fruit-sellers' (1919: 115). The deferent attitude of the hypocritical vendors is not enough to hide the inappropriateness of such products in this scene. Not only does the Arabian market offer a display of North African *terroir*, it also provides a mosaic of its different populations, as it is where Europeans, Jews, Muslims, Arabs, and Berbers convene. The market transports readers to the many corners of the North African landscapes. Here, colonial homogenization cannot take hold: the diversity of the North African landscape shines through.

The same effect is achieved diegetically when Saâda is brought back to the mountains of her village by contemplating a heap of black walnuts she cannot afford at the market. In the city of Blida where she is suffering from hunger, thinking back to her village landscape means more than gustatory nostalgia. It convokes a different understanding of her native environment, where nature is not exploitable soil but bountiful garden, whose bounty is granted by its ancestral connection to a people. There, food was not abundant but always sufficient for the needs of her family, where she could pick a fruit in the wild unattended trees every time she felt like it. Rhaïs writes of the homeland as Rousseau does of the state of nature: 'There, one only had to put one's hand out to satisfy one's hunger or fancy' (1919: 121). In colonial cities, the procrustean European agricultural model has resulted in widespread deprivation and hunger, denizens living separated from their homeland and thus from the satisfaction of their basic needs. Such food scenes as the one depicting Saâda's visit to the market, irrespective of their obvious romanticism, summon intimate geographies, connecting the women who shop, cook, and eat to a reimagined land.

Food and Landscape

Echoing the reimagined mountains of Rhaïs's novel are the private gardens of Jeanne Faure-Sardet's *Fille d'Arabe*. In this novel, mostly concerned with the difficulty of mixed marriages, characters are repeatedly presented in private gardens that, according to their dwellers, are simultaneously reminiscent of Arab and French landscapes. The 'delicious garden' of the main character Meriem, for instance, is in the same chapter compared to her Arab father's own childhood landscapes and to her French neighbours' native Anjou region (1935: 41-43). In this example as in many others, the adjective 'delicious', although obviously designating the garden's pleasantness, can also be read in relation to taste: gardens are as full of flowers as they are of fruit trees and meal scenes.

As Faure-Sardet's novel travels from one home to the next, from North Africa to France, from the city to the countryside, the narrative is woven together through its depiction of gardens. The blurry succession of jasmine bushes, cypresses, and olive, fig, and orange trees produces a feeling of sensuous continuity between various points. Landscapes mix with private gardens and orchards, creating a series of tableaux where the smell of flowers mixes with that of cooking. In one scene, for instance, Chaalal, the main character's father, and his friend are walking through an olive-tree orchard. There, they stop to smell some couscous being prepared by the women somewhere in the house: the weird sensuous juxtaposition of the visible olive trees with the invisible dish that almost makes the narration of the scene seem an incongruous anacoluthon. In this scene, couscous serves no utilitarian function; it is not even consumed. Instead, it is part of the environment, sensually tying the characters to the land.

Indeed, although fruit trees and gardens are omnipresent in the novel, characters are rarely depicted eating. Rather, they drink coffee or lemonade, smell dishes being prepared behind closed doors, or refuse to eat the traditional foods presented to them, out of grief. This intangible but ubiquitous presence of food, woven in the garden scenes, suggests the profound cultural and historical link between nature, the land, and its people through domestic practices. In Faure-Sardet's novel, landscapes are smelt and drunk rather than eaten, establishing an ethereal, sensual connection between land and people. In this regard, private gardens are but an extension of natural landscapes, not so much the spectacle of tamed nature, but rather a reflection of nature's coexistence with local people.

'*Le Couscous de la Paix*': Sharing *Terroir*, Fantasizing the Colonial Encounter

Just as food scenes stage a fantasized ingestion of the physical landscape – a compulsion to eat the landscape 'in a salad' as Noirfontaine puts it (1856: 177) – they also stand as a fantasized communion with the region's history and culture, the 'social' landscape. The desire to join this social landscape results in disparate consequences across these novels, revealing the authors' anxiety about sharing the land in a colonial setting. In its romanticized claim to reveal the private lives of the Other, female colonial literature is mostly concerned with staging an encounter between French and indigenous populations, translated through various motifs in the novels. One such literary motif is the repetition of meal scenes shared by settlers and locals that come to crystalize the fantasy of a non-exploitative, mutually beneficial, colonial encounter. A common trope in that regard is the sharing of couscous, a traditional Maghrebi meal – 'the soul of the Maghreb' in the words of Hadjira Mouhoub and Claudine Rabaa (2003) – directly linking the making of couscous to the fertile land where it originated.[7] Linking land, people, expertise, and taste, couscous seems to stand as a symbol of *terroir*, although the product of a conquered and still foreign land.[8]

Terroir is nevertheless a useful concept when studying food descriptions that appear in female-authored colonial literature, perhaps because of the genre's ethnographic pretensions. Pauline de Noirfontaine, who like many subsequent authors recounts a scene of couscous sharing, establishes an explicit connection between land, landscape, and local food habits when mentioning one of her travels into the Ben-Daoud region. There, she is invited to share a meal of 'Kous-Koussou' that she describes as 'the favorite dish of the Arabs' (1856: 70). The scene is an opportunity for the writer-narrator to display herself as integrated into the exotic world she depicts: by ingesting the dish, she is welcome into the world of her subjects. Indeed, the sharing of the 'Kous-Koussou', an act of 'patriarchal hospitality', propels the narrator into 'a marvelous dream' where she fancies herself part of the region's history, part of a desert caravan or capturing Christians (71). By sharing the meal, the narrator is able to symbolize the overcoming of gendered and cultural boundaries, successfully becoming part of the social landscape she describes.[9]

A similar scene is played out in Marie Bugéja's *Nos Soeurs Musulmanes*, a collection of assimilationist essays on the condition of North African Muslim women. Bugéja dedicates one entire chapter to the description of the meal served during an event in a Muslim household to which she has been invited. As she argues for the emancipation of Muslim women through their assimilation into European way of life, pro-colonial sentiments are readily detected in Bugéja's book. The attempt at creating a sense of solidarity (and even, as the title suggests, sorority) with the Other woman, displayed through her depiction of the meal, is nevertheless telling of female colonial literature's attempt to bridge the gap through the symbolical act of sharing food.[10] For Bugéja, however, this scene does not allow her to become the Other. Instead, she hopes that its transformative effects are to be felt by those women who prepared the meal, as the passage ends with the narrator commenting on the desire of her 'Muslim's sisters' to assimilate (1921: 87-88).

From Noirfontaine's fantasy of belonging to Bugéja's dream of assimilation, the tensions surrounding the sharing of the bounty of the land in a colonial context are taking shape. But it is once again in Elissa Rhaïs's work that these tensions are more fully articulated. *La Riffaine*, a novel recounting the conversion of a rebellious Berber to the '*oeuvre sublime*' of colonization is set in the context of the War of the Rif, which pitted Berber tribes against Spanish and French forces. Given the premise of the novel and the fact that Rhaïs's writing was supported by a grant from the French government the colonial message is certainly central.[11] However, as she articulates her vision of colonial cohabitation, Rhaïs proves a shrewd painter of colonial tensions and devotes a large part of the novel to defending and portraying the position of her rebellious Berber protagonist, an emphasis symbolized by a tense food scene. After M'silla's tribe has been forced to capitulate to the French, she is summoned to prepare a '*couscous de la paix*' to be shared with the victors. Seen through M'silla's perspective, however, the scene, far from a peaceful encounter or an acceptance of happy cohabitation, is one of humiliation and defeat:

> As she is telling her story, Aicha is brought back to that dreadful evening. Once more she sees, before the horizon of the Kiffane hills, the tent adorned to welcome the Frenchmen, the couscous of peace that she has rolled with her own hands, steaming and gleaming with butter, the vases overflowing with buttermilk, the carpets, the black-striped mats where the Frenchmen sat, looking content, at ease. And soon, Si Djellouli had come forth, that tall majestic old man, and extending a hand towards the Mouquim representative, he declared: 'Messieurs, before we bring to our mouth the bread and salt that shall unite us, you ought to know what is in our hearts. We surrender because we have no gunpowder left, no money, no men [...]. And when our children will be of age, they will kick you out!' (1929: 30)

The promise that concludes this scene is one of violence, a predestined rebellion even before peace has been formally sealed by the sharing of the meal. The meal ends with a murder that forecloses the possibility of peace. This scene of failed reconciliation is a pivotal narrative node that haunts the rest of the novel, crystalizing colonial tensions.

As emphasized by this last example, the colonial vision fashioned by female writers, the fantasy of a non-exploitative colonial encounter, often enacted through food scenes, is never simple. First of all, it is complicated by the mere premise of colonial literature: its attempts at establishing a connection with the Other while simultaneously emphasizing her irremediable difference and wishing for her assimilation. But, as their foray into the privacy of the home allows them to stage the quotidian lives of Maghrebi women, these writers also shed some light onto forgotten colonial figures: the women who shop, cook, and eat. In this corpus, these characters – although still largely exoticized – are revealed as part of the fabric of colonial society and woven into the bigger picture. From their seemingly private practices, these women are shown partaking in the making of culture. Exploring the possibility of colonial cohabitation, this corpus provides another cultural rethinking of women's role in colonial North Africa. The valorization and insertion of female practices into social life via food scenes transforms Maghrebi landscapes into generous gardens. More than a faithful ethnographic account of the lives of Maghrebi women in colonial times, this literature expresses the desire of French colonial women writers to not only penetrate Nature's garden, but also to feel welcome there, to feel at home.

From Nature's Garden

Beyond romanticism, food scenes betray an anxiety about sharing the land, an anxiety about the possibility of cohabitation, which might still hold true in a postcolonial context. For many years in a row, couscous was voted one of the 'favourite dishes of the French' in surveys published in *Elle*, *le journal des Femmes* and *le Figaro* Although this suggests France was somewhat successful in its campaign of postcolonial integration, we should remain suspicious of couscous's place in the culinary canon. Couscous might have made its way to school cafeterias, those factories of Frenchness, as the promise of a truly reconciled and fraternal France, but we should also remember that controversies often erupt in school regarding the availability of halal meals or of choosing payment options that take Ramadan into account. In many respects, it seems like what Elissa Rhaïs ironically designated as '*le couscous de la paix*' in 1919, almost exactly a century ago, is still very much a fantasy today.

Notes

1. The '*Société d'émigration féminine*' (what would later become the *Société Française d'Emigration des Femmes*) was created in 1897 by the *Union Coloniale Française*, eager to provide *colons* with French wives.
2. The word 'Maghreb' is used to refer to North African countries. In this paper, the use of this term is limited to its French usage, referring to Morocco, Tunisia, and Algeria.
3. Free land was given to new Algerian settlers until 1864. Because of its focus on food, this paper does not explore the complicated history of land possession and expropriation in North Africa during the colonial period that remained a point of contention amongst colons themselves.
4. In fact, Davis suggests that France was itself responsible for the acceleration of deforestation and desertification by its introduction in North Africa of modern exploitative farming techniques that did not take into account the particularity of the climate. Rather than recognizing its role in this environmental failure, France used it as a scientific justification for its exploitation of North Africa (2004).
5. Vicken Cheterian has observed that a very similar rhetoric is still used by Western powers to justify their interference in the Maghreb. The instrumentalization of environmental concerns, he suggests, serves often as a way to prompt 'economic reforms', 'democratization', and 'good governance' accordingly to hegemonic Western models that limit self-governance in the Maghreb and threatens what remains of traditional lifestyles (2010).
6. Elissa Rhaïs was the pen name of Rosine Boumendil. Originally from the city of Blida in Algeria, Rhaïs's career was launched in France by the publisher Plon who presented her as a Muslim Algerian woman who had escaped from the harem and was now telling her story in French. For an outline of Rhaïs's life and career, see Jean Déjeux (1985).
7. In a poetic article dedicated to his mother, Mustapha Marrouchi devotes an article to celebrating his childhood memory of couscous, where he explained the origins of the name (2008: 100).
8. Kolleen Guy remarks that, although a 'French' region, Algeria was denied participation in *terroir*, which remained intimately connected with the land that produced 'Frenchness', which is to say metropolitan France (2010: 150).
9. For a more recent but similar take on the nostalgic and evocative virtues of couscous see Mustapha Marrouchi (2008).
10. On the fantasy of a transcultural sisterhood in the Maghreb, see Denise Brahimi (1984).
11. See Déjeux (1985).

References

Brahimi, Denise. 1984. *Femmes arabes et soeurs musulmanes* (Paris: Tierce).
Bugéja, Marie. 1921. *Nos soeurs musulmanes* (Paris: La revue des études littéraires).
Chailley-Bert, Joseph. 1896. '*Où en est la politique coloniale de la France?*', in *L'âge de l'agriculture* (A. Colin & cie.).
Cheterian, Vicken. 2010. 'Environmental Pressure, Neoliberal Reforms, and Geopolitical Competition in the Maghreb', *The Journal of North African Studies*, 15: 255-64.
Cœur, Pierre. 1876. *La Fille du rabbin* (Paris: Plon).
Davis, Diana K. 2004. 'Desert "Wastes" of the Maghreb: Desertification Narratives in French Colonial Environmental History of North Africa', *Cultural Geographies*, 11: 359-87.
———. 2007. *Resurrecting the Granary of Rome : Environmental History and French Colonial Expansion in North Africa* (Athens: Ohio University Press).
Déjeux, Jean. 1985. '*Elissa Rhaïs, conteuse algérienne*', in *Le Maghreb dans l'imaginaire français La colonie, le désert, l'exil*, ed. by Jean-Robert Henry (Aix en provence: Edisud).
Deprest, Florence. 2011. 'Using the Concept of *genre de vie*: French Geographers and Colonial Algeria, c.1880–1949', *Journal of Historical Geography*, 37: 158-66.
Faure-Sardet, Jeanne. 1935. *Fille d'Arabe* (Paris: E. Figuière).
Guy, Kolleen M. 2010. 'Imperial Feedback: Food and the French Culinary Legacy of Empire', *Contemporary French and Francophone Studies*, 14: 149-57.
Halvorsen, Kjell H. 1978. 'Colonial Transformation of Agrarian Society in Algeria', *Journal of Peace Research*, 15: 323-43.
Janes, Lauren R. 2014. '*Curiosité gastronomique et cuisine exotique dans L'entre-deux-guerres: une histoire de goût et de dégoût*', *Vingtième Siècle. Revue d'histoire*, 123: 69-84.
Lebel, Roland. 1931. *Histoire de la littérature coloniale en France* (Larose).
Marrouchi, Mustapha. 2008. 'On Couscous', *Southern Review*, 44: 99.
Mouhoub, Hadjira, and Claudine Rabaa. 2003. *Les aventures du couscous* (Paris: Actes Sud).
Noirfontaine, Pauline. 1856. *Algérie: Un regard écrit* (Havre: A. Lemale).
Rhaïs, Elissa. 1919. *Saâda, la Marocaine* (Paris: Plon).
———. 1929. *La Riffaine* (Paris: Ernest Flammarion).

Coming in to Graze: The Fall and Rise of Hill-Reared Mutton

Jessica Fagin

'There's nothing like the meat from the sheep when they get up high. The heathers, the wild grasses. It's hard getting up there, and you can taste it. It's the most beautiful flavour. But the crofters, they're getting on now, some are hitting 90, they can't get up those hills anymore. They get older, the sheep get lower, and that flavour, it's not the same.'[1]

The transcendence of place into the flavours and textures of food is communicated through the concept of *terroir*: a confluence of climate, land, and species. *Terroir* has been explored through its rhetoric, politics, and social effects of its increased value in food production. Discourses promoting a food's unique *terroir* often focus on the non-human characteristics of place that producers capture rather than determine. This framing belies the human biographies which are as entwined into this taste of place as the land itself. Through *terroir*, time is valued as a moment and process. The harvest season, the ageing of a cheese, or the months animals have grazed on pasture are familiar in the language mapping the sensorial effects that identify a food as from somewhere.

However, the processual effects of time in the ageing of human producers and their labour is rarely configured into narratives of how place is transported onto taste buds. The crofters of Lewis and Harris, the northernmost of the Hebridean islands scattered off the west coast of Scotland, are now into their 60s, 70s, and 80s. As the younger generations leave the islands, the crofting community has transformed and dwindled. Following the local smallholding traditions, some of the remaining crofters put their sheep out onto the common grazings, the wild moors and hills, to produce hill-reared mutton. They work alone or in small groups in harsh climates on remote, steep gradients. Physical abilities change, and thus accessibility to the land – albeit common grazing land – is rendered inconsistent.

Simultaneously, food discourses which isolate *terroir* alongside localism and traditional farming practices are promoting hill-reared mutton to support the future of upland farming communities. The meat is celebrated for its complex, deep flavour attributed to the sheep's gradient faring bodies and diet of heathers and wild grasses found on the hills and moors. Framed around conversations with crofters in their homes and out on the moors and hills, their actions and biographies reveal that accessibility to land has been disrupted by shifting tastes and agendas both on and off the island. Considering the effects of human aging through the changing motivations and physical capabilities of crofters offers an opportunity to question crofters' connections to place as these connections are remade and abandoned throughout their lifetimes, reframing how, and for whom, a taste of place is constructed.

The Croft and the Common Grazings

> 'Back then in the village there were 30 men to 100 sheep, in the last 10 years, there were six of us with 200 sheep. Now it's just the three of us crofters, my dad is 78, another 64 and I'm 48. Just three, when once there were 30. We've given up the common grazing all together, it's unmanageable. It used to take 30 men three days to gather.'

Putting the sheep out on the common grazings, the moors and hills, in the highlands and islands of Scotland is deeply embedded in the history and cycle of crofting life. Though represented as a traditional form of agriculture, crofting has been shaped historically by external forces and markets. During the highland clearances that peaked in the 1840s, smallholding tenants were moved off estate-owned land in favour of commercial sheep farmers to profit from the increasing price of wool. T.M. Devine argues that Scottish crofting society emerged as a distinct social and economic system before the clearances, against the thrust of industrialization.[2] Whilst the lowlands were consolidated into large farms, the isolated Hebridean wilds were marginalized, resistant to intensive agricultural cultivation, suitable only for highland cattle and hill sheep. Crofting emerged as an uncommercialized rural practice because it did not have the resources or regularity to compete with the new waves of industrialized farming. Smallholdings, crofts, were occupied by single tenant families who were expected to survive as part self-subsistent agriculturalists and part paid labour force in the coastal fishing or kelp industries. The clearances, alongside the demise of the fishing and kelp markets, left crofters landless and without income.

After decades of poverty, the government-commissioned 1844 Napier Report instigated the Crofters Holding Act in 1886, which established centralized legislation of crofting. The act granted crofters with tenure from working on the land an apportionment to grow crops and access to the common grazings for a small souming of sheep. It connected the crofts politically to the mainland through legislation and symbolically as protected yet marginalized outsiders to capitalist progression. The Crofting Commission, initiated to mediate between landowners and tenants, continues today, allocating government and now EU subsidies and grants to crofters who continue with agricultural work. 'Going back in history,' a crofter recalls, 'you had half a dozen sheep, a milking cow, chickens, the right to cut peat on the common grazing, the right to sheep on the common grazings, the right to take seaweed off the foreshore for fertilizing your land, these things were put in the statutory books. Everybody was given an allocation of 3-4 acres of ground for a small rent.'

Crofting, then, is both a subsistence practice and an external, documented system of rights and rents. It marked geographical distinctions between the privately cultivated spaces of the croft and the wild common grazings. 'Putting sheep out' was knotted into living off the land as a part-time farmer. Native blackface sheep, with compact bodies and thick coarse coats, could withstand the harsh island winters, relentless winds, boggy moors, and steep gradients. Sheep were kept 'just the right side of wild', freeing the crofter of the responsibility of feeding. Distance generated time for other labour: tending to vegetable patches, weaving tweed in their houses, or leaving the island for temporary fishing and oil work at sea.

Gathering sheep from the commons punctuated the year, when men in a village would return and work together as a strategic group, guiding sheep in for lambing, tupping, shearing, or dipping. This system produced mutton, not lamb. Mutton, meat from sheep older than two years, was produced at a distance. It allowed the sheep time to mature and produce wool for sale. Before refrigeration, families killed a few mutton at the end of summer, after they had been fed on the grasses and heathers to recover from the draining winters and produce 'new meat' on their bones. Some cuts were eaten immediately, the offal and blood were used in puddings, and the rest was preserved through salting or drying and eaten into the following year. The meat was never sold off the island. Slaughtering lambs was unfathomable; it would disrupt the crofting cycle and curtail wool production. Small lamb bodies could not yield a year's supply of meat, and crofters still regard lamb meat as inedible, slimy, and tasteless.

In the villages across Lewis, crofting as a communal activity is visibly in decline. In a village of eight houses, one person may keep a few sheep close to the croft. Well-maintained, two-story, pebble-dashed or painted houses with planted front gardens were built in the 1960s with the support of government subsidies or social housing. They replaced the stone blackhouses; the traditional drystone walls, thatched roofs, and shared living for animals and families were condemned as unsafe and unsanitary. The main crofts, the land beyond the front gardens, have crumbling fencing combing fading ladders into the landscape. There are no vegetable patches, and overgrown reeds breach closer to the houses. 'Tourists come here and are blown away by the scenery, but to us it looks untidy now,' one crofter lamented. In the middle of lambing season, when ewes would have been bought closer to the croft to lamb, most are empty. A few sheep group together by the side of tarmacked roads on the accessible in-bye land between villages. The moors and hills in the core of Lewis, stretching towards Uist and Harris, are inhabited by either sheep or man.

The changes to the villagescape reflect the activities of those living within it: transitory holidaymakers, elderly crofters no longer able to work the land, or those that just don't want that work anymore. Crofting grants, for which any croft owner is eligible to apply, are awarded for technological improvements to the land and property to increase agricultural output. Indeed, residents must prove some form of crofting activity to retain their homes. Crofters speak with ambivalence about these grants: they have been both supportive of many and misused by some. Younger crofters, those aged under forty-one, are eligible for additional grants, but I didn't hear of, or meet, anyone who had received such grants.

Ethnographies of the Scottish Highlands, islands, and borderlands place crofters as marginalized. They highlight crofter actions in reproducing their identities as fierce outsiders, Celts, or Reivers.[3] S. Parman's rich 1990 ethnography of Lewis suggests that the continuity of crofting reflects 'the failure of economic rationality to suppress traditional Gaelic culture' because people retained an intense relationship with the land that maintained their symbolic and embodied identifications as Celts. Further, Parman argues that 'crofting continues to exist, despite various economically anomalous features, [because] crofters play an important role in the national symbolism and self-identity of Scotland as representatives of the modern Celt'.[4] These readings find ethnic and cultural continuity in the remaking of identities through an agricultural system and show how people are drawn to and hold onto the land where they feel they belong. For distant actors in mainland Scotland, these communities are perceived as maintaining traditions that hold value for the larger nation. However, the image of Lewis I have drawn appears instead emblematic of rural decline and cultural erosion in the face of migration, changing economies, and government intervention. The youth, I'm told, are no longer interested in the land or in crofts; those who remain committed to this lifestyle are too often hindered by their own increasingly limited physical abilities, and even so too few of them exist to share the necessary labour.

Pause and Return

'There isn't a country in the world where you won't find a Lewisman.'

'Lewis people like to come back home.'

The narrative of the elderly crofter, who can no longer continue the tradition of gathering on the moors, obscures an important stage in a contemporary crofter's life. It is also a stage that is often obscured by them when they contextualize their own desire for the continuity of their traditions. The crofters I spoke to range from their early 40s to their 90s. Some were still gathering in small groups; others, now physically unable to gather, have sold their sheep, given them away, or left them on the moors. They blamed age, limited physical abilities, and an absence of village community for why the common grazings are no longer accessible, but they rarely comment on their own disinterest.

One example of these crofters' conflicting desires is Angus. Now 63, Angus is one of a small group that holds onto the desire to practice crofting: 'They are hanging on to a life that is going, they want to hang on as long as they can and try and keep that type of life going. God knows why. I'm doing it too. God knows why. It's because I'm

Coming in to Graze

stuck. Well, I could change, I could change tomorrow, change anytime.' As with every crofter I spoke to, however, Angus left the croft in his twenties. As young, single men, they wanted to escape and explore. The temptations to leave were many: the sound of the Rolling Stones on a battery powered radio in the 1970s, a manufacturing job in the main town of Stornoway, the adventure of whale fishing in South Georgia or national service in Portsmouth, drunken nights out in Liverpool in the 1950s, or oil and aquaculture in the North Sea in the 1980s. Others tell me they just weren't interested: as one said, 'I needed to do something with my own life.' They left because they could not see themselves working in a subsistence agricultural community, with their time filled by weaving and mucking in, when they had access to a world beyond the island.

There has been a tendency, both in ethnography and in the larger symbolism of the marginalized crofter, to connect a sense of belonging to the land to the continuity of tradition. However, this connection has been staggered: the pull of the land has at times instead been a push away. Crofting was intended to be part-time; pauses were designed into its fabric and distance engrained in the semi-wild relationships with their sheep. The men I spoke to had returned to the island, but many hadn't. Those who returned say it was because 'it's where I belong'. There are now less than ten men who gather sheep from the moors across Lewis and neighbouring Harris. When they returned, their fathers had struggled to maintain sheep in their absence, and they needed to re-build the crofts, increase the number of sheep, and get them back out onto the moors. Most returned unmarried and without children to a village where very few were still crofting. They left a communal system to return to one of independent work.

In his ethnography of hill sheep farming in the Scottish borders, John Gray maps the spatial dimensions of social life through shepherds' encounters with the landscape as both a symbolic and sensuous activity where place – the hills – is produced through the embodied processes of being-in-the-world.[5] The crofting legislation physically and symbolically demarcates space, separating the tame space of the croft and the wilds of the common grazing, but the crofters' experience of being on the land and working with sheep shapes their own perceptions of place. Angus speaks about his skills handling sheep and traversing the moors as a kind of physical knowledge and ability that he has been learning since childhood. His body knows how to walk and balance on the island's irregular terrain, knows where to put his hands on a sheep's head so it doesn't charge, and knows which way the wind blows so that he can guide sheep who will walk towards it. He tells me:

> If I died this year, or next year, and in ten years' time somebody had this croft and wanted to have sheep on the hill, they wouldn't know where to gather them or how to go about it. That knowledge is gone and there are not many people to pass it onto that are interested, they are not even interested in accompanying me. This way of life is going to go, it will disappear, and I don't know what it will be replaced with, nothing, just a blank bloody space we are living in here.

Without knowledge embodied in crofters like Angus, place will have lost its identity, will be erased into nothingness. For Angus, continuing tradition rests not on verbally communicated, repeatable practices, but on being-in-the-world. His efforts to teach his nieces and nephews, whose family moved to Stornoway in the 1970s, proved unsuccessful because 'you can't avoid getting covered in sheep shit when you're gathering. They don't want to do dirty work nowadays'. Likewise, newcomers who move to the island with visions of a small holding 'usually leave after a year, once they've done a winter or realised you can't keep pigs here, sheep are the only animals for this place'. An existential question emerges that disrupts ideas about tradition as continuity: these men see nothing coming after them, but they do it anyway. For the older generation, the relief they first felt at getting rid of their sheep – because 'when you can't look after them yourself, when you're depending on someone else to do anything, it's not so good at all' – transforms into sadness when they look at the landscape and realise they are no longer active within it. One crofter in his 90s has a painting on his kitchen wall mirroring the view he can see through the window on the opposite side of the room. On both sides he is at a distance. The croft, for him, seems to have become symbolic of past activity rather than present meaning-making.

Don't Say the L-Word?

Despite the staggered crofting on Lewis, there are pockets of activity, people who keep sheep on the commons. Angus is part of a group of men working collectively and independently to gather, which complicates how many perceive traditions as lost or rejected. On a small scale, indeed, traditions are being recreated.

These recreated traditions both reflect and differ from those of the past. As Sandy, now in his 60s, puts it, 'We're just so old now, if you come to a gathering it's like a Saga holiday.' Sandy isn't originally from the island. Once a lawyer in London, he moved to Lewis a decade ago with no knowledge of crofting or raising hill-reared sheep, but his presence and entrepreneurialism has played a significant role in creating a market for Lewis mutton in southeast England, a market specifically for 'wedder' mutton (known as 'wether' in England), meat from males older than two years. He introduces the concept of *terroir* when he talks about the meat he produces, promoting the sheep's age and varied diet of grasses and heathers as bringing a flavour and a taste of place not present in commercial lamb. 'Don't mention the L-word,' he tells me. Having appeared on numerous TV documentaries about rural life, where he promotes this superior meat and denigrates lamb, he now struggles to meet the demand he helped create. He has built a new network of gatherers from the elderly crofters who had returned to the island, some from his own village, and some from others. Seeking out the men who still wanted to use the common grazing, he helped bring them together to teach him and to work as a cooperative. Individuals in this new group take up elements of crofting piecemeal: some still grow potatoes, and others keep only a few sheep. They have not returned to crofting in its entirety. But this new network,

Coming in to Graze

which represents a radical move away from the village-and-kin structure of crofting, is making the common grazings again accessible through creating a group tied to shared interest rather than to locality.

Sandy's is not the only way tradition is being recreated. Standing atop a blustery hill in the centre of the island with binoculars in hand, a crofter in his 40s and I are surveying the hill ahead, trying to spot sheep. I can't see any, even when they are pointed out to me, but Callum, who knows what to look for and where to look, is guiding my eyes across the smudge of a distant hill, identifying little white dots. Callum, a documentary maker, has returned to Lewis from Glasgow. His father used to put his sheep out to graze on this hill, and Callum hasn't seen this scene in over twenty years. Getting the sheep back out onto these common grazings has been a solo effort. If his plan works, the hill, isolated and fortress-like, will allow him to strategically gather with a team of just the wind and his Collie dogs. The hill will be the centre for a sheep's entire life cycle. Callum is retraining himself: he needs to know how not to do too much, how to encourage wildness to mould the sheeps' instincts to stay away from the croft. He too is challenging his instincts, keeping himself from bringing the lambs back in harsh weather: 'if some die, which they will, they die. If some sheep don't follow the others out to the hill, then they aren't good enough to be mutton, they die.' For both sheep and man in this cycle, hardiness and separation have value. Callum's return to hill sheep farming is processual, bit-by-bit developing new paths to tread and creating a new territory on the common grazings. He is continuing a tradition, by kick-starting it anew.

Crofting's decline has allowed a different practice of sheep farming to emerge in Lewis, the production of lamb. Enabled through a confluence of disinterest, crofting policy, and negotiation between sheep farmers, residents, and absentees, this new practice is limited by the availability of unused land in the immediate croft village. Iain returned to his family croft after twenty years working in aquaculture. Unable to continue using the common grazings because he and his father couldn't gather alone, he now uses the in-bye land and the crofts of others. The production of lamb requires different techniques, which he is teaching himself or making-do by tweaking existing practices. Without the grazings, Iain's labour has increased. He is now responsible for feeding his animals, so he grows more hay on the croft. Feeders have been created out of old church pews; the metal containers for synthetic dies used in Harris Tweed weaving have been repurposed into haylage containers. No longer needing the hardy characteristics of the blackface sheep, he breeds his ewes with a larger Texel ram: the crossbred lambs get a higher price at auction. He can lamb earlier because the sheep are on the milder in-bye land, which extends his lambing season from March to September. He can do all this work alone and make a profit. Despite his transition into commercial lamb farming, Iain remains deeply connected to his land. His ethos is still that of a crofter: he has a potato patch, he weaves, he produces as much on the croft as possible whilst earning income from the lambs.

The continuity of rearing sheep in any capacity on the island demonstrates that knowledge is not fixed into set traditional practices. These men, working alone or in small groups, are continually observing the social, economic, and spatial changes around them and adapting their practices to them. They are as much part of a crofting tradition as they are embedded in processes and markets away from the islands. What cannot be measured is how or when others may decide to return to the island. Despite the sadness that many older crofters feel, or the fact that, for some, the relationship with the land has changed, the adaptive practices of others and of newcomers suggest that crofting and keeping sheep for either lamb or mutton may continue after them in ways that cannot yet be predicted. It is unremarkable that perceptions and desires change alongside our aging bodies. If the flavour of the sheep meat from these islands has changed only because the crofters are older, it would presuppose the idea that it is only the characteristics of the land that stop their bodies being able to access it. These common spaces rely on other bodies and agendas to make them accessible.

The Future of Mutton

If place is temporally experienced, abandoned and recreated through the changing desires encountered throughout lifetimes, can we even think of it as producing a specific food or flavour? Over the past fifteen years, there has been an attempt to get the British public to return to consuming mutton, the type of meat produced by crofters on the hills and moors of Lewis. Headed up by Prince Charles's Mutton Renaissance campaign, we are told that consuming mutton is a way for us to support the 'continued life and soul of upland communities of Britain' and to connect with our British history.[6] Bob Kennard, a champion of mutton, tells us, 'The story of sheep and mutton is very much part of the story of the United Kingdom and indeed of our empire. Mutton fed our people through the upheavals of the industrial revolution, its fat lit our homes, it was served as the last lunch on the *Titanic* in 1912, and was the birthday meal on Captain Scott's last expedition.'[7] Kennard celebrates the power of Empire to characterize mutton as a remarkable meat, one that both elevates the commoner and feeds the elite.

Despite media attention, this traditional food has not moved from the menus of specialist chefs such as Fergus Henderson to butchers' cabinets or supermarket shelves. In 2008 and then again in 2014, the BBC4 *Food Programme* dedicated episodes to praising mutton's virtues even while discussing the disappearance of this onetime mainstay of the British diet. Whilst mutton is historically placed as being the food of both the king and the peasant, the inflection in its re-emergence is invariably on the tastes of the elite. The meat is more complex, more discerning; there is good mutton (which is aged well and has grazed on a diet of heathers and wild grasses) and there is bad mutton (the old sheep, no longer fit for purpose). Contradicting narratives describe it as a lost flavour and a new food, one that requires consumers to 're-educate' their palates to appreciate it.

To those who champion mutton's return, it is absurd that there is a potential food source from areas where nothing except solitude and sublimity is produced, whilst pigs and cattle require grain or animal feed in times of shortage. Competing accounts of sheep rearing claim that they are 'woolly maggots sheepwrecking' the landscape, over grazing on hillsides causing erosion and landslides.[8] This confusion about the ecological and financial merits of mutton is set to deepen at the precipice of Brexit. Upland farmers are being warned that they won't be able to compete with New Zealand or Australia. Currently, 40% of British-reared sheep are sold through the single European market, supporting the livelihoods of 10,000 farmers.[9] This figure collapses distinctions between lamb and mutton into a single substance, sheep meat, even though farming practices and markets are distinct. The fastest growing market for mutton is China (which the UK cannot access), the sharpest increase is in the cheaper cuts, not small-scale production mutton.[10] EU subsidies on which many of the crofters rely are currently uncertain. If lamb farmers refocus their markets to the UK, will the comparatively less popular mutton be able to compete if narratives of local food sovereignty become the norm? Or will the decreased costs of feeding see a return to the common grazings?

The Mutton Renaissance claims that it is 'vital to the continued life and soul of the upland communities of Britain that sheep farming remains financially viable, so having a flourishing market for good quality mutton is a way of ensuring that'.[11] Historically however, as we have seen, mutton production on Lewis existed outside of a commercial market. Mutton was a way for crofters to nourish themselves from the land whilst earning wages in other industries. Their access to the land was politicized, marginalized, and fragmented by the very British history of empire that Kennard celebrates. The narrative of its attempted reinvigoration has the potential to fetishize rural production without considering the diversity of contemporary crofting practices. It reconfigures the status of a food that was produced through part-time labour through the discernment of a different register: taste, and the taste of a dislocated consuming public. What these campaigns don't script as clearly is the taste of place for those who produce the mutton. Regardless of the different ways crofters have negotiated their relationships with the land, they all prefer to eat mutton. They too have a register of discernment for good and bad meat; for them lamb is inedible. To produce the taste of place of hill-reared mutton for any significant market away from the islands, whether on mainland Scotland, the EU, or beyond, would be to introduce new practices of sheep production on the island.

Conclusion

Lewis hill-reared mutton is currently in the process of being recreated as a meat which has a taste of place, a specific *terroir* which can be appreciated beyond the shores of the island. Crofting emerged as an agricultural practice because the islands did not have enough resources, access, or regularity to compete in the markets of industrialized agriculture. Its introduction into commercial markets is premised, paradoxically, on the fact that the meat is an antidote to industrialized food. Indeed, for those who have grown up on the croft, the mutton they eat tastes simply like sheep meat should taste. It isn't new; it isn't lost. The current campaigns to promote mutton as superior commercialize a food that, on the island, was never commercial. At the same time, they smooth over the differences and variables of producers' lives. The campaign hopes that a market-based approach can invigorate a traditional rural community. Indeed, the active sheep gatherers on Lewis demonstrate that adapting their networks beyond the traditional village structure is forming a new kind of community of gatherers alongside new economies. At the same time, the crofter who now raises lambs, but otherwise is actively working with the ethos of crofting, would be omitted from the narrative of mutton as traditional or supportive of rural upland community life. What the crofters of Lewis have demonstrated through the shifts in their lifetime, however, is that they don't always want to be the safe keepers of tradition, or to be stuck on this island. They pause, they explore elsewhere, and they may or may not return. Whilst the production of mutton has continued to exist on a small scale on the island, its availability rests on the presence of those who want to be there.

Notes

1. Quotations used as section epigraphs come from interviews conducted by the author.
2. T.M. Devine, *The Great Highland Famine: Hunger, Emigration and the Scottish Highlands in the Nineteenth Century* (Edinburgh: John Donald, 1988).
3. S. Parman, *Scottish Crofters: A Historical Ethnography of a Scottish Village* (Belmont, CA: Thompson Wadsworth, 1990); L. Fitzpatrick, *Croft and Creel: Harvesting the Land and Sea in West Highland Scotland* (Anstruther: Scottish Fisheries Museum, 2007); John Gray, 'Open Spaces and Dwelling Places: Being at Home on Hill Farms in The Scottish Borders', *American Ethnologist* 26.2 (19919), 440-60.
4. Parman, p. 3.
5. Gray.
6. HRH Prince of Wales, 'Foreword', in Bob Kennard, *Much Ado about Mutton* (Ludlow: Merlin Unwin Books, 2014).
7. Kennard, pp. 4-5.
8. George Monbiot, 'Sheepwrecked', *George Monbiot*, 30 May 2013 <http://www.monbiot.com/2013/05/30/sheepwrecked/> [accessed 28 April 2017].
9. Department for Environment, Food, and Rural Affairs, 'Leaving the EU would be a Major Threat to Sheep Industry', GOV.UK, 16 May 2016 <https://www.gov.uk/government/news/leaving-eu-would-be-major-threat-to-sheep-industry> [accessed 28 April 2017].
10. Agriculture & Horticulture Development Board, 'Chinese Demand for Sheep Meat Continues', *ADHB Beef & Lamb*, 1 June 2017 <http://beefandlamb.ahdb.org.uk/market-intelligence-news/chinese-demand-sheep-meat-continues/> [accessed 1 October 2017].
11. HRH Prince of Wales.

Dining Outdoors in Renaissance Art

Allison Fisher

In his 1498 essay, *De splendore*, the humanist Giovanni Pontano highlights the cultivation of gardens and convivial meals as activities appropriate for sophisticated elites. He writes that the prince of a state should 'have gardens, in which he can take exercise by walking, and in the right weather hold banquets'.[1] Pontano adds that a splendid man will have a table 'shine with gold and silver, so too will it be splendid in its foods'.[2] Through a series of case studies, I will explore this connection between food and landscape to demonstrate that in Renaissance imagery, as in life, the garden landscape and the refined meal acted as conduits through which social affiliations took place.

The highly contrived landscape of the garden, as well as natural landscapes such as forests, offered an ideal location for banquets during the Renaissance because of the health benefits it provided to diners. Common plants of Renaissance gardens, such as cedar, cypress, and citrus trees, were considered to emit 'beneficial fragrances' that would help restore appetites.[3] The sixteenth-century writer Petrus Crescentius noted that gardens 'preserve bodily health' because of their good air.[4] To dine in a healthful location fostered the well-being of both the host and the guests. Thus, many outdoor banquets celebrated important social events, including weddings and diplomatic meetings.

Further contributing to the zeal for dining outdoors was the revival of classical culture during the Renaissance. In the mid-fifteenth century, villa culture developed in Italy as learned elites sought to emulate the lifestyle of the ancients. Patricians commissioned *all'antica* villas where they could escape the stress and diseases of the city to instead pursue leisure activities, such as gardening, humanistic debates, and gatherings with friends.[5] At the Renaissance villa, as at the ancient villa, dining was an important pastime, particularly dining outdoors in the garden.[6] Gardens included many different spaces, such as grottos, fruit orchards, and terraces, where dinner services could be accommodated. Indeed, in his 1559 agricultural treatise, *La Nuova, vaga et dilettevole villa*, Giuseppe Falcone extolls the variety of locations where one could dine. At the villa, he explains:

> you can eat at any time, as much as it suits you, and in any place, including under a pergola, or in a loggia, or in a portico, or in the middle of an aisle, in the *orto*, the *giardino*, near the fountain, in the middle of the vineyard, under an apple tree, a pear tree, a beech tree, a cypress tree, sometimes in the middle of a beautiful meadow, the side of a fish pond, or along the river, or in the middle of a room.[7]

The range of spaces in the garden offered different sensory experiences for convivial entertainment. A fountain-side banquet would be refreshing in the summer heat, while a meadow might offer an ideal location for a spring meal.

Outdoor banquets appear in many paintings owned by the same elite members of society who retreated to villas. To examine the multivalent links between food and landscape in art, I will consider a series of case studies. The first is a depiction of one of the most famous literary works in Italy: Boccaccio's *Decameron*. In 1483, Sandro Botticelli was commissioned to paint four panels that illustrate the story of Nastagio degli Onesti, a didactic tale about the triumph of love told in the *Decameron* (Figure 1).[8] According to the tale, Nastagio wanders in despair through a forest after being rejected by his beloved. There, he encounters a phantom rider hunting down a woman. Nastagio speaks to the phantasm, who explains that he, too, was spurned by a woman, and subsequently doomed for eternity to hunt her down. Nastagio takes advantage of this tableau, and invites his intended to dine right where the ghastly vision will play out. After witnessing the violent scene, Nastagio's beloved realizes the error of her ways, and consents to marry him. For the Renaissance audience, the story served as appropriate imagery to decorate a chamber for newlyweds, and indeed the panels are linked to the 1483 marriage of Giannozzo Pucci to Lucrezia Bini, a marriage that was promoted by Lorenzo de' Medici, the de facto ruler of Florence at the time.[9]

Figure 1. Sandro Botticelli, The Story of Nastagio degli Onesti (Panel 3), c. 1483, tempera on panel, 84 x 142 cm. Museo del Prado, Madrid, Spain. Courtesy of Museo Nacional del Prado / Art Resource, NY.

The third panel in the series, the *Banquet in the Pine Woods*, represents the feast hosted by Nastagio in order to persuade his beloved to marry him. Although the banquet takes place in a pine forest, a wild landscape, the tables have been covered with the accoutrements of civilized society, including a white tablecloth, fine metalware, and glass carafes. For the most part, the foodstuffs remain in their natural state: whole, fresh cherries, plums, and cucumbers are scattered across the tables, perhaps as a compliment to the 'natural' landscape of the pine forest. Much of the food portrayed underscores the themes of love and marriage. Indeed, one of the comestibles on the table is cherries. Grown in Italy since the first century BCE, cherries often symbolized the blood of Christ in religious paintings. However, because cherry trees were the first tree to bear fruit after winter, they can also represent spring.[10] Boccaccio firmly situates the story in spring, specifically 'one Friday morning towards the beginning of May'.[11] As spring was traditionally considered to be the season of love during the Middle Ages and the Renaissance, the presence of cherries on Nastagio's table is particularly fitting.

In addition to the produce depicted on the banquet table, there are also small, rolled wafer cookies. These items would have required much time to make from luxury ingredients, such as sugar. Renaissance recipe collections, such as Bartolomeo Scappi's *Opera* (1570), include similar sweet delights. Although published a century after Botticelli's painting, Scappi's book includes recipes that would have graced elite tables such as Nastagio's. His recipe for wafer cookies uses flour, rosewater, sugar, and fresh egg yolks as ingredients, which are then cooked on special wafer irons and rolled up.[12] To offer such time-consuming and luxurious foods on one's table was an obvious mark of status, as only the wealthiest could have afforded such delicacies for a 'simple' banquet in the woods.

Botticelli illustrated the banquet in a pine wood, yet the space is a manufactured nature, not unlike the ordered landscape that a Renaissance noble would have encountered in a villa garden.[13] Renaissance gardens were spaces filled with natural flora, but arranged and ordered by the hand of man. Nastagio has created this landscape by felling pine trees, whose trunks are visible in the foreground of the scene. Moreover, the actual dining area is separated from the forest by a tapestry partition. To enclose the landscape in this manner echoes the late medieval artistic tradition of the *hortus conclusus*, the enclosed garden. This garden symbolized the Immaculate Conception of Christ, and derived from the Song of Solomon in the Old Testament, in which a bride was described by her beloved as 'a garden enclosed [...] a spring shut up, a fountain sealed'.[14] Just as the garden was enclosed, so was the Virgin Mary, who had not been penetrated when she conceived Christ.[15] Earlier artists painted devotional images in which Mary sits in an enclosed garden, filled with flowers that symbolize her pure and humble qualities.[16] The virtue of chastity, embodied by the Virgin Mary in her enclosed garden, was an important quality that Renaissance women should cultivate. The enclosure around the

Figure 2. David Ghirlandaio (David Bigordi), Banquet Scene from the Tale of Nastagio degli Onesti, in Boccaccio's 'Decameron', late 15th century, tempera on panel, 70.2 x 135.9 cm. John G. Johnson Collection, 1917, Philadelphia Museum of Art, Courtesy of The John G. Johnson Collection, Philadelphia Museum of Art, Cat. 64.

dining space in the woods would have reminded the newlywed viewer to be chaste like the Virgin, even in marriage.

A second version of the painting, now in the Philadelphia Museum of Art, has been attributed to Davide Ghirlandaio, a Florentine painter contemporary with Botticelli (Figure 2).[17] This painting contains many similarities to Botticelli's version, including the arrangement of the figures around an L-shaped table, and the arrival of the ghostly figures from the right. As in Botticelli's version of the narrative, a tapestry partition encloses the dining space, and separates the guests from the trees behind them. While both paintings illustrate food on the table, in the Philadelphia example the diners feast on bread loaves, small roasted fowl, and small yellow plums or apricots. Similar to cherries, yellow plums could be more than just a tasty comestible enjoyed by the guests. Yellow plums symbolized the chastity of Christ, and thus could further underscore the chastity of Nastagio's intended.[18] Chastity was considered such an essential quality for a Renaissance wife that the humanist Leon Battista Alberti proclaimed that '[c]hastity has always been worth more to anyone than beauty'.[19] During the late fifteenth century, many examples of imagery commissioned for marriages portrayed allegorical triumphs of chastity and other virtues as a reminder to the newlywed bride that she should cultivate virtuous behaviour in order to have a successful marriage.[20] The plums served by Nastagio in the Philadelphia painting highlight this same concern with marital behaviour, and they visually guide not just Nastagio's intended, but also the viewers of the painting, to be virtuous.

The roasted fowl on the table offer particular insight into the alimentary culture of the period, as poultry was considered to be a suitable food for the upper classes in Renaissance Italy. As Allen Grieco has shown, according to the Great Chain of Being in late Medieval and Renaissance thought, chickens and capons were considered to be appropriate food for people of higher social class because these birds were more aerial creatures than pork, sheep, or oxen, which belong to the earth.[21] Food reflected social status – the more superior your station, the more refined your food choices. It was believed that the working class and poor should eat mostly vegetables, especially beans and turnips, because they grew close to or below the ground.[22] In contrast, the elite should eat food that was higher up, such as fowl, or fruit that grew in trees. Nastagio, a young man from the

Figure 3. Workshop of Raphael, Feast of the Gods, c. 1518, fresco. Villa Farnesina, Rome. Courtesy of Scala / Art Resource, NY.

Figure 4. Workshop of Raphael, Venus on the Chariot, c. 1518, fresco. Villa Farnesina, Rome. Courtesy of Scala / Art Resource, NY.

upper class, and his viewers would have understood that the poultry he served on his table underscored the status of both himself and his guests.

A generation after Botticelli and Ghirlandaio executed their versions of the *Nastagio degli Onesti* tale, Raphael and his workshop portrayed a banquet set in a heavenly landscape rather than a terrestrial realm (Figure 3). The *Feast of the Gods* was created as part of the vault decoration of an open-air loggia in the suburban villa of the merchant-banker Agostino Chigi around 1518. The fresco depicts the marriage of the divine Cupid with the mortal woman Psyche, told by the ancient author Apuleius in *The Golden Ass*. In the story, food plays a central role. Apuleius relates that, after completing a series of near-impossible tasks imposed on her by Venus, Psyche was rewarded with immortality by Jupiter. At the divine feast on Mount Olympus, Psyche consumed ambrosia and nectar, the food and drink of the gods, and thus transformed her social status from mortal to divine.[23] Despite the landscape, the guests in the fresco do not dine on heavenly fare. Instead, the table is laid with silver platters of roasted birds, bread rolls, and the rounded tops of fruits, including an apricot and a pomegranate. The food on the table is not divine – rather, the artist illustrates foodstuffs that were recognizable to elite Renaissance viewers, including fruit and poultry.

Although the banquet is set in the cloud-like realm of Mount Olympus, Raphael's collaborator, Giovanni da Udine, painted festoons of lush fruit, vegetables, and flowers around the fictive tapestries that illustrate the narrative. These swags are not gardens in the traditional sense, but they add a naturalistic flavour to the fresco. Furthermore, the festoons also echo the variety of plants that grew in Chigi's gardens and the variety of food offered on his table.[24] While the swags are rendered with great naturalism, they are completely fantastical. The variety of produce would have never been ripe and available to human diners at the same time. For example, around a spandrel of Venus in her chariot are olives, grapes, cherries, and a quince above her head (Figure 4). Cherries are one of the first fruits to come into season, around May, while quinces are in season from October to December. Thus, for all their refined naturalism, the food in the festoons reinforces that this is a heavenly landscape, where fruit and vegetables are always ripe.

Food and Landscape

The Olympian realm is not bound by the earthly constraints of seasonal availability.

Agostino Chigi was one of papal Rome's most illustrious hosts, and he held sumptuous banquets for members of the papal court at his Villa Farnesina. As one of the richest men in Italy, Chigi treated his guests to opulent, exotic delicacies, such as eels imported from Constantinople and sauces made from parrots' tongues.[25] One of his most famous feasts took place in the summer of 1518 in his garden loggia, where Pope Leo X was present. After each course, Chigi amazed his company by having the servants throw the gold and silver plates into the Tiber River. Unknown to the guests, there were nets hidden in the water to retrieve his treasure.[26] The gardens at the Villa Farnesina were also famed, and humanists wrote laudatory poems describing their sensory delights.[27] In the 1511 poem *De Viridario*, written by Aegidio Gallo, the goddess Venus herself descends to earth to admire Chigi's estate, and to bless it with eternal spring.[28] The garden, Gallo writes, is embellished 'everywhere with golden ornamentations [...] most delightful flowers and the sweetest fruits, for the pleasurable and honourable recreation of [Agostino's] spirit'.[29] The description of Chigi's garden as an eternally fruitful landscape reflects the divine banquet and surrounding festoons in the *Feast of the Gods*. Moreover, both the poem and the illustration mirror the sumptuous banquets that Chigi hosted at the villa. The Olympian gods enjoy themselves drinking and dining, much as Chigi and his noble guests would have done in the loggias and gardens.

My final case study moves north to explore images created around the city of Venice. On the mainland, or *terrafirma*, members of the Venetian ruling class built villas and cultivated crops, such as grapes and grains. As is the case elsewhere in Italy, the villas were often designed by leading architects, such as Andrea Palladio, and the interiors were decorated with scenes of pleasurable pursuits, mythological stories, or illusionistic landscapes. During the late sixteenth century, some artists working around Venice began to also portray the past times of villa life as independent works of art. My final example, depicting a feast in a villa garden, provides the full manifestation of the linkages between landscape and food in Renaissance painting.

Lodewijk Toeput, also known as Lodovico Pozzoserrato, painted a series of outdoor banquets that highlight how the consumption of food and nature communicated the status of sophisticated elites in Renaissance Italy.[30] One version, now in the Kunsthistorisches Museum in Vienna, shows a banquet taking place in a verdant garden setting, while servants set up a table of sumptuous foods in the foreground (Figure 5). Unlike my earlier examples, in which the tables were sparsely laden or the food difficult to identify, in Pozzosearrto's work identifiable foodstuffs are rendered with great detail. Ripe fruit covers the table, while one servant picks up a block of cheese that resembles well-aged parmesan. Sugared sweetmeats cover the right side of the table, where a serving boy retrieves the trays to take to the diners in the midground. The table is set with a crisp white cloth, similar to the previous case studies, but under this tablecloth there is a luxurious oriental table carpet, which was a common feature of Venetian banquet paintings of this period.[31]

Dining Outdoors in Renaissance Art

The garden, too, is filled with a wealth of details that show off the splendour of the landscape. Behind a strolling couple, a bronze fountain gushes cool water. Leafy trees frame the scene, and, in the centre, diners sit under a pergola constructed of trained vines and classical caryatids. Pergolas, or arbours, were common features in Italian Renaissance gardens. The most common types were 'structures of latticework or crisscrossed wooden slats with vegetation trained against them', such as the one Pozzoserrato portrays.[32] Pergolas often defined areas of space in the garden, created axes, and directed vistas, as Claudia Lazzaro has noted.[33] Although Pozzoserrato's pergola may not delineate the garden space, by drawing the eye toward the centre of the painting, it emphasizes the refined guests dining within it.

Many of the foods in the painting allude to the earthly pleasures enjoyed by the guests in the garden. The grapes remind the viewer of the enjoyable intoxication induced by wine, which is also shown on the banquet table.[34] Melons, of which one is shown in the foreground, were a well-known symbol of earthly joys, particularly erotic pleasure, on account of their shape and sweetness. Cheese was an integral aspect of an elite banquet during the Italian Renaissance, and it was often served at the end of the meal to aid digestion.[35] Lobsters have been considered a luxury item since antiquity, when they were included in Apicius's recipe collection.[36] Lobsters often appear as reflections of *vanitas* in Northern European still-life paintings, which developed as an artistic genre around this time.[37] Pozzoserrato was born and trained in the Low Countries, and he would have been familiar with the Northern tradition of representing luxury objects and food delicacies as reminders of the fleeting pleasures of life. The painting may also have been informed by stories condemning the excess of riches, a theme that became popular in Venetian art during the mid-sixteenth century.[38] Pozzoserrato represented similarly decadent spreads of fruit, sweetmeats and cheese set in a landscape in his paintings of the *Vanity of Riches* and *Dives and Lazarus*, both themes that warn about the transient pleasures of life. Some Venetian audiences, particularly those interested in charitable reform, could have read allusions to the transience of worldly pleasures in this garden banquet; other viewers less concerned with moralizing meanings

Figure 5. Lodewijk Toeput (Pozzoserrato), Banquet in the Garden, c. 1590, oil on canvas, 120 x 197 cm. Kunsthistorisches Museum, Vienna. Courtesy of KHM-Museumsverband.

would have simply appreciated the delicious array of ripe and expensive foods displayed on the table.

The food on the table, however, has multivalent meanings. Indeed, the fruit offers particular insight into how social hierarchy was reflected in the alimentary choices of Renaissance diners. Pozzoserrato portrays platters bursting with lush fruit, including pears, peaches, and quinces. The variety of fruits reinforces the high status of the guests seated under the pergola, in the same manner as the fowl on the table of the Ghirlandaio example. During the Middle Ages and the Renaissance, fruit was considered a status symbol at wealthy tables. The Great Chain of Being made fruit, which grew above ground in trees, prized for the tables of the elite; the more aerial the origin of the food, the more appropriate that it be consumed by the highest members of society.[39] Thus, the fruit in this painting further communicated the wealth and elite status of the guests in the garden who are privileged enough to enjoy this produce.

In order to supply the owner's table with fresh produce, Renaissance gardens, especially those at villas, would include fruit trees and orchards. In his discussion of family life at the villa, Alberti declared that a gentleman 'should grow all kinds of good, rare fruit' in an ideal garden.[40] Fruit trees were so highly valued that they were even listed in inventories of the period. For example, the 1588 inventory of the Villa Lante at Bagnaia mentions pomegranate, quince, peach, and plum trees.[41] In the orchard of the Villa Barbaro at Maser, the architect Palladio describes the landscape as 'very large and full of superb fruit [trees]'.[42] In the painting, the viewer would have recognized the role that fruit played as an indicator of status through both its consumption and its cultivation in elite gardens.

Without archival information or documentation to determine the specific context in which the painting was produced, the food portrayed may just be a demonstration of the artist's virtuosity in still life painting, or the abundant display allude to moralizing messages popular in other paintings of the period. Regardless, the subject of a lavish garden banquet strongly suggests that the patrons were members of the same elite class that dine in the images. Moreover, the heavily laden tables hint at the agricultural production of the garden landscape. A Venetian patrician, the sort of individual who would have owned a villa and farmlands, would have appreciated the imagery. The paintings assert the wealth, both material and agricultural, of the patron and the viewers, who would have seen their own status and habits represented in this garden banquet.

Throughout this paper, I have explored how paintings of outdoor banquets are encoded with messages about social interactions through the food served, how it is served, and where the meal takes place. My first case studies demonstrate how the banquet acts as an element of didactic narratives to help instruct newlyweds about appropriate marital behaviour and social mores. In contrast, Raphael's *Feast of the Gods* fresco portrays a mythological meal that decorated a villa, where the owner could entertain noble guests and cultivate socio-political alliances. In my final case study, Pozzoserrato combined the familiar Italian motifs of villa life with the Flemish ability to render meticulous detail in order to create a painting of 'dining outdoors' that celebrates this cultured activity in its own right. His scene would have delighted the senses of the refined viewers through the verdant setting, the tastes of the sumptuous foods, the fragrances of the plants, and finally, though the overall visual splendour of the garden banquet.

Notes

1. Giovanni Pontano, *De splendore* (1498), qtd. in Evelyn Welch, 'Public Magnificence and Private Display: Giovanni Pontano's *De splendore* (1498) and the Domestic Arts', *Journal of Design History*, 15 (2002), 211-21 (p. 216).
2. Pontano, qtd. in Welch, p. 216.
3. D.R. Edward Wright, 'Some Medici Gardens of the Florentine Renaissance: An Essay in Post-Aesthetic Interpretation', in *The Italian Garden: Art, Design and Interpretation*, ed. by John Dixon Hunt (Cambridge: Cambridge University Press, 1996), pp. 34-59 (p. 36).
4. Petrus Cresecentius, *Opus ruraliam commodorum* (Basel, 1548), p. 377, qtd. in Wright, p. 35.
5. For a discussion of villa culture during the Italian Renaissance, see David Coffin, *The Villa in the life of Renaissance Rome* (Princeton: Princeton University Press, 1979).
6. Claudia Lazzaro, 'The Villa Lante at Bagnaia: An Allegory of Art and Nature', *Art Bulletin*, 59.4 (1977), 553-60 (p. 558).
7. Giuseppe Falcone, *La Nuova, vaga et dilettevole villa* (1559), fol. a 3r. Hervé Brunon cites this passage in his exploration of villa culture in sixteenth-century Italy: 'Imaginaire du paysage et "villeggiatura" dans l'Italie du XVIe siècle', *Ligeia*, 19-20 (1996), p. 59-77. I consulted the 1612 Venice edition; the English translation is my own.
8. The story is told on the fifth day in the *Decameron*. See Giovanni Boccaccio, *The Decameron*, trans. G.H. McWilliam (London: Penguin Books, 1972; rpt. 2003), pp. 419-25. Christina Olsen presents a fascinating argument for the four Nastagio panels as a metaphor for consumption in 'Gross Expenditure: Botticelli's Nastagio degli Onesti Panels', *Art History*, 15.2 (June 1992), 146-70.
9. Andrea Bayer in *Art and Love in Renaissance Italy*, ed. Andrea Bayer, exhib. cat. Metropolitan Museum of Art, New York (New Haven: Yale University Press, 2008), cat. 139, pp. 300-03 (p. 300).
10. Mirella Levi D'Ancona, *The Garden of the Renaissance* (Florence: Leo S. Olschki, 1977), p. 90.
11. Boccaccio, p. 420.
12. *The Opera of Bartolomeo Scappi* (1570), trans. Terence Scully (Toronto: University of Toronto Press, 2008), Book VI. 141, p. 588.
13. In her book, Lazzaro explains that 'order' distinguished a garden from nature through the conventions of planting (*The Italian Renaissance Garden: From the Conventions of Planting, Design, and Ornament to the Grand Gardens of Sixteenth-century Central Italy* (New Haven: Yale University Press, 1990), especially at p. 20, p. 30, and p. 69).
14. Song of Solomon 4.12.
15. K. J. Hellerstedt, *Gardens of Earthly Delights: Sixteenth- and Seventh-Century Netherlandish Gardens* (Pittsburgh, PA: The Frick Art Museum, 1986), p. 28.
16. Little scholarship exists on this painting, though Bernard Berenson and Barbara Sweeney do discuss the work at modest length: see Bernard Berenson, *Catalogue of a Collection of Paintings and Some Art Objects*, 3 vols (Philadelphia: 1913-1914), vol. 1, pp. 36-37, cat. 64; Barbara Sweeney, *John G. Johnson Collection, Catalogue of Italian Paintings* (Philadelphia: 1966), pp. 70-71. Thank you to Julia Valiela at the Philadelphia Museum for assisting with bibliographic and provenance information about the painting.
17. For example, Stefano da Verona's *Madonna in a Rose Garden* of c. 1420-1435, a painting which is now housed in the Castelvecchio Museum in Verona.
18. Levi D'Ancona (p. 311) cites the source of this connection as the *Reductorium Morale* by Petrus Berchorius, a fourteenth-century Benedictine writer who worked at the papal court in Avignon.

19. Leon Battista Alberti, *The Albertis of Florence: Leon Battista Alberi's Della Famiglia*, trans. Guido Guarino, (Lewisburg, NY, 1971), p. 221.
20. For example, a *cassone* (wedding chest) by Francesco Pesellino of c. 1450 in the Isabella Gardner Museum in Boston shows a triumphal procession of Love, Chastity, and Death. The imagery derives from Petrarch's fourteenth-century poem, *I trionfi*.
21. Allen Grieco, 'Food and Social Classes in Late Medieval and Renaissance Italy', in *Food: A Culinary History*, ed. by J.-L. Flandrin and M. Montanari (New York: Columbia University Press, 1999), pp. 302-12 (p. 311).
22. Grieco, p. 311.
23. Apuleius, *The Golden Ass, or Metamorphosis*, trans. E. J. Kenney (London, Penguin Books, 1998), Book 6, 23-24, p. 105.
24. On the botanical diversity of the produce represented in the festoons, see Jules Janick, 'Fruits and Nuts of the Villa Farnesina', *Arnoldia*, 70 (2012), 20-27.
25. Ingrid Rowland, *The Culture of the High Renaissance: Ancients and Moderns in Sixteenth-Century Rome* (Cambridge: Cambridge University Press, 1988), p. 242.
26. Rowland, *The Culture of the High Renaissance*, p. 242.
27. For a discussion of the poems written in honour of Chigi's villa gardens, see Ingrid Rowland, *The Roman Garden of Agostino Chigi* (Groningen: The Gerson Lectures Foundation, 2005), particularly at pp. 19-31.
28. Mary Quinlan-McGrath, 'Aegidius Gallus, *De Viridario Augustini Chigii Vera Libellus*. Introduction, Latin Text, and Translation', *Humanistica Lovaniensia*, 38 (1989), 1-99 (p. 5).
29. Aegidio Gallo, qtd. in Quinlan-McGrath, p. 14.
30. Luciana Larcher Crosato notes that there are at least four versions of garden banquet scenes by Pozzoserrato ('I piaceri della villa nel Pozzoserrato', in *Toeput a Treviso. Ludovico Pozzoserrato, Lodewijk Toeput, pittore neerlandese nella civiltà veneta del tardo Cinquecento, Atti di Seminario, Treviso, 6-7 novembre 1987*, ed. by Stefania Mason Rinaldi and Domenico Luciani (Asolo: Acelum Edizioni, 1988), pp. 71-77 (p. 76)).
31. Indeed, table carpets are seen in many feast images by sixteenth-century painters, including Titian, Veronese, Tintoretto, and Jacopo Bassano.
32. Lazzaro, *The Italian Renaissance Garden*, p. 30.
33. Lazzaro, *The Italian Renaissance Garden*, p. 30.
34. Silvia Malaguzzi, *Food and Feasting in Art*, trans. Brian Phillips (Los Angeles: J. Paul Getty Museum, 2008), p. 250.
35. In his fifteenth-century dietetic treatise, *De Honesta Voluptate et Valetudine*, Bartolomeo Sacchi, known as Platina, recommends that cheese be taken after the meal to 'seal the stomach' which will take away both the 'squeamishness of fatty dishes' and benefit digestion (*Platina's On Right Pleasure and Good Health*, ed. and trans. by Mary Ella Milham (Asheville, NC: Pegasus Press, 1999), p. 40).
36. See *Apicius, Cookery and Dining in Imperial Rome*, ed. and trans. by Joseph Dommers Vehling (New York: Dover Publications; reprint of Chicago: Walter M. Hill, 1936), 9. 398-402.
37. See, for example, Donna Barnes and Peter Rose, *Matters of Taste: Food and Drink in Seventeenth-Century Dutch Art and Life* (Syracuse, NY: Syracuse University Press, 2002), p. 140.
38. Philip Cottrell, 'Vice, Vagrancy and Villa Culture: Bonifacio de' Pitati's "Dives and Lazarus" in its Venetian Context', *Artibus et Historiae*, 26 (2005), 131-50.
39. Allen Grieco, 'The Social Politics of Pre-Linnaean Botanical Classification', *I Tatti Studies in the Italian Renaissance*, 4 (1991), 131-49 (pp. 131-34).
40. Alberti, p. 198.
41. Lazzaro, *The Italian Renaissance Garden*, p. 113.
42. Andrea Palladio, *The Four Books on Architecture*, trans. Robert Tavernor and Richard Schofield (MIT: MIT Press, 2002), ch. 14, p. 51.

Global Warming and the Changing Global Food Landscape: The Need to Preserve Diversity

Len Fisher

Global warming is a fact of life. Its effects on the distribution and nature of global food supplies are already being felt (Fisher 2015). According to a report of the World Economic Forum (2017), those effects are likely to be even more dramatic in the years to come.

Here I look at some of the changes that have already occurred in the world food landscape, examine predictions for future change, and ask what specific actions might be taken to mitigate the effects of global warming. One major practical action that has emerged from many research studies is to preserve and promote local and global diversity, individuality, and sound ecological practice. I consider how this might be achieved in practice, and what pitfalls lie in the way.

Climate-Induced Changes in the Global Food Landscape: Past, Present, and Future

The fact that global temperatures are on the increase is now well established (Intergovernmental Panel on Climate Change 2007), and is vividly exemplified by a NASA (2017) video depicting a century of climate change. The multi-factorial effects of this temperature increase on the global food landscape are, however, more difficult to assess, and the scenario is much more complicated.

Probably the most thorough study to date is that performed by David Lobell of Stanford University and his colleagues from Columbia University and the US National Bureau of Economic Research (2007). The authors studied the four largest global commodity crops (maize, wheat, soy, and rice), and found that declines of maize and wheat production by 3.8% and 5.5%, respectively, since 1980 could be attributed to climate change. For rice and soy, however, decreases in some countries due to climate change were offset by increases in other countries, also due to climate change. So the effects of climate change are already showing up, but just what those effects are depends very much on where one is sitting, and what food one is considering.

As for the future, we are dependent primarily on computer modelling projections, which are becoming increasingly sophisticated. A splendid example has been developed by the UK Met Office Hadley Centre (2018) in the form of an interactive tool that links food insecurity in less developed countries to various plausible scenarios for future climate change. The tool is an important adjunct for anyone wishing to follow the effects of climate change on our global food landscape.

One message from studies so far is that the predictions of most models to date have actually underestimated the effects of climate change. Unfortunately, there are still large areas of ignorance. On one hand, for example, there are no reliable data on the effects of climate change on livestock production (Vermeulen and others 2012). On the other hand, there is good evidence (Bakun and others 2015) that warming seas are encouraging, or even forcing, some fish to find new waters.

Nevertheless, there are some grounds for hope. The World Economic Forum, in its latest report 'Shaping the Future of Global Food Systems' (2017), has examined four broad scenarios, illustrated in the figure:

Scenario analysis of future food systems (World Economic Forum; reproduced with permission).

Global Warming and the Changing Global Food Landscape

The report looks at our behaviour as a complex, interconnected, consumption-driven society and comes to some strong conclusions – specifically, that our consumption must become more resource-efficient and less resource-intensive, and also that the increasing connectivity of the modern world is incompatible with long-term global food security. The report demonstrates that our main hope for the future is encapsulated in the phrase 'local is the new global'. What is needed is to encourage local farmers and local communities to produce local products, preserving and promoting diversity, individuality, and sound local ecological practice – themes dear to the hearts of many symposiasts. But why should these themes be so important for ameliorating the problems posed by global warming?

Why Do We Need Diversity?

The simple answer is that diversity is a key factor in promoting resilience and adaptability, both of which are essential elements in dealing with sudden and dramatic change in any complex system (Fisher 2013). The United Nations Food and Agriculture Organization makes the point with respect to climate change in its recent report 'How to Manage Biodiversity for Food and Agriculture' (2017). 'In particular', say the authors of the report, '[biodiversity] increases resilience of agro-ecosystems and is as such a means for risk reduction and adaptation to climate change.'

The experimental evidence that underpins this statement is overwhelming. It is summed up in a recent seminal review by Miguel Altieri and Clara Nicholls from the University of California at Berkeley (2017), who show that '[o]bservations of agricultural performance after extreme climatic events in the last two decades have revealed that resilience to climate disasters is closely linked to the level of on-farm biodiversity'.

This conclusion is at odds with the way in which intensive agricultural practices have been developed over the last few decades. But, as Atif Ansar and his colleagues in the business school at the University of Oxford have pointed out (2017), efficiencies of scale (common in world agriculture) are accompanied by dangers of inflexibility when conditions change. In the case of world agriculture, those dangers are now bordering on the extreme.

Altieri and Nicholls point out that biodiversity is a typical feature of traditional farming systems. One example, suggested to me by Dr José Tomás Ibarra from the University of British Columbia (2017), is that of Southern Andean home gardens, which his research has shown to be biocultural hotspots, where biodiversity thrives and food sovereignty is correspondingly strengthened.

Based on an accumulation of such evidence, 'various experts have suggested that rescuing traditional management systems, combined with the use of agroecologically based management strategies, may represent the only viable and robust path to increase the productivity, sustainability and resilience of peasant-based agricultural production under predicted climate scenarios' (Altieri & Nicholls 2017). But there are serious hurdles.

Problems in Maintaining Diversity

One of the main barriers to maintaining agricultural diversity is the effect of globalization. According to a very recent study (Cárdenas and others 2017):

> Smallholder farmers make a significant contribution to food security in developing countries. Those farmer communities are experiencing new challenges owing to integration with the broader economy (increasing price volatility) and climate change (increasing frequency of extreme weather events). [...] Experiments performed in 118 small-scale rice-producing communities in China, Colombia, Nepal and Thailand show that increasing the integration of those communities with the broader economic system is associated with lower investments in public goods when facing collective risks. As such, the provision of local public goods may be negatively affected by market integration and climate change.

In other words, attempts to catalyze change through small groups may be scuppered by the integration of those groups into the global economy.

The failure of the global economy to protect sustainable practices has been criticized in detail by Johan Rockström from the Stockholm Resilience Centre (2017). One particular problem, pointed out by food writer Eva Perroni (2017), has been the role of the World Bank and the International Monetary Fund. As Perroni notes:

> Agricultural policy was reconfigured in the thirty years between 1970 and 2000, through structural adjustment programmes (loans granted by the World Bank and International Monetary Fund to low income countries with the condition that governments reorient economic activity and policies toward repaying debt) and neoliberal trade policies. Under these policies, *countries were forced to abandon their national goals of growing traditional crops to ensure food self-sufficiency, and instead switch to non-traditional cash crops for foreign markets, in order to generate money to pay off their international debt* [my emphasis].

The Art of Persuasion

How can we change this situation, and promote a fresh (or, perhaps, old) approach to the development and protection of agricultural diversity?

One approach is political: to devise effective, research-based national and international policies, and to attempt to have those policies implemented through communication, education, and political pressure.

The research is certainly there, often already attuned to the political arena. To cite just two examples:

- Jonathon Foley and a large group of distinguished international colleagues have produced a seminal analysis 'Solutions for a Cultivated Planet' (2011), in which they argue that '[t]o meet the world's future food security and sustainability needs, food production must grow substantially while, at the same time, agriculture's environmental footprint must shrink dramatically. Here we analyse solutions to this dilemma, showing that tremendous progress could be made by halting agricultural expansion, closing "yield gaps" on underperforming lands, increasing cropping efficiency, shifting diets and reducing waste.' Hidden within this summary is a strong argument for increasing agricultural diversity as an integral part of the process.

- Joem Fischer and colleagues have produced a 'Plea for Multifunctional Landscapes' (2017), in which they quote chapter and verse of just why agricultural biodiversity is so important for our future.

There are many organizations (such as the Swiss-based International Risk Governance Council with which I have been involved (Fisher 2013, 2016)) that are working to have these important research insights implemented as political policy.

But there is another approach, grounded in changing the actions of individuals and small communities, aiming to catalyze large-scale change through small-scale innovation. It is exemplified by the work of Dr Charles Massy, an Australian farmer with a bachelor's degree in zoology and a powerful interest in sustainability. Massy has set out almost single-handedly to change Australian farming practices from their present mechanical and chemical bases to one that recognizes the dynamic biodiversity of the soil, vegetation, and other landscape functional components. He calls it 'transformative agriculture'.

In his PhD thesis (2013), Massy contends that such a change is necessary if food security (defined as 'the ability of the world to provide healthy and environmentally sustainable diets for all its people') is to be maintained in the face of climate change. It is a change where some seventy Aussie farmers have already acted as key innovators, with many more now joining in. Charlie has investigated how they changed their minds – and changed their practice. The lessons that he learned provide a concrete foundation for initiating vital changes across the wider spectrum.

Hope and Success

There is a growing movement (Gruber 2017) to preserve the variety of indigenous crops and bring these back into cultivation in order to promote agricultural biodiversity.

These are early days, but there are some signs that the message is getting through, often for purely pragmatic reasons. On a recent visit to Bali, for example, I found that the relative failure of rice monoculture practices has meant that there is now a return to the use of diverse varieties in rice production. Another example comes from the global wine industry, where new vineyards and new varieties are already being planted in new locations, in anticipation of climate change due to global warming (Yeamans-Irwin 2015; Mozell and Thach 2017).

Elsewhere, the Indian State of Sikkim has now become 'India's first fully organic state by converting around 75,000 hectares of agricultural land into sustainable cultivation as per guidelines laid down in [the] National Programme for Organic Production' (PTI 2016). 'Organic' does not necessarily mean 'diverse', but in this case it appears to, and the drive for the preservation of diversity underlies the move.

The Sikkim example, though, exemplifies the practical difficulties of promoting diversity in agriculture at the expense of short-term profits, since it now appears that local consumers are reluctant to pay the higher prices involved (Doshi 2017). The obvious answer is to provide government subsidies, and the example illustrates the point that governments must be prepared to underwrite such projects with more than just words in order to invest in the future at the expense of the present.

Whether many governments will be prepared to do this is a matter of conjecture. It is more likely that the initiatives will have to come from individuals like Charlie Massy, or through the instinct for self-preservation of such industries as the global wine industry. The signs are not necessarily favourable, but the fundamental point, backed by thorough scientific analysis, is that the maintenance of diversity, and the flexibility and resilience that it engenders, are key to dealing with the effects of climate change on food quality, food availability and other aspects of the changing food landscape. It is a message that food writers and other members of the foodie community can play a part in driving home, and one that we must drive home if we are not to face an increasingly bleak future in terms of the variety, quality, and availability of the foods that we now enjoy.

References

Altieri, Miguel A. and Clara I. Nicholls. 2017. 'The Adaptation and Mitigation Potential of Traditional Agriculture in a Changing Climate', *Climatic Change*, 140: 33.

Ansar, Atif and others. 2017. 'Big Is Fragile: An Attempt at Theorizing Scale', in *The Oxford Handbook of Megaproject Management*, ed. by Bent Flyvbjerg (Oxford: Oxford University Press), pp. 60-95.

Bakun, Andrew and others. 2015. 'Anticipated Early Effects of Climate Change on Coastal Upwelling Ecosystems', *Current Climate Change Reports*, 1: 85-93.

Cárdenas, Juan-Camilo and others. 2017. 'Fragility of the Provision of Local Public Goods to Private and Collective Risks', *Proceedings of the National Academies of Science of the US*, 114: 921-25.

Doshi, Vadhi. 2017. 'Sikkim's Organic Revolution at Risk as Local Consumers Fail to Buy into Project', *The Guardian*, 31 January <https://www.theguardian.com/global-development/2017/jan/31/sikkim-india-organic-revolution-at-risk-as-local-consumers-fail-to-buy-into-project> [accessed 28 May 2017].

Fischer, Joern, Megan Meacham, and Cibele Queiroz. 2017. 'A Plea for Multifunctional Landscapes', *Frontiers in Ecology and the Environment* <DOI: 10.1002/fee.1464>.

Fisher, Len. 2013. 'Preparing for Future Catastrophes', *IRGC Report*, 11 March <https://www.irgc.org/wp-content/uploads/2013/03/CN_Prep.-for-Future-Catastrophes_final_11March13.pdf> [accessed 28 May 2017].

Fisher, Len. 2015. 'Climate Change and Future Food Supplies', in *The SAGE Encyclopedia of Food Issues*, ed. by Ken Albala (Los Angeles: SAGE Publications), pp. 718-23.

Fisher, Len, Marie-Valentine Florin, and Anjali Nursimulu. 2016. 'Governance of Slow-Developing Risks in Socio-Ecological Systems', *Society for Chaos Theory in Psychology & Life Sciences Newsletter*, 24.1: 2-3.

Foley, Jonathon A. and others. 2011. 'Solutions for a Cultivated Planet', *Nature*, 478: 337-42.

Food and Agriculture Organization of the United Nations. 2017. 'How to Manage Biodiversity for Food and Agriculture' <http://www.fao.org/agriculture/crops/thematic-sitemap/theme/spi/scpi-home/managing-ecosystems/biodiversity-and-ecosystem-services/bio-how/en/> [accessed 28 May 2017].

Gruber, Karl. 2017. 'The Living Library', *Nature*, 544: S8-S10.

Ibarra, José Tomás. 2017. Personal communication.

Intergovernmental Panel on Climate Change. 2007. Fourth Assessment Report 'Climate Change 2007: Working Group I: The Physical Science Basis <https://www.ipcc.ch/publications_and_data/ar4/wg1/en/tssts-3-1-1.html> [accessed 28 May 2017].

Lobell, David B., Wolfram Schlenker, and Justin Costa-Roberts. 2011. 'Climate Trends and Global Crop Production Since 1980', *Science*, 333: 616-20.

Massy, Charles. 2013. 'Transforming the Earth: A Study in the Change of Agricultural Mindscapes' (unpublished doctoral thesis, Australian National University).

Mozell, Michelle Renée and Liz Thach. 2015. 'The Impact of Climate Change on the Global Wine Industry: Challenges and Solutions', *Wine Economics and Policy*, 3: 81-89.

NASA. 2017. 'NASA, NOAA Data Show 2016 Warmest Year on Record Globally', NASA Climate Change, 18 January <https://www.youtube.com/watch?time_continue=1&v=bCVXnrQfzgA> [accessed 28 May 2017].

Perroni, Eva. 2017. '21st Century Famine: A Long Time in the Making', *Sustainable Food Trust*, 27 April <http://sustainablefoodtrust.org/articles/21st-century-famine-a-long-time-in-the-making/> [accessed 28 May 2017].

PTI. 2016. 'Sikkim Became India's First Fully Organic State in 2016', *The Indian Express*, 31 December <http://indianexpress.com/article/india/sikkim-became-indias-first-fully-organic-state-in-2016-4452765/> [accessed 28 May 2017].

Rockström, Johan. 2017. '5 Reasons Why the Economy Is Failing the Environment, and Humanity', *World Economic Forum*, 10 January <https://www.weforum.org/agenda/2017/01/5-reasons-why-the-economy-is-failing-the-environment-and-humanity?utm_content=buffer2aaea&utm_medium=social&utm_source=twitter.com&utm_campaign=buffer> [accessed 28 May 2017].

United Kingdom Met Office Hadley Centre. 2018. 'Food Insecurity & Climate Change' <http://www.metoffice.gov.uk/food-insecurity-index/> [accessed 28 May 2017].

United Nations Food and Agriculture Organization. 2017. 'How to Manage Biodiversity for Food and Agriculture'.

Vermeulen, Sonja J., Bruce M. Campbell, and John S.I. Ingram. 2012. 'Climate Change and Food Systems', *Annual Review of Environment and Resources*, 37: 195-222.

World Economic Forum. 2017. 'Shaping the Future of Global Food Systems: A Scenarios Analysis', World Economic Forum *White Paper, World Economic Forum*, January <http://www3.weforum.org/docs/IP/2016/NVA/WEF_FSA_FutureofGlobalFoodSystems.pdf> [accessed 28 May 2017].

Yeamans-Irwin, Becca. 2015. 'The Effects of Climate Change on The Global Wine Industry: A Meta-Analysis for SOMM Journal' <http://www.academicwino.com/2015/06/climate-change-global-wine-industry-somm-journal.html/> [accessed 28 May 2017].

The Landscape of Food and Memory: Cuisine and Cultural Identity in the Sephardic Jewish Diaspora

Sara Gardner

In his most famous poem, the twelfth-century Spanish Jewish poet Judah Ha-Levi laments that 'my heart is in the East and I am at the edge of the West'. Even as he openly considers 'all the pleasures of Spain', Ha-Levi's personal longing for Jerusalem gives voice to the emotional undercurrent defining Jewish life in diaspora: the constant longing for homeland.[1] In the centuries following Ha-Levi's life, his wandering co-religionists would yearn for Spain. Before the Catholic monarchs expelled them in 1492, the Sephardim were an illustrious religious minority, contributing to all levels of medieval Spanish society and culture, especially through their lucrative mercantile role. It was this commercial legacy that enabled Sephardic resettlement in new lands after the community's early modern dispersal across the Mediterranean, allowing the Sephardim to literally put down roots in the landscape as they carried with them many of the cultivars essential to their cuisine in pre-expulsion Spain. As the diasporic Sephardim assimilated into new lands, they also integrated the indigenous culinary and agricultural terrain in their food, in so doing combining their familiar Iberian *terroir* with that of their new homes. Thus, analyzing the dishes of the Sephardic Jews in Morocco, Italy, and the Ottoman Empire for the distinct landscapes they literally and symbolically encompass enables a deeper understanding of Sephardic identity in the early modern diaspora.

Before their expulsion, the Sephardic Jews were involved in all levels of Spanish society, as viziers, literati, merchants, and more. While a great deal of scholarship has already been written exploring the historical influence of the Sephardim on the cultural landscape of medieval Spain, very little has analyzed their impact on the physical terrain of the Iberian Peninsula. In many ways, the Sephardic community's relationship with the Iberian homeland from which they would eventually be expelled corroborates Olivia Remie Constable's point that 'the diversities of Iberian history cannot be fully explained by either harmonious *convivencia* or hostile *Reconquista*'.[2] Even during the periods when the Sephardic Jews were prohibited from full societal participation, such as 'in Visigothic Spain', Norman Roth highlights, still 'Jews seemed to be mostly engaged in agriculture'.[3] Though the dominant political powers prohibited Spanish Jews from societal positions, the Sephardim could always interact with land; therefore, that relationship reflects the more minute considerations of Sephardic daily life. Due to the Jewish laws of *kashrut* –

root of the word *kosher* – that regulate the consumption of certain foods, the Sephardic community needed to control the production of most of the cultivated crops it ate. There was one such 'prohibition on drinking wine even touched, much less made, by a Gentile', meaning 'that Jews had to make their own wine'.[4] These religious stipulations created a uniquely Jewish relationship to the Spanish environment. Their successful adaptation of crops brought to Spain through Islamic influence – including 'a number of vegetables [that] proved particularly successful and quickly spread to Spain [...] at the head of the list was the eggplant', as well as spinach, beets, carrots, artichoke, leeks, and onions – demonstrated Sephardic acculturation especially within the pre-expulsion Muslim territories.[5] As Geniza documents show, Spanish Jewish land ownership was quite common:

> the Hebrew documents or formularies that have reached the Geniza from [Spain] show that private persons possessed vineyards and sold or leased them at liberty. Of particular interest is one deed of sale of half a vineyard, which [...] enumerates in Arabic [...] no fewer than fifteen defects and diseases that the vineyard might have [...] Another document from Spain [...] shows how minutely obligations of a tenant were fixed, including the exact number of loads of manure to be used; he had to look after everything, from the amelioration of the soil and of the stock of the vines to the pressing of the grapes.[6]

Sephardic land cultivation and ownership, as Shlomo Goitein highlights, were a main means of the community's involvement in their pre-expulsion context. The Sephardic relationship to the Spanish terrain, expressed through the production of comestible cultivars, thus offers a nuanced portrait of the pre-1492 Sephardic reality: simultaneously distinct through differentiation by their religious practice as well as fully integrated by dint of owning and cultivating land. By physically restructuring the Spanish countryside to suit their specific religious and gastronomic needs, the Sephardim left a lingering mark on the Iberian Peninsula that has lasted longer even than their profound impact on Spain's cultural heritage.

The Geniza documents are also significant because they signal the connections between the Sephardic community's agricultural production and mercantile role, for which the Sephardim were particularly prestigious in pre-expulsion Spain. Beyond merely reshaping the Spanish landscape through their trade in foodstuffs, the Sephardim also helped to transform the culinary terrain of medieval Spain, in the process cementing the community's illustrious position in society. As a ninth-century account of Radanite Jewish traders demonstrates, medieval Jewish merchants were particularly involved in the movement of valuable spices, returning 'from China [to] load musk, aloe wood, camphor, cinnamon, and other products of the eastern countries and they come back to al-Qulzum [...] from there they embark again on the Western Sea'.[7] Besides playing a role in the lucrative Silk Road spice routes, Sephardic Jewish merchants played an especially prominent role in 'the meager trade of the early Middle Ages [...] in the highly developed Byzantine and Muslim territories [... where] they were second to none in the scope of their travels'.[8] Even the most prominent Sephardic figures were involved in this culinary trade, including Samuel Ha-Levi the Nagid, a 'high-ranking personality [...] alleged to have begun his career as a merchant – of spices', and Isaac Abravanel, advisor to the Catholic monarchs, who 'took part in the major trends of the Iberian Renaissance: international trade with Flanders, Tuscany and North Africa'.[9]

Through these commercial interventions, the Sephardic Jews exerted their influence on the culinary topography of medieval Spain, as shown by Jewish recipes from a thirteenth-century Andalusian cookbook. While all the recipes listed as Jewish share a great deal with the other non-Jewish recipes of the period – particularly the elaborate presentation of the final dish – they do diverge ingredient-wise: Carolyn Nadeau cites 'the biggest variances [as] the central role of organ meat, the addition of citron and mint shoots'.[10] This difference in ingredients is significant: the citron, an important fruit used on the Jewish holiday of Sukkot, owed its dissemination across the Mediterranean to the Sephardic Jews.[11] Moreover, the abundance of spices – 'in addition to oil, vinegar, salt, and pepper, seasoning often includes cilantro or coriander' – gastronomically communicates the Sephardim's involvement in the medieval spice trade.[12] Here, it becomes evident that the culinary repertoire of the Sephardic Jews in pre-expulsion Spain expressed not only their integration into the physical landscape of Spain through its agricultural bounty, but also their role as key traders of the exotic flavours that perfumed Jewish and non-Jewish dishes alike. Thus, the Sephardic involvement in trade and agriculture before their expulsion from Spain helped to shape the terrain of medieval Iberian cuisine even as they manipulated the physical Spanish landscape; upon their expulsion, it was this culinary repertoire that the Sephardic Jews took with them – including physical cultivars and remembered recipes – as tokens of that land.

After expulsion, a majority of Sephardim traded Spain for a new-yet-proximate land: Morocco. Though Jewish migration to Morocco had started even before 1492, beginning around the aftermath of the 1391 Seville pogrom, Richard Hull explains that 'in the Maghreb, Morocco was arguably the greatest beneficiary of the epochal Sephardic diaspora of the 1490s'.[13] As Hull highlights, trade documents show that the relationship between the Spanish Jews and Morocco largely predates expulsion:

> Jews already figured importantly in the Catalan trade, and James encouraged Jewish merchants and professionals with their intimate knowledge of the Maghreb and its southern hinterlands to live in his kingdom [.... M]any prominent Moroccan Jews moved to Barcelona and Valencia, and historians believe the Moroccan-Jewish émigrés in Barcelona introduced their Christian associates to North African Muslim trading opportunities.[14]

Trade seemed the main communicative medium between medieval Spain and Morocco that made them, especially at the height of the Muslim reign of Southern Spain, nearly contiguous territories, with Moroccan and Sephardic Jewish traders as central actors in that commerce.[15] Geniza documents demonstrate that a great deal of this pre-expulsion trade was foodstuffs. In particular, in a letter from Isaac b. Baruch to Abu Sa'id Halfon b. Nethanel Ha-Levi, Abu

The Landscape of Food and Memory

Sa'id (incidentally acting as the silent business partner to the poet Judah Ha-Levi) explicitly mentions the delivery of important spices such as pepper, rose marmalade, and caraway seeds, used for both culinary and medicinal purposes.[16] Saffron, too, as Zohar Amar and Efraim Lev demonstrate, was shuttled by Sephardim between Spain and the Maghreb, having been 'cultivated in Muslim Spain [… and] according to many eleventh-century Genizah fragments, saffron was brought from the countryside to major towns in the cultivation areas and […] transported along the trade routes to other commercial centers of the medieval world', including North Africa.[17] In fact, as medieval Islamic agricultural texts demonstrate, the cultivation of certain crops like citron, almonds, and saffron were shared between Spain and Morocco, with Spain often being the gateway to the dissemination across the Mediterranean basin and Morocco as the first stop.[18] This food-based trade not only affected the physical topography of Morocco but also the mutually shared culinary landscape between the Iberian Peninsula and the North of Africa. For example, as Rachel Laudan explains, 'the Berbers are believed to have contributed a pie of layers of paper-thin pastry filled with a chicken ragout (*judhaba*) that still exists in Morocco (*bastilla*).'[19] After expulsion, this long-standing trade relationship took on greater meaning as the Sephardic Jews had now become diasporic transplants themselves; for many Sephardic exiles, the familiarity of Morocco's landscape – commercially, agriculturally, and gastronomically – acted as a draw.

Though its topography may have felt familiar to the Sephardic settlers, the cultural landscape of Morocco offered the exiles a new set of challenges. Particularly trying was the relationship of the Sephardim with their indigenous Moroccan co-religionists, most of whom Haïm Zafrani explains were Judaized Berber tribes in terms of ethnicity.[20] Mohammed Kenbib affirms that 'for centuries a feeling of difference existed between the *toshavim* (indigenous Jews) and the *megorashim* (lit. those expelled), namely Jews who fled from Spain after the fall of Granada in 1492'.[21] Though Zafrani takes a slightly more positive perspective on the interaction between the two Jewish communities, he concedes:

> the arrival of the Jews expelled from Spain caused some disturbance in the life of the local communities […]. For a long time [they] held conflicting views on certain points relating to the liturgy and the laws governing the ritual slaughter of animals for consumption; but in the end the newcomers took the lead in the communities where they had settled, particularly in the north of the country.[22]

Interestingly, as Zafrani points out, this conflict between the indigenous Moroccan Jews and the Sephardic exiles came to be expressed through different religious interpretations of food-based observances. In fact, it also occurred through the different relationships each community had to the physical landscape. As Abdellah Lahrmaid highlights, in Morocco 'cultivated lands held both a symbolic and material value that provided a means of distinguishing social categories', such that 'when it came to owning land, Jews in the Sous [and Morocco generally] were subject to rulings of Muslim jurists as implemented by Muslim political leaders'.[23] The mostly urbanized Sephardim, who came to resettle in the cities therefore had a distinct relationship to the Moroccan environment from their nomadic and rural Berber co-religionists, as they were often given greater influence over their environment. These differences also manifested clearly through the distinct culinary repertoires of the two Jewish groups. Returning to the episode of the halakhic debate between the indigenous Moroccan Jews and the new Sephardic arrivals, Zafrani explains that 'a serious conflict broke out between the[m] on a problem relating to the ritual slaughter of animals for consumption [… that] ended in victory for the megorashim and the adoption of common regulations for the communities'.[24]

Here, it becomes clear that these culinary differences were metonymic for each group's distinct perception of Jewish identity. Not only did this distinction occur in the general rulings of kashrut, but also for the more specific gastronomic observances of certain holidays, like Passover.[25] These divergent conceptions of Jewish identity were thus demonstrated through the different *terroirs* communicated through Moroccan Jewish versus Sephardic Jewish food. As Herbert Dobrinsky notes, 'an interesting distinction between Moroccan food and that of other Sephardic groups is that Moroccans have some sweet foods, similar to Ashkenazim. Thus, sweet and sour combinations are different from foods served among any other Sephardic group. Among the sweet foods they eat are squashes and humus […] which many eat on Shabbat.'[26] The differences are even apparent according to the types of fats used in their food preparations: Sephardic Jews stuck to the olive oil they were known for using on the Iberian Peninsula, which they had brought with them to Morocco, whereas Moroccan Jews preferred using their indigenous argan oil or 'the fatty hooves of cattle and of sheep in a sauce of chickpeas'.[27] While the cuisine of their indigenous Moroccan co-religionists telegraphed that community's rootedness, the continued use of certain ingredients gastronomically signalled the Sephardim's lingering connection to their Spanish homeland.

If in Morocco the Sephardim's changing culinary repertoire communicated their distinct relationship to the landscape from that of their local co-religionists, in Italy it demarcated the difference between Christian and Jewish communities. As in Morocco, Sephardic food-based trade with Italy had been established long before their expulsion, according to Francesco di Balduccio Pegolotti's account of the goods imported to Florence in *The Practice of Commerce*. His list of over two-hundred goods shipped into the port of Florence includes many foodstuffs for which the Sephardim were well-known traders, including 'fresh oranges', 'asafetida', 'cumin of Spain', 'cassia', and 'citrons'.[28] According to Francesca Trivellato, it was the Sephardim's prestigious commercial legacy that opened the doors for the Sephardic Jews to settle in Italy, as 'several Italian states tr[ied …] to attract Iberian refugees because of their perceived business skills and economic ties'.[29] This desire for Iberian Jewish exiles was particularly notable due to the often-unwelcoming attitude of Italian city-states towards Jews; it was this antagonism that served to dissuade

> many Sephardim [from] respond[ing] to the personal letters of invitation of the Duke [Cosimo de' Medici], especially because of his history of anti-Jewish

actions: complying with Pope Pius IV's directive to burn all copies of the Talmud in 1553, forcing Tuscan Jews to wear an identifying insignia in 1557, and revoking all privileges of Jewish moneylenders and forcing the Jews to leave the state or move to the ghettos of Florence and Siena in 1571.[30]

At the same time, the perceived commercial acumen of the Sephardic Jews acted to mitigate the negative consequences of their Jewish identity, especially under attack in those Italian city-states where the Inquisition was established. Further, as many of the Sephardim who made their way to Italy – including such notable figures as Doña Gracia Mendes – had been converted (often forcibly) to Catholicism before having left Spain, those who arrived in Italy in the century following expulsion did not seem 'Jewish' in the normative sense, instead passing as Christians or claiming a more secularized version of Jewish practice.[31] Indeed, such documents as the Livornine issued by Cosimo de' Medici in 1593 – which Stephanie Nadalo remarks had been 'specifically engineered to attract merchants from the Sephardic Jewish diaspora' – extended 'social, religious, and economic protections to new residents of Livorno and Pisa, including "all merchants of any nation, Eastern Levantines and Westerners, Spanish, Portuguese, Greeks, Germans, and Italians, Jews, Turks, and Moors, Armenians, Persians, and others"'.[32] By including 'Jews' among all the 'merchants of any nation', the Italian city-states, particularly Tuscany, signalled their desire for the commercial influence of the Iberian refugees, as long as they quietly fit into the Christian landscape. It did not take long for the Sephardim to take up this invitation and establish themselves as fixtures in the urban environment, as demonstrated by the growth of the ghettos in Rome, Ferrara, Ancona, and Livorno.

Sephardic integration into the Italian sociocultural context could also be seen through the physical landscape, in no small part due to the foods that the Sephardim brought with them. As Gil Marks explains, 'since Sephardim were at the forefront of medieval citrus cultivation and growing citrons for the Sukkot festival, the practice of using lemons in sauces first became widespread among them', and so, upon their expulsion, the citron and its citric variants including the lemon and orange came with the Sephardim to Italy. A sauce called *agristada*, made of lemons and egg, became quite popular 'in the ghetto of Pitigliano in southern Tuscany, established by Cosimo de' Medici in 1608, [where] the sauce was commonly tossed with egg tagliatelle or drizzled over cooked vegetables'.[33] The sauce's adoption is particularly notable because it was through de' Medici's influence that the Sephardim were allowed to come to Tuscany at all. Thus, the cuisine of the Sephardic Jews in Italy served as a reminder of their Spanish home, from whence they brought their taste for citrus, even as its absorption of elements like egg tagliatelle signalled the acceptance of their new social context.

The cultivation of these crops, too, in their physical adaptation to the Italian landscape underscores the establishment of the Sephardim, even if the impact was not explicitly acknowledged. The orange even became a noble landscaping motif, as 'the Medici created one of the greatest European citrus gardens in 1544 at the Villa di Castello near

Florence. The orbs on their escutcheon have variously been interpreted as pawnbrokers' balls, apothecaries' pills or, some say, *oranges*'.[34] Thus, the crops that the Sephardic Jews helped disseminate became part of the physical environment and even a symbol of the ruling class. Yet the cultivation of these crops, much like the legal acceptance of the Sephardic exiles, depended on the intentional silence around Jewish identity.

Unlike citrus, the eggplant, that 'Jewish exiles fleeing [...] from Spain and Spanish-controlled Sicily and southern Italy in 1492, helped to popularize [... by] bringing it and numerous eggplant dishes to northern Italy', experienced a delayed reception into the Italian culinary repertoire on account of its status as a 'Jewish' vegetable.[35] In his 1891 *La Scienza in cucina e l'arte di mangiar bene*, Pellegrino Artusi confirmed that Italian tolerance was fickle when he wrote that 'forty years ago you could hardly find either eggplant or fennel in the markets here in Florence, because they were considered a Jewish food and abhorred'.[36] Therefore, unlike the orange and other citrus, which expressed Sephardic assimilation into the Italian context through their agricultural dissemination, the eggplant retained its Sephardic Jewish provenance for much longer. While the Sephardim brought with them many crops that would affect the physical and culinary landscapes of Italy, the extent of that influence depended on how explicitly these ingredients expressed Jewish identity.

The Sephardic culinary repertoire from the Ottoman Empire offers a look into yet another experience of Sephardic identity in diaspora. Again, the commercial influence of the Sephardim paved their way to the Ottoman Empire, as Fernand Braudel highlights: 'the Jews, driven out by their religious beliefs not their poverty, played an exceptional role in these transfers of technology. Jews expelled from Spain, at first retail merchants in Salonica and Constantinople, gradually built up their businesses until they were competing successfully with Ragusans, Armenians, and Venetians'.[37] This commercial role enabled the Sephardim to more easily establish themselves within the multicultural social milieu of the Ottoman Empire; in fact, since 'the first half of the sixteenth century [especially] was a period of economic florescence in the Ottoman Empire – a prosperity in which the Jewish community shared [...]. [It enabled] the form of Jewish social life at the time'.[38] More than merely occupational, the Sephardic role in food-based trade actually aided in the construction of their Ottoman social landscape. Moreover, as it encompassed various far-flung geographic terrains and cultural groups, the food-based trade of the Ottoman Empire openly reflected the variety of *terroirs* within it. Rachel Laudan explains the diverse commercial environment:

> Ottoman cuisine depended on, and stimulated, commerce and agriculture. In the mid-seventeenth century, two thousand ships a year docked in Istanbul laden with wheat, rice, sugar and spices from Egypt; livestock, grain, fats, honey, and fish from north of the Black Sea; and wine from the Aegean islands [...]. American plants entered the Ottoman Empire as fast or faster than they did Spain, perhaps because networks of Sephardic Jews expelled from Iberia stretched from the Ottoman Empire to the Americas.[39]

The Landscape of Food and Memory

The Sephardic exiles functioned as critical actors in the movement of Ottoman agricultural bounty from one end of the Empire to the other. Thus, they could rebuild in the Ottoman Empire exactly the same prestigious legacy that had defined them within their Iberian homeland.

The Sephardic culinary repertoire also signalled this newfound sense of home felt by many of the Sephardim who settled there. As *dhimmi*, a protected minority, the Sephardic Jews were able to re-establish themselves in the Ottoman Empire more profoundly than occurred in other branches of the diaspora. Esther Benbassa and Aron Rodrique affirm that 'in the Ottoman lands [...] an eastern Sephardi heartland came into being that lasted as a distinct Judeo-Hispanic unit well into the twentieth century'.[40] As Mary Isin highlights, being a well-integrated community in the Ottoman Empire implied mixing culinary elements:

> untangling the complex threads of origin and influence is often impossible, since the Christian, Jewish, and Muslim peoples of the Ottoman Empire lived side by side and exchanged food ways for over six centuries. Further complicating the situation is the fact that the region was a hub of trade, receiving a steady stream of expensive spices and exotic foodstuffs [...]. Many previously unknown foodstuffs introduced from Asia, Africa, and America became so acculturated that memories of their distant homelands faded away.[41]

It is perhaps no wonder, then, that the most well-known elements of the Sephardic culinary repertoire reflected the mix of Ottoman traditions. As Gil Marks notes:

> among the foods the Sephardim brought with them [...] at the same time börek were developing, were half-moon-shaped turnovers called empanadas, made from an oil pastry and a rudimentary puff pastry. The newcomers, proudly clinging to their traditional foods and language, did not immediately adopt Turkish foods, but [eventually] Sephardim in Turkey and Greece merged the Iberian empanada with the *börek* adding the Spanish feminine ending a to create one of the favorite Ottoman Jewish pastries, the boreka.[42]

The fertile cultural context of the Ottoman Empire allowed for the preservation of key parts of Sephardic identity including their language, Judeo-Spanish, and, most importantly, their food. Through the culinary repertoire of the Sephardic communities, their nearly full integration into the Ottoman landscape becomes clear, as the dishes of the Sephardic culinary repertoire seamlessly encompass and join two *terroirs*: that of Spain and the Ottoman territories where they settled. There, the Sephardim were able to recreate the flavours of their lost Iberian homeland, even as they incorporated vibrant Ottoman flavours to create a uniquely Ottoman Sephardic culinary landscape.

The culinary repertoires of the Sephardic Jews, as they evolved in Morocco, Italy, and the Ottoman Empire, clearly display the multiplicity of landscapes – real, symbolic, and nostalgic – encompassed in diasporic Sephardic identity. Although they were forced from their Spanish homeland, their continued cultivation of familiar crops and preparation of traditional Sephardic dishes enabled the Sephardim to re-access the Spanish landscape even as their incorporation of local ingredients in their new homes symbolized the community's re-rooting in these foreign lands. The Sephardim cultivated their *terroir* of memory by grafting it onto that of their diasporic experience, proving that no matter where we find ourselves, landless in diaspora or deeply rooted in community, our food serves as a guide through that most compelling of all terrains: our identity.

Notes

1. Judah Ha-Levi, 'My Heart Is in the East', *The Dream of the Poem: Hebrew Poetry from Muslim and Christian Spain, 950-1492*, ed. by Peter Cole (Princeton: Princeton University Press, 2009), p. 164.
2. Olivia Remie Constable and Damian Zurro, *Medieval Iberia: Readings from Christian, Muslim, and Jewish Sources* (Philadelphia: University of Pennsylvania Press, 2012), p. xxxi
3. Norman Roth, *Medieval Jewish Civilization: An Encyclopedia* (New York: Routledge, 2014), p. 18.
4. Norman Roth, p. 257. For more on the subject of faith-based prohibitions on inter-religious commensality, see David Freidenreich, *Foreigners and Their Food: Constructing Otherness in Jewish, Christian, and Islamic Law* (Berkeley: University of California Press, 2011).
5. Bernard Rosenberger, 'Arab Cuisine and Its Contribution to European Culture', in *Food: A Culinary History*, ed. by Jean-Louis Flandrin and Massimo Montanari (New York: Columbia University Press, 2013). pp. 207-223 (p. 217).
6. Shlomo D. Goitein, *A Mediterranean Society: The Jewish Communities of the Arab World as Portrayed in the Documents of the Cairo Geniza* (Berkeley: University of California Press, 1967), p. 123. The Cairo Geniza was a store of Jewish documents found in the basement of a synagogue that included documents pertaining to the trade, religious practice, and daily life of medieval Mediterranean Jewish communities.
7. *Medieval Trade in the Mediterranean World: Illustrative Documents*, ed. by Robert S. López and Irving W. Raymond (New York: Columbia University Press, 2010), pp. 31-32.
8. *Medieval Trade in the Mediterranean World*, p. 30.
9. Michael Toch, *The Economic History of European Jews: Late Antiquity and Early Middle Ages* (Boston: Brill, 2013), p. 140; *Isaac Abravanel: Letters*, ed. by Cedric Cohen Skalli (Berlin: Walter de Gruyter, 2007), p. viii.
10. Carolyn A. Nadeau, *Food Matters: Alonso Quijano's Diet and the Discourse of Food in Early Modern Spain* (Toronto: University of Toronto Press, 2016), p. 115.
11. See Erich Isaac, 'Influence of Religion on the Spread of Citrus: The Religious Practices of the Jews Helped Effect the Introduction of Citrus to Mediterranean Lands', *Science*, 129.3343 (1959), 179-86.
12. Nadeau, p. 114.
13. Richard Hull, *Jews and Judaism in African History* (Princeton: Markus Wiener Publishers, 2009), p. 71.
14. Hull, p. 56.
15. Trade was certainly the most important, though not the only impactful, medium of cultural communication between medieval Spain and Morocco. As Haïm Zafrani explains of the Jewish community, this connection also occurred through Jewish religious scholarship: 'as is well known, during the Golden Age of Spain, a time when Andalusia and Morocco maintained close relations, the Moroccan communities of Fez, Salé, Sijilmassa, and Der'a had large yeshibot conducted by teachers who enjoyed an immense reputation in the Jewish world' (*Two Thousand Years of Jewish Life in Morocco* (New York: KTAV Publishing House, Inc., 2005), p. 4).
16. Goitein, p. 259.
17. Zohar Amar and Efraim Lev, 'The Significance of the Genizah's Medical Documents for the Study of Medieval Mediterranean Trade', *Journal of the Economic and Social History of the Orient*, 50.4 (2007), 524-41 (p. 532).
18. See Ramón-Laca, L. 'The Introduction of Cultivated Citrus to Europe via Northern Africa and the Iberian Peninsula', *Economic Botany*, 57.4 (Winter 2003), 502-514.

19. Rachel Laudan, *Cuisine and Empire: Cooking in World History* (Berkeley: University of California Press, 2013), p. 141.
20. Zafrani explains that the classification of these Judaized Berber tribes was occasionally difficult, because though they considered themselves fully Jewish, certain 'proselytes were not always converted according to the requirements of the law (halakhah)' particularly that som were uncircumcised (p. 2).
21. Mohammed Kenbib, p. 27.
22. Zafrani, p. 7.
23. Abdellah Lahrmaid, p. 66, p. 59.
24. Zafrani, p. 7.
25. Herbert Dobrinsky notes that 'in Sefrou [unlike in other parts of Morocco], they ate kitniyyot [on Passover]', a traditionally Sephardic practice, different than their Moroccan coreligionists, who did not eat kitniyot [legumes] implying the adoption of Sepahrdic practice (*A Treasury of Sephardic Laws and Customs: The Ritual Practices of Syrian, Moroccan, Judeo-Spanish and Spanish and Portuguese Jews of North America* (New York: Ktav, 1986), p. 261).
26. Dobrinsky, p. 236.
27. Stacy E. Holden, 'Muslim and Jewish Interaction in Moroccan Meat Markets, 1873-1912', in *Jewish Culture and Society in North Africa*, ed. by Emily Benichou Gottreich and Daniel J. Schroeter (Bloomington: Indiana University Press, 2011), pp. 150-68 (p. 156).
28. *Medieval Trade in the Mediterranean World*, pp. 109-13.
29. Francesca Trivellato, *The Familiarity of Strangers: The Sephardic Diaspora, Livorno, and Cross-Cultural Trade in the Early Modern Period* (New Haven: Yale University Press, 2014), p. 46.
30. Stephanie Nadalo, 'Populating a "Nest of Pirates, Murtherers, Etc.": Tuscan Immigration Policy and Ragion Di Stato in the Free Port of Livorno', in *Religious Diaspora in Early Modern Europe: Strategies of Exile*, ed. by Timothy G. Fehler and others (New York: Routledge, 2015), pp. 31-46 (p. 36).
31. Doña Gracia Mendes Nasi – Christian name, Beatriz de Luna – is particularly important to mention in this analysis for her family's importance to the early modern black pepper trade andfor her boycott that paralyzed the port of Ancona: see Cecil Roth, *Doña Gracia of the House of Nasi* (Philadelphia: Jewish Publication Society of America, 1977).
32. Nadalo, p. 32.
33. Gil Marks, *Encyclopedia of Jewish Food* (New York: Houghton Mifflin Harcourt, 2010), pp. 88-89.
34. Clarissa Hyman, *Oranges: A Global History* (London: Reaktion Books, 2013), pp. 27-28.
35. Marks, p. 618.
36. Trans. and qtd. in Joan Nathan, *King Solomon's Table: A Culinary Exploration of Jewish Cooking from Around the World* (New York: Borzoi, 2017), p. 60. Artusi's original Italian is: 'petonciani e finocchi, qurant'anni or sono, si vedevano appena sul mercato di Firenze; vi erano tenuti a vile come cibo da ebrei'. (*La scienza in cucina e l'arte di mangiare bene* (Milan: Giunti Editore, 1998), p. 275).
37. Fernand Braudel, *The Mediterranean and the Mediterranean World in the Age of Philip II* (Berkeley: University of California Press, 1995), p. 336.
38. Minna Rozen, *A History of the Jewish Community in Istanbul: The Formative Years, 1453-1566* (Boston: BRILL, 2010), p. 82.
39. Laudan, p. 161.
40. Esther Benbassa and Aron Rodrique, *Sephardi Jewry: A History of the Judeo-Spanish Community, 14th-20th Centuries* (Berkeley, University of California Press, 1993), p. xix.
41. Mary Isin, *Sherbet and Spice: The Complete Story of Turkish Sweets and Desserts* (London: I.B. Tauris, 2013), p. 2.
42. Marks, p. 256.

'Bigger Was Better?' The Interplay of New Technologies, Field Size, and Basic Commodity Production in the Roman Occupation of Britain from c. 100 BCE to 400 CE

Christopher Grocock

Introduction

The Roman occupation of Britain is often caricatured as one in which sun-loving Mediterranean invaders found themselves confronted by a cold, wet climate that they found both alien and hostile. The opposite appears to be the case – the 'green and pleasant land' was known for exporting wheat, cattle, and hides before the Roman occupation began in AD 43, and the island's good soils, together with the temperate climate with its potential for stock-rearing and arable production, contrasted positively with areas of the Mediterranean which were seasonally arid and where good soils were limited in area.

Many older views of Roman Britain are based on the survival of the larger pieces of evidence left behind by the occupation, such as villas, which are easy to map. Figure 1 indicates the spread of villas known when the map was drawn in the late 1970s: large areas of Britain lack any evidence of Roman occupation when this data is used as a basis for assessment. It was also fashionable (and still is, in some quarters) to regard the North and West of Roman Britain as some sort of 'militarized area' with limited civilian activity (such as farming, for example), as indicated by the shaded areas on the map. A.L.F. Rivet commented that the *Brigantes*, located in modern Lancashire and Yorkshire, 'lay in territory which was heavily garrisoned, where martial law was normal'.[1]

This paper focuses on a range of archaeological information which is far less romantic than the luxurious villas whose heyday came in the fourth century, though

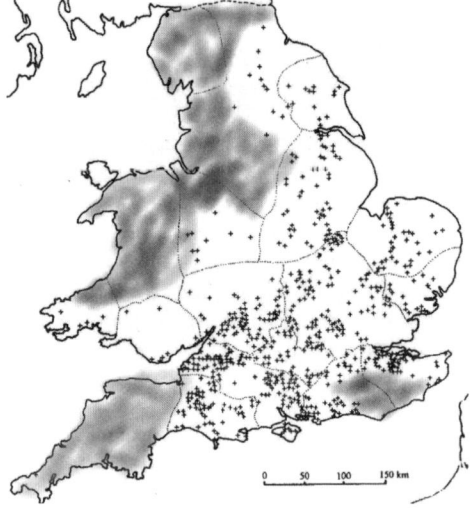

Figure 1. A traditional view of 'the Roman impact on Britain' (after Hill and Ireland, 1996); shaded areas show the absence of villas (more have been found since the 1970s).

these will have a part to play later in the discussion: it consists instead of the preserved remains of features such as ditches and field boundaries, less romantic but equally indicative of the changing impact on the landscape that occurred as the Roman occupation of Britain proceeded. The economic exploitation of the landscape during the occupation was not static: recent trends in archaeological research have focused on the large-scale evidence still extant in the large-scale developments of the landscape. Features such as field boundaries often remained unchanged until the recent industrialization of agriculture, and are still detectable through improved archaeological techniques.

Past Perspectives, Ancient and Modern

Roman writers confined their discussions of the peoples and landscape of Britain to matters which they and their anticipated audiences might have found interesting, drawn as they all were from the elite levels of ancient society. To be sure, some ancient authors discussed some practical matters relating to agriculture, but none ventured to discuss the peculiar local aspects of the exploitation of the landscape in such far-flung provinces as Britain. Indeed, there was an in-built snobbishness that saw these areas as distinctly inferior to others under Roman control.[2] The discussion that ancient authors do provide in the 'ethnographical' sections included in their works make no mention either of the landscape or of the human effect that the Roman presence had on it.[3]

The More Recent Picture

In the past thirty years or thereabouts, the picture has changed – in fact, it is fair to say that it has been stood on its head.[4] One scholar remarked to me that everything he had learned about Roman Britain thirty years before had been turned upside down.[5] From the perspective of a food historian interested in all manner of ancient foodways, it is heartening that the focus on Roman Britain has in recent years shifted quite noticeably from urban and elite centres to the vast majority of the territory of Britain and of the majority who occupied it – the rural landscape(s) and the farmers who shaped it.[6]

Multiple factors lie behind this. First, the involvement of archaeologists at the early stages of all building and infrastructure projects has meant that much more data is now available, especially since the introduction of PPG16.[7] Even in the 1960s, the programme of motorway construction across the heart of England and the West revealed the presence of Roman occupation – and occasionally more 'luxury villas' – in a much greater density than had been anticipated; the same occurred more recently during the building of the HS1 link from London to the Eurotunnel terminal.[8] Even greater advances have been made through the steady application of scientific processes in archaeology, which have meant that in some cases very large areas can be explored using non-invasive techniques such as aerial photography, ground-penetrating radar, magnetometry, and resistivity, which complement simpler tasks such as field-walking and contour surveys.[9] But perhaps the greatest shift has been one of attitude: rather than focusing only on elite art and structures, interest has shifted on to the 'wider picture' involving whole populations and economies, focusing on exploring the *pays* as a whole, and not just important or significant remains at the centre. The extent of Roman activity in Britain now known to have occurred up to the end of the second century can be seen in Figure 2, and it is mirrored by the spread of recent finds of Roman artefacts and activity in Britain recorded under the innovative and highly praiseworthy Public Antiquities Scheme up to 2003. This largely matches the distribution of farmsteads now known in the occupation period.[10]

Figure 2. *Rural Settlement in Roman Britain by the end of the second century AD.*

After all, it is generally accepted that in Roman Britain, some 85-90% of the population were rural dwellers directly involved in agricultural activity; many left no personal trace, but the overall appearance of the landscape shows definite changes, as we shall see. Even so, this changed picture of Roman Britain is probably still not final by any means. As Alexander Smith and Michael Fulford comment that 'it is, for the most part, those sites excavated and analysed during the past twenty years or so that are revolutionizing our understanding of the past', but they also note that 'a lack of standard ways of reporting data and a continuing emphasis in some quarters on central buildings rather than landscapes as a whole leaves room for taking our understanding of rural settlements and landscapes to a new level'.[11]

Landscape and Agricultural Activity in the Pre-Roman Iron Age (PRIA)

Strabo, a geographer writing at the start of the first century AD, provides some information that is interesting as it gives us something of a baseline to work from: 'Most of the island is low-lying and wooded, but there are many hilly areas. It produces corn [wheat], cattle, gold, silver and iron. These things are exported along with hides, slaves and dogs, suitable for hunting.'[12]

Strabo's comments are valuable because he has no apparent political or military axe to grind. At the same time, like all ancient writers, Strabo passes on items of tittle-tattle which neither he nor anyone else could verify, such as his assertion that some Britons 'are well supplied with milk but do not know how to make cheese'.[13] But the point he makes about the variety of different locations, of *pays*, in the island of Britain is a valuable one with considerable bearing on the development of the landscape in the Roman occupation.

Early Changes under the Influence of the Roman Occupation

The variation of land-types (*pays*) in Roman Britain is well known, being based on

'Bigger Was Better?'

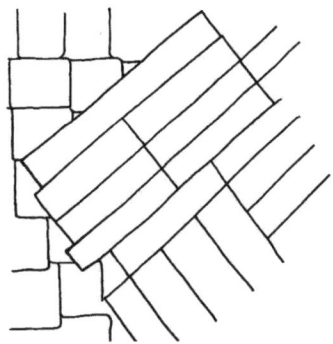

Figure 3. Changes in field systems (after Fowler 2002).

'natural areas' identifiable from the geology of soil structures and types, and climactic variations due to position and elevation above sea level.[14] 'Natural areas' of the British can be identified – for example, there is apparent underdevelopment compared to other areas around London and in the Sussex Weald which may be due entirely to the unsuitability of these areas for cultivation. Elsewhere there was rapid change: in the Middle Thames valley, for example, the PRIA pattern of small, open settlements located on the flood plain was rapidly replaced by the end of the first century AD by new settlement forms and co-axial field systems. These took the form of more complex or rectilinear field systems as shown in Figure 3, with lengths extended to 175-200m (the old-fashioned 'furlong' or 'furrow-long' of 220 yards) from 40-50m squares, and there is evidence that woodland was cleared to give more land over to improved pasture.[15]

At the site now occupied by Heathrow Terminal 5, the gap between these larger rectilinear layouts has been interpreted as a droveway; the longer fields to either side may have been meadow or arable (see similar fields in Figure 4). Changes like this can also be noted at Fullerton, in Hampshire.[16] The Roman field-system still survives as furlong-boundaries.[17] It is tempting to associate these early changes in land usage with the introduction (or imposition) of Roman land assessment that is clearly depicted in the writings of the *Agrimensores*.[18] As with so many aspects of Roman life, there is very little data to support this, though a unique piece of evidence for the early employment of a purely Roman form of transferring land ownership in Kent, in southeast Britain, comes from a wax tablet securely dated to 4 March 118 AD.[19] However, nothing is known for certain about the overall picture in Roman Britain. It has also been suggested that the orientation of some co-axial layouts of fields are not the result of deliberate allocation of land, but rather a way of making the landscape function effectively, allowing movement of wood as well as livestock efficiently in a 'strongly parallel banding of resources'.[20]

Rome's Impact on the Landscape

Allen comments that 'variations in field shape and size provide subtle indications of the differing ways in which the land was organized. Numerous small fields perhaps suggest that the land was more intensively managed, while larger fields may indicate a more extensive system of land management'.[21] Smaller settlements were abandoned in a more centralized organization of the landscape, and at the same time smaller fields seem to have been replaced by much longer, larger ones. This may have been the case at the Heathrow terminal 5 site, and it is shown very clearly by the extensive second-third century AD field system at Eye Quarry in Cambridgeshire, which also has evidence for lazybeds, a feature showing the persistent and careful attention paid to growing arable crops, which are quite common in the Central Belt area.²² These landscape changes may indicate a move from arable to pasture, though their existence might equally be due to the introduction of improved ploughing techniques, which will be discussed below.²³ What seems evident is that the replacement of earlier Roman fields with larger enclosures may have seen the abandonment of some settlements, but 'this was within the context of landscape reorganization, not landscape desertion'.²⁴ Examples include Knock Down East on Salisbury Plain.²⁵ Dominic Powlesland's work on the Vale of Pickering also shows intensive 'ribbon development' and village settlement along a major communication route.²⁶

This process continued into the second century, and by about AD 200 settlement numbers reached a maximum; the landscape was transformed to the extent that far more areas in the Central Belt were brought under the plough than was the case before the Roman period began. McCarthy makes the very valid point that re-arranging the land – and particularly clearing or draining land for agriculture – was not a 'five minute job', so to speak; elsewhere, even marginal areas were made usable by canalization in the Fens in East Anglia. Extensive drainage on the Severn Estuary, where some 235 hectares of land were reclaimed by drainage, and similar works on the Somerset levels 'perhaps implie[d] a military involvement […] with an investment in the region of 7-10 million man-hours, doubtless spread over a number of years'.²⁷ The Roman military presence in Britain undoubtedly had a significant impact on the landscape in this regard – much more so than the 'extra mouths to feed' argument often adduced in Romano-British studies but rarely quantified. In fact, the numbers are quite small when taken as a proportion of the actual population. In the invasion period, an army of 40,000 was introduced into a population of perhaps 1 million in the south – a 4% increase – but in the overall settlement period it represented about 30,000 (or even fewer) within a larger population – 1% of 3 million. The demands it made on supply became less significant over time. Nevertheless, the immediate impact of the Roman occupation of Britain – in the first twenty years – was of massive intensification of settlements right across the province. Housesteads Roman Fort, in the middle of Hadrian's Wall, is perhaps the most extreme example of such attempts to

Figure 4. Iron-Age (top) and Roman field layouts (bottom) compared.

adapt the landscape for agriculture. Here, attempts at arable cultivation were made on land adjacent to the *vicus* which were not farmed – except perhaps for grazing livestock – either before the Roman occupation or since, and the modern *pays* plays host to far more sheep than humans, even at the height of the tourist season.[28]

Changes in agricultural practice may have resulted as much from a cessation of inter-tribal violence and 'inadvertent' Romanization as from the presence of the military – more 'pull' than 'push' as farming methods developed. In essence, there was not much difference between PRIA Celts and Romano-British peasants. Smith and Fulford comment that 'while supply of the military might be guaranteed year on year, there were also the towns to feed, several only founded in the second century, the combination providing a clear context for the rapid development of farmsteads, particularly in the Central Belt'. In fact it is possible that a 'population peak' was attained at this time and not later, though they also assert that the landscape was never at its full 'carrying capacity'.[29] Notwithstanding this view, what now seems clear is that the population of the province – and thus the intensity of exploitation of the landscape that was needed (or permitted) to feed such a large number of human occupants – was far greater than often imagined in the past. The changes in settlement patterns are reflected in similar developments in northwest Gaul, and ultimately the *latifundia* of the literary sources.[30]

Iron and Improvements in Technology

Paradoxically, an area where there was little agricultural development illustrates what may have made the exploitation of other *pays* for arable production possible. The Sussex Weald, an area of poor agricultural land (birch and scrub, for the most part), was dominated by ironworking. Its best-known site is Beauport Park, now a golf course, and much of the evidence is covered in undergrowth or re-landscaped for recreational and sporting use. At the time, though, this was the third-largest ironworking complex in the whole of the Roman Empire. It has been estimated that about 100,000 tons of slag (waste product) were produced in ironworking on this site from the late first to mid-third centuries, a significantly greater amount than at any time during the PRIA (although as Strabo noted it was already being exported). Aside from the direct impact this production had on the landscape, it vastly increased the provision of raw material for tools.[31] The nature of the soil and its unsuitability for farming, as much as the regional concentration of ironworking, may have limited villa settlement in this area, but it is possible that the exploitation of the raw material it produced led to the wider availability of iron tools, and that this led to the possibility of much-improved technologies which exploited different areas of ground – hence the field-shapes.

The development of tools used in farming during the Roman occupation is beyond the scope and space of this paper.[32] One simple change may have made a huge difference, however: the ard required multiple cross-ploughing, as recorded in the myth of Ploutos, son of Iasion and Demeter, who conceived him in a 'thrice-ploughed field'. The technique was effective but time-consuming; it is still found in some parts of the world.[33] The

Roman plough was equipped with an iron ploughshare and a coulter, which may have reduced the time required to prepare ground for sowing by two-thirds; it also enabled heavier clay soils, as in the Central Belt area of Britain, to be exploited for the first time.

What about Cereals? Technology Changes the Landscape at the Centre

The heavier soils of the Central Belt area, stretching from south of the Bristol Channel to Lincolnshire and the Wash, were now suited for arable farming, to the point where it and parts of the south became the bread basket of Roman Britain. The ancient historian Zosimus states categorically that the short-lived emperor Julian used the extensive ability of Britain to supply grain to the continent following barbarian invasions in AD 359-360, building 800 boats 'larger than galleys' to transport grain from Britain to granaries in Germany to keep it safe.[34] The Central West area likewise demonstrates that there was a focus on cereals and cattle production. Some areas, including arable ones, have evidence of relatively permanent occupation while other sites may have been used for seasonal grazing and seem only to have been utilized occasionally.[35] Over the whole province, wheat remained the principal cereal, with barley very much secondary.[36] The emphasis on beef and wheat is taken to be typical of the Roman period market-based economy, with both the military and towns needing to be fed but not otherwise contributing to agriculture production (though it might be argued that military elites never did so, any more than they do nowadays).[37] Later developments saw more centralization but granaries and other buildings were re-used, indicating the continuity of cereal production.[38]

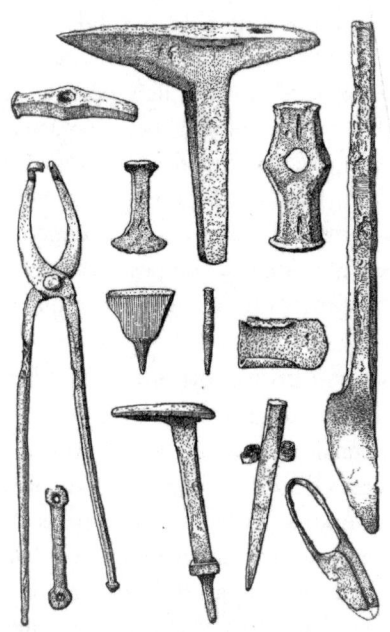

Figure 5. Roman iron tools from Silchester now in Reading Museum: on the right are an iron spade, a bar-coulter for a plough, shears for slipping or shearing, and a field anvil for straightening damaged tools.

Villa Estates in the Third and Fourth Centuries – Landscape Change in the South

Over the latter half of the Roman occupation period – the third and fourth centuries – villas become dominant in lowland areas, especially in the south. The term 'villa' covers a wide range of building types, sizes, and styles (in its original term it simply means 'farm' or 'farmstead'). The spectacular growth of villas during the later third and the fourth centuries is generally supposed to presume that sufficient income was being generated from agricultural production to allow this building to occur.[39] Some were 'palatial' in size, and their locations, like those of stately homes in a later age, were chosen with a view to impress just as much as the buildings themselves. The villas are found predominantly in the Wessex vales and on Wealden Greensand – areas suited to mixed farming.[40] Their location owes more to economics and to the geology of the landscape than to political or military considerations.

Changes in Landscape as Evidence for Changes in Food Production and Diet

In many southern areas, it seems that there was an increase in improved pasture, implying more cattle rearing, while other sites indicate either increased focus on, or perhaps more centralized processing of, arable products, particularly wheat.[41] It might seem obvious to farmers, but it has taken the community of ancient historians and archaeologists some time to recognize that different types of agricultural activity might be influenced by the potential offered by different land types! It is also noteworthy that about 40% of known villas lie within 400 metres of a watercourse; Martyn Allen comments that 'the seemingly close relationship of villas and rivers must at least in part reflect where the best agricultural land was, along with drinking water provision for cattle'.[42] Moreover, animal husbandry extends the 'range of activity' from a centre exponentially, allowing for greater dispersal of workers. Pastoral farmers may be away from a centre for weeks; for cereal processing, a working circle might be two or three miles; salads and herbs are cottage plants and are best grown closest to home.

Some indications of this activity come from pollen analysis, but while this technique represents a distinct advance in science, there are imitations to its use. Some arable crops, barley and wheat in particular, produce very little pollen, and many tree species do not produce any when they are coppiced or used for regularly laid hedges. Thus the results may not give a full picture by any means.[43] Vegetable and root crops are almost certainly under-represented, as most are harvested before flowering, but there is clear evidence for a number of fruit tree species, including cherry, plum, walnut, and apple.[44]

Pollen evidence from the south of Britain indicates that a wide variety of plant types were cultivated. Wheats (spelt and emmer) were ubiquitous; but alongside this there is evidence for more rye being grown in the London Basin than elsewhere, and free-threshing wheat, pulses, and flax are well represented on the South Coast Plain.[45] Oats (and some other grains) may have supplemented meadow grass grown for hay as cattle fodder.[46]

There is evidence of changes in meat production as well. Areas such as the Wessex Downs provide evidence from faunal remains (bones) of high proportions of pigs among the animals being reared, and there is some evidence for salt production at Ower on the Dorset coast; this may have been used for processing pork carcasses to make products such as bacon that could then exported from the immediate area.[47] From the second century AD onwards, cattle bones form a greater proportion of archaeological finds in the southern and Central Belt areas, while there is a change to sheep grazing in the Fens (East Anglia), which were systematically drained to provide seasonal grazing. This faunal evidence is corroborated by the re-organization of settlements into more complex farmsteads, suggesting a growth in systematic cattle rearing and management, including the development of hay meadows for increased overwintering of herds.[48] Cattle production seems to have dominated in the lowlands, and production steadily increased during the Roman occupation.[49] Clear evidence of animal processing (reflecting and reinforcing what Strabo had to say about the PRIA British economy) is also found in the Middle Thames Valley: at Staines, for example, cattle bones show evidence for distinctive cleaver butchery marks, most obvious of which are punctures in the shoulder-blade bone – found in numerous Romano-British sites – suggesting that large pieces of animal were hung for salting or smoking. Similar evidence from the bones of sheep/goat and pigs indicates the large-scale and rapid processing of livestock.[50] This is also true of some sites in the central belt, as at the site called Gill Mill, on the Thames gravels in Oxfordshire, and Fleet Marston, Aylesbury, Buckinghamshire, where evidence of regular, ditched, rectangular enclosure systems have suggested that the economies of the settlements were 'heavily geared towards cattle rearing and marketing'.[51]

Conclusion

There is no evidence that there was any kind of official, imperial policy to impel native Britons to change their farming practices, but cultural 'pull', a concept developed by the historian Greg Woolf, may have encouraged changes in landscape exploitation in two ways: first, larger fields came into being, perhaps a sign of improved farming efficiency and perhaps of a greater use of animal traction, a theoretical argument being explored by the author based on experimental archaeology; second, it became possible to exploit heavier soils for arable farming, and this too had a major impact on the landscape of key areas, particularly in central Britain. Increases in wheat production, among other factors, may have led to the overall population of Britain increasing by anything up to 400%, even while permitting the export of wheat from Britain to the continent in ever-greater quantities. Paradoxically, this development may have led to yet further landscape change: other areas which became comparatively less efficient for arable purposes were converted to large estates with luxurious villas at their centre which focused on wool production, an equally if not more lucrative source of revenue in a province and an empire which created a constant demand for it. For these

Figure 6. Landscape divisions of Roman Britain.

reasons, the interaction of humans and landscape during the Roman occupation of Britain makes a fascinating case study in examining the impact the natural desire for increased food production had on the countryside that provided it.

Notes

1. A.L.F. Rivet, *Town and Country in Roman Britain* (London: Hutchinson, 1964), p. 144. The map is based on the 'Distribution of Roman villas known in Britain in relation to the civitates', fig. 14 in S. Hill, S. Ireland, *Roman Britain* (London, Bristol Classical Press, 1996), p. 88; their 'distribution' is itself based on Rivet's work.
2. See for example Cicero's derogatory comments about British slaves in *Letters to Atticus* 4.16.7: 'there's no prospect of booty except slaves – and I don't imagine you are expecting any knowledge of literature or music among them!' (*Literary Sources for Roman Britain,* ed. and trans. by Y. Rathbone and D. W. Rathbone (London: London Association of Classical Teachers, 2012), p. 23).
3. See for example Caesar, *Gallic War* 5. 13-14; Tacitus, Agricola 10-13.
4. See for example Hilary Cool, 'Which "Romans", What "Home"? The Myth of the "End" of Roman Britain', in, *AD 410: The History and Archaeology of Late and Post-Roman Britain*, ed. by F. K. Haarer (London: Society for the Promotion of Roman Studies, 2014), pp. 13-22; James Gerrard, *The Ruin of Roman Britain: An Archaeological Perspective* (Cambridge: Cambridge University Press, 2013); on the earliest period of Roman occupation, see R.S.O. Tomlin, *Roman Britain's First Voices: Writing Tablets from the Bloomberg Excavations, 2010-14* (London: Museum of London Archaeology Monograph 72, 2016).
5. Personal communication with Dr Sam Moorhead, National Finds Adviser – Iron Age and Roman Coins, Department of Coins and Medals, The British Museum, London.
6. See for example M. McCarthy, *The Romano-British Peasant: Towards a Study of People, Landscapes, and Work during the Roman Occupation of Britain* (Oxford: Windgather Press, 2013); *The Rural Settlement of Roman Britain*, Britannia Monograph Series no. 29, ed. by A. Smith and others (London: Society for the Promotion of Roman Studies, 2016), henceforth cited as *RSRB*; S. Rippon, C. Smart, and B. Pears, *The Fields of Britannia: Continuity and Change in the Late Roman and Early Medieval Landscape* (Oxford: Oxford University Press, 2015), henceforth cited as *FOB*.
7. PPG stands for the British Government's document 'Planning Policy Guidance 16: Archaeology and Planning'; see *FOB* pp. 308ff. for comments on the positive impact it has had since its implementation.
8. A. Allen and A. Smith, 'Rural Settlement in Roman Britain: Morphological Classification and Overview', in *RSRB*, pp. 17-43 (p. 17). For finds associated with the HS1 line, particularly Ebbsfleet, see the series of reports by Wessex Archaeology <http://www.wessexarch.co.uk/publications/settling-ebbsfleet-valley-volumes-1-4> [accessed 24 March 2017].
9. See for example Sue Anderson, 'Introduction to Archaeology', *Spoilheap*, 2013 <http://www.spoilheap.co.uk/archae.htm> [accessed 24 March 2017].
10. See the *Portable Antiquities Scheme* website: <https://finds.org.uk/> (accessed 19.03.2018).
11. A. Smith and M. Fulford, 'Conclusion: The Rural Settlement of Roman Britain', in *RSRB*, pp. 385-420 (p. 420).
12. Strabo, *Geography* 4.5.1, in *Literary Sources for Roman Britain*, p. 33.
13. Strabo.
14. See M. Fulford and T. Brindle, 'Introduction', in *RSRB*, pp. 1-16, (p. 16, fig. 1.5); *FOB*, figs. 2.11 and 2.12, pp. 48-49; McCarthy, figs. 2.2, 2.3, pp. 17-30.
15. M. Allen, 'The South', in *RSRB*, pp. 75-140 (pp. 129, 131); Smith and Fulford, 'Conclusion', (pp. 418-19); *FOB*, pp. 182, 185.
16. Allen, fig. 4.76, p. 139.
17. *FOB*, p. 90.
18. See *The Writings of the Roman Land Surveyors: Introduction, Text, Translation and Commentary*, ed. by

B. Campbell (London: Society for the Promotion of Roman Studies, 2000).
19. 'Ownership of a Wood', *Roman Inscriptions of Britain*, ed. by C. Grocock, 5th ed. (London: LACTOR, 2017), entry H37, p. 141; *Britannia* 25 (1994), 302-04 n. 34.
20. *FOB*, p. 319.
21. Allen, p. 120. See also P. Fowler, *Farming in the First Millennium* (Cambridge: Cambridge University Press, 2002), pp. 127-60, esp. pp. 144-45, 150-51.
22. A. Smith, 'The Central Belt', in *RSRB*, pp. 141-207 (pp. 181-83).
23. Allen, p. 120.
24. *FOB*, p. 27.
25. *FOB*, fig. 3.6, pp. 85-86.
26. Allen and Smith, p. 41; see also (for his work on West Heslerton and the Vale of Pickering) Dominic Powlesland, 'The Heslerton Parish Project,' *The Landscape Research Centre* <http://www.landscaperesearchcentre.org/AA%20Tier%201%20Primary%20Headings/heslerton_parish_project.htm> [accessed 16 May 2017].
27. McCarthy, p. 70.
28. See J. Crow, *Housesteads: A Roman Fort and Garrison on Hadrian's Wall* (Stroud: Tempus, 2004), fig. 45, pp. 82-84.
29. Smith and Fulford, pp. 410, 416.
30. Smith and Fulford, p. 414.
31. See M. Russell, *Roman Sussex* (Stroud: Tempus, 2006), pp. 229, 242-47.
32. See K. D. White, *Agricultural Implements of the Roman World* (Cambridge: Cambridge University Press, 1967), and there is a good summary in McCarthy, pp. 71ff.
33. Including in the Mediterranean: see Hamish A. Forbes, 'The Thrice-Ploughed Field: Cultivation Techniques in Ancient and Modern Greece', *Expedition Magazine*, September 1976, <https://www.penn.museum/sites/expedition/the-thrice-ploughed-field/> [accessed 16 May 2017].
34. Smith and Fulford, p. 408, citing R. Ireland, *Roman Britain: A Sourcebook* (London: Routledge, 1996), p. 146 (*RSRB* incorrectly cites p. 149).
35. T. Brindle, 'The Central West', in *RSRB*, pp. 282-307 (p. 306); *FOB*, pp. 129-31.
36. *FOB*, fig 3.5, p. 81.
37. *FOB*, p. 315.
38. A. Smith, 'Buildings in the Countryside,' in *RSRB*, pp. 44-74 (pp. 58-61).
39. Smith, 'Buildings in the Countryside,' p. 73; Allen, p. 94.
40. Good examples of this are Woodchester and Great Witcombe: see Smith, 'The Central Belt', p. 176.
41. Allen, pp. 85ff., p. 137; for the 'Central Belt', see Smith, 'The Central Belt', p. 185. For details on mollusc evidence from the South Downs indicating extensive change from arable to pasture in the later Roman period, see also *FOB*, pp. 135, 139, 167.
42. Allen and Smith, p. 33; Allen, p. 116. See also C. Grocock, 'The Wroxeter Macellum: a Foodway in Every Sense', in *Food and Markets: Proceedings of the 2014 Oxford Symposium on Cookery*, ed. by M. McWilliams (Totnes: Prospect Books, 2015), pp. 163-76.
43. *FOB*, pp. 57ff., esp. p. 61.
44. Allen, p. 128.
45. Allen, p. 128.
46. Allen, p. 133; Smith and Fulford, p. 399.
47. Allen, p. 125.
48. Smith, 'The Central Belt,', pp. 201-02 and fig. 5.64, p. 205; Smith and Fulford, p. 402.
49. Smith and Fulford, p. 398; *FOB*, pp. 182-83.
50. Allen, p. 135.
51. Smith, 'The Central Belt,' p. 164.

Maple Moon: Landscapes of the Sugar Maple in a Time of Climate Change

Naomi Guttman

The sugar maple tree is iconic of eastern North America, the only place in the world where it grows; for centuries climate and soil conditions have made possible the springtime sap flow for which it is so famous. Not only is the maple tree a source of autumnal beauty and its distinctive leaf a national symbol for Canadians, but its syrup and sugar are also economic mainstays of the communities that produce it. In this essay, I will explore the many landscapes of the sugar maple: the physical, historical, economic, political, and personal, to reflect on the significance of its possible loss on the sense of identity in this corner of the world.

The Physical and Economic Landscape

The sugar maple, known by its Latin name *Acer saccharum*, grows across a region of northeastern North America that runs from Nova Scotia, New Brunswick, Québec, and all of New England, all the way west to southeastern Manitoba and western Minnesota, and as far south as southern Missouri, eastern Tennessee, and northern Georgia. That said, most of the world's maple syrup, 71%, comes from Canada and 91% of that is produced in Québec. In the spring of 2017, Québec's harvest hit an all-time high: the province's 13,700 producers collected enough maple sap to produce 152.2 million pounds of syrup, breaking the previous year's record of 148 million pounds.[1] One would think that these recent boom seasons would be a good sign for the future. However, the truth is somewhat more complicated. My research on the future of the maple syrup industry indicates that its current success is due to an increase in numbers of trees tapped as well as the adoption of new technologies, but that neither of these guarantees a bright future for the sugar maple.

For maple sap to flow, conditions must be such that tree roots are still covered in snow, night temperatures fall below freezing (0 degrees Celsius), and daytime temperatures rise to above freezing. In some years, such as 2017 in Québec, producers began tapping relatively early, in February. This period of flow was followed by 'several weeks of cold' during which the sap did not flow, followed by 'a new surge in March' that continued in some parts of the province until early May.[2] This earlier tapping season is characteristic of the challenges that lie ahead: scientists in Québec who have studied the shifting tapping season predict that by the late twenty-first century seasonal production will be 'displaced to occur 15-19 days earlier on average' than it is now and that 'in the southern part of Québec, very short periods of syrup production due to unfavourable conditions in the spring will occur more frequently in the future although their absolute frequencies will remain low'.[3] Still, these researchers conclude that more research is required to determine what effect these shifts and potential shorter seasons will have on maple sap harvests.

Throughout the region, research teams are focused on a variety of problems, and though they may not agree on precisely how things will change in coming years, they are certain that changes are already happening and will continue. The research group ACERnet (Acer Climate and Socio-Economic Research network), a team of academics from New Hampshire, Massachusetts, Québec, Montana, and Virginia, is doing a multi-year study to collect data on the timing and quantity of sap flow, sugar content, and phenolic concentrations over the course of the season. Another team at University of Montana, led by Selma Ahmed, is interviewing producers to find out what changes they have noticed over their careers. Their goal is to help predict the future so that 'growers can manage for the situation and manage risk'.[4]

What has helped mitigate the problems of early and erratic sap flow are more and improved taps, tubing systems, and the use of vacuum pressure so that the release of sap does not rely entirely on the trees' circulatory system. This means that even if the sap flow is erratic – which is to say that the season begins early and then experiences a lull – the vacuum system helps to continue sap extraction for as long as sap is being produced. In addition, the new spiles (or taps) make a very small hole in the trees and stay in place even when there are lulls in the sap run. Previously, when sap stopped flowing during the season, producers would remove taps to allow the tree to seal the hole, protecting itself from bacteria. Modern taps can stay in through the lulls in flow because they are as narrow as the tip of a pen and, while they allow the sap to flow out, they are designed to keep detritus and bacteria from entering the tree.[5] Re-tapping trees after a lull can stress the trees, so the new system protects tree health and reduces physical labour on the part of producers.

All the same, many scientists are working to chart the effects of climate change on the vulnerability of the maple forest and the possible effects to maple syrup production in North America. In their report, 'Northeast and Northern Forests Regional Climate Hub Assessment of Climate Change Vulnerability and Adaptation and Mitigation Strategies', Daniel Tobin's group forecasts that while certain boreal forest species, such as spruce-fir and aspen, will be more adversely affected by climate change than sugar maple, maples will still be affected.[6] This is not to say that the current population of maples in the northeast will suddenly die out, because normally maples live between 300 and 400 years. Still, the stress of increased temperatures, which may bring shorter seasons and exposure to dangerous pests, will mean less maple syrup. We might then assume that we should prepare for changes in seasonal temperatures by planting more maple stands further north. But even if climate change means locations with the right temperature range are occurring further north, appropriate soil conditions would take years to catch up; in other words, while it may be that maples will move northward as temperatures increase, to establish an ecosystem with the right soil conditions for the maple could take hundreds of years.

Scientists anticipate that northern states and provinces won't see the worst effects of climate change for some time, but the more southerly areas may be hard hit, and sooner. Ryan Huish from the University of Virginia says, 'we are finding that foresters and producers are concerned about the health of maple trees, in particular the effects of acid rain and pest outbreaks.' Still, Huish is confident that with good sugar bush management, maple sugaring will continue in the southern Appalachians for the foreseeable future.[7]

As one group who studies the decline of the sugar maple forests in Québec has pointed out, changes in soil acidification since the 1960s 'may have reduced the availability of [...] essential nutrients for forest growth'. This study of fourteen plots of the Forest Ecosystem Research and Monitoring Network in Québec came to the conclusion that 'soil exchangeable acidity were positively associated with stand decline rate' and they attribute that rate 'at least partially, to soil acidification and acid deposition levels'.[8] Another group studying the same phenomenon in New York's Adirondack range to the west and south of Québec has discovered the same regional growth decline, noting that '[s]ugar maple is calciphilic and therefore is vulnerable to effects of acidic deposition in poorly buffered soils'.[9]

Changing conditions on and in the ground will inevitably change the marketing of maple products. At Montana State University, researcher Selma Ahmed studies the effects of weather variability on maple syrup production and marketing. In the past few years, producers have noticed a decline in warmer years of the light-coloured 'fancy grade' syrup, associated with the early (cooler) days of the sap run, and an increase of the darker grade syrups. Not only are producers experiencing earlier sap flow caused by earlier springs, but the season ends earlier because trees respond to the warmth by budding, the point at which sap becomes unpalatable. Since producers will produce more quantities of darker grade syrup, which fetches lower prices in the marketplace than the light syrup, they will lose a significant chunk of income.[10]

As we can see, the economics of sugar bush farming are completely reliant on the physical landscape of the maple tree; what I will turn to now is the question of the political and cultural landscape of the maple tree, particularly as they inform community and identity in producing regions.

History, Politics, and Identity

In *The Maple Sugar Book*, twentieth-century Vermont homesteaders Helen and Scott Nearing consider the Native American relationship to the maple tree and its syrup or sugar. According to what we know today from early European visitors and settlers, maple sap collection was a women's occupation. The aboriginals made holes in the trees with a hatchet, fixed a piece of wood in the holes to channel the sap, and left birch vessels or hollowed logs below for collection. The sap itself was valued as a tonic, and the aboriginals enjoyed drinking it, but they also made syrup and sugar. Although no mention is made of the spiritual connection that might have been part of the sugar-making ritual, some observers remarked that the sugar-making season, when some tribes went to live in camps in the woods, was treated as 'a holiday for everybody'.[11] It makes perfect sense that American Indians, at the end of long winters that often ended in scarcity, would celebrate the spring by tapping trees for much needed calories. In addition, the oral history of multiple tribes in the maple regions records a culture of celebration and feasting that would ensue at camps, with storytelling, music, and dancing.[12]

Several early Europeans who lived among the indigenous American peoples, usually for the purpose of converting them, reported on the traditions of the sugar maple season. One of these is the early eighteenth-century Jesuit priest, naturalist, and ethnologist, Jean-Francois Lafitau, who describes the maple sugar operations of the Iroquois women he encountered. This is, of course, almost two centuries post contact, so that metal pots from Europe had been introduced. Like others, Lafitau notes that sap was collected in 'great bark vessels'. After collection, he explains:

> they boil this liquid over a fire which boils away all the water and thickens the rest to the consistency of syrup or even of loaf sugar according to the degree and quantity of heat which they wish to give it. There is no other mystery in it. This sugar is very healing, admirable for medicines but, although it is more healthful than that of the cane, it has not its charm or delicacy and almost always has a little burned taste'.[13]

A nineteenth-century traveller contends that the First People he encountered much preferred their own maple sugar to cane sugar – which they called 'French snow' – because they found its taste to be 'more fragrant – more of the forest'.[14]

Two methods were used to create sugar – or syrup – from sap. The first was stone-boiling, which is how American Indians cooked many foods: stones are brought to red-hot temperatures in the fire and then placed into 'pots' made from birch bark, hollowed wooden logs, and, sometimes, clay. Once stones lost their heat, they were replaced with others until enough water had evaporated to concentrate the sugars into a syrup. The second method was freezing: at night, tubs of sap were left to freeze and in the morning the ice water on top was removed. After several repetitions, the sugar would concentrate, producing a sweeter, darker syrup. In terms of the importance, cultural and nutritional, of the maple tree, W.J. Hoffman estimated that though the Ojibwa numbered fewer than 1,500, one spring they made almost ninety tons of sugar.[15] Lafitau wrote that '[t]he Indian women have their maize cooked like pralines in maple syrup and mix their crushed sugar with the stirred up flour paste of which they make their provisions for travelling,' and many contemporary European writers remark on the aboriginal taste for sugar as a seasoning and their disdain for salt.[16] So it shouldn't surprise us that maple-sugaring season found the aboriginal people well stocked with equipment to collect and conserve sugar. According to Nearing, a 'woman in good circumstances would possess as many as from 1,200 to 1,500 birch bark vessels [called *makuks*], all of which would be in constant use during the season for sugar making'.[17]

That said, because very early European explorers and missionaries left no record of the boiling process, there has been a great debate among ethnologists and anthropologists on whether Native Americans produced maple sugar – as opposed to syrup – before the introduction of metal kettles and thus whether they taught the Europeans about maple sugar-making or vice versa. At the end of the nineteenth century, in his essay 'Indian Origin of Maple Sugar', H.W. Henshaw critiques those who assume that, because there is no written record, the indigenous people were not making sugar long before contact:

> Considering the great familiarity of the Indians with the natural edible products of America, and the general ignorance of the European on this subject, it is fairly to be inferred that the a priori likelihood of the discovery of the properties of the maple sap is all in favor of the Indian. If maple-sugar-making in the Northern United States preceded the arrival of the European and if the latter derived the art from the Indians, it is reasonable to expect to find statements to this effect in the early French narratives. On the other hand, it is to be said that if the discovery of the saccharine juice of the maple and the simple art of boiling it down to sugar were made by Europeans, it is even more probably that this fact would have been duly recorded by the early chroniclers. I am not prepared to say whether the earliest chronicles, say 1600-1675, contain information as to the Indian or European discovery of maple-sugar-making. If the matter is not referred to, its absence cannot be taken as conclusive either as to aboriginal or European origin. Many customs of the Indians far more important than this received but the briefest mention by the early narrators or are not mentioned at all.[18]

As evidence that the French indeed learned to make sugar from the aboriginal women, Henshaw uses Lafitau's own words about this history: 'The French make it [the sugar] better than the Indian women, *from whom they have learned how to make it*; but they have not yet been able to whiten or to refine it'.[19]

Part of the debate is semantic: what do early writers mean by 'sugar' as opposed to 'syrup'? One anthropologist who goes to great lengths to solve this puzzle is Patrick J. Munson who published in 1989 the article 'Still More on the Antiquity of Maple Sugar and Syrup in Aboriginal Eastern North America'. Not only does Munson marshal the lack of written evidence that North Americans made sugar pre-European contact, but he also cites his own experiments to turn syrup into sugar with stone-boiling. These resulted in a charred – not sweet – bitter, and unappetizing product, and he concludes that 'it would be at best very difficult (I think impossible) to make sugar by this technique'. Thus, he believes maple sugar production did not begin before 1675.[20]

Presumably, once technology permitted by the end of the seventeenth century with the introduction of metal pots, sugar did become a dietary staple among Aboriginal Peoples. Munson believes that before metal pots were available, people made syrup during the sugaring season – a celebratory time known as Sugar Moon or Maple Moon – and consumed it on site. 'Syrup,' Munson points out, 'is difficult to store and transport. Furthermore, unless kept constantly cool, canned, or treated with preservatives [....] it will quickly mold and, at concentrations of less than 65% sugar, will ferment'.[21]

Whence the confusion between syrup and sugar? While the North American Indian word for cane sugar brought by Europeans, '*sukaw*', is clearly related to the French 'sucre', maple syrup and sugar are often etymologically related to one another. So it is confusing to distinguish the products, even though the techniques needed to produce them are distinct. As Munson writes, 'the oral traditions and the folklore of the Native Americans, which suggest an antiquity for "sugar," can be read equally as well for syrup. And the linguistic data, which I find the most compelling of the indirect indicators of a pre-European origin, very strongly suggest that the original product was syrup'. Munson includes a table of indigenous language terms that indicates all the aboriginal terminology for 'sugar' 'refers without exception to a liquid (e.g. 'wood, water,' 'tree juice,' 'sap') or syrup'.[22]

Whether or not maple sugar and syrup are synonymous, the descendants of eastern North American peoples have a close relationship to the maple tradition. Maple sugar connects them both to their ancestral traditions and its current nutritional and economic value. Autumn Brunelle, a Native American research associate with the ACERnet group, believes that '[c]ontinued tapping of maple syrup, and passing on its associated traditional ecological knowledge, is important for food sovereignty of Native American communities'.[23] Ryan Huron asserts that 'the aboriginal people, Metis and First Nations' produced sugar up until the early twentieth century when the handing down of all traditions was broken even more thoroughly by 'colonization and the residential schools' which removed children from their families in order to assimilate them. This destruction of 'indigenous knowledge' meant that aboriginal peoples lost the practice of maple-syrup-making and the techniques their ancestors once used.[24]

Researcher Selma Ahmed points out that '[m]aple syrup is an iconic non-timber forest product linked to regional identity', which has certainly become the case in parts of New England and the province of Québec.[25] No doubt, the loss of land and the erasure of aboriginal culture by settler populations made possible this transfer of the maple and its products to iconic status in the emergent white societies. The Canadian identity in particular is now focused on the symbol of the maple leaf. In her 1910 book *Maple Lore*, Annie L. Jack tells the apocryphal story that Ludger Duvernay, founder of the ultra-nationalist French-Canadian group, the St. Jean-Baptiste Association, proposed the maple leaf as the group's insignia in 1833. A few years later, in 1836, the Québec nationalist newspaper *Le Canadien*, which meant, and in some places still means, French Canadian, decorated its masthead with a wreath of maple leaves.[26] But

Maple Moon: Landscapes of the Sugar Maple

August Vachon on his website devoted to 'heraldic science,' documents that English patriots simultaneously adopted the maple leaf as their nationalist symbol and cites as one piece of evidence that in 1849, the '*The Maple Leaf or Canadian Annual*, a literary journal, described the maple leaf as "the chosen emblem of Canada"'.[27]

As the largest producer of maple syrup in the world, Québec is a good case study for how important maple products are to the image of what is called the 'distinct society' of French Canada. In his children's book *The Sugaring-off Party*, Jonathan London takes as inspiration his French Canadian mother-in-law's memories as she recounts her family's celebration of the sugar season to her grandson Paul. As with First Peoples, the Québecois sugaring-off ritual was a family affair, with relatives coming to help collect and transport sap from the woods. In this story, the girl's family arrives at Tante Loulou's sugar shack, or *cabane à sucre*, where they watch the sap boiled down into syrup, then further concentrating it for the maple taffy known as '*tire*' in Québec. The party included a feast, with traditional pork products, eggs, pancakes, and lots of syrup. There was live music and folk dancing. The illustrations, painted by Québecois artist Gilles Pelletier, offer a nostalgic and colourful portrait of farm life in 1930s Québec: horse-drawn sleighs, smiling barn cats, and beautiful landscapes.[28]

This idealization of the maple and its role in the Québecois family contrast with the current importance of maple as an important export product. While traditionally the Catholic Church supported what was called '*la Revanche des berceaux*', or 'the battle of the cradle' to counter via population the power of the ruling English-speaking elite, the Church has become much less powerful since Québec's 'Quiet Revolution' in the 1960s. In its stead has grown a large administrative and some would say protectionist culture, particularly when it comes to maple products. In fact, Québec's *Fédération des producteurs acéricoles du Québec*, which has been accused of being a cartel, has gone as far as fining individual syrup producers up to $400,000 for selling to outside parties. When the *Fédération* came under fire for insisting on its right to regulate the sales of individual Québec producers, Paul Rouillard, its deputy director, asked one reporter not to be 'too hard on us', saying, 'We know that economically it's not the best thing, but we want to protect our producers. It's our distinct society. A lot of anglophones don't understand us.'[29] This statement indicates that at least one sector of Québecois society believes maple and its products are essential to the '*patrimoine culturelle*' – or cultural heritage – and form an important part of regional and nationalist identity.

What does the future hold for the maple tree itself in an economic and social landscape such as this? Foresters will tell you that a maple needs forty to fifty years of growth before it can be tapped without compromising its health. However, in 2009, two researchers at the University of Vermont's Proctor Maple Research Center, 'were conducting research into the sap flow of maple trees and discovered an entirely new way to make maple syrup'.[30] By cutting off the tops of young maples, two inches in diameter, and using a tube and vacuum method, great amounts of sap can be collected. While these researchers hold that this new system has many benefits, they do not recommend it as a replacement for traditional maple syrup production. Instead, they recommend that it could be something that 'creates and expands opportunities for maple producers to increase their production and grow their businesses'.[31]

When I showed this research to Stephan Cantor, a Vermont producer who has worked her sugar bush in Vermont's Northeast Kingdom for over thirty years, she put her head in her hands. For her and her husband Howie, the forest is a spiritual experience and an environmental responsibility, a closed sustainable system she believes goes back to the roots of production by Aboriginal Peoples who discovered maple syrup and were its first producers. Cantor and her husband love 'being in the forest when winter moves to spring. This is a way to have a relationship with the trees and the seasons. It's a transformative time, an agriculturally sustainable cycle in which you use the deadwood and lumber collected from thinning the forest to cook the sap down into syrup.' 'It's funny how you can get to know every single tree when there's 5,000 of them in your bush,' Cantor says. On their sugar bush, they have always resisted technological innovations until they have been proved not to damage the trees. She and her husband 'fell in love with sugaring' in the 1980s and created a niche market for themselves, selling in New York City at Union Square Greenmarket and to several restaurateurs. Cantor insists that 'there's a *terroir* to syrup', and fears that producing more syrup more quickly with a higher sugar content is a mistake. 'There's a lot of low grade syrup in the U.S. market,' she says.[32]

It doesn't look like the plantation system, which requires a lot of investment in technology, will become ubiquitous any time soon. But the spectre of acres of lopped-off trees connected to vacuum pumps, like some kind of futuristic vineyard, is sobering when juxtaposed with the careful and sustainable forest management of producers such as the Cantors. I would prefer to return to the world of the Maple or Sugar Moon, when maple syrup was seen as a seasonal treat and its collection, or at least consumption, engendered a community festival, but in a world of seven billion people, this is a fantasy that can probably only be sustained in memory and children's books.

Notes

1. Laura Pederson, 'Québec Taps Record Amount of Maple Syrup', *Montreal Gazette*, 31 May 2017 <http://montrealgazette.com/business/local-business/quebec-taps-record-amount-of-maple-syrup> [accessed 31 May 2017].
2. Pederson.
3. D. Houle and others, 'Impacts of Climate Change on the Timing of the Production Season of Maple Syrup in Eastern Canada', *PLoS ONE*, 10.12 (2015).
4. Brian Kahn, 'Climate Change is Coming for your Maple Syrup', *Climate Central*, 28 March 2016 <http://www.climatecentral.org/news/climate-change-maple-syrup-20178> [accessed 20 May 2017].
5. Stephan Cantor, Interview, New York City, 13 May 2017.
6. Daniel Tobin and others, 'Northeast and Northern Forests Regional Climate Hub Assessment of Climate Change Vulnerability and Adaptation and Mitigation Strategies', ed. by T. Anderson, *Climate Hubs*, U.S. Department of Agriculture, 2015 <https://www.climatehubs.oce.usda.gov/sites/default/

files/Northeast%20Regional%20Hub%20Vulnerability%20Assessment%20Final.pdf> [accessed 20 May 2017].
7. Kahn.
8. Louis Duchesne, Rock Ouimet, and Daniel Houle, 'Basal Area Growth of Sugar Maple in Relation to Acid Deposition, Stand Health, and Soil Nutrients', *Journal of Environmental Quality*, 31, 1676-83.
9. D.A. Bishop and others. 'Regional Growth Decline of Sugar Maple (Acer saccharum) and Its Potential Causes', *Ecosphere* 6.10 (2015), 179.
10. Evelyn Boswell, 'MSU Researcher Studies Effects of Weather Variability and Market Dynamics on Maple Syrup Production', *MSU News*, 10 March 2017 <http://www.montana.edu/news/16779/msu-researcher-studies-effects-of-weather-variability-and-market-dynamics-on-maple-syrup-production> [accessed 20 May 2017].
11. Helen and Scott Nearing, *The Maple Sugar Book* (New York: John Day Company, 1950), p. 28
12. Nearing, pp. 22-39.
13. Jean-Francois Lafitau, *Customs of the American Indians Compared with the Customs of Primitive Times*, trans. by William Fenton (Toronto: The Champlain Society, 1974), vol.2, pp. 94-96.
14. Johann Georg Kohl, *Wanderings Around Lake Superior* (London: Chapman and Hall, 1860), p. 324.
15. Nearing, p. 37.
16. Lafitau, vol. 2, p. 96.
17. Nearing, pp. 30-31.
18. H.W. Henshaw, 'Indian Origins of Maple Sugar', *American Anthropologist*, 3.4 (October 1990), 341-35 (p. 342).
19. Henshaw, p. 343 (original emphasis).
20. Patrick J.Munson, 'Still More on the Antiquity of Maple Sugar and Syrup in Aboriginal Eastern North America', *Journal of Ethnobiology*, 9.2: 158-170 (p. 165).
21. Munson, p. 161.
22. Munson, p. 166.
23. Montana State University, 'Effects of Weather Variability on Maple Syrup Production Studied', *Phys.org*, 10 March 2017 <https://phys.org/news/2017-03-effects-weather-variability-maple-syrup.html> [accessed 20 May 2017].
24. Ryan Huron, 'Historical Roots of Canadian Aboriginal and non-Aboriginal Maple Practices', Wilfred Laurier University, 2014 <http://scholars.wlu.ca/cgi/viewcontent.cgi?article=1001&context=ges_mrp> [accessed 20 May 2017].
25. Kahn.
26. Annie L. Jack, *Maple Lore* (Montreal: A.T. Chapman. 1910), pp. 6-7.
27. Auguste Vachon, 'Canada's Coat of Arms: Defining a Country within an Empire Chapter 2: The Beaver and the Maple Leaf', *Heraldic Science Héraldique* <http://heraldicscienceheraldique.com/chapter-2-the-beaver-and-the-maple-leaf.html> [accessed 20 May 2017].
28. Jonathan London, *The Sugaring-Off Party, paintings by Gilles Pelletier* (New York: Dutton Children's Books, 1995).
29. Peter Kuitenbrouwer, 'Maple Sugar Rebellion', *National Post*, 23 April 2015 <http://business.financialpost.com/features/how-a-maple-syrup-rebellion-is-growing-in-quebec> [accessed 20 May 2017].
30. Joshua E. Brown, 'Remaking Maple: New Method May Revolutionize Maple Syrup Industry,' *University Communications*, University of Vermont, 6 November 2013 <https://www.uvm.edu/newsstories/news/remaking_maple > [accessed 20 May 2017].
31. Timothy Perkins and Abby van den Berg, 'Sap Collection from Small-Diameter Trees', University of Vermont Proctor Maple Research Center, 2016, p. 6 <http://www.uvm.edu/~pmrc/Perkins%20and%20van%20den%20Berg%202016_Sap%20Collection%20from%20Small-Diameter%20Trees.pdf> [accessed 20 May 2017].
32 Cantor.

Agriculture without Fences

Hilary Heslop[1]

A History Rewritten

'The myth that Aboriginal people had no knowledge of husbandry was a mistake based on prejudice.' – Robert Etheridge[2]

The hunter-gatherer tag was assigned to the Aboriginal Australians by the colonists, who arrived in Australia in 1788. It was a characterization designed to suit the European narrative of the time, claiming, in equal measure, dominance and possession of the land. The Aboriginal people had inhabited Australia for approximately 50,000 years prior to the colonists' arrival. Compelling evidence proposes that they used a land management system utilizing fire, water systems, and tree grass mosaics to ensure a constant food supply while granting them significant leisure time.

This system was the caretaker of an estate covering 7.7 million square kilometres encompassing huge diversity including tropical rainforests, deserts, and temperate terrains. They considered the whole land as single and universal, and this philosophy formed the basis of their land management system. They used fire to control growth, creating regeneration, which, in turn, allowed them to move grazing animals by carefully locating their feed and shelter. They dammed rivers and used weirs, carefully ensuring that some fish could still migrate, to allow stock to flow to allies and clans hundreds of miles away. As Bill Gammage writes, there were three rules to this system:

1. Ensure that all life flourishes.
2. Make plants and animals abundant, convenient, and predictable.
3. Think universal, act local.

The management of the land was not treated as an activity like farming but rather as a lifestyle allowing for mobility, which was considered more important. Mobility was important ecologically to allow the efficient exploitation of limited resources and socially to allow the maintenance of kinship networks. They tended the plants and animals in regions. They would leave the forest on poorer soils and clear the best soils to create pastures and croplands. Plants like kangaroo grass and lilies would flourish, protecting the thick mosses and lichens critical for holding water in the thin Australian topsoil.[3]

These practices were shaped by an understanding of the relationship and balance between the spiritual, moral, and natural elements of the world that the Aboriginal

Agriculture without Fences

people refer to as the Dreaming. The Dreaming is infinite, linking past and present to determine the future. The land a person belongs to acts as conduit between the people and the Dreaming. Stories from the Dreaming tell the truth from the past and, along with the code of law, dictates how to operate in the present. The spiritual parity of all life is decreed, enforced by the code of law. The Dreaming brings knowledge about the plants and animals – when to hunt, when to fish – and even the movement of the stars. It is often referred to as a complete guide to life and living.[4] This relationship with the land is critical in understanding how they managed it and how they considered the continent. It was the fundamental difference between their agricultural philosophy and that of the Europeans.

Figure 1. Botanist Dr Beth Gott with an Aboriginal hoe (Heslop, 2017).

To refine the land the Aboriginal people made templates through mosaics. Their aim was to create abundance, predictability, continuity, and choice. Tree breaks were formed to provide animal shelter. Clearings were developed to allow animals to graze. People tended animals and plants in regions. They manipulated the landscape through fire, using it to ambush wildlife and to create preferred conditions for plants to regenerate. They would leave after a harvest or hunt, allowing the land to find its balance, and they would know when to return. This management of the land left a distinct footprint on the continent. The open pastures and clumps of trees gave a parklike echo to the landscape.

On arriving in Australia the first explorers often noted this theme, as Charles Sturt wrote:

> As regards the general appearance of the wooded portion of this province, I would remark, that excepting on the tops of the ranges where the stringy-bark grows, in the pine forests, and where there are belts of scrub on barren or sandy ground, its character is that of open forest without the slightest undergrowth save grass [...]. In many places the trees are so sparingly, and I had almost said judiciously, distributed as to resemble the parklands attached to a gentleman's residence in England.[5]

But the colonists had arrived to claim a land. They believed it was their duty to spread civilization and religion to the world. Their reward would be the wealth generated from the lands they colonized. This sense of destiny blinded them to the achievements of other civilizations, and hence they discounted their observations. As author Bruce Pascoe writes, 'Few were here to marvel at a new civilization but to replace it.'[6] But the evidence was there. The question is not did it happen, but how did it happen?

Food and Landscape

How They Did It

The Aboriginal system was one of templates based on co-operative behaviour between communities, navigating often conflicting interests. Was it a template for harvesting, or a gathering or hunting? Was a fire due in one area, even though it had been a bad year for breeding in that area? The Law would determine which action would be taken. Some templates were left active whilst others were left dormant. As author Bill Gammage notes, 'Mobility made this possible: people walked not only to care for the country, but to leave it alone.'[7]

For the Aboriginal people, fire was their key tool. Fire burning had five principles:

1. Notating the mosaic pattern, to control the intensity, while allowing plants and animals to survive in refuge.
2. Deciding when to burn, dependent on the time of the year.
3. Working with prevailing weather conditions.
4. Advising neighbouring clans of the impending fire.
5. Avoiding the growing season of particular plants.

Burn times were controlled by the elders, and there was a planned program of fire stick burning. This was the knowledge, acquired over generations from the Dreaming. In Australia many indigenous seeds cannot geminate without hot ashes; plants that may have been dormant for years will grow after fire. Fire was the tool used to shape Australia, not fences. The most fertile land developed around the fewest trees, which was counterintuitive to those used to European agriculture, but burning in cycles promoted the perennial grasslands in Australia.

Fire allowed the Aboriginal people to control plants and animals and to control pests. As Bill Gammage writes:

> People think of what animals need. In 1788 people thought of what animals prefer. What animals prefer attracts them.
>
> As the term firestick farming suggests, the Aboriginal use of fire resembled agriculture in some ways: it yielded certain crops at certain times, suppressed weeds and was carefully controlled [...]. Aboriginal people are fiercely protective of their clan lands, excluding outsiders or inviting them in as conditions warrant. There are also clear rules about who has the right to what resources and highly evolved mechanisms to resolve conflicts and enforce penalties. This has enabled Australia's Aboriginal people to act as keystone species of the continent's ecosystems for forty-five thousand years. As the Europeans displaced them, Australia's fragile environment collapsed into a far less productive and diverse state.[8]

Fields were observed with lines of women digging for yam daisy tubers (*misroseris lanceolate*). This plant was used as food source. It grew high, across fields in Victoria, and was used for grain and feeding livestock. The high grasses protected mosses and lichens growing at their base. This spongy base retained moisture and kept the thin Australian

Agriculture without Fences

topsoil in situ.[9] Aboriginal people used seed propagation, irrigation, harvest, storage, and trading for other goods or giving as gifts. This trading effected the morphology of the plants across the continent.

Nardoo (*Marsilea dummondii*) could grow in the beds of shallow lakes; Aboriginals swept the seed after the lake had dried, processed them into flour, and stored the excess. Evidence of this labour has been found in Cuddie Springs, New South Wales where grindstones dating back approximately 30,000 years have been discovered. Others of a similar age have been found in the Northern Territory.[10]

In 1974, Norman Tindale documented grain belts that stretched over almost all of Australia. These differ vastly from grain maps of today where introduced European grains cover only the southern regions of Australia, due to rainfall and other climatic conditions.[11]

Across the Murray River, dykes were built to prevent it receding too much during the drier months; the retained water allowed fish to breed. Nets were used to catch specific species of fish and shellfish. The Brewarrina fishing traps in New South Wales were engineered using water races and a stone locking system. A yearly harvest would be held with up to 5000 people in attendance. Debate still rages on the age of the traps, but estimates put them between 3000-15,000 years old. The system was designed to allow some stock to pass upstream so that communities there could benefit.

The First Fleet arrived in 1788. The British originally hoped to absorb the Aboriginal people into British culture, supplying labour to the new colony. But as the colonists took more land, clashes with the Aboriginals become inevitable. The British put up fences, cleared land, restricted access, and put imported livestock on the land. The Aboriginal people began to retaliate as their Law was broken.

Expeditions of soldiers were sent out to punish any Aboriginal people who threatened settlers. Soldiers hunted and killed Aboriginals they thought responsible for stealing food or stock. Local government encouraged settlers to drive Aboriginals off British settlements. The Aboriginals resisted this activity, but without firearms it made the endeavour an unequal fight.

As the Aboriginal people lost family members and access to their lands, they became more reliant on the British for food, water, and shelter. Disease, including smallpox, measles, and tuberculosis, also decimated the population. Accurate numbers are challenging to confirm, but estimates suggest the population dropped by two thirds. Children and the elderly were particularly hard hit by disease. The loss of the elderly was a seminal issue for the Aboriginal people, as they were the keepers of the knowledge and the law. Their traditional way of life and land management was slowly eroded.

The decline of the Aboriginal people began to affect the land quickly too, aided and abetted by imported livestock. Indigenous mammals are all soft footed, and the hard-hoofed imported cattle and sheep impacted the thin Australia topsoil, causing soil compaction, erosion, and run off. They trampled over and ate plant life. The way they ate was a problem too: kangaroos nibble the tops of yam daisy (a key crop for the Aboriginal people), keeping the rootstock intact, but sheep pull the whole plant out of the ground, destroying it. Today, sheep are one of the most significant causes of chronic land modification in Australia, but by 1888 erosion was already being recognized as one of Australia's first environmental problems.

After 1788, colonists commonly banned fire, which allowed fire-sensitive species to run riot, creating fuel for wild fires. The lack of fire caused issues for animals as well. For example, ground parrots need fire every three to seven years to balance food and shelter. After 1788, infrequent fires caused their numbers to drop dramatically, and today they are an endangered species. Since 1788, thirty mammals in Australia have become extinct. Since 1940, almost a third of the world's mammal extinctions have been in Australia.[12]

In the Murray-Darling catchment, colonists drained water for pasture and crops which dried up swamps and stripped back sheltering scrub. The Murray-Darling Basin covers 1,062,025 square kilometres. Today it contains 40% of all Australian farms, producing wool, cotton, sheep, cattle, diary, rice, wine, fruit, and vegetables. It supplies one third of Australia's food supply and supports over a third of Australia's total gross value of agricultural production.[13] Overall, Australia is expected to be one of the worst affected regions of the world by climate change impacts upon future agricultural production and food exports.[14]

Culture in Colonial Australia

As the colonists overwhelmed the Aboriginal people, the diet of Australia began to change as well. The rations eaten by the First Fleet at sea – salted meat, pease/dried peas and rice, and sometimes sugar – influenced the diet on land. With the eventual success of grazing meat became ubiquitous at nearly every meal.

This success reflected a desire to re-create the land and diet of a land the colonists had left behind. Indigenous ingredients and livestock were rejected as unworthy of domestication. While kangaroos and wallabies were occasionally used as a meat source, they were quickly superseded by cattle and sheep.

Sheep and cattle were king in the colony. Their constant supply dominated menus and built an economically stable country. The growing middle class aspired to a new, more refined way of living. Entertaining at home, with lavish afternoon teas and spreads, was championed by social editors and embraced by emerging middle-class women. Improving economic conditions, new technologies, and opportunities were changing aspirations for, and the definitions of, success.

Food culture was also built by government policy, as part of nation-building initiatives. Subsidies were paid on the production of local foods – especially sheep, who created an Australian economy immortalized as 'riding on the sheep's back' – helping to develop overseas markets. The unseen, and largely unspoken, cost of this initiative was the yam daisy, other native tubers, and the Australian topsoil.

As Australia developed in the twentieth century a sense of nationalism evolved, and branding championing Australian-made became increasingly important. Brands such as Cherry Ripe, Milo, and Vegemite established themselves in the Australian psyche. Brand Australia was busily being constructed, without even a nod to its indigenous food past.

Waves of immigrant groups arriving in Australia bought their cuisines with them, embedding themselves into Australian cuisine. The Greeks, the Italians, and the Vietnamese all left marks – from espresso to pho – leaving little oxygen for an indigenous food culture.

The result was an outward focused nation, keen to shrug off the shackles of a monotonous colonial cuisine, always on the lookout for culinary salvation, yet never looking back to its own past. In 1993, author Cherry Ripe commented:

> There is a school of thought which holds that this shift in culinary emphasis – this adoption of the flavours and techniques of other cuisines – could have happened only in a post-colonial country, one without a strong cooking tradition of its own. By not having a culinary tradition that is tied to the soil, the land and the seasons, we are more open to suggestion.[15]

On occasion, indigenous food sources encountered cultural barriers in twentieth-century Australia. During a 1990 parliamentary debate to legalize kangaroo meat for human consumption in New South Wales, Ian Armstrong, the Agriculture Minister, declared, 'You can eat Bambi but you can't eat Skippy.' Skippy was a reference to the star of a local Australian television series, in which *Skippy the Bush Kangaroo* – unquestionably Australia's smartest kangaroo – consistently solved more mysteries than Hercule Poirot.[16]

Pioneer native foods chef Jean-Paul Bruneteau came to refer to what he called 'food racism', citing that indigenous foods were rejected just because they were Aboriginal, and that rejection reflected the many kinds of racism directed at the Aboriginal people.[17]

Modern Australia

The White Australian policy revealed the cultural intentions of successive governments through the early part of the twentieth century, which included views on the Aboriginal people. They may not have been directly affected by the immigration laws, but they certainly impacted its cultural intent. However, shifting social norms and protests began to have a positive impact on them too. A 1967 national referendum made two amendments to the Australian Constitution, removing Section 127 which stated that Aborigines would not be counted in the census and amending Section 51 to prohibit the federal government from making specific laws for the Aboriginal people.[18]

Change was coming, but it would be a sluggish journey. In 1966, the magazine *Gourmet Traveller* was launched in Australia. Highlights in the 1960s editions of the magazine were chicken vol-au-vents, lobster mousse, and crackers with cheese and pickles. In the 1970s, the theme was more cosmopolitan with an interest in nouvelle cuisine and the arrival – in significant numbers – of migrants from South East Asia and the Middle East. Recipes in that decade included French onion dip with cheddar biscuits, beef Wellington, and chilled zucchini, pea and buttermilk soup. In the 1980s, the term 'Modern Australian' started to take hold to refer to a kind of culinary freedom that still acknowledged the various cultures that had created it – with one notable exception: its own.

The 1990s set the tone for this new Australian cuisine, as restaurants such as Berrowa Waters

Inn and Rockpool opened that championed this new bent on Australian cuisine. Food was described as incorporating traditions from around the globe, but into this mix, finally, came some pioneers of indigenous food. Raymond and Jennice Kersch's restaurant Edna's Table started listing indigenous ingredients on their menus. Following his Rowntree's restaurant, Jean-Paul Bruneteau opened Riberries – Taste Australia in 1991. And Juleigh Robins founded her company Outback Spirit, which produces food products using indigenous ingredients, whilst helping fund indigenous food communities. Robins has developed numerous products over the years to help bring these ingredients into the mainstream.

Yet in *Gourmet Traveller* a strong Asian theme still resonated through their recipes, including coconut crab and green mango salad, soy-braised chicken with green bean sambal, and five spice duck and shitake pies.

The 2000s saw molecular gastronomy, Italian cuisine, and foraging highlighted. Recipes included such dishes as mussels in tomato broth, lobster and fennel lasagne, and asparagus and rice soup. Sustainability was now a major trend, but so was authenticity, which opened the door for indigenous ingredients.

In the current decade, growing produce and foraging both continue to trend, and the issue of sustainability continues to grow. From this base, more trailblazers of indigenous food have emerged.

Author Bruce Pascoe has written extensively about the history of Aboriginal agriculture, but he is also looking to the future. Pascoe has collaborated with Aboriginal groups on the New South Wales and Victorian border and set a crowd-funding campaign to 'support the recovery of our traditional food plants'. The funding would help commercialize the enterprise to provide employment and training.[19] In 2016, Bruce Pascoe was named by *Gourmet Traveller* as one of Australia's fifty most influential people in food.

Before Danish chef Rene Redzepi opened his pop-up version of Noma in 2016, he spent months in Australia learning from the Australian landscape and indigenous ingredients so that he could incorporate them into his menus. This indigenous angle featured heavily in media reports: copious copy queried why it took a foreigner to highlight this produce.[20]

Although these reports were not an entirely accurate account, as they failed to credit earlier pioneers of indigenous cuisine such as Jean-Paul Bruneteau, Raymond and Jennice Kersch, and Victor Cherikoff, they do mirror a dichotomy that has been evident throughout my own research.[21] For example, Jean-Paul Bruneteau was born in Vendee, France, and migrated to Australia. However, there are native-born, European-descended Australians on the list – though far too few – including brother and sister team Raymond and Jennice Kersch, Juleigh Robins, and Victor Cherikoff.

Figure 2. Outback Spirit Bush Tomato Sausages (courtesy of Outback Spirit).

Agriculture without Fences

Figure 3. Ruth Emery, Juleigh Robins, and Max Emery (courtesy of Outback Spirit).

From twentieth-century chefs searching for inspiration abroad to Juleigh Robins being asked why she would bother with indigenous food in the 1980s, from an Australian politician declaring we cannot eat kangaroo to a customer at Edna's restaurant claiming he doesn't want this 'Abo stuff', there is a common theme of rejection when it comes to indigenous food.[22] The reasons, I suggest, are complex; perhaps the cause for this lack of self-examination is that many of us would feel uncomfortable with the conclusion. Regardless, it is surely a reticence that must be overcome.

Conclusion

As Bruce Pascoe writes in *Dark Emu*, the history of Aboriginal people is not that of nomads barely subsisting in a formidable environment, but that of a cohesive and settled community, managing the land and wildlife. This assertion not only challenges our accepted wisdom but also forcibly begs the question whether a successful land management system was ignored because it was – an inconvenient truth – fatefully misaligned with the colonist's self-interest? The evidence and behaviour of the colonists, and unfortunately even today's Australians, would suggest so.

In Pascoe's vision of the future, he asks Australia to embrace Aboriginal agriculture. In accepting their methods and ideology, he claims there is a prize to be won for all Australians. The rediscovery of indigenous grains could revive staples – not just the exotics – from obscurity. Surely native grains that can survive across nearly all of Australia's unique terrain – as opposed to the present far smaller imported grain belt – makes sense? In addition, if we accept that the Aboriginal people did construct, in Pascoe's words, 'a system of government that generated peace and prosperity then it is likely that we will love and admire our land all the more; restoring Aboriginal pride in the past and allowing that past to inform the future will remove the yoke of despair from the Aboriginal people'.[23] It is difficult to argue against the optimism his words inspire.

Echoing Pascoe, Bill Gammage argues that today we champion a kind of sustainability that evokes merely surviving, whereas pre-1788, Aboriginal Australians assumed abundance. He claims we take more and leave the future less. The problems of degradation in the Murray Darling Basin underscore his narrative. With salinity, erosion, rising sea levels, and ocean acidification all set to worsen significantly, it has become imperative that we change our model of land management.

But there are green shoots. When Bob Purvis took over Woodgreen Station near Alice Springs in Australia in 1958, he encountered significant issues with land degradation. Most of the grazing country was eaten bare. Bob believes that central Australia carries up to four times more than it can sustain and that most drought is in fact man-made. To regenerate his own station, Purvis identified a buffelgrass his cattle preferred, and he adjusted his stocking rate to sustain them. Today he runs his herd at a third of 1958 levels. He stopped shooting dingos, netted off dams to keep kangaroo numbers low, and has sold most of his horses. He uses space, culling and adjusting to ensure a balance on the land for its future. Today the station thrives. Some of his work was trial and error, but he agrees that there are strong echoes of the Aboriginal land management systems in his work.[24]

Looking beyond such models of land action, Bruce Pascoe's crowd funding campaign to support the recovery of traditional food plants met and exceeded its target. In his words, 'our people were happy that the broader community showed so much interest in what we were doing. Aboriginal culture is obviously accepted a bit more widely these days than it used to be.'[25]

Government agencies are getting involved as well. The Department of Parks and Wildlife in Western Australia runs a controlled burning programme to reduce fuel, thus controlling wild fires. The Queensland Government manages prescribed burns for a large range of ecosystems with intervals ranging from a little over two to more than thirty years. Their guidelines include specifications on the best time of year and optimum intensity, mirroring Aboriginals traditions. The National Landcare Programme, another government initiative, builds on partnerships with indigenous people so they can participate in land and sea management using their unique knowledge and skills.

At the same time internationally acclaimed chefs, like Ben Shewry and Jock Zonfrillo, are helping to raise the profile of indigenous food. Placing it front and centre on the modern Australian plate demonstrates their commitment to sourcing, and growing these raw materials reminds diners of its heritage.

Bill Gammage believes there is no return to 1788, both because our modern society is too entrenched and because, above all, we do not think like the Aboriginal people. For us, the wilderness lies just beyond the fence, but for the Aboriginals the wilderness does not exist. Fences on the ground make for fences in the mind.

He may well be right, but perhaps there are new technologies that can help us create a new 1788. For example, new GPS devices allow for sheep and cattle to be farmed without fences. Trackers attached to livestock can be controlled via a smartphone, digitally managing the movement of the stock.[26] So, could sheep finally co-exist in harmony with murnong? Instead of being destroyed by sheep, murnong could grow alongside, safe from being uprooted and destroyed. If the past is prologue, could the demise of physical fences also signal an end to the present-day silo mentality of agriculture to take us back to the future? A future the Aboriginals managed and foresaw all those years ago?

After all, a land management system that reviews and manages a continent in its entirety is surely the only viable path for a sustainable future. Such a system would not only tell a story for this country but surely also represent a gift from the Aboriginal people of Australia to the world. It is time to give all Australians a past and a future to be proud of. To paraphrase John Newton who – in distinctly Australian vernacular – said it best: 'About bloody time mate.'[27]

Agriculture without Fences

Notes

1. My thanks to Jacqui Newling, for her guidance and help, on the history of colonial Australia, to Juleigh Robins for her friendship, time, and sublime lunch, to discuss her years of work in the indigenous food community. Dr. Beth Gott for giving me such insight into the native plants of Australia. Jana Hatfield for loaning me her copious back copies of *Australian Gourmet Traveller*. And of course, to the Aboriginal people of Australia, past and present, for 50,000 years of sheer genius. To them I say: 'Lest we remember.'
2. Robert Etheridge (1894), in *Rupert Gerristen, Australia and the Origins of Agriculture* (London: Archaeopress, 2008). p. 110.
3. Bill Gammage, *The Biggest Estate on Earth: How Aborigines Made Australia* (Sydney: Allen & Unwin, 2011) p. 1-4.
4. Gammage, pp. 123-53.
5. Charles Sturt, *Narrative of an Expedition into Central Australia* (London, T. & W. Boone, 1849), vol. 2, pp. 229-30.
6. Bruce Pascoe, *Dark Emu, Black Seeds: Agriculture or Accident?* (Broome: Magabala Books, 2014), p. 13.
7. Gammage, p. 213.
8. Gammage, p. 190.
9. Pascoe, p. 22.
10. Pascoe, pp. 30-34.
11. Norman Tindale, 'Adaptive Significance of Panara or Grass Seed Culture of Australia', in *Hunting and Gathering and Fishing*, ed. by B. Wright (Canberra: AIATSIS, 1978), pp. 345-49.
12. Australian Wildlife Conservancy, 'Wildlife', *Australian Wildlife Conservancy* <http://www.australian-wildlife.org/wildlife.aspx> [accessed 21 April 2017].
13. Discover Murray, 'Murray Darling Basin', *Discover Murray: Australia's Great River* <http://www.murrayriver.com.au/about-the-murray/murray-darling-basin> [accessed 20 April 2017].
14. Quentin Farmar-Bowers, Vaughan Higgins, and Joanne Millar, 'Introduction: The Food Security Problem in Australia', in *Food Security in Australia: Challenges and Prospects for the Future*, ed. by Quentin Farmar-Bowers, Vaughan Higgins, and Joanne Millar (New York: Springer, 2012), pp. 1-20 (pp. 1-2).
15. Cherry Ripe, *Goodbye Culinary Cringe* (Sydney: Allen & Unwin, 1996), p. 23.
16. Ripe, p. 211.
17. John Newton, *The Oldest Foods on Earth* (Sydney: NewSouth Publishing, 2016), p. X.
18. Ron Sutton, 'Myths Persist about the 1967 Referendum', *SBS News*, 11 March 2014 <http://www.sbs.com.au/news/article/2014/03/10/myths-persist-about-1967-referendum> [accessed 2 April 2017].
19. 'Sow the Seed: Aboriginal Agriculture', *Pozible.com* <https://pozible.com/project/202236> [accessed 11 March 2017].
20. Fran Kelly, 'Noma Puts Native Food Back on the Menu', *RN Breakfast*, Australian Broadcast Company, 27 January 2016 <http://www.abc.net.au/radionational/programs/breakfast/noma-pop-up-puts-spotlight-on-native-foods/7118496> [accessed 21 April 2017].
21. Vic Cherikoff, 'Be Creative with Authentic Australian Ingredients', *Australian Functional Ingredients*, 2011 <http://cherikoff.net/history/> [accessed 20 March 2017].
22. John Newton and Paul Ashton, 'Why Has Native "Grub" Been Ignored for So Long', *INDaily: Australia's Independent News*, 23 May 2016 <http://indaily.com.au/eat-drink-explore/2016/05/23/why-has-native-grub-been-ignored-for-so-long/> [accessed 21 April 2017].
23. 'Sow the Seed: Aboriginal Agriculture'.
24. Gammage, p. 321.
25. Max Allen, 'Did Australia Invent Bread', *Gourmet Traveller*, April 2016 <http://www.gourmettraveller.com.au/recipes/food-news-features/2016/5/did-australia-invent-bread/> [accessed 21 April 2017].
26. Emily Parkinson, 'Sheep and Cattle Could Be Enclosed by Virtual Fences', *Financial Review*, 9 March 2016 <http://www.afr.com/news/special-reports/sheep-and-cattle-could-be-enclosed-by-virtual-fences-20160307-gnch4a> [accessed 20 April 2017].
27. Newton, p. xiii.

Imaginary Landscapes and Virtual *Terroir*

Ben Houge

Introduction: The Landscape of Virtual Worlds

While the term 'landscape' has historically referred to a spatially articulated topography, we may also consider a new kind of virtual landscape in which the structuring determinant is not space but information. In a twenty-first century analogue to the historical genre of landscape painting, we can employ this network of dependencies to aesthetically depict not simply how something looks, but how it works. This forms the basis for the newly emerged creative practice of data visualization, for example, and it is a key concept in the development of video games and other forms of virtual reality.

Landscape architects, like game designers, create environments that support a range of potential activity and offer various affordances. Unlike the fixed sequence of a film or a book, these spaces allow for the emergence of infinite non-linear narratives. In addition, there is a new, networked landscape emerging as everyday devices become connected to the internet. These ubiquitous sensors, together with the powerful computing and sensing devices that many of us carry in our pockets every day, constitute a dynamic and rapidly expanding landscape of information.

Tremendous opportunity exists to incorporate these emerging technologies into the dining room to enhance and elucidate the various landscapes that converge in a meal, including the food supply infrastructure, the assembled community of diners, and the sensory domain of the meal itself. By highlighting these interdependencies and drawing their inner workings to the fore, we increase the potential of a meal to communicate ideas that extend beyond the walls of the restaurant.

A New Genre for Audiogustatory Expression

I come to the study of technology in relationship to gastronomy from a background in classical music composition, filtered through twenty-two years of experience developing virtual environments in the video game industry. In my practice as a composer, artist, and music technology professor, much of my work involves constructing digital, sonic landscapes, whether in museums in the form of sound installations, in the virtual worlds of video games, or in live performances that incorporate audience members' mobile phones. Since 2010, I have been collaborating with chefs to engage in an exploration of how music and food can be combined to enable multisensory dining experiences in an ongoing series of what I call 'food operas'.

Imaginary Landscapes and Virtual *Terroir*

The point of departure for this research was to consider a meal as a time-based art form and to posit that the reason we have no culinary equivalent to the genres of opera, ballet, or cinema that pair music with another form of expression is due to the technical challenges in synchronizing and siting sound in relationship to a meal. To address this, I developed a real-time music deployment system and a multichannel speaker array that positions a sound source at each seat in the dining area, allowing the music to conform to the unpredictable timings of each diner's meal. Rather than constrain the activities of diners, perhaps by requiring everyone to eat the same thing at the same time or to don headphones, I set myself the more challenging task of sonifying the dining experience as it typically is experienced in a restaurant setting: a room full of people eating different dishes at different times. The music from each of the speakers is coordinated in harmony and rhythm via a central computer server in a way that is somewhat analogous to the interaction of instruments of an orchestra, transforming the dining area into a lush, immersive soundscape. I feel that this format comprises a new genre for audiogustatory expression, enabling a wide range of possible narratives.

My work is part of a larger movement to reconsider what ideas can be conveyed via the chemical senses of smell and taste, as well as the social constructs that surround food consumption. The affordances of new technologies arrive at a moment when an increasing number of chefs (including Andoni Luis Aduriz, Heston Blumenthal, and Paul Pairet) have been exploring the narrative potential of a meal, while at the same time artists in a range of disciplines (such as Natalie Jeremijenko, Anicka Yi, and Rirkrit Tiravanija) have been investigating a meal's aesthetic potentialities. The environment is ripe for cross-disciplinary collaboration, allowing us to expand the conception of what a meal can communicate, encompassing aesthetic expressions, political statements, and addressing social issues such as climate change and sustainable food practices.

A Tour through Selected Digital Landscapes
Before examining applications of these ideas in my own work, it may be useful to consider some of the ways in which digital information can be read as a kind of landscape.

Sampling the Environment
If we look at a photograph of a landscape, we can immediately identify a number of attributes, such as the contour of the land, soil composition, the types of plants one finds there, different types of agricultural intervention, perhaps a glimpse of the weather, but many details are missing. Even if we visit in person, our ability to quantify aspects of the environment such as temperature or humidity are relatively coarse, and to track their change over time even more so. As a result we are accustomed to using different instruments to take more accurate measurements, and computers can accomplish this in a highly systematic way, with a high degree of precision and on a vast scale, capturing data that provides a richly multidimensional view of an environment. Just as one might take soil samples, we can create a large database of information samples in a way that

is akin to a film presenting twenty-four still images in rapid succession to suggest the illusion of movement, or the way in which the amplitude of an audio signal is sampled 44,100 times every second to reproduce music on a compact disc.

Since 2014, researchers in the Responsive Environments group at the MIT Media Lab have been taking this approach to recording data from Tidmarsh, a 600-acre former cranberry farm that is being restored to natural wetland. They have positioned small sensors throughout the property to capture temperature, humidity, ambient light, barometric pressure, motion, and sound, resulting in a richly detailed representation of how this environment changes over time. This approach to distributing data capture and processing across a large number of relatively inexpensive, networked devices is at the core of what is referred to as the 'Internet of Things', or IoT for short. As individual devices are connected in a network, a larger picture emerges that is far more detailed than what each individual device can detect. These devices don't need to be particularly powerful or intelligent, but instead need to be deployed in large enough quantity that, when their data is analyzed collectively, they can provide a new kind of insight into an environment.

Aesthetic Cartography

For an artist, one of the most alluring characteristics of digital media is that information is abstracted from its representation; the same data can be presented in a number of ways, as text, as a graphic image, or as a sound, for example. One of the most common and intuitive ways to navigate digital information is in a virtual 3D world, drawing on conventions that have been developed by the video game industry over the past few decades. Virtual worlds may be constructed to behave in ways that mirror our experience in the physical world, as when programming objects to get smaller and sounds to get quieter as they get farther away. This flexibility of representation is evident in the recent surge of interest in virtual reality technologies in which the same digital structures can be navigated via a different interface, replacing a mouse and keyboard or joystick with a motion sensing, strap-on visor.

A realization that these natural properties of the physical world are constructed phenomena in digital worlds may lead us to consider the many intriguing alternatives: what if objects don't get smaller as they get farther away? (In fact, in the fairly common perspective of an isometric video game, they do not.) Given that data and representation are decoupled in a digital system, how could sonic information be represented as images, or temperature information represented in sound? This is not unlike how, in an infrared image, temperature is mapped onto the range of visual light, showing cooler areas as blue or green, hotter areas as yellow or red. These kinds of questions are at the core of the practices of data visualization and data sonification.

The Tidmarsh project at MIT grew out of an earlier investigation into using sensors to build a multidimensional representation of a space known as the DoppelLab project. I contributed to this project myself as a visiting artist at the Media Lab in 2012, looking at ways to represent information captured from sensors positioned around the Media Lab building, in particular thinking about how certain types of information could be more readily apprehended by hearing than seeing (my thinking on this topic has been influenced by Princeton professor Perry Cook's 2002 book *Real Sound Synthesis for Interactive Applications*). For example, the density of a rhythmic pattern could be linked to the amount of activity happening in a certain area, or the brightness of a sound's timbre could be linked to humidity, while overall pitch could be linked to temperature.

The idea of 'mapping' is a core concept in digital art, and the way the term is used is really not so different from how it might be employed in the field of cartography. In rendering on paper the curve of a river or the boundary between boroughs, the scaled-down proportions may be replicated exactly, but often some creative reworking will transpire, showing the more interesting areas as being larger on a tourist map, for example, or flattening a globe into two dimensions. When we use colours to represent altitude, we are setting up an arbitrary correlation between two different parameters; these are not the actual colours of the mountains, but another axis of information represented within a two-dimensional plane. These links may be intuitive, or we may need a legend to decipher them. A sheet of paper conveys some information about a place, but it is not the place. Whether considering a conventional roadmap or a sonified weather system, the goal of the mapping process is the same: to simplify, clarify, or condense some collected or observed information.

The Networked Landscape

In the above examples, information is captured at various spatial intervals and then represented virtually in a proportional way, with the added digital benefits of being able to scale and rotate the representation, not to mention the ability to teleport instantaneously to another location. However more challenging data sets may not be organized as a function of three-dimensional space, which makes them more difficult to observe or conceptualize. Manuel Lima provides a range of examples in his book *Visual Complexity: Mapping Patterns of Information* (2011), showing how creative visual representation, i.e. data visualization as a creative medium, can provide insights onto complex sets of data; indeed, navigating large data sets and extracting meaningful analysis is one of the major challenges of the twenty-first century. Trends in the technology sector mirror this observation; a colleague of mine at Berklee College of Music leads a group of students to visit start-ups in the Silicon Valley every year, and he came back from the most recent trip declaring that what investors were looking for more than anything else in evaluating potential start-ups to fund was an exclusive data repository.

Examples of these types of non-spatial networks include relationships between people, such as a Facebook user's network of friends, resulting in a different kind of social landscape. While friends may be tagged with geographic information, location is not as important as the interpersonal links that allow a person to evaluate a friend request based on mutual friends. The same way of thinking has been used to map networks of terrorist cells, as Lima observes in his book. In the food industry, it is easy to think of a number of overlapping data sets, such as user reviews on a site such as Yelp, the pick-up and delivery logs of a shipping company, or a record of an individual's food purchases. Increasingly, people are volunteering personal information about themselves by virtually checking in to establishments or posting photos online, often with GPS information embedded. In this case, people use their phones as sensors, capturing and uploading information about their activities and their environments, and especially in situations where these overlapping data sets can be correlated (e.g. a person's Facebook profile and Yelp account), the amount of information that can be gleaned is vast. Networks that expose these correlations between different data sets recall the way in which combined forces such as climate, soil type, topography, continentality, hydrology, and other factors contribute to a vineyard's sense of *terroir*.

The philosophers Gilles Deleuze and Félix Guattari, in their book *A Thousand Plateaus* (1987), have put forward an appropriately botanical metaphor for these types of structures: a rhizome. Unlike the traditional tree of knowledge metaphor that embodies information in a clearly hierarchical organization, the rhizome does not inherently prioritize information, representing instead a structure that can be variably navigated with multiple points of entry and encompassing many, perhaps virtually limitless, trajectories through data. This metaphor is ideal for networks and other nonlinear systems, and as such it is particularly appropriate to many of the structures we encounter in the early twenty-first century; it reflects for example the way we read a web page, not from beginning to end, but by navigating our way to the information we need. As with the sensor networks discussed above, a rhizomic structure is as much about the relationships as about individual bits of information, perhaps even more so; the structure itself conveys meaning.

Modelling Terroir

While a traditional medium such as painting is ideal for showing how something looks, a digital model is capable of showing us how it works, which is a fairly radical shift in how we think of representation in the arts. This form of digital representation could even be considered truer to the nature of the thing being represented than merely depicting its appearance. Moreover, once a model has been developed, it becomes possible to modify its parameters, to explore alternate scenarios, rendering it not merely an object for aesthetic contemplation, but a site of active interrogation. As an example, for decades a branch of computer music has been involved in developing digital physical models of acoustic musical instruments, which allows for experimentation with impossible hybrids: what does it mean to blow a piano, or to bow a trumpet? Similarly, once you have a model of the various parameters in a landscape, it becomes possible to see what happens when certain parameters change. Some researchers are already using models to study the impact of climate change on winegrowing, crunching the numbers to see what happens in various 'what if' scenarios.

Imaginary Landscapes and Virtual *Terroir*

The gathering of data, as with the kinds of sensor networks described above, can be a useful starting point for developing a model, and this approach has grown in prominence in recent years as computer scientists employ sophisticated neural networks to explore machine learning, harnessing a computer's capability to rapidly sort, categorize, and analyze vast amounts of data to find patterns that describe various phenomena. The resulting models allow us to make predictions and to try out alternate scenarios. These models can have a wide range of applications, everything from developing hypothetical employee training simulations to performing highly targeted systems optimization, even exploring the potential of computers to create autonomous artworks.

Mapping the Senses

These concepts apply not only to geographical landscapes, but also the landscape of our own bodies. A growing body of research in the field of psychology allows us to speak about the relationships between the senses in ways that are increasingly precise and quantifiable. Psychologist Charles Spence leads the Crossmodal Research Laboratory at Oxford University, where researchers have published voluminously on the nature of perception and the links between the senses, showing how taste, for example, happens in the brain, not on the tongue, and how listening to music that emphasizes different frequencies can alter the perception of taste. The sensing mechanisms of the human body are parallel, interdependent systems that affect each other in the central processing unit of the brain.

Harvard professor Beth Altringer's Flavor Genome Project uses artificial intelligence to navigate data sets of flavour and recommend unexpected combinations. As data from investigations such as these is catalogued with increasing resolution, we can develop a model for how our interconnected senses map onto the world around us, allowing for the design of experiences to heighten awareness, focus, and perception.

'Imaginary Landscapes'

John Cage was a composer who had an incalculable influence on artistic discourse in the twentieth century, and among his many contributions was to introduce the notion of indeterminacy in the development and execution of an artwork. (He was also an accomplished mycologist.) While half a century ago his performances may have come across as provocations, today we can recognize his work as providing a very practical precedent to the challenges of building real-time systems, such as interactive video games, in which indeterminacy is a defining characteristic. Much of his work consists of putting a frame around a haphazardly observed phenomenon and upholding it as an object for contemplation, and we find echoes of this gesture in the way in which gustatory experiences are being considered beyond their purely hedonic potential.

Cage used the term 'imaginary landscape' to title a series of technologically mediated compositions, part of a body of work that has turned out to have a surprising relevance to a broad range of twenty-first century practices, from video game development to data visualization, interactive installation art to virtual reality. In the words of Cage, 'It's not a physical landscape. It's a term reserved for the new technologies. It's a landscape in the future. It's as though you used technology to take you off the ground and go like Alice through the looking glass' (Cage 1961).

This 'through the looking glass' allusion is a good metaphor for the ways in which this expanded concept of landscape can upend our customary views of the environment. With the ability to compress, extrapolate, and translate digital information, these imaginary landscapes exist, and they are all around us. The scale of processing and ubiquity of sensing devices, together with the sophisticated networked structures that link them, offer digital tools that give us new ways to perceive and understand them.

The Sonic Landscape of Food

As I mentioned previously, I consider these food opera events to represent a fertile soil for new kinds of expression, as I work with chefs, musicians, designers, and others to reimagine the communicative potential of a meal. I have presented a more general overview of this project in a number of other publications; here I would like to highlight the projects that engage most directly with the notion of landscape.

I consider several of my past projects to engage with a form of critical media practice known as sensory ethnography. In the words of sound artist Ernst Karel, former Visiting Lecturer on Anthropology at Harvard University and manager of Harvard's Sensory Ethnography Lab, sensory ethnography refers to a 'practice of making nonfiction work':

> sensory ethnography is based on the understanding that human meaning does not emerge only from language; it engages with the ways in which our sensory experience is pre- or non-linguistic, and part of our bodily being in the world. It takes advantage of the fact that our cognitive awareness – conscious as well as unconscious – consists of multiple strands of signification, woven of shifting fragments of imagery, sensation, and malleable memory. Works of sensory media are capable of echoing or reflecting or embodying these kinds of multiple simultaneous strands of signification. (Wright 2013)

In my work these strands have included olfactory and gustatory elements in addition to the audiovisual strands to which Karel refers, which range from pure music to field recordings of farms and interviews with farmers, plus visual and graphic design elements such as physical notecards, iPad displays, and various custom-built vessels and speaker apparatuses.

Sensing Terroir: A Harvest Food Opera (2012)

Sensing Terroir was my second collaboration with chef Jason Bond and the first to take place at his Cambridge, MA, restaurant Bondir, following our first event at the Harvard University Graduate School of Design. This project further developed the notion of pairing food with instrumental music to explore sensory perception, while at the same time it introduced a new, ethnographic element. Jason Bond is committed to supporting local farmers and sustainable food practices, and this event, timed to coincide roughly with the American Thanksgiving holiday, had as one of its prime objectives the idea of honouring the many, often invisible hands that are involved in bringing food from the fields to the plates in a restaurant. I visited several of the farms that provide ingredients for Bondir and recorded the ambient sounds of the environment, in addition to conducting interviews with the farmers, and I played these sounds back, incorporated into the music I wrote for each dish. By bringing the sounds of the farm to the restaurant table, we digitally compressed space and time to provide a new way of understanding the complex system of dependencies that conveys raw ingredients to a restaurant. This concept was later expanded in a subsequent work, *Beside the White Chickens: A Summer Food Opera* (2013) that featured Bondir's poultry providers Pete and Jen's Backyard Birds.

Santa Croce Food Opera (2016)
Some of my food opera projects have had gestation periods of well over a year, so it was refreshing to develop one in less than a week as part of the First Crossmodalist Symposium, held in a former convent outside the town of Batignano in Tuscany in late July 2016. Over the course of a few days, I made recordings of the sounds of the environment, the bells that called people to table, music being rehearsed on the piano, and the ambient sounds of the countryside, in this case compressing time more than space, so that the closing meal, a group effort led by chef Charles Michel, was a retrospective of the week's conversations and experiences and a snapshot of this special time together.

Workshop with Mugaritz and La Fura dels Baus (2017)
The original point of departure for my food opera project was the notion that real-time music deployment techniques from the world of video games could be used to synchronize music with a meal. The first few events accomplished this effectively, but still rather coarsely, as they depended on my observing the activity in the dining room to prod the music forward in my software. So in more recent projects I've been looking at how to increase the input from diners directly into the music system using sensors. In the summer of 2017 I participated in a workshop in Badalona (just north of Barcelona) with members of the R&D team at acclaimed San Sebastián restaurant Mugaritz and members of the Catalan theatre group La Fura dels Baus, who organize a summer theatre workshop for students. The Mugaritz team shared some of their concepts and techniques, and I presented a variety of wireless sensors that could be affixed to commonplace dining implements, such as silverware, allowing us to track and sonify diners' gestures. I also worked with designer Jutta Friedrichs to develop a smart chalice that plays sound and lights up when liquid touches a diner's lips.

These events incorporate techniques from the world of video game development to create real-time sonic environments that respond to the behaviour of diners; they can be thought of as a video game with a restaurant as an interface, as music is mapped onto and articulates the emergent rhythms of the dining room. Just as in the MIT Tidmarsh project above, these experiments show how sensors can make us more aware of activity that is already happening all around us, to see what we can learn not only about the individual responses of diners to a meal, but also from analyzing the aggregated activity of a busy dining room, allowing the gestures inherent in eating to drive the soundtrack to the meal. I am still working with Mugaritz, continuing a discussion that goes back to 2015, and we plan to unveil a new collaboration that incorporates some of these concepts in 2018.

Ploughman's Lunch: An Aural Reconsideration (2017)

For the 2017 Oxford Symposium on Food and Cookery, I collaborated with David Matchett, Market Development Manager of London's Borough Market, to present a reconsidered version of the ploughman's lunch to symposiasts. David proposed the idea of using the meal to encourage diners to consider the legal status of a protected designation of origin or protected geographic indication as it impacts England's food producers, especially in light of how these protections may change as Britain leaves the European Union. The meal was comprised of ingredients from Borough Market traders, and, as in some of my earlier events, I sought to use sound to compress space and bring the Market to Oxford. I developed a real-time soundscape that was played back on eight speakers surrounding the roughly 250 diners, which was built from recordings I made from around the Market, including the cries of vendors announcing fresh produce, characteristic sounds such as the passing trains, the ambient sounds of this lively atmosphere, along with interviews with some of the traders discussing protected food designations and the ways in which food products can evoke an environment. In addition, I developed a web application that allowed diners to contribute to the soundscape using their mobile devices to play the intermittent cries of vendors from the Market.

Summary: Fostering Community through Interdisciplinary Research and Practice

The overriding impetus behind all of my creative work is to forge new connections, whether between people, practices, cultures, disciplines, or ideas. Technology can provide new perspectives on historical data and traditional practices, even as the technology itself inexorably becomes part of that tradition. I am not interested in bringing technology into the restaurant simply for its own sake, but because I believe it can facilitate new forms of expression and modes of awareness.

In my food opera projects, I have observed that positioning speakers throughout the dining area fosters a sense of connectedness among diners. I believe that this is because people become dependent on the presence of others to complete their own experience, with a growing sense of how their actions affect those around them. In the course of one of these events, a new kind of network emerges between participants. I seek to apply my research towards the goal of nurturing a landscape of interconnected people, attuned to their environment and engaged in empathy towards their fellow humans.

References

Altringer, Beth. 2017. 'The Flavor Genome Project' <https://www.flavorgenomeproject.com/> [accessed 2 April 2018].
Cage, John. 1961. *Silence* (Hanover, NH: Wesleyan University Press).
Cook, Perry R. 2002. *Real Sound Synthesis for Interactive Applications* (Natick, MA: A.K. Peters).
Deleuze, Gilles, and Félix Guattari. 1987. *A Thousand Plateaus* (Minneapolis: University of Minnesota Press).
Houge, Ben. 2014. 'Food Opera: Transforming the Restaurant Soundscape', in Raquel Castro and Miguel Carvalhais (eds.), *Proceedings: Invisible Places, Sounding Cities* (Viseu, Portugal: Jardins Efémeros) <http://invisibleplaces.org/2014/pdf/ip2014-houge.pdf>.
Lima, Manuel. 2011. *Visual Complexity: Mapping Patterns of Information* (New York: Princeton Architectural Press).
Mayton, Brian and others. 2017. 'The Networked Sensory Landscape: Capturing and Experiencing Ecological Change Across Scales', *Presence*, 26.2 (1 May 2017): 182-209, < https://doi.org/10.1162/PRES_a_00292>.
Roads, Curtis. 1996. *The Computer Music Tutorial* (Cambridge: MIT Press).
Robinson, Jancis (ed.). 2015. *The Oxford Companion to Wine*, 4th ed. (Oxford: Oxford University Press).
Spence, Charles, and Betina Piqueras-Fiszman. 2014. *The Perfect Meal: The Multisensory Science of Food and Dining* (Oxford: Wiley Blackwell).
'Tidmarsh Living Observatory', *MIT Media Lab* <https://tidmarsh.media.mit.edu/> [accessed 2 April 2018].
Tissot, Cyril and others. 2014. 'Modeling of Vine Agronomic Practices in the Context of Climate Change', *BIO Web of Conferences* 3 <https://doi.org/10.1051/bioconf/20140301015>.
Wright, Peter Mark. 2013. 'Ernst Karel', *Ear Room*, 14 February 2013 <https://earroom.wordpress.com/2013/02/14/ernst-karel/> [accessed 2 April 2018].

From Kaluga to *Chak-Chak*: Eating Locally along the Trans-Siberian Tracks

Sharon Hudgins

The Trans-Siberian Railroad crosses some of the most diverse landscapes on Earth: the lush green forests of the Russian Far East, where subtropical plants mingle with subarctic flora; the bogs of Transbaikalia and the mountains of Buryatia; the rocky southern coast of Lake Baikal, a region home to 2500 species of plants and animals; the Siberian *taiga*, Russia's great boreal forest of coniferous trees; long stretches of birch forest famous in Russian literature; the grassy steppes of the West Siberian Plain and the fertile farmlands of the East European Plain. During much of the railway's 125-year history, most of the foods eaten by passengers came from the local or regional landscapes along each part of the 10,000-kilometre route – especially the foods served in station buffets and sold by platform vendors. But the railway also made it easier to transport foods over long distances, increasingly competing with local products. And globalization is now changing the 'landscape of eating' on the Trans-Siberian Railroad, oftentimes supplanting the local with the national or the international.

Introduction

Since its completion in 1916, the Trans-Siberian Railroad has remained the world's longest continuous passenger railway within one country. Linking two continents, Europe and Asia, Russia's legendary railway line crosses nearly 10,000 kilometres through seven time zones between Moscow, the capital, and Vladivostok, Russia's primary port on the Pacific Ocean. Along the way, the Trans-Siberian tracks traverse some of the most diverse landscapes on Earth: from forests to steppes, from mountains to the seacoast (Figure 1).

Figure 1. Commemorative postage stamp issued in 2002 for the centennial (in 2003) of the completion of the major portion of the Trans-Siberian route in 1903.

Each of these different landscapes has provided food for passengers on the Trans-Siberian route. Whether people were traveling long-distance across two

Eating Locally along the Trans-Siberian Tracks

continents or riding the train overnight to the next village, having food to eat on the journey has always been a primary concern. During the twenty-five years of the railroad's construction, from 1891 to 1916, a journey from Moscow to Vladivostok took at least two weeks, often much longer. Part of the trip east of Lake Baikal had to be made by boat and horse-drawn carriage, or by sleigh over packed snow and the 'ice roads' of Siberia's frozen rivers in winter, or through northern China on another line. Even today, travelling across Russia on a Trans-Siberian express train takes six to seven days.

A journey through Russia on the Tran-Siberian Railroad has often been described as 'the trip of a lifetime', literally or figuratively. For thousands of settlers in the nineteenth and early twentieth centuries, the Trans-Siberian was the route to a new life and better opportunities in the open lands of Asian Russia. For countless others, it has been a railway to exile, prison, or worse. But for most passengers, the Trans-Siberian has been, and still is, merely the most convenient, least expensive, and sometimes only way to travel by land from one place to another across the vast distances and varied terrains of Russia.[1]

Although the Trans-Siberian Railroad is associated in many people's minds with Siberia itself, it actually crosses the Eurasian landmass in an east-west direction between its northernmost point, latitude 58° N (northeast of Moscow, in European Russia) and its southernmost point, latitude 43° N (Vladivostok, in the Russian Far East). The mainline consists of 1777 kilometres of track on the European side of the Ural Mountains, the Russian boundary between Europe and Asia, and 7512 kilometres of track on the Asian side, in Siberia, a geographical area that constitutes 75 per cent of Russia's landmass.[2]

In the early years of the railroad, many thousands of passengers rode the Trans-Siberian from the European side of Russia to the Asian side: settlers, soldiers, businessmen, prisoners, exiles, and foreign travellers. Those who remained in Siberia, by choice or by law, lived mainly in the relatively narrow zone of arable land and more hospitable climate on either side of the railway tracks, in small villages, larger towns, and eventually major cities. Today, 75 per cent of Siberia's population lives along, or in close proximity to, the Trans-Siberian route.

The Europeans who settled in Siberia – Russians, Ukrainians, Belorussians, Germans, Poles, and Balts – all brought their food preferences with them. Many also brought their knowledge of crop cultivation, animal husbandry, foraging, hunting, fishing, food preservation, and the preparation of particular dishes. They also encountered the native peoples already living in Siberia, as well as ethnic Chinese, Koreans, and Japanese living in the lands that ultimately became known as Russia's Far East. For a number of reasons, however, 95 per cent of the people living in Siberia today are of European ancestry.

This dominance of Europeans or European descendants living near the Trans-Siberian tracks on both sides of the Ural Mountains, along with the characteristics of climate and terrain, greatly influenced the foods available to passengers on Trans-Siberian trains, although more so in the past than in the present. Local food producers in or near villages and towns supplied most or all of the ingredients for dishes served in railway station restaurants ('buffets') and sold by station platform vendors to passengers

Food and Landscape

on the trains. And although the trains carried some of the food supplies for their dining cars, they also purchased supplies locally along the 10,000-kilometre route.

The Trans-Siberian Landscape

For more than a century, travellers have commented on both the length of a Trans-Siberian rail journey and the 'monotony' of the landscape. Viewed from a train window, the landscape can, in some places, seem endlessly flat (especially in European Russia); at other places it seems claustrophobically dense with birch and evergreen forests. But a trip across the entire route of the Trans-Siberian Railroad brings into view a widely varied landscape, with many microclimates, that has also determined much of the foods available to railway passengers ever since the line was built.[3]

Figure 2. *Fishing in one of the many rivers of the West Siberian Plain* (©2006 Sharon Hudgins).

Traveling eastward from Moscow, the train traverses part of the huge East European Plain, with its continental climate and fertile *chernozem* ('black earth') agricultural region, known for large crops of wheat, buckwheat, barley, oats, millet, rye, peas, potatoes, and sugar beets, as well as for animal husbandry (cattle and sheep). The train also crosses the Volga River, the first of the great rivers on its route, all of which are important sources of fish.

As the train nears the Ural Mountains, forests begin to replace the steppes, and the low mountains are covered with pine, fir, spruce, larch, birch, linden, and oak. Between the Urals and the Yenisei River, the route traverses the West Siberian Plain, an extensive flatland of fertile steppe punctuated with small copses of birch, aspen, ash, and willow. The crops and climate are similar to that of the East European Plain, although with less rainfall. Gardeners grow apples, cucumbers, turnips, carrots, beets, cabbages, onions, and melons (in the south), as well as tending ducks, geese, pigs, and honeybees. Cattle, sheep, and goats are raised in this region. Game birds include capercaillie and quail; rivers and lakes provide sturgeon, sterlet, salmon, pike, perch, bream, and carp (Figure 2).

The train continues into Eastern Siberia, through the *taiga*, the great

Figure 3. *The dense* taiga *of the Eastern Siberia, source of many edible 'gifts of the forest', including pine nuts, mushrooms, and berries* (©2006 Sharon Hudgins).

Eating Locally along the Trans-Siberian Tracks

Figure 4. *The Selenga River and its tributaries flow through the mountains and steppes of the Transbaikal region (©2006 Sharon Hudgins).*

boreal forest of pine, spruce, larch, and fir. As in Western Siberia, rye, wheat, oats, barley, and millet are grown in arable areas; cattle, pigs, and goats are raised; and honey and pine nuts are abundant. Salt from local mines is used for preserving fish, game birds, and mammal meats. And Lake Baikal – the world's oldest, largest, and deepest lake – is famous for its *omul'*, a whitefish of the salmon family (Figure 3).

The Transbaikal territory, east of the lake, is a varied landscape of high, snow-capped mountains, grassy steppes, and thick forests that include juniper, Asian hazel, wild apple, wild apricot, and pine, all of which provide edible 'gifts of the forest'. Wheat is the primary grain crop, and vegetables flourish in this region. Cattle-breeding is important, and other meat comes from deer, elk, horses, sheep, goats, and pigs. Lakes and large rivers are the source of Siberian stone loach, salmon, and salmon trout (Figure 4).

Farther east, the Trans-Siberian route runs nearly parallel to the Amur River that forms Russia's border with China. The landscape ranges from grassy steppes to mountain ranges covered with larch, birch, ash, oak, elm, and Siberian 'cedar' (pine). Orchids, wild iris, and tiger lilies grow in profusion in the swampy lowlands. Birch, poplar, dwarf oak, Asian hazel, Siberian apple, hawthorn, linden, and acacia trees line the banks of rivers that are home to dozens of species of fish, including kaluga sturgeon, taimen, salmon, pike, trout, and carp. Wheat, barley, millet, maize, and buckwheat are cultivated, as are potatoes, cabbages, cucumbers, and onions; blackberry, currant, wild grape, and wild apple provide edible fruits (Figure 5).

The final 650 kilometres of the route to Vladivostok run through the southernmost part of the Russian Far East, whose dense, fertile forests boast an unusual variety of plants, unlike that in any other part of Russia. Subtropical vines curl around conifers, rowan trees grow next to lianas, cork trees tower over hot-pink orchids. Summer and early autumn are the seasons for many of the wild foods foraged by the locals: cherries, grapes, cranberries, and cloudberries; apples, apricots, plums and pears; fiddlehead ferns, horseradish, garlic, sorrel, and mushrooms; Manchurian walnuts and

Figure 5. *Potato patch behind a rural house along the Trans-Siberian route (©2006 Sharon Hudgins).*

Food and Landscape

Siberian filberts. Wild game includes deer, ducks, pheasants, quail, woodcocks, and hazel grouse; rivers run with salmon, and the sea provides herring, cod, king crab, sea cucumbers, and sea cabbage (Figure 6).

Eating Locally along the Tracks

The tradition of 'eating locavore' along the Trans-Siberian tracks extends from the railway's beginning to the present. Depending on the time period – Tsarist, Soviet, post-Soviet – food service in the

Figure 6. Vegetable garden in the lush Primorye region near the eastern terminus of the Trans-Siberian route (©2006 Sharon Hudgins).

dining cars and railroad station restaurants has been provided by the government or by concessionaires and franchisees. Dishes served at the early station buffets reflected the regional food products because those were more easily and cheaply available. And from the start, freelance vendors on the station platforms have also sold a range of local and regional foods to passengers all along the route.

During the initial phase of construction in the 1890s, when several sections of the tracks were not yet connected, there was passenger service on only some parts of the line and no dining cars on the trains. Travellers brought their own food in picnic baskets, or ate at the station buffets, or bought homegrown, home-prepared foods from vendors on the station platforms. When the Trans-Siberian section between Krasnoyarsk and Irkutsk opened to passenger trains in August 1898, Englishman Arnot Reid reported that '[e]xcellent refreshment rooms and buffets are placed at convenient intervals, while for the poorer passengers the country people have been

Figure 7. Platform vendors with samovars selling tea and fish along the Trans-Siberian route in 1901 (E. Burton Holmes).[5]

allowed to establish stalls beside the stations, where coarse black bread, meat, cooked chickens, and other such provisions are sold at cheap rates' (Figure 7).[4]

Traveling in the 1890s, Englishman Robert L. Jefferson vividly described one of those early railroad station buffets (Figure 8):

> Over on one side is a long bar, covered with smaller glasses and large bottles, mostly containing vodki [sic], as well as at least half a hundred dishes of the *hors d'oeuvre* style – sardines, bits of sausage, sprats, caviare [sic], sliced cucumber,

Eating Locally along the Trans-Siberian Tracks

Figure 8. *A Russian railroad station restaurant in 1901 (E. Burton Holmes).*

pickled mushrooms, artful dabs of cheese, raw radishes, smoked herring, and such like [... and] a kitchen-like arrangement in the corner where steams a heterogeneous mass of cutlets and 'Russian' beef-steaks. [...] Vodki is the lodestone of the arrived passengers. Each man gulps down a small glass of the fiery fluid, seizes a piece of fish, or sausage, or cheese, or whatever he may fancy or may be handy, and subsides to the big table, chewing vigorously. Energetic waiters pounce upon him, lay before him a big plate of the universal "stche", or cabbage soup, over which our Russian hangs his head and commences ladling away, apparently oblivious to its boiling heat or the feelings of people around him. The tables fill up. Great slabs of brown meat, floating in fat, are distributed with rapidity, and which with equal rapidity are demolished.[6]

John W. Bookwalter, an American industrialist who travelled through part of Siberia in 1898, noted that at station restaurants, 'You can get soup, as fine a beefsteak as you ever ate, a splendid roast chicken whole, cooked in Russian style, most toothsome and juicy, potatoes and other vegetables, a bottle of beer, splendid and brewed in this country.'[7] Referencing early travel on the train, the American writer Harmon Tupper also noted:

> Besides such eating places, there were rough board counters on station platforms where, in normal times, local women sold black bread, eggs, cooked chickens and game, meat pies, fried fish, milk, and kvass [a slightly alcoholic drink usually brewed from rye bread]… [While the] relatively affluent passengers crowded into restaurant or buffet, hoi polloi from third-class cars swept like a voracious Mongol horde upon the outdoor vendors, then rushed to the hot-water tap on every platform to fill kettles for tea-drinking on the train.[8]

In the summer of 1900 Reverend Francis E. Clark travelled from Vladivostok to Moscow by rail and river, a journey that took 38 days. His first meal on the train, in the Russian Far East – and in one of the earliest Trans-Siberian dining cars – included 'toothsome delicacies dear to the Russian heart, like caviare [*sic*], sardines, and other little fishes. [...] At the long table *table d'hôte* meals are served, consisting of three or four courses [...]. To be sure, one must get used to the greasy Siberian soup and to the chunks of tough stewed meat, which may be beef, mutton, or pork, one is never certain which'.[9] He also described the local vendors in European Russia, as the train neared Moscow: 'Peasant women stood on every platform with heaps of little wild strawberries…Others had the first red cherries of the season, and others yellow apples that had been kept in water for nearly a year and tasted as if baked' (Figure 9).¹⁰

In 1900 passenger service began on a continuous route between Moscow and Irkutsk, the capital of Eastern Siberia, approximately the halfway point on the line. To promote the Moscow-Beijing route that was being constructed as a branch of the main Trans-Siberian line east of Irkutsk, four luxury train carriages were displayed in a pavilion at the Universal Exposition in Paris in 1900, including two dining cars where visitors to the pavilion could eat. To create the illusion of a moving railway journey across Russia to China, a large, scrolling, painted-canvas panorama of the landscapes and landmarks along the route was installed outside the dining cars' windows. As the canvas panorama scrolled from Russian landscapes to Chinese, separate sections of cut-out figures and other scenery also moved at different speeds on rails in the foreground. The spectacle gave visitors inside the carriages the illusion that the train was rolling across the steppes of Russia, past towns with log houses and onion-dome churches, through forests and mountains, over mighty rivers, and finally into the exotic land of China. Diners in the restaurant cars could sip wine and enjoy a meal while imagining making that real journey themselves in the future (Figure 10).¹¹

Figure 9. Platform vendors selling plates of food to passengers along the Trans-Siberian route in 1900 (E. Burton Holmes).

Around 1900, upscale express trains began operating on the new Trans-Siberian line, in addition to the regular, slower, and less expensive local and long-distance trains on the route. An American who crossed Siberia several times by express train was favourably impressed: 'The food in the dining car was superb – an abundance of game, unlimited caviar which came from Lake Baikal en route, thick Siberian cream, rich sauces, brandy, good cigars.'¹²

In 1901, E. Burton Holmes, an American travel writer who also rode the early Russian express trains, wrote that the dining car was 'a stuffy little affair' where the meals were 'badly served, but surprisingly well-cooked and appetizing: good bread,

Figure 10: Poster advertising the Trans-Siberian Railroad exhibit at the Universal Exposition in Paris in 1900 (reproduced by permission of the Digital Magazine of Railway History, Design, and Photography).

Eating Locally along the Trans-Siberian Tracks

Figure 11. Passengers eating foods sold by vendors at a Trans-Siberian stop, 1901 (E. Burton Holmes).

excellent veal, and hearty soups, sometimes *frappés* with a clinking cake of ice floating on their chill depths, sometimes seething hot, with a hunk of steaming beef rising from them like a volcanic island'.[13] But another American traveller in the early 1900s complained about a station buffet meal at Chita, in southeastern Siberia: 'We reach Chita at 2 p.m., and have a wretched luncheon at the buffet, bad soup and steak that never was part of any beef. I think it was dog.'[14]

Foreign travellers were more likely than Russians to eat in the station restaurants and dining cars because foreigners usually had more money. Many Russians preferred their own foods brought from home or purchased from platform vendors. Foods sold by local vendors were freshly prepared, much less costly, and even offered more variety, depending on the wayside stop. Traveling on the Trans-Siberian Railroad in 1901, Scotsman John Foster Fraser noted that locals did a good business on the platforms selling 'cooked fowls, hot or cold [...] very hot dumplings with hashed meat and seasonings inside [...] huge loaves of new made bread, bottles of beer, pats of excellent butter, pails of milk, apples and grapes and fifty other things. Passengers loaded themselves with provender at the stall, and ate picnic fashion in the carriages until the next station was reached. There it began all over again' (Figure 11).[15]

After traveling third-class by train from Moscow in 1910, journalists Richard L. Wright and Basset Digby wrote:

> Our train did not boast a diner, but food you could buy at the buffets or at the row of booths in which the peasant women congregate [...]. The food at the booths was good and cheap – newly baked, fragrant rye bread [...] baked fish tarts, each as big as a plate [...] containing four small trout; whole roasted chickens [...] nearly a quarter of a roasted goose, tender and well-cooked [...] big jam turnovers [...]. Small wonder that the train to Siberia was one great picnic party during our waking hours![16]

World War I, the Bolshevik Revolution in 1917, and the Russian civil war that followed greatly affected railway services in Russia, including the foods served along the tracks. Traffic volume on the Russian railway system did not reach its pre-war level again until 1928.[17] But the days of upscale travel on the Trans-Siberian Railroad were long gone. During the Soviet era, from 1922 to 1991, railroad dining cars and station restaurants declined in quality. Especially in the first two decades of the new Soviet Union, the government focused more on the military and industrial uses of the railroad at the expense of passenger service, including food service.

Crossing Siberia by train in 1926, Junius B. Wood, European correspondent for the *Chicago Daily News*, wrote about the dining car food:

> At 3:30 a plate of soup appeared – greasy hot water poured over cold pieces of fish which had been cooked earlier in bulk. The next course was pre-cooked cauliflower warmed with a sauce of unknown texture. Roast veal, cooked weeks earlier and now dry and hard, smothered in warm brown gravy, without vegetables, was the main course. A compote of fruit completed the hurried meal.[18]

During this period, travellers continued the practice of buying food from private vendors on the station platforms. Sven Hedin, a Swede who crossed China and Russia by train in the early 1920s, noted:

> Buffets had been set up on the platforms of all the major stations, booths that were either open or covered with sackcloth or a few planks of wood. Farmers, both women and men, warmly wrapped up in furs, sold very fatty milk in bottles, cheese, butter, fresh bread, roasted duck, goose and partridge, eggs, and other assorted victuals. Several of the fellow travelers in my coach preferred the goods on offer at these booths to those available in the dining car.[19]

And in 1930, Englishman Malcolm Burr also favourably described the station vendors along the route:

> The station markets were allotted a substantial area on the platforms, arranged in crescent-shaped buildings open at the front; behind the counter were peasants selling their goods classified in groups; at one end large stacks of bread, black, brown and white, *kolachi* or rolls and great loaves in abundance and variety and all excellent; another group would be selling bottles carefully labeled "boiled milk" [...] at another, honey in homemade [wood or birch-bark] jugs [...]. Another again would have smoked sterlet, perch, pike and ide or burbot [...] also keta, the dog salmon of the Pacific, which makes such handsome big pink caviar; then there were great cauldrons simmering over wood fires with cutlets, tongues, whole chickens and ducks and game, as hazel hens, hares, blackcock and capercaillie. At others there were eggs [...] and at others fruit as apples, bilberries and whortleberries and great watermelons, an excellent investment on a railway journey.[20]

In the mid-twentieth century. World War II greatly disrupted much of the civilian passenger rail service in the Soviet Union. After the war, and up to the collapse of the Soviet Union in 1991, dining cars on most Soviet trains continued to have a bad reputation. Few people chose to eat in them because the food was usually poor, the staff surly, and the prices relatively high for the average Russian. Standard dining-car menus during the post-World War II period were up to ten pages long and offered a wide range of dishes – Russian appetizers, soups, main dishes, side dishes, and simple desserts – although usually only two or three of the listed dishes were actually available on the train. Meals commonly consisted of a piece of unspecified meat, often dubbed 'mystery meat' by the passengers, accompanied by potatoes or another starch (rice, pasta), maybe a sauerkraut salad, and perhaps canned peas. And the dining-car staff often ran a lucrative (and illegal) side business selling the trains' food supplies to locals at the stations where the trains stopped; hence, less food was left for serving in the dining cars.

As in the past, most travellers brought their own food to the train, or bought food from vendors at stops along the way. Traveling in the 1960s, Harmon Tupper wrote:

> Probably like their mothers, grandmothers, and great-grandmothers before them, kerchiefed peasant women stand behind board counters laden with bread, bottles of milk, roasted chickens, and such. Others walk past car windows with buckets of meat pies and plates of baked potatoes while small girls trail behind with pails of red currants or baskets of raspberries and wild strawberries in paper cones. Essentially, the scene at most wayside stops has changed very little from the descriptions by early rail travelers.[21]

When my husband and I travelled on Trans-Siberian trains in the mid-1990s, dining car fare was still very limited (and uninteresting). So we always carried food with us on those trips: cheese, bread, boiled eggs, smoked sausages, canned fish, packages of ramen noodles. At the end of each sleeping car was a big coal-fired water boiler, which the conductress used for making hot tea for the passengers, and which we tapped for hot water to rehydrate bowls of instant noodles in our cabin, as did many of our fellow travellers.

Like other passengers, we also bought food from vendors at the stations. Some stations had official kiosks where people were licensed to sell certain kinds of foods, such as alcohol and dairy products. At most stations there were also individual freelance sellers who cooked food at home and brought it to the station on sleds or in baby carriages (Figure 12). As our train rolled to a stop, the vendors quickly unpacked their wares and set up an instant outdoor buffet on the ground: hot *pirozhki* (little savoury pies filled with meat, potatoes, cabbage, or mushrooms); sauerkraut salads; pickled cucumbers and tomatoes; roasted potatoes and marinated mushrooms;

Figure 12. Platform vendor with homemade food brought to the station in a baby carriage, Trans-Siberian route, 1994 (©1994 Sharon Hudgins).

smoked or salted fish; fresh farmers' cheese and sour cream; fresh fruits and berries; jars of home-preserved jams; gingerbread cookies, sweet pastries, and yeast buns; salted sunflower seeds and Siberian pine nuts – all wrapped in newspapers or served in paper cones made from pages torn out of books and magazines.

Regional specialties were still featured by vendors at several points along the line: salmon caviar in the Russian Far East; Buriat-Mongolian fried savoury pies and meat-filled dumplings, steamed or boiled, in the Transbaikal area; smoked or salted *omul'* around Lake Baikal; *pel'meni*, boiled meat-filled dumplings in several parts of Siberia (Figure 13). And on later trips through Tatarstan, on the European side of the line, we ate regional Tatar foods: *chebureki*, half-moon-shaped, meat-filled, deep-fried pies, and *chak-chak*, small pieces of unleavened dough, deep fried, drenched with hot honey, and formed into balls, domes, pyramids, or other shapes. Buying foods from local vendors was a good way to sample regional specialties along the route, and regular travellers on the Trans-Siberian trains knew which private vendors had the best foods for sale at each station (Figure 14).

Figure 13. Fresh omul', a whitefish of the salmon family, endemic to Lake Baikal (©2007 Sharon Hudgins)

Between 2006 and 2008 I crossed Russia by train five times from Vladivostok to Moscow and noticed how much the food sold along the route had changed since my first trips in the 1990s. Major stations such as Vladivostok and Novosibirsk now housed attractive restaurants. Some of the larger stations also had little shops where travellers could buy anything from fancy boxes of candy to fresh breads and pastries, hamburgers and rotisserie chickens, sausages and cheeses. And most stations, even the small ones, had at least a kiosk or two where travellers could buy vodka, beer, cigarettes, and packaged snack foods.

The dining cars on Russian trains are now run as private franchises, instead of being operated entirely by the government as they were during much of the twentieth century – which also means that the foods vary widely depending on the rail line and the franchisee. Some dining cars sell no cooked food at all, just packaged foods and drinks. Others offer cooked food of varying quality. But it is still customary for many passengers to bring their own

Figure 14. Girl in Tatar costume with platter of chak-chak, pieces of fried dough drenched with honey, in Kazan along the Trans-Siberian route (2007 Sharon Hudgins).

Eating Locally along the Trans-Siberian Tracks

Figure 15. Vendor selling packaged foods on the platform of a Trans-Siberian station (©2009 Petar Milošević, reproduced by permission).

food for the journey, whether homemade or store-bought: cheese, sausages, ham, roasted chicken, canned fish, small savoury pies, boiled eggs, pickled cucumbers, bread, chocolate bars, cookies, fresh fruit, bottled fruit juices, and vodka.

The long tradition of platform vendors continues, too. Traveling from Beijing to Moscow at the turn of the twenty-first century, John Lee described the culinary scene on station platforms along the Russian segment of the route:

Chocolate, ice cream, and dark Russian beer are easy to find, but the best food comes from the droves of gnomish old babuskhas who descend on the train as it enters a station. Dressed in head scarves and thick woolen coats, most have red faces, bright blue eyes and strong, scarred hands. Many sell stews and boiled vegetables, cooked in their kitchen and warmed on their car engines for the trip to the station. Others walk the platforms with pale cheeses, curled brown sausages, smoked fish and leather-skinned rye breads. My favorite breakfast of the journey turns up in Omsk: a plastic bag of warm potatoes and onions drowned in butter and herbs.[22]

But after post-Soviet Russia started importing more foods from abroad, many vendors on station platforms began selling fewer home-cooked regional specialties and instead hawked more commercially processed products like Hungarian sausages, packaged German cakes and cookies, Chinese candies, and Korean 'Choco Pies' (Figure 15).

Another new development after the collapse of the Soviet Union in 1991 was that foreign investors were allowed to operate private charter trains on Russian territory,

Figure 16. One of the luxurious dining cars on the Golden Eagle Trans-Siberian Express (Golden Eagle Luxury Trains, reproduced by permission.).

reviving the standards (and nostalgia) of pre-Revolutionary luxury train travel with upscale dining. The most luxurious of those trains is the Golden Eagle Trans-Siberian Express, which has two elegantly decorated dining cars and a separate modern kitchen car with a food-service staff of twenty-one people. About 30 per cent of the food supplies for the twelve-day, cross-country trip are bought at the starting point of the tour (either Moscow or Vladivostok) and loaded into a special food-storage car equipped with large refrigerator and freezer compartments.

The rest of the food is supplied fresh along the way, some of it pre-ordered and delivered to the train at specific stops, other ingredients purchased at local markets by the chefs (Figure 16).[23]

The breakfast buffet is designed to appeal to Western tastes, while also showcasing Russian ingredients and dishes: a selection of ham, salami, and cheese; salmon caviar; fresh fruits and vegetables; hot and cold cereals; toast and jams; savoury and sweet pastries, baked daily; eggs cooked to order; yoghurt, fruit juices, kefir, coffee, and tea; and daily specials such as Russian *kasha* (porridge of buckwheat, millet, rice, or semolina), *bliny* (yeast-raised buckwheat pancakes) stuffed with *tvorog* (farmers' cheese), *ol'adiy* (smaller, thicker pancakes) with jam or sour cream, and *tvorozhniki* (curd cheese patties fried in butter) garnished with sour cream.

Lunch and dinner are three- or four-course meals. Traditional Russian appetizers, soups, and main dishes are often among the selections on the menu, accompanied by Russian vodka and good wines from abroad. When I travelled on this train in the mid-2000s, regional specialties were served in the dining car as the train rolled through various parts of Russia: Amur River sturgeon and Pacific salmon caviar while traveling through the Russian Far East and Siberian *pel'meni* dumplings in Eastern Siberia. And on the European portion of the tracks, one meal featured traditional Ukrainian specialties, even though the route doesn't go through Ukraine: an appetizer of *salo* (cured pork fat) with fresh hot red and green peppers, followed by Ukrainian *borshch* accompanied by *pampushki*, hot yeast buns topped with garlic, all washed down with spicy-hot *pertsovka* vodka – the same kinds of regional foods sold by vendors along train tracks in that former Soviet republic (Figure 17).

In conclusion, it is apparent that the many and varied landscapes along the Trans-Siberian tracks, as well as the culinary preferences of the Europeans who settled there, have, for much of the railway's history, been the prime determinant of the foods that passengers ate on the route. But the railroad has also made it easier to transport foods from distant regions, compared to the past when the lack of roads over often-difficult terrain meant that most foods were produced and consumed locally. And more recently – despite current economic sanctions against Russia, as well as Russian

Figure 17. Pel'meni dumplings, the "National Dish of Siberia," served in the dining car of the Golden Eagle Trans-Siberian Express (©2007 Sharon Hudgins).

restrictions on food imports from sanctioning countries – globalization has changed the 'landscape of eating' on the Trans-Siberian Railroad, oftentimes supplanting the local with the national or the international.

Notes

1. Some parts of this paper are adapted from Sharon Hudgins, 'From Caviar to Mystery Meat: Dining across Two Continents on the Trans-Siberian Railroad', in *Meals on the Move: Dining on the Legendary Railway Journeys of the World* (forthcoming from Reaktion Books, UK).
2. Historically, Siberia has been the general name for all of Asian Russia between the Ural Mountains and the Pacific Ocean, covering an area of 13.7 million kilometres and extending over eight of Russia's eleven time zones. This 'Greater Siberia' has three major geographic subdivisions: Western Siberia, Eastern Siberia, and the Russian Far East. In this paper I use the term 'Siberia' when referring to all of Asian Russia. When referring to specific geographic regions within Greater Siberia, I use the names commonly associated with those individual regions, such as Western Siberia, Urals, Transbaikal, Amur, Far East, etc.
3. A good source of information about the geography, plants, and animals at the turn of the twentieth century is *Guide to the Great Siberian Railway 1900*, ed. by A.I. Dmitriev-Mamonov and A.F. Zdziarski (St. Petersburg: Ministry of Ways of Communication, 1900).
4. Arnot Reid, *From Peking to Petersburg*, 2nd ed. (London: Edward Arnold, 1899), p. 194.
5. E. Burton Holmes, *The Burton Holmes Lectures, Vol. VIII* (1901), available at Michael Ward, Burton Holmes, Extraordinary Traveller, 2016 <www.burtonholmes.org> [accessed 18 May 2017].
6. Robert L. Jefferson, *Roughing It in Siberia: With Some Account of the Trans-Siberian Railway, and the Gold-Mining Industry of Asiatic Russia* (London: Sampson Low, Marston & Company, 1897), pp. 8-10.
7. John W. Bookwalter, 'A Ride on the Trans-Siberian Railroad in 1899', *Ainslee's Magazine,* May 1899 <http://www.digitalhistoryproject.com/search?q=siberian+railroad> [accessed 18 May 2017].
8. Harmon Tupper, *To the Great Ocean: Siberia and the Trans-Siberian Railway* (Boston: Little, Brown, 1965), pp. 262-63.
9. Rev. Francis E. Clark, *A New Way around an Old World* (New York: Harper & Brothers), p. 37.
10. Clark, p. 191.
11. Arjan den Boer, 'Panorama Sibérien', *retours*, November 2014 <http://retours.eu/en/22-panorama-transsiberien-expo-1900/#> [accessed 28 March 2015].
12. Qtd. in Tupper, pp. 354-55.
13. E. Burton Holmes, *The Burton Holmes Lectures: Vol. VIII* (New York: McClure, 1905), p. 246.
14. Michael Myers Shoemaker, *The Great Siberian Railway from St. Petersburg to Pekin* (New York: G. P. Putnam's Sons, 1903), p. 116.
15. John Foster Fraser, *The Real Siberia: Together with an Account of a Dash through Manchuria* (London: Cassell and Company, 1902), p. 28.
16. Richardson L. Wright and Bassett Digby, *Through Siberia: An Empire in the Making* (New York: McBride, Nast & Company, 1913), p. 3.
17. Russian Railways, 'The Company History', *Russian Railways* <http://eng.rzd.ru> [accessed 16 August 2014].
18. Qtd. in Tupper, p. 408.
19. Qtd. in Olaf and Anne Meinhardt, *The Trans-Siberian Railway, From Moscow to the Pacific Ocean* (Munich: C.J. Bucher Verlag, 2009), p. 100.
20. Malcolm Burr, *In Bolshevik Siberia: The Land of Ice and Exile*, excerpted in *The Trans-Siberian Railway: A Traveller's Anthology*, ed. by Deborah Manley (London: Century, 1988), pp. 183-84.
21. Tupper, p. 440.
22. John Lee, 'Beijing to Moscow: Six Days on the Trans-Siberian', *Russian Life*, 44.3 (2001), 38.
23. Author's telephone interview with Marina Linke, Golden Eagle Operations Manager, 27 April 2006.

Nice Day in the Driftless

Tom Hunter

Seven years ago, my wife and I bought a farm. I had retired from corporate life, but I was not putting myself out to pasture, to pick daisies or spend a lot of time in a hammock. It would not be the first time farming for my wife and me – we spent our first ten married years on my family farm in Illinois, raising corn, soy, beef cattle, and pigs, as well as three kids of our own. In the intervening years I had often vaguely imagined a return to farming. The development of the local, organic, specialty food market gave us an idea for an organic farm producing 100% grass-fed specialty meats from beef cattle and sheep. We found the ideal spot in southeastern Minnesota to bring this idea to reality. As we began our farming project, we also joined in a long and evolving story of the interaction between food production and the landscape around us. Our farm operation is shaped by the landscape we find ourselves in, but the landscape is also shaped by how we choose to farm. History is both a present force and clue to the future. Let's untangle these threads.

Stand with me in the middle of our farm, on top of a ridge, 2 April 2010, on the day we bought this farm. We can turn 360 degrees and see open farmland in the foreground and a tree line on the near horizon. The open land is fairly level to gently sloping, either side of a ridge that runs northwest to southeast. We have forty-eight hectares of open farmland; it has been producing corn (maize), oats, and alfalfa for a small dairy operation nearby. Beyond the farmland lies another forty-

Figure 1. Views of the near treeline and horizon from the ridgetop on our farm. Northeast horizon (top), Northwest horizon (middle), South horizon (bottom). Photos by Tom Hunter.

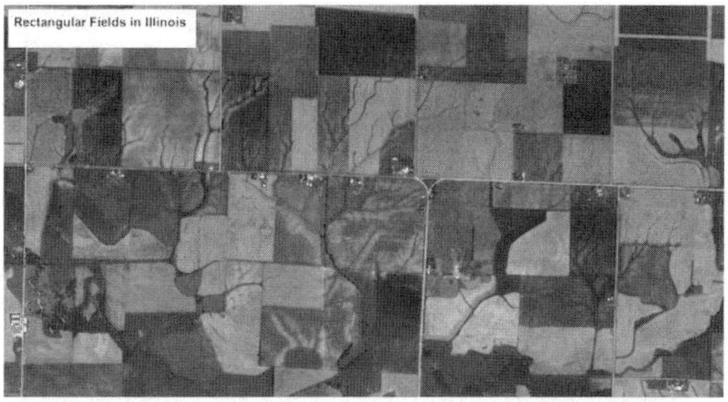

Nice Day in the Driftless

Figure 2a. Mostly rectangular fields in western Illinois, including the farm where I grew up. (Google Earth).

Figure 2b. Mostly rectangular fields in central Minnesota. (Google Earth).

eight hectares of much steeper slopes, heavily wooded. The slopes steepen abruptly and run down to narrow valleys. The woods are filled with oaks, elms, cedars, and black walnuts; the underbrush is so thick it's nearly impassable (Figure 1).

This farmland has a curious look to my eyes. My home farm in Illinois was made up of rolling prairie land cut into neat rectangular fields. An entire rectangle would be planted to corn or soybeans with a rare rectangular hayfield mixed in. Pastures were laid out along the small creeks and occasional steeper hillside. A farmer could be proud of planting those rectangular fields with arrow-straight rows (Figure 2).

But here, in our part of Minnesota, there are no square fields. Rather, the landscape is laid out in gently curving narrow strips maybe thirty metres wide. A strip of corn lies next to a strip of oats, and then a strip of alfalfa. As you walk from the peak of the ridge straight down the hillside towards the treeline, you cross from one strip to another every thirty metres or so. A farmer cannot plant straight rows; all the rows curve gently along the side of the hill, working across as the hills roll along (Figure 3).

On close inspection, the strips are not even consistently thirty metres wide. As the hills widen or narrow, and tuck into drainage ways or splay out over a gentle point, the strips flex accordingly, as required to keep the strips heading across the slope of the fields. Why would a farmer do this?

No doubt, these gentle, undulating curves give an undeniable beauty to the landscape. The roads and byways of southeast Minnesota curve and weave, climb and wend their way through the hills and valleys. As they go they reveal ever-changing vistas of these strip-cropped fields. But surely these farmers haven't complicated their ploughing and planting for the sake of regional aesthetics. What is the origin of this beautiful landscape? How and why did it come about, and where is it going? I want to use the perspective of this particular spot, on top of the ridge of our farm in southeast Minnesota, to unravel the story of this particular meandering landscape and to consider other landscape possibilities for this same spot.

Agricultural landscapes are a result of interactions between geology, agriculture, and the broader human culture. Geology sets the context for possible landscapes, both imposing limitations and creating possibilities. Human culture, through agricultural practices and the forces of economics, can work within those limitations to achieve various outcomes, some more successful and persistent than others. A widespread persistent landscape works within geological limits, exploits inherent possibilities, and relies on a food system that supports the farmers and food producers operating there. Let's start with the geological context.

Figure 3a. A typical landscape view in the Driftless Area of Minnesota. (Google Image capture).

Stand with me again on top of the ridge in the middle of our farm. It's a very different time; indeed, a different epoch. It's also the second of April, in the spring of the year, but there's an undeniable chill in the air.

Figure 3b. An aerial view of the Driftless Area including our farm. (Google Earth).

The ground is a bit muddy underfoot, with just a few blades of grass and odd patchy wildflowers trying to get started. There is no treeline in the middle distance – just muddy brown hillsides cascading down to bare valleys below. Everything seems raw and … new, like a newly scraped construction site. And, very oddly, there's a loud roar in the distance that seems powerful enough to shake the ground beneath our feet. But the sun is shining and a slight breeze feels pleasant despite the chill. It's a nice day. In fact, it's the first nice day in the previous 30,000 years.

Where we're standing, the date is 12,000 years before the present. The roar in the distance is the Mississippi River, just five kilometres away. But it's nothing like the meagre 'Mighty Mississippi' of today; it is the glacial Mississippi, running with perhaps one hundred times the present volume of water, draining the meltwater from the rapidly disappearing glaciers.[1] Just a few thousand years earlier, a layer of ice up to 1.6 kilometres thick covered the North American continent from the Arctic as far south as modern Saint Louis, Missouri, four hundred kilometres away. 30,000 years previous, the climate had cooled so much that ice began accumulating from endless snowfalls that never melted. This snow compressed into a vast sheet of ice that advanced from the north as a relentless tide across the continent. But eventually the climatic conditions changed, and the ice

Nice Day in the Driftless

began to retreat. After 30,000 years of really bad weather, we've finally got a nice day.

However, in an odd quirk of fate not completely understood by scientists today, the tide of ice split and left a large area uncovered. Over the millennia, the ice advanced and retreated, moved forward in one area while stagnating in another. Somehow, these fits and starts left 48,000 square kilometres of land in present day Wisconsin, Minnesota, Iowa, and Illinois uncovered. Certainly snow fell here as well; somehow it melted and ran off rather than becoming compressed into ice. The climate was brutal, cold, dry, and windy; the primeval forests and grasslands that had prevailed there before the glaciers advanced died out, not adapted to such extremes. The land was barren and uncovered for thousands of years.[2]

As the glaciers advanced through the millennia, they acted as bulldozers scraping the land surface, piling up soil, breaking up bedrock, grinding rock into sand and powder, and dumping these remains unceremoniously into mixed piles. As the glaciers melted and retreated, vast quantities of meltwater ran out of them, washing out this debris and leaving it in piles, fans, and sandbars. This mess left behind by the glaciers is called 'drift'. Glaciers utterly transformed the landscape of northern North America, leaving behind piles of drift and huge chunks of buried ice, to melt over thousands of years. This created the moraines and 'pothole lakes' of northern Minnesota and Wisconsin.[3]

But in the 48,000 square kilometres left untouched by the glaciers, there is no drift. There was no reshaping of the underlying bedrock. The shape of the landscape was left as it had been for hundreds of millions of years. Long after the glaciers had disappeared, the appearance of this area was so distinct from what surrounded it that it merited a name of its own, a name that denotes what is essentially lacking: the 'Driftless Area'.

So on that first nice day in 30,000 years, we are standing in the Driftless Area. The ridges and hillsides reveal horizontal layers of bedrock limestone and sandstone of unimaginable age – about 450 million years old. Rocks this age do not carry fossils; the primitive lifeforms thriving when these sediments were laid down were too soft to fossilize. The sediments were laid down at the bottom of a shallow tropical sea. Later the land rose and the seas retreated; millennia of rain and wind shaped the former seabed into a landscape with ridgetops and deeply cut valleys – a dendritic landscape, treelike.[4] Perhaps the best way to visualize the preglacial landscape is to picture today's American southwest: dry ridges, rocky, steep-sided ravines, and deep-cut streambeds (Figure 4).

The Driftless Area escaped the ravages of the mountains of ice. But as the glaciers retreated, the devastation left behind was transformed into a blessing. The grinding action of the ice on stone created vast quantities of very fine dust, silt and clay as fine as flour. The temperature contrast between the remaining ice and the warming atmosphere developed powerful, swirling winds that picked up this fine dust and whirled it away.[5] Finally the dust settled out, more in some areas than others, creating huge dunes across the centre of the continent. The Driftless received depths varying from a metre to as much as fifteen metres.[6] This wind-blown soil is known as 'loess' (pronounced 'luss').

On that first nice day in 30,000 years, on the ridge of our farm, we are standing on at least eight metres of loess. It's been many centuries since it blew in as dunes. The loess has settled and compressed, perhaps washed off the steepest hillsides down into the valleys, but generally remains as a thick carpet of fine particles, ideal material to transform into soil. The sharp-edged pre-glacial landscape seems eased by a thick layer of frosting. In the latest centuries, seeds have arrived, on the wind or carried by birds and other animals pioneering into this developing landscape. These plants and animals are beginning the process of transforming the mineral-rich loess into true soil. The original dunes of loess, the accumulation of fine minerals, was simply a layer of dirt. Soil is a complex structure of minerals, organic matter, agglomerated particles, air pockets, moisture, and, importantly, a rich and diverse microbial community. From this beginning point, these processes have a long way – and thousands of years – to go.

As we stand here on this first nice day, 12,000 years ago, we can see all the main geophysical limitations and possibilities that will set the parameters for future landscapes. The underlying ancient bedrock defines the shape of the landscape: hill, valley, and connecting slopes. The climate is settling into the long-term temperate pattern that prevails into modern times. The incipient soil has a good start on developing its structure, depth, and fertility. Plant and animal communities are moving in. The main missing impact is that of humans.

Stand with me on our vantage point again, not so very long ago. It's early fall, the year is 1855. From our spot on top of the ridge, let's look south – and we see a small group of people walking due north towards us. Carrying a compass and axes, they are using chains to measure their progress – a surveying crew. We shake hands with Thomas Gilmore, Deputy Surveyor, the leader of the crew. This crew is part of the first official land survey of Minnesota. Such crews will walk the edges of every square mile of Minnesota, marking every corner and 'quarter-corner' of every square mile, in anticipation of arriving settlers. We are standing on the quarter-corner of the boundary between Sections 33 and 34 of Township 111 North, Range 11 West of the 5th Principal Meridian, now known as Pepin Township, Wabasha County, Minnesota.

Thomas Gilmore made notes of

Figure 4a. Dendritic pattern in the Driftless Area, with the Mississippi River. (image: Google Earth).

Figure 4b. Dendritic pattern near the Grand Canyon, with the Colorado River. (image: Google Earth).

every corner he marked. We have those original field notes. Every corner was marked with a wooden post or a ditch and mound. Notes were made of nearby trees, with compass bearing, distance, and type of tree. On this spot, Thomas Gilmore 'set quarter section post'. And he noted that a burr oak was located just east of due north, at a distance of '156 links', or 31 metres. Another burr oak was southwest from this spot, about 7.5 metres away. Gilmore's men 'blazed' these trees, marked with an axe as reference trees (Figure 5).

These notes tell us what this landscape looked like when the earliest European settlers arrived. Along with reports from early travellers, we know that the hillsides and ridgetops in the Driftless Area were vast areas of grasslands with scattered trees, mainly burr oak trees. Early settlers called the grasslands with scattered trees 'oak openings' or 'barrens', revealing their experience with the dense forests of the eastern US. Today, such a landscape is called an 'oak savannah'.

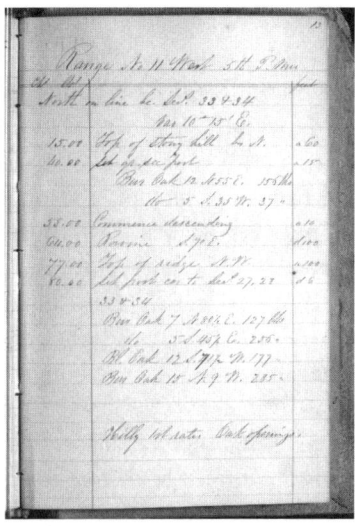

Figure 5. Original Surveyor's Field Notes by Thomas Gilmore, 1855 (US Bureau of Land Management, General Land Office Records).

Why mostly burr oak trees, scattered just so? The answer is fire. Burr oak trees are highly resistant to fire. Their thick, corky bark can resist hot fires. They develop large root systems that live underground for a long time, and shoot up tree sprouts when the conditions are right, giving burr oaks an ability to recover even if particularly hot fires damage older trees. Regular prairie fires eliminated other tree species, and kept burr oak trees from filling in too densely by killing sensitive small trees, creating the savannah.

What was the origin of such frequent fires? After much controversy amid historians, it is generally accepted today that American Indians managed the landscape with regularly-set prairie fires. The intent was to burn the prairie grasses, which stimulated them to grow tender new shoots, attracting bison, elk, deer, and other grazers. These animals provided a significant portion of the Indians' diet. The grazers then fertilized the prairies with their manure, cycling nutrients as my cows do today. Thus, the original oak savannah was a particular managed landscape which existed because it was the foundation of a successful food system. This landscape persisted for several thousand years, until European settlers arrived, pushed Indians out of the area, and stopped the fires.[7]

Now join me on another day on top of our ridge. Again it's early fall, 22 September, the year is 1938. Pioneer European farmers arrived about fifty years previous, and this farm now has a sturdy white farmhouse and a big red barn. The stone for the foundations was quarried on this farm from those limestone seabeds laid down 450 million years ago. The family has a nice herd of dairy cows that they milk twice a day in the barn; the cream is separated and stored in cans submerged in cold well water until picked up to go to the creamery. While some neighbouring farms now have tractors, this farmer still uses draft horses to plough and plant the corn, oats, and clover that feed the animals. High overhead, unnoticed by the farm family, an airplane soars; the pilot is snapping aerial photographs.

I have the photograph of our farm taken this day, by the US Department of Agriculture. Our farm of today is much like this photo. The treeline that we can see from our spot on the ridge remains. All the open land I have today was being cropped regularly in 1938. But there are differences. This black and white photo shows quite a lot of straight lines and rectangular fields (Figure 6).

The next aerial photo I have is from 1951. It looks quite different; by that time, narrow curving strips have been laid out. These strips remained essentially unchanged from this time until we bought our farm in 2010. A look at photos across the Driftless from 1938 shows very few strips; by 1951 most neighbouring farms were laid out in strips. What motivated such widespread change at the landscape level? Why did farmers almost completely change their farming practices in just over a decade?

Extensive crop farming developed in the Driftless Area in the 1880s. Farmers had arrived decades earlier, in small numbers, but mainly settled in the river bottom areas and near river towns. As the population grew, farmers moved to the open ridgetops and grew wheat in a great boom period of the 1880s and 90s. Eventually, the wheat boom moved further west, and farmers settled into diverse farming with dairy, pigs, and other livestock. Farming slowly intensified as population and the markets grew.

The farmers who settled the Driftless Area were mostly Americans from further east.

Figure 6a. 22 September 1938. Note straight field edges and rectangular shapes. (US Department of Agriculture).

Figure 6b. 28 July 1951. Curving contour strips now in place. (US Department of Agriculture).

Nice Day in the Driftless

Many of them had moved west more than once already, having farmed perhaps in Illinois, Indiana, and Ohio – or Britain, Germany, and Scandinavia. The settlers' previous experience was based on very different geology. While the soils in the Driftless were deep, the slopes were much steeper than their previous experience. Even rainfall was different in the Driftless Area, compared to the eastern US or northern Europe. Rainfall tended to come in much more concentrated and extreme rain events. Early farmers worked their Driftless land as they had in Illinois or Germany – ploughing straight up and down hillsides, planting the same way they had for generations.[8]

The first thing pioneer farmers did was to 'break the sod'. Teams of oxen pulled steel ploughs, cutting the mass of roots and turning the sod upside down. Once exposed to the air, the structure of the prairie soil began to degrade in a way that the pioneer farmers did not understand. Soil organic matter volatilized into the air as carbon dioxide, and the mass of roots disintegrated. This destroyed the soil structure and exposed bare dirt to driving rain. The impact of raindrops on bare soil is explosive, dissolving soil particles and setting them in motion as the rainwater drains away down the hillside. And once the soil structure was destroyed, the underlying fine particles of loess were highly vulnerable to deep erosion – all the way to ancient bedrock.

Longstanding farming practices conflicted with geological parameters, and from about 1915 to 1945, farmers in the Driftless Area unwittingly created catastrophic erosion. Entire towns were buried under eroded sediment and abandoned. Broad valleys were covered with sediment and changed from productive farmland to sandy unproductive barrens. Rainstorms produced such volumes of flowing mud that cars were trapped on highways. The town of Zumbro Falls had been located near a ten-foot high waterfall on the Zumbro River; so much sediment settled in the valley that the falls were buried and do not exist today. The Whitewater River valley was once a bucolic scene of small farms and villages. The marshy floor of the valley is now two to three metres higher than it was before settlement.[9] You can canoe the Whitewater River and look down through clear water to see the stumps of huge walnut trees that grew on dry land before the erosion occurred.

Huge ravines developed on farms seemingly overnight. Efforts to mitigate the problem were aimed at the effects of the erosion, rather than at the more subtle causes. Attempts were made in the valleys to

Figure 6c. 15 July 2015. Treeline is essentially unchanged from 1938. Contour strips are replaced with permanent perennial pastures. (US Dept. of Agriculture).

direct or control the runoff from the fields above; control structures of stone or concrete were promptly overwhelmed. There was little understanding at first that the origin of the problem began at the top of the ridges: the rainfall on the ridgetops broke soil loose and started it flowing down the hillsides. As the hillsides became steeper, the flow was concentrated into draws and drainage ways, building force; the runoff flowed from the tips of the dendritic landscape to the trunk. When the flow reached the valleys below, the volume was so great, and the content of soil in the runoff was so huge, that the devastation could not be avoided. 48,000 square kilometres of rich loess soil was being destroyed.

A few scientists and technicians working for the new Soil Erosion Service, a New Deal agency created during the Depression, had an inkling of the cause. They understood that the root of the problem was raindrops hitting bare soil, and the complicating factor was an unimpeded rush of that loose soil down the hillside. In the 1930s, the SES began a pilot project in Wisconsin using 'contour strips' to change the pattern of farming. The strips follow the 'contour', essentially remaining at the same elevation as they meander along the hillsides. Ploughing creates miniature ridge and valley patterns; if these patterns ran up and down hillsides, water flow was accelerated. Ploughing across the hillsides would tend to trap rainwater in the valley pattern and slow it down.[10]

Alternating the crops planted in adjacent strips created an opportunity to slow runoff further. The biggest erosion risk was from corn, which was planted in widely spaced rows and cultivated to control weeds. This left bare ground exposed for many months of the year. Oats and clover are planted densely and keep the ground covered most of the time. By alternating strips of corn with strips of oats and clover, any rain running down the hill carrying soil from the corn strips would be slowed down and trapped by the oats and clover strips. This approach addressed the core causes of the severe erosion at the source.

The concept of contour strips was implemented as a recommended practice by the Soil Erosion Service in Wisconsin in 1933. By 1955, the practice was widespread across the entire Driftless Area and other areas of the US facing severe erosion. The practice was simple in design, easy in execution, and did not require large capital investment or heavy earthmoving. It could be used equally well by farmers with tractors or horses. Farmers could see the results quickly and embraced it wholeheartedly.

The practice of contour strips remains widely in place in the Driftless Area today, giving the landscape its unique beauty. The long-term stability of this practice owes its existence to more than just erosion control. The practice of contour strips in the Driftless Area meshed particularly well with the style of agriculture in the region, and with the food system that became entrenched there for generations.

Dairy production has been a staple of the agriculture scene in the Driftless Area from early days. Both Minnesota and Wisconsin have been large dairy producers, and much of that has been concentrated in the Driftless. From the 1950s on, farmers were encouraged to feed corn to their dairy cows to increase milk production. Dairy cows also need protein to balance the energy from corn – clover and eventually alfalfa provided high protein. The strip rotation of corn, oats, and clover/alfalfa provided a complete dairy ration. The strips protected the slopes from erosion. This match of food system and farming practices sustained farm families in the Driftless for decades.

The persistence of the contour landscape has positioned farmers in the Driftless Area to take advantage of emerging consumer attitudes toward the modern food system. Consumers are developing new expectations for their food, looking for organic, grass-fed, humane, and environmental values in their food. This shift gives farmers in the Driftless area an advantage: the continued reliance on alfalfa and other forages in the contour strips makes it easier to transition away from reliance on corn to organic and grass-fed production. The Driftless Area today is brimming with innovation in the new values-driven food economy.

So, as I stood on our ridge on that spring day in 2010 when we bought our farm, I looked out on the contour strips. I could look across the countryside and see more strips on the neighbours' farms, an entire landscape of contour strips – the landscape where these strips were born and where they seemed at this point aboriginal. I knew enough about soil erosion to understand their importance on my new hillsides. Nevertheless, I looked around and decided: I would eliminate my contour strips (Figure 6).

There would be two themes of my new farming venture: certified organic and 100% grass-fed. Certified organic farming means not using herbicides, pesticides, synthetic fertilizer or genetically modified seeds. Rather, organic production relies on emphasizing natural cycles of fertility and pest control, farming in harmony with nature.

Grass-fed livestock production means not feeding starchy grains to ruminant livestock such as cattle and sheep. This approach is inspired by the savannah food landscape that prevailed before European settlers arrived. Our animals graze on diverse pastures of grasses and legumes, and eat hay from these pastures in the winter. We are mimicking the patterns of the bison and deer by closely grazing an area and letting it rest and regrow. By intensively managing the grazing process, nutrients are cycled from the pastures through the animals and back to the soil, building soil organic matter, sequestering carbon from the atmosphere, and increasing fertility in the process. Meanwhile, the meat from these animals develops a much healthier fat profile, high in Omega 3, conjugated linoleic acid, and antioxidants, as well as being delicious.

This farming system needs neither corn as a high-energy source nor alfalfa as a high protein source. Oats are needed only occasionally as pastures need to be re-established. So the rotation that fit so well with contour strips for conventional dairy does not fit with 100% grass-fed cattle and sheep.

With permanent perennial pastures, I take the soil-conserving benefits of contour strips to the next level. Rather than slowing runoff and trapping eroding soil on a few strips of hay mixed in with annual crops, my entire hillside is covered with a rich thatch of deep-rooted perennials, eliminating erosion. I don't plough, so I have no exposed soil, except when I occasionally renovate small areas used for winter feeding. Rainwater soaks into our soil rather than running down the hillside. Soil is conserved; water quality is improved; carbon is sequestered; livestock live natural lives outside on green grass. Human health is enhanced by improved nutrition.

Food and Landscape

Stand with me now, on the ridge top on our farm on a nice day in spring. All of our open land to the treeline is a diverse mix of grasses, legumes, and forbs – at least seventeen species growing together in profusion (Figure 1). It's early spring, and the cows are giving birth to their calves. They graze the pasture with a munch-munch-munch sound, tearing off large bites of grass and swallowing them, later to ruminate and chew their cud. I can see the shape of the ancient landscape that prevailed for millions of years before the glaciers surrounded this Driftless Area. I am standing on more than eight metres of fine loess that blew in as the glaciers retreated, but nearly washed away in the early years of modern farming. Seventy years of contour strips effectively protected the remaining soil from further erosion, and created 48,000 square kilometres of beautiful landscape based on a food system of dairying on small family farms. Now, a new landscape may develop as organic, grass-fed farming slowly takes hold. While it may not have the handcrafted beauty of the gentle contour strips, it is always green, is always covering the precious soil, and forms the basis of a healthful food system that's as good for the eater as it is for the soil. It can flourish here because of millions of years of bedrock formation; thousands of years of post-glacial loess deposition and soil development; centuries of Native American land management; a hundred years of modern farming and soil conservation; decades of attitude change among American consumers; and seven years of work building fences, herds, and markets. An agricultural landscape is an integration of food system, geography, and human culture; a new perennial landscape may emerge in the Driftless Area as more farmers and consumers come to appreciate the links between the new landscape and their values. What will this landscape look like in another decade, whether from a Google satellite image, a plane, a drone, or from the top of our ridge?

Notes

1. Thomas Madigan, 'The Geology of the MNRRA Corridor', in *River of History*, ed. by John O. Anfinson (Saint Paul, MN: Saint Paul District Corps of Engineers, 2003), <https://www.nps.gov/miss/learn/historyculture/upload/river_ch_1.pdf> [accessed 18 May 2017]
2. E.C. Pielou, *After the Ice Age* (Chicago: University of Chicago Press, 1992), p. 84.
3. John T. Curtis, *The Vegetation of Wisconsin* (Madison: University of Wisconsin Press, 1987), pp. 27-28.
4. Richard W. Ojakangas, *Roadside Geology of Minnesota* (Missoula, MO: Mountain Press Publishing Company, 2009), pp. 267-76.
5. Pielou, pp. 87-89.
6. John H. Mossler, 'Bedrock Topography and Depth to Bedrock' (Saint Paul, MN: University of Minnesota, 2001) COUNTY ATLAS SERIES ATLAS C-14, PART A Plate 4 <http://conservancy.umn.edu/bitstream/handle/11299/58557/plate4%5b1%5d.pdf?sequence=6&isAllowed=y> [accessed 18 May 2017].
7. Roger C. Anderson, 'Evolution and Origin of the Central Grassland of North America: Climate, Fire, and Mammalian Grazers', *Journal of the Torrey Botanical Society*, 133.4 (2006), 626-47.
8. Stanley W. Trimble, *Historical Agriculture and Soil Erosion in the Upper Mississippi Valley Hill Country* (Boca Raton : CRC Press, Taylor & Francis Group, 2013), pp. 5-14.
9. Trimble, pp. 85-105
10. M. Scott Argabright and others, 'Historical Changes in Soil Erosion' (Washington DC: US Department of Agriculture, 1996) <https://www.nrcs.usda.gov/Internet/FSE_DOCUMENTS/stelprdb1043907.pdf> [accessed 18 May 2017].

'A way of seeing which we learn': Food as Resistance

Fozia Ismail

How does a person of Colour navigate through landscapes dominated by White-centric thought and action? Let them eat *sambusa*.[1]

In this paper I will explore the theme of food and landscape from the perspective of race. I believe that the African food landscape is a dynamic and evolving scene, one constantly shaped by power relations. These power relations determine what is consumed, what is considered 'cuisine', who gets to decide, and importantly how knowledge about consumption is produced and shared – including the role that the digital landscape plays in making food knowledge more accessible for Sub-Saharan Africans across the diaspora.

In a country that is increasingly hostile to people considered not 'truly' British, this paper, more than anything, is about resisting that hostility and finding solace in food: in Somali food.

Introduction

I agree that 'landscape is a way of seeing which we learn', a way subject to the same hegemonic practices that exclude alternative narratives, particularly from people of Sub-Saharan African descent in the UK.[2]

This exclusion includes food itself: African food/cuisine is apparently invisible in the UK's food scene.[3] The invisibility of African food relates to wider issues around structural racism born out of British and European imperial history and the occupation of African lands. This occupation included a production of knowledge that framed White peoples as a superior race; the social construction of 'racial identity' justified actions like slavery and colonization. This construction in turn impacts how African peoples and their foods are seen or not seen or dismissed altogether in food history. As the historian James C. McCann says, '[t]he history of food as cooking and sensual experience overall is a new subfield that is growing rapidly. For Africa, however, the process has scarcely begun [...]. In the area of ethnic cuisine, African occupies the smallest of spaces in even the most innovative bookshops or library collections.'[4]

I would add that it is not just that the work has not begun, it's that the work has not begun within the framework of Western knowledge practice. African people across the diaspora eat a variety of African cuisines from their countries of origin; the techniques and knowledge of these cuisines are passed down informally through home environments.

Food and Landscape

There are African people eating their cuisines across the UK in cafes or restaurants, but these spaces have not historically catered to the Western (i.e. White) market and therefore seem invisible in the UK food scene. The exception is Ethiopian cuisine.

Interestingly Ethiopia was the only African country not to be colonized, and food was an important marker in the making of a strong Ethiopian national identity.[5] This identity went on to become the centre of a pan-African movement for Black people across the world.[6] I believe this is one of the reasons why Ethiopian restaurants flourished in cities across parts of Europe and North America and are an exception rather than the rule.

Context

My own journey to writing this paper starts, in part, with a move to Bristol in 2014. I noticed two significant things with the move: 1) I was Somali; 2) I missed my mother's food. It seems strange to say I noticed I was Somali, as if I did not know that to be the case before. Whilst I was aware of my racialized body, I had never lived in an almost all White neighbourhood (apart from a brief spell at Cambridge) until we moved. In Bristol I experienced regular interactions that reminded me of my Blackness; some explicit – 'people like you should not breed' – and others less so, like being ignored as the only Somali mum in playgroups, probably out of some kind of fear that English was not my first language. We hear the term micro-aggression bandied about, but what does it mean in practice? Let's define it as the small, incidental interactions of everyday racism. And these interactions of everyday racism shape our food landscape. Consider that peculiar British obsession, tea.

Tea and Britishness

I am at a playgroup, the only Black person in this space. The first interaction goes smoothly enough: I am starting to feel a sense of pride in my fledging East African food business, and people are always intrigued and want to hear more.[7] There is a queue for the tea hatch being run by two women in their seventies. When I get to the hatch, one of the women, who had been serving the other mothers perfectly well, with a smile and a chat, stopped short when confronted with me. Unable to bring herself to look at me, she pretended not to hear me when I asked politely for a cup of tea. Her eyes were filled with such unfriendly indignance at the thought of giving me a cup of tea, and her arms locked straight down her body, their hard rigidity making it clear that they were on strike, that these White arms will not serve you. There is an awkward moment before the other lady gives a me a friendly smile and makes me a tea, providing a momentary release of tension for which we are all grateful. I take my cup and walk away with a smile, forcing my body into a performance, a kind of dance my face has played many times before.

Always when this sort of awkward social interaction happens to you as a person of Colour you know it for the racism that it is, but calling it that sounds crude and unreal, the word too big and too blunt to encompass this banal scene. You cannot accuse

'A way of seeing which we learn': Food as Resistance

someone of being racist just because they are unfriendly to you. She did not say anything, but then we are more than words: her White flesh and rigid bone told me I was not welcome there. Such exchanges become an insidious and powerful form of social control. These seconds of interaction — really just a few seconds — leave such an impression. The powerlessness I feel is hard and made harder by the briefness of the moment. You are bound up in social conformities, the ropes squeezing hurt, anger, frustration, confusion, recognition inside, keeping your Blackness in check.

This is everyday racism in action, but even though it's common, inevitably this indirect and casual racism blind-sides far more than that of the far-right skinhead with the 'Britain First' t-shirt. Him you can prepare for, but an innocuous looking elderly White lady at a playgroup in a church hall, that is not the image of a bigot. The irony that the cup of tea's foreignness equals my own, and yet somehow has become more intrinsically British, is not lost on me.

How did this woman, and so many other White British people, come to feel this way? If landscape is a way of seeing which we learn, this woman has learned to see a British landscape that I do not fit into. How does this relate to food? It is everything and more, as this quotation from Stuart Hall encapsulates:

> I am the sugar at the bottom of the English cup of tea. I am the sweet tooth, the sugar plantations that rotted generations of English children's teeth. There are thousands of others beside me that are, you know, the cup of tea itself. Because they don't grow it in Lancashire [...]. Not a single tea plantation exists within the United Kingdom. This is the symbolization of English identity – I mean, what does anybody in the world know about an English person except that they can't get through the day without a cup of tea? Where does it come from? Ceylon – Sri Lanka, India. That is the outside history that is inside the history of the English. There is no English history without that other history. The notion that identity has to do with people that look the same, feel the same, call themselves the same, is nonsense. As a process, as a narrative, as a discourse, it is always told from the position of the Other.[8]

Here Hall calls out the fallacy inherent in British identity; how can a cup of tea come to symbolize such Englishness without any acknowledgment of the complex history that brought that seemingly safe and comforting cup of tea to our tables? I am aware that my Black body in this English landscape is irrevocably linked to the trade of spices, sugar, and tea, and yet the vast majority of the British public seem ignorant as to how I and so many others have come to be here. Everyday food items we now take for granted held such value in the fifteenth century that it set in motion the age of European exploration and colonization. How does this knowledge affect our understanding of African food in the UK?

The Structures that Frame Our Understanding of African Food

The colonial legacy of defining Black Africans as sub human has left its traces in insidious ways. If 'culture began when the raw got cooked', how can a supposedly uncultured people have a cuisine?[9] Representations of the African continent and its people are still on the whole negative. We talk about Africa as if it is a country, not a continent, caught in a seemingly endless cycle of famine and war. Its people are often compared with animals and considered primitive, exotic, savage, noble, and lazy. Boris Johnson's disgraceful descriptions, calling African children 'piccaninnies' alongside 'tribal warriors with watermelon smiles', did not stop him from becoming the Foreign Secretary. This reductive and dehumanizing way of describing the African continent and its people is part of a long legacy that includes a systematic erasure of African civilizations and their influence prior to European colonialism. A production of knowledge about 'Africa' was cemented in the eighteenth century and the Enlightenment period, when European philosophers, scientists, and thinkers reduced African peoples to nothing more than objects to be studied, classified, sold, and conquered, all for the benefit of the Empire.[10]

Such systematic erasures and reductions largely explain why it has taken so long for African food to gain prominence outside the African diaspora. Other reasons include:

1) The structural inequality that has resulted from racism has meant people of African descent tend to be amongst the poorest in the UK, so there are less resources for setting up food businesses.[11]

2) Remittances are a factor in how financial resources within African households are used. One 2006 study found 'that Black Africans had the highest propensity to remit, accounting for 34% of remitters […] while only representing 10.5% of the sample'.[12] Because remittances are a priority for many Black Africans in the UK, the pressure to support family and others in the country of origin is often behind the pressure to get a good education and a stable professional job. The remaining financial resources are unlikely to be used for something as risky as a food business.

3) Whilst food plays a vital role in maintaining the culture of African diasporic communities, it is not seen as a worthwhile vocation in itself (possibly for the two reasons listed above). From speaking to my family, there is a sense that it would not even be worthwhile paying for: the idea that you would go out and pay to eat something you could make at home seems astounding, even though Somali people will happily go out to a Lebanese restaurant or Italian etc. This attitude is slowly changing with a younger generation who are proud of their heritage and long for 'authentic' representations of African food within the British food scene.

4) There is an assumption that African flavours would not appeal to White British / European people; at the same time, a strong sense of what makes a dish more authentically Somali leads to reluctance to play around with presentation or creative interpretations.[13] My mother still thinks that my East African supper club does not make Somali food even though the Lamb *Sambusa* is her recipe: we have tweaked the presentation so in her mind it is no longer Somali. Despite

such reluctance to adapt the food to the European market, the development of the street food scene in the UK means there are now opportunities to serve food in a contemporary way, whilst maintaining the informality that is recognizable in street food markets in Africa.

5) There is some internalized racism at play which results in the food itself being simultaneously cherished and tarnished through its very association with Somalia and Africa. By tarnished I mean fear: a fear outsiders looking down on the food because of the presentation or smell, etc. This contradiction results in a complex relationship to our foods. Yemisi Aribisala captures this with brilliant humour: 'The relationship of the nouveau middle-to-upper income-earning Nigerian and their food is a mixture of love, snobbery, the passion that results from the snobbery, and social repression. It's like loving fat women but being compelled to marry a thin one to keep up appearances; it makes the clandestine meets with the fat one all the more scorching'.[14]

Foods between Landscapes

'We're never more intimate with the environment than when we actually eat it.'
– Felipe Fernandez-Armesto[15]

Complexities arise in the spaces that are produced between landscapes. I am made of Somaliland and England by way of Kuwait and exist in between them; it feels like standing on tectonic plates that are constantly shifting. Brexit was a huge quake, formalizing what we all knew as Somali people to be true: our foreign bodies are not welcome in a country that I thought was my home. I can just about balance and hold onto something stable through the making of my mother's *Xawaash* (pronounced *hawaash*) spice mix. *Xawaash* simply translates as 'essentials', and it is the essential spice mix that a Somali cook cannot live without.

Ginow (my mother) makes her mix with lots of cumin and coriander seeds, a small amount of cinnamon bark, cardamom, black pepper, turmeric, and a tiny number of cloves. It's not really measured: the bulk of the mix is made up of equal measures of cumin and coriander seeds with the rest of the spices making up a third of the mixture. The spices are lightly dry-fried in a pan and then ground up. I love the smell of it, I love the making of it, and I love how adaptable it is. It's used in so many dishes that my mother would make for us as children; from the seemingly mundane *Xawaash* beans on toast with fried onions and green pepper to the sublime lamb *sambusa*, a samosa by another name.

Ginow's spicy lamb *sambusa* is truly special, fresh and aromatic with a hint of fire. Fresh coriander, green chillies, a small amount of ginger, an amount of yellow pepper so small as to appear pointless (but makes a difference), and a big white onion. It sounds like it should not be delicate with those punchy flavours, but there is a lightness of touch which is surprising and comforting. Every family has its own *Xawaash* mix, and across the Somali diaspora there is a bit of home represented in each spice mix: in making and eating that *Xawaash*, it feels as if we are eating Somaliland itself and remembering our nomadic past. I believe this to be true for most people of the diaspora.

I interviewed Alicia Ama who set up Chalé! Eats (a street food stall selling contemporary Ghanaian food) and Nima Owino of *Nim's Din* blog and Cham Cham supper club (specializing in contemporary Sierra Leonean and Liberian food), both of whom run their stalls on the vibrant street food markets in Hackney. Food played a vital role in forming a connection with their African heritage. Alicia described it as the 'the umbilical cord to Ghana', and Nima was inspired to start her supper club as a way of raising money for the Ebola crisis that was affecting Sierra Leone. The food proved so popular she continued, and it is still going strong. Nima said she wanted to show more of Sierra Leone and Liberia than 'portrayed in the news [...] there is more than war and disease'. For Alicia it was about creating 'a space for me that I can work free of racism'. As women of African descent we have all come across lazy assumptions, casual racism, and ignorance about our separate places of origin. What struck me was how making this food became much more for us than just selling tasty grub for people to eat: it was also a way of resisting a wider racist narrative that so many people have about 'Africa' by educating them, starting with food. Alicia and Nima are part of an exciting vanguard of the African food renascence in the UK.

Reimagining the African Food World through the Digital Landscape

> 'We younger negro artists who create now intend to express our individual dark-skinned selves without fear or shame [...]. We build our temples for tomorrow, strong as we know how, and we stand on top of the mountain, free within ourselves.' – Langston Hughes[16]

I believe the digital landscape has played an enormous role in this African food renascence. It is democratizing the production of food knowledge in revolutionary ways, including making African food visible not just to African people but to a much wider audience. Take Eden Hagos, the inspirational Ethiopian food blogger who set up the *Black Foodie* blog. I spoke to Eden about what led her to showcase Black-owned restaurants in North America. After going through a negative experience at a restaurant in Toronto, where Eden and her Black female friends were made to feel unwelcome, she started to look more critically at how Black people navigated the food world. Eden realized that the incident she experienced was not just a one-off. This led her to create *Black Foodie*, an online platform showcasing the contemporary Black food scene. Her blog is revolutionary, not just to Canadians/Americans of African descent but to African and Caribbean diners across the diaspora.

The blog appeals to what Alicia from Chalé! Eats calls the 'Afro-Politian elite'. These are people of African descent across the globe, whether African American, Caribbean, or African. Young Black social media-savvy trendsetters are using Twitter, Snapchat,

'A way of seeing which we learn': Food as Resistance

Instagram, and other platforms in innovative ways, influencing fashion, art, and culture across the globe. In the UK, there are online magazines like *gal-dem*, *Black Ballad*, and *Media Diversified*; internationally there is *Okay Africa* – a whole world of Black excellence flying under the radar of the mainstream UK press.[17]

Although Black people are not just ignored by the White-dominated press but, worse, often represented in ignorant and dehumanizing ways, digital media has allowed a rebalancing. We are producing our own platforms for sharing information in our own ways, which places our experiences at the centre, not at the margins. Better still, we are sharing and connecting with each other; the everyday racism we experience has a creative and funny outlet on that cultural phenomenon known as 'Black Twitter'.[18] In April 2016, the first conference exploring 'Digital Blackness' was held at Rutgers University in New Jersey. Exploring the evolving role that the digital landscape is playing in Black people's lives, the conference reinforced that point by filming sessions that are available on YouTube, allowing revolutionary, even transformative, access to academia for Black people across the diaspora. Knowledge is power, and for so long that knowledge has been produced and controlled by people (who on the whole happen to be White) with resources: money to access education at a high level, contacts for work experience, and freedom to travel in a completely different way than any Black body, regardless of citizenship.

A Solution Is Found in Salt and Spice[19]

If landscape is a way of seeing that we learn, I see a Somaliland that is inextricably linked with England. I learned to make *Xawaash* in England, and yet it is also a reminder of a home, or at least of a landscape that is not English. When we as a family go for walks in the beautiful English countryside around Bristol, I always take a flask of *shaah* or chai. I grew up drinking *shaah*, the tea my mother made for guests. My boys now associate country walks with *shaah* as does my English husband; it is the only time I make it. I think there is something beautiful in this, a Somali trace of spiced tea in the rural English landscape. T.S. Eliot articulates the complexities of this migration well:

> The migrations of modern times […] have transplanted themselves according to some social, religious, economic or political determination or some peculiar mixture of these. There has therefore been something in the re-movements analogous in nature to religious schism. The people have taken with them only a part of the total culture [.... T]he culture which develops on the new soil must therefore be bafflingly alike and different from the parent culture.[20]

Wherever people migrate, there will always be gaps in the availability of foodstuffs, some seemingly essential items that cannot be transported or do not grow well in the new environment. For my mother, who grew up as a goat herder on the Ethiopian/Somali border, fresh camel milk has a strong association with the Somali landscape; since leaving Somaliland, this camel milk has become, for her, imbued with mystical powers. Camels are so important to sustaining Somali nomads that there are forty-six different words for camel. My mother firmly believes fresh camel milk cures all sorts of ailments, and she laments its loss. The loss is far greater than just camel milk: it is a loss of home, a loss so keenly felt that my mother (along with a generation of her peers) took up a recipe for camel milk, consisting of the following unlikely but available ingredients: a dash of 7-Up, natural yoghurt, salt, and water. Imagine our excitement each Ramadan when she brought out the 'camel milk'.

For children of the African diaspora this idea of home, of this 'parent culture', is entwined with food. If we are fortunate, our parents cooked food for us to pass this knowledge on. When I asked Yemisi Aribsala about the relationship between food, home, and identity, she said:

> 'I can't think of a topic more closely to heart than "home" [.... P]eople in the diaspora hold their food close to their hearts because it is tied intricately with identity. Especially for people like me who can be walking down the street in Somerset West and someone will say "that's the problem with 'you' Nigerians." You are not wanted. You go home to your house, you cook your meal with all the aromatics that are your old friends, you eat, you are consoled. It feels almost like carrying your true home around with you.'

If culture began when the raw got cooked, the making and eating of food becomes much more than nourishment. In a foreign land or in a hostile and racist world it becomes a safety net for your identity, a space where you can simply exist and recharge this sense of you as a human outside of the White gaze. When you leave this safety net you again become defined by your otherness.

As I write this paper I am aware of the famine that is devastating East Africa. I am aware because we are always aware of what is happening back home and do what we can to help. We are connected: my mother's sister, still a nomadic goat herd like many others, has seen her flock and way of life devastated. I have struggled to reconcile this reality with running an East African supper club. It's felt indulgent and wrong to be commodifying Somali food here while the very people who have inspired the food are struggling.

We live in a time of political uncertainty. The recent vote for Britain to leave the EU was rooted in an idea of Empire: making Britain 'great again' is a form of nostalgia, a longing for a past that unmakes people like me. Against such uncertainty I am finding solace in food. The setting up of Arawelo Eats has been in some ways a response to a gap in the food scene, in others an outlet for my own nostalgia for Somaliland, a land I never lived in but which frames so much of my world through its wonderful people and cuisine. I hope it will frame my children's world too: Somali spice tea fits the English landscape.

Notes

1. A *Sambusa* is a fried or baked triangular pastry with a savoury filling.
2. Gillian Rose, *Feminism & Geography: The Limits of Geographical Knowledge* (Cambridge: Polity Press,

1993), p. 87.
3. For the purpose of this paper, African/Africa refers to the Sub-Saharan African region.
4. James C. McCann, *Stirring the Pot: A History of African Cuisine* (Athens, OH: Ohio University Press, 2010), p. 181.
5. McCann, pp. 65-78.
6. Fikru Gebrekidan, 'From Adwa to OAU: Ethiopia and the Politics of Pan-Africanism, 1896-1963', *International Journal of Ethiopian Studies*, 6.1/2 (2012), 71-86.
7. When I moved to Bristol I co-founded an East African supper club with Edwina Bruford called The Matatu Kitchen. The Matatu Kitchen closed in October 2017 to make way for Arawelo Eats <www.araweloeats.com>.
8. Stuart Hall, 'Old and New Identities, Old and New Ethnicities', in *Culture, Globalization, and the World-System: Contemporary Conditions for the Representation of Identity*, ed. by Antony D. King (Minnesota: University of Minnesota Press, 1997), pp. 41-68 (pp. 48-49).
9. Davia Nelson & Nikki Silva, 'A Conversation with Felipe-Fernandez-Armesto', *The Kitchen Sisters*, August 2014. <http://www.kitchensisters.org/2014/08/07/a-conversation-with-felipe-fernandez-armesto/> [accessed 20 May 2017].
10. Julie Rivkin and Michael Ryan, 'Situating Race', in *Literary Theory: An Anthology*, ed. by Julie Rivkin and Michael Ryan (Oxford: Blackwell Publishing, 2004), pp. 959-64.
11. Kehinde Andrews, 'Racism Is Still Alive and Well, 50 Years after the UK's Race Relations Act', *The Guardian*, 8 December 2015. <https://www.theguardian.com/commentisfree/2015/dec/08/50-anniversary-race-relations-act-uk-prejudice-racism> [accessed May 2017].
12. Carlos Vargas-Silva, 'Briefing: Migrant Remittances to and from the UK, March 2016', p. 5. <http://www.migrationobservatory.ox.ac.uk/wp-content/uploads/2016/04/Briefing-Migrant_Remittances.pdf> [accessed May 2017].
13. This statement is backed by anecdotal evidence from speaking to my family and friends and on interviews with African food innovators such as Eden Hagos from *Black Foodie* (<blackfoodie.co>), Alicia Ama from Chalé! Eats (<chale-lets-eat.tumblr.com>), Nima Owino of *Nim's Din* (<nimsdin.com>) and Cham Cham supper club.
14. Yemisi Aribisala, *Longthroat Memoirs: Soups, Sex and Nigerian Taste Buds* (London: Cassava Republic, 2016), p.12.
15. Nelson and Silva.
16. Langston Hughes, 'The Negro Artist and the Racial Mountain', in *Small Acts: Thoughts on the Politics of Black Cultures*, ed. by Paul Gilroy (London: Serpents Tail, 1993), p. 172.
17. *gal-dem* is a creative collective and online and print magazine created by women and non-binary people of colour; *Black Ballad* is an online lifestyle magazine centred on the Black British female experience; *Media Diversified* seeks to cultivate and promote skilled writers of Colour by providing advice and contacts and by promoting content online through its own platform; *Okay Africa* is an online magazine that showcases the latest fashion, art, music, and culture emerging from Africa and the African Diaspora.
18. Black Twitter is a cultural signifier on twitter used by Black people, predominately in America but also increasingly in the UK and Africa. Humorous memes (ideas and concepts in visual formats spread in the digital landscape) are used in radical ways to poke fun at stereotypes and challenge racism. Black Twitter has also been an important platform for highlighting systematic violence against Black people through the #blacklivesmatter campaign and raising important debates about representation in the media such as the #oscarssowhite campaign.
19. Ethiopian proverb qtd. in McCann, p.1.
20. Homi K. Bhabha, 'Cultures In-Between', in *Questions of Cultural Identity*, ed. by Stuart Hall and Paul du Gay (London: Sage Publications, 1996), p. 54.

The Terraces of Kea: Producing Food for Subsistence Shaped the Cycladic Landscape

Aglaia Kremezi[1]

'Ceos is the queerest place imaginable,' wrote British traveller James Theodore Bent, who visited the island in the nineteenth century. 'The flat roof of the house beneath us fitted close up to ours, and this seemed to be the universal custom, so that most of the houses are entered by the roof of the house in front. Everybody walks on the roofs as being preferable to the dark, dirty alleys, arched over for the most part, which are given up to pigs.'[2]

This was what Bent experienced in crowded Chora, Kea's main town. Today, Chora is officially called Ioulis, a resurrection of its ancient name. Bent described with admiration the many stone wall structures of Ceos or Keos, as the island was called in antiquity. In later times the island was known as Zia, and today as Kéa or Tziá. Bent also described Kea's paved roads, their sides defined by low fortifications all along them, the numerous smaller and larger *stavlià* (stables) that dot the landscape, and the ancient watchtowers used for protection and communications with the neighbouring mainland of Attica.[3]

Chora is not densely populated today, as it is inconvenient to live in a place inaccessible by car. Pigs no longer wander its alleys, and the village is beautiful and clean, with whitewashed paths. But the peculiarities of having to live on a precipitous hill are still felt when visiting the once booming town. What is your 'below' is someone else's 'above'.

Figure 1. Kea terraces (Otzias).

This upstairs-downstairs culture is a perennial theme on mountainous Kea, and it is not solely observed in its main town. The whole island has been terraced to form flat cultivable strips of land over and beneath one another. Endless stonewall-supported terraces define the island's slopes and make a strong impression on today's

The Terraces of Kea: Producing Food for Subsistence

visitors. Very common throughout the Cyclades and other parts of southern Greece, their original purpose was to tame the land and provide precious soil for cultivation.

The Place

'A poor land in general, but with few stretches that can't be cultivated,' wrote Hara Georgiou and Nicolas Faraklas to describe Kea's arable land in a paper regarding research of the island's population in antiquity.[4] Their description could not be more accurate. Kea's soil is not great, but you can make do with it if you are stuck on this stony piece of land and try really hard. But let's take things from the top.

Set in the south Aegean Sea, Kea belongs to the group of islands called 'the Cyclades'. An infertile extension of mainland Greece, this group forms a circle that is roughly divided into two sub-groups. The outer group includes islands in the north east, from Andros to Delos and Mykonos, and the inner group starts from Kea and extends all the way south-southeast to Anafi, a neighbour of Santorini, and the Dodecanese. The inner group is thought to be an extension of the mountain ranges of Attica, the region around Athens.[5] Located about seventeen nautical miles off Lavrio(n) and the western coast of Attica, and forty-two miles from Piraeus, Kea's landscape is believed to resemble that of ancient Athens and its environs. It is greener and more fertile than many other islands. So close is it to the mainland that, when the weather is clear, the ancient temple of Poseidon in Cape Sounio(n) just a few kilometres south of the modern port of Lavrio, is a visible dot from Kea. About 128.9 square kilometres (49.8 square miles) – less than half the size of Martha's Vineyard (226.6 sq km) or a quarter of the Isle of Man (572 sq km) – the island is the sixth largest in the Cyclades and the twenty-fourth largest island in Greece. Today it registers about 2500 permanent inhabitants, a number that probably doubles or even triples during the high summer season.

It has been estimated that ancient Ceos had between 6500 and 10,500 permanent inhabitants to feed.[6] Before the days when ferries and refrigerated trucks brought all kinds of provisions from the mainland, here, as in many parts of southern Greece, there were not enough fields for the islanders to plough to produce sufficient food. Making use of local stone, usually quarried on the spot, stone walls were built to support terraces, which proved a successful solution that compensated for the island's lack of valleys. They retained soil-creating strips of land where crops could grow, and extended the island's pastoral capacity. Terraces turn erosion into an advantage. Torrential rains often hit the Cyclades in wintertime, gradually carrying good soil from the mountaintops to lower elevations. Kept in place by the terracing stonewalls, this fertile mud

Figure 2. Goats on the Kea terraces (Koukouvaya).

fills the endless manmade rows of terraces that decisively mark even the most desolate, rocky seaside slopes. From a distance, Kea's terraces resemble Southeast Asian rice patties, minus the permanently inundating waters and lush green. Precipitation was never as abundant here as in those tropical lands. It is a seasonal event only, but it is plentiful enough to fill the subterranean water reserves, hence the epithet *hydrousa* (water bearing) given to the island in antiquity. Kea is better off than many other islands of the Cyclades. With soil safely guarded in place by extensive agricultural terracing and plentiful water supplies, its poor but not uncultivable soil becomes almost fertile.

The History, Briefly

Johnathan Sandor explains that '[t]erracing constitutes some of humanity's strongest and most enduring efforts to manage geomorphic processes in agriculture and to conserve land resources'. He notes that the 'array of terracing strategies among past and present agricultural societies reflects the high degree of indigenous knowledge of soil and landscape processes'.[7]

Mostly in disrepair today, Kea's terraces are centuries old. They extend to its most remote and rocky eastern slopes, often reaching from the seafront all the way to the top of the mountains, to places that seem accessible only to goats. Who would ever even contemplate growing crops there? One can get a better idea of what they would have looked like in their better days observing those still in decent shape adjacent to some of the island's small valleys. Still in use in these more fertile spots, the terraces have been repaired again, again, and again through many years of existence. Who first built these terraces, why, and when are questions archaeologists and others have long been trying to answer.

Kea's long history, extending over some six millennia, may provide us with some clues. The earliest archaeological evidence dates to the Neolithic era. During historical times, we know, four cities thrived on the island. 'Foremost was Ioulis, inland, high on the northern hills, famous as the home of Simonides, Bacchylides, and Prodicus. It is the chief modern town,' writes John Caskey, who for many years excavated Kea's Agia Eirini site, active mainly during the Bronze Age, which may have had close ties first with the Minoans and then the Mycenaeans.[8]

Later evidence points to the island's importance in the classical era, with its contribution of four ships to the allied fleet of Athens during the Persian Wars. The island probably continued to do well during the Hellenistic period. Not much is known, but, as part of the Ptolemaic kingdom of Egypt, its proximity to Athens and the mainland couldn't but contribute to its importance. The Ptolemies seem to have established a colony on Keos to serve the needs of travellers along the main marine routes – and of course the needs of the Egyptian fleet.[9]

In other words, Kea was not unimportant. It had to sustain a good number of people, both permanent inhabitants and visitors of all sorts, and, at times, it may also have had to contribute to the sustenance of various fleets. It needed to produce sufficient crops.

Romans, Venetians, and Ottomans dominated Kea for centuries after that. In more recent

The Terraces of Kea: Producing Food for Subsistence

Figure 3. Central eastern slopes of Kea covered in snow.

times, the island has seen an influx of Arvanites, people of Albanian descent who started moving south to Greece around the eleventh century CE. For the island to attract these newcomers, it must have had something to offer, and that something was probably cultivable land. Are we to think that much of the infrastructure necessary to survive on Kea was already mostly in place, with the terraces already being there and only in need of some repairs? Possibly.

Terraces were an indispensable part of the island terrain, wonderfully adapted to the inhabitants' agricultural needs, enabling them to enjoy crops, some of which could even be exported for some much-needed cash. Western European travellers writing around the eighteenth century never fail to comment on the island's impressive agricultural terracing. J.A. van Egmond, who sailed around the islands and the Middle East in 1759, writes that Kea was 'industriously cultivated'. Indeed, as archaeologist T. M. Whitelaw concludes, within thirteen square kilometres in the island's northern part, '84% of the land preserves evidence of having been terraced at some point in the past'.[10]

Dating the Terraces

Johnathan Sandor, who has researched the impact of agriculture and other land use on soil formation, believes that 'ancient and traditional agricultural terraces encompass a broad range of forms and functions, occurring in diverse environments on five continents and Oceania [...]; likely centers of origin are southwestern and southeastern Asia, and the Americas'.[11] Sandor thinks that 'it is more difficult to date ancient agricultural land than crop remains which can occur in several archaeological contexts', and believes that the earliest evidence for terracing in most regions is similar, around two to three thousand years ago.

By contrast, J. E. Spencer and G. A. Hale claim that terracing began five to nine millennia ago in the Near East.[12] Stone placements cannot be accurately dated, and, although archaeologists are very careful in their statements, there seem to be ways of telling with certainty that many of the terraces that continued to be cultivated over the years were indeed constructed in antiquity. Lynne Kvapil, who has studied the terraces in Korphos, writes that 'the results indicate that early terraces were contemporary with the development of the Mycenaean harbor site of Kalamianos [...] during the Late Bronze Age' (from 1200 to c. 500 BC).[13] As archaeologist Hara Georgiou mentioned in an email exchange, the terraces on Kea 'were constructed and maintained over a very long period of time, as they are to some extent even now; and the same is true for farm buildings and structures. Many of the abandoned nineteenth century ones have earlier foundations and much earlier datable potsherds in and around them'.

Such foundations can be especially evident around Kea's four ancient cities. Cultivable land must have been in great demand in antiquity, when up to 10,500 people lived on the island, bringing intense pressure on agricultural resources.[14] Constructing those terraces would require an enormous workforce, and could not be accomplished without free workers or slaves – and considerable wealth.[15] Let's take the example of Karthaea, the best preserved of Kea's four ancient cities, in the south-easternmost part of the island. The impressive ruins on Karthaea include an archaic temple of Apollo, a classical temple of Athena, a Hellenistic theatre, and Roman baths. The terraces around the now deserted site suggest that a significantly large population lived here in antiquity. Archaeological evidence dating to the late fifth or early fourth century BCE shows that public land was being leased to individuals in Karthaea, as also in Poieessa, the neighbouring south-western ancient city, known today as Poisses, and also further up the hill, near the village of Katomeria.[16] Notably, these places have small valleys with fertile flatland still cultivated to this day. Most of Kea's seasonal vegetables, tangerines and other citrus fruits of excellent quality come from the Poisses gardens.

Besides material evidence about the terraces, collected and dated from archaeological surveys, Simon Price and Lucia Nixon research ancient texts, focusing on the word αἱμασιά, one of the terms that seem to refer to agricultural walls.[17] The earliest references to such walls comes from the *Odyssey* (18.357-359, eighth century BCE): 'Stranger, I wonder whether you would like to work my land, if I took you on, on some marginal fields, at a proper rate of course, assembling *haimassiai* and planting tall trees.' The landowner mentioned in Homer's verses evidently is extending his cultivable land to far away, 'marginal' areas. Elsewhere in the *Odyssey* (24.222-225) we find servants assembling such stone walls to protect cultivated land. Such references concur with archaeological research. And there are also parallel examples from North Africa and the Middle East, Kea's not-too-far away neighbours.

In their quest for sustainable agricultural developments, FAO scientists have studied 'level terraces for dry land farming, [which] have been extensively used in the past, for example in Ethiopia, The Yemen Arab Republic, and in the Maghreb countries of North Africa (Algeria, Morocco, and Tunisia). Most were built in the past and nowadays are increasingly not maintained or abandoned as the

Figure 4. A donkey on the Kea terraces (Koukouvaya).

The Terraces of Kea: Producing Food for Subsistence

maintenance becomes uneconomical or impossible because of labor shortages'. The study cites as an example Yemen's Haraz mountain area that 'until recently has been one of the most densely populated high-mountain regions in the world, with virtually all slopes being terraced or used as rainwater collection areas. Mainly since the end of 1970, large areas of this man-made ecosystem have been abandoned. […] Several similar examples are recorded on the north coast of Africa where the migration has been across the Mediterranean to Europe'.[18]

The Crops

In antiquity, but also to some extent today, terraces were used to cultivate trees, grains, vegetables, and grapes. Different crops seem to have been planted in various parts, often depending on the microclimate and soil. Based on a study of the terraces in Sphakia, Crete, but also elsewhere in Greece, Price and Nixon conclude that terraces dating to the Roman and Late-Roman period are generally constructed on gentler slopes because their main purpose was the cultivation of grains or legumes. Terraces from the Venetian and Ottoman periods are on steeper slopes: their purpose was likely the cultivation of vines.[19]

Unlike the terraced rice paddies of Southeast Asia, the terraces on Kea and other parts of the Mediterranean were surely never all cultivated simultaneously. The soil in our part of the world is quite poor, and while rains are usually sufficient, they are never too abundant or predictably regular: 'Dry hot summers with mild winters [usually] providing plentiful rainfall. The irregularity of annual rainfall did mean that crop failure was a regular problem,' writes Mark Cartwright.[20]

We can assume that alternating terraces was the case in ancient, as in more recent, times. Cartwright notes that throughout Greece, 'there is evidence of crop rotation, and fields were left fallow to allow soil nutrients to regenerate and moisture to build up […]. Crops as [fava] beans and lentils were also grown and re-ploughed back into the field to fertilize it, or weeds could be left to grow as food for grazing animals'. In antiquity, much like today, people ploughed and sowed in the late fall or early winter, after the first rains of November and December, and '[i]t is interesting to note that there were no distracting [ancient] religious festivals or records of Assembly meetings in Athens during this crucial and busy period'.[21]

Kea's southern slopes, those that face north, are the ones that are more fertile. The cool northern winds bring precious moisture which is captured in the island's many ravines. In most cases, these fertile patches of land were kept for the more demanding annual crops, such as grains and legumes, which are still planted in rotation. And, of course, sheep and goats grazed on the patches of land that were left fallow, as they still do. The milk of the goats and sheep was used to make cheese and yogurt. Occasionally a young lamb or kid would be slaughtered for Easter or other important family feasts and religious celebrations.

For many centuries, Kea was self-sufficient; Bent, our favourite traveller, observes that the island produced 'far more than is needed for home consumption'. This, he thought, was a mixed blessing: it made things too easy for Keans, who did not have to strive for more, and missed the chance of making their island an important commercial centre: 'With complacency they watch from their town the steamers plying east and west without a regret that they do not stop at Keos; they cultivate their oaks and their fields, and retain far more of the old-world life that the busy Syriotes, for only a weekly steamer touches here and a few *caïques* [...] making its winters, in particular, not a season for the faint at heart.'[22]

Barley and Legumes

Barley was the island's staple grain, as it has been in most parts of southern Greece and many areas around the Mediterranean.

Gruel from barley and barley cakes were the basic foods of common people in antiquity, while *paximadia*, twice-baked barley rusks, were still a staple on Kea and other Cycladic islands until the mid-twentieth century.[23] White bread didn't reach Kea until the mid-1960s, and even wealthy islanders consumed dark bread, baked with a combination of local barley and wheat from the mainland. Not only did the island produce enough barley for its inhabitants' needs, but there was also an occasional surplus to export. Kea is dotted with numerous stone threshing floors, where the harvested crop was crushed and winnowed to separate grain from fodder, which was used as animal feed. Many of these threshing floors were in regular use until recently.

In alternate years, instead of barley, legumes were planted. My neighbour, Zenovia Stefa, told me that in the small gardens and terraces around Otzias, where we live, her late father used to plant grass peas (*Lathyrus sativus*), a legume for which the generic name 'fava' is used throughout Greece. This primitive, drought-resistant pea 'originated from the Balkan Peninsula in the early Neolithic age. It may have been the first domesticated crop in Europe around 6000 BCE'.[24] Zenovia told me that she and her siblings helped harvest and separate the peas from the pods after the stalks had been threshed on the stone-paved floor, much like barley. The discarded stalks and peelings were a much-appreciated feed for sheep and goats during the dry summer months, when fresh grass was not available. Hand stone mills were used to grind off the peas' hard skins, splitting them, so that after a brief cooking they would be easily mushed into the yellow purée also called 'fava', a poor islanders' staple since antiquity. Anya Anastasia Sarpaki writes that a unique archaeo-botanical material of 'crops in the latest stage just before consumption' was identified among the archaeological finds at Akrotiri, the Bronze Age settlement on the volcanic island of Santorini (Thera). It 'includes split legumes, bulgur-type cracked barley, and flour'.[25] Fava, especially the type from Santorini, is today considered a delicacy, served in taverns all over Greece, although the purée is now usually made from imported yellow split-peas (dal).

Wine

Kea was once famous for its red wine. Bent mentions that the island had extensive vineyards, many on terraced corridors in its northern slopes. Considerable amounts

The Terraces of Kea: Producing Food for Subsistence

Figure 5. Barley threshing on the terraces c. 1920 (Photo: Nikos Alexandrou).

of wine were being produced throughout the island's history. There was enough wine for local consumption, and until the early twentieth century some was also exported. Bent writes that Michael Psellos – the eleventh century monk, scholar, and politician – describes Kea's wine as 'sweet to the scent, and black in colour', and 'much sought after in Constantinople. [...] The wine of Keos is still of great repute'. Bent observes that 'even the shepherd in his "stable" had an excellent draught to give us out of his gourd'.[26]

Photographs taken at the end of the nineteenth and beginning of the twentieth centuries bear witness to serious wine-producing activity, especially in the northern part where we live. The old abandoned, overgrown winepress I see from my office window, half-way up the terraced hill, is proof that vines must have been cultivated on the grounds around our house. There are many old winepresses all over the island, indicating extensive vineyards.

These precious old presses – some in covered stone shacks, others just simple open-air cisterns carved in rock, or built with stones and plastered – are the sole remnants of the once thriving viticulture. Santorini and other Cycladic islands never gave up on their vineyards and managed to revive their unique grape varietals, putting their exquisite local wine production on the international map. Kea doesn't even manage to produce enough decent wine for local consumption these days, and the same is true for the island's once plentiful cheese production. Bent playfully remarks that, unlike other islanders, Keans, complacent with their beautiful and relatively fertile island, are 'not an ambitious race', and this does not seem to have changed much.[27]

At some point, after the vines were gone, the abandoned narrow terraces were invaded by goats and sheep who graze climbing up and down, often adding to the stone walls' deterioration. Throughout the winter and spring, the animals consume every piece of edible green, uprooting most vegetation. This is the reason why precious few plants survive, apart from some thorny bushes, asphodels, and the hearty wild sage,

Figure 6. Threshing floor (Photo: Nikos Alexandrou).

thyme, and savoury, Kea's iconic fragrant shrubs. Even if the old, abandoned vines had managed to survive neglect, disease, and the goats' teeth, they would have been consumed by the November fires set by shepherds on the terraced hills.

Acorn Caps

Another interesting, unusual crop that peaked in the mid-nineteenth century was acorn caps. On the slopes that were not planted with vines or legumes grew oak trees: 'over all but the northern slopes', Bent writes – in other words, not in places where vines grew. The traveller adds that even 'the poorest Keote possesses a few oak trees, and from August to October the oak harvest keeps them all employed. The acorns are huge things, as big as eggs, astonishing to our eyes; but it is the cap only that they export, the acorns are, as with us, eaten by the pigs'.[28] The *velani* oak tree variety (*Quercus aegilops*), was mainly grown on Kea not as animal feed but as a cash crop.[29]

Figure 7. Open-air Wine Press.

The large acorn caps, rich in tannins, were quite a valuable export in the old days because they were an essential element of the leather tanning process.[30] As for the acorn nuts that were left behind, they were not wasted. Acorn-fed pigs produce wonderful meat, and pigs once roamed around, feasting on the leftover nuts. In the early twentieth century, as modern chemicals started to be used, acorn caps were no longer valued. But pork meat is still one of Kea's delicacies. Not many people cook now with pork fat, as in the old days, but they still feast on pork. Every year, most households raise at least one pig to slaughter, usually in early winter. Besides sausages and the local delicacy *loza*, smoked pork loin, all parts of the slaughtered animal were preserved in many ways, to complement and flavour the predominantly vegetarian dishes islanders consumed.

This 'abundance of oak trees has caused an absence of olives in Keos', Bent states.[31] This fact has puzzled many European travellers of the eighteenth and nineteenth centuries. Although there are a few very old olive trees on Kea, most have been planted quite recently. At some point, when acorn caps lost their industrial value, almond trees were planted all over the island, for local consumption but also as a cash crop. Older Keans remember earning one golden British sovereign for each *oka* (1.3 kilos) of almond kernels! Kean almond trees are never irrigated so their fruit is not plentiful, but it is intensely delicious.

The Present

The inhabitants of Kea often had an easier life than other islanders. They exported their agricultural produce, wine, and acorns, while in antiquity they were also blessed with milt,

The Terraces of Kea: Producing Food for Subsistence

a naturally occurring red iron oxide that was much valued for its use in painting and the marine industry.[32] In the last few decades, around the turn of our century, they were once more exceptionally lucky: land on Kea, this time not the fertile parts but even the rocky, wind-ravaged hillsides, became particularly precious. Just an hour by ferry from Athens, the island has become a trendy upscale resort, and properties have gained a lot of value, making many poor inhabitants rich. On top of that, construction has provided jobs to many, even now during the tough economic times. It is not uncommon to see a bulldozer parked on some terrace, near a big oak tree next to an on-going construction site.

For the past sixteen years, my husband and I have been living in a small valley on the north-eastern part of Kea, surrounded by terraced hills. The way terraces meticulously follow the hills' curves is truly amazing, reminiscent of the cornrow braids that adorn modern heads. It would not be an exaggeration to say that these manmade structures enhance the beauty of the Aegean landscape. Terraces do not become a blight to the eye the way modern construction often does, with ugly, imposing frames of unfinished houses destroying the serene landscape.

Terraces are still built on the island, and new supporting dry-stone walls are created, albeit for a different purpose. Now their function is to capture the eroding soil around Kea's modern cash crop: vacation villas. The stone wall style has also changed, adapted to the skills of modern masons used to squaring the stones and following straight lines that seldom respect a hill's curves. Terraces now make beds for the fancy, thirsty, imported decorative plants that drain the island's water bed. They expand verandas, creating swimming pool space and other guest areas for the villas that hang over the steep, rocky cliffs above the sea, where once sheep and goats grazed. Modern villa owners get incensed at the locals whose goats sneak into their unsustainable yards, invitingly green as they are to the hungry animals. They complain about the sheeps' odour and annoying night bleating. These new Greek and foreign vacationers don't care about locally grown produce, as they seldom cook at home. They eat out in the island's taverns, and for their fancy parties they order from Athenian caterers. The prepared foods arrive by ferry, in refrigerated vans....

Notes

1. I am grateful to Hara Georgiou and Nikos Alexandrou for their invaluable help, and also to my husband, Costas Moraitis, and my friend, Dr Maxine Ain, for their comments and edits.
2. James Theodore Bent, *Cyclades, or Life among the Insular Greeks* (London: Longmans, 1885), p. 155.
3. Bent, p. 157.
4. Hara Georgiou and Nikolas Faraklas, 'Ancient Habitation in Kea; the Northern Part of the Eastern Side', *Ariadne, Yearbook of the University of Crete* (Rethymno: University of Crete, 1993), in Greek (all translations by the author) <https://elocus.lib.uoc.gr/php/pdf_pager.php?filename=%2Fvar%2Fwww%2Fdlib-portal%2Fdlib%2F0%2Fd%2Fd%2Fattached-metadata-dlib-ca44d62ba718d90ab232568f5269d5d1_1277112096%2FAriadne_06_1993r.pdf&rec=&do> [accessed 20 April 2017].
5. Anaya Anastasia Sarpaki, 'Palaeoethnobotany of the West House Akrotiri, Thera: A Case Study'

(unpublished doctoral dissertation, Sheffield University, 1987), p. 2.
6. Georgiou, pp. 38-39, p. 48.
7. Johnathan Sandor, 'Ancient Agricultural Terraces and Soils', in *Footprints in the Soil: People and Ideas in Soil History*, ed. by Bruno P. Warkentin (Amsterdam: Elsevier, 2006), p. 505.
8. John L. Caskey, 'Notes on Keos and Tzia', *Hesperia* 50.4, 320-26.
9. G.M. Cohen, *Hellenistic Settlements in Europe, the Islands, and Asia Minor* (Berkeley: University of California Press 1995), p. 51, p. 133.
10. J.F. Cherry, J.L. Davis, and E. Mantzourani, *Landscape Archaeology as Long-Term History: Northern Keos in the Cycladic Islands*, Monumenta Archaeologica 16 (Los Angeles: Cotsen Institute of Archaeology Press, 1991), p. 405.
11. Sandor, p. 5
12. J.E. Spencer and G.A. Hale, 'The Origin, Nature, and Distribution of Agricultural Terracing', *Pacific Viewpoint* 2 (1961), 1-40.
13. Lynne Kvapil, 'Untangling Mycenaean Terracing: Landscape Modification and Agricultural Production at Korphos-Kalamianos', paper abstract for Archaeological Institute of America annual conference, Department of Classics, McMicken College of Arts and Sciences, University of Cincinnati <http://classics.uc.edu/index.php/news-5/132-2011apaaia> [accessed 20 April 2017].
14. Georgiou and Faraklas.
15. Lina Mendoni: Structures Rurales Et Sociétés Antiques: Actes Du Colloque de Corfou.
16. Cherry, Davis, and Mantzourani, p. 320. See also Simon Price and Lucia Nixon, 'Ancient Greek Agricultural Terraces: Evidence from Texts and Archaeological Survey', *American Journal of Archaeology*, 109.4 (October 2005), 665-94 (p. 671).
17. Price and Nixon.
18. Norman W. Hudson, '4. Soil Conservation', *Soil and Water Conservation in Semi-Arid Areas* (Rome: Food and Agriculture Organization of the United Nations, 1987) <http://www.fao.org/docrep/t0321e/t0321e-10.htm> [accessed 20 April 2017].
19. Price and Nixon, p. 681.
20. Mark Cartwright, 'Food and Agriculture in Ancient Greece', *Ancient History Encyclopedia,* 25 July 2016 <http://www.ancient.eu/article/113/> [accessed 20 April 2017].
21. Cartwright.
22. Bent, p. 154.
23. Aglaia Kremezi, 'Paximadia: Barley Biscuits' Past and Present', *Aglaia's Table on Kea, Cyclades*, 9 June 2015 <http://www.aglaiakremezi.com/paximadia-barley-biscuits-past-and-present/> [accessed 20 April 2017].
24. V. Heuzé and others, 'Grass pea (*Lathyrus sativus*)', *Feedipedia: Animal Feed Resources Information System*, INRA and CIRAD, 19 April 2016 <http://www.feedipedia.org/node/285> [accessed 20 April 2017].
25. Sarpaki, p. 232
26. Bent 157. Dried gourds were used to store and sometimes serve wine.
27. Bent, p. 154
28. Bent, p. 154
29. C.C. Lacaita, 'Quercus Aegilops', *Bulletin of Miscellaneous Information* (Royal Botanic Gardens, Kew), 1920.3 (1920), 100-05.
30. *Vegetable Substances: Materials of Manufactures* (London: Charles Knight and others, 1833).
31. Bent, p. 154.
32. E. Photos-Jones and others, 'Kean Miltos: The Well-Known Iron Oxides of Antiquity, Annual of the British School at Athens, 92 (November 1997), pp. 359-71 <https://www.cambridge.org/core/journals/annual-of-the-british-school-at-athens/article/kean-miltos-the-wellknown-iron-oxides-of-antiquity1/6FEB377A4E260C7445A9592DC5898619> [accessed 20 April 2017].

Ghosts in the Cane Fields

Michael Krondl

What remains of the culinary landscape of St John, the smallest of the U.S. Virgin Islands, is little more than a ghostly echo. The visible absence of thriving foodways is not only evident in the scrub forest, dotted with ruins of sugar plantations, and in the wandering feral goats and donkeys, but even in the town supermarket where nothing is even remotely local – instead, there are piles of Costa Rican pineapples and freezers full of kingfish from Florida.

Perhaps because most the island was preserved as a national park some sixty years ago (prior to the full-blown development of jet tourism), the phantoms are more in evidence than elsewhere in the Virgin Islands. Here, the traces of the landscape's colonial past were not bulldozed to make room for beach resorts, unlike next door St Thomas, or ploughed under, as on St Croix where the old plantations now conform to twenty-first-century ideas of agriculture. Yet if the St John's landscape is still haunted by the past, that past, to use Lévi-Strauss's formulation, is very much a floating signifier. Visitors mostly just look for a perfect sandy hideaway, National Park rangers envision a pre-colonial ecosystem, and the few remaining locals see an abandoned larder.

St John's foodways prior to the establishment of the Virgin Islands National Park in 1956 had certain commonalities with other Caribbean islands, but there were also notable differences. The challenging landscape had much to do with it. As a rugged mountainous island that was never an especially profitable location for sugar cane cultivation, St John did not become as fully enmeshed in eighteenth-century slave provisioning routes as more lucrative slave economies in Jamaica or Barbados, or even nearby St Croix. Even before the abolition of slavery here in 1848, the population saw little of New England cod and beef, those staples of the slave economy, but instead became almost wholly dependent on eating what the land and sea could provide. Similarly, for medicine they turned to the curative shoots, roots, and bark of the dense inland forest. These peasant, place-based foodways lasted for generations but quickly began to lose their rationale as the island reconnected to the outside world in the 1940s. The cuisine became definitively disconnected from its locale once it lost its provision grounds, something that occurred when some 60% of the island was set aside for the national park. Yet it wasn't just the removal of the land from cultivation (and the sea from commercial fishing) that transformed the subsistence economy but rather a massive influx of non-locals, to whom the landscape meant either an income stream or a place of leisure, but certainly not a source of sustenance. In some ways, it was an echo of 1492. If the first wave of globalization here destroyed indigenous civilization and replaced it with an African diaspora culture, the second wave – spearheaded by Bermuda-shorts-clad Americans armed with Kodak instamatics instead of Conquistadors bearing muskets and disease – so overwhelmed the local foodways that today little remains except stories and memories, as fleeting as the ghosts that haunt the cane fields.

Sugar Island

As on other Caribbean islands, the foodways of U.S. Virgin Islanders were a legacy of the so-called Age of Discovery. Enslaved Africans replaced the decimated natives, adopting many of their foods, while adding other items from the transatlantic larder. Depending on the productivity of the sugar island, the enslaved workers developed a diet that was more, or less, dependent on the currents of the triangular trade of sugar, human beings, and overseas provisions. In terms of cookery, topography turned out to be destiny. In general, the more fecund the cane fields, the more the diet depended on food from abroad. Since neither St John nor its immediate neighbours had a landscape especially suited to the sweet cane, sugar plantation workers depended more on local fish than imported salt cod, more on manioc bread than wheaten loaves.

St John belongs to an archipelago first identified by Europeans during Columbus's 1493 expedition. The Spaniards eventually introduced hogs, goats, and chickens to feed passing galleons and caravels, and also fatefully left behind deadly microbes that soon all but wiped out the indigenous Taino population, but otherwise the islands were left in peace during Europe's initial land grab. When Denmark finally joined the West Indian sugar rush in the eighteenth century it had to settle for St Thomas and neighbouring St John. The former, with its well-endowed harbour, would prosper from the passing trade even as the latter remained a backwoods stepsister.

A ragged inkblot of bays and promontories, St John covers about twenty square miles, making it a little smaller than Manhattan. Its steep hills and coral-sand-rimmed inlets make for pretty postcards, but from an agricultural standpoint they leave a lot to be desired. Christian Georg Andreas Oldendorp, a representative of the Moravian church who visited in the 1760s, described both islands as having 'mountains and valleys [that] alternate in the landscape to such an extent that there is only very little flat land in between'.[1] The island's soil was especially stony and thus poorly suited for cane cultivation. Not that the Danes didn't try.

Whereas St Thomas was seized by the Danish crown as early as 1666, no comprehensive effort to settle St John was attempted until 1718, when cotton and tobacco estates were established. Sugar cultivation followed. By 1796, 1863 acres (almost 15% of the island's landmass) were planted with cane, producing some 850,000 pounds of sugar for export; by the 1820s, this had gone up to 1,100,000 pounds.[2] (To put that in context, St Croix, the next island purchased by the Danes in 1733, produced up to 17 million pounds in the late 1700s; meanwhile on the English colony of Barbados some

80% of landmass was devoted to sugar cultivation.)[3] Like many other cane-producing islands, the only way of making the sugar business viable on St John was with enslaved labour; accordingly, following emancipation in 1848, sugar production collapsed. The African-diaspora population that had grown as sugar production increased, from a little more than a 1000 in 1833 to a peak of almost 2600 in 1808, now dropped rapidly on the eve of emancipation to some 1800 in 1846. By comparison, the island's European population was always minuscule and left little impact on the local culture, culinary or otherwise.

Fish and Fungi

The foodways of the island can broadly be divided into four periods, with some more reliant on the local environment than others. When humans first migrated here, perhaps as early as the ninth century BCE, they introduced exogenous plants and some limited domestic animals, but largely depended on local food for sustenance.[4] During slavery, the African-diaspora diet was at least partially embedded in a global network of foodstuffs traded or brought from abroad. Then, once sugar cultivation all but ceased in the second half of the nineteenth century, the inhabitants returned to a diet that, for several generations, was as removed from the global trade networks as the foodways of Russian peasants. Over the last seventy years, since the advent of the national park and the tourist economy, the dinner plate has been increasingly filled with food entirely disconnected from the local landscape.

By the time the Danes took possession of their Caribbean toeholds, the local Taino population had largely been wiped out through European predation and disease. Archaeological records on St John indicate an indigenous diet similar to that found in other aboriginal settlements on the islands of the Lesser Antilles, which is understandable given the active pre-Columbian trading networks across the West Indies. Cassava (manioc) and sweet potatoes formed the backbone of the diet supplemented by helpings of fish and other sea life, most notably whelk, conch, and sea turtles. The Tainos had also introduced guinea pigs and hutia (a raccoon-sized rodent, of the family *Capromyidae*), though these were extinct by the time the Danes arrived.

With the advent of slavery, St John, like other islands, became a node of global trade network, which meant that the cuisine not only included local Taino foods but also African ingredients and preparation methods, as well as imported ingredients in the form of cornmeal and preserved meats and fish. Ask a native St Johnian about a defining local food and an oft-repeated refrain is 'fish and fungi' (pronounced FUN-jee), that is, locally caught fish, typically boiled, served with a side of (imported) cornmeal mush with an admixture of that African vegetable, okra.

Mostly though, enslaved workers on sugar plantations here had to depend more on food they could obtain through their own devices than on provisions provided by plantation owners. Given that St John lacked the soil, topography, or rainfall ideal for cane cultivation, only the largest plantations were willing to buy imported foodstuffs.

Food and Landscape

Instead, the planters expected their workers to provide their own sustenance, mostly by cultivating the bush at the edge of plantations. Oldendorp had this to say on the arrangement:

> On each plantation, the Negro houses form a kind of village. Often fifty, sixty, or even more of them are constructed in a row. Each family is given a piece of land by their master, which they cultivate. From this, they are to produce their own means of sustenance. The yield is generally great enough that it provides the diligent cultivator with a surplus beyond his basic needs, and from this he can provide himself with other commodities. This arrangement relieves the master of any further cares concerning the upkeep of his slaves, and it is much more agreeable and advantageous to the slaves than when the essentials for their sustenance are handed to them in kind, as is the case on several English plantations on St Croix. The Negro, therefore, enjoys a kind of freedom on his little plantation, wherein he cultivates the soil according to his own free choice.
>
> [... T]he Negro plants his garden with cassava, potatoes, and yams. The former serves as his daily bread, whereas the latter two replace it in time of emergency. Maize, or Welsh corn, also belongs to the Negro's essential crops. In addition to those crops [...] the wild bush provides him with a quantity of fruit [... and] with even slighter effort and skill, he can provide himself with fish, crabs, and shellfish from the sea. Piskets [reef silverside, *Hypoatherina harringtonensis*], in particular, are to be had in such quantities from July to October that one can merely scoop as great a supply from the sea as deemed necessary for future consumption. These small fish can be nicely preserved once they have been dried. In addition, industrious housewives raise poultry and fatten swine, which they sell for cash to acquire other kinds of food and necessities.[5]

Needless to say, this paradisiacal idyll seldom reflected reality. Frequent droughts and regular hurricanes disrupted the provision grounds as much as they did the cane harvest. Scholars have largely attributed a 1733 slave uprising (suppressed only with French assistance) to famine. And the reason the slave owners allowed their workers to grow their own food in the first place was that their plantations were insufficiently lucrative for the planters to afford to feed their workforce, as they did elsewhere in the Caribbean. In this narrow respect, a labourer on St John had more in common with a medieval peasant than with a cane worker on English Barbados. Or, as Karen Fog Olwig points out in her study of St John, 'The slaves were essentially leading a double life as plantation labourers and as small farmers and fishermen; as chattels of the planters and as members of large family networks.'[6]

Traditional rural foodways are everywhere a negotiation between population and landscape, the product of culturally-inflected *terroir*. On St John, due to the limited success of cane cultivation, the Africans had to depend on the landscape, precisely because of the limits of the landscape.

Nowhere is this clearer than in the consumption of fish and other seafood. Archaeological excavations at several Jamaican sites, for example, reveal an almost complete absence of local fish during the pre-emancipation period. The protein remains are primarily from pigs and cattle, most likely salted imports. On St John, in excavations at Cinnamon Bay Plantation and on the East End (a mostly free African community), fish predominate, supplemented by a variety of molluscs and turtle.[7] This is not to say that no food arrived from New England or other slave provisioning locations – there is evidence, for example, of salt cod and herring remains as well as some salted pork and beef remains – but this was the exception rather than the rule. Occasionally, the foreign provisions became a barter good for slaves on the larger plantations, so that cornmeal or salt pork might be traded for local food or even services. Records from the first half of the nineteenth century document a slave from Hope Estate (in the hilly central plateau) trading cornmeal for rum with a free coloured woman, and slaves on Carolina Plantation (near today's Coral Bay) hiring free coloured women to sew clothes for them in exchange for cornmeal.[8]

Poor and Free

The always-tentative sugar cane economy of St John did not survive the effects of emancipation. Despite coercive efforts to make the workers stay on the plantations, many chose not to continue a life that seemed little better than slavery. The island's population rapidly decreased in tandem with the plantations. The 800 or so acres planted with cane in the year of emancipation shrunk to 126 twenty years later, and by 1902 only 7 acres were planted with sugar cane![9] By 1880, the population had diminished from a height of some 2500 to little more than 900 and kept gradually shrinking so that by 1950 only some 750 St Johnians remained on the island.[10] What commercial agriculture lingered on was in the form of cattle ranches, since these required little labour.

Unable to afford foreign trade goods, the people who remained turned to the land and sea for sustenance. At least in retrospect, it wasn't such a bad life. Olivia Christian, who works for the Park Service demonstrating traditional foodways, tells me, 'We were poor, but our parents never let us feel that way,' recounting her childhood in the 1960s. Admittedly, by that point the connection between food and land had already begun to attenuate.

Up until the Second World War, St John's population was almost entirely rural, with a population density of 36 people per square mile, one tenth the density of next door St Thomas. St John's main town of Cruz Bay could count 88 inhabitants. What jobs there were could mostly be found on St Thomas. The foodways remained more or less as they had been a couple of generations earlier: with limited cash, the local diet depended on substance agriculture and fishing. A plot would be cleared and planted with sweet potatoes, tannier (*Xanthosoma sagittifolium*), cassava, and pigeon peas, then once the soil was exhausted in three or four years it would be left to revert to bush.[11] Not only did this itinerant agriculture provide a subsistence crop – what the locals still call 'provisions' – but the initial clearing provided wood to make charcoal, a commodity that could be sold in St Thomas and exchanged for such necessities as cornmeal. The staple ground crops were supplemented with greens from kitchen gardens and fruit trees. The fruit was eaten in multiple ways, as Ms. Christian explains:

> Every 'provision,' say papaya, [we] find [many] ways to prepare it. You [an 'American'] might just eat it ripe but we might peel it and eat it green as a side dish or cut it up with the meat to tenderize it. The sugar apple, most people eat it ripe, but you can eat it green as a side dish. You boil it, you cut the green part off and cut it up and you boil it, and it's sort of like a potato [...]. So, most fruit you eat ripe as well [...] a green banana you do the same thing, the plantains you can eat it green or ripe so every type of fruit you name it we found a way to boil it and use it as a side dish.[12]

Combining a lack of cash with the complex extended kinship network that developed in such a small population resulted in an economy where food exchange was common and expected. Fish might be exchanged for 'provisions'; whelks might be traded for cornmeal. In a series of interviews recorded by the St John Historical Society in 2009, residents recalled life in the middle part of the twentieth century when food was a community bond. Eulita Jacobs, a retired nurse, recounted how her grandfather and his neighbour both had provision grounds, and when the 'reap crops' came in they would share them. 'We had love in this island, we share with each other [...]. Whatever you have, you shared with them, they shared with you, even the bread, bacon and so on,' she recalled. Another respondent remembered how her grandfather would go fishing and she, as a girl, was expected to deliver the fish to a family acquaintance.[13]

Beyond this reliance on the landscape for food, the absence of even a single doctor made the island's residents dependent on so-called bush medicine. On the more populous islands, women might specialize in collecting, prescribing, and selling these indigenous remedies. A 1958 study identified several of these 'weedwomen' on St Croix and St Thomas, though none on St John.[14] Presumably the small population couldn't support such a specialist. But the use of bush medicine was hardly limited to experts. A 1997 University of the Virgin Islands publication, the *Traditional Medicinal Plants of St Croix, St Thomas and St John*, received several entries from St John informants, including the retired nurse Eulita Jacobs.[15] Soursop (*Annona muricata* L.) might be used to treat colds or to calm babies, eye bright (*Heliotropium indicum* L.) in compresses for sores or teething pain to control inflammation, and maiden apple (*Momordica charantia* L.) as heart and diabetes medicine.[16]

America's Paradise

The first significant rupture between the indigenous population and the island's landscape came in 1945 when a government-sponsored program sold plots of land in the vicinity of the village of Cruz Bay. As people relocated to the port town they left behind their agricultural heritage. Visiting St John in the mid-1950s, anthropologist Robert Manners found that the locals could now only survive due to the contributions received from absent relatives: 'No more than 10-15 families of some 175 resident on the island had even modest kitchen gardens [...]. Fishing provided partial support for about a dozen families on the eastern end of the island. But all St Johnians were dependent upon cash for their survival, and almost all cash [...] derived from the wages of family members working in St Thomas or the United States.'[17] This is not to say that agriculture disappeared entirely, but it no longer had a central role.

Yet if the relocation of St John's population from rural to semi-urban locations was given a gentle nudge in the 1940s, it received a violent shove a decade later when some 60% of the island was transformed into Virgin Islands National Park. This preserved the landscape for a more populous (off-island) public but simultaneously removed the land from its former role as provisioning ground. Yet it wasn't so much the fencing of public land that transformed the island's cuisine but rather the park's impact on St John's demography, the transformation of which would soon drive a wedge between the island's foodways and its landscape.

The origins of the park date to 1952 when Laurance and Mary Rockefeller bought a cattle estate on the north side of the island that still contained the ruins of the Danish Caneel Bay Plantation. The same year, the scion of the Rockefeller clan began to buy up land all over the island with the intention of donating it to the U.S. Parks Service to create a national park, a desire that was realized in 1956.[18] He retained Caneel Bay, which was developed into a low-key, exclusive retreat for well-heeled tourists, but continued to enlarge the parkland through additional purchases in the early 1960s. Eventually the park would consist of 7259 terrestrial acres and as well as 5650 acres below the water line.[19]

The effect of the resort and park would prove fateful for the local population, which was soon flooded with 'down islanders' (migrants from the Lesser Antilles) and 'Americans' from the continental United States. Whereas in 1950 all but two score of the island's 749 people were native Virgin Islanders, by 1970 the population had more than doubled, with virtually all the growth from migrants from other Caribbean islands or the United States.[20] The trend has continued apace. So even as St John's younger generation seeks work off-island, the island's gentle climate and low-key lifestyle attracts American settlers, and the tourist economy brings in workers from Haiti, Puerto Rico, and former British possessions. By 2010 the local population had almost disappeared: out of 4170 residents, only 277 were native born.[21]

Again, you can learn a lot about the island's relationship – or rather disconnect – to place through fish. It's still possible to eat fish and fungi if you know someone. On St John, an informal market in local fish continues to exist. Restaurants serving a West Indian clientele often buy them from local fishermen. Hercules's paté stand, located a spitting distance from the St Thomas passenger ferry in Cruz Bay, for example, fries up local fish and serves them to labourers arriving from off-island for the morning shift.

Customers later in the day, he tells me, are more likely to be tourists who want to buy beef or saltfish-stuffed 'patés'. The ubiquitous West Indian patty is fried in the Virgin Islands, but there isn't a single local ingredient in it. Arthur Hercules originally hails from St Kitts and like many early transplants first came to St John to work at Caneel Bay before buying into the paté business. Just down the street, home cooks can also buy fish from local fishermen who regularly sell their catch out of a cooler in a parking lot across from the post office. But most 'Americans' won't buy it, and neither will diners find local fish at the tourist restaurants. The fear is of ciguatera, a potent neurotoxin that builds up in the flesh and viscera of certain reef fish and the predators that consume them. Some fish are more prone to the condition as are particular locales. Locals tend to know their fish and always inquire where it is caught, since the reefs north of the island, for example, are less dangerous than those to the south.[22] But not everyone knows to ask. The disconnect between food and place is hinted at by a 2013 St Thomas study that found the likelihood of succumbing to ciguatera poisoning was higher among Caribbean migrants than among locals, who presumably knew the local fishermen.[23] But how much longer will they know what or whom to ask?

Today, for locals and migrants alike, the primary provision ground is increasingly the Cost-U-Less. Comparing the food sources of her childhood in the 1960s and 1970s, Olivia Christian paints a picture of a very different landscape than today: 'When I was a child it was pretty much what you catch as far as getting meat, chicken. There was always chickens in people's yards [...] wildlife [...] goats, pigs were always in abundance.' But now if people want chicken, she tells me, they go to the supermarket.

She maintains a connection to her St John ancestry by demonstrating how to make dumb bread and johnnycake in the cookhouse at the site of the Annenberg plantation. Dumb bread is a sort of kneaded quick bread, here cooked by setting a Dutch oven over a charcoal fire and piling more glowing coals on the lid. The same dough can be fried into what the locals call johnnycake. 'This bread here,' she tells me, referring to the dumb bread, 'was the life saver withal. This bread here is like a dumpling bread – heavy – it stays in your stomach all day. So, we have slice in the morning, first thing in the morning, then [at lunch] we'd have one meal a day which is meat, potatoes and veg and we'd finish up the night with this bread and bush tea [herbal tea].' And her children? 'My kids don't really eat West Indian food anymore [.... I]t's easier to go to the supermarket and microwave pizza, microwave hamburger.'

Floating Signifiers

The disappearance of the provision grounds can not only be attributed to population shifts and a tourist economy but also to a peculiarly European vision of landscape, shared by both the plantation owners and Rockefellers. Even if the former wanted to replace bush with farmland and the latter wanted to return the land to an imagined edenic forest, what they had in common was a dialectical distinction between cultivated, that is food-producing land, and wilderness, a distinction without meaning in many traditional societies. Neither could imagine that it could be both and that uncultivated land could be both wilderness and provision ground, that you need not clear away the existing ecosystem in order to live off the land.

But there's hardly anyone left who looks at the green hills and sees provision grounds. National Park naturalists see an ecological system under threat, while tourists arrive to bathe in the coastline's unspoiled pleasures. Certainly, neither of these groups associate the land with agriculture or food. The plantations are historical curiosities; the wandering goats present an Instagram moment. And St Johnians are increasingly no different. When I ask several locals how they feel about the park they tell me that opinion is split. Some see it as an intrusion, an impediment to profit, but others look across the water at the unfettered development on St Thomas, and praise Laurence Rockefeller's beneficence. But as a source of food? Hardly.

One thing the park has done is to make today's disconnect between food and landscape clear, perhaps more transparent on St John than elsewhere. Peasant societies everywhere have gradually become disconnected from their *terroir* as urbanization has depopulated the countryside. (The loss shouldn't be over-romanticized – many had good reason to cut and run – yet there is a loss nonetheless.) For those seeking to roll back a literally displaced relationship to food, there is perhaps a lesson here, but maybe not an entirely satisfactory one. In a place like St John the local and global have repeatedly chafed against each other for centuries. The result, at least for a time, was a food culture that was not only embedded in the landscape, it was actually constructed of the landscape. This cannot be replaced by market gardens, professional foragers, and sustainability-minded fishermen, no matter how locally-based or well-meaning. The former comes out of necessity and need, the latter out of choice and privilege. Both can be delicious (or not), but each has a very different meaning.

Postscript

Less than two months after presenting this paper, I watched the news with horror as Hurricane Irma tore through St John with devastating winds. The aftermath of the category five storm, the worst in over a century, left most houses roofless, boats scattered across the shore, and virtually all trees denuded of foliage. Given the likely exodus of St Johnians and the probable influx of off-islanders seeking construction jobs, the trend outlined in this paper is only likely to accelerate.

Notes

1. C.G.A. Oldendorp, *History of the Mission of the Evangelical Brethren on the Caribbean Islands of St Thomas, St Croix, and St John* (Ann Arbor: Karoma Publishers, 1987), p. 51.
2. Judith A. Sichler, 'Historic Period Foodways in the Danish West Indies (1718-1917): The Zooarchaeological Evidence from Cinnamon Bay and the East End, St John, Virgin Islands' (unpublished doctoral thesis, University of Tennessee, 2003), p. 55 <http://trace.tennessee.edu/utk_graddiss/4296/> [accessed 25

April 2017].
3. Isaac Dookhan, *A History of the Virgin Islands of the United States* (St Thomas, USVI: Caribbean Universities Press, 1974), p. 81. For the Barbados statistics, see Philip D. Curtin, *The Rise and Fall of the Plantation Complex Essays in Atlantic History* (Cambridge: Cambridge University Press, 2010), p. 83.
4. Sites in St Thomas have yielded radio-carbon dates as early as 880 BCE for human settlement: see Irving Rouse, *The Tainos: Rise & Decline of the People Who Greeted Columbus* (New York: Yale University Press, 1992), p. 62.
5. Oldendorp, p. 222.
6. Karen Fog Olwig, *Cultural Adaptation and Resistance on St John: Three Centuries of Afro-Caribbean Life* (Gainesville: University of Florida Press, 1985), p. 81.
7. Sichler, pp. 190–200.
8. Olwig, p. 51.
9. Olwig, p. 90.
10. Department of Commerce, Bureau of the Census, 'Census of the Virgin Islands of the United States' (Government Printing Office, 1918), p. 37.
11. Olwig, p. 108.
12. Interview with Olivia Christian, 2017.
13. St John Historical Society, 'Ladies' Storytelling at Bethany Church Hall, November 10, 2009', *St John Historical Society*, 2009 <http://stjohnhistoricalsociety.org/ladies-storytelling-at-bethany-church-hall-novemember-10-2009-by-robin-swank/> [accessed 29 May 2017].
14. A. J. Oakes and M. P. Morris, 'The West Indian Weedwoman of the United States Virgin Islands', *Bulletin of the History of Medicine*, 32 (1958), 164.
15. Toni Thomas and others, *Traditional Medicinal Plants of St Croix, St Thomas and St John: A Selection of 68 Plants* (Saint Croix, USVI : University of the Virgin Islands, Cooperative Extension Service, 1997).
16. Oakes and Morris, p. 164.
17. Qtd. in Olwig, p. 100.
18. Robin Winks, *Laurance S. Rockefeller: Catalyst for Conservation* (Washington, D.C.: Island Press, 1997), p. 63.
19. 'Frequently Asked Questions – Virgin Islands National Park (U.S. National Park Service)' <https://www.nps.gov/viis/faqs.htm> [accessed 29 May 2017].
20. '1950 (from '100 Years of U.S. Consumer Spending') – 1950.Pdf' <https://www.bls.gov/opub/uscs/1950.pdf> [accessed 21 May 2017].
21. U. S. Census Bureau, 'Profile of Selected Social Characteristics: 2010 U.S. Virgin Islands Demographic Profile', *American FactFinder* <https://factfinder.census.gov/faces/tableservices/jsf/pages/productview.xhtml?pid=DEC_10_DPVI_VIDP2&prodType=table> [accessed 30 May 2017].
22. David A. Olsen, David W. Nellis, and Richard S. Wood, 'Ciguatera in the Eastern Caribbean', *Mar. Fish. Rev*, 46.1 (1984), 13-18.
23. Elizabeth G. Radke and others, 'Ciguatera Incidence in the US Virgin Islands Has Not Increased over a 30-Year Time Period despite Rising Seawater Temperatures', *The American Journal of Tropical Medicine and Hygiene*, 88.5 (May 2013), 908-913.

Pasture and Pastoralism: The Inextricable Links between Food, Culture, and Landscape in Samburu District, Northern Kenya

Jane Levi and William Rubel

Pastoralism Relies on Pasture. No Pasture? No Problem.
In a paper for the 2010 Symposium on Smoked, Cured, and Fermented Foods that was co-authored with one of our Samburu friends, Elly Loldepe (now a local politician and too busy to write this latest paper with us), we discussed the techniques, language, and aesthetics of Samburu milk culture. At that stage, it was already clear that the traditional pastoralist way of life of these Maa-speaking people was under threat from global climate change, changes in land ownership and management (especially disintegration of the commons), recurring drought, land erosion, economic challenges, and the human migration that goes with all of the above. We were engaged with our local friends in an effort to understand in detail and record in full the practices, techniques, and traditions associated with milk, the Samburus' unexpectedly varied and complex prime staple food. Seven years later, we are still working on the project, documenting milk-related processes and language and collecting artefacts for preservation and future display in the county capital, Maralal – and working with increasing urgency. For whereas in the past it seemed possible to recover from the occasional extreme climatic episode, it is now clear that in vast areas of this particular landscape it is not. And with this realization comes another equally clear – and perhaps equally obvious – fact: without the landscape that supports it, there is no pastoralism; without the pastoralism, there is no traditional way of life; and without either pastoralism or traditional life, there is no Samburu milk.

It is not an exaggeration to say that the underlying ecology that supported pastoralist life in Northern Kenya has collapsed. Around the town of Wamba in the Samburu Lowlands, where William Rubel began visiting and documenting in 1995 (joined by Jane Levi in 2010), a landscape that once supported vast herds of cows now supports no cows at all. Whereas photographs from the 1990s show grass beneath the acacias, as befits a grand African Savannah, what one now sees is red gravel and sand. Increasingly larger herds of camels browse the higher branches of the acacia; goats browse the lower branches and compete with the few cows for what little scrub is left beneath them. Now, even in the rainy season, there can be so little scrub that even the hardy goats die of starvation. When the rains come, the bare land is ploughed into ever deepening erosion gullies, massive scars on the landscape, many of which are metres wide and deep. They are too large to be filled in by debris during future rains, and instead the rushing water simply widens and deepens them. What used to be a long, straight walk across the flat lowland Savannah has become a hike of multiple up-and-down scrambles through new mini ravines, and leaps across the various smaller trenches.

The landscape and the Samburu culture were always deeply intertwined. Social relations were organized according to very clearly delineated gender roles and, while there were few material objects, those that existed were organized in support of the social system. It is fair to say, however, that most anthropologists and ethnographers of the Samburu (and their cousins, the Maasai) have dwelled on the masculine elements of their culture. This is hardly surprising. Even for the most experienced researcher, it is, as in so many other cultures, much more difficult to gain access to and communicate effectively with women, whose lives are more domestic than public. Furthermore, Samburu men are so very glamorous and photogenic. At every stage of their lives from young adolescence onwards boys and young men participate in fascinating rituals and adopt complex and highly decorative styles of dress. They carry weapons, colour their hair, festoon themselves with beads, and mark their flesh with decorative scars. The women, too, wear remarkable beads, but it is the young men who are most on display. All of these visible expressions of Samburu culture and practices are worthy of record and study. However, if our purpose is to develop a deeper understanding of the people and their lives, we suggest that to focus only on the artefacts and rituals of the warrior culture is to miss the point: while dominant in the culture, they are only one of the products of it. In fact, we would argue that the masculine Samburu culture grew up to support and effectively manage the underlying pastoralist system, which, far more than being about warriordom and display is actually synonymous with the food system – all other aspects of which are managed by women. In their daily lives both genders are engaged in work and rituals that support the production and consumption of milk. Food, culture, and landscape are thus inextricably linked and mutually supportive, with landscape as the foundation. Without landscape, none of it can exist, except as a shadow, as a ghost or memory.

In the context of landscape, it is important to consider this people's general approach to land access and ownership. Traditionally, the Samburu lands were held in common, an approach to land custody essential for successful pastoralism. It is worth pausing to consider what this really meant: the Samburu people agreed that this vast geographical area was held in collective ownership. It is no accident that the name of the geographical district and the name of the people is one and the same: it was understood that all of this land, their land, was part of one continuum, common to all Samburu people. There were, literally, no fences. While clan structures meant that there were chiefs, assistant chiefs, and heads of families with more or less sway over the specific movements and behaviours of their groups and sub-groups, each with nominal responsibility for and entitlement to specific areas, none of them 'owned' it in the way we modern people of the global North would understand it. Under British colonial governance this district beyond the northerly settlement of Archer's Post was a closed area, subject to tight management, and for long periods of time it was effectively isolated from the more southerly parts of northern

Kenya. Within the district itself, the British imposed strict limits on land access, such as disallowing human and livestock movement between the Highlands and Lowlands. While some of these strictures were genuine attempts to tackle legitimate issues of excessive herd size and resultant over-grazing, the denial of the practice of this long-standing form of transhumance over major distances, fundamental to the success of Samburu pastoralism and their long-standing land management practices, should be further investigated as a root cause of some of the issues exacerbated by the recent acceleration of climate change.

Eating the Landscape

Cow milk, *kule*, sits at the core of Samburu identity. Cow milk is the traditional staple food of the Samburu and other pastoralist peoples of the sub-Saharan savannah. They also consume goat, sheep, and camel milk, but not in the same way as cow milk. These other milks are consumed in sweetened tea, rather than enjoyed as a stand-alone food or beverage. While *kule* is translated as milk, in a sense it should be understood as principally meaning 'cow's milk' even though the word is also used to denote milk from any animal. An analogue is probably that of wine. In France, a country where wine is a central cultural product, it is understood that by 'wine' one means grape wine. If, in the space of twenty years, all the grapevines in France were to die, and under circumstances that preclude them ever growing again, France might still continue with a wine culture, but it would have to be wine from other fruits – apple, plum, pear, and so on. These products could still be wine in some senses, but there would be no grands crus, no Bordeaux, no champagne, no Château Laffite Rothschild. In other words, there would be a great cultural void. There would be further distance from an understanding of the ancient European myths of Dionysus and Bacchus, and the countless ways that drinking grape wine are integrated into French culture would be lost. That is, on one level, what is happening in the Savannah lands of Northern Kenya with respect to milk – except that in this case it is even more extreme.

The Samburu are semi-nomadic pastoralists. They live within the landscape their animals feed on, both in semi-permanent communities that typically have a few years duration and include all of the women and children, and in seasonal camps associated with dry season pasture that are inhabited by male warriors (*muran*), guardians of the cattle. Until very recently, there were always at least a few cows left behind at the semi-permanent settlements (*manyatta*) to provide cow milk for these residents and the *muran* roaming the district providing security, and to supply blood to mix with milk for the children. This was a separate milk supply from that of the camels, sheep, and goats also being kept with the women and children. Until recently, it was the more significant milk supply in terms of its dietary contribution.

There is a way of looking at Samburu culture as one with the cow at the centre. Nomadic pastoralists have few possessions. Milk being the staple food, most of the objects owned by Samburu pastoralists are related to milk production, and when cows were plentiful the material culture revolved around them. Besides treasured possessions held in a leather bag called a *samburu*, plus (by the time that we began visiting) a few other possessions stored in a small metal trunk, the dominant household possessions were the containers that the milk was stored in. These milk containers existed in many forms, each having a specific use, often highly constrained and with a distinct shape identifying the container's proper use within the Samburu social hierarchy. Generally referred to by researchers as *calabash*, which tends to imply a dried gourd, almost all Samburu containers are carved from wood (although there are a very few that are woven from tree roots such as the *ntutua* or made from gourds such as the *nkirrau* and *nyatio*). These wooden containers are known in Maa as *lmala* (plural *lmalasin*). We have so far documented fifteen different *lmalasin*, each one specifically dedicated to a different gender, age group, and purpose. For example, the *nkoiting* was a small *lmala*, for children, while the much larger *seenderi* was for the husband only. A man would receive this new *lmala* on marriage, and whenever he came into his own house he would drink milk out of that one container, but no other; and no one else in the household would take milk from it. Some containers change for ceremonial purposes. Before a wedding the small *nkilip* generally used by the young woman who was to be married was decorated with white cowrie shells and red ochre. She would carry it on her back in the wedding ceremony during which it is called *lmala enkoriong*, while her husband's best man would carry the groom's larger *nkilip*, known as the *mala nailiori* during the wedding. After marriage, both *lmalasin* revert to being household *nkilip*, though the female one retains its wedding decoration throughout the rest of its useful life.

In our latest visit in July 2016, it became clear that since the containers are now rarely (if ever) used to store cow milk there no longer any purpose in maintaining all the previous distinctions between vessels. One particularly dramatic symbol of this collapse is found in the use of one particular *lmala*. In the past there was a large container, the *lmala loolmuran*, that held milk for *muran* (the young warrior cow-herds and community protection force). Any *muran* could come into the house – a hut a few metres in diameter with a roof too low to permit occupants to stand – at any time and take milk. These colourfully dressed *muran* moving through the landscape on the community's shared business was central to the Samburu social structure and to the social contract that held its social system together. As the land dies that container is now either empty, or, if it has milk, it is needed either to nourish the family or to be taken to a market to be sold. It is now possible for a warrior to drink the milk he finds in the container and to be thought of as stealing, a notion unthinkable even a year or two earlier.

Landscape and Flavour
When picturing Savannah it is easy – especially in its current state – to forget the place of trees in the landscape. But the trees are fundamental to the expression of Samburu culture, and they form the basis of many of their food practices. Far from simply being fuel for cooking fires, wood is used (as discussed here) to make food containers, especially for milk, and used (as discussed in our previous paper) as flavouring medium for cooked foods and preserved milk products. The different qualities of different woods – their grain, hardness,

fragrance, sterilizing properties, fragrance, and flavour – are well known to all Samburu and form a fundamental part of their interaction with and use of their landscape.

What Is Pasture?

For those of us that grew up in the global North, especially in Northern Europe, the word 'pasture' conjures up a very specific notional landscape: a verdant green one, rich with grasses. The dominant colour is green. While in the Samburu Highlands it is still sometimes possible to see these kinds of stretches of green grass across rolling hills (after the rains), for most of the region 'pasture' includes many plants other than grasses. The sheep, goats, cows, and camels all eat the leaves of multiple bushes, shrubs, and trees.

Samburu people are as intimately connected with this variety of plants and foliage as they are with every other aspect of their landscape. When the elders sit together tasting their milk they know from its smells and flavours where the animals have been foraging, and which plants they have been eating. A bitter (*kodua*) taste in the milk might come from the leaves of the *loduaporo*, so sharp that they say even ticks will jump off cows when they taste it in their blood. In the lowlands, a strong taste and smell (unpleasant to some) might mean that the animals have been grazing on *sukuroi* or *lopitara*. For these elders, who no longer manage the cattle herds or follow the flocks on their daily roamings, the state of the wider landscape is made visible to them through the flavours they find in their milk.

The animal forage is not the only flavour of the landscape to be found in the milk. As described in our previous paper, the *lmala* are subject to a cleaning and sterilization process that involves the insertion of burning sticks. The woods used in this process are carefully selected by the woman whose task it is to prepare for and conduct the milking according to the properties they give the milk stored in the container. These effects on the milk range from impacts on long-keeping (some 'bitter' woods apparently make the milk last longer) to a broad range of flavours that our untrained palates mostly identify as smoky but which the Samburu identify along a range of bitterness, sourness, and sweetness in the cured milk.

Commons and Landscape

The land and the food culture that goes with it is dying owing to two converging forces, both different, but both stemming from the same problem: the problem of the commons. While commons have a place in utopian thinking, in practice commons are difficult to manage, particularly once they come under threat from multiple factors. One of the reasons this particular land is dying is that the industrialized world has altered the composition of the earth's atmosphere – something that all humans share but none of us own – in a way that has increased the severity and frequency of droughts throughout sub-Saharan Africa. These difficulties are compounded in Northern Kenya, and throughout the region, as land that was only fit for grazing is itself damaged through overgrazing. The only lands that can really now support cows are the game parks, as they are no longer part of the commons. The other lands that can support cows are properties that are fenced. Fenced properties are, as of this writing, very few and very far between.

But the Samburu common lands are in the process of being evaluated for at least some privatization. In fact, courtesy of our local politician friends we are now partial owners of seven and a half acres of largely destroyed land – land that is little more than a series of erosion gullies – and if we follow local advice our first investment will be a fence.

The warriors' magnificent beading and hairstyles are now much less common. During a recent field visit, when we came upon a previously splendid *muran* we know, Mori, herding goats dressed in trousers and a shirt with no beaded jewellery, he explained that there is no honour in dressing up to herd goats. Goat herding is child's work. Even though instead the children might go to school, leaving the goats to be tended by the young men, if there are no cows, there is no need for warriors. If there is no need for warriors then the entire social structure collapses.

Which is where we are, today.

The Samburu no longer enjoy their national food: urban Samburu are not drinking *kule*, and they have not shifted from drinking their smoke-cured fermented cow's milk to drinking boxed milk. Samburu still living in the Savannah only drink inferior goat or camel *kule* boiled up with their sugared tea, and urban Samburu use packaged cow's milk for the same purpose. In other words, they are no longer even eating (drinking) their proper meal. The children growing up there today are increasingly growing up as mainstream Kenyans, which means, like us. They are shifting from a pastoralist culture to today's world-dominant culture of the farmers – the Cain side of the Neolithic revolution.

There are always reasons to mourn the death of another unique human culture. In this case, there is no time to mourn. It is time to feel fear.

Grassland turns into a parking lot – this is really the best way to imagine the current state of most of the Samburu Savannah – a car park landscaped with acacia and a few shrubs. The consequence is that the people who evolved their culture to support their animals, and whose foodways were inextricably linked to those animals, especially their cows, will meld into the population of a modern state. We are talking about a quarter of a million people. They will join the many cultures that are now known only from the works of anthropologists and documentary photographers. But we should probably not read the passing of the Samburu as yet another passing of a niche culture in a globalized world. It probably makes more sense to hear the bell tolling for us, too.

For all food-producing landscapes are increasingly under stress from problems of the commons. The ocean, like the Samburu savannah, is owned communally and nearly every fishery is being fished faster than the fish can reproduce. The commonly owned atmosphere continues to be poisoned by our carbon-based economy which itself impacts the ocean and also the farmland. When we think food and landscape we tend to think about the landscapes where food is produced. But, there is another way to think of food landscapes. Instead of looking at the fields of grain, the habitats where fish live, range land, and feed lots, we should look to the cities.

There were no cities before the invention of agriculture. NASA recently posted a photograph on their website of the southern portion of the US eastern seaboard at night.

Pasture and Pastoralism

Florida's east coast is a string of lights running for hundreds of kilometres. The landscape that supports the food that supports the social system that underpins the Florida coast is hundreds to thousands of kilometres away. Wherever you see a city, you should ask where are its farms, ranches, oceans. The urban landscape and the rural landscape are paired, even if in today's world the pairing may be in part between London and Kenya, Spain, Israel, Holland, Greece, and north Wales. As changing rain patterns affect our local agricultural production in ways as extreme as we see now in Northern Kenya, and as at the same time rising seas will stress our many coastal cities, our own social structures will be severely tested.

The Samburu culture has not proved resilient to the change in their food-producing landscape. Their culture was woven around them being the producers of their own milk and meat. Eating cornmeal mush produced in distant cornfields keeps their bodies alive but ends their ancient culture. Perhaps our more complex societies will manage to survive the many food substitutions that are likely to emerge in our shared future. Perhaps, because so many of us already live in cities eating food that comes through an industrial food system, it won't make a material difference to how our societies operate what foods that system produces for us, as long as they produce enough calories to keep us healthy. However, while it may not matter to us urbanites whether our meat comes from an actual cow or from a lab, that does matter to the ranchers.

Last July, we stayed in the bush with Marissa, the mother of a friend. It had been a good rainy season, and it had rained the day before our visit. The bare ground was dry. There was no grass, but there were a few nightshades. They were wilted. Camels, standing on bare ground, were eating from the acacia. The goats were thin, and two had recently died of starvation – and this during a good rainy season. Their community of five huts was looking to move, but the only places they could go, places with better pasture, were in contested areas – meaning they would probably be killed. Marissa, a vibrant, flexible woman who is probably around sixty years old, has started raising chickens. She has thirteen. Her little community of five stick and iron huts (the walls had been made of cow dung but as there is no dung the walls, which are under two meters high, are now made of a piece of corrugated iron) consists largely of old women, old men, and a few children. In a general conversation about life and their future the consensus was that they were trapped. The land is dead. They have no place to go. They will stay where they are, and starve.

That is not what we think will really happen. They will move to one of the growing villages, live in a shack, and get by somehow, while the land will continue to wash away. It is possible that, relieved of the burden of the humans, some of the land will revive, the animals will return (the zebras, the giraffes, the lions, more elephants), and a new balance will be established. At the same time, we can already see some of the Samburu becoming ranchers, selling goats and highland cows, prized for being 'organic', into the increasingly affluent Nairobi market. But the milk and meat based culture of the Samburu is finished. Their story, one that we are documenting, is a contemporary *memento mori* demonstrating that as the landscape dies its associated culture and foodways die with it, and when this death spiral begins the most likely outcome is acceleration.

Steps Toward an Ecology of the Cookbook: Landscape in the Cookbook and the Cookbook in Its Landscape

Don Lindgren

Introduction

Julia Child's *Mastering the Art of French Cooking* (1961), one of America's most-beloved cookbooks, sought to introduce, or really re-introduce, French cuisine to an American audience. Yet Child avoids directly addressing issues of the French landscape and tells us why: 'We have purposely omitted cobwebbed bottles, the Patron in his white cap bustling among his sauces, anecdotes about charming little restaurants with gleaming napery, and so forth. Such romantic interludes, it seems to us, put French cooking into a never-never land instead of Here, where happily it is available to everybody.'[1]

Child chooses to consciously ignore the landscape and other descriptive aspects of place to focus on Here, since it is Here where the reader will be cooking and not in the landscape of distant France. Despite this declaration, this text appears within the twelfth line of the first paragraph on the first page of the introduction of the first edition, later to become the first of two volumes, written in Cambridge, Mass, published in Boston, printed and bound in Kingsport, Tennessee. The surface of the page, the page within the book, the locations of the book's separate authorship, publishing, and printing histories all speak to elements of place and landscape beyond the text itself. Despite Child's intention, landscape is, in at least this way, an inescapable feature of her book.

The coexistence of landscapes, explicit or implicit in the text in some cases, extra-textual in others, is the subject of this essay. It is an attempt to briefly survey the myriad ways in which landscape might manifest itself in a cookbook, historical or contemporary. The various elements of the cookbook – recipes and their attendant parts, supplemental texts, illustrations, and publisher's information – will be examined for expressions of landscape, as will physical materials used in production of the cookbook itself and, finally, the accumulated evidence of use. I seek to show the presence of additional landscapes beyond the text, some of it familiar, some of it less so, asking how the readers and cooks who use cookbooks address place through marginalia, inscriptions, criticisms, edits and additions, vernacular bindings, and other modifications to the physical book. Finally, I will briefly consider the landscape in which the cookbook lives or may live, how the book itself reveals that landscape, and how that specific place contributes to the unique nature of the cookbook as an object of study. The cookbooks in this survey appear as examples that reveal landscape in at least one manner. It is unlikely that any single cookbook contains all of the elements considered here, and some may have precious few, but it is my hope that this birds-eye view of the landscape of the cookbook provides useful clues to all who turn to cookbooks as objects of study and pleasure.

Landscape in the Cookbook

Current Expectations

It has become commonplace for contemporary cookbooks to offer promises of travel, to transport the reader and cook to new cuisines, new cultures, and new landscapes. It is not enough that a cookbook provide satisfying, nutritious, and economic recipes, we now expect it to describe the geographies of food production, to evoke the atmosphere of a place, to invoke human activity within the landscape, and to do so using all the parts of the book: recipes, supplemental text, illustrations, design, etc. When all these elements are brought to bear, a cookbook may allow a reader to conjure a landscape with remarkable specificity: the topography of the land, the angle of the sun, the smell of the rain, the feel of soil in one's hands, the bustle of the market, music on the radio in a kitchen as a meal is cooked. This contemporary landslide of landscape is not found solely in cookbooks that address foreign cuisines. Landscape can be found readily in domestic cookbooks, particularly in those that address what is broadly called 'farm-to-table' cooking. In some, landscape is present right down to the soil, extending the French concept of *gout de terroir* through imagination to imply that taste of place is attainable through the cookbook.[2]

Three deservedly-praised books of 2016 exemplify this: Naomi Duguid's *Taste of Persia, a Cook's Travels Through Armenia, Azerbaijan, Georgia, and Kurdistan*; Laila El-Haddad and Maggie Schmitt's *The Gaza Kitchen, A Palestinian Culinary Journey*; and Ronni Lundy's *Victuals: An Appalachian Journey, with Recipes*.[3] All excellent cookbooks, they extend well past providing recipes to take readers on a journey to deeper understandings of food cultures and new landscapes. Beyond the evocative place-filled titles, all three of these books use illustration (here photographic) and supplemental text to connect the food to the landscape. Farms, markets, and kitchens are discussed and depicted, connecting the recipes and the landscape. The authors of *The Gaza Kitchen* write in their introduction, 'this is a hybrid sort of book. It is mostly a cookbook that recovers and compiles both traditional and contemporary elements of a rich and little-known cuisine. But it also attempts a little history, a little political analysis. Cuisine always lies somewhere at the intersection of geography, history and economy.'[4] This intersection of the recipe, culture, history, and the landscape, explicitly articulated by the author, is what we've come to expect of contemporary cookbooks.

Landscape in the Historical Cookbook

Cookbook authors of the past have not always concerned themselves with issues of place; certainly not to the extent we see in many of today's cookbooks. Broadly speaking, authors of historical cookbooks, from ancient times right through the middle of the twentieth century have often sidestepped descriptions of landscape and instead have focused on providing the practical knowledge of cookery for sustenance and celebration. Two categories of cookbooks can help demonstrate this lack of explicitly stated landscape. By their natures each addresses place, but each also nearly completely fails to include overt descriptions of landscape.

Cookbooks that Introduce Foreign Cuisines. A survey of cookbooks that introduce English-language readers and cooks to Chinese, Japanese, Mexican, Italian, South-Asian, and Middle-Eastern recipes includes only one that explicitly celebrates the landscape of the homeland.[5] Otherwise, these cookbooks promote their recipes as tasty, nutritious, economical, etc. For example, in the *Italian Cook Book*, one of the earliest Italian-American cookbooks, Maria Gentile elaborates, '[o]ne of the beneficial results of the Great War [WWI] has been the teaching of thrift to the American housewife. For patriotic reasons and for reasons of economy, more attention has been bestowed upon the preparing and cooking of food that is to be at once palatable, nourishing and economical.'[6] Not a word about Italy as a place, its farms and topography, its people and landscapes. Certainly, these books were published for a variety of reasons including product marketing, promotion of a specific diet, or to meet growing demands for more subject-specific cookbooks, a significant market by the turn of the twentieth century. In some cases, the authors had little connection with the countries of origin for these cuisines. As such, landscape was not a primary concern. Despite the variety of purposes and approaches within this small category of books, the lack of landscape in almost all of these books is striking. The exception to this lack is the first book to introduce Syrian recipes to the United States, George Haddad's *Mt. Lebanon to Vermont* (1916). First and foremost an autobiography of George Haddad, the book is a tale of immigration and success, accompanied by significant descriptions of travels in Syria and Lebanon. All of this precedes thirty-seven pages of recipes provided by Mrs. George Haddad, who sadly is not credited on the title page. The recipes are a pleasant extra for those of us inclined toward Mediterranean cookery, but seem something of an afterthought.

As an English example of this pattern, the indomitable traveller Janet Ross might be expected to wax poetic about the landscape of Tuscany in her *Leaves from Our Tuscan Kitchen* (1899), generally accepted as the earliest collection of Italian recipes published in Britain.[7] Many of Ross's other works are classics of travel writing, including *Italian Sketches* (1887), *Florentine Palaces and Their Stories* (1905), and *Old Florence and Modern Tuscany* (1904).[8] But in her cookbook, landscape is barely mentioned. She does describe fantastic historical meals, the perfumed scent of ancient kitchens, and the sixteenth-century introduction of pastry into Tuscany by the Lombards, but no descriptions of rolling hills, farms, vineyards, markets, or dappled sunlight; nothing of, as Frances Mayes calls it in her *Tuscan Sun Cookbook*, 'the *bellissima* landscape'.[9]

Community Cookbooks. Community cookbooks form a second category in which one might expect to find an abundance of landscape. Community is the umbrella category for church, charitable, and fundraising cookbooks produced by civic and social groups (overwhelmingly women's organizations), such as grange halls, parent associations, and campaigners for temperance, suffrage, and others.[10] Community cookbooks, especially those produced from 1865 to 1940, were compiled, edited, and printed locally, often substantially funded by advertisements for local businesses. From start to finish, the community cookbook is a local endeavour: recipe compilation, project finance, printing, binding, and sales to the expected audience of readers are all likely to have been done in the same municipality or somewhere nearby. Pride of place then, alongside civic duty and aspirational competitiveness, is a prime motivation of the community groups that produced these books.[11] Yet place as landscape, once again, is substantially missing. A collection of nearly eight hundred American community cookbooks, dating from the 1860s through the Second World War, has occupied much of my research and cataloguing for the last sixteen months; of the eight hundred books, only a handful explicitly address landscape: in introductory remarks, or within recipes, or with illustrations other than images of churches, grange halls, and the like. One exception is *The Lebanon Valley Cook Book*, compiled by the Church of Our Saviour Ladies' Guild, Lebanon Springs, N.Y. Published in 1926, this book illustrates how we might expect a cookbook so grounded in a specific place to express landscape. The title includes the place of origin, the Lebanon Valley, and an introduction describes the landscape in glowing terms:

> In the Westerly fold of the Berkshires lies the beautiful Lebanon Valley, with its famous healing spring on the mountainside [...]. High on the eastern slope of the range the dignified old buildings of the Shaker Community stand, embowered in sugar maple and locust trees, with tall sentinel spruces about the domed meeting house [...]. Since Charles Dickens immortalized the scenery of this region [...] it has not only grown more lovely, because more wooded, but also far more accessible.[12]

The editors speak of trout-filled creeks, 'woods full of wild flowers, and wild life'. Supplementary text joins photographs, not of a charred church building, or a new pipe organ – frequent subjects for fund-raising cookbooks – but with half-tone illustrations of shepherds on Lebanon Mountain, and a panoramic view of Lebanon Valley in 1880 (Figure 1).

Figure 1. Panoramic view from the Lebanon Valley Cook Book *(1926).*

A second exception is *The Sierra Madre Souvenir and Book of Recipes*, compiled by the Woman's Club of Sierra Madre, California. As much a real estate prospectus as a cookbook, nearly half of the text is dedicated to descriptions of '[t]he Wisteria Town, namesake of 'The Mother Mountains' that brood above her; beautiful for fragrant orchards, wide vistas, and sheltering oaks: satisfying for city comforts, country quietness and friendly, welcoming hands, all accompanied by images of homes and beautiful gardens, and an aerial photograph of the city'.[13] Uncharacteristically, the book also includes supplementary text considering the benefits of the fruits and vegetables grown in its subtropical climate.[14]

While the *Sierra Madre Souvenir* encouraged development, which certainly affected the landscape, another southern California community cookbook sought to preserve elements of the landscape, albeit human elements. *The Landmarks Club Cook Book* was published to raise money for the preservation of Spanish missions in southern California. Nineteen photographs by Charles Lummis depict decaying missions in need of repair, some viewed from a distance and situated within their landscapes, and appear with an artist's rendering of mission 'San Juan Capistrano in its prime'. Lummis' chapter, 'Spanish-American Cookery, with the Most Famous Dishes of Old California, Mexico, and Peru', places the dishes, among the earliest descriptions of Mexican cooking in an American cookbook, in the landscape of Mission-era California the Landmarks Club sought to preserve.[15] But again, these books were outliers amongst hundreds of other community cookbooks whose authors stand mute on the subject of landscape.

Figure 2. The San Fernando Mission in The Landmarks Club Cook Book *(1903).*

Finding Landscape in the Cookbook

Despite the limited attention paid to landscape by authors of historical cookbooks, landscape remains present and discoverable. Cookbooks, even those with no explicit goal of discussing place, contain landscape implicitly: within the recipes of the authors and compilers, in the supplementary writing, in the illustrations, and in the physical book itself. Place is visible if we know where and how to look for that landscape.

Landscape within Recipe Names

Place is frequently included in recipe titles and ingredients. A single page-spread from the Offal section of the *Larousse Gastronomique* contains dishes in '*Allemande sauce*', '*à l'italienne*', '*Clamart*', '*à l'anversoise*', '*à la lyonnaise*', '*à la milanaise*', and '*à la hongroise*'.[16] Here, the place-names refer to various cities and countries, acting as shorthand for sets of ingredients or techniques associated with those places, thus allowing cooks to quickly and easily distinguish between multiple versions of a dish. In contrast, some authors tie numerous recipes under a single geographic assignment, as in Bill Petersen's *Treasurer's*

Cactus Barrel Full of Arizona Recipes (1940). While not every dish in the book has 'Arizona' in the name, a preponderance do: 'Arizona Strawberry Shortcake', 'Arizona Figlettes', 'Arizona Cantaloupe', and five more 'Arizona' recipes grace a single page-spread.[17]

Landscape within Illustration

Cookbook illustration has mostly held the landscape at arm's length. Instead it has focused on other subjects: author portraits, carving instructions, table settings, equipment and utensils, process, and finished dishes. Forms of landscape do appear in some of these subjects of illustration, including the landscape of dining in the table setting, the landscape of the meat animal in carving instructions, and most notably in the landscape of the kitchen, a topic explored in depth by Deborah Krohn in her *Food and Knowledge in Renaissance Italy*.[18] Other illustration types may also contain landscape. A frontispiece portrait from the *London Art of Cookery* of 1792 pictures chef John Farley atop a view of his handsome London Tavern.[19] The frontispiece from a popular nineteenth-century middle-class German cookery book, *Supp', Gemüß'und Fleisch, Ein Kochbuch*, sports a split image with burghers, all men, sumptuously dining and drinking in an upstairs room while female domestics toil below (Figure 3).[20] In Albert's *L'Art du Cuisinier Parisien*, a professionally attired *Cuisinier Parisien* taste-tests from a saucepan amidst an extensive *batterie de cuisine*, while behind him a woman worker plucks a chicken, a cat and dog at her feet.[21] The illustrations of Marie-Antoine Carême's *piece monté* are imaginative landscapes in miniature.[22] All of these depict place and contribute toward an understanding of different landscapes: the street face of a restaurant; the upstairs/downstairs of a German bourgeois household; the professional kitchen of a French chef; an idealized landscape of ruins and follies.

Figure 3. Frontispiece from Supp', Gemüß'und Fleisch, Ein Kochbuch *(1792).*

The Landscape of Ingredients

In the previous examples, the cookbook authors, or perhaps publishers in the case of illustration, address landscape explicitly. Beyond that, landscape appears within the text of every cookbook implicitly. No matter an author's intention, every cookbook does indeed contain at least one landscape through its list of ingredients. That landscape may be constructed through a methodology taught by Barbara Wheaton as part of her annual seminar, 'Reading Historic Cookbooks: a Structured Approach', which I attended in June 2011. On the first day, we were asked to record the name of each ingredient found in a cookbook's text. Ingredients were recorded and then grouped and mapped, taking into consideration the origins of the ingredients and their distances from the household. My assigned text was the fifteenth-century manuscript, Harleian ms. 279, later edited by Thomas Austin (1888).²³ By the close of the seminar's first day, the book had yielded a list of ninety-two ingredients. Grouped with like items, their probable source locations were revealed: pantry, larder, herb garden, kitchen garden, farmyard, well, orchard, grains fields, hedgerow, pasture, forest, lake, river, sea, shore, town market, and from the market to the trade routes and to the other side of the globe.

Figure 4. Ingredient map from the author's seminar notebook from 'Reading Historical Cookbooks' (2011).

By mapping these ingredient groups and their locations, distances between the kitchen and source areas become clearer, and a sense of space emerges. Ultimately, the groups and distances begin to reveal a picture of a landscape containing not only different terrains, but also humans toiling in those landscapes, doing the work of gathering the foodstuffs. And so, through the cookbook's ingredients, an author has unintentionally walked us from the kitchen, through the pantry and the larder, outside to the kitchen garden, past the dairy barn, the bee skeps, to the hedgerows and through the fields. We see the hunter in the forest, the clam diggers on the tidal flats, the poacher in the hedgerow. We shop the town or city market, and gather food from locations on the far end of the Spice Route.

In the case of Amelia Simmons' *American Cookery* (1796 second edition), recipe names and specific ingredients have helped uncover the landscape in which the author compiled what is generally recognized as the first cookbook written by an American.²⁴ Little is known of the personal history of Simmons, but a few ingredients in *American Cookery* speak to the landscape in which she worked. In her introduction to a modern edition of *American Cookery*, Karen Hess states, '[t]he presence in her work of a number of Dutch words lends further support to my maverick notion that perhaps we should look to the Hudson River valley rather than to Connecticut for possible traces of her existence. Chief among these words is slaw, from *sla*, meaning salad, and cooky, from *kookje*, meaning, well, cookie.'²⁵ Hess uses the linguistic origins of ingredient or dish names to place the author in the Hudson Valley, at the time a region with a significant German/Dutch speaking population and with a culinary vocabulary different from that of Connecticut, which had been established by English-speaking Massachusetts

Puritans. Another ingredient, ambergris – a prized excretion of the sperm whale – offers further evidence of potential Hudson Valley origins of Simmons. *American Cookery* contains a recipe for 'Whipt Cream' in which Ambergris appears as 'amber gum'.[26] Why would an ingredient associated with luxury perfumes and royal recipes appear in this humble book aimed at a readership of 'American orphans', a work with only two of sixteen printings from large cities: Boston (1819) and New York (1822)? It is presumed that Simmons saw the ingredient in Susannah Carter's *The Frugal Housewife*, where it appears in a recipe nearly identical to Simmons's as 'Ambergrease'.[27] The recipe for 'Whipt Cream' first appeared in Eliza Smith's *Compleat Housewife*, and from there was copied by Hannah Glasse in *The Art of Cookery*.[28] *The Frugal Housewife* appeared in three American printings (1772, 1792, and 1795) prior to *American Cookery*, and was a significant recipe source for Simmons' work, so it is very possible the recipe, like others in Simmons' book, was copied. But Simmons doesn't simply copy: she changes the word to 'amber gum', a common usage for the sticky substance in the whaling communities of the Hudson River valley. Hudson, New York was established as a whaling town in 1783 by Nantucket whalers escaping the disruption caused by the Revolutionary War.[29] If Simmons was writing in the Hudson Valley, as Hess asserts, ambergris or 'amber-gum' would have been a more familiar, available, and potentially affordable ingredient.[30]

Landscape in Publication Data

Hess uses one more element of *American Cookery* to place Simmons in the Hudson Valley: place of publication. Six of the early editions were published in five towns on or near the Hudson River, including Albany, Troy, Salem, Poughkeepsie, and New York City, creating a clear cluster on a map of all of her printings.[31] To that, I would add that Simmons's second edition of 1796 was published in Albany, NY; it is the one edition for which there is evidence of Simmons's direct editorial control. Albany lies one-hundred-twenty miles upriver from the Atlantic, and just thirty-five miles from Hudson, the whaling town. And so patterns of publication emerge, and patterns of word use become apparent, and evidence builds that the mysterious Simmons may indeed have created the first American cookbook in the Hudson Valley. While the author has remained mute regarding her whereabouts, the evidence we have, though still inadequate to mark Simmons' location definitively, does allow us to begin to read and study her work through the prism of landscape.

Landscape in the Materials of the Physical Book

Printers, binders, papermakers, and others who contribute to the production of physical cookbooks offer us parallel narratives to that of the author. These narratives may touch on issues of landscape told through the materials of the cookbook itself: paper, leather, ink, or book cloth. Of course, this is not confined to cookbooks; all books through all of history contain narratives in their materials: narratives of the technology of printing and book production, of the dissemination of information through commerce and distribution, and of the social reception of ideas. Not all of these material narratives are significant, but for some cookbooks our understanding of the landscape of production and consumption is expanded. In the best cases this new element of landscape may inform our larger understanding of the book. Each material employed in the book provides numerous indications of place: paper may contain watermarks which, when identified, reveal a location and timeframe for a papermaker; book cloth witnesses the changing technologies of textile manufacture as commerce and industry spread. During the American Colonial era, the unavailability and expense of book cloth and paste-board – both common materials used for bookbinding – led to the use of cheaper scrap-paper, wooden scaleboard, and bindings with tawed leather backstrips.[32] In this case leather is not a luxury item for higher-class households, but a simple product made from scrap skins to be found in any town with a cobbler or butcher. In March of 1808, a pirated edition of Amelia Simmons' *American Cookery* was published by a Lucy Reed Emerson in Montpelier, Vermont.[33] When the book, re-titled *The New-England Cookery*, was issued, Montpelier was barely twenty years old, its first permanent settler having arrived in 1787. As a frontier town, goods and materials were scarce. So it should come as no surprise that many of the materials used to bind the book were simple scavenged scrap, likely gathered from the butcher shop (leather), the baker (sugar paper), or the sewing box (cord for hanging) (Figure 5). All of these materials contribute to our understanding of a landscape of production in a small town on the early American frontier.

Figure 5. Binding materials visible on Lucy Emerson's New England Cookery *(1808).*

Landscape in a Single Material: Sugar Paper

Sugar paper provides an example of a common scrap material that through its use ties a book to a landscape in a significant way. Many books published in England and America in the late eighteenth and early nineteenth centuries left the printer's shop in a simple binding: a paper spine with a handwritten label, and over the boards, 'sugar paper' or 'sugar blue paper', a dull but saturated indigo-coloured paper.[34] In the eighteenth and nineteenth centuries sugar was shipped, either from the source in the Caribbean or after some degree of refining, from cities like New York in cones or loaves wrapped in sugar paper.[35] The rough blue paper, manufactured in England and Europe since at least 1665, had a special characteristic that made it attractive to confectioners and bakers.[36] Made with a high level of ash, the paper would not fix natural pigments well, and the high alkaline reactivity of blue plant-dyes created a paper that would change colour when exposed to different types of sugars, including grape and beet sugars, revealing potential adulteration of the preferred cane product.[37] Confectioners and bakers preferred sugar packed in sugar paper as it implied a more pure product. Once its original purpose was served, sugar paper was scraped clean and sold on a secondary market, where it was sought as a cheap material used

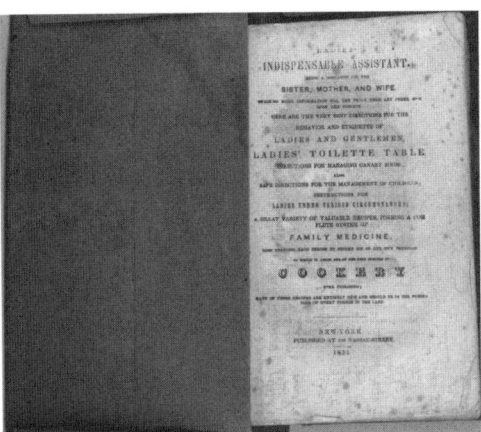

Figure 6. A vernacular binding of sugar paper on the Ladies' Indispensible Assistant *(1853).*

in bookbinding, particularly in America. The nascent American papermaking industry was focused on the production of newsprint and other standard papers, and specialized sugar paper scrap remained a welcome and useful material in the printer's shop (Figure 6). Housewives also treasured sugar paper as it was a source of indigo dye and useful in baking. Sheets of sugar paper travelled west from New England with housewives as a convenient source of colouring for cloth. Sugar paper has even been credited as the source of the blue doors and window frames of Taos, New Mexico.[38] Thus a simple piece of coloured paper, used as part of a printer's binding or later in a vernacular binding, can connect a cookbook to a number of landscapes simultaneously, including that of the sugar industry: the slave-powered Caribbean cane plantations, the shipping routes of the triangle trade, the early sugar refineries of New York, and the bakeries and confectioners shops throughout the Colonies. Sugar paper also connects the book to the landscape of the printer's or binder's shop where books were being made despite scarce materials in the new nation, and to the landscape of the household, where women valued this material for domestic applications in baking and dyeing.

Landscape in Evidence of Use

Upon leaving the printer's shop, a cookbook enters a life of use, and begins to accumulate evidence of that use. Evidence of use may include purposeful changes made to a book by owners over time, such as ownership marks and signs of presentation, manuscript revision and criticism expressed in marginalia, navigational aids, and protective or preservative vernacular bindings. Recipes may be added by handwriting, or clippings and slips of paper may be laid-in, tipped-in, pasted-in, pinned-in, sewn-in, or even attached with wax seals. Incidental change occasioned by environmental exposure is a separate type of evidence of use, and may include smoke, stains (splatternalia), predators, and other abuses. Both intentional and incidental changes are evidence that can be gathered to build a new narrative of how and where a cookbook is used.

The Kitchen as the Landscape of the Cookbook

By examining accumulated evidence of use we come to recognize that cookbooks inhabit a specific landscape in or proximate to the kitchen or pantry, and very separate from the home library. Margaret Wooley White, in *The Kentucky Cookery Book* (1891), wrote, 'I have always regarded a cookery book as a book for the kitchen.'[39] In other words, cookbooks are for cooking. By nature, they deliver practical knowledge, and the need to consult cookbooks before and during cooking places them in a category different from most books found in a home. Cookbooks are objects of everyday life, to be consulted and perhaps abused. They live adjacent to other objects of use and to domestic activity. Evidence of that use displays the material nature of that landscape; not just of pots and pans, stains and smoke, but also the other materials of domesticity: of pins, linen, cotton and silk thread, sealing wax, ink and pens, scraps of linen, canvas, and wallpaper, the paper clip and the Post-It – all speak individually to the domestic or professional environment in which the cookbook lives. In the household, they speak of cooking but also of housekeeping, of sewing and mending, of letter writing and educational exercises. In a professional environment, they speak of ownership, succession, navigation, and reference. In both, damage from smoke and stains, and ad hoc efforts to protect or mend a binding, speak of the rough use to which books are subject and the harsh environment in which many cookbooks live. That cookbooks of all eras have lived in and around kitchens is undeniable. The signs are unmistakable, and this we know solely by what remains of historical cookbooks today. For centuries, well-meaning booksellers, collectors, and librarians disregarded or discarded cookbooks with significant evidence of use. Had more cookbooks survived that exhibit this accretion of life experience, we would have rich new narratives to study, and our confidence that cookbooks are kitchen objects would be redoubled. The place of the cookbook in the kitchen environment – that landscape at the intersection of printed, rational instruction and domestic folk practice – is what sets cookbooks apart. By the nature of their use and the landscape they inhabit, cookbooks remain unique witnesses to history and to the culture of their times.

Notes

1. Julia Child, *Mastering the Art of French Cooking* (New York: Alfred A. Knopf, 1961), p. viii; original emphasis.
2. Amy B. Trubek, *A Taste of Place, A Cultural Journey into Terroir* (Berkeley: University of California Press, 2008).
3. Naomi Duguid, *Taste of Persia, a Cook's Travels Through Armenia, Azerbaijan, Georgia, and Kurdistan* (New York: Artisan, 2016); Laila El-Haddad and Maggie Schmitt, *The Gaza Kitchen, A Palestinian Culinary Journey* (Charlottesville: Just World Books, 2016); Ronni Lundy, *Victuals: An Appalachian Journey, with Recipes*, second edition (New York: Clarkson Potter, 2016).
4. El-Haddad and Schmitt, p. 15.
5. Vernon Galster, *Chinese Cook Book in Plain English* (Joliet, IL: Joy Sing Lo Co, 1907); Sara Bosse and Onoto Watana, *Chinese-Japanese Cook Book* (Chicago: Rand McNally, 1914); Gebhardt Chili Powder Co., *Mexican Cooking* (San Antonio: U.S. Print and Litho. Co, c. 1911); Antonia Isola, [Mabel Earl McGinnis], *Simple Italian Cookery* (New York: Harper Brothers, 1912); Maria Gentile, *The Italian Cook Book* (New York: Italian Book Company, [1919]); K.D. Shastri, *Hindu Dietetics, Hints on Cooking and Recipes* (Minneapolis: Indo-Aryan Publishing, 1917); George Haddad and Emily Marie Haddad, *Mt. Lebanon to Vermont* (Rutland, VT: Tuttle, 1916); Ardashes Keolian, *The Oriental Cook Book* (New York: Sully & Kleinteich, 1913).

6. Gentile, p. 3.
7. Janet Ross, *Leaves from Our Tuscan Kitchen* (London: J.M. Dent & Co, 1899), pp. xii ff.
8. Ross, *Italian Sketches* (London: 1887); *Florentine Palaces and Their Stories* (London. 1905); *Old Florence and Modern Tuscany* (London: 1904).
9. Frances Mayes, *The Tuscan Sun Cookbook* (New York: Potter, 2012), 14.
10. Margaret Cook, *America's Charitable Cooks* (Kent, OH: [the author], 1971).
11. Janice Bluestein Longone, '"Tried Receipts": An Overview of America's Charitable Cookbooks', in *Recipes for Reading: Community Cookbooks, Stories, Histories*, ed. by Anne Bower (Amherst: University of Massachusetts Press, 1997), pp. 17 ff.
12. [Ladies' Guild, Church of Our Saviour], *Lebanon Valley Cookery* (Lebanon Springs, NY: Church of our Saviour, 1926), pp. 5 ff.
13. Sierra Madre Woman's Club, *Sierra Madre Souvenir and Book of Recipes* (Sierra Madre, CA: Sierra Madre Press, 1929), p. [3].
14. Sierra Madre Woman's Club, p. [27].
15. Landmarks Club (Charles Lummis), *The Landmarks Club Cook Book* (Los Angeles: The Out West Company, 1903), pp. 1 ff.
16. Prosper Montagné, *Larousse Gastronomique* (New York: Crown Publishers, 1961), pp. 678-79.
17. Bill Petersen, *Treasurer's Cactus Barrel Full of Arizona Recipes* (Phoenix: 1940), pp. 46-47.
18. Deborah Krohn, *Food and Knowledge in Renaissance Italy* (New York: Routledge, 2015).
19. John Farley, *The London Art of Cookery*, seventh edition (London: Scatchered and Whitaker, 1792), frontis.
20. *Supp´, Gemüß´und Fleisch, Ein Kochbuch* (Darmstadt: Lange, 1792), frontis.
21. B.Albert, *L'Art du Cuisinier Parisien* (Paris: Emile Babeuf, 1822), frontis.
22. Marie-Antoine Careme, *Le Pâtissier Royal Parisien* (Paris: J. G. Dentu, 1815).
23. *Two Fifteenth-Century Cookery-Books*, ed. by Thomas Austin (London: Early English Text Society; Trubner, 1888).
24. Amelia Simmons, *American Cookery* (Albany: Charles R. and George Webster, 1796; repr. Bedford, MA: Applewood Books, 1996).
25. Karen Hess, 'Historical Notes on the Work and Its Author, Amelia Simmons, an American Orphan', in Simmons, p. xi.
26. Simmons, p. 40.
27. Susannah Carter, *The Frugal Housewife* (New York: G&R Waite, 1803), p. 171.
28. Eliza Smith, *The Compleat Housewife* (London: Pemberton, 1727); Hannah Glasse, *The Art of Cookery Made Plain and Easy* (London: Mrs Ashburn's, 1747).
29. Margaret B. Schram, *Hudson's Merchants and Whalers: 1783-1850* (Hensonville, NY: Black Dome Press, 2004).
30. Stephen Schmidt, 'Ambergris, the Perfume of Whales that Once Scented Foods', *Manuscript Cookbooks Survey*, July 2015 <http://www.manuscriptcookbookssurvey.com/ambergris-the-perfume-of-whales-that-once-scented-foods/> [accessed 28 May 2017].
31. Hess, p. xi.
32. Julia Miller, *Books Will Speak Plain* (Ann Arbor: Legacy Press, 2014), pp. 45 ff.
33. Lucy Emerson [Amelia Simmons], *The New-England Cookery* (Montpelier, VT: Josiah Parks, 1808).
34. Nancy Cox and Karin Dannehl, 'Sugar loaf – Surfeit water', in *Dictionary of Traded Goods and Commodities 1550-1820* (Wolverhampton, 2007), *British History Online* <http://www.british-history.ac.uk/no-series/traded-goods-dictionary/1550-1820/sugar-loaf-surfeit-water> [accessed 28 May 2017].
35. Joy Santlofer, *Food City* (New York: Norton, 2017), p. 143.
36. Richard Leslie Hills, *Papermaking in Britain, 1488-1988* (London: Athlone Press, 1988), p. 49.
37. Ferenc Szabadváry, *History of Analytical Chemistry*, trans. by Gyula Svehla ([Burlington, Vt]: Elsevier; repr. Oxford: Pergamon Press, 2014), p. 239.
38. Michael Wigley and Mimi Sloane, *Eric Sloane's America* (Mineola, NY: Dover, 2009), p. 35.
39. Margaret Woolley White, *The Kentucky Cookery Book* (Chicago: Belford-Clarke, 1891), p. 3.

Terraced Landscapes: Farming and Performing on Balconies

Morna Livingston

During twenty-five years of photographing medieval water buildings in Yemen, Spain, and the classical world, a link between mountain cisterns and farming turned my attention to terraced fields. Terracing's epicentre appeared to be Yemen, but it had spread to the Alpujarras in Spain, the Atlas Mountains in Morocco, and to Mallorca around Banyalbufar. Yemen had impressive slopes, but the West held channels, basins, trellises, wind breaks of cane, and pergolas adjacent to reservoirs. *Acequia* channels were plastered with lime for water tightness, and where they crossed were tiny bridges, or tunnels. Tim Macintosh-Smith says the Yemenis travelled to the West long before Islam, while Spanish authors argue that change was afoot before Mohammad, driven by a fancy for plants of the wet-tropics introduced along old trade routes. These plants all needed irrigation, which was easier to manage uphill. Gravity-fed water systems sourced from above created a pleated universe linked by small diagonal roads, ramps, and stairs, an infrastructure that required the close attention we might associate with preparing Slow Food. One had to tread lightly on the land when opening it, or risk landslides on the slopes, and keep walls intact from the top down. The verticals alternating with the flats made it easy for men and animals to work in fields at once in the open, yet protected; visible from afar, yet a refuge. Most dramatically, terraces slow down water because it loses energy when it falls and only gradually builds up speed again. Today terraced farming gets less attention and fewer subsidies than large farms because it is 'low-tech'. It resembles a still life, not a history painting in being what Norman Bryson would call 'low-plane reality', meaning a part of the domestic world lying far from the expansive landscapes where battles were fought, stags were hunted by kings, or parks full of fountains were enjoyed by the rich.[1]

This paper will look at the transformations that created these elegant, spare, virtually fireproof, and almost chemical-free landscapes, and then at changes occurring in them today. The magnetism of terracing, with its narrow strip of edibles against a stone backdrop, is theatrical in the sense that a section cut through its balconies is almost indistinguishable from a section through a *teatro di verzura*, or outdoor theatre in a private garden of the Baroque. This is not to say that the makers of either of these landscapes was conscious of the other, but rather that terraces and 'green theatres' hold

Terraced Landscapes: Farming and Performing on Balconies

Figure 1. Terraces in Estellencs, Mallorca (Photo: Morna Livingston).

everything formal in common. Not only do they share tight masonry and fine acoustics, their stones enhancing sound, but the terraces are a stage for plants needing extra attention or more sun, since the wall acts as a radiator.[2] In Yemen that includes qat, coffee, melons, and raisins; and in the West, wine grapes, limoncello lemons, fruit, perfumed flowers, and high-end vegetables marketed as 'bio', or organic. In Banyalbufar pigs foraged along the high forest edge; lower came olives and cereals under almond trees and sheep; finally were irrigated terraces for vegetables. Tomatoes adore irrigation: from Ramallet, Mallorca, and France to Vesuvius, clusters weighing several kilos hang ready for winter. But in the West, vineyards form the backbone of the terraced landscape, thriving on rock, slopes, and good drainage. Thus terraces are stone theatres for fine vegetables as much as for Bacchus, places where, as Dan Stanislawski assures us, 'the appearance of the landscape is enough to soften a heart of stone'.[3]

Rock, Rain, and Soil

Where the earth's slope is steep and land is scarce, rock-walled terraces can create levels for planting. Building flat fields on hills above a river plain began in the Neolithic, followed by later examples on most continents, but should one place lay first claim to terracing, it would be Yemen's highlands. Here endless stonewalled fields serve for dry or irrigated farming, which the Yemenis either discovered, or, linking terraces they invented, watered using knowledge from the Nabateans. Iran might share in this unwritten history, but its myriad *qanats* channelling snowmelt to water fields in the desert almost certainly came from somewhere else. In what seems more than coincidence, early *qanats* were also built in southern Yemen, for Yemenis tried out everything they could with water.[4]

Hillside terraces require such labour to build that people make them only where pressed by over-population, civil unrest, or brigands. Since hills often hold poorer soil than valleys, wall construction is but a first step, followed by clearing stones, enriching topsoil, grading, then cutting eyebrow-like channels, called *cilioni* in Italian, that permit water to sink in. In spite of millennia of use, no one has found a way to make or cultivate terraces by machine. Instead, along thousands of kilometres of terraced landscape, each wall speaks of one mason's skill and each field shows the green thumb of one farmer. Field shapes are also unique, paralleling a particular curve. That terraced walls are dry-stacked adds elegance. Renate Löbbecke, a noted authority on corbelled domes, admits that, arriving in a landscape of stone, 'I always find myself in a state of great sensory and mental alertness [...] mindful of the structure of the rock.'[5] The stone *trulli* and *cabanes* she describes provided storage and shelter for workers on terraced land, especially in wine country. Small buildings and exquisitely paved paths, or *calades*, co-existed with terraces everywhere but in Asia, where plant materials replaced them, while Yemen and Europe terrace in stone.

Even with lengthy construction, terraces can hold only light machinery or a few animals, although over time they teem with lizards, spiders, alpines, moss, and lichen. For the walls to remain stable, their thickness and footings must be calibrated to counteract soil pressure of fields swollen with rain. The stones have no mortar, but weep holes are also left to drain them. Where there is no stackable stone, some hills are planted *rittochino*, or 'straight as a backbone', up and downhill; but where terraces work, the precision of their walls imposes great clarity on the view, outlining each precise contour in distinct greens. The most perfect terraces are sharply cut and noticeably more architectural than a grassy slope left to slide into a comfortable angle of repose, yet thousands of olive and fruit terraces, never firmed with stone, do shape themselves like this in southern Italy and Greece.

To control erosion, terraces must be built all at once from the top down, including their complement of rapid-drainage channels, steps, and ramps. Paths must be separated from the main drains and firmly paved. Unlike farms in flatter land, mountain topography guarantees that every terrace will be keyed to its *genius loci*. Banyalbufar in Mallorca shows this rhythmic stratification of a hill: the wooded top, where men still hunt; the un-watered olives; then further down, irrigated fruits and vegetables on their own terraces, accompanied by stone cisterns with rounded corners tucked into the margins of the principal channels, fed by winter rain and used during droughts. In summer these turn a shiny blue against the dense browns and greens of the earth. The authors of *Paysages et Terrasses* explain that irrigating these terraces 'is simple enough in its methods, but very refined in its meticulous and garden-like character'.[6] The complication of watering justifies a terrace for thirsty plants like rice, wheat, cane, cotton, eggplants, watermelons, artichokes, and saffron. Only sorghum in Yemen is drought tolerant, like the olive. The others crave water.

Worldwide, woody plants can also thrive in the limelight of terraced living. Shelves are ideal for plants that hate wet feet, or prefer a warm wall to ripen. Thus, costly wall construction provides a logic for costly plants, leading to vineyards throughout the Mediterranean, and qat and coffee

Figure 2. Terraces in northern Yemen (Photo: Morna Livingston).

Terraced Landscapes: Farming and Performing on Balconies

Figure 3. Terraced Baroque 'Green Theatre', Valec, Bohemia (Photo: Morna Livingston).

trees in Yemen. Tim Mackintosh-Smith calls Yemeni terraces hanging gardens, 'contouring voluptuously round the flanks of mountains, or perched, sometimes dinner-table sized, in what are often no more than vertical fissures'. Wedged in, 'they act like a cross between the pores of a giant sponge and the locks of a canal', releasing torrents as they calm kinetic energy.[7] Water falls down terraces not as if on a water slide, but instead slows at the lip of each wall to fall majestically. Plant roots then grasp the soil like rubber bands, with vines roots extending to fifty feet. Even today, lemons thrive on the Amalfi coast, capers fruit on dry Pantelleria, pendulous tomatoes thrive in the dusts of Vesuvius, while citrus and flowers for essences bloom from Grasse to Calabria. Olives, hazelnuts, almonds, walnuts and chestnuts also find terraces congenial, and with a little care, each can now be designated as organic. The authors of *Paysages et Terrasses* observe that beyond growing distinguished plants, terraced sites 'induce a great variety of landscape effects, sometimes contradictory, according to the axis of vision, or the situation: verticality-horizontality, mineral-vegetal, overture-closure, effects of a labyrinth, of a balcony, of a lure, the possibility to show up and work, or to hide, resonate', further stressing that 'this kaleidoscope of potentialities could not have escaped the creators of gardens'.[8] When Italians in the Baroque first explored the links between landscape and garden for private outdoor theatres, they devised a new theatre type, not strictly classical, that they called them *teatri di verzura*, and in them the vivid paradoxes of terraces served well.

Terraces Inspire *Teatri di Verzura* in the Renaissance

Almost in synchrony with early *arboreal* theatres, in 1576 Andrea Palladio re-envisioned the Villa Rotonda as an agricultural temple on a stone terrace overlooking its property.[9] When, some four hundred years later, David Losey filmed *Don Giovanni*'s wedding scene in the villa's ground-floor kitchen, he marked the upstairs-downstairs link to its fullest. In the vaulted kitchen, to suggest the vulnerability of women servants to abuse from their lord, he shot the maid Zerlina in white muslin against white hens and rabbits as she appeals her innocence in the matter of her employer's attentions to her furious fiancé Masetto. He is laced in tan leather, while cured sausages and hams hang from beams above him. Foods enhance the character, and by inference Palladio's design, since the architect described the air vents in this kitchen in detail. While Zerlina appeals to Masetto, we look for the concealed vents that removed smoke and smell, leaving clean air in the *piano nobile* and the lower kitchen.

By the Baroque, farm terraces, being at much the same scale, began to be constructed for *teatri di verzura*.[10] In drawings, their stepped sections even read similarly, although they met different purposes. Both shared excellent sightlines, much improved over open fields, with acoustics allowing sound to resonate better than most ancient theatres. From Greece to Yemen, the need to project voices across valleys gave early training in the performance of the chanted poems exchanged at gatherings, when host and guest challenge and answer each other. Since terraces lie like the steps of one giant ladder against the ramp of their supporting hill, they ease interactions up and down the slope. Still, linking mountain terraces with theatres would have been the last thought of farm people in European hills, much less in a terraced haven like Yemen, which never imagined theatres at all. It was the West, inspired by printed books and the rediscovery of all things classical, that set the stage for introducing terraces into Baroque gardens. Naomi Miller writes that, from Meudon to Tivoli, 'terraces were not only interwoven with the terrain, they facilitated the installation of fanciful grottoes'.[11] Scale may have suggested this logic, since farm terraces are compact, but hilly Italy took the lead over France as terraces edged their way toward villas, serving secular drama as opposed to Church festivals. For indoor theatres, northern Italy added wings to large rooms with a raked floor ending in a wooden set of an ideal city in perspective. These theatres blossomed outdoors – the urban backdrop was clipped into hedges and pollarded trees, with the sky as ceiling. This new scene suited Arcadian dramas populated by shepherds, nymphs, satyrs, and Bacchus, while classical Herms placed among the trees mediated in silence between live actors and audience, and the green architecture. Urban sets metamorphosed into topiary framed a compressed landscape – at once stage and garden room – with the audience placed above the stage, or the actors above the audience.

Occasionally, a villa borrowed the round form of the small Greek theatre or assembly, with seat-like stairs in grass or stone to serve either the actors or the audience, but when hemicircular, or elliptical, most were walled with box, bay, linden, or hornbeam, referring to the metamorphosis of Daphne. The compact intimacy could also transform the audience into shepherds, dancers, or nymphs by proximity to the acting professionals, opening new social avenues for women and encouraging elegance in men. The smallest 'green' theatres were termed 'cabinets', meaning closets or rooms, but these rooms had to withstand wind and rain and not ruin fine footwear. Here, the drainage of farm fields offered solutions, and it was not long before successive garden terraces were connected by diagonal stairs and ramps along which actors could appear from a distance, hide from one another, or pantomime simultaneous events. At the close of a performance, the players could mix, dance, or dine with the audience, while the traverses, or *traversières*, the French term meaning connections across the hill, allowed the terrace sweeps to become *coulisses*, or tree-filled theatre wings, by night while remaining delightful gardens by day. Although garden owners might doctor the season by tying silk flowers or ripe fruit on trees, all green theatres were meant to undergo the scrutiny of an audience, which meant their reality as a garden could not be faked. This uniquely appealing quality was one alfresco theatres never shared with theatres indoors.

Terraced Landscapes: Farming and Performing on Balconies

The earliest unrecorded links between farm terraces and theatres became explicit with Claude Mollet's 1616 *Le Théâtre d'agriculture et mesnage des champs*. Gardener and nursery man to three French kings, Mollet's work was published around 1669 by his son, André. It focussed on planting, especially trees, more than on the structure of gardens, but made mention of planted allées on terraces, along with the placement of sculpture and fountains. Mollet's parterres were meant to be viewed from high terraces, and in that they resemble stages, or the diagrams for courtly dance. By 1709, a more critical figure for the terrace-theatre link, Antoine-Joseph Dézallier d'Argenville discussed design for specific land surfaces in his *Theory and Practice of Gardening*. It was a new concern for the garden theorist. With his book, a garden could be read step by step, from its choice of site to its parterres. Born in 1680 to a family of booksellers and editors, Dézallier, flourishing in this cultivated milieu, assembled a *cabinet de curiosités* while studying law, collecting shells, learning the cello, and mastering architectural drawing. Yet, gardening was his first love. In 1711, in advance of his inheritance, he received the Argenville estate with its garden in Bezons.[12] Being near the Seine, it lacked terraces, but encouragingly, it had a *buffet d'eau*, potted orange trees, pomegranates, and bay laurels.[13] A few years later, he sold Argenville to buy the hermitage at Bièvres, acquiring his first theatre, a wall fountain, and a court called *La Tabagie* for smoking.[14]

In his *Theory*, Dézallier explains in unpretentious language garden design and water systems based on first-hand experience in a royal garden he helped design, plus countless hours spent drawing the king's gardens at Versailles, Marly and Chantilly.[15] The *Theory* shows amphitheatres, classical doorways made entirely of greenery, and diagrams of walled terraces, plus calculations for slopes and wall thickness.[16] Here, perhaps for the first time, his interests put the social elite in touch with artisans by connecting their two landscapes. It is worth mentioning that French garden literature is so extensive because the French located gardens along rivers and in wetlands, which constantly required earth moving, drainage canals, piping, and a grasp of optics to create height, while the Italians and Bohemians sought steep sites in the first place. Only the Parisian St. Cloud has its hunting park on a hill, while its gardens, gravity-fed water theatre, and parterres descend on terrace after terrace to the Seine.

The Water Buffet: Stepped Landform in Miniature

As the origami folds of terraces were being reconfigured to structure garden rooms, links to food served after performances occurred naturally. In the seventeenth century, new metal technology enabled the use of stronger pipes and valves to supply water buffets. This new garden furniture – part sideboard, part cascading fountain – offered a place to cool wine, exhibit prize porcelain, or moisten basins of fruit. In a theatrical gesture, a patron might pour wine through a fountain to dramatize a candlelit supper in open air. Soon the green theatre shared more than the term *cabinet* with the Baroque fashion for *cabinets de curiousités*, special collections of weapons, fossils, shells, instruments, and books, as well as still lifes, many of which recorded their owner's plant collections. The Medici commissioned dozens of luminous fruit, vegetable, and insect still lifes on parchment from Giovanna Garzoni, along with huge canvases detailing their citrus, cherry, and pear collections from Bartolomeo Bimbi. These minutely observed fruit and vegetable portraits give us a context for understanding food consumed in gardens, and, though seeming remote from farm landscapes, soon caught French garden owners growing rare things.

In 1563, Bernard Palissy, an odd combination of rustic potter and sophisticated scholar of natural science, proposed two completely glazed grottoes of fish, turtles, and frogs cast from life in clay. His major patrons, Anne de Montmorency and Catherine de Medici were offered an outdoor room, and later in *La Recept Veritable* Palissy described it: ceramic rocks, glazed like real ones, 'would form some sort of a buffet, to hold the glasses and goblets of those who feast in the cabinet. And by the same means, certain enclosures and receptacles would be formed in this rock to chill the wine'.[17] As part of the water theatres in gardens designated by various names, water buffets were striking. Gushing water and on occasion filled with dishes and bottles of wine, they come close enough to suggest one of Palissy's amphibian platters enlarged for a garden, its structure of rocks in semi-precious jasper, like stones mentioned in the *Hypnerotomachia Polifili*, held a table, but on the supporting wall snakes nestled and ferns grew, all realistic down to the snakeskin, and glazed in a ceramicist's technicolour dream. Instead of the more usual shell and pebble paving, Palissy engineered the water in his grottoes to flow over the ceramic stones, but remain so pure and cold that if you wanted to dilute your wine with it, you could dip your glass directly in a raised pool, while the water running over his ceramic fish and frogs made them shimmer as if moving.

Such elaborate conceits were not part of older terraced landscapes, but they were desired in gardens. The waterworks behind them needed piping that was often fiendishly complicated to lay out, as for example for Le Nôtre's lovely Salle de Bal, his last work at Versailles. The Salle's water cascades, confined to breaks in the terraced seating, flow beneath a path to emerge around a marble island used for plays, suppers, and dancing. This unusual shift from landscape to garden art was even more special because on the Salle terraces were suspended chunks of volcanic pumice on wires that rang in harmony with the orchestra. Gradually, pergolas, raised plantings, tension wires, and trellises were found as useful for rigging ephemeral garden theatres as they had been on farm terraces. In France, terraced gardens and green theatres tend to celebrate water and greenery over plants, although oranges, pomegranates, and grapes appear on sculpture.[18] Water was enjoyed as often for its ability to mirror landscape as for its playfulness in the wind, so designers like Le Nôtre delighted in marrying landscape to water.

Among early descriptions or drawings of green theatres, most striking is the mention and illustration of a 'theatre of memory and of nature' in the 1499 *Hypnerotomachia Poliphili* (*The Strife of Love in a Dream*), a book the Boston literati would call an 'odd volume'. This beautifully designed and illustrated work describes a lover wandering through a wood while discovering symbolic architecture as he looks for his ideal partner. Notable among the buildings is a woodcut of the Temple of Venus, on whose parapet,

Terraced Landscapes: Farming and Performing on Balconies

three stories in the air, cypresses curve to form green arches. Under each arch, a clipped tree is flanked by two smaller topiaries. The airborne garden image bears a startling similarity to gardens atop the frontispieces of two eighth-century Yemeni Korans. In *The Mediation of Ornament*, Oleg Grabar suggests these idealized mosques and rooftop gardens form an interface mediating between us and the text that follows. The illuminations lead, like a doorway, to writing more important than they are.[19] As for the gardens at the top of each page, we question where they are in relation to the mosques, probably not on top. But Grabar's theory could apply to the *Hypnerotomachia*'s 'theatre of memory and nature', to which all green theatres are later relations. These three peripheral images present utopian prototypes of architecture with gardens that artists drew before any practical gardener tried to realize, much less plant, one. Palissy offers confirmation that this might be a valid connection to follow, as, entranced by written descriptions of how ripples veiled marine life, and observing how water could animate the glazed crayfish in his grottoes and cause the skin of snakes and lizards to glisten, he provided animal-embossed ewers for his basin-sized ceramic wetlands, so their owners could pour water over his work to test the ripples at their pleasure.

Terracing the Rust Belt

Renaissance archaeology hoped to appropriate the classical world through a treasure hunt for its buried sculpture, capitals, and columns. As Protestant critics forced the Church into disapproval of much that was classical, arguing that it was pagan, the nymphs and erotic statuary in gardens had to go, especially from gardens of prelates. While previous adaptations of terraced agriculture carried no such legacy, even in gardens, most playful uses of grottoes were submerged. As cave-like rockeries based on classical nymphaea, although still a joy for their cool water and rock-filled decor, could no longer serve nymphs, even poetically, they lost interest for garden patrons, and the ever-graceful nymphs were sidelined. These changes would not have happened if the classical urban nymphaea, consisting of a fountain on a building facade, like the one on the Library at Ephesus, had been known, for that might have served as an alternative to the cave. But due to the Ottomans, Europeans were unsafe in western Turkey and had never seen Ephesus. Pirro Ligorio, a classical scholar and architect from Naples, did sense this. Studying classical remains in Italy, primarily Hadrian's Villa, the terraced Temple of Fortune at Palestrina and the circular, terraced Tomb of Augustus in Rome, he designed the fountains of the Villa d'Este at Tivoli. Revisiting that theme, he then sketched a five-storey terraced villa with water 'flowing and jumping successively' down its facade before pouring into a basin beside its entry. Trees crowned the villa above a terraced pergola with more trees above those, while the whole green building backed up against a hill.[20]

Ligorio, a contemporary of Palissy's, also designed the Casino Pio IV in the Vatican garden, which he then finished for the next pope along very different lines. Conceived as a classical pleasure pavilion on two hillside terraces, it offers respite from the formal life of the Vatican. Still in use, it has an apartment with a vaulted loggia for quiet dinners uphill, and nymphaeum and pool downhill, with the two joined by an elliptical terrace giving a view toward the Tiber. Almost as it was being built, the nymphaea was felt to be insufficiently Christian, and along with dozens of well-chosen classical statues crowning the Cascino terrace, any narrative of nymphs was replaced with art on the theme of Christian baptism, and the sculpture removed. Only a few charming lobsters, turtles, and fish, friendly to nymphs, remain suspended on mosaic ribbons behind the pool, reminding visitors of Palissy's grotto dioramas, in which 'reptilian species and crustacea cohabited dark and watery caves with lizards and lobsters, curled-up snakes and vipers, and fish moving as if alive'.[21] Palissy, potter and scientist, and Ligorio, scholar and classicist, designed works their contemporaries found both fascinating and problematic, and both men were neglected by later history. Why this was the case, and its connection the Council of Trent, give some indication of the complex meanings that would curtail the building of green theatres.

Beginning with terraces and the high-value plants on them, we have watched how carefully hand-crafted terraces spawned smaller versions of themselves in Renaissance villas, only to flower more fully in the Baroque when people built green theatres in their gardens. These were spaces that could not be traced back either to theatres or to gardens of the classical world. The Romans shaped grottoes where nymphs could be appeased, but these were never structured as successive terraces, and probably none had open cascades. The green theatres, amphitheatres, and green ball rooms of the Renaissance and Baroque become settings for masques, ballets, pantomimes, and serious theatre, followed by meals that were often staged like performances, offering visual and taste cornucopias for all the senses. It cannot be a coincidence that the meals among the hedges were often staged scenographically by professional theatre designers. One charming example occurred in Le Nôtre's garden at Chantilly at the end of August in 1688, when the Dauphin was welcomed in the middle of a hillside forest for a meal. On an enormous table was a citrus tree, in the middle were baskets of fruit in graduated sizes, baskets that were woven to fit like puzzle pieces. The display looks surprisingly like the pear collection Bartolomeo Bimbi would paint eleven years later for Cosimo de Medici, for Bimbi too grouped the pears on trays and baskets according to the season when they ripened.[22] Back at Chantilly, the theatre and meals continued for days, in the middle of which the guests were told they had to find their dessert in the garden's labyrinth.[23] This jest on the part of the host, Prince Henri-Jules de Bourbon, has to be close to the ultimate in linking a garden's plan with set design, as the host forced his guests and the Dauphin into the topiary scenery to finish the meal.

The longevity of terraces still inspires the twenty-first century, for from their compactness we slowly but consistently derive new ideas. One includes the recent sprouting of vertical gardens in industrial Newark.[24] Here, a rusty factory was reconfigured into vertical terraces, similar in principle to those of tradition, in that each floor provides luxurious living for plants under timed lighting, with precise irrigation, and no soil. The firm in charge grows microgreens bringing in five times per pound the cost of chicken. Their stacked urban terrain ignores New Jersey geology and Newark's *genius loci*. But it requires the extra care almost always needed to maintain what we must probably identify, due to an accumulated history of several thousand years, as a clear and durable 'terrace' culture, one that shines on a balcony.

Notes

1. Norman Bryson, *Looking at the Overlooked: Four Essay on Still Life Painting* (London: Reaktion Books, 1990), p. 14.
2. David B. Williams, *Cairns: Messengers in Stone* (Seattle: The Mountaineers Books, 2012), p. 45.
3. Dan Stanislawski, *Landscapes of Bacchus: The Vine in Portugal* (Austin: University of Texas Press, 2014), p. 197.
4. Conversation with Professor Ingrid Hehmeyer, Yazd, 16 November 2015.
5. Renate Löbbecke, *Corbelled Domes* (Cologne: Verlag der Buchhandlung Walther Konig, 2012), p. 13.
6. R. Ambrose, P. Frapa, and S. Giorgis, *Paysages de Terrasses* (Aix-en-Provence: Edisud, 1989), p. 65.
7. Tim Mackintosh-Smith, *Yemen: Travels in Dictionary Land* (London: Picador, 1999), p. 133.
8. Mackintosh-Smith, p. 20.
9. *Theatergarden bestiarium: The Garden as Theater as Museum*, curated by Chris Dercon (Cambridge: MIT Press, 1990); Naomi Miller, 'Domain of Illusion: The Grotto in France', in *Fons Sapientiae: Renaissance Garden Fountains*, ed. Elisabeth B. MacDougall (Washington: Dumbarton Oaks, 1978), p. 80.
10. Vicenzo Cazzato, Marcello Fagiolo, and Adriana Baculo Giusti, *Teatri di Verzura* (Florence: EDIFIR, 1993).
11. Miller, p. 200.
12. Erik Orsenna, *Portrait d'un homme heureux: André Le Nôtre* (Paris: Librairie Fayard, 2001), p. 182.
13. 'Une galerie d'arcades isolées, deux importants allées plantées donnant sur la campagne, un bassin, au centre du parc, des fontaines jaillissantes, un buffet d'eau sont les principaux ornements de ce jardin' (Sabine Cartuyvels, 'Préface', in Antoine-Joseph Dézallier d'Argenville, *La Théorie et la Pratique du Jardinage* (Arles: Actes Sud, 2003), p. 15).
14. Cartuyvels, p. 17
15. André Le Nôtre, *Fragments d'un paysage culturel* (Sceaux: Musée de l'ile-de-France, 2006), p. 230.
16. Antoine-Joseph Dézallier d'Argenville (1521), qtd. in Philippe Blanchemanche, *Batisseurs de Paysages* (Paris: Éditions de la Maison des Science de l'Homme, 1990), p. 96.
17. Bernard Palissy, qtd. in Marie-Dominique Legrand, 'Les Fontaines d'après la Recepte véritable et les discours admirables de Barnard Palissy 1510-1590', in *Sources et fontaines du moyen âge à l'âge baroque. Actes du Colloque tenu à l'Université Paul-Valéry (Montpellier III) les 28, 29 et 30 novembre 1996* (Paris: Honoré Champion, 1998), p. 267, trans. by the author.
18. For a charming, imaginary tale of Mozart and bitter oranges in a Bohemian garden in 1787, while the composer was en route to Prague to perform Don Giovanni, see Eduard Mörike's 1855 *Mozart's Journey to Prague* (London: Penguin, 2006)
19. Oleg Grabar, *The Mediation of Ornament* (Washington DC: Princeton University, 1992), pp. 156-60.
20. Marcello Fagiolo and Maria Adriana Giusti, *Lo Specchio del Paradiso* (Milan: Silvana, 1996), illus. p. 153.
21. Miller, p. 186.
22. Lucia Tongiorsi Tomasi and Gretchen A. Hirschauer, *The Flowering of Florence: Botanical Art for the Medici* (Washington: National Gallery, 2002), p. 92.
23. André Le Nôtre, *Fragments d'un paysage culturel* (Sceaux: Musée de l'ile-de-France, 2006), p. 230.
24. Ian Frazier, 'The Vertical Farm: Growing Crops in the City without Soil or Natural Light', *The New Yorker*, 9 January 2017 <https://www.newyorker.com/magazine/2017/01/09/the-vertical-farm> [accessed 25 April 2017].

Cuscuz Paulista: How an African Staple Became the Gastronomic Symbol of São Paulo

Sandra Mian

My father always told me, my son take care:
When I think about my future, I never forget my past.
– *Dança da Solidão*, traditional samba by Paulinho da Viola

It is a well-known fact that couscous is an African dish, nowadays mainly associated with North Africa. But less known is that, after the discovery of the New World, couscous was often prepared with maize and was widely consumed also in Portugal, where it was spelled *cuscuz*. This paper discusses the consumption of *cuscuz* in Portugal and its introduction in Brazil, and then focuses on how the landscape and historical context of the province of São Paulo caused *cuscuz* to undergo a total transformation to *cuscuz paulista*: a special type of corn flour mixed with fish, shellfish, and hearts of palm cooked in sauce and then steamed over boiling water. *Cuscuz paulista* is now one of the most emblematic dishes of São Paulo.

Couscous in Africa

The history of couscous has been widely described by scholars like Charles Perry and others.[1] Couscous was a staple broadly consumed in Africa, such a staple that couscous and food were synonyms. While this paper does not discuss that history again, it is important to understand how and when maize started being used to prepare couscous.

The research of A. Teixeira da Mota and António Carreira details the introduction of maize in Africa: the first Africans that were sent to Brazil had probably already been exposed to maize and, in some regions, may have even eaten it in the form of couscous.[2] Maize, along with manioc, peanuts, and hot pepper, were the first products of the New World to be introduced in Africa with great success.

The Portuguese, deeply involved in the triangular commerce of slaves, introduced those products to Africa early in the sixteenth century, and they became so common that they surpassed local ingredients like millet and Bambara groundnuts. Because these were also the foods newly enslaved Africans ate at the slave outposts and on the ships during the terrible Atlantic voyages from to Brazil, they were often used to these local foods when they arrived in Brazil.

Cuscuz Paulista: Gastronomic Symbol of São Paulo

Couscous Arrives in Portugal and Becomes *Cuscuz*

The Muslim conquest of the Iberian Peninsula had a great influence on local foodways; among the new products and techniques that came with the Muslims was one dish that became quite popular in Portugal: *cuscuz*.

Cuscuz was so popular among the Portuguese that it continued to be consumed even after the Moors left the Peninsula after the Reconquista. For instance, Gil Vicente in *O Juiz da Beira* (1525) makes the Squire complain about Ana Dias spending his money on *cuscuz*: 'Because the money you gave me / She ate all in cus-cuz.'[3]

João Brandão de Buarcos does not mention maize as a staple in his *Grandeza e Abastança de Lisboa em 1552*. However, in one of the most beautiful passages of his account about Lisbon, he does mention the popularity of *cuscuz*:

> And I say that in this city there are fifty women, white and black, freed and slaves, and in the morning they go to Ribeira with pots full of rice, and *cuscuz*, and garbanzos, crying. And when the children listen to them from their beds, they wake-up and beg for money to their parents. And in reality this is not so bad as doing so they give breakfast to the children. And the same do the young men that work on the streets, whites and blacks, that way they eat their breakfasts and warm their bellies. And with that they sell very fast the contents of their pots.[4]

From this passage, we understand that many slaves and freed women were street food sellers in sixteenth-century Lisbon. *Quitandeiras*, street food sellers, was an ancient tradition in Africa, and the slaves brought to Portugal continued this tradition. *Cuscuz* was a staple in Africa as it was in Portugal. This pattern, of *quitandeiras* and a liking for cuscus, would later be reproduced on the streets of São Paulo.

This desire for *cuscuz* crossed class lines in Portugal. During difficult economic times, the government tried to control the expenses of the nobility and of the bourgeois classes through sumptuary laws; in Portugal those laws mainly concerned clothing and food. For instance, the sumptuary law of 28 April 1570 stipulated: 'Nobody could eat nor serve on his table more than a roast and a stew and a chopped dish or rice or *cuscuz*, and no sweets like blancmange, wedding cakes or egg custards, or other things of this quality, etc.'[5] Such restrictions make clear that the lower classes were emulating royal tables, using *cuscuz* as accompaniment for *ollas podridas* and meat cooked in broths. *Cuscuz* was, like rice, thin pasta, or bread, a way of soaking up the liquid of those dishes. Portuguese cuisine is often based on wet-dry combinations: wet main dishes accompanied by dry foods used to absorb the sauce or broth. This combination later became important in the creation of *cuscuz paulista*.

In his *Arte de Cozinha* (1680), royal cook Domingos Rodrigues describes how to prepare the grains for *cuscuz*, rolling the flour mixed with water and continuously sifting the grains and then putting them to dry, so it can keep. This point reveals that *cuscuz* was not only a dish but also a method of preservation. He also mentions that *cuscuz* could be savoury or sweet. Both ways were served in Portuguese nunneries and monasteries, but the sweet version became associated with the famous convent sweets. The names of several recipes in Rodriques's book – terms like *albardada, mourisca, turca,* and *moura* are common through it – show that the Arabic influence was still quite present in Portugal at that time. In another chapter, Rodrigues describes the list of dishes for a banquet in March: among them there are two dishes of *olhas pudridas* and ten small dishes of *cuscuz* or *letria* (angel hair pasta). Later on, for a banquet on Thursday, he advises that hens cooked in broth should be sent to the table one day over *cuscuz*, on another day over thin pasta, on another over rice, and so on.[6] It is clear that *cuscuz* was not eaten by itself on noble tables, but as a dry accompaniment for wet dishes.

In the monasteries and nunneries, friars and nuns reproduced the delicacies so prized by the noble classes and also created new ones. Fortunately some of these pious people wrote down those recipes to give us a glimpse of the way they ate. In one of those manuscripts, the *Livro de Receitas de Cozinha, de Cosméticos e de Mezinhas* (*Book of Recipes for the Kitchen, Cosmetics, and Medicines*) compiled by Fray Manuel de Santa Teresa in the eighteenth century, we find two very interesting mentions of *cuscuz*. One of them offers advice on how to prepare *cuscuz* and the other is a detailed recipe.

> Coscus is done like rice, with butter or good oil and then put sugar and cinnamon and send them to the table.[7]
>
> Coscus how to season and cook it: to cook cuscus you have to grind sugar and add a small amount of cinnamon and then put the cuscus in a earthenware or metal dish in layers, one layer of cuscus and in between the layer put sugar and cinnamon and don't fill the dish too much as it grows three times and when the dish is complete pour over some well-seasoned broth not too fatty and then put the dish over a pot of boiling or very hot water and when the cuscus be well moistened and fluffy you could put something over it like a neck of mutton boiled or roasted or a poultry buried inside the cuscus, roasted or boiled, and its yolks hardened over it, and if it is a hem that you have to send to the table with the cuscus, put it first on a earthenware dish and after it is cooked you cover it with the cuscus and then wet with the broth and put the hardened yolk on the top, and cuscus can be done without sugar, only pouring the broth and if it is a fat day you wet it with the broth of chickpeas and add good fresh cow's butter.[8]

Two points are really striking in these two passages. First, the recipe as described resembles *cuscuz paulista*. Second, *cuscuz* has a history similar to blancmange: it was a savoury dish made with sugar and spices that gradually became only a sweet dish. It was as a sweet dish that it has arrived in Brazil.

As early as 1515, there is evidence of the introduction of maize in Northern Portugal, the Azores, and in Africa.[9] Maize replaced cereals like wheat and was soon used to make *cuscuz*. This change can be seen through the definition of *cuscuz* in dictionaries from different periods. In 1783, the word is defined as 'little grains of wheat flour'; by 1813, *cuscuz* is 'a kind of pasta reduced to little grains that is consumed cooked with the vapour of hot water'; and in 1874 *cuscuz* 'is a kind of pasta made of maize or rice, which is cooked in the vapour of hot water, in an earthenware vase of high sides, with the bottom smaller than the top and pierced with small roles'.[10]

Cuscuz Arrives in Northeast Brazil

In early European descriptions of Brazil, chroniclers wrote about the importance of manioc for the natives. Notably, to describe the products made with the manioc, they usually compared them with *cuscuz*: 'they are just like *cuscuz*', 'they are soft and as tasty as cuscuz', 'white and fluffy as *cuscuz*'.[11] We have no precise information on when *cuscuz* was cooked and eaten for the first time in Brazil, although we can imagine that it was soon after the Portuguese started the production of sugar cane in the northeast.

In the first half of the sixteenth century, the Portuguese started colonizing the country and introducing the first sugar plantations. Very soon they were using enslaved African as the workforce. Manioc was the staple, not only for the workers but also for people of all walks of life, as it still is in this part of the country. Not surprisingly, *cuscuz* was cooked in Brazil with tapioca and sugar, sometimes with water, other times with cow's milk or coconut milk. Sugar was omnipresent in this region. So, tapioca *cuscuz* was and still is most often a sweet dish, served as breakfast food, a light meal in the evening, or as a snack. When corn was used, it was usually steamed with a little salt and nothing else as food for the poor. Indeed, in the hinterlands of Bahia this version was known as the 'bread of the poor'.

Nowadays *cuscuz* is still much prized in this part of Brazil, using both tapioca and, more often, a special type of corn flour. It is served as breakfast or as accompaniment for a main dish. Alone, it is eaten with milk and sugar, and much appreciated by everyone and especially children. *Cuscuz* is so popular with the northeastern population that works by authors like Jorge Amado frequently mention it in all its forms: simple, made of maize flour, from *tapioca de caroço* or *carimã*, steamed or raw (some tapioca *cuscuz* can be eaten raw as the flour is already cooked), with or without cow's or coconut milk, and so on.

Cuscuz Goes to São Paulo and Becomes *Cuscuz Paulista*

The colonization of southeast Brazil followed a very different pattern from the rest of the country. São Paulo was the only city not located near the sea. Being much further from Portugal than the other cities up north, the Paulistas were largely left on their own until the middle of the eighteenth century.

São Paulo was founded by the Jesuits on 25 January 1554, in a plateau of Serra do Mar, a place the natives called *Piratininga*. José de Anchieta, one of the founders, explained the name: '*pirá* in Tupi is fish and *tininga* is dry, so Piratininga is the place where fishes are dried.'[12] São Paulo at that time was crossed by more than two hundred rivers and creeks, the most important being the Tietê and the Tamanduateí. Now most are hidden beneath the city or have been made into sewers, but until the beginning of the twentieth century those rivers were full of fish and crustaceans. They were a great food source, as seen in the 1765 census that showed that the neighbourhood of Pari had seventy-two inhabitants, most of whom were fishermen.[13] The accounts of the São Bento Monastery show that the friars and monks consumed all kinds of fresh fish from the surrounding rivers.[14] Salted fish only came to the monastery from the port of Santos along with enslaved Africans.

The inhabitants of São Paulo de Piratininga, the Paulistas, had to deal with very difficult geographical conditions and constant conflict with native tribes. They had few economic resources and had to deal with what nature provided. They often adopted many native habits; as in the rest of the country, manioc reined supreme in the beginning of the colonial period.

From the middle of the sixteenth century until the beginning of the eighteenth, Paulistas started entering the inhospitable lands of southern Brazil to capture natives in order to enslave them. Those expeditions were called *entradas* and *bandeiras* when by land and *monções* when they used the rivers. During the Iberic Union (1580-1640), Paulistas also searched for gold, emeralds, and diamonds, which was the origin of the states of Minas Gerais and Goiás, where foodways are quite similar to those of São Paulo.

As Rachel Laudan explains in *Cuisine and Empire*, manioc was not a good source of food for those expeditions: the roots are too heavy to transport, rot easily, and take too long to produce, sometimes almost two years to yield a good crop (small plots were planted from place to place to feed the members of the expeditions). In addition, the production of manioc flour is a very specialized task.[15] As a result, following a very different path of the rest of the country, Paulistas also started using maize as their staple. Maize is easy to transport, very resistant to deterioration if kept dry, and can be harvested in five months.

Another thing that helped Paulistas switch from manioc to maize was the introduction of a very simple but effective technology: the *monjolo*, a primitive hydraulic machine used for processing and grinding the grains. Instead of simply grinding the dry grain to make flour, the germ and skin were removed, the grains soaked in clear water until slightly fermented, and then ground to a paste. This wet paste was cooked over a very hot plate. The final product is a kind of flour that resembles corn flakes: it is light, durable, and, most important, a kind of instant, ready-to-eat food.[16] It is this flour that would later be used to prepare *cuscuz paulista*. Perhaps Paulistas should even claim to have invented the first breakfast cereal.

Until the end of the eighteenth century, São Paulo was a small and monotonous city. As in the rest of the country, São Paulo always had enslaved Africans but proportionally fewer than in other regions. With the discovery of gold and diamonds in Minas Gerais and Goiás in the eighteenth century, São Paulo became an important trading post for both goods and slaves for the mine regions. But what was about to change São Paulo completely in the beginning of the nineteenth century was a drink: coffee. When coffee became popular in Europe, new production regions were needed, and the fertile soil of the countryside was perfect for this culture. At this point, Paulistas started bringing much larger numbers of slaves to work in the coffee plantations. Most were sent to the countryside, but some, for many reasons, stayed in the city. Another turning point for São Paulo was on 11 August 1827 with the inauguration of the first law school in the country: the Faculdade de Direito do Largo de São Francisco. Many rich families had sent their sons to study in Europe, but now many of those young men flocked to the São Paulo instead. Those events completely changed São Paulo – and were the catalysts for the creation of *cuscuz paulista*.

Cuscuz Paulista Sold on the Streets of São Paulo

To own a slave in Brazil was not just the privilege of the very rich. People with fewer means used their slaves as a source of income, sending them to work on the streets or renting them to other people. They were called *negros de ganho*, the earning blacks. One of the most popular activities done by those slaves was to sell food on the streets: most of these sellers were women who came to be called *quitandeiras* (from *quinda, kinda*, the basket used to sell food on the streets, and the Kimbundo *kitanda*, market). All the Brazilian cities had *quitandeiras* selling goods on the streets, often from door to door.

Since the middle of the nineteenth century there was an abolitionist movement in Brazil, and many slaves escaped from the plantations and hid in the cities. Laws made some of them (the elderly and the very young) free until finally slavery was abolished on 13 May 1888. Meanwhile, a massive wave of European immigrants, many Italian, began to arrive. As plantations shifted from enslaved to paid labour, in São Paulo many new manufacturing jobs were created, almost all filled by the Europeans immigrants. The blacks, *pardos*, and *mulatos* – including women with young children, the elderly, fugitives, all of those forgotten by Paulista society – had to live in some way or another. For the women, there were only four possibilities to earn their living: to be a washerwoman, a maid in a private house, a prostitute, or a *quitandeira*.

Exactly how and when those women started cooking and selling cuscuz paulista is not known. What we do know is that in São Paulo all the conditions for creating this dish were present: the city had many rivers and creeks full of fish and crayfish; there was an active fishing community, usually fishing for subsistence but also selling part of the catch; small plots of land were cultivated and vegetables like onions, tomatoes, and herbs were commonly grown; and the omnipresent corn flour was easily available. Often hearts of palm could be found in the forests nearby. All those ingredients were – and still are – the elements of a good *cuscuz paulista*.

Another important factor was the existence of a ready market. In the heart of São Paulo, in a region called the Triangle (an imaginary triangle delimited by Direita, São Bento, and 15 de Novembro streets), there was a busy confluence of people from all walks of life: government officials; students and teachers from the law school; clerks, owners, workers, and clients of the area's many stores and businesses; peddlers and manual labourers among others. It was the ideal part of the city to find a good spot to set one's tray and start selling food to hungry passers-by.

By the end of the nineteenth century, São Paulo was already called 'the city that never sleeps' and 'the city that never stops'. Maybe because of that, in São Paulo street foods were easy and quick. There *quitandeiras* never sold the angú that we see in Debret's drawings of Rio de Janeiro. Angú is soft and hot and needs to be eaten with a spoon from a plate: it cannot be eaten on the go. In Salvador, *quitandeiras* generally sold food for their peers, as the concentration of Africans was greater than in São Paulo; perhaps as a result, the street food of Salvador is typically African. In São Paulo those women had to please all kinds of clients, from the arriving Italians to the rich law students and intellectuals, so the food they sold was varied, often including local favourites or using local ingredients. Among them *cuscuz paulista* proved to be a crowd pleaser.

In *Rótulas e Mantilhas – Evocações* (1931), Edmundo Amaral details the commerce of one famous *quitandeira*. The year was 1840 and she was Maria Euphrasia Rufina da Conceição Velozo, better known as Sinhára. She had four slaves working for her. The food was prepared in Sinhára's kitchen early in the morning (even the fried food), and then the women sold the food in the evening by the stairs of the Misericórdia Church. Amaral mentions *cús-cús de bagre*, of which he says Sinhára's preparation was unparalleled. There were also hearts of palm *cuscuz*, fried catfish and cod cakes, peanuts, and all kinds of sweets and pastries. He also tells us about Sinhára's origins and those of other slaves who met at the same place to sell their goods: they came from Guinea, Congo, Bahia, Cabinda, and Cassangue (Angola). The origins of the food they sold varied as well, including Portuguese and African, but also the typical food of Bahia and São Paulo, many with ingredients obtained for free from the rivers and woodlands around the city.[17]

Another chronicler of those times, Antonio Egydio Martins, talks about *quitandeiras* selling tasty crayfish and catfish *cuscuz*. Interestingly, among many dishes he describes, only *cuscuz* merited the adjective 'tasty'.[18]

When they could, the *quitandeiras* rented a place to live and work, so that they could sell their goods without wandering the streets. This was the case of Nhá Maria Café, who used to sell catfish and crayfish *cuscuz* by night.[19] Favourite locations were often nearby churches.

In his doctoral thesis about street foods in São Paulo from 1826 to 1900, João Luiz Máximo da Silva has observed that only three foods were constantly present throughout this period: *araucaria* pine nuts, *pastel* and *cuscuz*.[20] *Pastel* (fried turnover) and *cuscuz* are still among the favourite foods of Paulistas, but *pastel* is fried and, as we have seen, the *quitandeiras* fried all the food beforehand, carrying everything already prepared to the streets. Of course, fried food is at its best just after being fried, eaten while still hot, which was not possible with fried fish, fish cakes, or *pastéis*. However, *cuscuz* maintains its properties for much longer, is easy to portion, to serve, and to eat. Besides that, cuscuz perfectly fulfils the wet-dry combination typical of Portuguese and Brazilian cuisines. *Cuscuz paulista* was thought the perfect street food.

In the beginning of the twentieth century, São Paulo became the economic centre of Brazil, surpassing even the capital, Rio de Janeiro. The idea of modernity was everywhere. The influx of European immigrants had transformed São Paulo in a city more European than Brazilian, according to many travellers and locals. For a while Italian was spoken as often as Portuguese on the streets of São Paulo, and for the positivist thinking of the ruling elites this was the way to go. With hygienist principles as their guide, the rulers of São Paulo tried to clean the city – and that meant getting rid of the *quitandeiras* and their street food. The effort has been only partially successful: the old *quitandeiras* have disappeared, but not their creation! *Cuscuz paulista* entered the kitchens of the middle and upper classes, probably made by women who worked in those houses as cooks and maids. The poor immigrants living side by side with the *quitandeiras* have probably also learned how to prepare *cuscuz paulista*. The first half of the twentieth century even saw the dish offered by some restaurants, as witnessed by some newspapers of the time.

Cuscuz in Brazilian cookbooks

In the nineteenth century, two cookbooks guided the elites in Brazil: the *Cozinheiro Imperial* and, after independence, the *Cozinheiro Nacional*.

In the *Cozinheiro Imperial* the recipe for *cuscuz* is almost identical to the one found in Domingo Rodrigues's early nineteenth-century *Nova Arte de Cozinha*. This recipe offers the technique for preparing the cuscuz properly, the grains, from wheat flour.[21]

In the *Cozinheiro Nacional*, though, there are three recipes for cuscuz in the chapter of desserts: seminarian cuscuz, a variation on that, and fried cuscuz. The first recipe resembles the one in Fray Manuel de Santa Teresa's manuscript without the savoury additions. Perhaps it was transmitted from monastery to monastery, and in Brazil the main ingredient changed – maize instead of wheat – and the savoury ingredients were eliminated altogether, although sometimes fresh cheese was added. This is basically the way cuscuz is done in northeastern Brazil up through today. The second recipe is richer and uses milk, cheese, raisins, and nutmeg; the final taste is more like a pudding. The last one, fried *cuscuz*, is a way to use leftovers, which is still a common practice.[22]

Many cookbooks were published in Brazil in the beginning of the twentieth century, but none has lasted so long as *Dona Benta – Comer Bem*. *Dona Benta*, as it is affectionately called, was published in 1940 by a group of well-known gourmets and has become the most successful cookbook in Brazil with more than seventy editions. The *cuscuz paulista* recipe in *Dona Benta* is the one that has taught generations of Paulistas and Brazilians how to prepare it at home.[23]

There are no more crayfishes and catfishes in the rivers that cross São Paulo. There are no more hearts of palm to be harvested around the city. Nowadays *cuscuz paulista* is done with shrimp and fish from the sea, or sometimes with salt cod or tinned sardines. Hearts of palm come in a can or glass jar. Other times chicken is used instead of fish and many people have simply left the steamer pot behind. But *cuscuz paulista* is still very much alive.

Cuscuz paulista was the result of a unique landscape in a unique historical period. Created by poor people under harsh living conditions: it was a rich food of a poor people. Almost two centuries have passed, and it is still alive, thanks to all those women, most of them not recorded by history, who have created a masterpiece. *Cuscuz paulista* is more than a traditional dish: *cuscuz paulista* is edible history.

Notes

1. See for example M. Rodinson, A. J. Arberry, and C. Perry, *Medieval Arab Cookery* (Totnes: Prospect Books, 2006).
2. A. Teixeira Da Mota and António Carreira, '"Milho Zaburro" and "Milho Maçaroca" in Guinea and in the Islands of Cabo Verde', *Journal of the International African Institute*, 36.1 (January 1966), 73-84.
3. G. Vicente, *Obras Completas de Gil Vicente* (1562, repr. Lisbon: Oficinas Gráficas da Biblioteca Nacional, 1928), Livro Quarto, folio XXCCIII.
4. J. Brandão, *Grandeza e Abastança de Lisboa em 1552. Organização e notas de José da Felicidade Alves* (Lisbon: Livros Horizonte, 1990), p.72.
5. M.A. Coelho da Rocha, *Ensaio sobre a história do governo e da legislação de Portugal para servir ao estudo do direito Pátrio* (Coimbra: Imprensa da Universidade, 1851), p. 139.
6. D. Rodrigues, *Nova Arte de Cozinha* (Lisbon: Officina de Antonio Rodrigues Gualhardo, 1814), pp. 134, 174, 205.
7. Fray Manuel de Santa Teresa, *Livro de Receitas de Cozinha, de Cosméticos e de Mezinhas, in Sabores & Segredos – Receituários Conventuais Portugueses na Época Moderna*, ed. by I. Drumond Braga (Coimbra: Imprensa da Universidade de Coimbra, 2015), p. 175.
8. Manuel de Santa Teresa, p. 136.
9. Teixeira Da Mota and Carreira, pp. 73-84.; J. Jules and G. Caneva, 'The First Images of Maize in Europe', *Maydica* 50 (2005), 71-80; *Food: A Culinary History From Antiquity to the Present*, ed. by J.-L. Flandrin and M. Montanari, trans. by Clarissa Botsford and others (New York: Penguin Books, 1999), pp. 355-56.; L. Camara Cascudo, *História da Alimentação no Brasil* (Belo Horizonte: Editora Itatiaia Limitada, 1983), vol. 1, p. 124.
10. B. L. E Melo Bacelar, *Diccionario da Lingua Portugueza* (Lisbon: Offic. de José de Aquino Bulhoens, 1783), p.130.; A. De Moraes Silva, *Diccionario da Lingua Portuguesa* (Lisbon: Typographia Lacerdina, 1813), vol. 1, p. 506.; J. Maria de Almeida and A. Corrêa de Lacerda, *Diccionario Encyclopedico ou Novo Diccionario da Lingua Portugueza* (Lisbon: Escriptorio de Francisco Arthur da Silva, 1874), vol. 1, p. 831.
11. Camara Cascudo, vol. 1, pp. 104, 210.; G. Soares de Souza, *Tratado Descriptivo do Brasil em 1587* (Rio de Janeiro: Typographia Universal de Laemmert, 1851), pp. 164, 166, 168, 191.
12. P. J. De Anchieta, *Cartas Inéditas* (São Paulo: Typ. da Casa Eclética, 1900), p. 7.
13. 'Maços de População', *Arquivo do Estado de São Paulo* <http://www.arquivoestado.sp.gov.br/uploads/acervo/textual/macos_populacao/030_001.pdf> [accessed 27 March 2018].
14. E. Silva Bruno, *História e Tradições da Cidade de São Paulo* (Rio de Janeiro: Livraria José Olímpio, 1954), vol. 1, pp. 257-58.
15. Rachel Laudan, *Cuisine and Empire: Cooking in World History* (Berkeley: University of California Press, 2013), p. 28.
16. Francisco de Carvalho Dias de Andrade, 'A presença dos moinhos hidráulicos no Brasil', *Anais do Museu Paulista*, 23.1 (January-June 2014), 133-93.
17. E. Amaral, *Rótulas e Mantilhas – Evocações do Passado Paulista* (Rio de Janeiro: Civilização Brasileira Editora, 1932), pp. 73-77.
18. A.E. Martins, *São Paulo Antigo, 1554-1910* (São Paulo: Editora Paz e Terra, obra de 1911/12, 2003), p. 198.
19. Martins, p. 198.
20. J.L. Maximo da Silva, *Alimentação de Rua na Cidade de São Paulo (1828-1900)* (unpublished doctoral thesis, Universidade de São Paulo, 2008).
21. R.C.M., *Cozinheiro Imperial ou Nova Arte do Cozinheiro e Copeiro*, 10th ed. (Rio de Janeiro: Laemmert, 1887), p. 295.
22. *Cozinheiro Nacional* (Rio de Janeiro: Livraria Garnier, [between 1860 and 1870]), p. 406.
23. *Dona Benta – Comer Bem*, 58th ed. (São Paulo: Companhia Editora Nacional, 1982), p. 242.

The Contested Origins of the *Presniz* between Myth and Reality

Giulia Nicolini[1]

Italian foods, particularly those which are most strongly associated with national cuisine, are often the subjects of imaginative and implausible creation myths. For example, the invention of the *Panettone* is supposedly owed to a scullery boy, Toni, whose improvised cake saved a Christmas banquet from disaster when the original dessert caught fire on the morning of the celebrations. Stuck for a name when the guests asked what to call the delicious bread-like cake, the chef mumbled something about Toni's bread, '*Pan del Toni*', and so *Panettone* was born through a mixture of happy accidents and misheard phrases.

The *Presniz*, a typical dessert of the Italian city of Trieste, has been the object of a similar folk tale that lays claim to where and when the cake was invented, and to how it got its name. Sometimes there is some element of truth in these stories – be it the place of invention or the inventor – although usually it is difficult to distinguish fact from fanciful fiction. However, the significance of such stories arguably lies less in what they say – the finer details of the story – than what they do. How do competing myths and narratives about traditional foods contribute to the construction and (re)invention of the landscape to which they are attached? What role do traditional foods play in shaping and reshaping the imaginative geographies of a place?

The concept of *Mitteleuropa*, which is strongly associated with the Habsburg reign over Trieste (1382-1918), is central to the self-presentation of the city and to the imaginaries that food producers, along with the tourism and commerce industries, construct through marketing. While there are clear Germanic gastronomic influences in the cake, the origins of the *Presniz* lie much closer to home, in the Slavic hinterlands.[2] However, the Slavic component is at best inadequately acknowledged, and at worst ignored, in the promotional and public-facing materials about the cake. This erasure reflects a broader trend in local history to neglect the influence of the Slavic community on the Triestine landscape, including its cuisine. This paper will therefore discuss the competing narratives surrounding the origins of the *Presniz* and explore their broader meaning in the collective memory and imaginative geography of the city.

Trieste: A City on the Border
Trieste lies on a narrow strip of coastline in the northeast of Italy, sandwiched between the

Food and Landscape

Adriatic Sea to the west and Slovenia to the east and south. Maura Hametz has remarked that, looking at a map of the region, it is not immediately obvious why Trieste is in Italy at all.³ Indeed, throughout its history, Trieste was frequently the object of territorial claims by competing regional powers, namely the Republic of Venice and the Habsburg Empire. The city's location on the Gulf of Trieste and its proximity to Venice rendered Trieste attractive to the Habsburgs as an outlet on the sea, connecting landlocked central Europe to the Mediterranean. In 1719, after several centuries under Habsburg rule, interrupted only by occasional and short-lived Venetian occupations, Trieste was granted the status of free port, thereby assuming its new role as a trading hub of the Austrian Empire.

Under the reign of Maria Theresa of Austria (1717-1780), Trieste was transformed into a booming, cosmopolitan port. The exemptions from taxes and levies on trade that came with the free port status attracted merchants from across the Austrian empire and beyond. The area around Trieste, which includes parts of modern-day Croatia and Slovenia, had always been inhabited by both Romans and Slavs; now Jewish, Greek, and Turkish merchants began to trade and settle in the city, along with German, Hungarian, and Austrian imperial officials and merchants. While German was the language of bureaucracy and imperial administration, local dialects, initially the Friulan *Tergestino* and later the Venetian *Triestino*, were dominant among the wider populace. The influx of foreign merchants shaped this new Trieste, and the advent of different 'nationalities' was felt both demographically, in the growing and diversifying population, as well as culturally. The impact of this period remains visible in the architecture of historic neighbourhoods, but is also clearly discernible in the regional cuisine and typical foods of the city.

Trieste's traditional cakes are said to be a result of, and strongly reflect, the 'melting pot' character of the city under Habsburg reign.⁴ Recipe books for local desserts frequently evoke this trope, as in the title of Mady Fast's 1989 *I dolci di Trieste: punto d'incontro di civiltà* (*Desserts of Trieste: Point of Encounter among Civilizations*).⁵ Possibly no dessert is more emblematic of the city's cosmopolitan character than the *Presniz*, which is presented as a kind of gastronomic metaphor for the city, a culinary embodiment of the local identity. However, as Triestine intellectuals Angelo Ara and Claudio Magris suggest, the cosmopolitan city is both a 'reality and also a myth'.⁶ Despite the co-existence of multiple nationalities in the city and its superficially multicultural appearance, the integration and mixing of people has likely been overstated. Furthermore, the positive image of ethnic and cultural mixing conjured up by the 'melting pot' trope has also obscured the unequal status of the 'ingredients'.

The proximity of the city to the historically Slavic countryside has meant that there was always contact between the two groups; however, as the Slavic community in the city grew at the turn of the twentieth century, there was increasing tension between Italian irredentists on the one hand and on the other the Slavic migrants who saw Trieste as 'naturally' belonging to its rural surroundings. Under fascism, these national and ethnic tensions turned violent; the Narodni Dom, a Slovene cultural centre, was burned and looted in 1920, with little to no consequence for the perpetrators.

The Contested Origins of the *Presniz* between Myth and Reality

Historians such as Hametz and Glenda Sluga have cautioned against reading the history of Trieste through the lens of this ethnic-national conflict, instead arguing that 'the binary view of Italian and Slavic culture does not fit the reality of Triestine experience'.[7] However, I am wary of the way in which the alternative to this binary, the 'cosmopolitan melting pot', has excluded and obscured the influence of Slavic culture on the Triestine landscape. It is crucial to keep in mind that in the 1980s Trieste witnessed a period of economic decline, out-migration, and an ageing population that triggered a nostalgic desire to rediscover the city's former glory. This nostalgia is reflected today in the desire to paint the *Presniz* as a Habsburg delicacy, and, by extension, to present Trieste as a unique landscape shaped by its ties to the old Empire. Narratives about the landscape, which are reproduced in and through portrayals of the *Presniz*, should therefore be understood in the context of modern Trieste as a city on the margins of Italy.

The *Presniz*

The *Presniz* consists of a spiral of flaky or puff pastry wrapped around a rich filling of nuts, dried fruit, and chocolate. It can be found year-round in pastry shops and bakeries but is traditionally consumed at Easter and Christmas. Cesare Fonda, who has authored a number of cookbooks on Triestine cuisine, provides this recipe from a mid-nineteenth-century manuscript from Petrinje (modern-day Croatia), describing it as the oldest recipe he knows:

> 'Trieste-style Strudel' (*Strudel uso Trieste*)
> Having rolled out the flaky pastry and spread over it butter and an egg, cover one half with toasted almonds and the other half with ground blanched almonds, then sultanas, candied citrus peel, pine nuts, grated lemon peel, chocolate, rum and plenty of sugar. After rolling up the pastry, place on a buttered metal sheet and cook in a fairly hot oven.[8]

While, as the name of the recipe hints, the *Presniz* has ties to Germanic culinary traditions, including the strudel, the *Presniz* is thought by Fonda to have 'evolved' from two other Triestine specialties, the *Putizza* and before that the *Strucolo*. In fact, in a series of cookbooks published in 1989, Fonda gives this very same recipe for the *Putizza*.

Pellegrino Artusi famously provided the recipe for a *Presnitz* (note the different spelling) alongside that for a strudel in his *La scienza in cucina e l'arte di mangiar bene* (*Science in the Kitchen and the Art of Eating Well*), first published in 1891.[9] The recipe's introduction, as well as its positioning near that for a strudel, is telling: 'here is another Germanic dessert and how delicious!'[10] Similarly, the 1892 edition of Katharina Prato's *Die süddeutsche Küche* (*South-German Cooking*), published in Italian as *La cucina della Mitteleuropa* (*Mitteleuropean Cuisine*), included a recipe for '*Strucolo alla goriziana (Presniz)*'. The *Strucolo* is another Triestine specialty that is thought to have been inspired by the strudel and, in turn, to have provided the inspiration for the *Presniz*. But if Prato and Artusi sought to present the cake as uncomplicatedly Germanic in their cookbooks, the origins of the *Presniz* have been the object of considerable debate among Triestine food writers.

The Mythical Origins of the *Presniz*

The first source of contention concerns when and how the cake was invented. There is a folk story surrounding the invention of the cake. The story, which is printed on the packaging of the cakes sold by more industrial distributors, traces the origins of the *Presniz* and its name to the Austrian Empire. Supposedly, the cake was invented on occasion of the visit of Empress Elisabeth (known colloquially as 'Sissi') and Franz Joseph I to Trieste in the first half of the nineteenth century. To celebrate the royal visit, a contest is said to have been held among the bakers and pastry chefs of the city, with the winning cake being crowned with the title *Preis Prinzessin*, 'Princess Prize', in honour of the visiting royal. The name would then have been shortened over time to 'Presnitz' by the locals.

The story is implausible in a number of ways: the date of the visit is uncertain, but had it been held in 1832, as some sources indicate, then Empress Elisabeth could have been no more than a twinkle in the eye of Duke Maximilian Joseph, in light of the fact that she was only born in 1837. But even if the visit had taken place in 1856, as other sources indicate, then by this time Elisabeth's titles would have been Empress of Austria and Queen of Hungary, making 'Princess' a rather inappropriate choice. Fonda also notes that it would have been odd to give the cake a German name considering that, as I have already mentioned, the dominant language at the time was an Italian dialect. It is unclear where the myth originated, although Fonda suggests that an unspecified Triestine producer of *Presniz* might have been behind it.[11] This producer could be the current La Bomboniera, a patisserie founded in 1836 by migrants from Hungary, the Eppinger family. Indeed, it is in Trieste's first patisserie (thought to be La Bomboniera) that Artusi claims he tasted the famed *Presniz*.

The legend is probably of recent fabrication and little more than a marketing ploy, a romantic backstory dreamt up by an imaginative baker to sell his goods. However, Fonda argues that the cake itself most likely was first developed and sold by a Triestine *pasticciere* in the nineteenth century, even if not for the occasion of a royal visit. He further claims that at the time, all the pastry chefs in the city spoke Slovenian, and that this likely explains the real origins of the cake, including its name; it is to the latter that I will now turn.[12]

The Linguistic Origins of *Presniz/Presnitz*

As Anthony Buccini has observed, food studies abound with instances of invented and 'thoroughly unscientific' etymologies from which many an 'otherwise unsupported historical tale is spun'.[13] The most incontrovertible evidence against the 'princess story', and in support of the Slavic origins of these regional desserts, is the actual etymology of *Presniz*. Far from being a contraction of the German *Preis Prinzessin*, the name derives from the Slovenian *presenec*, the diminutive form of *presen*, meaning 'uncooked' (or in this context, 'unleavened'), and *kruh*, 'bread'.[14] One of the earliest descriptions of the *Presniz* has been found in a book by a Slovenian aristocrat, scientist, and writer, Janez Vajkard Valvasor (1641-1693), titled *Die Ehre des Hertzogthums Crain* (*The Glory of the Duchy of Carniola*) and published in 1689 in Ljubljana; in the book it is referred to as *presenc*.[15] While most local cookbook authors opt for the spelling '*Presniz*', every pre-

The Contested Origins of the *Presniz* between Myth and Reality

packaged cake sold in supermarkets uses '*Presnitz*'. The final 'tz' in this variation of the spelling hints at Germanic origin, especially when the 'princess story' is also printed on the packaging; the two myths support one another.

The debate over the spelling was recently taken up by Nereo Zeper in a brief article entitled 'The Importance of Being Called *Presniz*', published in April 2017 in the local daily paper, *Il Piccolo*. Zeper highlights the tendency in Triestine dialect to adopt Italian spellings for imported foreign words, such as *bisù* for the French *bisoux*, which he claims is not a rule per se, but an '*uso carino*', a 'cute' custom. The tendency to Italianize foreign names is actually rather problematic in light of the fact that, under the Fascist regime of the 1920s, the Slavic place names of localities in the region were replaced with Italian ones, and residents with foreign-sounding surnames were coerced and sometimes even forced into 'restoring' their family names to an Italian form. As a result, the Slavic community of Dolina became San Dorligo della Valle, and Sredipolje (also known as Rodopolje) became Redipuglia, which translates to 'King of Puglia' – misleading given that there was never a kingdom, never mind a king, of Puglia.

It is difficult to say whether the names of these cakes were victims of a 'linguistic habit' or a later policy of forced Italianization. What we can say with more certainty is that the Germanic 'misspelling' of the cake contributes to the construction of a particular image of Trieste. Zeper is in fact far more critical of the apparent custom in Triestine dialect of needlessly adopting foreign spellings in order to 'seem more cosmopolitan'; continuing to use a spelling which appears German despite having very local roots, as in '*Presnitz/Presniz*', is a case in point. In a similar vein, Fonda has lamented the bad habit of Triestini to seek the unusual or eccentric in their culture and traditions, something which he argues has led them to interpret Trieste's gastronomy as the offspring of *Mitteleuropean* cuisine, rather than taking rightful credit for it themselves.[16]

The Geographic Origins of the *Presniz*

A third source of debate is the gastronomic 'lineage' of the dessert: the relationship between the *Presniz* and other regional specialties, and where each was born. The *Presniz* in fact bears a striking resemblance to the *Putizza* and the *Gubana*. The *Putizza* has a similarly rich filling, but its pastry is leavened and therefore has a more bread-like, fluffy texture. The *Gubana* contains a less rich filling in smaller quantities, and has a similarly doughy, leavened pastry.

Both the *Putizza* and the *Gubana* are different from the *Presniz* in that the filling is spread onto the dough and then rolled together like a swiss roll, rather than simply being wrapped around a thick roll of filling and closed at the seam. The similarities between the fillings and preparation techniques of these traditional cakes clearly hint at some degree of 'contamination', although it is seemingly impossible to determine which of these desserts came first and where each one was born, given that they would not have evolved in a linear way, but likely co-existed across the region, perhaps known by a range of names in different localities.

However, the *Putizza* is incontrovertibly Slavic, the name coming from *potica*, or *potice*, which is still widely consumed in Slovenia today. While some authors would have the *Presniz* originate in Gorizia, and derive from the *Gubana*, Fonda argues most convincingly that the *Presniz* was born in Trieste, evolving from the *Putizza* and the *Strucolo*, while the *Gubana*, with fewer and more simple ingredients, is more likely to have been adapted from a luxury food to suit rural peasant cooking.[17] The explanation is that exotic ingredients such as rum, chocolate, and sugar needed for the rich filling of the *Putizza* and the *Presniz* could only be found easily and cheaply in the city at the time, due to the industries that had grown in Trieste's port since 1719. Moreover, it is difficult to imagine that anyone other than a *pasticciere* would have derived a *Putizza* and then a *Presniz* from the *Strucolo*, and at the time, the only pastry shops in the area were to be found in the city centre.[18]

The *Strucolo*, from which the *Presniz* and *Putizza* are supposedly derived, is thought by a number of authors to be a local adaptation of the Austrian *strudel*. This fits with the name of the recipe, supposedly one of the earliest in print, of the 'Trieste style Strudel'. Indeed, I do not wish to wholly reject the influence of Viennese tastes and traditions on local pastry making in Trieste, something that is highly probable; rather, my aim is to acknowledge the undeniable roots of these cakes in Slavic gastronomic traditions. Equally, we cannot exclude the possibility that early cookbook authors, in choosing names for desserts that they had come upon in their travels, merely drew on their existing knowledge. Therefore, it is plausible that bakers in the Friuli countryside had come up with a strudel-style dessert without ever having seen the Viennese pastry, as is suggested by the source from Carniola in 1689. In fact, a local tourism and culture magazine, *Tiere Friulane/Terra Friulana*, recently featured the *Gubana*, and noted its similarities to the *Kärntner Reindling*, or Carniolan Reindling, which is not mentioned in any of the cookbooks I consulted.[19]

Ultimately however, one must keep in mind that these cakes are all variations on a common theme: wrapping a filling of fruit and nuts in some kind of pastry casing. As such, speculation on the similarities, differences, connections, and diversions between these foods may remain just that: speculation.

An Indication Label for the *Presniz*

These discussions have taken on greater significance in light of the creation of a geographical indication label for the 'Presnitz of Trieste' by the city's Chamber of Commerce. The choice of spelling for the label and the accompanying guidelines lends legitimacy to the cake's mythical origins, and, at the same time, obscures the history of the *presenec* and the influence of Slavic culture on the city's cuisine. Geographical indication labels may involve both the 'mystification' as well as a 'problematic retrieval' of a food's history.[20] Despite the fact that the specification for the indication label does acknowledge the Slavic etymology of the cake's name, no mention is made of it on the promotional, public-facing leaflet; instead, the 'princess story' is the only historical reference included, alongside two mentions of the impact which the Habsburgs had on the city's culture.

The heading on the promotional leaflet for the cakes reads '*Com'è dolce Trieste: scopri i suoi dolci tipici*' ('How sweet is Trieste: discover its typical desserts'). Within the leaflet, Trieste

The Contested Origins of the *Presniz* between Myth and Reality

is described as a 'meeting point between North and South, East and West, Mediterranean and Central Europe', as a 'crossroads of culture and flavours', and as 'Mitteleuropean, multicultural, Mediterranean'. In these materials, the *Presniz* functions as a kind of culinary metaphor for the landscape, as a place where exotic ingredients mix and integrate with one another to produce something new and desirable. Moreover, the language used to describe the cake is applied to the landscape, so that Trieste is described as 'sweet', in the sense of 'sugary', further contributing to the positive images of peaceful cultural and ethnic mixing.

The *Presniz* in the Cosmopolitan Imaginary of Trieste

> 'Foods do not simply come from places, organically growing out of them, but also make places as symbolic constructs, being deployed in the discursive construction of various imaginative geographies.'[21]

Ian Cook and Philip Crang are among the anthropologists, geographers, and food studies scholars who have paid increasing attention to the role of food in constructing place, both materially and symbolically. The concept of *Mitteleuropa* has been central to what I have suggested is a dominant imaginary of Trieste as a cosmopolitan port and 'melting pot' of culinary and ethnic influences. I have argued that this over-emphasis on cultural affiliation to Central Europe has overshadowed the role of the neighbouring Slavic culture on the city's cuisine. In light of the longstanding tension between Slavs and Italians in the area, I have also suggested that the narrative which constructs the *Presniz*, and therefore Trieste, as Austrian or Mitteleuropean, contributes to the marking of boundaries, both symbolic and geopolitical, between Italians and neighbouring Slovenians and Croatians.

The very use of pastries to evoke the cosmopolitan character of the Empire is seen by Hametz to be a common practice in Central Europe; for example, the appropriation of the originally Hungarian *Dobish Torte* as a metaphor for the city of Munich. In fact, Hametz suggests that if the *Presniz* really was inspired by the visit of Empress Elisabeth, then 'it likely was developed on the same impulse that inspired the invention of the *Mozartkugel* […] in Salzburg in 1890', the chocolate confection created as a nostalgic reminder of the city's musical heritage.[22]

Hametz has argued that in the aftermath of the Second World War, the focus on nations and national affiliations obscured the 'enduring attachments to Central Europeanness and cosmopolitanness' in Trieste. Due to the ethnic-national tension that had fuelled much of the violence in the area, the dominant 'political imaginary' came to be a binary one: Italians or Slavs, Italy or Yugoslavia. Hametz argues that such a binary does not reflect the experience of Triestines, and that centuries of Habsburg rule rendered affiliations among locals much more complex. Although the movement for Trieste to be 'returned' to Italy was strong, the incorporation of the city into the new state was not premised on the destruction of its existing ties to previous administrators; Triestines could be both Italian and cosmopolitan. The 'cosmopolitan' identity of the locals therefore provides an alternative political imaginary that goes beyond the restrictive container of nationalism.

However, Hametz has also acknowledged the role of nostalgia in this cosmopolitan imaginary, which she interprets not as a 'rejection of history', in the sense of a regressive return to nationalism, but rather a 'selective remembrance' of the sometimes violent local history: 'Memory of this golden age [...] provides a vehicle for selective historical amnesia – enhancing the ability to forget the city's history of fierce Italian irredentism and Fascist nationalism [...] contested "Slavic" (primarily Slovene and Croatian) contributions to local culture, and bitter resistance to Nazi occupation.'[23] Pamela Ballinger suggests that 'mythologizing' about the Habsburg past is part of a 'prospective nostalgia'.[24] The cosmopolitan imaginary therefore 'provides a vehicle to reconcile the city's Central European past with its position on the geographic periphery of Italy and western Europe', as well as a vehicle for reinventing the city 'beyond the confines of Italy, a state that Triestines, rightly or wrongly, see as neglectful of their needs'.[25]

The decision – by individual producers and pastry shops as well as by tourism and commerce entities – to promote the *Presniz* as an enduring symbol, or even a remnant, of the Empire under which the city blossomed and thrived could be interpreted in the context of this 'prospective nostalgia'. The marketing of the *Presniz* as a Habsburg delicacy is part and parcel of the post-war efforts to reinvent the city through its associations to the old Austrian Empire. It is to this end that the 'princess story' has been mobilized by the Chamber of Commerce, as a means of accessing foreign markets through the creation of an EU Protected Geographical Indication label. Therefore, it is clear that when it comes to branding the city's material cultural objects, it is the romanticism of Empires, royalty, and internationalism which sells, not the stereotypically 'backwards' associations to Slavic peasant culture.

Conclusion

My aim in this paper has not been to reject the undeniable influence of more than five centuries of Habsburg rule on the cuisine of Trieste, but rather to demonstrate how, in Trieste, food is a site in which conflicts over imaginative geographies are played out. The *Presni(t)z* has been mobilized by different actors in support of particular narrative constructions of 'Trieste' as a place. Therefore, the history and origins of the *Presni(t)z* are part of an ideological project aimed at the hegemonic definition of local identity.

While the 'cosmopolitan' imaginary of the city helps to overcome a dominant ethnic-national binary, it nevertheless obscures and minimizes historical realities. Although there is ample evidence of the historical existence of different cultures and ethnicities in the city, the integration of, and mixing between, different peoples has likely been overstated. Moreover, the concept of cosmopolitanism is problematic in itself, insofar as it exalts the positive aspects of the intermingling of cultures and ethnicities at the expense of recognizing the unequal nature of the different components. The Slavic population in Trieste has historically been stereotyped as poor, uncivilized, and lacking culture in contrast to the wealth of the Austrians, under whose guidance Trieste grew and prospered and felt important. Cosmopolitanism is therefore loaded towards the powerful and privileged, and does not adequately represent Trieste any more than the Italian/Slavic binary.

The Contested Origins of the *Presniz* between Myth and Reality

In this context, the *Presni(t)z* is made to appear, like Trieste itself, many things at once. Its origins are both fixed and malleable, singular and multiple, monolithic and cosmopolitan, hegemonic and marginal, myth and reality. And insofar as it has been moulded in support of the political projects of different local actors, the *Presni(t)z* remains a powerful cultural, material and symbolic tool in the construction and reinvention of Trieste as a fragmented, yet dynamic and constantly changing, landscape.

Notes

1. My heartfelt thanks go to Chris Wilson and Davide Nicolini for their comments on the conference proposal and paper; to Renzo Nicolini for his research assistance and for accompanying me in the field; and to June Cattonar for all her support and encouragement, her unwavering enthusiasm, and our many animated discussions about *Presniz*.
2. I will use the word 'Slavic', which is accepted in the literature, to refer to people living in present-day Slovenia and Croatia, as well as those who historically lived in areas which are now part of Italy but would have been Slavic-speaking at the time.
3. Maura Hametz, *Making Trieste Italian 1918-1954* (Suffolk: Boydell and Brewer, 2001), p. 1.
4. Roberto Zottar, *Dolce Gorizia: Pasticceria dell'Antica Contea* (Gorizia: Libreria Editrice Goriziana, 2015), p. 13.
5. Mady Fast, *I Dolci di Trieste: punto d'incontro di civiltà* (Trieste: Edizioni Italo Svevo, 1989).
6. A. Ara and C. Magris, *Trieste: un'identità di frontiera* (Torino: Einaudi, 1982), p. 21.
7. Hametz, *Making Trieste Italian*, p. 8; Glenda Sluga, *The Problem of Trieste and Italo-Yugoslav Border: Difference, Identity, and Sovereignty in Twentieth-Century Europe* (Albany: State University of New York, 2001).
8. Cesare Fonda, *Ocio a la Jota: storia de Trieste e de la sua cusina* (Trieste: Italo Svevo, 2004), p. 288 (translations my own).
9. Pellegrino Artusi, *La scienza in cucina e l'arte di mangiar bene*, (1891; repr. Torino: Einaudi, 1970).
10. '*Eccovi un altro dolce di tedescheria e come buono!*', qtd. in Zottar, p. 26.
11. Fonda, *Ocio a la Jota*, p. 287.
12. Fonda, *Ocio a la Jota*, p. 288.
13. Anthony Buccini, 'The Anatolian Origins of the Words 'Olive' and 'Oil' and the Early History of Oleiculture', in *Food and Language: Proceedings of the Oxford Symposium on Food and Cookery 2009*, ed. by Richard Hosking (Totnes, Devon: Prospect Books, 2010), p. 52.
14. See Fonda, *Ocio a la Jota*, p. 288; Zottar, p. 30.
15. Qtd. in Zottar, p. 27, n. 44.
16. Cesare Fonda, *Trieste in Cucina* (Trieste: Edizioni Italo Svevo, 1989), p. 524.
17. Fonda, *Trieste in Cucina*, p. 524.
18. Fonda, *Ocio a la Jota*, pp. 286-87.
19. Regione FVG, *Tiere Furlane/Terra Friulana: rivista di cultura del territorio*, 8 (2016), 113-14 <https://www.regione.fvg.it/rafvg/export/sites/default/RAFVG/economia-imprese/agricoltura-foreste/tiere-furlane/allegati/TF24D.pdf> [accessed 28 May 2017].
20. Dwijen Rangnekar, 'Remaking Place: The Social Construction of a Geographical Indication for *Feni*', *Environment and Planning A*, 43 (2011), 2054.
21. Ian Cook and Philip Crang, 'The World on a Plate: Culinary Culture, Displacement and Geographical Knowledges', *Journal of Material Culture*, 1 (1996), 140.
22. Maura Hametz, 'Presnitz in the Piazza: Habsburg Nostalgia in Trieste', *Journal of Austrian Studies*, 47 (2014), 148.
23. Hametz, 'Presnitz in the Piazza', p. 137.
24. Qtd. in Hametz, 'Presnitz in the Piazza', p. 135.
25. Hametz, 'Presnitz in the Piazza', p. 131.

Mapping Food in France under the First Empire

Guillaume Nicoud

Introduction

As a proud French art historian, I was sure that I knew the geography of France very well. I thought I even knew its borders and limits during the French Empire, until the day I happened upon a large print incorrectly registered at the French National Library in Paris. This document is currently quite well known, but in the year 2000, when I chanced upon the print, no one had really taken an interest in it yet.[1] Upon a second look, I understood that this particular sample was in fact a poster, more precisely an advertisement for a book released in 1809. Nevertheless, the print includes a map, and not a common map, but the *Carte gastronomique de la France*: the Gastronomical Map of France, according to an inscription – that appears in an oval wafer being chewed by a little boy! – on the left side of the print (Figure 1).

This may well be the first thematic map of such kind ever made, based on ideograms. By starting a cultural-historical study of this exceptional topographical testimony, in this paper I will try to clarify its context, its origin, and its cultural meaning.

Context

The map is a masterpiece by itself, even if it was first printed to help to sell and illustrate a book, *Cours gastronomique, ou les dîners de Manant-Ville* (*Gastronomical Lesson or The Manant-Ville Dinners*), as it is written at the top of the poster.[2] The name of the book's author is not mentioned on the map; however, the title page of the publication mentions 'deceased Mr. C***, former lawyer at the Paris Parliament'.[3] Today we know that the author was Charles Louis Cadet de Gassicourt, and I will return to the matter of the book's authorship shortly.

Figure 1. Jean François Tourcaty, Carte gastronomique de la France, 1809 (Ithaca, Cornell University Library, Division of Rare & Manuscript Collections, Inv. Nr. 1030.01 (Wikimedia Commons)).

Mapping Food in France under the First Empire

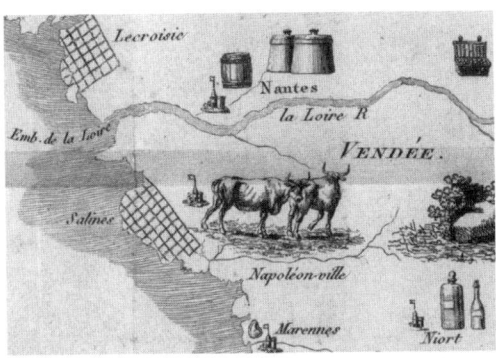

Figure 2. Detail of Figure 1.

According to the map and the book, it is said to be a second edition of a compendium of *'ouvrage anecdotique, philosophique et littéraire'* ('anecdotal, philosophical, and literary') matters according to the subtitle written on the title page. Actually, some of the text had been previously published not as book chapters but as articles in issues of a review called *L'Épicurien* (*The Epicurean*) published by a Parisian gourmet society. Cadet de Gassicourt was a prominent member, which helps explain why the wafer-chewing child is standing at the top of a grotto inside of which is a dressed dinner table.

The map's draftsman and printer was Jean-François Tourcaty (born 1763) according to the inscription (*'Torcaty del. et sculp'*) on the stone in front of the grotto. One year before, he had illustrated the well-known *Manuel des Amphitryons*, a culinary handbook by Alexandre Balthazar Laurent Grimod de la Reynière (1758-1837), also an active member of the gourmet society.[4] Both books were published by Capelle and Renand, booksellers and commissioners in Paris.

The map itself has no legend, but it does include the names of geographical locations. It includes cities (Paris, Montpellier, Grasse, etc.), regions (like Puy de Dôme, in the middle of France, or Vendée, in the west), and rivers, even pointing out some of their deltas (e.g. for the Loire river – *'Emb[ouchure] de la Loire'*); the map also highlights unique locations, such as the Islands of Hyères in the Mediterranean Sea and even three *'salines'* (salt gardens) on the Atlantic shore (Figure 2). Including the salt gardens does not make the map more geographically precise, because there is no particular location associated with such a generic term, but it does help explain the related grid design: the grid is supposed to roughly resemble a salt garden. Other than that, the naturalistic representations on the map are easy to understand: even when they are quite schematic, these icons or ideograms are drawn so nicely that we can recognize what they represent, even today.

These images of food products reveal that this is a treasure map, describing a geography of culinary specialties made entirely on French soil, and which, all in all, seem much more interesting than the products on display at a contemporary show of similar products such as the *Salon de l'agriculture* in Paris (the annual National Agricultural Fair).

Origin

The map offers an invitation to a virtual journey to discover French geography through its most highly praised local foods. It was probably initiated during a meeting of the *Société du Caveau moderne* (the Modern Vault Society), a group of Frenchmen who loved popular songs, comic theatre, wines, and food. Their society recreated two former eighteenth-century Parisian societies called *Société du Caveau*, which met in various locations in Paris between 1729 and 1789, which helps explain why the names of the most illustrious members of these societies are carved on the rocks in the poster. For example, the names of the writers and chansonniers Gallé and Panard (the creator and the most prominent member of the first society) can be found next to those of Piis and Grimod de la Reynière (major members of the modern society). Furthermore, the musical instruments, the mask, and the joker's stick decorating the entrance of the grotto are typical signs of *goguettes*, the eighteenth-century societies known for singing and drinking – a bit too much – wine (Figure 3). In the new *Société du Caveau*, food occupied an equal place to song during their monthly evening banquets (traditionally held on the twentieth day of each month, because *vingt*, French for twentieth, sounds like *vin* – wine).

Figure 3. Detail of Figure 1.

Between 1805 and 1815 (during the First Empire up to the second abdication of Napoléon), the new Society met at dinners called *Diners du Caveau moderne*, as written on a book in the poster's bottom left-hand corner. The dinners took place at the well-known Parisian restaurant *Rocher de Cancale*, on the east bank of the Seine. The poster represents this location through the rock cave next to the map; the name Balaine, for Alexis Balaine, the cook and owner of *Rocher de Cancale*, is written on the tablecloth inside the grotto (Figure 3).

The author of the book, Charles Louis Cadet de Gassicourt (1769-1828), a pharmacist and a writer, was an important member of this group. Likely through discussions with his comrades during their banquets, he compiled gastronomic information and then reassembling it as object lessons. In the book, he dramatized these lessons, structuring them into a narrative of a young man who must integrate himself into Parisian society. As the son of a provincial nouveau riche father, the young man, Manant-Ville, needs these lessons because he lacks the urban education needed to succeed in the city.

Among the thirty chapters, we find ones titled 'Oysters and Sauces' ('*Les Huîtres et les Sauces*'), 'Measurement of the Belly' ('*Mesure de la Panse*'), and 'One Can Bad-Mouth the Turtledoves' ('*On peut médire des Tourterelles*'). Inside, in the review *L'Épicurien*, one can find useful information to use among *compagnies* during dinners in town. For example, the book explains how garlic was known by the Ancients, despised by the Greeks, but cherished by the Egyptians and details how the British make fish soup (*savon de poisson*). The book also includes practical information about various culinary matters ranging from how to make polenta to how to tell the difference between Burgundy, Champagne, Arbois, Aurillac, Pomard, and Vougeot wines. Last but not least, the book offers a geography lesson in chapter twenty-eight, '*Sachons un peu de géographie*' ('Let's Learn a Bit of Geography'), for which the map was created.

In this chapter, as in the other ones, the scene takes place in Paris. Manant-Ville takes the opportunity to visit a certain Captain Durfort – possibly a real person I have yet to identify (according to the book, he is 'the son of a honest innkeeper of Nantes').[5] Durfort is described as one of Manant-Ville's friends who tries his best to transform Manant-Ville into a well-educated man, exactly the kind of knowledge that Manant-Ville's father's new-found wealth cannot buy.

They know well that, to gain success in Paris, one had better study food history, and, if one likes eating, one of the best ways to become better educated is through object lessons. Manant-Ville finds the captain at home, working on the map. Durfort explains:

> You already have access to quite a well-furnished gourmet library, inside of which you will find, with a bit of research, the origins of foods which could appear on your table, but nevertheless I would like, if it is possible, to keep you from needing to conduct such research, or at least to abbreviate it. I very much like synoptic tables: they make study easy, and let us see at a glance all the parts of a science and the relationships between them. [...] This is the map of France, where I put the dishes in their birthplaces: you will find here no big or small cities which do not produce delicacies, but I highlighted modest villages that built their names thanks to gourmet products. At first glance, this map looks like a fragment of a celestial sphere covered with constellations, but instead of the Big Dipper, of Perseus, of the Coma Berenices, Scorpio, etc., you can see beef, sheep, terrine, barrels, fishes, fatten hens, cheeses, in short everything that charms the palates of people fond of food, and locates these in the area where they come from: capons next to Le Mans, sardines next to La Rochelle, truffles next to Périgord, pig's head in the city of Troyes.[6]

Thus, based on a memory of a celestial atlas, with figures to identify constellations, Captain Durfort created a new sort of map, a geographical one of France, to help Manant-Ville, and possibly every gourmet of the time, improve his gastronomic knowledge. Indeed, 'this idea immensely pleased Manant-Ville, who thanked the captain, and praised him as if he made a discovery'.[7]

The possibility that the so-called Captain Durfort could be a real person is strengthened by his quite precise explanation of how he got this idea:

> I recall that, in 1786, being at Le Havre at the time when Abbot Dicquemare was preparing his big book on polyps, Mrs Masson le Golft, his niece, let me see a geographical map that she had just finished drawing that looked to me to be

very ingenious. With the help of around a dozen of signs, and five or six colours, she indicated for each country its type of government and religion, the nature of its commercial or agricultural wealth, the size and colour of its inhabitants, its population, and its dominant character: this gave me the idea to create for you, my dear Manant-Ville, a gourmet atlas.[8]

Marie Le Masson Le Golft (1749-1826), a unique French naturalist and teacher from Le Havre, was not the niece of her mentor, the naturalist and astronomer Jacques-François Dicquemare (1733-1789), but she nevertheless worked with him and, most of all, really did create such a map, not in 1786 but instead around 1778. Entitled *Esquisse d'un tableau général du genre humain* (*Draft of General Table of Mankind*), it may well be considered one of the most concise pedagogical publications of the French Enlightenment.[9]

It is not clear if there was a real person behind Durfort's character. We don't know if the author of the book, Cadet de Gassicourt – who could also be describing someone like himself – had known these Norman scientists and cartographers, but the story is accurate enough to suggest some connection. In addition, another member of the *Caveau moderne*, the geographer Edme Mentelle (1730-1815), may have also had a connection with this chapter and the map. Notably, there seems to be common interest in pedagogical mapping from both real people and the book's characters. For example, Mentelle, who was in charge of teaching geography in the royal household in the 1780s, had designed a globe of both the earth and the sky that is still on display in Versailles. Furthermore, he continued to publish lessons in geography and other sciences after the French Revolution. In 1804, for example, he published the fifth edition of his *Geography Taught According to a New Method [...] a Work Intended for Secondary Schools*.[10]

Interpretation

As a thematic map related to food, this print is probably the first of its kind. While it cannot be considered a standard geographical map because it involves signs that aren't topographical, it does show a peculiar geography. Nevertheless, all topographical maps are made with signs and symbols, and this 'gourmet atlas' might have been created for didactic purposes. As such, it is not intended to develop a better understanding of French culinary specialties, but rather to improve the knowledge of French geography for those more curious about food than geography.

The map may also be considered as an invitation to a culinary tour through France. If that is the case, one wonders if it is connected with other writers and members of the society such as René de Chazet (1774-1844), A.-M. Lafortelle (1769-1851), and the so-called Francis (the pseudonym of Marie François Denis Thérésa Le Roi d'Allarde, 1778-1841) who together in 1804 wrote a one-act comedy entitled *L'École des Gourmands*.[11] In this play, Mr Gourmandin tries to educate his son by relating culinary specialties to basic geographical knowledge. Therefore, to give a lesson of geography, he questions his son about the origins of some foods:

Mapping Food in France under the First Empire

GOURMANDIN. Very well, my little Bibi. Let us now move to geography. Where do you get the best foie gras terrine?

BIBI. From Strasbourg.

GOURMANDIN. And the best ham ?

BIBI. From Mayence [at this time in the French Empire]

GOURMANDIN. And what about the lark terrine ?

BIBI. From Pithiviers.

GOURMANDIN. So, there are three main cities in France, Strasbourg, Mayence, Pithiviers. Now, where do the stuffed tongue *à la mode* of Troyes ['*langues fourrées de Troyes*'] come from?

BIBI. The stuffed tongue *à la mode* of Troyes…

GOURMANDIN. Yes, Mister, where do they come from ?

BIBI. From Bologna !

GOURMANDIN. Fool!

BIBI. No, no, from Cancale [from where oysters actually come from].

GOURMANDIN. Shut up, foolish child. The tongue of Troyes comes from Troyes. This little funny boy will make me die of grief.[12]

Then, he gives him some classics ('*quelques livres classiques*') to read, including only one dedicated to food, the important review called *Almanach des Gourmands* by Grimod de la Reynière.

In this way of thinking and representing France, one can also decipher the general political issues of the time. Literally covering the entire French territory, and sometimes even beyond its borders, through images of culinary production, the map shows how wealthy and powerful the country might be. In these depictions France looks like a country overflowing with natural wealth and celebrated for the quality of its domestic production – almost the real land of milk and honey!

Conclusion

In the period when the map was made, France felt strong, felt like the most powerful country in Europe. But what happened when it lost its strength after 1815? In periods of crisis, even today, many French people find comfort in the fact that at least 'we still have kept our cuisine', and this claim was heard after the fall of the First Empire. The quality of French culinary specialties were so well known around Europe in 1815 that a French gourmet and diplomat like Charles-Maurice de Talleyrand-Périgord (1754-1838) made it possible for France to win at least one complete victory at the Congress of Vienna. While the Congress's official chef, Marie-Antoine Carême (1784-1833), left no record on the subject, the official painter, Jean-Baptiste Isabey (1767-1855), recalled:

> I remember that at a dinner given by the Prince of Bénévent [Talleyrand], the discussion opened on cheese. England claimed priority thanks to its Stilton, Chester, etc. A supplicant voice, which should have been Italian, whispered the name of strachino; but the arrogant Albion didn't give in, and she was on the road to victory when a courier from France was announced. – What does he bring? Important dispatches? – Better than that: a cheese from Brie. To uncouple, and cut it by removing the upper part ['chapeler'] was a matter of an instant. And the Congress decided, by a majority vote of voices, that France was the promised land of cheese.[13]

This Brie cheese is probably one of the most interesting French specialties because it is made not for its region of origin but for the nearby city of Paris. Parisians were looking for sweet cheese and helped the Brie farmers, who often depend upon the city, to develop the sweet, full-fat cheese. After the Congress of Vienna, a deluxe Brie was even named 'Talleyrand' to celebrate the victory he won with this specialty which is still known today as 'the king of cheese'. According to Eugène Sue's book *Les Sept péchés capitaux* (*The Seven Deadly Sins*), Talleyrand's Brie came from a farm called Estouville, in the municipality of Villeroy near Meaux, which apparently still exists; the cheese is even said to have been made by a farmer named Baulny.[14] As with this famous cheese, more research is required to verify the history of all the products presented on our special map, and mapping food in France under the First Empire promises to be full of discovery.

Notes

1. For example, the map is not mentioned in Anne-Marie Nisbet and Victor-André Massena's *L'Empire à table* (Paris: A. Biro, 1988).
2. [Charles L. Cadet de Gassicourt], *Cours gastronomique ou Les dîners de Manant-ville: ouvrage anecdotique, philosophique et littéraire. Seconde édition dédiée à la Société épicurienne du Caveau moderne […]* (Paris: Capelle et Renand, 1809).
3. 'Par feu M. C***, ancien avocat au Parlement de Paris' Cadet de Gassicourt, title page.
4. A.B.L. Grimod de la Reynière, *Manuel des amphitryons, contenant un traité de la dissection des viandes à table, la nomenclature des menus les plus nouveaux [...] et des élémens de politesse [...]* (Paris, Capelle et Renand, 1808).
5. *'fils d'un honnête aubergiste de Nantes'* (Cadet de Gassicourt, p. 229).
6. 'Vous avez une bibliothèque gastronomique assez bien meublée, dans laquelle vous trouverez avec un peu de recherche l'origine de tous les mets qui peuvent paraître sur votre table; mais je voudrais, s'il est possible, éviter ces recherches, ou du moins les abréger. J'aime beaucoup les tableaux synoptiques; ils rendent l'étude facile , et font voir d'un coup d'œil toutes les parties d'une science et leurs rapports entre elles. [...] Voilà la carte de la France, où j'ai placé les mets dans le lieu de leur naissance : vous ne trouverez ici aucune des villes grandes

ou petites qui ne produisent pas des alimens recherchés ; mais j'y ai placé avec honneur de modestes villages quand ils se sont fait un nom par leurs productions gastronomiques. Au premier coup d'oeil cette carte a l'air d'un fragment d'une sphère céleste chargée de constellations ; mais au lieu de la grande Ourse, de Persée, de la chevelure de Bérénice, du Scorpion, etc., vous y voyez des boeufs, des moutons, des pâtés, des tonneaux, des poissons, des poulardes, des fromages, enfin tout ce qui charme le palais des friands, placé dans l'ordre du pays qui fournit chaque objet : les chapons à côté du Mans, les sardines près de la Rochelle, les truffes dans le Périgord, les hures dans Troyes' (Cadet de Gassicourt, pp. 299-300). To better understand the map, Durfort also gives Manant-Ville a list of places associated with their culinary specialties (Cadet de Gassicourt, pp. 300-04 <https://archive.org/stream/b22033208#page/300/mode/2up>.

7. '*Cette idée plut infiniment à Manant-Ville, qui remercia le capitaine, et le loua comme s'il avait fait une découverte*' (Cadet de Gassicourt, p. 300).
8. '*Je me souviens qu'en 1786, étant au Havre, dans le temps que l'abbé Dicquemare préparait son grand ouvrage sur les polypes, mademoiselle Masson le Golft, sa nièce, me fit voir une carte géographique qu'elle venait de dessiner, et qui me parut fort ingénieuse. Au moyen d'une douzaine de signes environ, et de cinq à six couleurs, elle indiquait pour chaque pays l'espèce de gouvernement et de religion, la nature des richesses commerciales ou agricoles, la taille et la couleur des habitans, leur population et leur caractère dominant : cela m'a donné l'idée de composer pour vous, mon cher Manant-Ville, un atlas gourmand*' (Cadet de Gassicourt, p. 299-300).
9. Marie Le Masson Le Golft, *Esquisse d'un tableau général du genre humain où l'on apperçoit [...] les religions et les moeurs des différents peuples, [...] et les principales variétés de forme et de couleur de chacun d'eux / par Mademoiselle Le Masson Le Golft, du Cercle des Philadelphes, etc. ; Exécuté par M. Moithey* (Paris, Moithey, [ca 1778]) <http://gallica.bnf.fr/ark:/12148/btv1b530934317>.
10. Edme Mentelle, *La géographie enseignée par une méthode nouvelle [...] ouvrage destiné aux écoles secondaires* (Paris: the author, 1804).
11. R.Chazet, A.-M. Lafortelle, and Francis [Marie François Denis Thérésa Le Roi d'Allarde], *L'École des Gourmands, vaudeville en 1 acte [...]*, (Paris: Mme Cavanagh, 1804).
12. '*GOURMANDIN. Fort bien, mon petit Bibi. Passons maintenant à la géographie. D'où tire-t-on les meilleurs pâtés de foie gras? / BIBI. De Strasbourg. / GOURMANDIN. Et les meilleurs jambons? / BIBI. De Mayence. / GOURMANDIN. Et les pâtés d'alouette. / BIBI. De Pithiviers. / GOURMANDIN. Il existe donc trois principales villes en France, Strasbourg, Mayence, Pithiviers. Maintenant, d'où viennent les langues fourrées de Troyes? / BIBI. Les langues fourrées de Troyes [...]. / GOURMANDIN. Oui, monsieur, d'où viennent-elles? / BIBI. De Bologne. / GOURMANDIN. Imbécile! / BIBI. Non, non , de Cancale. / GOURMANDIN. Taisez-vous, petit sot. Les langues de Troyes viennent de Troyes en Champagne. Ce petit drôle me fera mourir de chagrin*' (Chazet, Lafortelle, and Francis, p. 14).
13. '*Je me souviens qu'à un dîner donné chez le prince de Bénévent, la discussion s'engage sur les fromages. L'Angleterre réclama la priorité pour le stilton, le chester, etc. Une vois suppliante, qui devait être italienne, prononça tout bas le nom de strachino ; mais l'arrogante Albion ne cédait pas ; elle allait triompher, quand on annonça un courrier de France. – Qu'apporte-t-il ? Des dépêches importantes ? – Bien mieux : un fromage de Brie. – Le déboîter, le chapeler fut l'affaire d'un instant. Et le congrès décida, à la majorité des voix, que la France était la terre promise des fromages*' (Edmond Taigny, *J.-B. Isabey: Sa vie et ses œuvres* (Paris: E. Panckoucke, 1859), pp. 39-40.
14. Eugène Sue, *Les Sept péchés capitaux* (Paris, J. Rouff, [1849 ?]), p. 1436.

Moveable *Terroir*: From Liquid Stability to Rock-Solid Ephemerality

Thomas Parker

The notion of *terroir* provides stability to the fleeting, ephemeral, and subjective quality of food. It situates flavours geographically and provides benchmarks for tasting and speaking about a particular product from a particular place. *Terroir* allows for grounding in terms of time as well, with the promise that eaters can expect to rediscover, on a perennial basis, characteristics in food and wines that reflect a given set of physiographic growing conditions. Better yet, *terroir* channels what would otherwise be fleeting sensorial impressions by offering an alternate philosophical medium for interacting with the landscape, allowing it to be contemplated through taste. That is to say, food via its geographic origin is perceived intellectually and corporally in a more visceral modality than the visual, aural, or tactile means with which we usually engage the landscape. Finally, *terroir* provides what tasters often construe as an objective grounding for the appreciation of something as personal as food, allowing alimentary productions to be translated into an aesthetic language that both facilitates the communication of pleasure between enthusiasts and offers standards for markets wishing to commoditize agricultural productions.

Yet, despite the appearance of stability and connotations such as 'grounded', 'rooted', or 'terra firma', the construct of *terroir* is fundamentally unstable. Indeed, instead of an anchoring force, *terroir* is perhaps more akin to Pangaea, the landmass that appears cohesive at a glance, though its pieces are imperceptibly drifting apart. In each case, though we may not feel it, the Earth is moving beneath our feet. In the following pages, I examine how *terroir*'s interminable flux belies the ideas of constancy and objectivity that we have attributed to it. I also look at the notion from an ethical perspective. *Terroir* is viewed favourably when it comes to questions of ecology in land management, and has been successfully adduced, for example, to redirect an autoroute away from the vineyards of Corton in Burgundy. But I reveal *terroir*'s darker side, a side that preserves established hierarchies and even represses efforts toward ecological conservation. Finally, I suggest that the illusion of *terroir* has led consumers to a damaging set of unrealistic expectations about the Earth's productions. We essentialize the earth in *terroir* foods and wines in order to provide reference points. In using this fantasy to understand and frame nature, however, we paradoxically move it further afield. We might ultimately do better to reject dreams of immutability and taste the landscape in a way that features *terroir*'s ephemerality.

Moveable *Terroir*

I will begin by looking at some ways in which *terroir* has occurred as a trope for stability and been presented as an objective natural phenomenon, and then describe how market forces worked to codify and objectify *terroir* in the last 150 years. I will then oppose what have become conventional standards for tasting *terroir* to the recent trend of natural wines, explaining how the latter destabilize the taster by presenting *terroir* as an unsettled, changing value. In the last part of my reflection, I will reveal the broader implications of two diametrically opposed ways of translating *terroir* while querying how and why European natural wine was paradoxically embraced in Japan, and resisted by Anglo-Saxon markets.

Terroir as an Anchor for Earth, Sky, and Soul

In a 2012 essay, Steven Shapin, the history of science professor, examines the origin of the flowery descriptions in wine language that have become prominent in recent times.[1] Shapin traces wine descriptions from the pedestrian, non-aesthetic lexicon used in the Renaissance, when wines and foods were principally understood for their medical properties, to contemporary society, where changing social and economic circumstances have produced the current abundance of florid tasting accounts. Most of what Shapin posits is on the money, but the suggestion that flowery language is a new construction could stand some nuance. Though culinary magniloquence is prevalent now in its use by markets to commercialize valued-added products, it has existed since antiquity.

Wine, for the Ancient Greeks, was saddled with the mundane charge of preserving and transporting supplementary calories, but also served as a symbol of elegance and Greek superiority over non-wine-drinking cultures.[2] Furthermore, the Greeks acknowledged the influence of origins on wines in general terms. Notwithstanding the fact that *terroir* lacked the expanded sense the word possesses today, descriptions could be as verbose and improbable sounding as modern ones. Hermippus described the wines of the island of Chios, in the Northern Aegean, as possessing a 'smell of violets, a smell of roses, a smell of larkspur, a sacred smell through all the high-roof hall, at once ambrosia and nectar'.[3] The flavours here are putatively referential, grounding the wine in a naturalistic register: they smell of violets, roses, and larkspur (related to the delphinium, and native to the Mediterranean). The wine is thus a reflection of regional natural flora and, ostensibly, of the '*terroir*' of Chios. Yet, there is also a connection to the divine, since the wine is 'sacred', tied explicitly to the gods through the terms 'ambrosia' and 'nectar'. The second observation of note is the metaphorical significance of the descriptors. Roses were prestigious in antiquity, associated with the goddess Aphrodite. Violets were affiliated with Persephone and Orpheus. Larkspur was linked to the god Apollo and the hero Ajax. To top it off, the wines possess extraordinary power, filling 'the high-roof hall' with their fragrances. Chios wines were thus both naturally grounded and seemingly ethereal, rooting the drinker simultaneously in the naturalistic causal power of the *terroir* it grows in and associating him metonymically with the Gods.

This convergence between eater and eaten (or drinker and what is drunk) is how the notion of *terroir* continued to develop in the French imagination in the Middle Ages and Renaissance.⁴ Wine descriptors were qualified in pre-modern Europe in mostly medical contexts, based on the Hippocratic and Galenic notion of humours and a notable interest in the soil. It was thought that one ought to drink wine from a *terroir* that corresponded to one's own predominant humours or, if one's humours were out of equilibrium, one ought to correct the imbalance with foods containing counteracting humours. In the *Maison Rustique,* a widely-read guide on estate management, Charles Éstienne wrote that, while wine from foreign lands is exotic and appealing, it could be dangerous; it is better to drink wines from the *terroir* where one lives, since the latter are better suited to the drinker's personal constitution.⁵ *Terroir* was a force used for situating one's own identity and constitution, uniting the consuming subject and the consumed object in physiological terms. By drinking wines from one's region, a person framed and performed their physiology according to a static image of the landscape.

In pre-modern times, the use of *terroir* to construct the identity of the consuming subject occurred not only in physiological terms, but also according to a spiritual and intellectual perspective. Claude Arnoux, from Burgundy, opens his 1738 *Dissertation sur la situation de la Bourgogne* with a prolonged discussion on Burgundian *terroir* by focusing on the military history of Beaune dating back to Roman times.⁶ He suggests that the greatness of Beaune's history and the courage of its people cannot be monumentalized by ruins from the time of Caesar, as is the case in Autun (the '*ancienne capitale des Gaules*'), which lies fifty kilometres to the west of Beaune, simply because Beaune's ruins have not been preserved. Rather, the wines of Burgundy provide a living testimony of past human accomplishment and current greatness, which Arnoux attributes to the perfection and purity of Beaune's *terroir*. Here, *terroir* provides both a geographical and temporal anchor. Ruins, Arnoux points out, are constantly being beaten down and destroyed by elements. *Terroir*, manifested through the glory of Beaune's wines, does just the opposite. It springs up, providing a perennial reminder that monumentalizes and disseminates the story of human greatness in a glass. Here again, landscape is objectified as an external causal force with certain natural attributes that merge and provide a self-referential image of the wine-consuming subject.

The Commercial and Aesthetic Objectification of Wine

In the above examples, from the Ancient Greeks to the early modern French, *terroir* provides stability through a framework that connects humans to the land through wine. The drinker then assimilates the wine, incorporating the potable object and appropriating its values, be they 'natural' (medical humours) or the transcendent sort attributed to the agentic force of landscapes in Chios and Beaune. That paradigm changed in the nineteenth century as wines increasingly became consumer objects, indexed and priced in order to make them quantifiable and marketable. The process displaced the direct unmitigated identity that *terroir* shared with the human subject.

The watershed moment arguably occurred with the 1855 *Exposition Mondiale* in Paris, in which France displayed its regional goods, technologies, and advancements in manufacturing to the rest of the world. In preparation for the event, the Bordeaux Chamber of Commerce opted to create a hierarchal ranking of its wines in order to simplify the market for international visitors and French consumers alike. Several propositions on how to create the hierarchy were proposed, including electing a panel of experts to conduct a comparative tasting. In the end, however, it was deemed that the most efficient and least controversial method would simply be to rank the wines according to the prices they had brought at market over the roughly 150 years preceding the classification.[7]

Although the 1855 classification of Bordeaux is often legitimized (or disputed) with references to the intrinsic qualities of the *terroir*, the classification from the outset was derived from prices related more to pragmatism and human-related contingencies than to an objective reflection on the quality and complexity of flavours. In fact, generally speaking, before railways and systems of commerce, the 'best' wines were those located in areas accessible for transport on waterways, or close to Paris.[8] Along with the location being a determinant, wine reputations were linked to the prestige of the people who owned the property, with prices dependent on the status of the grower. Rather than taking the objective measure of the *terroir*'s qualities, it was if the drinker were turned inward, seeking to appropriate metonymically the prestige of the human intercessor. Indeed, much of Bordeaux's original rating system was based on the perceived social success of the proprietor and the elegance of the chateau, rather than the wine itself. Moreover, there was nothing to prevent the owner of a highly-rated estate from purchasing surrounding properties and adding to the chateau's holdings, subsuming potentially inferior land under the umbrella of a more prestigious name. Yet, when Bordeaux was organized according to a classification system, the appearance of subjectivity gradually disappeared, and the *terroir*'s quality at any one estate was presented as a naturalized value.

That perceived objectification greatly facilitated marketing and allowed Bordeaux to gain international ascendancy as the world's most prestigious wine region. It also set the stage for the advent of wine connoisseurs and rating systems based on the aesthetic contemplation of wines. In the last third of the twentieth century, Anglo-Saxon wine critics, such as Jancis Robinson and Robert Parker, challenged Bordeaux's 1855 classification by conducting blind tastings. They used a rating system and an established wine-tasting vocabulary, positing that they were applying a meritocratic system to wine ratings. By using a systematic approach and a specialized scientific vocabulary (e.g. employing 'benzaldehyde' instead of the layman's 'cherry flavour', 'brettanomyces' instead of the amateur's 'barnyard smells', 'yeast 71b' for 'bananas', etc.), they conveyed the illusion of objectivity and supported the pretention that there was indeed a right and wrong way to perceive and describe wine. These tasters admitted personal preference, but also suggested that their analyses were based on an objective typicity emanating from wines from a specific geographic origin. Steven Shapin explains with the analogy of a dog show: the best beagle is not the biggest beagle, nor the beagle with the floppiest ears, but the beagle closest to the beagle type. Similarly, wines from a grape, region, and *terroir* should correspond to an imagined ideal type. In fact, a prominent methodology for wine evaluation detracts points for each imperfection (based on a twenty-point system) from the standard imagined for the perfect wine from a given origin.

Shaking *Terroir* to its Roots

Though sometimes challenged, *terroir* helped legitimize a system that provided stability on which to establish markets and a platform on which to construct meaningful conversations about wine as an aesthetic object. Yet, recently a trend has surfaced that reimagines *terroir* by offering it as trope for movement rather than stability, reversing the model that critics and commercial markets have established in the last 150 years. In this new regard, wines are no longer seen as mere objects of appreciation and appraisal, but as living agents that help to reimagine the subject-object duality expressed above.

One of the best examples is the wine made by Frank Cornelissen on Sicily's Mount Etna. Vineyards have existed on Etna for centuries, and the volcanic soil lends itself quite well to the pursuit.[9] Nevertheless, growing vines on Etna is a complicated affair. The volcano rises 10,000 feet above sea level and, most importantly, erupts often, burning property with its lava flows. Even when it is not actively erupting, it is impossible to forget you are on a volcano. It rumbles, shakes, and hollowly booms regularly. Even on a silent lazy day, water vaporizes while passing over the crater, giving the impression that the mountain is idly smoking, contemplating its next eruption.

When Etna wine was rediscovered about fifteen years ago, big firms rushed in only to discover that the *terroir* could not be managed on a large scale. The terrain could not be negotiated by tractors, and the spaces were too small for ample enough productions to cover costs. Instead of the relatively flat and straight lines of Bordeaux, Etna wines are grown on disparate sections of the mountain, with steep vertical slopes and sharp glass-like pumice adding to the punishment. More importantly, though vines can be grown up to an altitude of 1000 meters, the weather patterns are violent and unpredictable. There is more annual variability on the various parts of the mountain than in most places in the world. Still, the impetus to try remains since, at their best, the wines possess the appeal of grand cru burgundies. Moreover, ironically, the eruptions and the dynamism are precisely what makes for interesting wines. The lava flows that have destroyed and burned various places decompose over the following decades and centuries, becoming perfect for wines. They are called 'contradas', and are Sicily's equivalent to *terroir*, each possessing different characteristics.

Frank Cornelissen, a Belgian wine importer turned wine grower, has held property on Etna for nearly two decades. He produces 'natural wines' with minimal intervention, letting the wild climate of Etna fashion the wine. His reds can be superb when they don't re-ferment in the bottle or otherwise spoil. The whites are intellectual, angular, and often oxidized. The pleasure is in merely trying to understand them in comparison to more conventional white wines. Moreover, although Cornelissen's wines are expensive (the cost is explained by high demands, low yields, and how labour-intensive making good wine on Etna is), opening one amounts to a game of Russian roulette for the consumer. They are 'living products', not preserved by sulphur dioxide, and one never knows what to expect. Yet, that risk somehow makes sense since the very danger of a bottle erupting in an explosion of infelicitous biologic activity is the experiential corollary of living on Etna. One understands nature and *terroir* not as stability, but as molten mutability. Cornelissen is the first to admit these factors, but the mercurial nature of the wines is part of the ethos he seeks to convey. He does not set out to control the environment, but to act, insofar as possible, in harmony with it. As one critic writes, Cornelissen's wines are a sort of 'self-made unknown'.[10]

Cornelissen wines challenge temporal stability from one year to the next, but also from one bottle to the next, and even from one minute to the next. Instead of progressively opening and unfolding as one typically expects, the wines offer a fleeting, ephemeral experience, running the gamut from one set of funky, unappetizing smells to another. In the middle, if you're lucky (see Figure 1), the wine hits a moment of fleeting beauty and pure drinking pleasure. To drink Cornelissen wines is to embrace the aesthetic of precarity, fragility, and changeability. And yet, though Etna offers a perfect example of moveable *terroir*, the wines are not at the extreme end of the aesthetic.

In a 2014 article, *Der Spiegel* magazine reported on the ravages of climate change in the wine world.[11] Its author noted a certain propensity among winemakers to deny the effects of global warming. When faced with the topic, properties like the prestigious Chateau Ausone in Bordeaux were prone to skirting the question, or resorting to anecdotes about the vineyard's reputation for centuries of greatness. Other producers, such as Guigal, were more forthcoming, admitting that appellations like Chateauneuf-du-Pape were feeling the effects of global warming, with the grenache grape becoming progressively harder to harvest successfully. Growers could plant earlier, at higher altitudes, or use different grapes. Yet, these measures upset the tradition, destabilizing origins as points of reference in the natural world. There is a loss of typicity, and a loss of the stable, essentialist paradigm *terroir* provides.

Isabelle Frère, a grower in the Languedoc-Roussillon whose general approach is different than that of her conventional peers, offers an alternate solution. For one, rather than objectifying vines, *terroir*, and wine, Frère draws them in closer, making them a part of her own subjectivity: 'She talks to her grapes while working, sings during the harvest and ultimately sees winegrowing as a lifestyle and not a business.' The vines 'have to sleep, just like anything that's alive', *Der Spiegel* paraphrases breathlessly.[12] This anthropomorphic perspective might seem misguided insofar as it gives a characterization of the Earth in human terms, but the opposite view is that Frère is doing

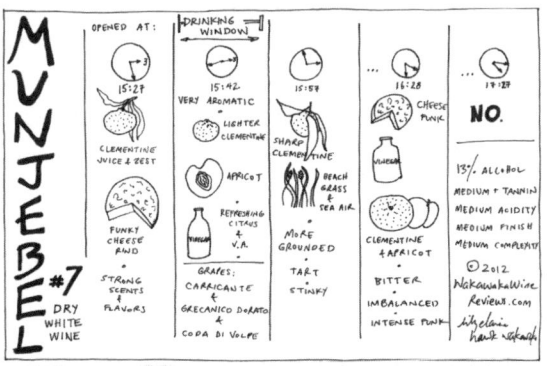

Figure 1: Cartoon describing the drinking window of a Cornelissen wine (Elaine Brown, Hawk WakaWaka Wine Reviews).

more good than harm by recognizing nature as an active player, instead of coldly objectifying it. Indeed, Frère is not alone in the anthropomorphic tendency. RAW, the international trade fair promoting natural wine, describes 'wines with emotion. Wines that have a humanlike, or living, presence'.[13]

Furthermore, in anthropomorphizing wines, Frère does not domesticate them or negate their agentic capacity, but instead depicts an inclusive biome uniting all things great and small, human and non-human. Instead of representing wine as a commodifiable object derived and mastered from inanimate rock and soil origins, there is a synergism and immediacy with the domain's natural world happily shared by Frère, fungi, beetles and flies, and the other members of the farm (there are three dogs, many cats, the father, a chain-smoking aunt, and a domestic partner). Yet, as *Der Spiegel* explains, there is no shortage of charisma: Frère has 'five helpers who are […] dashing, carefree characters with dreadlocks, tattoos and a lot of metal in their ears and noses. Both the wines and the people are outside of the mainstream and forge their identities together'.[14]

Producers like Frère and Cornelissen destabilize conventional wine aesthetics by making organic wine without the use of chemical fertilizers or pesticides, allowing the microbiome to express itself freely. The lack of control that accompanies such practices amounts to thumbing the nose at an established wine culture that attempts to commodify and homogenize nature. Conventional winemakers would view much of Frère's inclusive biome as a threat to the *terroir,* whereas, for Frère, they are the *terroir.* Moreover, by her own admission, she is not seeking to make wines that conform to a set of standards, nor even that are 'objectively' good (*Der Spiegel* describes her *cuvée* Scarabée as 'a dry, unsettled wine').[15] Rather, she is looking to make wines that are true. The Earth is getting warmer, and Frère and other likeminded winemakers choose not to intervene in ways that would somehow mask the reality of climate change. *Terroir* does not here connote stability and perfection, nor does it incarnate the 'perfect beagle type'. *Terroir*-driven wine, is this sense, is the three-legged, split-eyed beagle who pees on the floor. But it is a loveable beagle, Frère would argue, and it is our beagle.

Japanese Visions of Mountains and New Translations of *Terroir*
The conventional connoisseur rationalizes wine through mappable appellations, vintage charts, numeric ratings and objective-sounding scientific language. The process helps translate and universalize an experience of nature, but also demystifies it and even detracts from our freedom by suggesting that there is a right and wrong way to perceive food and wine. On the other end of the spectrum, instead of putting the accent on wine and *terroir* as static objects, the natural movement portrays wines as dynamic subjects, disrupting expectations and the mechanisms used to aestheticize and commodify wine. The two methodologies offer radically different ways of translating nature through the culinary experience that are as much culturally driven as anything else.

Until recently, natural wines have been mostly ignored by the Anglo-Saxon markets and rejected by critics. Robert Parker, for example, compared them to a 'jihadist movement' in a Tweet on 1 May 2013. But natural wine has been immensely popular in Japanese culture, with Japan consuming up to 75% of exports.[16] This taste for natural wines in Japan goes back to the birth of the movement in the 1990s when the influence of Parker was at its height, and it has been suggested that the popularity of natural wines owes to the fact that certain Japanese consumers were intimidated by the specialized lexicon and snobbism that went with conventional wine culture. Certainly, Tokyo's natural wine bars are often themed more on popular culture than high-culture motifs. Traditional reference points (extensive wine lists, special stemware, the pomp and erudition of the sommelier, the moment when the customer tastes the wine) are missing, and clients often drink standing up. A recent article in *Saveur* magazine described a natural wine bar: 'Kaneko poured me the 2014 Tsugane chardonnay from Beau Paysage in Yamanashi prefecture. It tasted like an oxidative white from the Jura and paired nicely with thin slices of mackerel and lotus root wheels [...]. Animal Collective blared on the speakers, the natty young creatives downed glass after glass [...], and Kaneko began doing a compact rhumba behind the bar with Sophia Burger, also from Noma.'[17] A countercultural element reminiscent of Isabelle Frère's vineyard workers pervades here, challenging the status quo, charging the atmosphere with carefree pulchritude, and jamming would-be pretension with unpredictability.

A recent article in the *Japan Times* offers an additional rationale, suggesting that the Japanese gravitate toward natural wines because the latter draw 'from elements of the traditional Japanese diet, which respects nature and uses ingredients with little intervention, resulting in delicate and simple flavors [...]. This is revealed through each wine's pronounced *terroir* – imparted by the natural environment in which it is produced'.[18] Others explain Japan's proclivity for natural wines by evoking the aesthetic of *wabi-sabi*, billed as important to Japanese culture as the idea of the beautiful was to the Greeks. *Wabi-sabi* is, however, the opposite of the perfect beagle. Nature is not appreciated for what it could or should be, but enjoyed for its transient, impermanent, imperfect qualities. The analysis is relevant both in the context of Cornelissen's wines, drinkable for a short window of time before becoming disagreeable, and with respect to wines transformed by global warming. *Wabi-sabi* is not tied exclusively to imperfection, but it is far from the bankable, stable, objectified qualities that conventional wines incarnate, and even farther from the search for the mythical 100-point wine.

A third way to explain the Japanese proclivity for natural wines lies in the Japanese notion of nature itself, and how it differs from Western standards. That is the subject of a 2015 book by the anthropologist Shiho Satsuka, *Nature in Translation: Japanese Tourism Encounters the Canadian Rockies*. Satsuka contemplates the tension that Japanese culture has felt when faced with the Western understanding of nature, noting that the Japanese originally possessed no word for nature that portrayed it as a separate entity from the human subject. In order to translate the Occidental notion of 'nature', the Japanese used the noun *shizen* to reproduce the binary framework designating human beings as subjects and nature as an object. Yet, *shizen* already existed in the language as an adjective and adverb with roots in the Taoist word *ziran* meaning 'artlessness' or 'without human intention'. That Taoist meaning did not separate human beings from the natural world. From within the same word, there therefore emerged a 'hybrid indeterminacy' wherein *shizen* alternated between a Western subject/object duality and a Taoist or Buddhist merging of the two into one.[19]

The phenomenon became relevant when Japanese travellers visiting the Canadian Rockies learned to apprehend nature in an American way. For one, there was a clear objectification of the mountains and a duality wherein the subject was an agentic force acting upon the objectified body with his regard. For Americans, mountain lakes were 'pristine' or 'hidden gems', waiting to be discovered by the detached human observer who framed nature through personal observations and scientific interpretations. Japanese tour guides, having learned this novel dualistic American appreciation of nature, delivered the landscape to Japanese tourists as if through American eyes, teaching them to 'do nature' as Americans do. The guides told Japanese tourists what to see, hear, and feel, in a way not completely dissimilar to how a Robert Parker or Jancis Robison might instruct novice drinkers to perceive *terroir* through flavours in a glass of wine. The experience of viewing nature as a separate object was empowering, allowing the tourists to act upon nature through the gesture of translating it, but it was also limiting since the pretention of objectivity ultimately curtailed subjective freedom of perception.

Ultimately, Japanese guides realized that they were not free at all. Unlike their Canadian counterparts, the Japanese did not have backgrounds in forestry and environment. They were thus compelled to pass a test administered by the Mountain Parks Heritage Interpretation Association certifying they were sufficiently conversant in the study of ecology and environmental stewardship to lead tours. The impetus derived from the MPHIA's mission to impart an understanding of responsible stewardship of the land to the park's visitors. That stewardship divorced the subject from the natural surroundings, since the guide was meant to analyze the landscape with a sort of disconnected scientific objectivity, disseminating verifiable facts to tourists without being swayed by cultural biases. Yet, due in part to the Japanese dual understanding of *shizen*, certain Japanese guides had difficulty sticking to a detached narrative. They thought that the message should be experiential, coming neither wholly from the guide, nor from the tourist, nor even from the wild surroundings themselves. The understanding of nature would be based on the interaction occurring between all of these variables, including the disposition and mood of the customers, the specific things encountered during the walk, and even the weather of that day. The corollary in terms of wine would be like coming to understand by allowing the entire experiential moment to shape the perception. The guides thought the idea of nature should be spontaneous, emerging 'naturally in intersubjective and embodied reactions' through a fluctuating lived interspecies experience, rather than through a one-side pedagogical mediation delivered by guides objectifying the mountainous *terroir*.[20]

The anecdote helps explain a Japanese proclivity (and Anglo-Saxon aversion) to natural wine. It also provides an impetus for a more prolonged discussion. Satsuka underscores the tension in the Japanese vision of *shizen* that contrasts nature as a culturally embedded intersubjective understanding to an object of universal scientific knowledge. If she is correct, the success of natural wines in Japan might be explained as pushback against pressure in the wine world to stabilize nature through an objective lens. The natural wine experience rejects this duality in the same way some Japanese tourists disavowed *shizen* as an objective construct. *Terroir* in this context can be flawed, transient, and even human, corresponding more to the aesthetic of *wabi-sabi* than that of the perfect 100-point wine. Paradoxically, as the Earth faces the threat of global warming, it is not an objectified, scientific view of *terroir*, but rather an intersubjective experience and recognition of the land's mutability that might prove most compelling.

Notes

1. Steven Shapin, 'The Tastes of Wine: Towards a Cultural History', *Rivista di Estetica*, 51 (2012), 49-94.
2. Peter Garnsey, *Food and Society in Classical Antiquity* (Cambridge: Cambridge University Press, 1999), pp. 118-19.
3. Hermippus fr. 77, qtd. in Andrew Dalby, *Siren Feasts: A History of Food and Gastronomy in Greece* (London: Routledge, 1996), p. 100.
4. Thomas Parker, *Tasting French Terroir: The History of an Idea* (Berkeley: UCP, 2015), p. 5.
5. Charles Estienne and Joseph Liébault, *L'Agriculture ou la Maison Rustique* (Paris: Jacques Du-Puys, 1637 (1578), p. 351.
6. Claude Arnoux, *Dissertation sur la situation de la Bourgogne* (London: Jallasson, 1728).
7. Dewey Markham Jr, *1855: A History of the Bordeaux Classification* (New York: Wiley, 1998).
8. Roger Dion, 'Querelle des Anciens et des Modernes sur les facteurs de la qualité du vin', *Annales de Géographie*, 61 (1952), 417-31.
9. Bill Nesto and Frances Di Savino, *The World of Sicilian Wine* (Berkeley: UCP, 2013).
10. Hawk Wakawaka Wine Reviews, 'Thinking Frank Cornelissen: Considering Wine's Natural Drinking Window via Munjebel 7 White and Red, and Contadino 8' <https://wakawakawinereviews.com/2012/03/14/thinking-frank-cornelissen-considering-wines-natural-drinking-window-via-munjebel-7-white-red-and-contadino-8/> [accessed 26 October 2017].
11. Ullrich Fichtner, 'The Grapes of Wrath: France's Great Wines are Feeling the Heat', *Der Spiegel*, 30 October 2014 <http://www.spiegel.de/international/zeitgeist/climate-change-threatens-french-viticulture-a-1000113.html> [accessed 26 October 2017].
12. Fichtner.
13. Eric Asimov, 'Wine That's Not Only Natural, It's Alive', *New York Times*, 17 November 2016 <https://www.nytimes.com/2016/11/23/dining/natural-raw-wine-fair.html> [accessed 26 October 2017].
14. Fichtner.
15. Fichtner.
16. Sarah Crago, 'Natural Wine is a Natural Fit in Tokyo', *Japan Times*, 28 August 2015 <http://www.japantimes.co.jp/life/2015/08/28/food/natural-wine-natural-fit-tokyo/#.WTqfHRPyuRs> [accessed 26 October 2017].
17. Alex Halberstadt, 'Drinking Wine in Tokyo', *Saveur*, April-May, 2017 <https://issuu.com/mimimi980/docs/saveur_aprilmay_2017/19> [accessed 26 October 2017].
18. Halberstadt.
19. Shiho Satsuka, *Nature in Translation: Japanese Tourism Encounters the Canadian Rockies* (Durham: Duke University Press, 2015), pp. 19-20.
20. Satsuka, p. 178.

Climbing Butter Mountain: How Food Law Has Affected British Landscape, In and Out of the EU

Olivia Potts

This paper looks at the role food law has played in the formation of the physical landscape of Britain. It briefly looks at food law's influence on landscape throughout history, and then examines in more detail the trajectory of European agriculture and food policy and legislation, from the European Union's inception, through the Common Agricultural Policy, to the present day, and the effect that this has had on rural Britain. It concludes by setting out the likelihood of the different scenarios following Brexit, and what these changes may mean for British landscape.

Laws have changed our landscape, and the way we eat, for centuries. From taxation to regulation, quotas to subsidies, food and farming laws have influenced urban planning, agriculture, defence, and conquest. Laws have operated at the macro scale – think of India's great tea plantations, which spread across the subcontinent after the British East India Company lost its Chinese tea monopoly – and the micro: the meandering hedge at the end of your road, maintained thanks to EU grants, that keeps the sheep in and the rustlers out.

The Birth of British Food Law

When the Romans came to Britain, they levied a grain tax – the *annona militaris*. The *annona militaris* had begun life as a hand-out to Roman citizens, but by the time the Romans invaded Britain, 200,000 individuals were eligible for this grain. Previous attempts to suspend or do away with the *annona militaris* had led to rioting, so in order to supply the vast amount of grain needed, it was taken from British farmers. It was taken 'from the top' of the farmers' produce, meaning farmers were obliged to overproduce in order to feed their families.[1] This tax, coupled with a general influx of people after the Roman invasion, meant Britain suddenly had many more mouths to feed: a considerable challenge for a nation that had largely farmed for subsistence up to this point. Inevitably, more of the British countryside was cleared for arable land. The *annona militaris* was the first major food law that shaped the British countryside. It would not be the last.

The English countryside is a farmed landscape: 70% of Great Britain is farmland. The irregular patchwork of meadows and fields, bordered by copses and woodlands, gave rise to the pastoral tradition, immortalized in Gainsborough and Constable, written about by poets from Wordsworth to Ted Hughes. As much as we are inclined to romanticize it as organic in the most literal sense, growing wild, untouched by human hands, the vast majority of it is farmed.[2]

No law has played a bigger role in creating this patchwork than the Enclosure Acts. We think of enclosure as one event: a transition from wild common land to neatly hedged fields, that took place somewhere in the eighteenth century and set the stage for Britain's Agricultural Revolution and, subsequently, the Industrial Revolution. Actually, various enclosure laws were enacted over some 300 years, between 1604 and 1914, with the effect of gradually moving Britain away from the feudal system of the Middle Ages, in which tenant farmers farmed individual strips on large open fields. The reality was that the old system wasn't very good at producing food. The Enclosure Acts allowed farmers to improve their efficiency, and 6.8 million acres of land were enclosed: inevitably, physical boundaries were needed: the manifestation of the Enclosure Acts were the drystone walls and hedgerows that now typify rural Britain.

But it wasn't until 1875 that English food law was formalized as a distinct field, with the passing of the Sale of Food and Drugs Act. The impetus for this was food safety: the Act sought to protect the consumer from rampant tampering, fraud, and adulteration.[3] At this stage, the understandable priority was the consumer, and there was little interest in what the production of food meant for Britain and its landscape as a country dependent on farming, but this would change.

European Food Law and the Birth of the Common Agricultural Policy

The UK's entry into the European Economic Community in 1961 brought powerful new force to bear on the British landscape. Instantly, the UK became part of a huge – and highly regulated – international market. The result was a mushrooming of food law. The Food Act 1984 was the most comprehensive set of food regulations ever introduced into English law.[4]

Agriculture remains the primary use of European land; some 42% of the EU's land area is devoted to farming, and few EU regulations have had a bigger influence than the Common Agricultural Policy. The CAP now dictates and regulates all kinds of things, from how much milk a dairy farm can produce to who's responsible for building and maintaining drystone walls. However, the original CAP, set out in the Treaty of Rome in 1957, was far narrower. There was no mention whatsoever of rural maintenance, landscape, or stewardship. The creation of the CAP came at a time of food shortage when, shortly after the end of World War II, a number of countries still rationed certain food items. Food security was the priority – not surprising, after a war that had brought starvation to millions. The nations of Europe were perfectly happy to adopt extensive interventionist measures, if those measures ensured that everyone could eat. Hence, Article 39 of the Treaty of Rome reads:

Article 39
1. The common agricultural policy shall have as its objectives:

(a) to increase agricultural productivity by developing technical progress and by ensuring the rational development of agricultural production and the optimum utilisation of the factors of production, particularly labour;

(b) to ensure thereby a fair standard of living for the agricultural population, particularly by the increasing of the individual earnings of persons engaged in agriculture;

(c) to stabilise markets;

(d) to guarantee regular supplies; and

(e) to ensure reasonable prices in supplies to consumers.

In its original incarnation, the Common Agricultural Policy sought to achieve these objectives by creating a common market for several agricultural products. It did so by guaranteeing minimum prices on some of those products, including dairy products such as milk, butter, and milk powder. For each qualifying commodity, there was a base price that was set for intervention. If the market price fell below this base, the European Agricultural Guarantee and Guidance Fund (EAGGF) bought up the product at that base price level.

The policy was successful – too successful. By the 1980s, vast surpluses had built up the famed 'butter mountains' and 'wine lakes'. In 1986, for example, 1.23 million tons of unsellable butter were bought up by the European Union.[5] There are differing accounts as to whether the butter mountains and milk lakes of legend were real, or merely colourful descriptions of food waste. The truth is prosaic: they existed, but in enormous warehouses, filled with unsellable pats of butter and vats of milk and wine.

In 1984, in an effort to put an end to overproduction, the EU instituted milk quotas, which placed a hefty levy on member states that produced in excess of their allocation. The quotas achieved what they set out to, but were resented by farmers who felt they were unable to compete with African and Asian dairy markets. In April 2015, these quotas were abolished. By January 2016, butter mountains had returned, and once again the EU were compelled to step in and buy up surplus.

These unsellable surpluses have historically been dumped on non-European countries, with unsurprisingly profound effects on its recipients. For example, subsidized milk powder has so undercut domestic production in Jamaica that many local farmers have had to abandon production; most local processors use the cheaper imported milk powder instead.[6]

There are issues with biofuel production from surplus wine too. Thanks to EU subsidy, the Languedoc-Roussillon region of France consistently overproduces wine. When this happens, the surplus is 'crisis distilled' into ethanol to be used as biofuel. While there is merit in the use of biofuel, and producing it from wine is certainly preferable to simply dumping the surplus, the process is inefficient and encourages production of sub-standard wine in the knowledge it will be bought up by the EU. Later laws have therefore sought to remedy the blunt instrument of subsidy; these include financial incentives to abandon vines and permission required to plant new vines.[7]

Along with creating metaphorical mountains and lakes, the subsidy system has had profound effects on the physical landscape. By incentivizing overproduction and rewarding productivity, intensive farming became irresistible. The land unsurprisingly suffered as a result. Particularly high levels of pesticides, fertilizers, tillage operations, and mechanical weed control were utilized by many farmers, and the land paid the price: soil erosion and degradation, visual homogeneity and lack of biodiversity, as well as constant use of land that had been previously unused.

For the first twenty years, the CAP remained almost completely divorced from environment and landscape. Coupled payments and market support gave incentives to increase the size of the farm and to grow the eligible supported crops.[8] As unintended results, the policy reduced crop diversity and rotation and homogenized the agricultural landscape.[9] It also contributed to livestock intensification, which was in and of itself detrimental to land.

In 1988, the EEC introduced 'set-aside payments', a scheme that paid farmers to set-aside portions of their land for set periods.[10] During that period, farmers were not allowed to use the land for any agricultural purpose except cultivation of non-food crops. The set-aside policy was designed to reduce production, improve land quality, and protect the environment. Soil, flora, and fauna would be given time to recover, in a similar way to standard crop rotation. In 1996, there were 7,259,000 hectares of set-aside land, which gave a significant portion of the landscape an opportunity to recover from intensive over-farming.[11] This policy was abolished in 2008.

Such changing policies led to questions about the very idea of subsidies. In their January 2002 report on 'Farming and Food: A Sustainable future', the Policy Commission on the Future of Farming and Food, led by Lord Donald Curry, found that subsidies tied to production under the CAP had 'become part of the problem rather than the solution'. They argued that the subsidies distorted pricing, divorced producers from the market, and 'mask[ed] inefficiency'.[12] But, truly, this was only half the problem. Much of the damage done by the direct payments was to the very landscape; 'CAP payments as they stand are still in some areas encouraging damaging practices, such as overgrazing in hill areas and inappropriate rotations on arable land.'[13] Environmental groups agree with this assessment, as an Oxfam report argues:

> The idea that existing industrialised-country agricultural policies are good for rural development and the environment is a myth. On the contrary, current subsidy patterns, with their emphasis on expanding production, have encouraged the industrialisation of agriculture, with a premium on the heavy use of chemical inputs. The most immediate consequences include extensive environmental damage.[14]

Such criticisms led, in 2003, to the introduction of decoupled aid: known as the 'Single Farm Payment', it subsidized the farmer on a per-hectare basis, literally decoupling aid from production. Instead, the full payment of direct aid was linked to 'compliance with rules related to agricultural land, agricultural production and activity', and those rules would incorporate basic standards for 'the environment [...] and good agricultural land environmental condition'.[15] The objective, explicitly stated of these Standards of Good Agricultural and Environmental Condition (GAEC), is to ensure that all agricultural land, especially land which is no longer used for production purposes, is maintained in good condition.

The rubric for this is set out in Annex III Council Regs (EC) No 73/2009: member states define these standards individually on the basis of optional and compulsory standards. There's a wide range of applicable conditions amongst the member states, and occasionally within them, as it's possible for different standards to be imposed in different regions: the standards must 'take into account the specific characteristics of the areas concerned, including soil and climatic condition, existing farming systems, land use, crop rotation, farming practices and farm structures'.[16]

The GAEC standards specifically aim to retain distinctive and traditional landscape features. Italian farmers must preserve and prevent the degradation of terraces and protect olive groves and vines. In France, farmers must place a minimum amount of arable land under environmental cover alongside watercourses and hedgerows and on slopes. Meanwhile, in the UK, the GAEC prohibited the removal of drystone walls.

Thus, EU farming law came full circle. Early EU regulations had affected the landscape in large, unanticipated, and devastating ways. Policymakers learnt from these mistakes, if slowly, so that later rules were explicitly designed to preserve and protect Europe's distinctive landscapes.

Pillar II Payments and Rural Development

The EU's agricultural regulations go beyond single-farm payments. Pillar II payments fund rural development: unlike the single farm payments, these are not directly paid to farmers, but instead paid to the member states' governments. It is then for that government to apply European criteria and distribute money accordingly, since all spending on rural development must be co-financed by the member state.

From 1975, the EU has introduced varying supports designed to help those who farm in areas where the land itself is 'handicapped', due to climate, or lack or rain, or altitude – conditions which tend to cause lower yields, and higher production costs. The EU's stance is that it is sufficiently important to ensure that land which might otherwise be abandoned remains maintained and farmed.[17]

This 'less-favoured areas' scheme has had a number of different manifestations since its introduction: it began as the Hill Livestock Compensatory Allowances, based on the number of livestock farmed, and remained so until 2000. That approach was replaced in 2001 by the Hill Farming Allowance, which was paid according to area. Seven years ago the scheme was revised again through the Uplands Entry Level Stewardship Scheme. As the name suggests, the UELSS places a heavier emphasis on countryside maintenance to promote more sustainable farming. In the UK, the main effects are to prohibit overgrazing and limit soil erosion. As of last year, there are 2.2 million hectares of LFA-designated land in the UK, and modern hill farmers are often heavily dependent on this form of subsidy.[18]

Despite the EU's interventionist role in the aesthetics and biodiversity of landscape, the role of the livestock that grazes there was largely ignored until recently. Yarwood and Evans have described the recalibration of policy as 'the new animal geography'. As well as a contribution to local identity and cultural landscape, the presence of traditional and rare breeds can affect the landscape beyond their sheer presence.[19]

To support indigenous breeds, commission regulation 445/2002 (Article 14) outlined how member states can draw on funding from European Agricultural Guidance and Guarantee fund. Rare breeds are funded differently: while payment has been decoupled from quantity for most livestock production, rare breeds are the exception, and can be paid per animal reared.[20]

Many traditional breeds are not suited to intensive farming, but are suited to non-intensive farming; they graze in different ways. If these breeds are supported financially, they can positively influence the landscape. For example, longhorn cattle – unlike modern, softer-mouthed cattle – can graze on limestone pastures in Derbyshire, reducing tough plant species that choke others and reduce biodiversity.[21]

Should funding disappear, and those breeds and crops go, so too will the landscapes with which we associate rural Britain. The reality is that there are much cheaper labour and production costs in Brazil, Argentina, Thailand, and elsewhere for cattle farming. Without financial protection – in other words, subsidy – British farmers will struggle. So what would this mean for the landscape? If, without subsidies or emergency intervention, the bottom drops out of the British livestock market, there are a number of consequences for the English countryside and its landscape. *Landscapes without Livestock*, an independent report commissioned by the Agriculture and Horticulture Development Board in 2011, looked at the likely effects on our land if market prices for cattle and sheep decline to such an extent that farmers reduce grazing densities. As well as the aforementioned degradation of dry stone walling, there would be an increase in bracken and scrub in upland areas, like the North Yorkshire moors. Now the moors, 'smooth pastoral fields of varying shades of green standing out against a backdrop of textured bronze and golden bracken and heather moorland habitats', are 'a varied upland mosaic reflecting patterns of land management activity.' In just a few decades, however, 'the spread of bracken, scrub and rough grassland along with new woodland planting [will result] in a more roughly textured landscape'. Rolling farmland areas like Pickering, again in North Yorkshire, will be dominated by continuous arable cropping, with larger farms and more intensive methods: 'species-rich grasslands, which depend upon low levels of grazing, [will be] replaced by taller, rank grasslands with lower species diversity. Subsequently, several rare butterflies and moths [will be] adversely affected.'[22]

So what does this actually mean? Well, in essence: homogeneity. The report makes no comment on the merits or otherwise of these likely landscape changes, but other studies do, and show that the general public sees homogenization as a reduction of visual beauty.[23]

There is the possibility of farms being sold as smallholdings to those who have little practical experience but an interest in rare breeds and self-sustainability.[24] Although it may begin to feel a little like *The Good Life*, this may be something we see an increasing amount of following Brexit: allotments and beekeeping have seen a resurgence over the last ten years, and if fresh produce prices increase as a consequence of European trade tariffs, it is likely to continue. Such practices will no doubt help urban dwellers feel connected to the land and put some fresh seasonal vegetables on their tables. But we're dealing with a different scale of production and interest: such changes cannot replace traditional farming.

What Does Brexit Mean for British Landscape?

It is clear that much of the legislation that has formed the modern British landscape has come directly from Europe: subsidies, quotas, and rural preservation mandates. When Britain exits the EU, these laws, for better or worse, will disappear. The government will need to take control of farming and fishery law, production, and agriculture.

At this stage, no one really seems to know how this is going to happen. Beyond the fabled but opaque 'hard brexit' – that is, withdrawal from the single market – there is no coherent idea of what an independent British agricultural policy would look like. There are over 12,000 EU laws, regulations, and statutory implements that will need replacing. Of course, there is the possibility that the UK will simply adopt the substance of EU regulations into English law, including market support, direct payments, rural investment, and insistence on good environmental standards, but this is no small undertaking. The likelihood of our government being willing to take on a raft of European legislation without quibbling seems unlikely.[25]

The most concerning reality is that there will come a point when the UK is responsible for funding UK agriculture and country stewardship. There are agreements in place that mean that this won't be immediate, but such a possibility looms large over the near future. The early days of the EU show what can go wrong when laws unbalance food production. In theory, given the contribution that the UK makes to the EU, and therefore the CAP, the money saved by giving up EU membership could be channelled into British farming. This would do much to maintain the status quo of our landscape.

However, the reality is that Pillar II payments are likely to remain more protected than Pillar I within a post-Brexit UK for two reason. First, for over ten years, DEFRA have been clear on the policy: 'Our vision for agriculture within the next 10 to 15 years' is for it to be 'internationally competitive without reliance on subsidy or protection'.[26] This is not a government who want to subsidize agriculture directly. Second, since Pillar II payments come through national governments and are in part funded by those governments, there are separate contracts in place that must be honoured in or out of the EU. Alongside those negotiated by Natural England on behalf of DEFRA, some legacy schemes have been contracted until 2024, and new agreements running from 2016 are in place under Countryside Stewardship: these will all need to be funded until their respective expiries.

Unsurprisingly, farmers will want direct payments to continue, and they will likely argue that they represent a protection against both market volatility and a subsidized European market. Evidence shows there are many farmers who are predominantly or wholly dependent on direct aid and subsidies to survive. Figures from the National Farmers Union show that, in 2015, the UK received £2.4 billion in direct payments: this means that almost 55% of the UK farming income was coming from the Common Agricultural Policy.[27]

Much EU food law has revolved around preserving the landscape of member states. For Britain this has chimed with how the British public think the landscape should be: patchwork fields full of cows and hills covered in sheep. But, arguably, this is an unsustainable picture: not just in terms of economics without the same level of subsidies, but also in terms of the environment. Bare uplands covered in sheep mean flash floods in flood plains.[28] Dairy farming has an enormous carbon cost.[29] So, is it desirable to maintain the status quo? Should our landscape not change?

Since the Romans and their taxes, the British landscape has always reflected not just domestic food needs, but the reality of Britain's role in the world. It is a product of trade, of tariffs, of taxes. So is the food we produce and eat. Now, our role in the world is changing. Our laws are definitely changing. The question for those making our food laws is not just how will the landscape change – but how should it?

Notes

1. Michael E. Jones, *The End of Roman Britain* (Ithaca: Cornell University Press, 1996), p. 215.
2. Ann Bermingham, *Landscape and Ideology: The English Rustic Tradition, 1740-1860* (Berkeley: University of California Press, 1986).
3. Bee Wilson, *Swindled: The Dark History of Food Fraud, from Poisoned Candy to Counterfeit Coffee* (London: John Murray, 2009), p. 145.
4. Caoihin Mamoalain, *Food Law: European, Domestic and International Frameworks* (London: Bloomsbury, 2015).
5. Stephen Castle, 'Europe to Buy 30,000 Tons of Surplus Butter', *New York Times*, 22 January 2009 <http://www.nytimes.com/2009/01/23/business/worldbusiness/23butter.html> [accessed 23 May 2017].
6. Clare Godfrey, *Stop the Dumping! How EU Agricultural Subsidies Are Damaging Livelihoods in the Developing World* (Oxford: Oxfam, 2002), p. 4 <http://policy-practice.oxfam.org.uk/publications/stop-the-dumping-how-eu-agricultural-subsidies-are-damaging-livelihoods-in-the-114605> [accessed 23 May 2017].
7. European Commission, 'Preparation Agriculture/Fisheries Council of November 2007', *European Commission*, 23 November 2007 <http://europa.eu/rapid/press-release_MEMO-07-497_en.htm> [accessed 23 May 2017].
8. Marianne Lefebvre, Maria Espinosa, and Sergio Gomez y Paloma, *The Influence of the Common Agricultural Policy on Agricultural Landscapes* (Luxembourg: Publications Office of the European Union, 2012), p. 17.
9. Centre d'Analyse Stratégique, *Rapport: Les aides publiques dommage ables à la biodiversité*, Republic of France, 2012 <http://www.ladocumentationfrancaise.fr/var/storage/rapports-publics/124000434.pdf> [accessed on 23 May 2017].
10. Commission Regulation (EEC) No 1272/88 of 29 April 1988 laying down detailed rules for applying the set-aside incentive scheme for arable land.
11. Michael Winter, 'The Arables Crops Regime and the Countryside', in *CAP Regimes and the European*

Countryside: Prospects for Integration Between Agricultural, Regional, and Environmental Policies, ed. by Floor Brouwer and Philip Lowe (Oxfordshire: CABI Publishing, 2000), p. 122.
12. Lord Donald Curry, 'Farming and Food: A Sustainable Future', Report of the Policy Commission on the Future of Farming and Food, January 2002, p. 20 <http://webarchive.nationalarchives.gov.uk/20100807034701/http:/archive.cabinetoffice.gov.uk/farming/pdf/PC%20Report2.pdf> [accessed 23 May 2017].
13. Curry, p. 73.
14. Godfrey, p. 4.
15. Council Regulation (EC) No 1782/2003 of 29 September 2003 establishing common rules for direct support schemes under the common agricultural policy and certain support schemes for farmers.
16. Council Regulation (EC) No 73/2009 of 19 January 2009 establishes common rules for direct support schemes for farmers under the common agricultural policy and establishing certain support schemes for farmers, Article 6(1).
17. David Harvey and Charles Scott, 'Farm Business Survey: 2014/2015 Hill Farming in England', Newcastle University Rural Business Research, March 2016 <http://www.ncl.ac.uk/media/wwwn-clacuk/agriculturefoodandruraldevelopment/files/Hill%20Farming%20in%20England%202014_15.pdf> [accessed 23 May 2017].
18. Harvey and Scott, p. 7; Peak District Rural Deprivation Forum, 'Hard Times: A Research Report into Hill Farming and Farming Families in the Peak District' (Hope Valley: Peak District Rural Deprivation Forum, 2004) <http://oxfamilibrary.openrepository.com/oxfam/bitstream/10546/126048/1/hard-times-010104-en.pdf> [accessed 23 May 2017].
19. Richard Yarwood and Nick Evans, 'Livestock, Locality and Landscape: EU Regulations and the New Geography of Welsh Farm Animals', *Applied Geography*, 23.2-3 (2003), 131-37.
20. Commission Regulation (EC) No 445/2002 of 26 February 2002 laying down detailed rules for the application of Council Regulation (EC) No 1257/1999 on support for rural development from the European Agricultural Guidance and Guarantee Fund (EAGGF), Article 18 (2).
21. Nick Evans, Peter Gaskell, and Michael Winter, 'Reassessing Agrarian Policy and Practice in Local Environmental Management: The Case of Beef Cattle', *Land Use Policy*, 20.3 (2003), 231-42.
22. Robert Deane, 'Landscape without Livestock: Visualising the Impacts of a Potential Decline in Beef and Sheep Farming on Some of England's Most Cherished Landscapes', *LUC*, 12 December 2011, p. 11 <http://beefandlamb.ahdb.org.uk/wp-content/uploads/2013/06/Landscapes-without-livestock-report.pdf> [accessed 23 May 2017].
23. M. Arriaza and others, 'Assessing the Visual Quality of Rural Landscapes', *Landscape and Urban Planning*, 69 (2004), 115-25.
24. Deane, p. 22.
25. Tim Lang, 'Food, Brexit and the Consequences: What Can Academics and the UK Food Movement Do?', Food Research Collaboration, July 2016 <http://foodresearch.org.uk/foodvoices/food-brexit-and-the-consequences-what-can-academics-and-the-uk-food-movement-do/> [accessed 29 May 2017].
26. HM Treasury and Department of Environment, Food, and Rural Affairs, 'A Vision for the Common Agricultural Policy' (London: 2005), p. 3.
27. Emma Downing, 'EU Referendum: Impact on UK Agriculture Policy', Briefing paper number 7602, House of Commons Library, May 2016 <http://researchbriefings.files.parliament.uk/documents/CBP-7602/CBP-7602.pdf> [accessed 29 May 2017].
28. George Monbiot, 'Why Britain's Barren Uplands have Farming Subsidies to Blame', *The Guardian*, 22 May 2013 <https://www.theguardian.com/environment/georgemonbiot/2013/may/22/britain-uplands-farming-subsidies> [accessed 29 May 2017].
29. Agriculture and Horticulture Development Board, 'Greenhouse Gas Emissions on British Dairy Farms', *DairyCo*, February 2012 <https://dairy.ahdb.org.uk/media/623464/greenhouse_gas_emissions_on_british_dairy_farms.pdf> [accessed 29 May 2017].

A Creature of Salty Estuaries and Glacial Till: The History, Remarkable Qualities, and Incomparable Flavour of the Wild Peconic Bay Scallop

Charity Robey

Figure 1. Peconic Bay scallops at dockside (photo: Charity Robey).

Introduction
The Peconic Bay scallop is one of Nature's most appealing creatures. A 7.5-centimetre hermaphrodite with an adductor muscle that tastes like a briny gumdrop and seventy blue eyes arranged like sapphires along the edge of its waffled shell, the bay scallop has a two-year lifespan that winds down a few months after it reproduces. Then we eat it.

People who taste a wild Peconic Bay scallop often describe its flavours (sweet, umami), its aroma (redolent of the sea), and its mouthfeel (firm, tender) as unlike – and as better than – those of any other scallop they have tasted.

How the Peconic Estuary Gives Its Scallops Flavour
There are over three hundred species of scallops in the world, ranging from animals the size of a dinner plate (the Weathervane, a sea scallop found in the Pacific Northwest and

Alaska) to 2.5-centimetre scallops so small they are of no commercial value as food. The wild bay scallop species of the Peconic estuary is *Argopecten irradians irradians*.[1]

The Bay Bottom: Sand, Grass and Mud

Naturalist Ernest Ingersoll's vivid account of the Peconic Bay scallop's home in his 1886 article 'The Scallop and its Fishery' still rings true today: 'The proper home of this species seems to be in fairly deep water on a firm bottom – either sand or tough mud: yet in many localities grassy beds are resorted to by it, especially when young.'[2]

The East End of Long Island is a landscape of hills and ridges, kettles, eskers, bays, creeks, and enormous boulders left behind when the glacier of the last Ice Age receded. The bottoms of the harbours and 'creeks' (pronounced 'cricks' by old-timers; actually narrow, tidal inlets) of Peconic Bay are covered in grass, sand, or mud, and the organic and mineral compounds of the bay bottom find their way into the body of the bay scallop, a filter-feeder that constantly sifts and ingests particles of its environment.

James Hayward, a commercial fisherman and restaurant owner on Shelter Island since the 1950s, is one of the handful of men who have fished these waters for decades. He has a succinct way of summing up how the bay bottom and its mineral composition affect scallop flavour: 'Everything tastes sweeter on mud.'[3]

Another expert on the question of mud is Charlie Manwaring, the owner of the Southold Fish Market, an East End institution. Manwaring buys Peconic Bay scallops from local baymen, sells them in his fish market, and distributes the rest to restaurants and consumers in New York City and Long Island, and he's not so sure he can ascribe their wonderful flavour to mud. 'Some guys say they can tell the difference between an Orient scallop and one from elsewhere, that Orient scallops taste better,' he says, referring to a muddy and popular scalloping spot. 'Some say they can tell the difference in taste from scallops that are found on mud versus sand.'[4]

It's not just a romantic notion that the scallops are what they eat. Stephen Tettelbach, a biologist at Long Island University who studies the Peconic Bay scallop, has pointed to research that suggests that bay scallops will even eat organic aggregates: organic matter held together by a kind of mucus – food they would get from a muddy bay bottom.[5]

Water Salinity, Temperature, and the Scallop Life Cycle

Bay scallops live in brackish waters that are only slightly less salty than seawater (27-31 parts per thousand (ppt)). Like many sea animals, scallops produce amino acids that help them tolerate higher concentrations of salt in the surrounding seawater than in the cells of their bodies. These amino acids also make the shellfish taste good to us. Two amino acids are largely responsible for bay scallops' flavour: glutamate gives scallops the savoury flavour known as umami, and glycine makes them taste sweet.[6]

Unlike oysters, whose flavour varies according to levels of water salinity, scallops are almost impervious to this effect because they don't tolerate low salt conditions. Oysters will grow in a wide range of salinities, from 10-30 ppt. In contrast, bay scallops tolerate

A Creature of Salty Estuaries and Glacial Till

Figure 2. Peconic Bay scallop with a string of blue eyes along its shell (photo: Charity Robey).

a salinity range of only 27-31 ppt.[7]

Another source of the very sweet flavour in scallops can be found in the simple sugars present in their tissues after glycogen breakdown.[8] Unlike animals that store fat (an important source of flavour in meat), molluscs store energy in glycogen, especially in the adductor muscle and the digestive gland, until it is needed for spawning in May and June. By the end of the summer months, the scallops' glycogen, along with the flavour, is restored.

Baymen are experts in the life cycle of the Peconic Bay scallop because getting the largest, sweetest, most marketable scallops depends on understanding the physiological changes that take place over the molluscs' two-year lifespan. By November, when the scalloping season opens, the adult bivalves have recovered from spawning, developed a deeper and more globe-shaped shell with a slightly raised ring, grown to almost 7.5 centimetres, and are ready to eat. It's this growth ring that baymen look for when they bring up a dredge-full of scallops. Juvenile scallops without a growth ring go back into the bay to grow another year and spawn.

Peconic Bay scallops only spawn once, and the adults die of old age during the winter months. There is no guilt in eating an adult bay scallop.

The sweeter the flavour of a scallop, the more calories it provides when eaten, and the better it is as an energy source. It is an evolutionary adaptation in humans to prefer sweet flavours, and in that way the bay scallop has played a role in the evolution of human taste preferences. As an energy-rich food, bay scallops conferred an evolutionary advantage on early humans who liked to eat them.[9]

Bay Scallops and the 'Taste of the Sea'

Scallops are filter feeders who strain sea water containing phytoplankton, the microscopic plants and organic matter that constitute their food. The flavour compounds that contribute the 'taste of the sea' to wild seafood and enhance the other flavours are bromophenols, and the varieties of plankton that create bromophenols can change from one bay or harbour to the next.

Levels of intensity of flavour depend on the species of plankton the scallop feeds on. Biochemist Joseph Provost gives this explanation of the mechanism by which bromophenols make flavour: 'Depending upon the combination and the number and placement of bromines, you can get different levels of intensity of flavor, and that depends on the species of marine organism the animal feeds on.'[10] In addition to plankton in the water, scientists think that bay scallops eat organic matter from slipper shells that attach themselves to the shells of adult scallops, as well as the algae that grows on the surface of their own shells.[11]

All of these different factors partly account for the fact that attempts to farm Peconic Bay scallops have produced animals of the same species, *Argopecten irradians irradians*, but without the same 'taste of the sea' flavor.[12]

A Muscular Mollusc that Is More than a Mouthful

Scallops are the only bivalves that move, and the adductor muscles of scallops are huge compared to other molluscs. The adductor muscle opens and shuts the shell, forcing water and creating something resembling jet propulsion to elude crabs, sea stars, whelks, and other predators. Scallops also use this capability to orient their shells toward the best flow of water for feeding.[13]

Movement gives scallops clear survival advantages, but it can also be a sign of distress. The tendency of scallops to move when under stress is something every bayman experiences upon loading freshly caught wild bay scallops onto a table for shucking and hearing the sound of clapping shells fill the air. As scallop farmers can tell you, scallops seem to be particularly stressed when they are crowded. Farmed scallops are held close together as they develop and as a result do not reach the size of wild scallops.

Gregg Rivara, an aquaculture specialist with the Cornell Cooperative Extension of Suffolk County, NY, helped develop a cultivated scallop industry in Peconic Bay waters. Called the Empire State In-shell Bay Scallops, this initiative, launched in September of 2012, has had mixed results. Cornell provides seed scallops, which hang in mesh nets similar to those used in oyster cultivation. Scallops raised this way are under stress, are said to be less sweet, and have much smaller adductor muscles than wild scallops. Farmed bay scallops are usually steamed and eaten whole like soft clams or mussels.

The History and Technology of Scalloping and Its Effects on the Physical and Economic Landscape of the Peconic Bay

In 1881, Ernest Ingersoll was a 26-year old naturalist when he wrote a series of monographs for the US Fish Commission and the Census Bureau on the state of US shellfishery. The series included interviews with settlers and Native Americans alike and documented how the earliest explorers of North America observed Native Americans on Atlantic shores eating a variety of shellfish, including bay scallops, and leaving huge heaps of discarded shells as evidence of their enthusiasm.[14]

Archaeological evidence of scallop consumption on Shelter Island in the area around Fresh Pond suggests that Native American settlement on Shelter Island was not just seasonal, but year-round and much more established than previously thought.[15]

A Creature of Salty Estuaries and Glacial Till

Mountains of Scallops, 1885-1985

For a century, Peconic Bay scallops on Long Island accounted for about half of the fishing economy.

The Shelter Island Historical Society Archive holds a 130-year old invoice for the sale of 10.5 kilograms of scallops by C.A. Congdon to John Elsey, a New York seafood distributor, on 2 December 1884.[16] The sale took place five months after the Long Island Railroad linked New York City and Greenport in July of 1884, and it marks the beginnings of large-scale commercial scalloping on the East End, made possible once men like Charles Congdon had access to the New York market.

The molluscs were so plentiful on Long Island in those days that their impact on the landscape mirrored their profound effect on the economy. A US Fish Commission Report described scallop shacks in New Suffolk, NY, in the 1880s this way: 'Piles to the height of 8 or 10 feet [2.5 to 3 meters] and covering a quarter of an acre [1000 square meters] were alongside the opening houses.'[17]

'From the 30s until 1985, it was a basic part of many a family's living,' explained Skip Tuttle, a bayman now in his 70s. 'You could take 10 bushels [a third of a cubic meter] a day every day for the whole season, and many did. The price was 25 cents a pound [about 1/2 a kilogram] when I was 14 years old. If the price went up a nickel, it was the talk of the town.'[18] Hoot Sherman, Shelter Island Town Supervisor in the early 1980s, remembered the extent to which scalloping took over the life of the Island every fall: 'Every year for the first weeks after opening day, I couldn't find anybody to work the ferry. They were all out scalloping.'[19] With virtually everyone old enough to hold a knife opening scallops for the better part of the day, the Island exuded the aroma of a seafood processing facility, and people greeted each other with the cheery words, 'It smells like scallop season around here,' as bayman Roland Clark recalls.[20] There were so many scallops, they were even canned, a practice that is unheard of today.

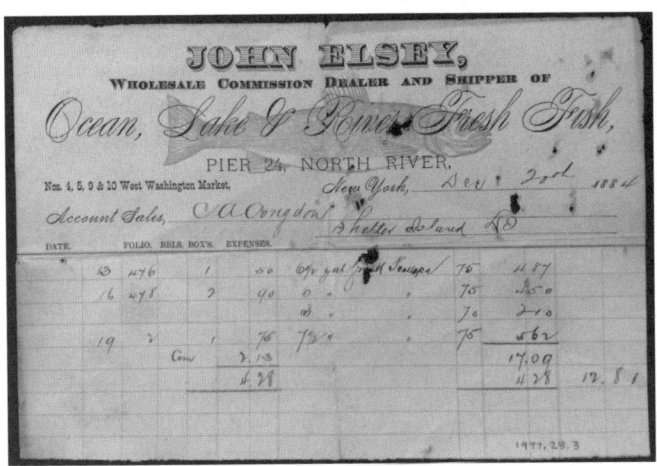

Figure 3. An invoice from 1884 for the sale of 10.5 kilograms of scallops marks the beginnings of commercial scalloping (photo: Charity Robey, courtesy of the Shelter Island Historical Society).

Scalloping Technology

Today catching scallops is done largely as it was in the 1880s: a bayman pulls a dredge – an iron frame with a bag attached – along the bottom of the bay from an open boat.

The lower edge of the dredge hits the scallop and the current pops the scallop into the bag. The bayman then hauls the 25-kilogram dredge – full of scallops, whelks, seaweed, etc. – onto a culling board, where the catch is sorted by hand. The mature scallops are tossed into bushel bags on deck, and the rest of the load is returned to the sea.

Although Paul Nossolik retired in the late 1980s, the dredges he made by hand out of his blacksmith shop on Fifth Street in Greenport, NY, for sixty years are still the state of the art for harvesting bay scallops. Known to every bayman on the East End as 'Paul the Blacksmith', Nossolik made dredges sized for each of the different waters where the molluscs were found. Smaller dredges, designed for a 'soft bottom' (mud), were generally used in the more sheltered 'inside waters', such as Coecles Harbor, while larger dredges with a sharp edge were used on 'outside waters' with a sandy or hard bottom. The smaller dredges were also lighter, and many a bayman gracefully aged into pulling a smaller dredge.

Figure 4. A can of Shelter Island scallops (now empty) in the collection of the Shelter Island Historical Society (courtesy of the Shelter Island Historical Society).

Keith Clark of Shelter Island, who still uses dredges made by Nossolik, recalls watching Nossolik work at his forge with bellows, hammer, and anvil: 'It was amazing to watch [...]. Every dredge was custom made, a lost art today. His fingers were black and there was soft coal all around the shop up to your knees [...]. You came out of there smelling like a smoked eel.'[21]

Skip Tuttle was twelve when he began scalloping with his father, Maurice, in the late 1950s. 'I got a commercial license when I was fourteen,' Tuttle said. 'So young that my father had to sign for me.'[22] Tuttle's scalloping days started around the time that the first significant labour-saving device came into use – the motor. Prior to that, scallop boats could be powered only by man or wind.

Baymen in rowboats used manpower and a technique called a warp line. In an interview, Tuttle gave this description: 'Put down an anchor, let out 400 feet [122 meters] of line, the bayman hauls the boat along the line, with the dredges pulling along behind. It took a lot of strength to haul the boat and the dredges, before there was power.'

A type of sloop called a catboat was the vessel of choice for baymen who used wind power to drag dredges before motors were permitted in the late 1950s. With the mast very close to the bow and no jib, just a mainsail, they were stable and drew very little water. 'They were fat, almost round, and you sailed on the beam,' Keith Clark pointed out. According to Clark, catboats were the perfect platform for work because they didn't draw any water: 'In Menantic Creek you could put the nose up on shore and open scallops on the beach.'[23]

A Creature of Salty Estuaries and Glacial Till

Figure 5 (left). Peconic baymen in the 1950s, like scallopers today, used dredges made by hand by Paul Nossolik (courtesy of the Shelter Island Historical Society). Figure 6 (right). Alfred Tuthill scalloping from a catboat, 1949 (courtesy of the Shelter Island Historical Society).

Scallop-Processing, a Family Affair

Captain Ed Clark has been scalloping for most of his eight decades. For much of that time, his wife, Ann, has been at his side: 'My job is to cull them and put them in the bushel baskets. It can be very cold. Standing in one spot you tend to get colder. The men are pulling dredges, so they get warm.' Scalloping is woven into the fabric of the Clarks' marriage. (As Ann Clark points out, 'I wear a gold scallop shell around my neck all the time [...]. My husband gave it to me.') It also governs the rhythm of their family life. One of the most important family traditions is going out on the opening day of scalloping season: 'It gets in your blood. You've got to go.'[24]

Scalloping was an important source of income for the Clark family for many years. It helped them pay for their house and raise their five children. Ann Clark is proud of the fact that everyone in her family knows how to wield a scallop knife. 'We open our own scallops [...]. There is a certain technique. Some people don't know how to open a scallop anymore. My children were opening scallops in second grade, standing on a stool.'[25]

Roland is Ann and Ed Clark's middle child and the only member of his generation of the Clark family who is still a full-time commercial fisherman. He remembers his scallop training well: 'By age ten, most kids were fast shuckers. Everyone helps shuck.' After the shucking, the shells went into the driveway, or to the dump.

Ed Warner Sr, a commercial bayman and trustee in the Town of Southampton, NY, remembers having so many scallops to open that he once fell asleep while shucking. He bragged that his daughter could shuck four litres of scallops an hour.[26]

Food and Landscape

The Great Scallop Catastrophe of 1985 and Its Impact on Efforts to Improve Water Quality in the Peconic Estuary

Considering the small system of 'creeks' and harbours that produce them, Peconic Bay scallops have had an outsize influence on food history. They have not only given rise to an industry and way of life – they ultimately motivated the movement to improve water quality in the Peconic estuary.

A devastating brown tide (an algae bloom fuelled by water pollution, especially nitrates and phosphorus associated with human waste) essentially wiped out the Peconic Bay scallop population in 1985. Stephen Lenox, a Shelter Island bayman, remembered opening day that year, when he, his brother, and every other bayman on the East End headed out early to throw out their first dredge of the year precisely at dawn: 'It was my brother's 50th birthday. We went out and everything was dead except the hard clams. Brown algae killed everything.'[27]

It was an environmental and economic calamity for the region, but it got the attention of legislators and spurred a number of clean water initiatives that are improving water quality by reducing levels of nitrates and phosphates in the estuary. Although there have been other harmful algae blooms, there has been no repeat of the brown tide in Peconic Bay since 1995.

Peconic Bay scallops became one of the disappearing foods brought aboard the 'Ark of Taste', an endangered species list of sorts established by the Slow Food organization. This addition was a clear indication of the widespread concern for the preservation of this unique wild food. According to Brady Wilkins, baykeeper for the Peconic Estuary Program, the scallop harvest in the years prior to the brown tide was in the range of 227,000 kilograms annually but then plummeted as algal tides fuelled by pollution fouled the water. In 1996, the harvest was 24 kilograms for the entire year.[28]

In 2006 a reseeding program headed by Stephen Tettelbach at Long Island University began to support wild bay scallop populations by planting millions of larval scallops in the Peconic estuary. Shell colour is hereditary among scallops, and those with striped shells (called 'skunks') are very rare in the wild. Biologists selected them as seed scallops since their shells are easy to identify. When after a period of years skunks became more common in the wild, the scientists had an early indicator that the seeding was working.

In 2014 baymen harvested 40,000 kilograms of scallops, thirty times more than the annual average landings for the twelve years prior to the beginning of the restoration work. The sharp increase in bay scallops was sustained

Figure 7. John Kotula and his son Wade on opening day, 2015 (photo: Charity Robey).

Figure 8. *A bayman unloading scallops at Congdon's Dock, Shelter Island (photo: Charity Robey).*

in 2015, 2016, and 2017, although the harvests are still not equal to the huge annual landings of the early 1980s. As Tettelbach commented, 'Obviously we'd all like to get back to what it was before the brown tide in 1985. That's what we are shooting for.'[29]

Peconic Bay scallops are farmed in great numbers in the coastal waters of Peru, China, and Korea, then frozen and sold in supermarkets everywhere. Most of the now-enormous Chinese aquaculture business started with bugs (juvenile scallops) from wild Peconic Bay scallops. Graham Homan, whose family runs Braun's Seafood in Cutchogue, NY, has carried bay scallops from China in his store from time to time but admits that 'they never really taste as good as Peconic Bay scallops'.[30]

Conclusion

There are many reasons to love the blue-eyed, sustainable, sexually ambiguous bay scallop, a creature that lives fast, dies young, and leaves a very good-tasting carcass. Whether you are eating a freshly opened scallop dockside or enjoying a plate of scallops seared on one side and barely cooked on the other at a cloth-covered table, the first taste is the sweetness of energy-rich nutrients, an evolved flavour preference that has worked out very well for the human race.

Every flavour of this perfect food reflects an aspect of the bivalve's habitat: the temperature and salinity of Peconic Bay waters; the local plankton of the estuary; and the bay bottom, which provides a hint of mineral mud. All of these factors produce flavours that are unique to the scallop and the place and time from which it came.

Figure 9. *Scallop shell colour is hereditary, and the dark shells with stripes, known as skunks, were very rare in the wild before they were seeded to restore the Peconic Bay scallop population (photo: Charity Robey).*

The Peconic Bay scallop has made its mark on the culture and economy of the East End of Long Island, building the homes and livelihoods of families who fished and processed scallops and shaping a way of life on Long Island that has endured for centuries and continues still among the area's baymen.

Notes

1. Interview with Dr Stephen Tettelbach, Professor of Biology, Long Island University, 15 May 2017.
2. Ernest Ingersoll, 'The Scallop and its Fishery', *The American Naturalist*, 12.20 (1886), 1002.
3. Interview with Steven Hayward, bayman, Shelter Island, NY, May 2016.
4. Interview with Charlie Manwaring, Owner, Southold Fish Market, Southold, NY, January 2016.
5. Tettelbach.
6. Harold McGee, *On Food and Cooking* (New York: Scribner,1984), p. 188.
7. Tettelbach.
8. Joseph Provost and others, *The Science of Cooking* (Hoboken: Wiley, 2016), p. 297.
9. Interview with Dr Joseph Provost, Professor of Chemistry and Biochemistry, The University of San Diego, 25 January 2017.
10. Provost.
11. Tettelbach.
12. Provost.
13. Tettelbach.
14. Ernest Ingersoll, '1881a. The Oyster-Industry', *The History and Present Condition of the Fishery Industries*, ed. by George Brown Goode (Washington, DC: US Government Printing Office, 1881), p. 251.
15. John Charles Witek, 'Archaeological Investigations at the Fresh Pond Locus on Shelter Island', *The Bulletin*, 115 (1999).
16. Invoice for the sale of scallops to John Elsey, Courtesy of the Shelter Island Historical Society, 23 December 1884.
17. Ernest Ingersoll, 'Quoting Mr. O. B. Goldsmith of Cutchogue', *The Fisheries and Fishery Industries of the United States*, Volume 6, ed. by George Brown Goode (Washington, DC: US Government Printing Office, 1887), p. 573.
18. Interview with Skip Tuttle, bayman, Shelter Island, NY, November 2014.
19. Interview with Hoot Sherman, former Shelter Island Town Supervisor, June 2017.
20. Nancy Solomon, 'Roland Clark, September 11, 1997', Voices from the Fisheries, NOAA Fisheries, <https://www.st.nmfs.noaa.gov/vff/search/VOFComplete.jsp?inputInterviewId=214> [accessed May 27, 2017].
21. Interview with Keith Clark, bayman, November 2014.
22. Tuttle.
23. Keith Clark.
24. Interview with Ann Clark, wife of bayman Captain Ed Clark, October 2014 and March 2017.
25. Ann Clark, October 2014.
26. Nancy Solomon, 'Ed Warner Sr, July 24, 1997', Voices from the Fisheries, NOAA Fisheries, <https://www.st.nmfs.noaa.gov/vff/search/VOFComplete.jsp?inputInterviewId=211> [accessed May 27, 2017].
27. Interview with Stephen Lenox, bayman, November 2014.
28. Interview with Brady Wilkins, baykeeper, Peconic Estuary Program, October 2014.
29. Tettelbach.
30. Interview with Graham Homan, Employee, Braun Seafood Company, Cutchogue, NY, November 2016.

Americans and the Landscape of Wine

Laura Shapiro

We have a founding myth in the United States, taught to every schoolchild, that tells of the seventeenth-century visionaries who crossed the Atlantic in search of freedom and built a new nation in its name. There's truth to the story, of course, but among numerous omissions is the fact that many English, French and Dutch voyagers were struck by something else about the New World – not quite so soul-stirring as its promise of liberty, but inspirational nonetheless. They noticed the grapevines. Flourishing everywhere in wild profusion, those masses of grapevines turn up constantly in the reports that document the early colonial era. Never had the newcomers seen a landscape that appeared to be so rich with the potential for huge grape harvests, and they weren't thinking about fruit bowls, they were thinking about wine. It took longer than anyone had expected – nearly 400 years – but the dream of a land criss-crossed with fine vineyards eventually came true. Today the US is the world's fourth-largest producer of wine, after Italy, France, and Spain.

But look for a wine glass on a typical American dinner table and you won't find one. Most Americans wouldn't dream of buying a bottle, and if they do it's for a special occasion. Statistics vary, but according to recent figures on global wine consumption per capita, the US now ranks 62nd in the world, a standing that places us well above Tuvalu but not quite on a par with Equatorial Guinea.[1] 'High frequency drinkers', to use the wine industry's terminology – those who drink more than one glass a week – appear to constitute about 12% of America's adult population, and they're the ones who drink more than 80% of the wine.[2] In other words, despite centuries of concerted effort on the part of a wine industry once personified by Thomas Jefferson himself, the US has never become a wine-drinking nation. By this I mean a nation where a bottle is plunked down next to the hamburgers as inevitably as the mustard and ketchup, and where parents acquaint their children with wine by serving them a taste of it, watered down, at family dinners. The physical landscape of America has fulfilled its promise so abundantly, it's as if we've got wine flowing right out of the earth. But the cultural landscape keeps us dry.

How did this happen, in a land that once seemed to have 'WINE' written across the hills like an early version of the 'HOLLYWOOD' sign? It's tempting to blame the Puritans – or at least our favourite stereotype of the Puritans – for handing down a legacy of grim and strait-laced values that leave no room for pleasure. But it was drunkenness that the Puritans hated, not alcohol. Ten thousand gallons of wine accompanied them on the *Arabella* when that ship sailed to Boston in 1630, and Governor John Winthrop himself made an unsuccessful attempt at establishing a vineyard. It's also easy to blame the nineteenth-century temperance movement, which attacked wine as well as all other forms of alcohol and culminated in Prohibition (1920-1933), leaving a streak of anti-alcohol sentiment that's still discernible in American culture. But even within the world of alcohol, wine has followed a peculiar trajectory of its own, quite independent of beer or hard liquor. Wine has been a home-grown product in the US since colonial days; it belongs to the land as surely as cattle, corn, and oranges do. Yet when the Roper organization surveyed a cross-section of adults in 1955, asking them if they thought wine was a beverage for Americans, 90% of the respondents said no. They said wine was for foreigners and rich people.[3]

More than half a century later, little seems to have changed. 'Stop Being Intimidated by Wine, America', pleads an article in *Bon Appétit*; it's full of tips on how not to feel 'embarrassed and clueless' in the presence of wine.[4] The idea that most Americans perceive wine as 'an elitist beverage', that consumers are 'intimidated', and that the industry should try to 'democratize' its image has dominated both trade and popular writing on wine for many years.[5]

The extraordinary degree of wariness that characterizes America's view of wine is unique. No other alcoholic beverage has been forced to justify its claim to citizenship – certainly not beer, despite the fact that it had a relatively minor presence in America until German immigrants set out to establish an industry in the mid-nineteenth century. What's more, the effort to 'democratize' the image of wine has been going on for decades. By now wine is available in boxes and cans; it's available with fruit flavourings and funny names and cute labels; it's available at Walmart and Target; it's available for less than $10 a bottle and sometimes for less than $5. Democracy hasn't worked. I've come to believe that the reason so many Americans can't be tempted to pour a glass of wine has nothing to do with alcohol or taste or cost or packaging; in fact, it has nothing to do with wine. It's about class and American identity, a toxic combination that has bedevilled the wine industry in America for more than a century like a serpent in the vineyards.

*

André Simon, a Frenchman long based in Britain, sailed for New York in 1934 with a mission that struck many of his colleagues as ludicrous: he wanted to create a wine-drinking culture in America. Prohibition had ended a year earlier, but the nation's vineyards were in shambles and the Depression was still underway, making the US a poor bet for a surge in sophisticated new drinking habits. But Simon was optimistic. He had worked in the London wine trade for decades, and most recently had convinced more than a thousand British gastronomes to join a fledgling organization he called the Wine and Food Society, dedicated to staging elegant culinary events with appropriate fine wines – a far-fetched venture considering Britain's economic doldrums at the time, but he pulled it off. His trip overseas was sponsored by the French wine industry, which was eager to take advantage of Repeal to open up a new market among affluent Americans. In a memoir, Simon insisted that he was not traveling as a commercial spokesman for French wine, but simply hoped, as he put it, 'to pass on to a few of the more cultured and influential American citizens in each of the great cities my own faith in Wine […] as the fairway of a truly civilized mode of living'.[6]

The best approach, he decided, was to establish American branches of the Wine and Food Society. Hence he was on the lookout for what he termed 'the "right" people'.[7] New York was a disappointment – the only connoisseurs willing to devote themselves to the Society were those in the wine business, and he felt that 'anybody commercially interested in the sale of wine was unsuitable'.[8] What he wanted was gentlemen. He had better luck in Boston, San Francisco, Los Angeles, and New Orleans, where he was able to meet 'true lovers of wine who welcomed the idea of starting a branch of the Wine and Food Society without any thought of personal gain'.[9] Chicago, alas, was a washout, despite the fact that a professional chef named Arnold Shircliffe had already enrolled in the Society months earlier, becoming its only American member. Shircliffe's friends – 'chefs, stewards and hotel people' – were eager to set up a Chicago branch, but Simon backed off. They were, he wrote, 'all good fellows, keen and intelligent, but, unfortunately, they just did not happen to belong to the right social group to suit my purpose'.[10]

Simon's perspective – that wine was best entrusted to 'the right social group' – was a familiar one in the US, though it was usually expressed more discreetly. 'Happily for us all, wine-drinking is largely on the increase among Americans, and as it is an acquired habit, only traveled and cultivated Americans know how to drink wine,' explained the journalist Frona Wait Colburn in *Wines and Vines of California*, published in 1889.[11] In truth there were quite a few other wine-drinkers around at the time, including the immigrants from Europe who readily poured cheap or homemade wine whenever the family gathered for a meal; but these didn't interest Colburn. The purpose of her book was to infuse California wine with prestige, not to make it popular among the working classes. Unfortunately, however, the supply of 'cultivated Americans' was quite a bit more limited than she suggested, and those who had what she called 'correct tastes' were even scarcer, so she devoted a big chunk of her book to a sternly authoritative essay called 'How to Drink Wine', contributed by a member of one of California's most prominent winemaking families, Arpad Haraszthy. He made it clear that there was nothing easy or natural about drinking fine wines at dinner; on the contrary, it was a rarefied pleasure available only to those who understood its subtleties. 'To drink wine with any degree of satisfaction it should be done with the proper surroundings, in the proper frame of mind, from the right kind of glasses, and at the right temperature,' he counselled.[12] The instructions on decanting alone went on for pages.

Haraszthy firmly believed in wine-drinking for the lower classes – he felt that 'the American laborer' would be much better off with a bottle of cheap table wine than with his usual whiskey – but he confined this observation to a section of the essay called 'Wine as a Temperance Agent'. Workingmen in Italy, France, Germany, and Spain drank plenty of wine, he pointed out, but always with meals and not just for the alcohol. As a result, they were 'healthy, good natured and jolly, free from dyspepsia and drunkenness'.[13] How the labouring classes were able to extract all the pleasures of wine without ever setting the table with proper claret glasses – 'very thin, of medium size, blown from crystal, cut sharp, and absolutely colorless' – or pairing the soup with 'a dainty glass of rich-flavored, full-bodied, oily Sherry' was an achievement Haraszthy didn't attempt to explain.[14]

A carefully constructed barrier of rules and rituals became a standard feature in discussions of wine, as if to make sure drinkers never lost sight of the fact that their social standing was at risk every time they lifted a glass. Etiquette guides, which sold briskly to the aspirational middle class, went into considerable detail on the correct way to offer, accept, sip, and even talk about wine. 'In inviting a gentleman to take wine with you at table, you should politely say, "Shall I have the pleasure of a glass of wine with you?" You will then either hand him the bottle you have selected or send it by the waiter, and afterwards fill your own glass, when you will politely and silently bow to each other, as you raise the wine to your lips,' instructed the author of *Good Manners: A Manual of Etiquette in Good Society*: 'Do not praise bad wine, for it will persuade those who are judges that you are an ignoramus or a flatterer. At the same time, avoid noticing that it is bad, unless the host calls attention to it himself.'[15]

Ladies, too, participated in the ritual of wine-drinking, but their roles were largely passive: 'It is expected that every lady will be properly helped to wine by the gentleman who takes her to the table, or who sits next to her. Do not offer to help a lady to wine until you see that she has finished her soup or fish.'[16] According to these authorities, a lady would never drain her glass, she would never ask for more, she would never accept a glass of wine with dessert, and she wouldn't drink wine at all unless she were a married woman of a certain age. Even displaying knowledge of wine was inappropriate for a female. 'When serving wine a man-servant may mention what it is,' ruled the author of *The Etiquette of New York Today*. 'A waitress seldom does this.'[17]

Most of these formalities disappeared under the pressure of Prohibition. When wine-drinking emerged in public again, the Depression and then the upheaval of the war years made it impossible to revive such arcane rules. Yet the air of mystery and high-class clubbiness that had marked wine-drinking in earlier times proved surprisingly difficult to eradicate in the era of suburbs, electric blenders and Bermuda shorts. Americans in the postwar years didn't worry about most of what had seemed so momentous in the old etiquette books – how to eat an artichoke or identify the salad fork. They used the same fork for everything except dessert, and canned artichoke hearts presented no difficulties whatever. But wine seemed immune to shortcuts, and it resisted the informality that was a hallmark of American social life. Even in Italian-American households that treasured their heritage, reverently passing down the family cannelloni recipe from generation to generation, wine was becoming identified with special occasions rather than everyday meals.

The challenge facing the industry in the postwar years was similar to the one that had faced Frona Wait Colburn: how to rustle up more drinkers and change the way they perceived wine. The Fifties and Sixties should have been a perfect time for a transformation of America's relationship with wine, since the economy was booming and millions of people were able to spend money on pursuits traditionally confined to the rich, including restaurant dinners and travel to Europe. Crucially, too, the start of a food revolution was underway. Despite the lure of convenience foods, many homemakers were experimenting with French, Italian, even Chinese dishes. Cooking classes were popular, cookbooks aimed at every level of expertise were abundant, and women's magazines were publishing recipes for quiche, guacamole, chicken kiev, and pizza from scratch. Wine had a natural place in this picture – if people could be persuaded to try a bottle.

The elaborate scaffolding of class, the aura of exclusivity that André Simon and similarly high-minded advocates had so carefully nurtured, plainly had to be demolished. The industry had been trying somewhat feebly to project a more inviting image since the late 1930s, but the annual crowning of a 'Vintage Queen' was not having the impact California winemakers had hoped. During the Fifties a flood of new promotional materials including ads, pamphlets, handbooks, graphics, lists, and pronunciation guides ('Bow Joe lay', 'Poo yee Fweesay')[18] began to appear, all of it aimed at rejuvenating the image of wine and assuring people they would love it if they got to know it. This wasn't hard for companies like Garrett & Co., in business since 1835, which called itself the most successful winery in the country and probably was. Garrett specialized in the intensely sweet wines that had always characterized popular American taste, selling them under such reassuring labels as Virginia Dare, Minnehaha, and Pocahontas. 'Only 1 out of 6 like wine well enough to serve regularly,' announced an ad for Virginia Dare in 1950. 'But 9 out of 10 like Virginia Dare. Once you taste the wine with that 100-Year Flavor YOU, TOO, WILL LIKE WINE!'[19]

But more ambitious branches of the wine industry, especially the wineries producing higher-quality, European-style wines, were forced to negotiate a great many cultural nuances that Garrett & Co. were free to ignore. The biggest problem was that these lighter table wines were made specifically to enhance food, and middle-class American meals were getting along just fine with milk, coffee, and lately soft drinks. What could convince ordinary, unpretentious folks to try wine instead? 'Wine Comes to the Family Table', a first-person account published in *American Magazine* in 1953, purported to describe how a regular guy made his way into the world of wine and found that it was just the right place for regular guys like him. It's likely that the wine industry itself was behind this story, which ran under the byline 'John Carleton', for every detail reflects the industry's preoccupations at the time. 'Until a few years ago I hardly knew a sauterne from a sarsaparilla, and didn't much care,' declares Carleton at the outset. 'Having occasionally tried in vain to translate unreadable French menus and "cartes de vin," and having listened to fancy Dan "connoisseurs" prattle preciously about "delicate bouquets" and "vintage years," I had developed a violent allergy to the whole silly business.' When he discovers, however, that 'home-grown vintners, in typical American fashion, have been stripping off most of the froufrou and super-snobbish folderol', he picks up the courage to start learning and tasting. And now? 'I love it! Red, white, or blue! And red, white and blue is just what it is – because wine has gone American.'[20]

This conversion narrative is centred on Carleton alone. His wife, Nancy, is supportive but strictly on the sidelines. One day she plans a dinner party to which wine-loving neighbours have been invited and sends Carleton out to buy something that will go with roast beef. Carleton is nervous, but happens to meet a couple of knowledgeable folks in a wine store who gladly educate him. (Here the article name-drops Bill Mauldin, the World War II cartoonist, and Frank Schoonmaker, the most famous authority of the day and a champion of American wines). Ultimately Carleton chooses an inexpensive California cabernet and serves it in plain goblets from the dime store. Everyone at the party is impressed, Carleton gains a reputation as a wine expert, and the evening is a triumph. 'I'd proved to myself that you can enjoy wine without being chichi and without becoming a walking encyclopedia!' From then on, he says, he and his 'fellow hobbyists' have been having a great time swapping their favourite wines. 'Our wives swap, too,' he adds. 'They swap recipes for cooking with wine.'[21]

Every wine enthusiast in Carleton's story – including his neighbours 'Henry Mitchell' and 'Bill Doyle', as well as Mauldin and Schoonmaker – is male. Indeed, he refers to his friends as 'the local wine fraternity'. This language is deliberate, for the role assigned to women in the new American wine world was the same as it was in every other sphere of their lives, namely to be a charming and subordinate wife. Obviously women had to be involved in some way, if the goal was to put a bottle of wine on ordinary suburban dinner tables. After all, it was women who were reading the cookbooks, choosing the recipes, doing the cooking, arranging the dinner parties, and in general creating the family's culinary identity. And yet, it didn't sit easily with advertisers to depict respectable women, much less Mom, in close proximity to alcohol. The old etiquette-book conventions governing ladylike behaviour were gone, but they left a residue, and stereotypical femininity was not supposed to show up with a glass of red in her hand and a slight stumble.

What's more, while women were at the centre of everyday meal-planning, the situation was very different in the realm of *haute cuisine*. Here wealthy Americans were doing just what wealthy French and British food-lovers had done for centuries: they defined great food and wine as male. Men were the chefs, men were the critics, men had the expertise, and men founded the gastronomical associations, frequently restricting them to men. The industry had no wish to lower the status of wine by associating it with women or, worse yet, housewives, but it was also the case that rich, sophisticated Americans didn't need any encouragement to buy wine. They were already on board. If wine-drinking was to have a significant future in the US, it had to be a middle-class future. Which meant the promotional material had to start bringing women into the picture, and placing them in a relationship with wine that had the least potential to offend anyone.

'Which wine will please him most?' ran the headline on a 1958 newspaper ad. 'Clip out this 'Wine Taste Chart' and take it shopping with you today ... *Then let your man taste and choose.*' A chart alongside listed thirteen wines and described their flavours, from 'Cocktail Sherry ... *Brilliantly dry*' to 'Champagne ... For your joyous occasions'.[22] A photograph showed the husband in an easy chair, smiling as he holds up two different glasses of wine and gazes at them appreciatively. The wife, leaning over the back of the chair with her hands clasped under her chin, is also smiling; but her gaze is fixed on her husband. Or, as Milton put it, 'He for God only, she for God in him'.

Wine-centred households like this one, with its sharply defined gender roles, turned up again and again in the ads and pamphlets. 'COOK WITH WINE!' exclaimed the caption under a picture of two women conferring at the stove. Behind them, a man is intently focused on his glass. Meanwhile, '[w]hile their men sip California Sherry, the women (above) add 2 *tsp. Sherry per serving* to Black Bean Soup'.[23] Similarly, numerous authorities advised homemakers that they could prepare Jell-O, cake mix, powdered salad dressings and all sorts of other convenience products with wine instead of water and carry them with pride to the table. 'And to make your good living complete, adopt another pleasant custom: serve the great wines of California with your meals,' suggested one pamphlet.[24]

It seems unlikely that the stereotypical housewives who were a staple of the promotional literature in these years inspired many real-life women to rethink the nature of dinner. The sort of women in the 1960s who travelled and dined in restaurants – the target audience for these ads – were also the women who were getting restless and reading *The Feminine Mystique*. If they had a role model in the kitchen, it was far more likely to be Julia Child, who hated the very word 'housewife' and couldn't abide Jell-O. Julia was one of the most trusted and beloved figures in the history of television, a sensation ever since the official launch of 'The French Chef' in 1963. Although she became famous demonstrating French recipes, her larger message was simply that Americans should learn to enjoy food the way the French did – relaxed and convivial and at the family table. At the end of each episode of 'The French Chef', she stood next to a dining table arrayed with the food she had just prepared and poured a glass of wine. She said a few words about why she had chosen it, and then she lifted her glass and gave the sign-off that became legendary – 'Bon appétit!'

And yet, even Julia couldn't turn Americans into everyday wine-drinkers. She may have had better luck with women, who constitute some 57% of wine-drinkers today; but on the whole, the pleasure she took in wine was never as contagious as the pleasure she took in cooking. People did start drinking more wine in the Sixties, and tastes began shifting to the lighter table wines; but the fundamental imbalance of the American wine market didn't change. Relatively few people were consuming most of the wine, and they still are. Julia once remarked that McDonald's – where she appreciated the fries but thought the buns were a little too soft – should be serving a good house red by the glass. 'Why not!' she exclaimed.[25] There are many reasons why not, but the only one that matters is the simplest: it's inconceivable. Most Americans don't want to be French. Even the ones who drink wine regularly don't see it the way the French do, as an intrinsic part of a meal. According to a survey of frequent wine-drinkers, less than half the wine they pour is meant to accompany lunch or dinner. The rest is consumed with no food at all, or while they're snacking or cooking.[26]

Is there any hope for such a misguided nation? Since the last election, many of us have been asking that question in a different context. But maybe it isn't a completely different context. Let's look back at an event that made headlines in July 2009, just seven months into Obama's first term. One night that month an eminent Harvard professor named Henry Louis Gates, Jr., who is African-American, was having trouble unlocking his front door. He lives in a very nice Cambridge neighbourhood, so when somebody saw a black man trying to get into a house there, they called the police. By the time Sgt James Crowley arrived, Gates was inside the house. He told Crowley he lived there, and he produced his driver's licence, which had his home address on it. Nevertheless, there was apparently a loud argument, and Crowley, who is white, arrested the black professor for disorderly conduct. A story appeared in the *Harvard Crimson*, then many other news outlets picked it up; and finally a reporter asked Obama what he thought. The president said the police had 'acted stupidly'.[27]

This prompted an even bigger explosion of publicity, and now the White House had a problem on its hands. Racism is the evil undercurrent in America's history and still taints daily life. Obama always tried to maintain a calm, moderate, bring-us-together tone when he talked about race in public, but this time he had exposed his own feelings. What was the White House to do? How could it cancel the image of an ugly, divided America and replace it with an image everyone could take pride in? Obama invited Professor Gates and Sgt Crowley to join him and Vice-President Joe Biden for a casual get-together at the White House. Needless to say, plenty of photographers were also invited. So the four men – two black, two white – sat down at a table in the Rose Garden, and while the cameras clicked away, the guys drank beer. They even lifted their mugs and toasted their new brotherhood. This event is remembered as 'the beer summit'.

One gender, male; two races; and four beers – it all adds up to America, or at least the America that many people choose to believe in. Substitute a bottle of wine, however, and the picture goes right out of focus. Perhaps you've noticed that whenever you see a reference in an American news story to the kind of people who 'sip white wine', it's clear that the writer is evoking phony, aloof, liberal elites who don't care about real Americans. In short, we have the landscape, just as the first settlers hoped, and we have the science and the weather and the know-how. But the cultural *terroir* may be all wrong for wine.

Notes

1. Wine Institute, 'Table 7 (Revised November 2015). Per Capita Wine Consumption By Country' <https://www.wineinstitute.org/files/World_Per_Capita_Wine_Consumption_Revised_Nov_2015.pdf> [accessed May 24, 2017].
2. Liz Thach and Janeen Olsen, 'Profiling the High Frequency Wine Consumer by Price Segmentation in the US Market,' *Wine Economics and Policy* 4 (2015): p. 53, <doi.org/10.1016/j.wep.2015.04.001>. See also press release, 'Wine Market Council Unveils New Stats on Consumer Wine Consumption Habits', 9 February 2016 <https://www.winebusiness.com/news/?go=getArticle&dataid=164519> [accessed 24 May 2017].
3. Jay Stuller and Glen Martin, *Through the Grapevine* (San Francisco: HarperCollinsWest, 1994), p. 62. See also Andrew Barr, *Drink: A Social History of America* (New York: Carroll & Graf), 1999 and Thomas Pinney, *A History of Wine in America*, 2 vols. (Berkeley: University of California Press, 1989-2005).
4. Kate Thorman, 'Stop Being Intimidated by Wine, America', *Bon Appétit*, 12 November 2015 <https://www.bonappetit.com/drinks/wine/article/demystifying-wine> [accessed 24 May 2017].
5. See, for example, Bill Swindell's coverage of a Gallo executive underscoring her company's success with a new line of sweet, fizzy wines ('Gallo: Consumers Don't View Wine as an Elitist Drink', *Santa Rosa Press Democrat*, 6 December 2016 <http://www.pressdemocrat.com/business/6397950-181/gallo-consumers-dont-view-wine> [accessed 24 May 2017]).
6. André Simon, *By Request* (London: The Wine and Food Society, 1957), p. 110.
7. Simon, p. 111.
8. Simon, p. 112.
9. Simon, p. 114.
10. Simon, p. 113.
11. Frona Wait Colburn, *Wines and Vines of California* (San Francisco: The Bancroft Company, 1889), p. 10.
12. Colburn, p. 49.
13. Colburn, p. 82.
14. Colburn, pp. 56, 71.
15. *Good Manners, A Manual of Etiquette in Polite Society* (Philadelphia: Porter & Cotes, 1870), pp. 163, 164.
16. *Good Manners*, p. 162.
17. Ellin Craven Learned, *The Etiquette of New York Today* (New York: Frederick A. Stokes Col., 1906), p. 89.
18. Advertisement for B&G, *The New Yorker*, 10 November 1956, p. 134.
19. Advertisement for Virginia Dare, *Chicago Tribune*, 16 November 1950.
20. John Carleton, 'Wine Comes to the Family Table,' *American Magazine*, September 1953, p. 39.
21. Carleton, p. 92.
22. Advertisement for Wine Advisory Board, *New York Herald Tribune*, 7 October 1958.
23. Advertisement for Wine Advisory Board, *The Hartford Courant*, 11 October 1957.
24. Wine Advisory Board, *How to Cook with California Wines*, n.d., Washington, D.C., Smithsonian Institute, National Museum of American History Archives Center, Warshaw Collection of Business Americana, Box 6, Folder 4.
25. Julia Child to Janet Helm, 7 January 7 1991, Cambridge, Harvard University, Radcliffe Institute for Advanced Study, Schlesinger Library, Julia Child Papers.
26. Eric Asimov, 'Wine Divorced from Food? Let's Be Adults About It', *New York Times*, 6 April 2011, p. D6.
27. Helene Cooper, 'Obama Criticizes Arrest of Harvard Professor', *New York Times*, 22 July 2009, p. A20.

'Le mariage entre mets et vins': On the Geographical and Historical Origins of Pairing a Food with a Particular Wine in France

Richard Warren Shepro

Vast portions of the landscape of France are defined by vineyards, many dating to Roman times, and French cuisine has such an emphasis on regional dishes and wines that it is natural to assume that what the French refer to as a marriage between a dish and a wine is a straightforward matter of geography and history, with regional dish and local wine dancing together, influencing each other's development, and growing old and comfortable in each other's company.

There is much truth to this simple narrative, but the question of why a dish is viewed as marrying with a particular wine – and why those not respecting the rules might be regarded as unrefined or ignorant – is far more complex and intriguing and has not yet been told in any comprehensive manner. It turns out that most of the ideas about these 'marriages' are not so very old at all.

Even such a broad and simple idea as 'red meat with red wine' – the rule typically but erroneously understood today as the most immutable and consistent of all wine pairing rules – has an elusive and not ancient origin. Works on French regional cooking and on the history of French wine treat their subjects with precise French rigour, but rarely have analyzed food and wine together. Most experts have a focus on food or wine, not both. Evidence of what was eaten with what wine in what region at what time is scarce. It may be that certain food and wine customs were so thoroughly agreed upon that no one needed to mention them. Important cultural norms of manners or behaviour are often left unmentioned because they are so universally accepted as to be obvious: the obvious or implicit is ignored. As the French literary critic Bernard Pivot has noted, French literary works often have vivid descriptions of food at meals but then merely say that the wines were exquisite without revealing what those wines were.[1] Still, deviance from established norms is often imagined or commented upon, and I am still in search of examples from French literature of characters feeling anxious or humbled for choosing the wrong wine.

Paintings can occasionally be more illuminating. Although paintings rarely illustrate the pairing of *un mets* with *un vin*, there are some intriguing examples: for example, the 1735 painting, *Le Déjeuner d'huîtres: le saute-bouchon* (*The Oyster Lunch: The Flying*

'Le mariage entre mets et vins'

Figure 1. Le Déjeuner d'huîtres: le saute-bouchon (The Oyster Lunch: The Flying Cork), *by Jean-François de Troy (1735) (Wikimedia Commons).*

Cork), by Jean-François de Troy (Figure 1).

Another complication is that many wines in earlier eras had names similar to wines produced today, but they were classified, produced, or consumed in different ways, making analysis of how wines were paired with food difficult. As late as the end of the nineteenth century the colour of wine was viewed as a rainbow of colours including green and blue, instead of the dichotomy of 'white' and 'red' prevalent today.[2] The grand cru Burgundy *Le Chambertin*, deservedly prominent today, owes some of its prestige to its reputation as the favourite wine of Napoléon, yet the wine Napoléon drank did not come exclusively from the small parcel of land that produces *Le Chambertin* today, or even from the commune of Gevrey-Chambertin. It was vinified in different ways, and Napoléon did not savour it as a profound part of a complementary dish: he drank it as a refreshing beverage, mixed with chilled water and ice.[3]

The intensity with which the pairing of food with wine has long been viewed in France is dramatically revealed in the anonymous Enlightenment 'philosophical' novel *Thérèse Philosophe* (1748), in which the main character refutes the idea of free will on the basis of wine pairing rules. 'Am I not free to drink with my dinner either Burgundy or Champagne?' she asks, but only rhetorically. Only in 'a far-off haze' could one imagine one had a choice, because if a person actually 'sits himself down at the table and orders oysters: the dish demands Champagne'.[4] (Given the context, it is clear she is referring to effervescent Champagne, although most 'Champagne' from the sixteenth until well into the nineteenth century was a still wine, red or white.[5] *Le Déjeuner de huîtres* shows the popularity in fashionable mid-eighteenth-century aristocratic circles of pairing oysters with the relatively new, formidably expensive, and frequently explosive sparkling beverage that had begun to resemble the Champagne we know today.)

Two hundred years later, Roland Barthes emphatically described the deep importance within French culture and the French psyche of having rare beef with red wine: 'Steak participates in the same sanguinary mythology as wine [...] whoever eats it assimilates a taurine strength.'[6] Moreover, 'knowing *how to drink* is a national technique which serves to qualify the Frenchman, to prove at once his performative power, his control, and his sociability'. A 'collective morality [...] embellishes [...] the *gros rouge* with a piece of Camembert'. And 'absence of wine is shocking, like something exotic'.[7] If certain dishes and certain wines go together so intimately that they form a 'marriage', then, just as with a marriage, can the bond be so tight that the food and the wine should be considered an inseparable entity? The wine is surely not a mere beverage or accompaniment if its absence is shocking.

The 'national technique' of knowing 'how to drink' celebrated by Barthes can also constitute a considerable burden. A curator at an important wine museum in France told me recently that she feels sorry for young men today: they are expected to have the sophistication to select the right wine yet few today learn this skill from their fathers. There is a certain degree of pressure in a country where people quote Paul Claudel as saying, '*Le vin est un professeur de goût*' (Wine is a professor of good taste).[8] Like the art of carving, learning to select '*le meilleur accord*' has long been viewed as a male rite of passage, but perhaps this was not so before the nineteenth or late eighteenth century.[9] Certainly before individuals began to host meals in restaurants, beginning just before the French Revolution, any coordination of food and wine could all be done for the host by professionals.[10] In a restaurant, however, a patron acting as a host would be confronted with a choice of wines, written or oral, subject to some time pressure, and the potential for performance anxiety. Some could take pleasure navigating these rapids. In Tolstoy's novel *Anna Karenina*, the character Oblonsky acquits himself well in the face of a French-speaking waiter, hesitating for the match for his *poularde à l'estragon* only momentarily between a 'Nuits' (red Burgundy) and 'the classic Chablis' that a modern sommelier might advise for poultry because of the soft, aromatic qualities of the tarragon.[11] Marcel Proust, often an acerbic chronicler of manners, was not so self-assured, and wrote a bit plaintively to a female confidant before hosting a dinner party, 'tell me what I ought to order [...]. Do you know about wines?'[12] Although choosing the right wine can be a test of 'breeding' and 'taste', it can also cut across class lines as part of the national identity cited by Barthes. Although the *vins des ouvriers* may be viewed as lesser wines, Pierre Bourdieu, the pioneering sociologist of 'taste', found in France in the 1970s that manual workers devoted more time and interest to gastronomy than did executives and professionals.[13]

The origin of food and wine pairing is, of course, geographical. Before food and wine were generally transported long distances within France, wine and food evolved together.¹⁴ In some cases, a local wine is used for cooking and, whether used in a dish or not, it is natural to use the same local wine to accompany the local food. *Boeuf à la bourgignonne* is made with red, originally Burgundy, wine.¹⁵ *Coq au vin* in Burgundy uses red wine, while in Alsace, where most of the wine is white, a local dish is *poulet au Riesling*. More surprising combinations emerge geographically as well. The eel stew known as *matelote* in Bordeaux is made and paired with red Bordeaux wine, a concept that nowadays might shock those who think they are classicists because they pair seafood and river creatures only with white wine. In other regional combinations where wine was not a cooking ingredient, I would argue that the qualities of the wine, the selection of ingredients, and the cooking techniques evolved together so that the wine and the dish enhance each other. An example is *agneau au pré-salé*, lamb that grazes on nearby salt marshes, drunk with red Bordeaux wine, especially Pauillac, grown and produced nearby. Another regional tradition some might find surprising is the association of the assertive chitterling sausage *andouillette de Troyes*, with its regional wine, Champagne.

On the other hand, Thérèse's oysters-and-Champagne and Barthes' emphatic embrace of red wine with rare meat are in no way geographical, yet the pairings they represent are presented as definitive, immutable rules. It is worth considering what other factors are at work, and why? Methods of pairing – or reasons pairing might be irrelevant – have appeared and disappeared at different places and in different historical periods.

I posit that French history reveals that there are four essential methods of analysis for pairing food with wine, each unique and each needing to be placed in its historical context: I will refer to them as (1) the geographical pairing, (2) the sequential pairing, (3) the analytical, intrinsic, or even 'alchemical' pairing, and (4) pairing the wine with the person rather than the dish.

First, the geographical pairing. Although this is undoubtedly the oldest sort of pairing of wine and food, because wines were of course drunk locally, there are issues with historical continuity in large part because, as discussed below ('pairing the wine with the person rather than the dish'), it is not necessary to pair food and wine at all, and people have not always considered that gastronomy was a consideration in the selection of wines. Since medieval times, Paris has been the place in France where the broadest selection of wines was available, but I have seen no evidence that Parisians eating in Paris tried to match regional dishes with wines of the same region prior to the twentieth century.¹⁶ The pairing of oysters with sparkling wine from the landlocked region of Champagne is just one counter-example to the geographical pairing.

In his celebrated 1826 book, *Physiologie du gout,* Brillat-Savarin – the lawyer who was one of the earliest French chroniclers of gastronomy – describes some dinners he experienced while travelling, including a regional pairing that might be criticized today: good dinners in Lausanne, Switzerland, where he had 'fine game from the neighbouring mountains' and 'excellent fish' from Lake Geneva, both 'moistened, according to our own wishes,' with a simple local white wine.[17] If today's 'rules' had been extant but implicit when he wrote, he would never have admitted to eating game with a white wine without some sort of explanation. However, Brillat-Savarin may have been following a regional tradition based on the evolution of a local cuisine to complement that locally available simple white wine.

The regional marriage is still presented in best-selling French manuals as a 'grand principle' of pairing:

> *La façon la plus spontanée d'accorder mets et boissons consiste à marier les produits d'une même région. Ici, c'est le contexte culturel qui est mis en avant. La gastronomie française, compose d'une multitude de cuisines régionales, est un modèle du genre. Cassoulet et rouges du Sud-Ouest, choucroute et blancs d'Alsace, huîtres et muscadet, les exemples ne manquent pas.* (The most natural method of matching dishes and beverages consists of marrying products from a single region. Here the cultural context comes first. French gastronomy, made up of a multitude of regional cuisines, is a model of this method of pairing. Cassoulet and reds from the Southwest, sauerkraut and Alsatian whites, oysters and Muscadet: there is no shortage of examples.)[18]

In fact, as usually described today, the geographical pairing has many of the qualities of an invented myth, akin to other received histories of the nineteenth and twentieth centuries for things that appear ancient and respect older traditions but may not be authentically old, such as Scottish tartans (product of Victorian England), Viollet-le-Duc's medieval French churches (often imaginative reconstructions), the châteaux of Bordeaux ... and the French *cuisine bourgeoise* itself.[19]

My research suggests that the regional pairings viewed today as so essential in France became important outside their particular regions only as a result of two parallel changes in French culture: the growth of automobile tourism and of writings aimed at gastrovoyagers. The earliest examples of the latter may be the influential series of booklets on the regional food of France, *La France gastronomique,* that Curnonsky and Marcel Rouff wrote beginning in 1921. During the same period, the Michelin tyre company's guidebooks encouraged motoring and exploration. Michelin gradually added restaurant ratings from 1923 (the first listings) to 1933 (when the new three-star rating system was extended to cover all of France) and these proclamations of merit also encouraged visitors to consider dining a reason to travel.[20] It is no wonder these meanderings caught the imagination of the French and created a feeling that a wine is best in its (food) milieu: strict regional pairings created a correct marriage. But there was something else new: the idea that these marriages could be celebrated and renewed back home, following the regional tour. Appreciation of food and wine builds on memory and imagination, and if regional dishes are paired with regional wines, every meal becomes an adventure, whether while motoring through a new region or back at home. The regional marriage becomes part of the almost mystical appreciation in France for 'regional dishes', however modest, and a confirmation that these dishes constitute, for the nation and not merely for the inhabitants of the region, 'our communal roots, the mysterious *patrimoine du goût* buried in our collective unconscious'.[21]

Traditions related to some regional pairings can be so obscure and narrow that they become revealed only when someone writes to criticize them. In his influential 1997 book, the Parisian restaurateur/sommelier Philippe Bourguignon wrote that it is important in the search for harmonious alliances not to be too categorical: 'Since no one can distinguish a *médoc* from a *Saint-Émilion* in a blind tasting, why impose a *médoc* rather than a *Saint-Émilion* on a rib steak?'[22]

An extreme example of regional pairing influencing the development of the regional cuisine is the food of the city of Lyon and the region just outside, sometimes viewed as the gastronomic capital of France, where, from the early twentieth century, '*pots*' of humble Beaujolais (and its more refined *cru* Beaujolais cousins), made just north of Lyon, became the unique accompaniment for almost all dishes. If a cook always knows what wine will be drunk, she or he will easily and perhaps unconsciously adjust the cooking so that the wine and the food always work in synergy; and, conversely, dishes that might not go well with the universal wine may fall into disfavour. That is the essence of regional pairing. But wine styles are not static. From 2011 to 2014, a series of legal changes have allowed Burgundy style wines to be made in the Beaujolais region, and Burgundy *négociants* have begun to invest there.[23] Will the new wines cause the regional style to evolve?

Second, the sequential pairing. The goal of the dominant pairing principle at formal dinners in the late eighteenth and early nineteenth centuries was to create a 'crescendo', by requiring light wines before heavier wines, less precious wines before more precious wines – and, generally but not necessarily, white wines with seafood, red with meat. It was not possible in most cases to have more precise pairings, because formal dinners followed the principle of having many dishes within a broad category on the table at the same time (*service à la Française*).[24] At formal dinners, the idea of serving one dish at a time (*service à la Russe*) only appeared in the nineteenth century.[25] At the same time, wines had become more consistent, in part because bottling and consistent storage became prevalent after stronger bottles that allowed better aging were developed.[26] In order to pair precisely it is necessary to have wines whose qualities can be predictably anticipated before the bottle is opened. These developments were prerequisites for allowing a particular dish to be paired with a specific wine, with predictable results, thus paving the way for the third type of pairing.

Third, the analytical, intrinsic, or even 'alchemical' pairing, which requires analysis rather than geography (although it will often validate the wisdom of a geographical pairing). The history of analytical pairing can be illustrated by looking at the successive editions of one of France's key culinary reference books, the *Larousse Gastronomique*.[27] The following passage appears as a subentry under '*Vin*' in the three most recent editions: 1996, 2007, and 2012:

> ***Mariage des mets et des vins***. *Marier un vin et un plat est une aventure toujours exaltante mais souvent aléatoire. L'accord parfait demande de la modestie, de l'intuition et de l'expérience pour que naisse le 'troisième goût' qui fera la fusion entre les arômes et les saveurs des mets et du vin.* (**Marriage of dishes and wines**. Marrying a wine and a dish is an adventure that is always exhilarating but often random or unpredictable. The perfect match demands modesty, intuition and experience to create a 'third taste' that will blend the aromas and flavours of food and wine.)[28]

This statement has no parallel in earlier editions of the *Larousse Gastronomique*. The first edition (1938), by Prosper Montagné, does contain an exhaustive chart of pairings, as do the editions of 1960, 1967, and 1984, but they contain no notion of 'fusion', or as some others have said, '*alchimie*' (alchemy), a term that may have started in the 1990s with Alain Senderens, the three-star pioneer of the Nouvelle Cuisine who said in 2004, '*Je ne peux plus concevoir un plat sans un vin*' (I can no longer design a new dish without having a particular wine in mind).[29]

Senderens worked closely with Jacques Puisais, a chemist who became an advocate of encouraging restaurant patrons to choose their wine first and then select the dishes to go with it. He believed that the education of 'taste' in food and wine takes time and humility.[30] Drawing on unstated but understood '*accords priviligiés*', not rules but favoured ideas from the past, Puisais gently suggested slight deviations from received tradition in hopes of occasionally creating felicitous marriages and 'moments of happiness' that were precious, rare, and mysterious.[31] Soon after, Patricia Wells, writing about a series of meals at Senderens's restaurant, Lucas-Carton, in Paris, announced a new era of synergistic creation. Wine pairing was no longer a matter of good taste and decorum but the creation of something new. Senderens, she wrote,

> looks for notes in a wine – whether one of fresh or dried fruit, of toasted nuts, of wood or the woods, of herbs of the garrigue of Provence (fennel, thyme, bay leaf). When you find these elements in wines, he asks, why not match them up with the real thing? [...] When a single wine and single dish seem to merge as one, we are forced to pause, taste and think about the interplay of wine and food [...]. Weeks later, what my memory recalls most vividly [...] is the puddle of creamy polenta laced with white truffles from Italy, a dream of smooth textures, intense fragrances, rounded out by the cool Corton Charlemagne 1990 from Domaine Bonneau du Martray, rich with truffle and woodsy essences of its own.[32]

'Le mariage entre mets et vins'

Despite Wells's claims of new-found synergies (I, too, was dazzled by the pairings of that phase of Senderens's career, especially with his *lièvre à la royale,* paired with a thirty-five-year-old Chateauneuf-du-Pape Château Beaucastel, which Senderens said recapitulated the scent of the stomach of the hare), Puisais and Senderens were classicists, describing and executing combinations based solidly on tradition, using all their knowledge and good taste to describe or create something memorable to the experienced connoisseur.

A new world of analytical or intrinsic pairing has emerged since then, perhaps spurred on by scientific investigation or, more likely, by the introduction into French cuisine of foreign or novel dishes for which there are few traditional pairings. François Chartier, a French-Canadian, has poured decades of research into analysis of underlying tastes, deliberately with no concern for tradition or geography, and teamed up with the highly original chef Ferran Adrià to arrive at entirely novel solutions. Although rare, roasted cuts of beef he sees as in harmony with the traditional pairing with 'red wines matured in oak barrels' (geographically unspecified), he implores diners to eat boiled beef with 'a rather generous white wine that's moderately acidic' because he believes the volatile flavour molecules of the pair complement each other. Lamb with Pauillac (Bordeaux) is wrong because the volatile compound thymol is found in both thyme and lamb; in his view, Mediterranean wines with the aroma of wild herbs are more appropriate.[33]

Chartier and others seem to have had a real impact on French attitudes toward cheese, formerly (except for certain goat cheeses) the *domaine,* as Roland Barthes notes, of red wine. Chartier writes, 'Does the pairing of tannic red wines and cheeses almost always leave you, as it leaves me, with a disagreeable bitter taste in your mouth? That's normal! White wines do much better [...].'[34] Switching to white wine for a cheese course, which comes just before dessert in a traditional French meal, is increasingly accepted in French households (though still shocking to many) and now is a common recommendation of French sommeliers, breaking long-standing traditions about cheese as well as key rules of wine progression, which do not allow white wine after red except for sweet wines with dessert. At the same time, neurological research suggests a need for a healthy scepticism about the scientific bases for what are, at base, aesthetic judgements.[35]

Although generally more modern, this experimental approach, tied to rigorous analysis and never cavalier, was suggested by Brillat-Savarin in 1825: he occasionally mentions having a particular dish with a particular wine but doesn't really comment on the relationship between the two. He makes an exception for *faisan farci* (stuffed pheasant): '*Ce mets de haute saveur doit être arrosé, par préférence, de vin de cru de la haute Bourgogne; j'ai dégagé cette vérité d'une suite d'observations qui m'ont coûté plus de travail qu'une table de logarithmes.*' (These dishes of high flavour must be drunk with the best wines of Burgundy; I uncovered this truth from a series of observations which took more work than a table of logarithms.)[36]

Comments like this have led some to think of Brillat-Savarin as the father of wine pairings, but it seems to me that this claim is more an example of the wit reflected also in his story about a magistrate who was asked whether he preferred Bordeaux or Burgundy and replied, 'Madame, [...] that is a trial in which I so thoroughly enjoy weighing the evidence that I always put off my verdict until the next week.' Brillat-Savarin is a chronicler, not an inventor, for the most part, and through his notes we get a sense of how people ate and drank during his lifetime, but he does not set rules. While some of his comments fit a modern pattern ('We drank *à la française*, which is to say that wine was served from the very beginning: it was a really good claret [Bordeaux]' served with an 'enormous' roast beef and a turkey'), others seem unusual, such as the tuna omelette he suggests be consumed 'thoughtfully and slowly' with 'a fine old wine'.[37]

Fourth, pairing the wine with the person rather than the dish. This turns out to have been the principal approach to wine pairing in the seventeenth and early eighteenth centuries. Medical advice, not gastronomic advice, was the norm. Red wine was too rough for women and aristocrats but provided useful nourishment to labourers.[38] Louis XIV's wines were selected by his physicians. As the king's health was a matter of national concern, detailed records survive chronicling the long struggle between two of his doctors as to whether the king should continue to drink (still) Champagne or switch to older bottles of red Burgundy. The leading physicians of Paris, Reims, and Dijon engaged in extensive debates. Guy-Crescent Fagon, the doctor arguing for Burgundy, won the battle, became chief physician to the king, and the king began to drink aged, full-bodied Burgundy – a major blow to the Champagne region and a major boost to Burgundy, particularly after the court followed the king's example.[39] What foods might marry, or even complement, the wine was not discussed. It is conceivable, however, that the preference for fuller-bodied red Burgundy wines, together with the king's diet, may have helped to further the association of red wine and red meat.

After the king died and France began to be ruled by the Regent, Philippe, duc d'Orléans, from the Palais Royal, a new fashion emerged that again did not relate to the qualities of the food: the new style of expensive, sparkling Champagne. Fashion dictated drinking it with everything.

Did Thérèse, seemingly so contemporary in thinking a red Burgundy would clash with the oysters, really think sparkling Champagne intrinsically better, or, succumbing to fashion, would she have drunk Champagne with roast beef? From the passage quoted above, she appears to be making the point that the selection of the oysters was what made drinking the Burgundy impossible, so it is likely she is not merely a lover of Champagne.

Medical advice pairing a person to a wine gradually disappeared, but as late as 1934, Escoffier, who made very few comments about wine in his books, advised in *Ma cuisine*, '*Les vins jeunes contiennent trop d'acidité: les estomacs délicats et les vieillards doivent donc s'en abstenir ou les sucrer légèrement.*' (Young wines have too much acidity: those with delicate stomachs and the aged must avoid or lightly sweeten them.)[40]

One might think I should go on to say, **Fifth, just drink what you like.** But this fifth category would be antithetical to French history and the patterns of rigour and categorizing that are at the heart of French culinary traditions. And it would seem dreadfully American. In any case, this would be in some sense a modern version of pairing to the person and not the dish. There are people who feel bonded to their particular favourite type of wine ('I'll have a glass of Chardonnay') and feel it has no connection to the enjoyment of their food, nor do they feel they are missing an alchemical reaction or a third taste; but those people are not usually French. I have a worldly friend, a prominent American food critic revered in many countries, who told me, 'I choose the wine I like, I drink water with the food and in between courses I drink my wine.' This does evoke a time before wine and food were considered spouses. The Greeks and Romans did not take their wine with food. Even in the late eighteenth century, Thomas Jefferson, a serious early connoisseur of the then new style of dark and tannic Bordeaux wines, saved his best wines to have after his meal, without food. In a letter to the U.S. Secretary of Foreign Affairs, John Jay, Jefferson wrote about a dinner consisting of mutton drunk with (presumably sparkling) Champagne and Burgundy, with 'Bourdeaux' consumed 'after dinner'.[41] It seems worth noting that, for most people in France during the period when most modern styles of wine developed (mainly the eighteenth and nineteenth centuries), 'drinking what you like' simply meant drinking the local wine that was most available, and we are back once again to the landscape.

A final mystery: the gradual emergence of drinking red wine with red meat. One reason it is so difficult to determine the origin and history of what Roland Barthes proclaimed the 'sanguinary mythology' of red meat and red wine is that there was no clear event or process that created the association, which had a slow, winding path to the definitive position it had assumed by the time Barthes wrote in the 1950s. Perhaps the shift has been rarely written about because it was so gradual. Yet, simply because there was a gradual process does not mean the association remained weak. At the monumental new museum of wine in Bordeaux, *La Cité du Vin*, there is a small and clever virtual reality exhibit, intended to be light-hearted, where visitors can pair on screen up to ten dishes with ten wines and hear commentary on their choices in their language from a pre-recorded 'sommelier', who does not necessarily insist on a single correct answer but at times leaves no doubt that this subject involves right and wrong. If a visitor has the misfortune to pair rare beef with sweet Sauternes, he or she receives a scolding: 'Oh, dear! I won't give you the keys to the cellar!'

However, by contrast, through much of the nineteenth century, sweet wines had been acceptably drunk with everything – sweet Champagnes, sweet Constantia imported from South Africa (one of the only wines Napoléon, exiled to St. Helena, believed his stomach could handle). Somehow, this taste for sweet wines with savoury foods gradually disappeared.

One aspect of the association of red meat with red wine has to do with the Eucharist, implicit in Roland Barthes's phrase, 'sanguinary mythology'. Blood is red, but red wine was not red in the modern sense until Bordeaux began to produce the new French clarets during the eighteenth century – and Communion wine is often white. Red wine came to be formally associated with blood at events toward the end of the French Revolution, but this was a mythic connection, not a practical gastronomic tool.[42] Both sides of this mythology have been often in flux: red wine was not always red and neither was red meat, because fashions in how thoroughly to cook meat come and go. Although, roughly speaking, eighteenth-century lists of dishes are likely to show roasts and game dishes clustered later in the meal at the point when the more assertive wines – principally red wines – would be appearing, there simply seems to be no overt discussion of drinking red wine with red meat. France's first gastronomic chronicler, Grimod de La Reynière, insisted on white and red wine to be present at all meals and expressed no interest in what sort of wine to serve with what food.[43]

Eventually the menus and records of banquets begin to reveal the ascendency of red Burgundy and Bordeaux. By the end of the nineteenth century it becomes harder to find menus or descriptions of meals that do not match red wine with game and red meat.[44] There is still no discussion of this association by any of the leading chroniclers of gastronomy before the 1930s, although it appears the rule was already in place and followed. Beginning in the 1930s, there are a few books giving advice on *l'accord parfait* … the perfect match. There is an inexhaustible supply of such books now, but even without them today in France the unwritten rule is essentially law.

Notes

1. Bernard Pivot, 'Quel vin?', in Bernard Pivot, *Dictionnaire amoreux du vin* (Paris: Éditions Plon, 2006). pp. 337-40. The earliest reference I have so far found suggesting a requirement that red meat combine with red wine is in Émile Zola's novel, *Le ventre de Paris* (1873), in which a woman speaks of the expense of providing red meat and Bordeaux wine for her invalid husband. I expect there are many earlier references and would be delighted to hear from any readers who have suggestions. Fashion is a related area where devotees who understand the genre have strong feelings about what goes with what, and the synergies created by certain combinations of clothing, but where the rules are merely 'understood', and understood in different ways by different people, and rarely written down.
2. Gilbert Garrier, *Histoire sociale et culturelle du vin*, 2nd ed. (Paris: Larousse, 2008), p. 612. Green, for example, is a shading of the largely colourless wine we call white; blue is a deep purple that would be considered red today. In vogue today there are also light-coloured red wines known as rosé, the 'yellow' wines of the Jura, and an increasing vogue for 'orange' and 'black' wines.
3. Moreover, the ice Napoléon placed in his wine would not have been neutral in taste, having been stored for up to a year after being cut from glaciers – ice-making machines not having been developed (Jean-Robert Pitte, *Dictionaire amoureux de la Bourgogne* (Paris: Éditions Plon, 2015), pp. 186-87).
4. *Thérèse philosophe ou mémoires pour servir à l'histoire du P. Dirrag et de Mlle Eradice* (various editions, beginning in 1748). I thank the great historian of France, Robert Darnton, who told me about this passage over oysters (with, as he recommended, Champagne) at dinner some years ago. He comments on this Enlightenment passage in Robert Darnton, *The Forbidden Best-Sellers of Pre-Revolutionary France*

(New York: Norton, 1995), p. 107; I quote Darnton's translation, p. 251. 'Philosophical' in this context means that the book is a story of sex and metaphysics.
5. See Thomas Brennan, *Burgundy to Champagne: The Wine Trade in Early Modern France* (Baltimore: The Johns Hopkins University Press, 1997).
6. 'Le bifteck et les frites', in *Mythologies* (Paris: Éditions du Seuil, 1957), p. 72. ('*Le bifteck participe à la même mythologie sanguine que le vin [...] et quiconque en prend, s'assimile la force taurine.*')
7. 'Le vin et le lait', in *Mythologies*, p. 71. ('*savoir boire est une technique nationale qui sert à qualifier le Français, à prouver à la fois son pouvoir de performance, son contrôle et sa sociabilité [...] .l'absence de vin choque comme un exotisme.*')
8. I am not certain this is an authentic quotation but it is treated as such by people in France and included in lists of famous quotations. See, e.g., "Citations avec Dico-Citations', *Le Monde.fr* <http://dicocitations.lemonde.fr/citations/citation-58682.php> [accessed 15 May 2017].
9. See Robert Lowell's description of carving at his home in Boston: '"I have always believed carving to be the gentlemanly talent," mother used to proclaim' (*Life Studies & For the Union Dead* (New York: The Noonday Press, 1956-64), p. 34).
10. See Rebecca Spang, *The Invention of the Restaurant: Paris and Modern Gastronomic Culture* (Cambridge: Harvard University Press, 2000).
11. Leo Tolstoy, *Anna Karenina*, trans. by Richard Pevear and Larissa Volokhonsky (New York: Penguin, 2000), p. 35.
12. Letter to Madame Straus, end of June 1907, in *Letters of Marcel Proust*, trans. by Mina Curtiss (London: Chatto & Windus, 1950), letter no. 105. The sophisticated Geneviève Straus, née Halévy, the widow of the composer Georges Bizet, was a model for the Duchesse de Guermantes in *À la recherche du temps perdu*.
13. Pierre Bourdieu, *Distinction: A Social Critique of the Judgement of Taste*, trans. by Richard Nice (Cambridge: Harvard University Press, 1984), p.187.
14. Yes, wine was imported and exported over long distances even by the ancient Greeks and Romans, but French government statistics show that in France local consumption of local wine was at the heart of regional economies in most wine growing regions until the late twentieth century, with only Champagne, Burgundy, and Bordeaux having significant export markets. And in those areas, known for their exports, the local wine was still the most consumed in the region itself.
15. At least this is the myth. As with all regional dishes, questions of origin and authenticity are subject to debate.
16. See Roger Dion, *Histoire de la vigne et du vin en France des origins au XIXe siècle* (Paris: Privately printed, 1959) and Marcel Lachiver, *Vins, vignes et vignerons: Histoire du vignoble français* (Bordeaux: Fayard, 1984).
17. Jean-Anthelme Brillat-Savarin, *Physiologie du goût* (Paris: A. Sautelet, 1825), repr. *The Physiology of Taste*, trans. by M.F.K. Fisher (New York: Knopf, 1972), p. 382. Brillat-Savarin worked on this book for much of his long life and published it just before his death.
18. Olivier Bompas, *Et avec ça, Qu'est-ce qu'on boit? 400 idées pour accorder parfaitement vos mets et vos boissons* (Paris: Hachette, 2015), p. 9.
19. See, for example, Philippe Meyzie's description of the contrast between the idea that the food of Southwestern France in the early nineteenth century fulfilled the medieval myth of the '*pays de Cocagne*', a land of plenty (with, in this case, plenty of truffles), and the idea that the people were so deprived of food that they survived mainly by eating garlic ('Construction et diffusion d'une image contrastée de la culture alimentaire régionale', in *La Table du Sud-Ouest et l'émergence des cuisines régionales (1700-1850)* (Rennes: Presses Universitaires de Rennes 2007), pp. 337-61).
20. Jean-François Mesplède, *Trois étoiles au Michelin: Une histoire de la haute gastronomie française* (Paris: Éditions Grund, 1998). Bill Buford has pointed out to me that Curnonsky, '*prince élu des gastronomes*', needed Rouff in part because he did not drive.
21. '*L'important, c'est que cette cuisine constitue nos racines communes, mystérieux patrimoine du goût enfoui dans notre inconscient collectif [...]*' (Jacques Puisais, in *Le goût juste des vins et des plats* (Paris: Flammarion, 1985), p. 133).

22. Pictured with a bottle of Chateau Angelus (St. Émilion), a blazing fire, and an evocative large piece of beef, in *L'accord parfait* (Paris: Éditions du Chéne, 1999), p. 11. '*Dans l'exercice si difficile qu'est la recherche de l'alliance harmonieuse entre des mets et des vins, il ne faut pas être trop catégorique. Puisque personne ne distingue un médoc d'un saint-émilion dans une dégustation à l'aveugle, pourquoi imposer un médoc plutôt qu'un saint-émilion sur une côte de bœuf?*
23. *Le Guide des Meilleurs Vins de France* (Paris: La Revue du Vin de France, 2017), pp. 102-05.
24. Jean-Louis Flandrin, *L'Ordre des mets* (Paris: Odile Jacob, 2002).
25. Jean-Pierre Poulain and Edmond Neirinck, *Histoire de la cuisine et des cuisiniers: Techniques culinaires et pratiques de table, en France, du Moyen-Âge à nos jours* (Paris: Éditions LT Jacques Lanore, 2004), pp. 71-79.
26. It is hard to overemphasize the importance of the development of wine bottles, for both still wines designed for aging and for the development of sparkling Champagne: see Jean-Robert Pitte, *La Bouteille de Vin: Histoire d'une revolution* (Paris: Tallandier, 2013).
27. Known as the *Grande Larousse gastronomique* for the two most recent editions.
28. *Larousse gastronomique* (Paris: Larousse 2012), p. 894.
29. 'Des mets à la rencontre des vins', *L'Humanité*, 18 December 2004. See also Alain Senderens, *Le vin et la table* (Paris: Éditions de La Revue du vin de France, 2000).
30. Puisais, p. 33. Bee Wilson describes Puisais's more general food taste education classes in French primary schools in the 1970s (*First Bite: How We Learn to Eat* (New York: Basic Books, 2015), p. 244).
31. Puisais, p. 7.
32. Patricia Wells, 'Dining: Alain Senderens and the Triumph of the Wines', *New York Times*, 22 November 2002 <http://www.nytimes.com/2002/11/22/style/dining-alain-senderens-and-the-triumph-of-the-wines.html> [accessed 15 May 2017].
33. François Chartier, *Papilles et molécules: La science aromatique des aliments et des vins* (Paris: Les Éditions La Presse, 2009), repr. *Taste Buds and Molecules: The Art and Science of Food, Wine, and Flavor*, trans. by Levi Reiss (Hoboken, NJ: Wiley, 2012) , pp. 89-93.
34. Chartier, p. 114.
35. A recent book by Gordon Shepherd, a professor of neuroscience at the Yale School of Medicine, explores the science of tasting but concludes that the state of current science is not sufficient to recommend what to pair with what (*Neuroenology: How the Brain Creates the Taste of Wine* (New York: Columbia University Press, 2017)).
36. Brillat-Savarin, p. 375. I remember reading some decades ago, but have been unable to find my source, that Escoffier understood the magical effect the right wine could have with his food, and said that during his career in England when he served Albert Edward, Prince of Wales, and the Prince complimented the wine, he knew he had cooked well. I would be grateful for any leads to this missing anecdote.
37. Brillat-Savarin, pp. 393, 353, 349.
38. Thomas Parker, *Tasting French Terroir: The History of an Idea* (Berkeley: University of California Press, 2015).
39. The primary source material as to the debates over Louis XIV's health as regards wine have been published in *Journal de santé de Louis XIV*, ed. by Stanis Perez (Grenoble: Éditions Millon, 2004). Vivid descriptions of the controversy are found in Jean-Robert Pitte, *Bordeaux Bourgogne: Les passions rivales* (Paris: Hachette, 2005), pp. 63-72 and in Garrier.
40. Auguste Escoffier, *Ma Cuisine* (Paris: Ernest Flammarion, 1934), p. 692. Escoffier is often said to have codified, some would say ossified, French cooking at the beginning of the twentieth century in his comprehensive *Le Guide Culinaire* (four editions, 1902, 1907, 1912 and 1921). But it does not discuss wine or pairing.
41. John Hailman, *Thomas Jefferson on Wine* (Jackson: University Press of Mississippi, 2006), p. 85.
42. Garrier, p. 198.
43. Jean-Robert Pitte, *Les accords mets-vins, un art français* (Paris: CNRS-Éditions 2017), pp. 16-17.
44. See examples collected by Garrier, pp. 265-81.

Lines in the Landscape: How the Olive-Line, the Date-Line, and the Vine-Line Have Defined Mediterranean Culture

David C. Sutton

Introduction: Dates, Olives, and Vines: Three Food Frontiers

The traveller voyaging north from the Sahara Desert arrives at the Mediterranean zone, in the classic definition of Fernand Braudel, on leaving the landscape of the palm tree and entering the landscape of the olive tree. In many traditions, the olive is seen as the plant whose cultivation-limits naturally provide the boundaries of the Mediterranean landscape.[1]

This essay examines food frontiers and cultural identity, following the three (mostly east-west) lines which Braudel drew across the map of Europe and North Africa: the date-line, the olive-line, and the vine-line. Dates and olives in particular provide defining landscapes, which are accompanied by food patterns and lifestyles, within their lines of demarcation.

The three zones do overlap, but they are distinguished above all by climatic factors, especially the limits of hot and cold, and by access to water. For example, in order to initiate good quality flowers and fruit, olive trees need a two-month period of cool weather (below 10°C). This means that olives require a winter – although only a Mediterranean winter.[2] Although olive trees may benefit from watering, they are

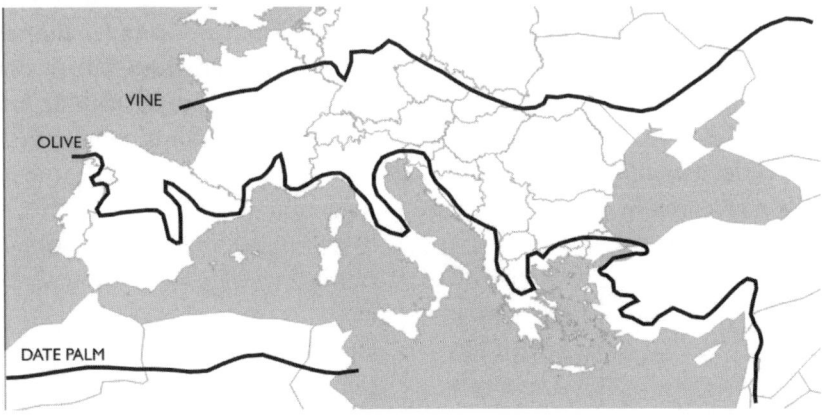

Figure 1: The three northern-limit landscape lines, after Fernand Braudel.

generally more drought tolerant than palm trees and do not demand the complex systems of irrigation which date palms need, other than in oasis locations.

Water, climate, and rainfall are thus determining factors for the three zones. In studying the cultivation of the date in particular, water systems and irrigation can be seen as vital features in the landscape. The shift from oasis dates and palms near rivers to systematically cultivated dates has been one of the major agricultural changes in the landscape of the Maghreb and the Near East in the past fifty years.[3]

Approaching the history of European food by way of these three food frontiers may provide new insights into the differing zonal food cultures, in respect of both the food of the rich and the food of the poor.

*

Tim Ingold, in his highly original book about lines, tells us that lines on maps may serve to separate 'the space inside' from 'the space outside'.[4] This is especially true of the way first the Greeks and then the other peoples of the Mediterranean world saw themselves. For them, the core of the civilized world lay inside the olive-line.

It may be significant, therefore, that one etymology of '*Keltoi*', the Greek word for the Celts from Hecataeus and Herodotus onwards, derives from a word stem signifying 'outsiders' – natives of the outer (non-olive) regions. This etymology is plausible when we recall that the earliest writers considered 'Celtica' to extend from the Danube Valley to both sides of the English Channel and down as far as Portugal.[5] The Barbarians and the Celts were historically defined, in respect of the lines of this essay, as those with the misfortune to live outside the olive landscape.

In addition to the geographical and climatic lines of demarcation, therefore, there are social and cultural lines of identity. These lines are fundamental to the perceived distinction between Greeks and Barbarians (or Celts), and to the nature of Hellenism. This was primarily a food-based identity, with a strong belief that cereals, olives, and vines defined Greek life, while dairy products, red meat, and cheese were typical of Barbarians. The bread-oil-wine self-definition underlies, for example, the story of Odysseus and Polyphemus the Cyclops, the epitome of Barbarianism. Polyphemus was unfamiliar with wine (Odysseus easily made him drunk); his cave stank of milk and cheese; he not only ate meat but ate meat in its most extreme form, human flesh.

We can offer a preliminary summary of such food oppositions by using the pairings presentation favoured by structuralist anthropologists:

olive oil	:	butter
wine	:	ale
dried figs	:	cheese
breads	:	porridges

Table 1. South-north food oppositions.

In reality, despite the strength of belief in this self-defining lifestyle, supposed to have a uniquely strong focus on bread, olive oil, and wine, it always contained a significant part of popular mythologizing. Non-Greeks from surrounding cultures produced and loved bread, and the Greeks ate a range of cheeses and yogurt-like products, especially from the milk of sheep and goats.[6]

Nonetheless, the Greek notion that the limits of civilized society were formed by the limits of olive cultivation has proved very durable, and the associated veneration of olives and their oil is well attested. It also has, as we shall see, many parallels with the veneration of dates and the date palm in the Arab world.

The Olive Zone

The olive zone (in its landscape, its patrimonies, and its food norms) defines the culture of a wide area of Mediterranean lands in three continents which share a generally uniform benign maritime climate – ranging from Andalucía to Croatia to Palestine to Tunisia,[7] and including many of the Mediterranean islands. The role of the 'central sea' appears to be essential in this homogeneous zone and its food culture. With the exception of a few parts of central Spain, all the principal olive territories are within a 100-mile distance from the sea.

The islands, littoral areas, and hinterlands of most of the countries with a Mediterranean coastline comprise the essential historical olive zone. There may then be marginal questions of inclusion. For example, despite successful recent initiatives in Herzegovina and the Republic of Macedonia, the Balkan area has no historical tradition of olive production beyond the coastal strip of Croatia and Montenegro. Northern Greece, on the other hand, especially Thrace and Boeotia, has strong reasons for being considered to be within the 'olive zone' as part of its cultural identity. At the other end of western Europe, there are small numbers of olive oil producers in northwest Spain (Galicia), who can adduce a historical tradition dating back to the Romans, but it is implausible to place Galicia within the historical olive zone. Southern Portugal has a much stronger claim, with a location between the Atlantic and the Mediterranean, and a way of life that is clearly 'Iberian-Mediterranean'.

As well as islands, the olive zone is characterized by Mediterranean peninsulas, which notably include Tunisia and the Crimea. The food

Bozcaada	Korčula
Brač	Krk
Corfu	Lefkada
Corsica	Lesbos
Cres	Mallorca
Crete	Malta
Cyprus	Menorca
Djerba	Pag
Dugi Otok	Pantelleria
Elba	Porquerolles
Euboea	Rhodes
Gökçeada (Imbros)	Sardinia
Ibiza	Sicily
Kefalonia	Zakynthos

Table 2. Some Mediterranean islands with long historical traditions of olive oil production.

history of the Crimea has always included figs, olives, oranges, and pomegranates, although these crops have scarcely extended beyond the limits of the peninsula.⁸ The lifestyles and food traditions of the islands and peninsulas provide archetypes of olive oil cookery in olive-tree landscapes.

*

The drought-resistant nature of the olive tree is illustrated by the history of olive oil in Biblical Palestine. It is now known that a major factor in the great crisis in the Near East around the year 1200 BCE was climate change and the culmination of a period of global warming which had been continuing for around 800 years. In this period the Syrian-Palestinian climate gradually transformed from Mediterranean to desert-arid; and yet the pre-existing plantations and groves of olives continued to thrive, as we know from the Biblical account of the tribute paid by the Jewish King Shlomo (Solomon) to the Phoenician King Hiram, around 950 BCE: 'And Shlomo gave Hiram 100,000 bushels of wheat as food for his household and over a thousand gallons of oil from pressed olives – this is what Shlomo gave Hiram each year' (I Kings 5. 25, *Complete Jewish Bible*). The eastern olive line was thus robust and durable, and was sustained by its history and pre-history (a number of sources suggest that the olive tree was in fact first cultivated in Syria and Palestine) despite the impact of climate change and desertification.

By contrast, Egypt had a history of importing olive oil (notably from Palestine, but also from Crete) and, lacking a history of olive groves, was unable to begin its own olive production until after the later cooling of the climate that began around 300 BCE. The same would apply to Libya, despite the fact that only a decade ago Libya was the twelfth-biggest producer of olive oil in the world, with over eight million olive trees. In terms of historical landscape, geographical culture, and food culture, Egypt and Libya (unlike Tunisia) cannot be said to be part of the Mediterranean olive zone nor of its long and self-aware olive-oil-based food history.

In seeking to define the lifestyle and food-culture characteristics of the olive zone, one is quickly drawn into the entertaining but treacherous territory of north-south prejudices and caricatures, and care is needed in separating history from mythology. Nonetheless some classic characteristics and distinctions can certainly be identified:

- After the great heat of the southern summer, which often requires a good deal

Catalunya (Arión)
Corsica
Crete
Israel and Palestine
Lebanon (Bechealeh)
Mallorca
Malta
Montenegro
Provence (Roquebrune)
Puglia
Sardinia (Olivastro di Luras)

Table 3. Locations of fruiting olive trees said in 2017 to be over 1000 years old

of daytime indoors, the olive harvest is a social and community event in the temperate month of November.

- Hand harvesting produces the best results, but is the most labour-intensive technique. Other traditional methods include trunk beating, shaking, and branch raking. Ladders are essential to these processes, sometimes ten ladders or more to a tree.

- Olive oil transcends social class; it is beloved of rich and poor alike; it takes its place in southern gastronomy, but it is also integral to peasant foods such as the mashes and pastes of beans and oils that became the staple food of the mighty Roman armies.

- Olive cultivation has a harvesting time, but less year-round field working than many other crops. This gives rise to a perception of a lifestyle (associated with olives, figs, lemons, pomegranates, and chestnuts)[9] containing a significant amount of 'waiting for the ripening': a slower, more leisurely cycle.

- The Mediterranean olive zone, comprising islands, peninsulas, and littoral lands to the north, east, and south of the Sea, is remarkably unitary as a set of landscapes. This unitary nature is further underlined by the universal style of the historical olive mills found throughout the zone.[10]

- The roles, both social and culinary, taken in the north of Europe by butter and beer were taken in the south by olive oil and wine. There is no mention of butter in Apicius, and in later times there is ample evidence of the southern horror at northern use of butter, with its vile smell of rot and animal origin – notably during the Spanish occupation of Flanders and the Netherlands around the year 1500. Alonso Vázquez described Flanders as a land with no lavender, no thyme, no figs, no olives, no melons, and no almonds, a land where the parsley, onion, and lettuce had neither juice nor flavour, and where, unbelievably, food was prepared with cow-butter instead of oil. The Cardinal of Aragon, who arrived in the Netherlands in 1517, expressed his disgust by suggesting that the universal use of cow-butter and dairy products would surely be the reason why leprosy was so widespread.[11]

- This north-south cultural contrast may also distinguish mountain and littoral lifestyles and, in some cases, religious affiliations. Using the structuralist style once again, this could be presented as:

butter	:	olive oil
north	:	south
cool	:	warm
mountain	:	littoral
protestant	:	catholic
daily work	:	cyclical work

Table 4: Further oppositions, expressed as north-south.

Food and Landscape

Figure 2. A fine example of the Mediterranean style of olive mill, preserved amongst the Roman remains in Volubilis, Morocco (Wikimedia Commons).

- On the other side of the olive-line in eastern France, we find a food culture (from Haute-Provence to Burgundy) based not on butter but on walnut oil, which is generally closer to olive-oil-based than to butter-based styles of cookery: a transitional region between south and north, inside the wine zone but outside the olive zone.

- Caricatures must be treated with caution, as opinions or prejudices rather than facts, but they are not to be ignored: they include the northern caricature of southerners lazing in the shade under trees, and the southern caricature of northerners working themselves to death, in impossible weather, eating impossible food – an attitude nicely captured by Norman Douglas's Count Caloveglia in *South Wind*, talking principally about England and New England: 'That a man should wear himself to the bone in the acquisition of material gain is not pretty. But what else can he do in lands adapted only for wolves and bears?'[12]

- Olive oil has an aura of life-giving healthiness, whether consumed or (as in Ancient Egypt) rubbed into the skin. This has evolved into admiration for the 'Mediterranean diet', associated with olive oil, fish, and vegetables. (The close association with fish follows naturally from olive oil's status as a littoral product.)

- Olive oil has been venerated in the Mediterranean area, and closely associated with the gods. This high luxury value attributed to an everyday product can be compared with the history of butter further north and of dates further south and east, but there is nonetheless a clear distinction in the historical texts between northern butter, which is relished, and southern olive oil, which is revered.

Lines in the Landscape

In summary, people who live in the olive landscapes, in the lands of olive oil cuisine, have, throughout history, been proud of their superior diet and linked it very specifically to the fruit of the olive tree, often by way of the beneficence of the gods. In the twenty-first century many nutritionists have confirmed this dietary superiority under the heading 'the Mediterranean diet'.

The Date Zone

The veneration of dates as a foodstuff is characteristic of the lands which lie to the south and east of the olive landscape, and has an even longer history than the veneration of olives, going back at least as far as the story of Gilgamesh. *The Epic of Gilgamesh* has its written origins around 4000 years ago and describes events that may have occurred around 4700 years ago. In the verses of the Gilgamesh story, we find dates described as products which are cultivated by gardeners who specialize in working with date palms, and which are highly regarded and loved: 'You loved Ishullanu, your father's date gardener, / who continually brought you baskets of dates, / and brightened your table daily.'[13] (Other translations of these lines suggest 'baskets filled with dates without end'.)

The love of dates is clearly as geographically specific as the love of olives. Ancient writers from Mediterranean lands make little or no mention of dates. Even in the work of Herodotus, for all his interest in Egypt, there is not a single reference to dates. In the Koran, by contrast, references to dates abound, and are included in some of the most beautiful sections.

This geographical specificity is illustrated by the maps of date production, both historically and up to the present day. At the end of the twentieth century, the world's premier producers of dates were Iraq and Iran, and this had probably been the case for more than three millennia. Following the wars and embargoes that have recently afflicted those countries, the leading producers are now said to be as shown in Table 5 (although figures from war-torn countries should, of course, be treated with some caution).

Table 5 also shows how the countries of the date zone tend to be just on the other side of a food-frontier that separates them from the olive zone. Even in Tunisia, which

1.	Egypt
2.	Saudi Arabia
3.	Iran
4.	Algeria
5.	Iraq
6.	Pakistan
7.	Oman
8.	United Arab Emirates
9.	Tunisia
10.	Libya

Table 5. Date-producing countries in 2017, in approximate order of importance.

Medjool	Morocco
Deglet noor	Algeria
Barakawi	Sudan
Barhi	Palestine
Derrie	Iraq
Halawi	Arabia
Kenta	Tunisia
Khadrawi	Arabia
Khalabash	Arabia
Mazafati	Iran
Thoory	Algeria
Zahidi	Arabia

Table 6: Some of the most highly-regarded dates, with their countries or areas of origin.

features in both zones, olive trees tend to grow closer to the Mediterranean and date palms closer to the Sahara Desert.

Dates are known for their range of flavours and qualities, for their regional and national associations, and for their hierarchies of value. Few would dispute the supremacy of Medjool, and most would allocate second place to Deglet noor.

The most highly-regarded dates of all, and especially the Medjool, warrant a form of harvesting which is accorded to not even the most highly valued olives (which might include, for example, the Royal de Cazorla variety in southern Spain). Individual Medjool dates are hand picked as they each achieve their perfect ripeness, leaving the dates which are not quite ripe on the palm.

Whilst venerated, the date is also a vital staple in the Arab lands, regarded often as lifesaving and life-giving:

> For the nomad, the date meant survival. It is a good food, of very high nutritive value and – as Westerners know well – keeps almost forever when dried. The date has a further property: a sugar content so high – up to 80 per cent – that it inhibits most germs and so provides a healthy food, unlike much fresh fruit which, in the tropics, is apt to spread disease.[14]

In the harsh desert regimes near the date zone, a combination of camel's milk and dried dates (or camel-milk cheese and dried dates) is one of the most frequently reported staples – from the Touareg lands of north and north-west Africa to the Bedouin lands of Arabia and the Near East. This staple is much more typical of everyday Bedouin life than the occasionally reported extravaganzas, such as camel stuffed with mutton, which in turn is stuffed with goat, which in turn is stuffed with chicken. This is celebration food of the desert elites, not regularly eaten food.

Cathy Kaufman's book *Cooking in Ancient Civilizations* underlines the importance of dates in Arabian cuisine between 4000 and 5000 years ago. Notable examples include the 'palace cakes' of Ur, with ingredients including white cheese, dates, and raisins; a funeral meal, also from Ur, with ingredients of goat, dried dates, dried apples, and flatbread; and a compote of dried fruit (dates, figs, and grapes) offered to the gods in Uruk.[15]

As with olive oil in the Mediterranean region, dates were regarded as a wonderful and magical food for the rich, for the poor, and for the gods: 'To Muslims, the date palm and its fruit was a God-sent gift, a miracle food capable of healing body and soul. According to a famous saying by the Prophet, "A house empty of dates is a poor house indeed." It was their livelihood and Tree of Life. The forbidden tree in paradise was said to be a date palm.'[16] The earliest date palms cropped by man would have been naturally irrigated, in locations in oases or in river flood plains. Improvements in irrigation in such sites evolved over many centuries. More sophisticated approaches to irrigation have been developed recently and have sometimes failed or disappointed precisely because of their sophistication. This is a summary by the irrigation scholar M. K. V. Carr:

1. Since early times, flood irrigation has been used to irrigate date palm and, in many countries, it is still the most commonly used method.

2. In oases, most of the water for crops comes from natural groundwater, and in some coastal areas rising tides push water into date palm plantations.

3. Since the 1980s, localized irrigation (e.g. drip, micro-sprinklers and bubbler systems) has been promoted by governments to date palm farmers as a means (in theory) of saving water.

4. Considerable water savings, as well as yield advantages, have been recorded from subsurface drip irrigation, compared with a conventional system.[17]

The Vine Zone

The European vine zone extends from Jerez de la Frontera to Champagne, and from Portugal to Bulgaria and Hungary, and, despite its greater extent, like the other two zones has some homogeneity of appearance, lifestyle, and food culture.

Extending further north and east in particular, the vine zone almost completely envelops the olive zone so that many of the characteristics of olive foodways and landscape also apply here, and, indeed, many of the recipes, meal descriptions, and adages explicitly link olive oil and wine.

The typical landscape of vineyards was brought into being by early civilizations, notably the Syrian-Palestinian, the Phoenician, and the Greek. Between 3000 and 2000 years ago, the characteristic landscape of vineyards spread along the Mediterranean routes colonized first by the Phoenicians and then by the Greeks, and then outwards into lands where the Visigoths, the Gauls, and others became wine producers in the landscapes immediately to the north of the olive zone.

As with olives and dates, wine was considered to be such a wonderful product that it was offered also to the gods. Pliny the Elder singled out wine from the hillsides of the Lebanon (home to the Phoenicians), with its flavour of incense, as being an especially appropriate divine offering.[18]

The southern veneration of wine is often described in a dualist contrast with the historical Mediterranean contempt for beer, a close parallel of the contempt for cow-butter that we saw as characteristic of the olive zone.

However, as was suggested in the brief mention above of the walnut oil zone, the area between the northern olive-line and the northern vine-line may be regarded, in terms of landscape and lifestyle, as a transitional zone between the Mediterranean and the North.

Many of the wines in this transitional zone are in fact quite different from the wines in the olive zone. For example, the olive zone has no equivalent to the heavy and herbal-flavoured Gewürztraminer white wines of Alsace or the very similar Traminec white wines of Macedonia.

Landlocked wine-producing areas such as Alsace, Austria, Burgundy, Hungary,

Food and Landscape

Serbia, and Macedonia have their own non-Mediterranean lifestyle and historical food culture, most obviously in the absence of Mediterranean fish such as mullet, turbot, or rascasse from their diets and recipes. In several cases the food culture of this transitional upper vine zone also reflects the influence of the centuries of occupation by the Ottoman Empire.

There is a marked similarity in the food cultures of different areas within the upper vine zone. In the absence of Mediterranean fish, common ingredients including carp, trout, and eel are shared by the food traditions of Macedonia, Hungary, and Alsace, together with cherries and plums (and their alcohols), shredded cabbage, soured cream, and fiery grape alcohol (schnapps / rakija), within a lifestyle which is neither Mediterranean nor Northern.[19]

Typical and traditional recipes from these regions reflect this transitional nature: the *ajvar* (red pepper pâté) of Serbia and Macedonia; the *baeckeoffe, choucroute*, and *fleischnacka* of Alsace; the *Csirkepaprikás, Császármorzsa*, and goulash meals of Hungary. The styles and tastes may reflect Mediterranean influence to a certain extent, but they are quite distinct from Mediterranean foodways.

The foodstuffs used are also distinct from those typical of the olive zone. Table 7 shows the characteristic foods of the twelve months of the year as perceived in the Republic of Macedonia, but also applying elsewhere in the southern Balkans.[20] Again, we see that they are not Northern, but not quite Mediterranean either:

January	Chestnuts
February	Squash
March	Cucumbers
April	Radishes
May	Tomatoes
June	Cherries
July	Water melons
August	Maize
September	Grapes
October	Red peppers
November	Aubergines
December	Apples

Table 7. *The transitional zone between the olive and vine zones: illustrated by the Macedonian fruit and vegetable calendar.*

The vine zone can thus be regarded as two separate areas, in the context of food frontiers. These are the Mediterranean (wine and olive) food zone and the upper vine zone (characterized by wine without olive products).

Conclusion

The concept of food frontiers has provided some of the most original themes of research in recent food history.[21] Fats and oils used in regional cookery have been seen as among the strongest lines of demarcation, but food frontier definitions have also been used in studying topics as varied as the eating of horsemeat; attitudes to cereals such as wheat, barley, spelt, and oats; areas of coffee production and consumption; and historical food exclusions between Normans and Saxons.

In this essay, the clear demarcations seen on either side of the date-line, the olive-line and the vine-line have provided 'ways of seeing' within the food cultures of many countries. In particular, they illuminate the ways in which residents of the respective zones define and describe their own food cultures. These self-definitions, as we have seen, tend to include some strongly judgmental attitudes towards those who are outside the food zone in question (Barbarians, Celts, Anatolians, etc.). They also present what has been well described as 'food pride' – a strongly-held belief (especially in the olive-growing lands) in the superiority of their own food-ways.[22] In some respects, this superiority has been factually confirmed by recent nutritional research, and the health-giving properties of olive products and date products in particular have now passed from the domain of traditional folk beliefs to that of confirmed nutritional science.

The landscapes of olives, dates, and vines present visual images that evoke the popular affection for the three products. Olives, dates, and grapes appear in popular culture and beliefs in ways that are almost universally positive and laudatory. Dates are used in the Near East as tropes for sweetness and for health and happiness. Grapes and wine are widely associated with civilization, knowledge, and cultured lifestyles. The peaceful olive branch remains a widely-used metaphor, and a pair of Antigone's lines about 'some god's grove' from Sophocles' *Oedipus at Colonus* are also worth quoting in these concluding remarks: 'This place must be sacred – thick-set / With laurel, with olives and with vines; and nightingales, / Thronging within it, make sweet melody.' The food-frontiers of olives, dates, and vines offer conceptually useful dividing lines between different food cultures, *terroirs,* and traditions, and the concepts of date zone, olive zone and vine zone can enhance our understanding and appreciation of the cultures and lifestyles of a historically significant sector of the world.

It is hoped that this essay has demonstrated that the lines in the landscape chosen by the great social historian Fernand Braudel, and described by him in summary form, are, when analyzed in more detail, found to be very clearly the right lines.

Notes

1. Fernand Braudel, Fig. 19: 'La "vraie" Méditerranée, de l'olivier aux grandes palmeraies', in *La Méditerranée et le monde méditerranéen à l'époque de Philippe II*, 8th ed., vol. I. (Paris, Armand Colin, 1987), p. 212. There is also a second and more recent olive-line, not part of the subject of this essay, running through Argentina, South Africa, and Australia.

2. See *El cultivo del olivo*, ed. by R. Fernandez Escobarand others, 6th ed. (Madrid: Mundi-Prensa, 2008) and 'Royal Horticultural Society', The Royal Horticultural Society, 2018 <www.rhs.org.uk> [accessed 15 May 2017]. On the botanical history of olive oil more generally, see three good sources: Paul Vossen, 'Olive Oil: History, Production and Characteristics of the World's Classic Oils', *HortScience*, 42.5 (August 2007), 1093-100; Sophia Rhizopoulou, 'Olea europaea L.: A Botanical Contribution to Culture', *American-Eurasian Journal of Agricultural and Environmental Science*, 2.4 (2007), 382-87; and *Ode to the Olive Tree*, ed. by The Hellenic Folklore Research Centre of the Academy of Athens, the Hellenic Ministry of Culture, and the General Secretariat for the Olympic Games (Athens: Academy of Athens Hellenic Folklore Research Centre, 2004).
3. The Food and Agriculture Organization of the United Nations (FAO) provides useful data on date-palm irrigation, including flood irrigation, pipe irrigation, sprinkler watering, and drip watering (P.J. Liebenberg and A. Zaid, 'Chapter 7: Date Palm Irrigation', *Date Palm Cultivation: FAO Plant Production and Protection Paper 156*, ed. by A. Zaid (Rome: Food and Agricultural Organization of the United Nations, 2002) <http://www.fao.org/docrep/006/Y4360E/y4360e0b.htm#bm11.3> [accessed 15 May 2017]).
4. Tim Ingold, *Lines: A Brief History* (London: Routledge, 2007), p. 87.
5. Alice Roberts, *The Celts: Search for a Civilization* (London: Heron Books, 2015), pp. 28-31.
6. See *Les frontières alimentaires*, ed. by Massimo Montanari and Jean Robert Pitte (Paris: CNRS Éditions, 2009), especially pp. 13-19.
7. See Philippe Leveau: 'L'olivier et l'oléiculture dans l'histoire et le patrimoine paysager de la Tunisie', in *L'olivier en Méditerranée: entre histoire et patrimoine*. Manouba: Laboratoire Régions et ressources patrimoniales de Tunisie, 2011, vol. II, pp. 409-431.
8. Braudel, p. 215.
9. In an earlier paper I referred to the indignation of northern French authors attributing the alleged laziness of Corsican peasants to the fact that their favourite staple, the chestnut, simply falls out of the trees for them to eat (David C. Sutton: 'Nefs: Ships of the Table and the Origins of Etiquette', in *Material Culture: Proceedings of the Oxford Symposium on Food and Cookery 2013*, ed. by Mark McWilliams (Totnes: Prospect Books, 2014), pp. 304-13.
10. Braudel, p. 216.
11. Braudel, p. 217. Revulsion to butter had become rare, in the south as well as the north of Europe, by the end of the eighteenth century (Jean-Louis Flandrin, 'Et le beurre … conquit la France', *L'Histoire*, 85 (January 1986), 108-11).
12. Norman Douglas, *South Wind* (Harmondsworth: Penguin, 1935), p. 69.
13. *The Epic of Gilgamesh*, Tablet VI, Academy of Ancient Texts, June 2001 <www.ancienttexts.org> [accessed 15 May 2017].
14. Paul Lunde, 'A History of Dates', *Saudi Aramco World*, 29.2 (March/April 1978), 20-23.
15. Cathy K. Kaufman, *Cooking in Ancient Civilizations* (Westport: Greenwood Press, 2006), pp. 31-34.
16. Nawal Nasrallah, *Dates: A Global History* (London: Reaktion Books, 2011), p. 84.
17. M. K. V. Carr, *Advances in Irrigation Agronomy: Fruit Crops* (Cambridge: Cambridge University Press, 2014), pp. 123-24.
18. *Histoire de l'alimentation*, ed. by Jean-Louis Flandrin and Massimo Montanari (Paris: Fayard, 1996), p. 89. See also Roger Dion, *Histoire de la vigne et du vin en France, des origins au XIXe siècle* (Paris: CNRS Éditions, 2010), especially pp. 77-94.
19. Edward Lear reported eating 'broiled and boiled salmon trout' in the Macedonian plains in September 1848 (*Journals of a Landscape Painter in Albania etc*. (London: Richard Bentley, 1851), p. 44).
20. See *Skopje: Capital of Seven Gates* (Skopje: Gradot Skopje, 2008).
21. See Madeleine Ferrières, 'Une frontière de l'huile d'olive: le midi français, 1500-1800' in *Les frontièrs alimentaires*, pp. 201-22, and other essays in the same volume.
22. See essays in *Food Tourism and Regional Development: Networks, Products and Trajectories*, ed. by C. Michael Hall and Stefan Gössling (London: Routledge, 2016).

Turkish Tea for Liberty: Changing the Landscape of a Region and Drinkscape of a Nation through Political Choice

Aylin Öney Tan

This paper will delve into the history of tea in Turkey to explore how the country switched from a coffee-drinking nation to a tea-obsessed one. The landscape of the eastern coast of the Black Sea was transformed by tea cultivation within just a few decades. The most striking aspect of this dramatic change was that it stemmed solely from a political decision to introduce tea as an alternative to coffee: coffee was imported, but tea could be grown in Turkey. The switch was seen as part of becoming a self-sufficient country; the only way to confront imperialism was to grow your own food and drink.

Starting from the early days of the Republic after 1923, Turkey quickly became a tea growing country and now ranks among the top five producers in the world – and the foremost in per capita consumption. The country's tea comes from the narrow strip of hilly territory along the Black Sea coast, and the entire annual yield is locally consumed. Today, tea and Turkey can hardly be considered separately. Even daily eating patterns are affected by the tea addiction: one could argue that the Turkish breakfast phenomenon was developed along with the tea drinking habit. Turkey also developed its own particular tea paraphernalia, the foremost items being the iconic tulip-shaped glass nestled on a saucer, and the stacked brewing kettle-teapot combo. The tea initiative of the early republican years surely succeeded beyond the wildest expectations: a nation's drinkscape was totally altered to the point where the iconic tulip-shaped tea glass seems almost as instantly reminiscent of Turkishness as the national flag.

Early Encounters with Tea Cultivation
In the mid-1920s, the plant that was supposed to offer a miracle rescue looked completely useless: a shrub with green leaves and no fruit. Even the leaves seemed inedible; one could neither use them in wrapped dishes nor pan-fry them with onions. The locals were not convinced. In the mountainous Black Sea region, covered with thick forests, there was an old saying that 'whatever the bear eats is good – we should eat the same' – and the bears did not even seem to notice this strange plant. When the new crop was introduced to the people of Rize, a town at the eastern end of Turkey's Black

Sea coast, nobody was willing to plant tea, as even the bears would not eat it!

This is the story of how tea cultivation began in Turkey almost a century ago. It did not start smoothly, but the people living on the steep hills of the Black Sea coast had little choice. After the 1917 Bolshevik revolution in Russia, the region was heavily affected by an economic crisis caused by the loss of business and trade across the border. The Ottoman Empire had crumbled, and the young Turkish Republic was founded in a land completely dilapidated by the Turkish War of Independence from 1919 to 1922. At the turn of the century, most of the region's men had been itinerant workers far from home, or had businesses in Russia, leaving the women, the elderly, and the children behind to tend the small patches of gardens they owned, cultivating mainly corn as the only sustenance crop. The land did not offer many other choices: wheat and other cereals could not be grown due to the lack of flat land and the unfavourable climate, with too much rainfall and too little sunshine. In the damp, steep hills by the Black Sea, only corn, hazelnuts, collards, brassica varieties, and green beans could be grown. The region desperately needed to find a staple crop, preferably one that could help them survive when food was scarce, but people were sceptical of the newly introduced plant, since one could not eat tea if it did not sell.

This general picture of the early days of tea cultivation in Rize emerges from the memoirs of Asım Zihnioğlu, one of the pioneers of tea cultivation.[1] Zihnioğlu served as the director of the tea factory in Rize from 1949 to 1954; he was sent to India and Sri Lanka for extensive visits to tea plantations and to England for training as a tea expert. Despite the many concerns and obstacles, tea would soon rescue the people on the Black Sea coast and come to be synonymous with the town of Rize.

Ottoman Coffee versus Republican Tea

In the nineteenth century, the Ottoman Empire led the world in coffee consumption. Coffee was the national beverage and played a pivotal role in daily routines; Turkish coffee had – and still has – cultural significance in society. On the contrary, tea had no such place and was not even available to a great portion of the population; where available, tea drinking did not have the same ritualistic aspect as coffee. By the end of nineteenth century, both coffee and tea had to be imported; while coffee was no longer grown within the shrinking boundaries of the Ottoman territory, tea cultivation was limited to small patches of experimental plantations. Yet tea drinking was spreading, in part because a glass of tea was almost four times cheaper than a cup of coffee. War also brought great coffee shortages, leading people to invent coffee substitutes by roasting and powdering chickpeas, wild pistachios, cardoons, and the like.

Turks first learned of tea through China, and hence named both the plant and the hot beverage *çay* (pronounced *chai*) after Chinese *chá* (茶). In the twelfth century, Ahmed Yesevi, a distinguished Sufi master, mentioned tasting it for the first time and praised its restorative qualities.[2] Exhausted from travelling in the scorching heat, he took rest in a farmer's house in Turkestan; upon drinking the tea offered to him, he sweated and found relief from his fatigue, and he advised everyone to drink this healing beverage. Turkic tribes in Asia are known to have consumed tea as far back as the sixth century, during the Tang Dynasty in China. Despite the early encounter of Turks with tea, in Ottoman times its earliest mention appears in the seventeenth century in the *Book of Travels* by the great Ottoman traveller Evliya Çelebi. He mentions it twice. First, he tells of the tea trade in Istanbul in 1631, mentioning the health benefits of tea and noting that the servants at the Customs Office serve visiting officials tea in addition to *salep* and Yemeni coffee.[3] Second, he mentions it as part of the lavish feast he was served in Bitlis: when he was hosted with his patron Melek Ahmed Pasha by the Kurdish Khan, he was served tea along with other beverages like spiced Yemenite coffee, *salep*, *mahaleb*, fennel, rice-water, sweet sherbet, hot flour-water, and milk in jewelled cups.[4] He notes that he tasted the stuff for the first time: tea remained a novelty even though coffee had already become a part of daily routine in Ottoman territory after its first arrival in Istanbul in the mid-1500s.

During Ottoman times recordings of tea remain scarce. There are a total of three tea treatises in the Ottoman period, the earliest written by Şeyhülislam Damadzade Ebu'l-Hayr Ahmed Efendi in 1711.[5] Few other sources mention tea: there is an apothecary notebook dated 1774, and a few customs accounts in 1816. In the early nineteenth century, tea becomes more recognized, but its distribution in the empire is still quite uneven. In 1838, Helmuth von Moltke gave Russian tea and sugar to his host in return for the guard dog (probably the infamous Kangal of Sivas) given to him as a gift in Alacahan, south of Sivas. He notes that they had tasted tea for the first time and liked it.[6] Around the same time, Julia Pardoe writes that she was served tea in both Istanbul and Bursa; the first in the Russian fashion by two negro servants in the military college, the latter in the Greek Archbishop's place, supposedly in the English style, but sweet, weak, and without milk, indicating that tea was not really a part of their own culture but rather something seen as favoured by foreigners.[7] By contrast, Pardoe mentions coffee served at almost all occasions wherever she goes. These sources indicate that tea was seen as a new foreign culture, and tea service as part of western etiquette, and thus it was considered polite to serve tea to foreign visitors and missions. By the second half of nineteenth century, tea was becoming more widely known and consumed in certain regions of the empire. Teahouses began popping up here and there, and tea was imported by individual traders on a small scale. Historian Soraya Faroqhi thinks that tea first became known in places that were in contact with Iranians and Azeris. Even today, cities that used to have trade relations with Iran and Russia have strong tea drinking traditions. Meanwhile, after the 1838 Balta Limanı Treaty between the Ottoman Empire and Great Britain dropped import taxes, more foreign goods started to enter the Turkish market, including tea.

The first attempts at tea cultivation started in the 1870s, following the Sultan's decree on tea production in Trabzon. Attempts made with seeds from Japan proved unsuccessful in Bursa in 1878. The same year, the governor of Adana, Mehmet İzzet, wrote a treatise on tea, *Çay Risalesi*, highlighting the health benefits of tea. In 1894, Sultan Abdul Hamid II received a report from his agricultural minister, Selim Pasha, suggesting the importance of tea growing in Ottoman lands, which led to further attempts in tea cultivation despite the failure in Bursa.

By the end of the 1870s, some individual farmers also tried to grow tea around Artvin, the easternmost town on the Black Sea coast. According to historian Kemalettin Kuzucu, tea growing proved to be successful and profitable in the villages of Hopa and Arhavi, so much so that the Ottoman authorities tried to tax tea grown there as forest. After hearing complaints about this practice, the Trabzon governor, Yusuf Ziya Pasha, persuaded the Sultan to promote tea cultivation instead of taxing it, and the forest tax was lifted in 1879.

The first official attempt to bring tea to Rize was made in 1912 by Hulusi Bey (Karadeniz), Head of Chamber of Agriculture.[8] Observing the similarities in climate between Batumi and Rize, he brought tea seeds from Batumi (then under Russian siege) and successfully planted them in his experimental garden. However, with the outbreak of World War I and the Russian occupation of Rize, he had to leave, only to return in 1919 to continue his experiments with tea growing. After the founding of the Turkish Republic in 1923, he promoted growing tea in Rize to Ali Rıza Erten, a tutor at the Halkalı Agriculture School (Halkalı Ziraat Mektebi), where the efforts were expanded.

Late Ottoman attempts to cultivate tea were soon embraced by the young Turkish Republic that arose from the ashes of empire. Both the country and the region were heavily disrupted by the collapse of the Ottoman Empire and the consequences of World War I, a situation worsened by the most unfortunate inheritance of '*Düyun-u Umumiye*', the Public Debt Administration, from the last decades of the Ottoman Empire. In order to rejoin the world economy, the Republic of Turkey had to pay foreign creditors the debts of the Ottoman dynasty for several decades, despite the country's war-ravaged economy, after the founding of the republic in 1923. In attempting to revive the shattered economy, the first Izmir Economic Congress (*İzmir İktisat Kongresi*) held in 1923 was a turning point for Turkish agriculture. It decided to focus on local produce in an attempt to make the country totally self-sustaining.

Following the congress, Law No. 407 (1924) called for the cultivation of tea, citrus fruits, and hazelnuts (filberts) in the Black Sea province of Rize. With steep hills and high precipitation levels, the region was not suitable for the cultivation of staple crops like wheat, but attempts to grow tea on a larger scale began in 1937, again using seeds from Batumi. The first yield was a mere 30 kilos; persuading locals to grow an alien crop that seemed uselessly inedible required strenuous efforts, mostly by dedicated bureaucrats like Zihni Derin, the first director of 'Garden-culture Stations', and Asım Zihnioğlu, the first director of Rize Tea Plantations unit.

In 1935, Prime Minister İsmet İnönü visited Rize and was briefed on the tea growing attempts; back in the capital, Ankara, he formed a technical team from the Faculty of Agriculture to support tea cultivation. Campaigns were carried out under leadership of a schoolteacher, Yusuf Ziya Kotil, to convince locals to grow tea instead of corn. With increasing cultivation by 1940, a new Tea Law regulated cultivation and production, and all tea lots were now required to get a license. Eventually, as the yield of tea grew each year, a tea factory was designed with the help of two British experts. The first tea factory was established in 1947 by the state. Between then and 1950, in just three years, tea consumption in Turkey tripled.

The success of tea production coincided with a period of economic crisis after World War II. Because Turkey could not afford to import coffee, tea drinking surged. By the 1950s and 1960s, tea became the foremost product of the Black Sea region and was widely consumed by the Turkish citizenry. There was no turning back. Tea cultivation became so successful that it has become a symbol of identity. Some towns were even renamed inspired by tea: Mapavri became Çayeli and Kadahor became Çaykara.

In 1971, Çaykur, the Directorate of Tea Enterprises, was founded to coordinate and expand tea cultivation and processing, and it maintained monopoly control until 1984, when tea processing was opened to private enterprise. This marked the end of state control of tea production, allowing private companies to produce tea. A new era in the history of tea in Turkey was about to commence.

Years	Produce, tons	Import, tons	Consumption	Export, tons	Cons/capita g
1938	0.030				
1939	0.081				
1940	0.191				
1945	54		625		35
1950	208	1,744	1,744		85
1955	1,196	2,450	3,574		150
1960	5,815	3,919	7,754		280
1965	14,391		12,206	4,100	390
1970	33,431		18,114	7,864	520
1975	56,463		46,098	24	1,100
1980	95,889		85,550	6,500	1,900
1983	100,782		95,936		2,100
1984	132,561		110,623		2,400

Table 1. Turkish tea production, consumption, import, and export during monopoly years.

Changing Drinkscape: A Tea-coholic Nation

It is amazing that the country has now become so synonymous with tea: a swift offer of tea to a complete stranger is a usual act of hospitality, and ironically the *kahvehane* (coffeehouse, usually just called *kahve*), now predominantly serves tea. Tea is now an essential part of daily life in Turkey. The first thing to do in the morning is to brew tea for breakfast, where several glasses are consumed.

Turkey has developed its own genre of particular tea paraphernalia, the foremost items being the iconic tulip-shaped glass nestled on a saucer, and the *demlik/çaydanlık*, the stacked brewing kettle-teapot combo. This locally developed tea equipment is essential to a Turkish kitchen. Originally the Russian samovar was also much-loved, especially in leisurely tea gardens, but in homes the basic essential utensil used is the *demlik/çaydanlık*. (Lately, electric versions have also become common.)

Brewing tea strong, and diluting it by half in the glass with hot water, is a typical way to serve tea, often with two cubes of sugar, and less common with slivers of lemon. Milk is never added to tea. The tulip-shaped glass displays the bright scarlet colour of the tea, strangely and lovingly called *tavşankanı*, rabbit's blood; the wide brim diffuses the aromas easily to the nose; and the curvy form is good for handling and cupping with the hand to feel the tea's warmth. This curvy form led one particular voluptuously round glass to be nicknamed after the pop singer Ajda. In the early years of the Republic, tea sets with cups and saucers were popular at Western-style tea parties, but Turks never really liked the cups, and always preferred the glasses for tea. The tea glass is also sometimes used to drink rakı, the anise-infused grape-based distilled spirit that is the national drink, and interestingly the tulip glass is now being internationally promoted as the ideal glass for savouring whisky.

Tea gardens, often called *Aile Çay Bahçesi* (family tea gardens), have become vital parts of every cityscape in the country, and spending long hours there playing backgammon, gossiping, and watching children run around is now an essential pastime.[9] Another phenomenon is women's gatherings at homes, in a neighbourhood or a friend's circle, with each woman taking her turn inviting others to her home for tea drinking, eating, and of course gossiping. Tea has become a way of communication everywhere: in shopping, in business, and especially in the bureaucracy, no discussion starts without initial small talk over a glass of tea. People often joke that in government offices the only hard-working employee is the tea-man. Offering tea is the first act of hospitality in most cases. Experiencing this hospitality and sense of sharing deeply affected influential American chef Alice Waters when she was in Turkey: in 'Tea & Cheese in Turkey', she says that her experience there influenced her decision to become a chef.[10] Tea can be served anywhere, even on the ferries. The accessibility of tea has made it democratic, something that belongs to the masses. It dissolves class distinctions: the ubiquitous *çay & simit*, tea with *simit*, the bread rings studded with sesame seeds and perhaps a wedge of cheese, is a poor man's feast and a much-loved breakfast on the go for all. Tea is humble in comparison to the sophistication of coffee. In today's Turkey the two drinks co-exist, both having their unique places in daily life, both loved and cherished, but tea became so wildly popular due to its very approachable democratic standing. Everyone can have tea, anywhere, anytime. In addition to helping the country feel free from relying on other nations, it has enormously empowered the people. It allows the people to express themselves, and one might even say that tea liberated the nation. In short, anyone who visits Turkey is obliged to take a sip from the tea offered in the trademark tulip-shaped glass. There is no escape!

Controversies beyond Two Leaves and a Bud

Tea in Turkey seems like a true success story. But of course, real life is complicated, and there has been a series of mistakes and deliberate or unconscious wrong turns in the country's tea policy. From picking to base-price application to excessive use (and wrong choice) of chemical fertilizers – not to mention environmentally threatening disasters like Chernobyl – the tea story that had been an epic of rags to riches has shifted back to rags.

Under the command of corrupt politicians, the early idealistic bureaucrats were replaced by more obedient ones, and governmental parties, hoping for votes, ignored the ever-declining quality of tea. The bad practices started with the picking. Ideally, only the top two tender leaves and a bud must be picked. At the initial peak years of tea production, this was successfully implemented with the close watch of scrutinizing directors of *Çaykur*, but political pressure led to new cutting equipment that, instead of picking two leaves and a bud, lopped off two or even more whole branches with many tough leaves in one go. With the new harvest scissors, picking only the finest top leaves was practically impossible. Most of the crop purchased by the state monopoly was useless, despite being paid for by public money, and the bad-quality crop usually ended up being burnt.

The Chernobyl disaster raised many questions about whether the tea was safe to drink. Swept by the wind, clouds laden with radioactivity hit the Black Sea Mountains, resulting in radioactive rain falling all over the tea shrubs. Although many people still remember certain ministers drinking tea in front of television cameras to prove that it was perfectly safe to drink, cancer cases in the region increased after the disaster.

Approximately 210,000 families are sustained by tea cultivation. However, the early ideals of being self-sufficient and anti-imperialist are long forgotten; Turkey is now confronted with the recent possible privatization of *Çaykur* tea monopoly that has been the most successful in creating a self-sustaining model. In 2012, Turkey's Privatization Board declared that *Çaykur* would not be included in the privatization scheme. In 2013, over 10,000 *Çaykur* workers went on strike, but *Çaykur* was still the country's largest tea buyer. It bought 653 tons of tea the year before the strike, more than half of the country's total production. It continued to act as a market regulator despite the growth in the number of private tea firms. In 2017, *Çaykur* is said to be transferred to Turkey's Sovereign Wealth Fund / TVF *Türkiye Varlık Fonu*; rumours hold that the directorate is to be sold to Qatar, but parliamentary questions submitted by the leading opposition party still remain unanswered, and the case has not yet been made public.

Recently, in December 2016, another controversy was sparked over removing a statue of Turkey's founder, Mustafa Kemal Atatürk, at a major public square in Rize and replacing it with a tea glass-shaped statue instead. The opposition blamed the Mayor from the ruling pro-Islamist party with trying to erase the legacy of Atatürk from the town. Atatürk, as the leader who founded the secular state separate from religion, is not much favoured by the ruling AKP. The city has a considerable ability to change, as it has shown by adapting to tea. Today, many in Rize seem to have forgotten that their vital signature crop was envisaged by the independence policy of Atatürk. Nevertheless, symbolized in a modern statue of a tea glass, the city still takes pride in its tea.[11]

Notes

1. Asım Zihnioğlu, *Bir Yeşilin Peşinde* (Ankara: Tübitak, 1998), pp. 7-23.
2. Fuad Köprülü, *Türk Edebiyatında İlk Mutasavvıflar* (Ankara: Diyanet İşleri Yayınları, 1976), p. 45.
3. Evliya Çelebi, *Evliya Çelebi Seyahatnamesi*, ed. by O. Ş. Gökyay, (Istanbul: YKY, 1996), pp. 240, 263.
4. Robert Dankoff, 'The Relevant Section of the Seyahatname Edited with Translation, Commentary and Introduction', in *Evliya Çelebi in Bitlis* (Leiden: Brill, 1990), part 1, p. 119.
5. Kemalettin Kuzucu, 'Tea as a New Flavour in the Ottoman Culinary Culture', in *Turkish Cuisine*, ed. by Özge Samancı and Arif Bilgin (Ankara: Ministry of Culture, 2008), pp. 243-59.
6. Helmuth Graf von Moltke, *Moltke'nin Türkiye Mektupları* (*Unter dem Halbmond*), trans. by H. Örs (Istanbul: Remzi Kitabevi, 1969), pp. 149-50.
7. Julia Pardoe, *The City of the Sultan and Domestic Manners of the Turks in 1836* (London: Henry Colburn, 1838), vol. 2, pp. 196, 274.
8. In the Ottoman Empire people did not have surnames, but were addressed with titles, so Hulusi Karadeniz appears as Hulusi Bey in former documents; later in the Republic period after the acceptance of surname law in 1934, he was given the surname Karadeniz (meaning Black Sea) for his efforts for the development of the Black Sea region.
9. Sharon Wohl, 'The Turkish Tea Garden: Exploring a "Third Space" with Cultural Resonances', *Space and Culture*, 20.1 (2017), 56-69.
10. Alice Waters, 'Tea and Cheese in Turkey', in *The Kindness of Strangers*, ed. by Don George (Melbourne: Lonely Planet, 2003).
11. Choosing the tea glass as an alternative symbol to replace that of Atatürk reflects Rize's history of supporting the ruling party. In a recent referendum, the city voted for AKP, the governing Party, with 76% in favour despite rumours of privatizing the tea enterprises and other controversial decisions, including plans for environmentally questionable hydroelectric power plants.

Brandenburg-Prussia's Cultivated Natural Food Landscape

Molly Taylor-Poleskey

Friedrich Wilhelm of Brandenburg-Prussia (r. 1640-1688) became Prince Elector in the midst of the Thirty Years War and during the lowest moment in the history of the Hohenzollern family. However, by the time of his death in 1688 he had laid the foundation of the family's rise on the European political and cultural stage.[1] Much of this change in fortunes was due to the cultural program orchestrated by Friedrich Wilhelm and his servants to rebuild the depopulated city of Berlin and territory of Brandenburg. The young Friedrich Wilhelm and his Dutch wife, Luise Henriette (1627-1667), defined and expressed their cultural values through their food, and their choices had long-term effects on the landscape of Berlin and its surrounding countryside.

Although the war officially ended in 1648, it took years for Berlin to recover and take its new form. Luise Henriette only saw Berlin for the first time in 1652. Already, though, Friedrich Wilhelm had hired a Dutch landscape architect, Johann Gregor Memhardt (1607-1678), to devise a plan for reshaping the royal holdings in Berlin to suit the stature he wished to attain. The palace garden and the hunting park (*Tiergarten*) had fallen into decay over the course of the war. Both were key pieces in building an image of strength, dependability, and Teutonic noble heritage. The produce of these two spaces in Berlin ended up on the court table where they continued the sensuous expression of Friedrich Wilhelm's ideals. This paper explores these two sites where, paradoxically, intentional alterations to the Berlin landscape were touted as bringing forth the 'natural produce' of the realm. This concept of the constructedness of nature is nothing new to environmental historians, who since the 1970s have elucidated the ways that humans have created the idea of nature and therefore deprived nature of its autonomy.[2] Two seemingly opposite but, in reality, connected values of wildness and cultivation dictated the food culture in the Brandenburg-Prussian court.

The *Tiergarten*, as the site of the hunt, is a particularly potent case of the mythology of 'natural' food. The *Tiergarten* underwent an image makeover under Friedrich Wilhelm. In the early years of his reign, the park had to be reclaimed from Berliners who had squatted on the land and cultivated farms there when the fences fell down while the ruling family was absent during the Thirty Years War.[3] Friedrich Wilhelm bought back the *Tiergarten* land piecemeal, and it likely was not forested early in his reign, since an alternative name at this time was *Schöneberger Wiesen*, or 'Schöneberg meadows'.⁴ Friedrich Wilhelm fenced in the area again to keep the 'wild' (the German word for game) animals from snacking at the surrounding private farms. The term *Garten* originally referred specifically to a fenced in area or to a fence itself, which underscores the constructedness of the space (Figure 1).⁵

Man-made changes to the landscape did not always guarantee a desired effect. Johann Christoph Bekmann, in his extensive chronicle of Brandenburg, noted an episode in the Oranienburg *Tiergarten* when fallow deer escaped through a damaged fence. They reproduced better than in their enclosure – a discovery which led to the rest of the deer being let free, even into lands that had been leased to others.⁶ This episode certainly would not have endeared the ruling family to the neighboring farmers!

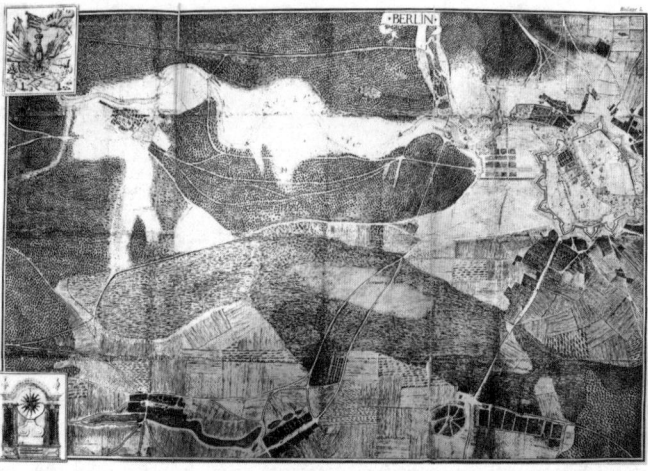

Figure 1. La Vigne plan of Berlin from 1685 showing the road connecting the electoral palace to the Tiergarten *(Wilhelm Gundlach,* Die Geschichte der Stadt Charlottenburg *(Berlin, 1905), Wikimedia.commons).*

Hunting parks were, of course, a standard feature of European palace complexes since the Middle Ages. But they carried particular meaning in German royal households because they referenced the savage heritage of the barbarian conquerors in Italy, who subsequently became the elite of Europe. The forest represented the wildness of Germania in juxtaposition to the civilization of Rome and Italy.⁷ After the invasion of the Barbarians, this was no longer seen as necessarily a bad thing: the forest and hunting became associated with masculinity and power. Central Europe and particularly Prussia were the last parts of Europe deforested in the Middle Ages, which meant that eventually the forest became a strong symbol of Teutonic identity. Forest animals such as wild boars that had been forced from their habitats in other parts of Europe migrated to the last vestiges of virgin forests in Poland and Prussia, which explains how the last known wild cows, the aurochsen, ended up there. These animals were often used in heraldic motifs for German noble families.⁸ The *Tiergarten* became a miniature forest in the centre of the city that connected the ruling family to their more wild domains in Prussia, where they ruled as fiefs to the King of Poland from 1618 and as sovereign rulers after 1657.

As Massimo Montanari points out, though, this vision of the wilderness was not actually any more natural than the presumed culture of the Mediterranean.⁹ Rather, it

Brandenburg-Prussia's Cultivated Natural Food Landscape

was another, equal part of the European food culture. This is abundantly clear in the administration of the Berliner *Tiergarten* and the great efforts that went into reshaping it in the seventeenth century. For one thing, the game animals had to be purchased and brought to the *Tiergarten*.[10] Bekmann notes that Elector Friedrich Wilhelm had fallow deer brought from abroad for the hunting parks of Berlin, Potsdam, and Oranienburg. On 4 April 1657, shortly after the fence was completed, the head hunting master, Jobst Bernhard von Hertefeld, reported to the elector that ducks and three different kinds of deer had been established in the *Tiergarten* and that a ton of oats had been left for them.[11] The delivery of feed for the game was not a singular occurrence to establish the new population: a later record from 1673 indicates a delivery of two tons of oats for the game.[12] At times, the game animals even shared this space with recognizably domesticated animals: in 1661, there were seventy cattle and horses grazing in the *Tiergarten*.[13]

This space was an urban escape for the Hohenzollern where they participated in their favourite pastime of hunting. It was close enough to the palace on Cölln that Friedrich Wilhelm could work a full morning at the palace and hunt in the afternoon. In 1647, the elector called for the first linden tree to be planted along the thoroughfare to shade him as he moved between the two spaces. Urban development grew up to fill in the area around this thoroughfare instead of continuing eastward as it had been previously. Thus, the electoral palace moved from the periphery of the city to the centre.[14] The demarcation of the *Tiergarten*, the importation of animals both native and exotic, and the delivery of harvested agriculture to sustain those animals left a permanent impression on the landscape of Berlin (Figure 2).

The hunting and forest custodians (*Jagd- und Forstmeistern*) employed by the court were not just charged with monitoring the flora and fauna of these parks, but also for ensuring that the palace's head cook had the meats necessary for the court's meals. From the few surviving menus (*Küchenzetteln*) from Friedrich Wilhelm's reign, we know that midday and evening meals had about twenty-six dishes and centred around a number of roasted meats brought in mainly from the elector's own hunting grounds. Friedrich Wilhelm suffered from gout later in his life, which also suggests a strong personal taste for meat. The *Küchenzetteln* include other meat dishes as well, with a variety of sauces, such as boiled chicken with endives, roasted

Figure 2. Johann Stridbeck, watercolor of the prospect from the Tiergarten *towards the palace (*Die Stadt Berlin im Jahre 1690 *used by permission of Staatsbibliothek zu Berlin).*

apples with removed egg yolks, beef with turnips, boiled chicken in butter with lemons, kale with bacon-cooked mutton with egg yolks and cow blood, and brown mutton roast with wine and limes.[15] This is just a sampling of the types of dishes usually listed first in the *Küchenzetteln* (indicating a loose order to the dishes). Already though, this list gives us an idea not just of how the non-roasted meats were prepared, but also of the mixture of local and imported ingredients. The fruits and vegetables might even have been more local than the meats because there was a kitchen garden in the lavish pleasure garden Friedrich Wilhelm had built on the palace island of Cölln.

Like the *Tiergarten*, the palace gardens were an embodiment of the elector's ideals. And, even more than in the case of the *Tiergarten*, the elector concentrated money, time, and effort in transforming the landscape of the island of Cölln to support his showpiece garden. Renaissance and Baroque gardens were metaphors for the order of nature and the perceived natural hierarchies that justified hereditary systems of rule. These gardens contained a paradoxical 'collaboration of art and nature'.[16] Embodying this paradox, the emblematic feature of early modern palace gardens was strict geometry, both in the arrangement of the flower beds and the linear axes that implied symmetry. The most famous example, of course, is the radial Baroque masterpiece in Versailles, where the Sun King could view his kingdom from his bedroom down the long garden axes. The ability to replicate the natural world in miniature emphasized the garden creator's divinely privileged status. Palace gardens, such as the type in Berlin in the seventeenth century, were 'testaments of power and prestige' (Figure 3).[17]

The abundance of edible produce from these gardens likewise sent a

Figure 3. Frontispiece of a popular Brandenburg gardening manual depicting Friedrich Wilhelm and Electress Dorothea as Apollo and Luna (with the Prussian eagle) ascendant over the landscape of Berlin-Cölln (Johann Sigismund Elsholtz, Vom Garten-Baw: Oder Unterricht von der Gärtnerey auff das Clima der Chur-Marck Brandenburg/ wie auch der benachbarten Teutschen Länder gerichtet/ und in VI. Bücher abgefasset. Der dritte Druck: Welcher so wol an Figuren/ als am Text/ abermahl vermehret und verbessert worden *(Berlin: Autor, 1684), p. [7] used by permission of Staatsbibliothek zu Berlin).*

message of the ruler's paternalistic ability to provide for his court and metaphorically for the wider care of his people. Renovating the garden was particularly tied to Friedrich Wilhelm's reign; it was an expression of his generation's yearning for stability and recovery following the destruction Brandenburg had suffered in the previous war-torn decades.[18] Laying down roots in such a public fashion was one of the marks of the 'struggle for stability' that characterized Europe in the wake of the brutal wars of religion.[19]

Re-establishing and expanding the gardens after the war mobilized a tremendous amount of labour and specialized knowledge. The island of Cölln was not a naturally fertile sliver of land; extensive and constant efforts made it so. Luise Henriette and Friedrich Wilhelm grew up in the Netherlands of the Dutch Golden Age, and it is not surprising that they hired a Dutch-trained designer for their showpiece garden. Johann Gregor Memhardt drew up a complex plan for the run-down plot that included fountains, floating gardens, and bridges. This 'fanciful' plan utilized the latest in Dutch hydraulic engineering and underscored the elector's commitment to innovation as well as stability.[20] Both were emblems of power in early modern political culture (Figure 4).

The kitchen garden grew at the northernmost point of the palace island in a wheel form with eight beds between the spokes and one at the hub. This part of the garden was not the most important – that was Friedrich Wilhelm's beloved tulip bed right in front of the palace. Nevertheless, the kitchen garden was prominent at the pinnacle of the island. Boats travelling upriver on the Spree or pedestrians on the opposite shore would have seen this point of the palace compound first.[21] The court physician and botanist Johann Sigismund Elsholtz (1623-1688) described the gardens in detail in his 1657 *Hortus Berolinensis* and intimated that Memhardt's intention with this design was that the kitchen garden would bring forth a variety of excellent produce every day (Figure 5).[22]

Again, although the underlying principle was to display a microcosm of the natural world in the elector's domain, the production of that green space involved manipulation of the existing landscape. The region of Brandenburg has sandy soil, and much of the topsoil had to be brought from elsewhere. Buffalo from the *Tiergarten* were paraded around the island to fertilize the soil with their dung.[23] Elsholtz, too, described this process in a tone of instruction for other Brandenburgers

Figure 4. Johann Stridback drawing of the palace pleasure garden in Berlin. Stridback (Die Stadt Berlin im Jahre 1690 used by permission of Staatsbibliothek zu Berlin).

to follow the example of the elector and increase the amount of food grown in the desolate region.[24] Elsholtz reported the process by which the *Lustgarten* became fruitful in Berlin:

> In order to reap the harvest of a garden, healthy air or harmless weather are not enough if the earth is not naturally blessed with fertility. If this be the case, the skill of the gardener must be applied to overcome this helpless situation. Additionally, in such a garden, if many different breeds of plants will be planted, it might be impossible to find every plant the appropriate spot in the same earth, in this case, instead, a considerable change is necessary. This is what was done in our garden, where, even though we are on a low-lying and northern-facing site that is very damp and wet, and in other places naturally dry and sandy. Now, fertile soil has been mixed with dung brought from elsewhere by the cartload and spread over the infertile sand with such tremendous success, that the flower sprouts, which before were so wispy and thin, now sprout with full flesh and strength.[25]

Besides the changes to the soil itself, keeping many of these plants alive through the cold, grey Brandenburg winters meant building greenhouses with ovens to mimic the plants' native climates. As Elsholtz rightly emphasizes, such efforts were necessary to accommodate the many non-native plants being brought to Cölln.

Every attempt was made to make this an encyclopedic garden where every plant known to Europeans could be found.[26] Elsholtz's own catalogue of the garden from 1656 indicates this goal with circa 1350 plants. Around 15% of those were recognizably edible, including many foreign plants.[27] In 1656, another letter announces which foreign trees will be brought from gardens at the fort city of Cüstrin for Berlin. This letter is signed by Elsholtz; the head gardener, Michel Hanff; and Georg Heinrich Boltzmann, the court apothecary and mayor of Cüstrin. These three figures likely confirmed what the different plants were, and their signatures suggest the coordination among different officers of the court who shared an interest in the gardens. These plants included twenty-four bitter orange trees, three lemon trees, five pomegranate trees, jasmine, yucca, and 'eight crates of rare clove blossoms with 50 shrubs', among other plants.[28]

Although not all of the palace's fruit and vegetables came from the island of Cölln (there was another kitchen garden by this time in Schöneberg), much of the produce from the *Lustgarten* ended up on the court's tables. After noting all of the effort that went into maintaining a fruit and vegetable garden on a sandy island, it is somewhat surprising to see that members of court use the term '*in natura*' to describe the source of much of their food. This expression, and the related word *Naturalien*, are peppered throughout the archival records of the kitchens of Friedrich Wilhelm's court. Court servants might have some or all of their salaries paid *in natura*. In 1683 Friedrich Wilhelm instructed the bursar, Michel Matthias, to account for all of the salary payments in cash, allowance in kind, and *in natura*.[29] Later that month, he also wrote to the chamber of the electoral domains (*Amtscammer*) ordering better accounting for goods *in natura* that were paid

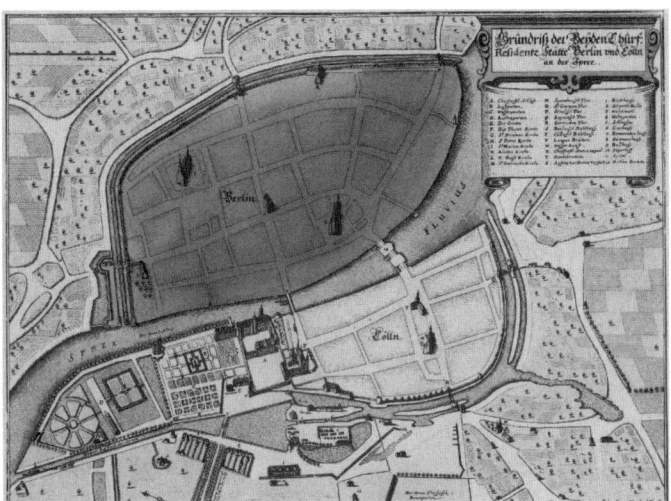

Figure 5. Johann Gregor Memhardt plan of Berlin and Cölln with the palace kitchen garden visible in the circle at the tip of the palace garden (Grundriss der beyden Churf. Residentz Stätte Berlin und Cölln an der Spree ([1650]; repr. [Berlin]: Verein f. d. Geschichte Berlin, [1888]) used by permission of Zentral- und Landesbibliothek Berlin).

to court servants. Some servants had received double payment because they had gotten both their cash salaries and goods *in natura*. The elector emphasized that servants were welcomed to receive their payments *in natura*, but they should get a receipt for the cash value.[30]

It becomes clear from kitchen account books, however, that this attempt at monetizing the palace garden produce was unusual. Typically what distinguished food *in natura* from other foods in the court records is that they were not tracked with as much care. While the kitchen clerk (*Küchenschreiber*) meticulously accounted for all foods purchased for the court household, foods from the elector's own properties (fisheries, gardens, and forests) were not exchanged for money and were only loosely recorded in accounts. For example, in 1652, the kitchen master in Berlin, Erdman Schmoll, drew up a detailed budget for a half a year down to the last pfennig. He listed the estimated quantities for eighty-five items with unit prices and sums. After this detailed table, Schmoll added vaguely that 'the need for all kinds of plant foods shall be filled from the gardens'. There are other foods on the list that Schmoll claimed were too unpredictable to estimate. These might also be considered the 'natural' foods like fish, which he says would be coming in from the leased fisheries and accounted for as they arrived. For the seven different types of fish he foresaw cooking, he estimated a lump sum of 135 thalers. The same is true with livestock and game, for which he did not estimate any expense.[31]

The expressions *in natura* and *Naturalien*, though, refer to foods that were anything but natural. One early modern definition for *in natura* is 'everything that is provided in its raw state by nature, as long as it is not changed overmuch artificially. One calls the grains, the wool, etc, the *Naturalien*, or the natural products of a particular place'.[32] This definition signals an appreciation for native plants as well a division from things affected by human interference. Another definition emphasizes the supernatural aspect of the natural: 'We Christians understand nature as everything made by God at the creation, including giving the Earth powers to bring forth everything at the right time that is necessary for the sustenance of all mankind and all other living creatures.'³³ This definition emphasizes that nature serves mankind. Both of these definitions overlook the many ways that foods found *in natura* were manipulated to suit human needs and desires.

Nature is extremely marketable in modern food culture. The myth of natural food, however, is nothing new. Furthermore, the idea that traditional food was natural is also not accurate. Even in the early modern period, people modified their environments to get the food that they needed and desired – albeit not on an industrial scale. The court cuisine of seventeenth-century Berlin modified the local landscape so there were bountiful gardens in sandy soil, forests where farms had been, foreign animals that adapted to Berlin and in turn made their impressions felt there, and non-native plants that survived thanks to the labour and experiments of gardeners and botanists. Some changes from Friedrich Wilhelm's reign, such as the Unter den Linden boulevard with a park at the end, are still prominent in the landscape of Berlin. Others, like the city palace and its gardens, are long gone and any attempt to recreate them reflects twenty-first century values more than seventeenth-century ones. The political culture of Friedrich Wilhelm's court encompassed and connected concepts of rule, environment, and taste.

Notes

1. See for example Heinrich Gerd, *Ein Sonderbares Licht in Teutschland: Beiträge zur Geschichte des Grossen Kürfursten von Brandenburg (1640-1688)* (Berlin: Duncker & Humblot, 1990) and Christopher Clark, *Iron Kingdom: The Rise and Downfall of Prussia, 1600-1947* (London: Allen Lane, 2006).
2. See for example Richard White, 'American Environmental History: The Development of a New Historical Field', *Pacific Historical Review*, 54 (1985), 297-335.
3. Folkwin Wendland, *Der Große Tiergarten in Berlin: Seine Geschichte und Entwicklung in fünf Jahrhunderten* (Berlin: Gebr. Mann Verlag, 1993), p. 19.
4. Wendland, p. 19. Anyone visiting current-day Berlin can see this same phenomenon of the 'renaturalization' of some parts of the city that have been abandoned, become overgrown, and then reimagined as wild natural spaces.
5. Johann Georg Krünitz, 'Garten', *Oekonomischen Encyklopädie Oder Allgemeines System Der Staats- Stadt- Haus- Und Landwirthschaft* (1773) <http://kruenitz1.uni-trier.de/> [accessed 23 February 2018].
6. Johann Christoph Bekmann, *Historische Beschreibung der Chur und Mark Brandenburg 1* (Berlin: Voß, 1751), vol. 1, p. 779 <https://digital.ub.uni-potsdam.de/content/zoom/70309> [accessed 23 February 2018].
7. Massimo Montanari, *Food Is Culture* (New York: Columbia University Press, 2006).
8. I have seen many examples of the boar in heraldic shields, but the aurochsen seems less common.
9. Massimo Montanari, *The Culture of Food* (Oxford: Blackwell Publishers, 1994).
10. Wendland and Anton Balthasar König, *Versuch einer Historischen Schilderung der Hauptveränderungen, der Religion, Sitten, Gewohnheiten, Künste, Wissenschaften [et]c. der Residenzstadt Berlin seit den ältesten Zeiten, bis zum Jahre 1786; Enthält die Regierungsgeschichte Churfürst Friedrich Wilhelms des Großen von 1640 bis 1688* (Berlin: Wilhelm Dehmigke dem jüngern, 1793), p. 87 <http://opacplus.bsb-muenchen.de/search?oclcno=643896277> [accessed 23 February 2018].
11. Bekmann, p. 779.
12. Geheimes Staatsarchiv Preußischer Kulturbesitz (GStA PK) I. HA Rep. 36 40, p. 23.
13. Felix Escher, *Berlin und sein Umland: zur Genese der Berliner Stadtlandschaft bis zum Beginn des 20. Jahrhunderts* (Berlin: Colloquium, 1985), p. 59.

14. *Palace. City. Berlin. The Residence Shifts to the Center (1650-1800)*, ed. by Paul Spies, Dominik Bartmann, and Peter Schwirkmann (Berlin: Holy Verlag, 2016).
15. Midday menu for 2 January 1652 at the electoral residence in Kleve (Hessische Staatsarchiv Marburg Bezeichnung 117 Nr. 2170).
16. Luke Morgan, 'Design', in *A Cultural History of Gardens in the Renaissance*, ed. by Elizabeth Hyde (London: Bloomsbury 2013), vol. 3, p. 26.
17. Andrew Cunningham, 'The Culture of Gardens', in *Cultures of Natural History*, ed. by Nicholas Jardine, James A. Secord, and E.C. Spary (New York: Cambridge University Press, 1996), p. 39.
18. This point about the island of Cölln being a showpiece of the values of each generation of rulers is borne out by the actions of his grandson, King Friedrich Wilhelm I (r. 1713-1740), the so-called Soldier King, who tore up the Baroque masterpiece garden for a military parade ground.
19. Theodore Rabb, *The Struggle for Stability in Early Modern Europe* (New York: Oxford University Press, 1975).
20. The court botanist described Memhardt's plan as being '*einfallsreiche*', which might also be translated as imaginative, inventive, or resourceful; Johann Sigismund Elsholtz, *Hortus Berolinensis: = Der Berliner Lustgarten: lateinisch/deutsch: liber primus: erstes Buch*, trans. by Thomas Fischbacher and Thomas Fink (Weimar: Verlag und Datenbank für Geisteswissenschaften, 2010), p. 81.
21. It is not clear when or how high the walls were around this part of the island.
22. Stridback.
23. Paul Seidel, '*Der Lustgarten am Schlosse in Berlin bis zu seiner Auflösung im Jahre 1715*', FBPG 3 (1890), 94.
24. Elsholtz's *Hortus Berolinensis* was not published until 2010, but he published similar pieces of advice for a Brandenburg audience in his other popular works. This type of paternal care from the ruler also fit with Friedrich Wilhelm's mercantile efforts to increase production and self-sufficiency in Brandenburg (*Palace. City. Berlin.*).
25. Elsholtz, *Hortus Berolinensis*, p. 83.
26. Elsholtz first gained his employment under the elector by advertising his services to catalog and publicize the diversity of plants of Friedrich Wilhelm's palace garden (Letter of J.S. Elsholtz to Friedrich Wilhelm, 1656, GStA PK I. HA Rep. 36 2879, p. 49). The plant catalog from 1657 is available in manuscript: Staatsbibliothek zu Berlin Ms. boruss.qu 12.
27. See Molly Taylor-Poleskey, 'When the Tomato was Purely Ornamental: Considering New World Foods in Seventeenth-Century Berlin', in *From the 'New World' to Europe. Transfers Since the Sixteenth Century*, ed. by Martina Kaller and Frank Jacob (forthcoming).
28. GStA PK I. HA Rep. 36 2879.
29. Letter of Friedrich Wilhelm to Michel Mattias, 6 April 1683 (GStA PK I. HA Rep. 36 50, p. 164).
30. Letter of Friedrich Wilhelm to the Amtscammer in Berlin, 30 April 1683 (GStA PK I. HA Rep. 36 50, p. 196).
31. Erdman Schmoll to the Berlin Amtskammer, 22 July 1652 ('*An allerleÿ Gartten gewächs, kömbt die Noturfft, aus den Gärtten*', GStA PK I. HA Rep. 36 1066, p. [104]).
32. Johann Christoph Adelung, 'Naturalien', in *Grammatisch-kritisches Wörterbuch der Hochdetuschen Mundart mit beständiger Vergleichung der übrigen Mundarten, besonders aber der oberdeutshen* (Leipzig, 1793–1801), vol. 3, p. 443.
33. Paul Jacob Marperger, 'Natur/Natura', in *Paul Jacob Marpergers... Vollständiges Küch- und Keller-Dictionarium: In welchem allerhand Speisen und Geträncke, Bekannte und unbekannte, gesunde und ungesunde, einheimische und ausländische, wohlfeile und kostbare, nothwendige und entbehrliche... Beschrieben, Ihr rechter Einkauffs- u. Erziehlungs-Ort, Zeit und Preiß... Gewiesen; Ferner allerhand nützliche Haushaltungs- Gesundheits- Lebens- und Policey-Regeln, mit Moralischen Anmerckungen gegeben...* (Hamburg: Verlag Benjamin Schillers seel. Wittwe, 1716), p. 820-22 <http://nbn-resolving.de/urn:nbn:de:bvb:12-bsb10228972-9> [accessed 23 February 2018].

Minnesota's Hardy Plums: The Story of a Fruit and Its Ties to Rural and Urban Landscapes

Emily S. Tepe

There are some areas of the United States that are renowned for growing fruit trees. Georgia is famous for its peaches. Washington and New York pride themselves on being top apple producers. In California, just about every fruit tree is right at home. Even Michigan is known for its cherries. And then there's Minnesota, a state in the Upper Midwest on the border of Canada. The famously frigid winters make Minnesota about the last place one would expect to find fruit trees, which is the reality settlers faced when they began arriving in the mid-1800s. The determination of a handful of fruit growers who vowed to change this fate helped establish the University of Minnesota fruit breeding programme in 1878. Since then, the programme has developed over a hundred hardy fruit varieties, including apples, grapes, plums, cherries, apricots, pears, and berries. In this state where early settlers lamented the lack of fresh fruit, commercial orchards are now abundant, and home gardens are dotted with lovingly tended fruit trees.

In recent years, the University of Minnesota fruit breeding programme has focused on apples and grapes, yet the programme's early work on plums effectively changed the food landscape for people in northern regions. For almost 140 years, these plum varieties have played an important role in the story of cold-climate fruit production: from early settlers seeking food to survive to today's consumers seeking a return to locally produced food.

A Picture of Minnesota's Climate

Minnesota's continental climate means cold winters, hot summers, and variable precipitation. During the winter, it is common to see as many as fifty days below -17°C accompanied by harsh, drying winds that accelerate across the open plains. The state averages 140cm of annual snowfall; however snow cover varies dramatically from year to year. Historically, it has snowed in every month of the year except July. Spring consists of drastic temperature fluctuations and inconsistent moisture. Frost is common across the state well into May, and in some areas until mid-July. This equates to an unpredictable start to a short growing season that averages from 90 to 160 days. The hot summers commonly bring temperatures above 35°C accompanied by damaging storms with high winds and hail. On average, over half of the annual precipitation occurs between May and September (MN DNR 2017).

Each season presents its own challenges for farmers and gardeners, but it is primarily the severe cold that limits the success of perennial plants like fruit trees. When settlers encountered their first few Minnesota winters, they wondered about the practicality of choosing this harsh landscape for their homes.

Driven to Grow Fruit Trees

Around 1850, settlers from the eastern United States and Europe began arriving in Minnesota with hopes of striking gold through agriculture. Even more made the trek with the passing of the Federal Homestead Act in 1862, which gave 160 acres of land to any adult citizen, under the condition that the land be improved with dwellings and crops. Between 1862 and 1880, over 62,000 homesteads were established on 7.3 million acres in Minnesota. Settlers were drawn to the state by the rich prairie land that promised ample harvests of wheat, oats, and corn (Granger and Kelly 2005). The land was flat, the soil fertile, and the water plentiful. These crops grew vigorously, and rewarded farmers for their willingness to endure the harsh environment of the northern plains. Ample wheat harvests did not, however, mean that life was easy. Food was extremely limited, and fresh fruits and vegetables were scarce. Settlers were encouraged to establish gardens and orchards, thus many planted seedlings of their favourite fruit varieties from back east only to be disappointed when, after a few typical Minnesota winters, the trees died. Threat of malnutrition and scurvy was accompanied by heartfelt disappointment: 'A majority of our citizens have lived in the Eastern States, and been accustomed to an unstinted supply of apples, peaches, pears, plums, cherries, etc. To be deprived of them and to have no hope of ever seeing or using them more, takes all the poetry out of their lives' (MN State Hort Soc 1873: 87).

At the time, the apple was prized as the symbol of a fruit-growing state. The dispiriting proclamation from *New York Tribune* founder and editor Horace Greeley, 'I would not live in Minnesota […] you cannot raise apples there', gave weight to the general sentiment that it was 'useless to attempt to raise fruit in such a cold country' (MN State Hort Soc 1873: 87). As immigrants and settlers sought out land to call their own, many were hesitant to consider Minnesota because of this very fact.

However, some new Minnesotans were driven to change this fate. Amateur horticulturists set forth to determine which fruits might survive, hoping that their beloved apple would stake its own claim on Minnesota soil. But as much as they longed for the apples of the East Coast, it would be some time before the apple would become Minnesota's prize fruit. Rather, it would be the plum that cemented the possibility of cultivating tree fruits in Minnesota.

A Plum from the Prairie

Scattered amid the forest openings of the Minnesota prairie grows a humble, shrubby tree – the American plum (*Prunus americana*). Native Americans made good use of this tree, eating its fruits fresh, preserved, and dried (Hamel and Chiltoskey 1975). The bark was used for medicines, dyes, and disinfectants. Branches were employed as domestic tools, and even the seeds were used as game pieces (Gilmore 1913, 1991).

This abundant tree was greatly valued by early settlers as a source of nutrition. Fresh plums could be preserved for a few weeks by storing in cold well water. According to reports of the time, the water also served to 'remove all harshness from the skin and pit' (Goff 1897: 39). For longer preservation, settlers followed recipes that remain virtually unchanged today:

> Plum butter, jam or marmalade – Boil the fruit in clear water until nearly done. Remove from the stove and put through a colander to remove the pits. Then rub through a sieve to make the pulp fine. Place pulp in kettle with about half as much sugar as pulp – or if you wish to have it very rich add nearly as much sugar as pulp – and boil down to the desired thickness. Stir almost constantly to prevent sticking to the kettle. (Goff 1898: 449)

Helpful, though sometimes questionable, tips were shared by those who deemed themselves experts on the preservation of these fruits: 'The earlier in the morning and the clearer the day, the better will be your jelly. A cloudy day makes dark jelly, and if not made early in the day the juice requires boiling so much longer that the jelly is dark, and sometimes it is almost impossible to get it to jelly' (Goff 1898: 449).

Prunus americana, one of several native North American plum species, is the most prominent one in Minnesota. The trees are tolerant of extreme cold with dormant flower buds surviving temperatures as low as -30°C (Dorsey and Strausbaugh 1923). This moderately sized tree has variable growth habits, ranging from multi-stemmed shrubs to single stemmed trees reaching 4m to 7m. The species suckers readily, sending up new growth as far as 3m from the tree, which in time forms dense, shrubby thickets. The branches have short, lateral twigs that resemble thorns (Fryer 2010).

Flowers bloom in mid-April, when freezing temperatures are still likely. Each year it is possible that the flowers could be killed by freezing, in which case no fruit would be produced. Bees are the primary pollinators, and during spring's typically cool, wet, windy conditions bee activity can be minimal. In a good year, if the flowers manage to escape freezing, and the weather is warm and dry enough to promote bee activity, then the trees produce a heavy crop.

The fruit of *Prunus americana* are highly variable from tree to tree. The skin may be thin and tender, or more commonly thick, tough, and astringent. The flesh is only marginally sweet, and more often bitter. The small amount of flesh clings to the large pit, or stone. Ripe fruit readily drops from the tree, which promotes the spread of diseases as the fruit rots and releases fungal spores that can overwinter in the soil. Dropped fruit also encourages the proliferation of insect pests and weedy growth of seedling trees: all things that would not be desired in an orchard. As a naturally occurring source of fruit *Prunus americana* served a purpose, but it was far from the quality that settlers were used to and not well suited to a managed orchard.

Minnesota's Hardy Plums

The Promise of Better Fruit

In 1866, after a small display of homegrown fruit was presented at the fledgling Minnesota State Fair, a group of two dozen horticulture enthusiasts established the Minnesota Fruit Growers Association. Until that time, growers had been toiling alone experimenting with fruit varieties from the east coast, and quietly hypothesizing about failures. Now a concerted effort was made toward improving the outlook for fruit production in the region. This group established a governing council, and drafted a constitution, the first article of which read: 'The object of the Association shall be to encourage fruit culture in the State of Minnesota: to collect and disseminate correct information in relation thereto, and to promote friendly reunions and community interest, and a spirit of generous emulation among the amateur and professional fruit growers of the State' (MN State Hort Soc 1873: 22). Incidentally, the Fruit Growers Association would later become the Minnesota State Horticultural Society, which is still active today and has close to 15,000 members.

Early meetings of the Fruit Growers Association consisted of much lamenting: 'Here [...] we have to encounter at the outset the strongest doubts whether fruit, or apples at least, which constitute the great essential of a fruit country, can be raised at all; or, at the best, can be produced in sufficient quantity to justify our claim to be a fruit growing State' (MN State Hort Society 1873: 25).

However, it was not long before discussions turned more practical and members recognized that their efforts might be better spent exploring opportunities with fruits that were native to the region. And so, the Association's second meeting in 1867 resolved:

> That while we would by no means discourage experiments for the introduction and cultivation of all varieties of domestic fruit, we would earnestly urge upon all fruit growers in the state, the importance of further efforts for the careful testing and improvement of the fruits indigenous to our soil, especially plums, cranberries, raspberries, and blackberries. (MN State Hort Society 1873: 35)

Through the effort of this group, an approach to developing fruits for Minnesota was established. By 1868, members were identifying wild *Prunus americana* trees with desirable traits including larger and redder fruits with tender skin, sweet flesh, and a smaller stone. Awards were distributed annually for the best selections, and this spurred so much interest that just about anyone who discovered a tree of moderate quality was quick to name it. Thus, at the 1901 Minnesota State Fair, 910 displays of plums were submitted, representing over 100 named varieties of debatable quality (Latham 1901). Society leaders determined that a more controlled effort led by professionals was needed to refine the varieties.

Collaboration was key during this period, and growers from Minnesota, Wisconsin, Iowa, and South Dakota shared notes and planted each other's varieties to determine their suitability to areas throughout the Upper Midwest. Three in particular, the De Soto from Wisconsin and the Wolf and Wyant from Iowa, were recognized as reliable in quality and hardiness. De Soto was noted for its large purple-red fruit, despite its large clinging stone and tendency to overbear; Wolf was valued mainly for its free stone and attractive tree form; and Wyant was known for its productivity of large, semi-clingstone fruit, though the flavour was somewhat astringent. These became the most popular varieties grown in the region during the late nineteenth and early twentieth centuries (Goff 1897).

Enthusiasm for these plums hit a speed bump in the early 1900s as transportation methods improved and greater shipments of California plums began appearing at markets in the region. Consumers were delighted by the large, sweet, juicy fruit, and interest in local plums diminished. Local growers resolved that Minnesota's plums could only compete if higher quality species could be incorporated into breeding efforts.

A State-Supported Fruit Breeding Programme Is Born

The Minnesota State Horticultural Society lobbied the state for funds to support a fruit breeding programme, and in 1878 the legislature established an experimental fruit farm. This farm was administered by the University of Minnesota, and marked the official beginning of cold hardy fruit breeding in the region. Later, a larger property was acquired and officially became the State Fruit Breeding Farm. This same property is currently the Horticultural Research Center, where fruit breeding efforts continue to this day.

Early in its existence, fruit breeders continued selecting and hybridizing native plums until a major boost to the programme arrived in the early 1900s by way of California. Famed botanist Luther Burbank had acquired seedlings of an Asian plum species, *Prunus salicina*, commonly called the Japanese plum. Burbank hybridized seedlings of this species and released 113 varieties (Karp 2013). The University acquired several of these varieties and in 1908 began hybridizing Japanese plums with the native varieties. Most of the work was done in a greenhouse, because the tender California trees could not withstand the Minnesota climate. Breeders were thrilled to discover that their hybrid trees produced fruit that matched California quality. Large, intensely coloured, sweet, juicy fruit with small pits was borne on trees that had the cold hardiness of the native species. The excitement was such that the programme introduced several named varieties from the very first cross made in 1908 (Alderman 1926).

The first varieties were released in 1920 with names like Mendota and Waconia honouring Minnesota's landscape and early inhabitants, the Dakota Sioux. Mendota, which is Sioux for 'meeting of the waters', and Waconia, meaning 'fountain' or 'spring', depicted the natural features of the landscape (Bright 2004). The University recognized the significance of these places and people, and by bestowing their names to these varieties made a statement that Minnesota's new fruits were deeply connected to the land.

The Process of Breeding Plums

The breeding of plums is similar to that of other plants. Two parent plants are selected in the hopes that if their genes are blended a superior plant will result. Pollen is collected from one parent's flowers and applied to the other parent's flowers. These flowers are tagged and isolated so no other pollen is introduced. This process is repeated on many flowers of the tree, so breeders have a large quantity of resulting seeds. This is especially important with plums, as each fruit contains only one seed. In late summer, the ripe fruit is harvested. The seeds are removed and stored until the following spring when they are planted in the nursery. Each tree grown from those seeds will have unique characteristics, and may not necessarily resemble either parent. It is this genetic variation that allows for the wide range of colours, flavours, and sizes of plums, along with differing levels of tree vigour and cold hardiness.

During the first few years of growth, some percentage of seedling trees are eliminated due to lack of hardiness, disease, or poor growth. Beginning in the third year, the remaining trees reach maturity and begin bearing fruit. Out of thousands of seeds that are planted, only a handful of trees make the cut to be propagated and grown on for further evaluation.

A plum tree is propagated by grafting in order to maintain the exact combination of genes that gave it successful characteristics. Cuttings of one-year-old twigs, called scions, are taken from the tree and grafted onto a rootstock (the lower portion of a tree containing the roots). Rootstocks themselves are bred for certain qualities they can bring to the resulting grafted tree: cold hardiness, pest resistance, drought tolerance, and even dwarfing. Once propagated, the trees are further tested to ensure their quality. If the trees propagated from a particular seedling perform well over multiple seasons and reliably produce high quality fruit, the variety is named and released for sale. From seed to a named variety can take up to twenty-five years.

Plums Have Their Day

After the initial excitement of the new hybrid plums, the University fruit breeders continued their work to improve upon their first successes. A testing system was established in which promising seedlings were propagated and distributed to growers throughout the state. Trees were also grown at University agricultural experiment stations for evaluation under different conditions. Cooperators reported annually on the success of the trees and the quality of the fruit. These reports were compiled, and final determinations were made about which trees merited naming.

From 1920 through 1949, the University released 21 plum varieties, including 18 that combined the Japanese and American species. Colours, flavours, and textures of these varieties were delightfully diverse. La Crescent's small, delicate, golden fruits contrasted sharply with the deep crimson, meaty fruit of Redglow. Nicollet had tender skin which yielded easily to the bite, while the thick, tough skin of Pipestone and Radisson held the tender flesh captive until, with a sudden burst, it split and sent forth a spray of sweet juice. Breeders had undoubtedly achieved their goals of larger fruit with exceptional flavour that could easily compete with the plums from California.

To promote the new hybrid plums, local nurseries dubbed them as "mammoth" and "jumbo" in their catalogues, while tantalizing descriptions undoubtedly sent people running to purchase trees: 'Monitor Plum – The large and beautifully formed upright spreading tree is a delight to the eye and the luscious, richly colored fruits offer an irresistible temptation to the palate' (Alderman 1926: 14).

The new hybrid plums were popular with commercial and home growers. Production grew significantly across the region, increasing 300% between 1909 and 1939. Ten years later, the agriculture census of 1949 reported over 167,000 plum trees were being grown throughout the state on 25,530 farms (NASS 2017). Commercial and home growers were encouraged to plant a diverse mix of plums and other newly developed hardy fruits to provide an assortment of fruit throughout the season and to reduce the potential of failure from disease, insect damage, or early spring frosts. Some farms had several acres of fruit, while some homesteads had just a few plants. The result was a rather pastoral picture of a rural landscape dotted with plum trees and other fruits, providing fresh food for communities across the northern plains.

The University published bulletins that provided detailed instruction to fruit growers across Minnesota and the Upper Midwest. These publications were encouraging and practical, offering advice on site selection, planting, pruning, pest management, and winter protection. The persistent challenge was the early bloom of plum blossoms, something breeders had not been able to solve even with the new hybrids. Each spring, commercial growers held their breaths in hopes that the blossoms would survive the fluctuating temperatures, but after a few too many crops were lost to frozen flowers, growers started to lose faith in plums. Despite the outstanding fruit quality, this inherent lack of reliability was discouraging. Coupled with the facts that the tender fruit did not stand up to shipping and that the tree lifespan was quite short, it became clear that plums would never be a major commercial crop. Production peaked in 1940, when 78,000 bushels were harvested. By the end of the 1960s, that number had dropped to 1300 (NASS 2017).

Even home production dropped off significantly during this time. The University continued to encourage homeowners to include fruit trees in their landscapes, but interest waned as ever-improving transportation saw more fruit coming in from around the United States and overseas. Fresh plums were readily available without the effort of managing trees and suffering the disappointment of crops lost to poor weather. Homeowners planted lawns, flowers, and shade trees to enhance their landscapes, and left fruit to the professionals, however distant they may have been.

Between the 1950s and early 1980s no one in Minnesota was talking much about growing plums. A brief survey of selected Minnesota Horticultural Society publications during this time shows very few mentions of this fruit. However, a few trees remained on some farmsteads and in the gardens of enthusiasts, and a small research block of trees was maintained by the University. In 1985, interest was briefly reinvigorated by the unexpected introduction of a new variety, Alderman, named for one of the programme's most influential leaders. This variety resulted from a cross that had been made many years before known only as MN416. A few trees had been growing in the yard of a University employee but hadn't gotten much attention until the early 1980s when it was suddenly noted that the trees were quite handsome, and each year produced exceptional fruit with deep burgundy skin and sweet, golden flesh. The introduction renewed interest among plum enthusiasts, but the reach was limited and short-lived.

The Future of Minnesota's Plums

From the early days when growers were satisfied with any tree that survived the winter to the introduction of the Honeycrisp apple which put Minnesota on the world fruit map, the University of Minnesota has been labouring to ensure people in cold climates have access to fresh, local fruit. Unfortunately, consumers lost sight of local fruit for much of the mid to late twentieth century. Grocery stores were piled high with fruit from all over the world. There was little to no recognition of where fruit came from as long as it was always available. In recent years, however, a marked change has taken place. The buy-local movement is shifting consumer focus back to its own landscape. Consumers want to know where their food comes from and how it was grown. The demand is encouraging. Farms are responding by growing more hardy fruit, and consumers are delighting in the flavours that come from their local landscape.

A handful of growers have started planting Minnesota's plums again, and they've enjoyed the shocked, ecstatic response when customers taste the fruit for the first time: 'Plums grow in Minnesota?' Plum wine is a hot seller for one local grower. 'Plums make spectacular wine if not overly sugared', says Scott Wardell of Montgomery Orchards in South Central Minnesota. He freezes and thaws the fruit twice before fermenting the juice to get the rich colour and flavour of the skin into the wine. Scott says, 'our biggest problem is we don't have enough plums to keep up with demand for our wine'.

So far, for most new Minnesota plum growers, pests and diseases aren't too much of a problem, but early bloom still is. One farm in North Central Minnesota destroyed all their plum trees a few years back because of the frustration. Some growers say they get a bumper crop every third year, while others see good harvests four out of every five years. For these few growers, the interest in Minnesota plums is growing so quickly that they plant more trees each year to meet the demand. They use email blasts and Facebook posts to inform their customers when the plums are ripe, and those lucky enough to be in the know don't waste any time claiming their share.

Plum trees are starting to appear in home landscapes again too. Urban dwellers with a little spot of sun reach out to the University and local nurseries to learn which fruit trees would be best for their location. Most come into the conversation with apples in mind, but when they find out about plums and how easy they are to manage with few pests, they're easily sold on the idea. The risk of frozen flowers doesn't alarm most home growers, because they're not relying on the fruit for income. An occasional year without a harvest isn't a big worry.

The University isn't planning to breed any new varieties, because there are several that have endured the test of time. Superior, a fiery red plum introduced in 1933, is a top pick. 'The fruit is big and sexy', says Scott Wardell. One of the very first 1920 introductions, Underwood, is considered to be one of the best flavoured. Alderman, the 1985 release that has become synonymous with the University of Minnesota breeding programme, is very popular as well. A few varieties from neighbouring states have also endured. Toka, from South Dakota, is a heavy bloomer and often planted as a pollen source since its pollen is compatible with most other varieties. A new release from Wisconsin called BlackIce™ is also becoming popular. Mount Royal is one of the only European plums that was found to be cold hardy, and is popular for its ability to produce fruit without cross pollination – a good feature in a yard where there's only room for one tree. So, the collaboration between northern states that began more than a century ago continues to this day, as plums from these states intermingle in orchards and gardens across the Upper Midwest.

The expanding interest in Minnesota's plums has led the University once again to focus on helping growers have success, especially home growers who may have no experience with fruit trees. New publications offer encouraging advice aimed at simplifying management and maximizing satisfaction. The renewed interest has also inspired new research. The University recently investigated seed germination rates of varieties to determine the potential for unwanted seedlings popping up as the result of dropped fruit (a trait held over from *Prunus americana*). Another study was conducted to determine if cuttings from trees could be grown on their own roots rather than being grafted, investigating the hypothesis that trees grown on their own roots might be even more hardy and longer lived. Results indicated that grafting is still the best method of propagation (Anderson 2016). A study on jam made from Minnesota's plums, which included sensory evaluation panels, determined several to be of exceptional quality. The results of these studies will provide commercial and home growers practical information they can use for selecting varieties and managing their trees well into the future.

There is no longer any doubt that Minnesota is a fruit growing state. Early settlers could have only dreamed of the present reality in which a vast array of tree fruits and berries grow on farms and in home gardens all across the state. And though they were virtually forgotten for decades, Minnesota's plums are now coming full circle. Finally, after almost 110 years, people are seeking out these delicious plums and enjoying the rich, sweet flavour of fruit grown close to home.

References

Alderman, W.H. 1926. *New Fruits Produced at the University of Minnesota Fruit Breeding Farm* (St. Paul: Agricultural Experiment Station, University of Minnesota).

Anderson, N.O., and others. 2016. "Cutting Type and Time of Year Affect Rooting Ability of Hardy Minnesota Prunus Species", *Journal of the American Pomological Society*, 70: 114-23.

Bright, William. 2004. *Native American Placenames of the United States* (Norman: University of Oklahoma Press).

Dorsey, M.J., and P.D. Strausbaugh. 1923. 'Plum Investigations I: Winter Injury to Plum during

Dormancy', *Botanical Gazette*, 76: 113-43.

Fryer, Janet L. 2010. 'Prunus americana', *Fire Effects Information System* (Washington: United States Forest Service).

Gilmore, Melvin R. 1913. *Some Native Nebraska Plants with Their Uses by the Dakota* (Lincoln: Nebraska State Historical Society).

Gilmore, Melvin R. 1991. *Uses of Plants by the Indians of the Missouri River Region* (Lincoln: University of Nebraska Press).

Goff, Emmet S. 1898. 'Recipes for Use of Our Native Plums', *Annual Report of the Minnesota State Horticultural Society*, ed. by A.W. Latham (Minneapolis: Harrison and Smith).

Goff, Emmet S. 1897. *The Culture of Native Plums in the Northwest, Bulletin No. 63* (Madison: Agricultural Experiment Station, University of Wisconsin).

Granger, S., and S. Kelly. 2005. *Historic Context Study of Minnesota Farms, 1820-1960* (St. Paul: Minnesota Department of Transportation), Appendix A.

Hamel, P.B., and M.U. Chiltoskey. 1975. *Cherokee Plants and Their Uses* (Sylva: Herald Publishing).

Haralson, Charles. 1920. 'The Commercial Value of the New Plums', in *The Minnesota Horticulturist*, ed. by A.W. Latham and R.S. Mackintosh (Minneapolis: Harrison and Smith), p. 44.

Karp, David. 2015. 'Luther Burbank's Plums', *HortScience*, 50: 189-94.

Latham, A.W. (ed.). 1901. *Trees, Fruits and Flowers of Minnesota: Embracing the Transactions of the Minnesota State Horticultural Society from December 1, 1900, To December 1, 1901* (Minneapolis: Harrison and Smith).

Minnesota Department of Natural Resources. 2017. 'Climate of Minnesota', <http://www.dnr.state.mn.us/climate/index.html> [accessed 14 May 2017].

Minnesota State Horticultural Society. 1873. *History of The Minnesota Horticultural Society: From the First Meeting Held at Rochester in 1866 to the Last at St. Paul in 1873* (Saint Paul: Office of the St. Paul Press).

National Agricultural Statistics Service (NASS). 2017. 'Census of Agriculture' (United States Department of Agriculture) <https://www.agcensus.usda.gov/> [accessed 23 May 2017].

Reading the English Countryside: A Thousand Years of English Agriculture Etched on the Surface of the Land

Malcolm Thick

Introduction
This paper will examine, albeit briefly, some of the ways in which food production over many centuries has shaped the landscape of England. I will use examples from Oxfordshire wherever possible, which may enable Symposiasts to visit the areas I mention. Landscape is the result of a two-way, 'chicken and egg' process because, although undoubtedly men and women fashioned the landscape, their activities were shaped by the underlying rocks, the soils, the rivers and streams, as well as climate, altitude, and aspect. For the most part, people have changed, and continue to change, the landscape while producing food. In the words of the distinguished agricultural historian Joan Thirsk, 'Through the centuries, every corner of the landscape has been altered many times over, and layer upon layer is hidden from sight by modern developments. Yet innumerable traces remain of the past, if only we train ourselves to see it.'[1]

Argument
As my examples are mostly from the nineteenth century or earlier, I am using a map of Oxfordshire as it was in 1916, before more recent boundary changes. Oxfordshire then was a long, thin county, slanted northwest to southeast (Figure 1). The county had two areas of relatively high ground: the Cotswolds in the northwest and the Chilterns in the southeast. Both are composed of calcareous rocks, limestone in the Cotswolds and chalk in the Chilterns. Covered with a relatively thin, free-draining, and alkaline soil, these areas are in contrast to the swathe of lower land between them covered in a mixture of soils: clays of various degrees of stiffness; lighter loams – mixtures of sand and clay; as well as alluvial soils and gravel near to the rivers. In the words of the natural historian Robert Plot in 1676, these lowlands had soils 'being in some places black, or reddish earth; in others a clay or chalky ground, some mixt of earth and sand, clay and sand, gravel and clay etc'.[2]

People suited their settlement patterns and agriculture to the landscape of Oxfordshire. In the lowlands, between about a thousand or more years ago until two or three centuries ago, one would be likely to find arable farming carried on in many small strips of land scattered amongst big open fields, with farmers living next to their neighbours in nucleated villages beside the fields. Those in the hills, in contrast, were

Figure 1. Topography of Oxfordshire, 1916.

more likely to live on isolated farms or in a loose collection of houses. Many of these latter farmers had carved out their holdings from woodlands, in the form of small, irregular shaped fields, often with strips of the original woods in between as hedges. They grew crops in their fields but were as likely to keep sheep or cattle in them, allowing their pigs to root in the woods and making many other uses of the woods in their economy. I will, using local examples, elaborate on these settlement patterns and show how some traces of early landscapes remain as living fossils from the past. We will attempt to peel back more recent layers of farming landscape to get to earlier ones. The first thing to observe about the present rural landscape around us is there is nothing left which can be termed a natural landscape – everywhere has been shaped by agriculture. Even the sward of open downland has been nibbled by grazing animals – keeping it short and chopping off any shoots of trees or bushes. So, the land has all been shaped by man or man's beasts.[3]

The most obvious feature of English rural landscapes today is fields – areas of land separated by fences, walls, or hedges – mostly hedges around Oxford. In the nearby Cotswolds field boundaries are often dry stone walls, composed of blocks of limestone, originally picked up from the land where they lay exposed and dragged to the side of the field. Making these walls, by fitting different shapes of stone together without mortar, is a skilled occupation. If you had ridden out into the countryside from Oxford two centuries ago, travelling say east or north, you would have noticed areas of the countryside devoid of hedges. Suppose you rode east over Magdalen Bridge, then took the right hand of three roads on offer, the Iffley Road. After a few strides, you would be in the country, but you would not see a hedge, either by the side of the road or for some distance to right and left of you, until, after a mile, you came to the turning for Iffley. Similarly, if you took the left-hand road from St Clements towards Headington – once at the top of Headington Hill you would find an area devoid of hedges. If you left Oxford northwards from St Giles along either the Woodstock or Banbury Roads you would see no hedges for some time. This absence of hedges is because you would be passing through arable areas known as open fields. Their openness is emphasized on a large-scale map of Oxfordshire of 1797, which shows open fields as sizeable voids – blank areas of the map which emphasize the lack of field boundaries. Such voids occur frequently on the map; one example is the area around Bampton, a village in West Oxfordshire (Figure 2).[4]

Open fields were vast areas of cultivated land made up of furlongs, patches of land subdivided into narrow strips with drainage gutters between them which from the air looked rather like a patchwork quilt made of pieces of corduroy.⁵ This type of agriculture was practised in many areas of southern England until the nineteenth century. Typically, a village would have two or three of these enormous fields next to it. Farmers in the village would own or rent strips of land scattered in some or all of the fields. Usually there was also waste or common land where animals could graze and wood, hay, berries, etc. could be gathered. Sometimes wet meadow by a stream was also split up into sections so individuals could mow their respective patches for fodder. What was grown in the fields was usually decided communally – a two field system might have a two-fold rotation with grain crops sown one year followed by beans in year two, a three field system might also include a fallow year when no crops were grown in one field to rest the ground but at certain times animals were allowed to graze on any weeds growing there. Similarly after the harvest, all eligible animals could graze on the stubble in an open field. This is a simplified version of what was often a complicated system, regulated by the Lord of the Manor (the major landowner), his steward, and a manorial court with a jury made up of villagers. The court decided disputes or changes to custom. It was capable of some flexibility: new field crops such as turnips were incorporated into open fields by agreement in the eighteenth century, and some manors allowed strips to be temporarily enclosed with hurdles and laid down to grass for several years, but the system did not give a farmer complete control of his land and this lack of control was a major argument for ending the system – by a process called enclosure.⁶

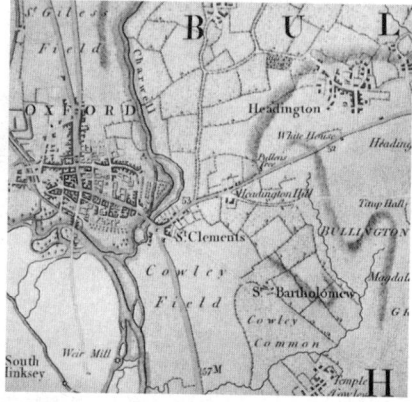

Figure 2. Open fields to the North and East of Oxford, 1797.

The characteristic narrow strips of cultivated land which made up the open fields, humpbacked with shallow ditches on each side and usually a curving into a slight S-shape along their length, were formed over many years by ploughing. The ploughman started ploughing along the outside long-edge of the strip, laying the furrow inwards. He then crossed to the other side of the strip and repeated this, gradually moving inwards towards the crown of the strip, ever laying the furrow inwards. Over time this built the land up into its characteristic shape, known as ridge and furrow.⁷

My own village of Harwell was not enclosed until very early in the nineteenth century. Prior to enclosure it had a two field system – West Field and East Field – on either side of the village, plus meadow and common land. It was, as is typical for open-field areas, a nucleated village – houses and farmyards forming a relatively tight group, with rights of way radiating out to the various parts of the fields – a sensible arrangement

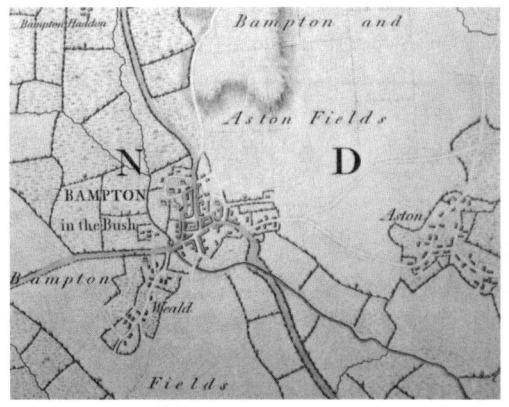

Figure 3. Bampton – a typical nucleated village with open fields to North and South.

when each farmer's strips are scattered in several directions. This layout reflects the communal nature of the agriculture. The shapes of villages in many parts of southern England today conform to this pattern, and have therefore been formed by open-field agriculture. Open fields first appeared slightly over a thousand years ago. How and why has vexed agricultural historians for many years, and there are still many theories. The motivation may have been to increase agricultural efficiency by coordinating the farming operations of every farmer in the village. Some systems seem to have been carefully planned – Mears Ashby in Northamptonshire had houses neatly sited in rows on identical plots and the farmers all had identically-sized holdings – giving weight to the theory that the scattered strips were a way of allocating land fairly.[8] In the course of many centuries, manors modified, or even abolished, open fields and common lands piecemeal. Informal agreements were made consolidating holdings by exchange of strips, and partial or total enclosure might occur by the agreement of landowners and holders of common rights, a private Act of Parliament, or by the coercive power of landlords. Many fields, however, remained open until the nineteenth century when general Acts of Parliament made the process of enclosure easier (Figure 3).[9]

Why spend time considering a landscape that has disappeared? Because it has left many nucleated villages and other traces that can still be seen, preserved by later agricultural trends. In the Midlands, some enclosure took place in the sixteenth century in areas of heavy clay soils, more suited to pasture than arable. Cattle grazing was more profitable in these areas because transport was difficult and it was easier to drive cattle to market than to cart arable crops overland. Many of the new farms created on enclosure were put down to grass immediately and were never ploughed again. The new grass fields were superimposed on the old furlongs and strips, and the characteristic pattern of ridge and furrow was fossilized and is still clearly visible today. The nearest example of this ridge and furrow topography you can see is barely half a mile from the Symposium in Headington Hill Park – visible particularly in the early morning when the sun is low and one is looking east up the slope of the hill (Figures 4, 5, and 6).[10]

Figure 4. Faint traces of ridge and furrow in Headington Hill Park, Oxford (Photo: author).

The process of enclosure involved dividing up the open fields, pasture, and common land in a way that recognized the rights all interested parties had over the land. Thus, landowners were allocated land based on the acreage they held in the common fields, its quality, and their rights over the commons. Others who had rights over the common were compensated by land when the commons were split up. The result was compact holdings that could then be divided, as the owners wished, into individual fields. New farm buildings outside the villages were built on these newly-created farms. Often country roads were diverted round the new holdings – resulting in right-angled bends and zigzagging roads. In Oxfordshire the new farmsteads are usually red brick structures, some with names that indicate their nineteenth-century origin – one near me is called Zulu Farm.

Figure 5. Ridge and furrow at Overthorpe, near Banbury, Oxfordshire (Photo: author).

Figure 6. Ridge and furrow at Overthorpe, near Banbury, Oxfordshire (Photo: author).

Enclosure could be complicated exercise. I purchased recently a notebook containing the proceedings of the enclosure commissioners for one manor and parish, that of Wellesford in Lincolnshire, in 1774. This appears to have been a relatively straightforward enclosure, but even so numerous meetings were held – a good percentage of them in the fields – supervising the staking-out of the new enclosed farms. To help the process, the commissioners tabulated: the names of landowners and their claims to lands in the open fields (measured in oxgangs – approximately six hectares or fifteen acres); the numbers of cattle, sheep, and horses they, or their tenants, were allowed to graze on common lands; and the names of their tenants. Rights to graze animals were complicated. The commissioners recorded:

> Lord Melbourne also claims a Right of Common belonging to his Hall farm for Two hundred & fifty Sheep upon a certain Walk all the Year, & one month over & upon all the fields & Commons from Lammas or Open Tide – But all the Commonable Beasts in the Parish have a Right to go & depasture upon the Sd. Sheep Walk from three in the morning 'till nine from Old may Day to Open Tide & then all the Commonable Cattle in the Parish have a Right of Common on the same Sheep Walk.[11]

The whole process started in May 1774 and was not completed until the following August. Today only one parish in England retains an open-field system, Laxton in Nottinghamshire, kept as a living museum. Comparing modern maps with the 1797 Oxfordshire map, one can see the results of enclosure on the landscape. I have superimposed modern field boundaries on one part of the open fields of Bampton and Aston as depicted on the 1797 map. This is the topography we are familiar with today (Figure 7).[12]

Some parts of England were never part of the open-field system, and sometimes they were cheek by jowl with those that were. For instance, look at the area in southwest Oxfordshire between Watlington and Chinnor in 1797 – a swath of open-fields. Notice the hachured line bordering it to the southeast: the slopes of the Chiltern Hills. Beyond this line up into the hills we have a very different topography. Here there are no open fields. Fields are small, irregular in shape, and interspersed by pieces of woodland. In the area near Stoken Church, you can see fields rounded in shape, patches of woods, and a couple of isolated farms south of the village (Figure 8).[13]

The northwest of the county shares some of these characteristics – exemplified by the parish of Leafield. Today this village straggles along a road and has several isolated farms, all set in a collection of small irregularly shaped fields, some bounded by scrubland.[14] On the 1797 map, Leafield is a circle of cultivation surrounded by woodland. What is the origin of the Leafield landscape? The clue is in the name 'Field Assarts' seen on the map. An assart is a field carved out of an area of woodland. Leafield was once part of the forest of Wychwood, the remains of which surround the village. Enterprising peasants cut down trees and made small fields, leaving bits of the woodland as field boundaries. They built farmhouses on their holdings rather than in the village. Living without firm manorial control, these inhabitants developed a sense of strong independence. In the late nineteenth century, Tory election canvassers would not set foot in Leafield; the villagers were staunch Liberals and would not tolerate opposition. Until recently the locals called their village by the Saxon name Fieldtun, rejecting the Norman translation of Leafield. The area was summed up succinctly in Volume VII of the *Agrarian History of England and Wales* thus: 'Leafield in Oxfordshire... grew up as a squatter settlement on the forest waste, with no 'persons of quality' to lord over it, and without even a church until the 1850s. Here a mixture of woodland trades, smallholding and poaching supported a community which was thought of as wild and lawless until the 1930s.' The small, irregular fields and isolated farms of the Chilterns were also for the most part originally assarts (Figure 9).[15]

Incidentally, just a couple of miles south of Leafield

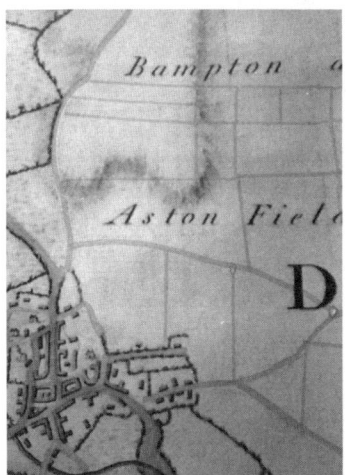

Figure 7. Modern hedges superimposed on part of map of Bampton open field of 1797.

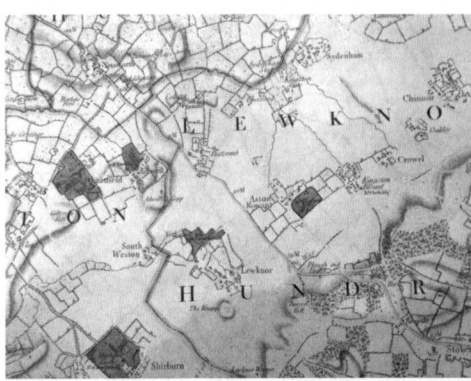 

Figure 8 (left). Contrast between low land open fields and small irregularly shaped fields in the Chilterns. Figure 9 (right) Leafield in 1797.

is an unusual rural landscape shaped by radical nineteenth-century politics, the area of Minster Lovell called Charterville. It is comprised of cottages on either side of the road, each on a smallholding. Many have been rebuilt and their land converted to gardens, but some original cottages remain. Charterville was an experimental colony created by the Chartist Feargus O'Connor in 1842. He set up the National Land Company, which bought 244 acres (99 hectares) and created Charterville. O'Connor:

> hoped to take families away from factory-living or unemployment in towns and to set them up to be self-supporting on land in the country, thereby also giving them sufficient property to enable them to vote. The Minster Lovell estate was built by national subscription... being divided before 1847 into around 80 regular plots each comprising between two and four acres of arable and a small cottage.

The experiment was unsuccessful: the smallholdings were too small, and the occupiers were not used to agriculture. Maybe the lack of a pub in the colony was an additional hindrance. But it has left us with an unusual landscape (Figure 10.)[16]

I have mentioned commons, which were part of most open-field systems. These were usually divided up as part of any general enclosure. It is a misconception to think that common land belonged to everybody (or nobody). The ultimate owner was the lord of the manor who usually received a large part of any common or enclosure. Other inhabitants made use of the common, for pasture or the right to take wood, turf, berries, nuts etc. Those who could establish such rights over the common were also allocated land in compensation upon enclosure. But many poor villagers who used commons had no legal right to do so, or could not establish a right and suffered from their disappearance. Commons still remain, but they have been steadily eroded: in Surrey, for example, in 1800 there were 96,000 acres (38,850 hectares) of commons, 43,000 (17,404 hectares) in 1873 and 26,900 (10,886 hectares) by 1958.[17]

Parishes which had streams or rivers running through them often had wet meadows as part of their communal agriculture – rich grassland bordering the streams

Figure 10. A relatively unimproved cottage at Charterville, a Chartist agricultural colony (Photo: author.)

which benefitted from spring flooding, enriching the soil and encouraging early growth of grass. These meadows were sometimes mowed several times in a season and were a valuable addition to the food available for farm animals. Like the arable fields, they were divided up amongst those eligible to share them. Individual strips were often demarcated by stone or wooden markers. One such system of meadows still exists in Oxfordshire, just north of Oxford, off the A40 at Yarnton – the Yarnton Lot Meads. As their name suggests, these long areas of grassland bordering the Thames are divided into strips allocated each year to landholders by lot – numbered holly wood balls which are annually drawn out of a bag. The survival of this communal land has left a pleasant landscape by the Thames, and, because the mead has never been ploughed or had artificial fertilizer spread upon it, it is rich in plant and insect species and of considerable interest to ecologists. The grass is mown in July, and in the autumn a common flock of sheep is put on the meadow; they are the white dots which can be seen in the background of my picture (Figure 11).[18]

One type of common was not tied to an open-field system, and many have survived to this day: commons owned by towns and originally set aside to allow citizens to graze livestock. We have a prime example here in Oxford – Port Meadow to the northwest of Oxford, accessible from Walton Street or Heyfield Road. On the map, and from my photograph, you can see it is a large, open area, over 300 acres (120 hectares) in extent, which flanks one side of Oxford. It is over a thousand years old, and the right of certain citizens to run cattle and horses on the meadow is greatly prized. Note the absence of trees or bushes. This open landscape is the result of animals grazing on it. Low-lying parts often flood in winter, and, if we have a heavy frost, Oxford has a vast ice-rink (Figures 12 and 13).[19]

Southampton Common is another example of an urban common that has survived. It is now totally surrounded by the town and forms an area of 326 acres (132 hectares) of woodland, parkland, rough grassland, ponds,

Figure 11. Yarnton Lot Mead in winter (Photo: author).

and wetlands as well as sports grounds. It was acquired by the town in the thirteenth century and enabled the citizens to pasture animals and take fuel and wild food from the Common. A cowherd was employed to keep watch over the beasts.[20] Several public parks within the built-up area of London owe their existence to the need for grazing land for people who lived in what were once villages. Clapham Common, Wimbledon Common, Barnes Common, Wandsworth Common, Chiswick Common, Old Oak Common, Streatham Common – the list goes on, all originating as landscapes formed by the need to graze animals for milk, meat, or haulage.

Unlike a town common, medieval deer parks were exclusively for deer owned by their rich owners. Very large fields, usually surrounded by fences and ditches, they provided recreation, chasing and shooting deer, and obtaining thereby a source of lean meat. Almost all such parks have disappeared in England, but one of the survivors is five minutes walk from the Symposium, Magdalen College's deer park.

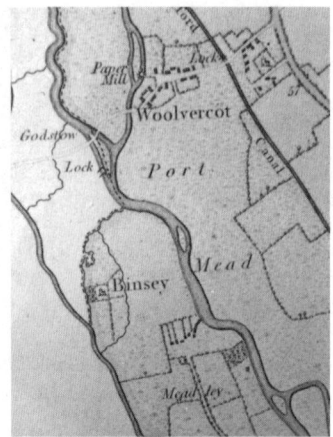

Figure 12. Port Meadow on the 1797 map.

Enclosure changed the landscape by adding many more hedges, but modern farming methods have, until curbed by recent legislation, removed many miles of them from the English countryside – thousands of miles of hedgerows were destroyed after the Second World War in Britain. In just three years, from 1990 to 1993, 33,740 miles (54320 km) were lost in England and Wales, and in the ten years to October 1996 an estimated 110,000 miles (177027 km) disappeared. This sustained removal of hedgerows has, of course, resulted in larger fields – to quote one authority: 'In pastoral Somerset and Dorset, average field size increased from 5.5 ha to 9.5 ha between 1945 and 1994, whereas in arable Cambridgeshire, where stock-proof boundaries are generally no longer required, the increase has been from 6.5 ha to 16 ha; hedgerow density in arable counties may now only be 20–30% of that in pastoral counties.' Removing hedges increases the area of a field that can be cultivated or grazed; modern machines employed on farms are more efficient in large fields – they do not have to waste time turning round (Figure 14).[21]

Finally, a ghostly outline of a garden at least eight centuries old

Figure 13. Port Meadow looking North towards Wolvecote (Photograph by author).

Figure 14. Hedge removed, leaving only the mature trees (Photo: author).

can be found in London not far from Victoria Station. The Abbots of Westminster enjoyed, until the dissolution of the monasteries in the 1530s, a country retreat at the sub-manor of Le Neat. This consisted of a manor house surrounded by about four acres (1.6 hectares) of garden, enclosed by a four-sided moat. Seed purchases for the garden in the thirteenth and fourteenth centuries indicate that cabbage, skirrets, onions, leeks, parsley, spinach, and beets were grown there, as well as hemp, flax, and herbs. This retreat was about a mile from the Abbey, accessed by a long straight road called the Willow Walk. This road is still there, now called Warwick Way. At the western end of it is a small estate of low rise flats and other buildings called The Abbot's Manor: roads there – namely Warwick Way, Winchester Street, Cumberland Street, and Sunderland Row – form three sides of a neat square. These roads follow the line of the original moat, so the vegetable garden of the Abbot's country house has imposed itself on today's street map (Figure 15).[22]

Conclusion

This is a very brief outline of some of the ways farming has shaped the English landscape over the last thousand or so years using mainly Oxfordshire examples. There are many things I have not touched upon – surviving royal forests such as the New Forest, the dramatic landscape produced by fenland drainage in the seventeenth century, the fruit trees in neat rows which until twenty years ago surrounded my home village of Harwell in Oxfordshire, nineteenth-century field drainage systems, old water meadows, and the disastrous effects of modern mechanical flails on hedgerows. But I hope I have given you a few pointers on reading the effects of agriculture on the English landscape we have today and how to peel back successive layers of agriculture to see how the past has influenced the present.

Figure 15. Author's sketch map of Abbots Manor Pimlico, London showing modern streets following outline of moat round the site of the original house and garden of the Manor of Neat.

Food and Landscape

Notes

1. *The English Rural Landscape*, ed. Joan Thirsk (Oxford: Oxford University Press, 2000), p. 9.
2. John Orr, *Agriculture in Oxfordshire* (Oxford: Oxford University Press, 1916), frontispiece map, pp. 172-74; Robert Plot, *Natural History of Oxfordshire* (Oxford, 1676), p. 52.
3. *The Victoria History of the Counties of England*, vol. 18, ed. by Simon Townley (London: Boydell, 2016), pp. 4, 42-45, 276, 284-85 (henceforth cited as *VCH*).
4. R. Davis, *A New Map of the County Of Oxfordshire from an Actual Survey* (J. Cary, 1797); Thirsk, pp.79-80.
5. There are numerous manorial surveys showing the complex plans of strips in open fields; an impressive one is the survey of Benson, Ewelme, and Berrick Salome in 1788 (*VCH*, Colour Plate 7).
6. Thirsk, pp.78-82.
7. 'Ridge and Furrow', *Wikimedia.org* <https://en.wikipedia.org/wiki/Ridge_and_furrow> [accessed 23/3/2017]. Not all strips were ridged – on light soil the strips were ploughed flat, sometimes with a narrow grass strip between them.
8. Thirsk, p. 80.
9. Berkshire Record Office, T/Pka4.
10. Thirsk, p. 82.
11. *Proceedings of the Commissioners appointed by an Act of Parliament passed in the 14th year of the reign of king George the Third for dividing & enclosing the Common & Open Fields Meadows Pastures Heath & Waste within the Manor & Parish of Werford otherwise Wellesford in the County of Lincoln* (1774-1775) (mss in the author's possession).
12. Davis; http://www.laxtonvisitorcentre.org.uk/ , accessed 23/3/2017. For a fuller discussion of enclosure see Chapters from *The Agrarian History of England And Wales*, vol.3, *Agricultural Change: Policy And Practice*, ed. by Joan Thirsk (Cambridge: Cambridge University Press, 1990), pp. 54-109. A superb book on enclosure of an Oxfordshire village is Anthony Parsons and Sandra Millikin, *Landcape Reinvented: The Uffington Enclosure Award 1778* (Uffington: Uffington Museum Trust, 2014).
13. Davis.
14. *OS Explorer*, vol. 180 (Southampton: Ordnance Survey Maps, 2015).
15. Davis; John Field, *The History of English Field Names* (London: Taylor Francis, 1993), p. 19; Chapters from *The Agrarian History of England And Wales*, vol.7, 1850-1914, ed. E.J.T. Collins (Cambridge: Cambridge University Press, 2000), part 2, p. 1305.
16. 'Former Chartist cottage and plot in Charterville Allotments', *Wikimedia Commons* <https://commons.wikimedia.org/wiki/File:Former_Chartist_cottage_and_plot_in_Charterville_Allotments_-_geograph.org.uk_-_1549901.jpg> [accessed 2 April 2017]; Christina Colvin and others, *VCH*, vol. 3: *A History of the County of Oxfordshire*, ed. by Simon Townley (London, 2006), pp192-99, *British History Online* <http://www.british-history.ac.uk/vch/oxon/vol15/> [accessed 2 April 2017].
17. Thirsk, p. 223.
18. Alison W. McDonald, 'Oxford Meads', *Floodplainmeadows.org* <http://www.floodplainmeadows.org.uk/sites/www.floodplainmeadows.org.uk/files/files/AMcD%20Flood-meadow%20history%20for%20web%20sm.pdf> [accessed 30 November 2016]; R.H. Gretton, 'Lot-Meadow Customs at Yarnton, Oxon', *The Economic Journal*, 20.17 (London: Royal Economic Society, 1910), 36-45.
19. Davis; 'Port Meadow, Oxford', *Wikimedia.org* <https://en.wikipedia.org/wiki/Port_Meadow,_Oxford> [accessed 23 March 2017].
20. 'Southampton Common', *Wikimedia.org* <https://en.wikipedia.org/wiki/Southampton_Common> [accessed 23 March 2017].
21. Robert A. Robinson and William J. Sutherland, 'Post-war Changes in Arable Farming and Biodiversity in Great Britain', *The Independent*, 26 October 1996.
22. Malcolm Thick, *The Neat House Gardens* (Totnes: Prospect Books, 1998), pp. 79-81.

Tejate, Tejateras, and the Taste of Place: A Sensory Excavation

Amy B. Trubek

Introduction

To drink *tejate* is to consume Mexican civilization. This claim seems too bold, bordering on the ridiculous. Well, perhaps, to drink *tejate* is to do a sensorial excavation, to use taste, flavour, and texture to uncover crucial eras in the history of Mexico, a reflection of constantly intersecting cultures through conquests. Excavations in the archaeological sense, however, involve material objects that in turn help explain the course of human events. So, perhaps to drink *tejate* is to taste the layers, more than one, of multiple human engagements with terrains that now exist within the borders of a nation called Mexico – borders that had no name during the early conquests of the small remote valleys lying along the foothills of the Sierra Norte mountains. The sensory strata might tell such tales, a reflection of the waves of conquest over the millennium, the result of broad historical transformations. First, the Olmecs. There is evidence of their presence in these regions by 1000 BCE (Bernal 1969). Then there were the Mixtecs, Mexicans and Aztecs. And, for the history to be recounted here, above all there were the Zapotecs, who long inhabited the region and built a grand city-centre on top of a hill (now just outside the main city, first established in 1528 as a Spanish colonial centre) over two thousand years ago. At Monte Alban, they had command over three main valleys (or Valles Centrales), the region understood as the birthplace of *tejate*.

Tejate (pronounced *te-hah-tay*) is a traditional gruel made in what is now the southern Mexican state of Oaxaca. It is similar to *atole* (pronounced *ah-tohl-lay*) – a daily dish throughout Mexico, often eaten in the mornings – but there are stark contrasts too. Both *tejate* and *atole* rely primarily on freshly ground corn masa mixed with water. Rachel Laudan identifies *atole* as a dish fundamental to maize cuisine, one of the grain cuisines crucial to world civilizations (2013: 28-29). The Olmecs made *atole*; corn gruels are thousands of years old. *Tejate* is unique among corn gruels (*atole*, *champurrado*, etc.), and uniquely a product of this region due to the recipe's inclusion of hard to locate ingredients (the flower of the *Rosita de cacao* and the seed of the mamey fruit) and difficult to replicate techniques (roasting ingredients, the creation of an *espuma*, or foam) combined with the more typical Mexican ingredients for gruel (corn masa, water, cacao, and increasingly sugar or sugar syrup). Investigating each ingredient and technique individually, in order to tell the whole story of *tejate*, builds a case for the worlds we humans create as we navigate the natural environment, seeking to not just nourish our bodies but also our identities. It is also a story of how natural and social landscapes always intersect. If we adopt the archaeological stance, drinking *tejate* is tasting the complexity of Mexican civilization and cuisine, telling a story about time and place through the layers of objects, while also acknowledging that each layer exists due to human imprints. With tejate, each ingredient and technique is part of the dig: masa, cacao, *Rosita de cacao*, seed of the mamey, sugar syrup, roasting, grinding, stirring.

First Layer

Archaeological excavations are long-term affairs; for now, my focus will be on the layers that differentiate *tejate* from other maize gruels: the use of the *Rosita de cacao* and mamey seed as ingredients and the creation of the foam, or the *espuma*. *Tejate* used to be a daily dish among the Zapotecas residing in the Central Valleys, but particularly the Zapotec pueblo located in San Andres de Huayapam (subsequently just called Huayapam), uniquely situated just at the start of the Sierra Norte range and next to a natural spring. This location creates a lush landscape straddling cultivated and uncultivated lands. The *Rosita de cacao* tree, *Quararibea funebris*, is native to Mexico and was once found throughout Oaxaca but became increasingly rare due to deforestation. The tree only grows in neo-tropical and tropical environments; if the ambient temperature goes below zero degrees Celsius, the tree will die. Traditionally, the Zapotecs would go into the forests to harvest the flowers (and also wood) from these trees. At some point (no one really knows when) some tree saplings were brought down into the pueblo and cultivated. Huayapam is the sole Zapotec pueblo where the tree has been actively cultivated for centuries. There is a tradition that when a woman from Huayapam gets married and moves to another pueblo, she is given a *Rosita de Cacao* sapling, but the story goes that those trees never thrive. Plenty of water and a cool climate allow the tree to best flourish in Huayapam, resulting in beautiful and fragrant white flowers that, when roasted, impart a sweetness and vanilla aroma to the finished *tejate*. Most residents of Huayapam have a tree or two on their property; the flowers are picked, dried, and roasted all year round.

The mamey seed is a layer brought from afar, a product of the many trade routes between civilizations that emerged in regions of what is now the Mexican nation; it comes from the *Pouteria sapote* or mamey zapote of the *Sapotaceae*. It is native to Southern Mexico, needs to be grown in the full sun, and flourishes in tropical climates in locations with more than 190 centimetres of rainfall a year. Most Mexicans consume the fruit, either as fresh fruit, in desserts, or in drinks; only in *tejate* is the large seed of the fruit used. The seed is dried, roasted along with the cacao seeds, and ground on a *metate* (large stone mortar). People who make the dish/drink think that the seed provides fats that bring texture to the liquid and help create the foam.

The techniques for making *tejate* are more complex than for making *atole*. The recipe for *atole* involves grinding corn into a paste (or masa) and then whisking in water. Sugar and cinnamon are sometimes added but are not necessary. Making *tejate* is more complex. First the cacao, mamey seed, and *Rosita de cacao* flowers are roasted on a *comal*, a wide and flat ceramic platter used for such tasks as well as making tortillas. The ingredients are moved around the *comal* rapidly with a woven palm mat, usually for a few minutes. The

Tejate, Tejateras, and the Taste of Place

Rosita de cacao is moved to the outsides of the *comal* to avoid burning, while the cacao and mamey seeds remain in the centre. The roasting process is complete when the cacao starts to pop and the *Rosita de cacao* flowers turn brown and release aromas.

Next, the roasted ingredients are moved to a *metate* and ground into a paste. Once all the ingredients are fully ground into a uniform paste, it becomes the *masita de cacao*, and will be used again later on in the process. At this point in the process the corn masa is combined with the *masita de cacao*. Once the *masa de maiz* and *masita de cacao* are combined, water is added to the mixture. The dough has to be the perfect temperature for the *tejate* to achieve the correct texture and foam, and all great *tejateras* can identify it by touch and taste. The water is mixed into the dough very slowly in a circular motion; this is done by hand, with a hand moving the liquid from the top to the bottom of the large bowl and back around again. The unique mixture of ingredients along with the addition of water added in a slow and precise manner ensure that there is a large amount of foam (or *espuma*) produced on the surface of the *tejate*. The *espuma* is a key feature – a good *tejate* has a good *espuma*. As the *tejate* is served, the *tejatera* fills and empties scoops of the *tejate* to create more *espuma*. The quality of a *tejate* is judged by the combination of flavours – floral, roasted – and textures – smooth, creamy, foamy.

Layer Two

Drinking *tejate* is also engaging with *terroir*, or, as I have translated it, the taste of place (Trubek 2008). This gruel, this dish/drink, this crucial form of nourishment to multiple generations of peasants and villagers, has identifiable strata: certain bands involve unique tastes and flavours that come from unique locales. There is the more universal masa, the generally ritually significant cacao, the regionally sourced seed of the mamey fruit, and finally the crucial local ingredient: the flower of the tree that only grows at a certain altitude and that has only been domesticated in two Zapotec villages. But there is another way *tejate* intersects with *terroir*. That is clear if one accepts that *terroir* can never be simply or solely about the soil. Somehow, *terroir* also involves some type of human collective: collective property, collective identity, and collective aspirations. *Tejate* also reflects *terroir* because the people in this region have the know-how to cultivate the *Rosita de cacao* and correctly prepare the gruel.

This social stratum is crucial to understanding what gives *tejate* a taste of place. The main premise of my work on the taste of place is that it always concerns a relationship between a social group and a natural environment. Anthropologist Mary Douglas famously said that to define 'dirt' is to make sense of matter out of place, because there can only be dirt and dirtiness when matter has been classified (1985). *Terroir*, by extension, is dirt in a certain place, and what this dirt signifies is a human matter; sensory evaluations mediate between natural and social conditions.

In this characterization, *terroir* happens due to the interdependence between humans and landscapes: how do our desires for the taste of a piece of cheese or a bowl of *tejate* build these layers, creating strata that reveal the creation of cuisines and civilizations?

Food and Landscape

More recently, the import of collective property and identity has become more pressing in my considerations of *terroir*. Although this concept is often cast as either solely intrinsic (in the soil) or solely extrinsic (a marketing claim), my explorations in Vermont and Oaxaca reveal another possibility: the taste of place involves cultivating a unique landscape, and seeking to promote and preserve what the cultivator identifies as their unique dish, unique due to the ingredients, the techniques, and the link to landscapes, both near and far. *Tejate* is known to have a home in a Zapotec village and to be the provenance of a group of Zapotec women. Their story is about the 'we' in the taste of place, and working with the *tejateras*, the women who make this dish, not just in their homes for their families but also in the marketplaces for sale, is helping me craft the taste of place in a broader register. *Tejate* reflects landscapes, but in the unique ingredients and complex techniques it also reinforces a certain reality: landscapes are made via the hearts and minds of human communities, and food is central to allowing such communities to thrive and survive. Thus, cuisines and civilizations are made not born. And, *terroir* is always in the making, an integration of intrinsic and extrinsic sensory and social circumstances.

Layer Three

The field site, the place best to excavate *tejate*'s layers, is the purported birthplace of the dish/drink. The highway you take to get to Huayapam from Oaxaca City is busy, dusty, and full of life. The road is lined with stores, ranging from a small room selling paper products to a brand-new, three-storey mall housing a WalMart and a multiplex cinema. There are cars, large and small, *collectivos* (or shared taxis), and buses both staying local and travelling long distance. After about ten minutes, there is a major intersection, made unusual by the large mosaic mural dedicated to the life of Benito Juarez. Juarez, the only indigenous president of Mexico (from 1858 to 1872), was born and raised in the Sierra Norte, an hour up north of Huayapm. This is the road you turn onto to get to the village.

When you make the left turn and start up the hill, what appears before you is the Sierra Norte mountain range. Dark green, spiked triangles dominate the horizon. There is a sharpness in the air, and the traffic and surroundings are less cacophonous. After a mile or so, you take another left into the town of Huayapam. In terms of the landscape, this small place is complex. As you move into the town, there is a verdant park encircling a reservoir. Water is a scarce commodity in this region, so the town already seems unique, and uniquely green. As you move toward the centre of town, the houses are a mix of free standing, multi-storey, and multi-coloured structures and brown adobe walls with large wooden doors. Behind these walls are the typical houses of Oaxacan pueblos – a large central courtyard with rooms around the edges. Huayapam is a Zapotec village. At the same time, Huayapam has become a desirable place for wealthy Mexican and American and European expatriates to settle. The quiet and subdued quality of the traditional houses dominates as you walk down the quiet, cobblestoned streets. But all around, especially on the outskirts of town, are the signs of other residents, of a village with many complex stories to tell.

Tejate, Tejateras, and the Taste of Place

A central plaza dominates the centre of Huayapam, like in most Oaxacan towns. The plaza houses the municipal building and the church. Here the colonial legacy is clear and present: the church the tallest building in town, scrupulously clean and well tended. Bright yellow plaster, hedges of pale yellow oleander, and bright pink bougainvillea vines all add a festive air, in contrast to the adobe walls that line most of the streets of Huayapam. The streets are laid out neatly and nicely in a grid, and most simply end in a field, or a person's *milpa* (or fields), or onto another larger road. Walking down the streets there are a few scrubby empty lots interspersed with brown walls. And always, what dominates as you look up the streets to the north are the mountains. From the town, the green is more nuanced. There are folds to the land and the landscape, various peaks and valleys. A few large houses can be seen in the foothills. Higher up, a funny concrete structure turns out to be a new water catchment system. Small, quiet, and orderly, the town seems cultivated, a bridge between the urban chaos of Oaxaca City and the wilderness of the Sierra Norte mountains.

Huayapam is a Zapotec village (or pueblo) and also a suburb of the cosmopolitan Oaxaca City. My excavations have been done in collaboration with a Zapotec family that lives in Huayapam, proud makers and promoters of *tejate*. They work their *milpa*, they run a small pizza restaurant, and they make and sell *tejate*. The pizzeria consists of a small, enclosed building made of mud bricks with a terrace and then a small garden area. The building houses the lovely large wood brick oven, a three-bay sink, a refrigerator, several shelving units, and a worktable. There are tables to seat about twenty to twenty-five people on the covered patio. The pizza restaurant is only open for *cena* – it opens at 8pm, after all the other *comedors* and restaurants in town have closed. Miguel spent fifteen years on and off working in Poughkeepsie, New York – on a dairy farm, doing landscaping, and working in restaurants. Rosy stayed in Huayapam, working in the pizzeria and also with her mother to make *tejate*. They have four children between the ages of eight and sixteen.

In discussions with Rosy and Miguel, their relationship with *tejate* is really a reflection of their relationship and commitment to their community. All the functions of the town are performed by members of the Zapotec community. Much of the land is communally held. Much of their work is with members of the community. Their sense of place and sense of communal purpose is integrated. The strength of their connections in Huayapam, for better or for worse, are rooted in the history of Mexico. The Zapotec community in Huayapam predates Spanish colonial rule and even the invasions of the Mixtecs and the Aztecs. Settlement patterns were disrupted by the Spanish, who built churches and administrative offices at the center of most communities, orienting physical space towards God and man, and away from the mountains and fields. Over time, with the end of colonial rule and the creation of the *eijodos* land tenure system after the Mexican Revolution, the town centre and fields of the pueblo were unified, and administered by the Zapotec villagers.

The daily life of Rosy and Miguel revolve around their obligations to family and pueblo. Rosy, like her mother, is a *tejatera*. The drink reflects the sense of place held by the Zapotec community but also reaffirms Huayapam's identity. Since pre-Hispanic times, the tradition of making *tejate* has been passed on through the women in a family. This intergenerational *tejatera* identity is unique to the families of Huayapam. Through the lineages of two sides of Rosy and Miguel's family, and the different relationships each family member has to *tejate*, we can begin to understand how the taste of place is made for the product – *tejate* – for the people – Zapotecs – and for the place – Huayapam.

Rosy was born into a family of producers. Their family home is adorned with a giant, 150-year-old *Rosita de cacao* tree where they harvest and dry the small, fragrant, white flowers to make *tejate*. Her father, Maximino Martinez Mendoza, seventy-five years old, continues to tend the family *milpa* without the use of chemicals. Her mother, Paula Santiago Ruiz, sixty-five years old, has produced *tejate* all of her life. To this day, her mother makes *tejate* and travels to Mexico City for about four months each year to sell her *tejate* at cultural festivals and markets. Rosy helps her mother with this business, preparing the dough and assembling the necessary ingredients necessary for her mother. In an outdoor kitchen at their home, Paula Santiago roasts the mamey seeds for *tejate* on a large clay *comal*, and Maximino removes grains from dried corn mazorcas to make masa for *tejate* and *tamales*.

Rosy learned to make *tejate* as a little girl. Learning to make *tejate*, Rosy explains, was a coming-of-age process in Huayapam. When she was young, all girls began to make *tejate*, usually at about six years old. She learned informally, helping her mother and observing the methods of production. Little by little, Rosy gained responsibility as she mastered the art of making *tejate*. She is now a part of the cooperative of *tejateras*; they work to promote and preserve the practices, selling in markets in Oaxaca and Mexico City and also doing demonstrations for tourist groups. The main time that she makes *tejate* is for the *tejate* festival, when thousands of people come to the village to experience *tejate*; for her it is not an everyday event, but certainly it gets made for special occasions. Rosy's daughters have not learned how to make *tejate* yet; they are in school, and their mother hopes they will attend university. Their grandmothers have offered to teach them, though, and Rosy believes that *tejate* is still a viable way for families to make a living. Many women in Huayapam now use their education to develop new ways to promote the dish and make it as much a commercial as household product.

Miguel is one of the only men in the pueblo who learned how to make *tejate* as a boy. Though making *tejate* is normally reserved for women, Miguel's mother, Maria Ester Santiago Rafeal, taught him when he was twelve. Though Miguel has never sold *tejate*, he understands the process and is skilled at making the *masita de cacao* paste. Miguel sometimes accompanies his mother-in-law to Mexico City where she goes to make sell *tejate* while he sells *tlayudas* at the markets.

Maria Ester, now seventy-nine years old, continues to drink *tejate* every day. She has made and sold *tejate* for the past forty-eight years, and she still takes her *tejate* to sell most days at the large indoor market in Oaxaca City, the Central de Abastos. Although it's difficult to carry the prepared cacao paste and large clay containers all the way to the market each day, Maria Ester is still committed to her work as a *tejatera*; it is a meaningful part of her life and gives her valuable role in her community. Maria Ester works closely with the other women in town to organize the annual *Festival de Tejate* each year in Huayapam; this event draws thousands of locals and tourists from farther afield. The festival creates a strong connection between the town and an identity as the place to find an 'authentic' *tejate*. For Rosy and Miguel, they hope this event allows the connection between a certain place, people, and elements of the landscape to persist into the future.

Conclusion

The *tejateras* of Huayapam believe in the taste of place. Their pride in their practices, their willingness to bring thousands to the town for the yearly *Festival de Tejate*, and their commitment to selling 'authentic *tejate*' in the markets are a testament to how and why *tejate* continues to be made and shared over thousands of years and despite so many conquests and disruptions. Their taste of place involves a 'we'. This is our land. These are our ways in making the right *espuma*. *Terroir* can never be simply or solely about the soil, as many would have it. Somehow, *terroir* is also about the collective: collective property, collective identity, and collective aspirations. If I consume *tejate*, I don't just taste the smokiness from the roast cacao and smell the vanilla aroma of the flowers. I taste a 'we' – Rosy and her family, the *tejateras* of Huayapam, the Zapotec pueblo, the Oaxacans in the Tlacalula market. Of all my decisions about the taste of place, the one to emphasize the 'we' remains the most important and also the most difficult to articulate and justify. To insist on not just human influences to the taste of place but to also insist that the piece of cheese or bowl of *tejate* is more than the work of individuals but of a collectivity, or collective belief, or collective tradition, goes against so much current common sense – food is a commodity to be bought and sold – but not so for Rosie and the other *tejateras*. As Rosy says, 'The hand of a *tejatera* needs to know the right temperature. Because if it does not know then it is just corn-water dough. There is no machine that can do this.'

I continue to believe that to taste *terroir*, in any food and drink, is to taste the 'we'. However, as modern technology is introduced and the younger generations seek work in other places, the future of *tejate* and the knowledge of how to produce it are in question. Now, what are we to do, those of us committed to preserving foods, dishes, meals, and even cuisines in the face of an ever more dominant (and homogenous) industrial and global food system? It seems to me, as much as documenting the necessary ingredients and recipes, the task at hand is to ensure that in places like Huayapam, the members of this community still work together as a 'we', and keep making *tejate*, for themselves and for others.

Bibliography

Bernal, Ignacio. 1969. *The Olmec World*, trans. by Doris Heydon and Fernando Horcasitas (Berkeley: University of California Press).
Douglas, Mary. 1985. *Purity and Danger: An Analysis of Concepts of Pollution and Taboo* (Boston: Ark Paperbacks).
Laudan, Rachel. 2013. *Cuisine and Empire: Cooking in World History* (Berkeley: University of California Press).
Trubek, Amy. 2008. *The Taste of Place: A Cultural Journey into Terroir* (Berkeley: University of California Press).

Fratelli Ingegnoli: Reshaping the Landscape of Italian Cooking in the Late Nineteenth and Early Twentieth Centuries

Anne Urbancic

Who are the Fratelli Ingegnoli? How did their firm effect long-term changes on the food landscape of Italy? The firm is cited as the sole outside source consulted by Janet Ross in her ground-breaking *Leaves from our Tuscan Kitchen*, the first English-language Italian recipe book. An immediate bestseller when the first edition appeared in October of 1899 and almost continuously in print ever since, Ross's book contained recipes primarily for vegetable dishes, also an unusual departure from other British cookbooks.[1] Why did she consult the Fratelli Ingegnoli and not any other Italian cookbooks, such as the ubiquitous and popular 1891 volume by Pellegrino Artusi?[2] At her farming estates in Tuscany, how did she even know about the Ingegnoli nurseries in Milan?

No comprehensive history of the Fratelli Ingegnoli has yet been published. This study, therefore, will describe the sociocultural impact of this firm on Italian farmers and the urban bourgeoisie in the years between Italian Unification (1861) and the First World War. It will focus particularly on the late nineteenth and early twentieth centuries, when the company, recognizing Italy's rapidly changing social and political landscapes, published a book of recipes, *Come si cucinano i Legumi* (*How to Cook Vegetables*), the small volume acknowledged by Janet Ross in her own cookbook.[3] The book appeared in 1895, indicating the firm itself as publisher. I retrace the history of the firm, highlighting its commitment to changing the agricultural and agronomical landscape of Italy. I also review their marketing strategies, which included the innovative, ingenious, and judicious use of catalogues and other print materials to ensure that their name and products were recognized across the peninsula and beyond. Even today, the pride and dedication that the firm demonstrates in its catalogue and website reflects how their approach to the Italian landscape has been welcomed by both Italian farmers in rural areas and by small urban terrace gardeners. I will also briefly touch on some of the work that the firm is involved with today. Finally, my study is an academic celebration of the longevity of the Fratelli Ingegnoli firm that in 2017 celebrated two hundred years of horticultural innovations in Italy: in plants, landscape, tools, and marketing.

The Fratelli Ingegnoli began with Francesco Ingegnoli, an engineer, who moved to Italy in the late 1700s from the Ticino region of Switzerland. He settled in Sesto Calende (Varese) where he grew *barbatelle*, the small grapevine tendrils from healthy vines that, once planted, produce little rootlets (*barba*) from which new vines will grow. In 1789, Ingegnoli decided to move to Milan. There, he opened a nursery in the area of today's central train

Fratelli Ingegnoli: Reshaping the Landscape of Italian Cooking

station. Even in those early years, Ingegnoli recognized the importance of plant research, and the nursery developed specialized genetic selections to produce cereals for forage.[4]

Francesco's primary competition, the Burdin family, had similar nurseries nearby, where via Vivaio is now located in Milan. The Burdins, originally from the Savoy region of northern Italy, had come to the city to establish a retail business for ornamental plants and fruit trees. Additionally, they supplied mulberry trees for the silk trade, still continuing in the late 1700s. The political upheavals of 1848 and several bad investments wreaked havoc on the Burdin nursery; they sold unwisely, and the firm's subsequent owner was close to bankruptcy. In 1879, the Burdin enterprise was purchased by their revitalized rivals, the Fratelli Ingegnoli, who marked the merger by monumentalizing the date of the Burdin firm's founding, 1817, in the Ingegnoli motto: *Dal 1817, di padre in figlio, al servizio dell'orto-floro-frutticoltura italiana*.[5]

By the 1879 purchase, a new generation of the Ingegnoli family, three young brothers, had returned to the family business despite the fact that they were neither horticulturalists nor botanists. The second Francesco was only twenty-three; his brothers, Vittorio and Paolo, even younger. Each of the brothers took on a different role in the new business. Francesco had studied business in Paris; he also had a passion for agronomy. The merger of the two nurseries allowed him to integrate his avocation and his shrewd commercial acumen. More importantly, he had a vision for the enterprise, a *mission* according to the Ingegnoli website, one that extended beyond financial profitability and that led to profound changes on Italy's food landscape.[6] Together the brothers officially became the *Società commerciale in nome collettivo Fratelli Ingegnoli* in 1884.

Francesco's visionary approach comprised a multifaceted campaign. First, he sought excellent selections of healthy plants and seeds intended for the immediate market in Italy. Second, the brothers initiated a concentrated effort to open that market up to the rest of Italy through their seed catalogues. In both these endeavours, Francesco, Vittorio, and Paolo were aided by the new rail system that could deliver seeds, plants, and catalogues across the peninsula more rapidly and efficiently than in previous times. Thirdly, Francesco's vision encompassed on-going research and innovation in agronomy in order to produce new hybrids of vegetable and flower seeds and plants of the highest quality.

While Paolo sailed for Buenos Aires, taking seeds to sell to the Italian immigrants who had settled there, Francesco travelled to the Far East in search of new seeds and new varieties of plants to bring back to Italy and, in this way, to add to and strengthen indigenous plants. The well-known Italian *cachi* (persimmons) are one result. It was Francesco who discovered these while in Japan and introduced them to Italy. In a relatively short time, careful genetic hybridization by highly specialized botanists in the employ of Fratelli Ingegnoli ensured that Italy boasted at least twenty-five varieties of *cachi* which, in 1888, were even lauded in a letter of thanks from composer Giuseppe Verdi, an avid gardener himself.[7]

Other innovations followed. Francesco developed hybrids of the Japanese grain named *kakomugi* that soon increased yields of animal fodder along the Italian peninsula.[8] By 1890, British horticulturists praised two new offerings, a legume and a chestnut tree, also successfully adapted from Japan.[9] In 1893, Francesco attended the Chicago World's Fair, where he met with representatives of the *Canadian Horticulturalist* who reported that 'Francesco Ingegnoli of Milano, Italy, called. He is the Secretary of the Italian Horticultural Society, and took careful lists of our more valuable fruits, for trial in Italy'.[10] Many decades later, in 1965, Fratelli Ingegnoli was also at the forefront of bringing kiwi to Italy, and of adapting Italian techniques used in successful vineyards to nurture the kiwi, so much so that today Italy is second only to New Zealand in kiwi exports.[11] The brothers understood that to make their nursery essential and beneficial to Italian farmers and horticulturalists, they had to innovate constantly, developing new technologies and continuing consultations with the most respected botanists and horticulturalists from around the world. Their conceptual framework did not change, even as they progressed from plant nursery in the early years to being one of Europe's first agro-botanical businesses.[12]

Their first expansion saw their facility move to Corso Loreto (now Corso Buenos Aires) in Milan where a special nursery, warehouses, and a retail area were built. Paolo wisely diversified their offerings to meet the complete needs of gardeners of all interests and abilities, and the company began offering gardening tools as well.[13] Branches were opened in Rome and Naples, as well as in Argentina (Ingegnoli Hermanos of Buenos Aires). Later, in the years of Italian colonialist expansion, Paolo's son (another Francesco) founded an agricultural enterprise in Tripolitania which comprised 1000 hectares of terrain and lasted from 1927 to 1950.[14] (Tripolitania, a province of Libya, was a separate Italian colony from 1927-1934.)

Perhaps most importantly, Francesco Ingegnoli understood that he could substantially, and literally, alter the landscape of Italy through a concentrated effort to promote gardening and horticulture as a hobby. For this he turned to making the name Fratelli Ingegnoli well known even when seeds, plants, and tools were not involved.

The Fratelli Ingegnoli company already benefitted from their wide distribution of seed catalogues, which had been in existence since 1870. Train travel greatly facilitated distribution, especially after the Unification of Italy in 1861. Unification also led to the gradual standardization of the Italian language, which made their print materials more accessible to readers throughout the country.[15] Fairly early, Francesco realized the value of printing the covers in colour, making them more attractive to the eye of the potential consumer.[16] At times his catalogues also included street scenes of Milan and images of well-dressed ladies and children of the bourgeoisie; in this subtle way, he successfully instilled the connection between hobby gardening and urban dwellers, and happy families. Colour advertisements for the Fratelli Ingegnoli began to appear in the *Domenica del Corriere* as early as 1903.[17] By 1925, the company had even produced animated film shorts, directed by Guido Presepi, to advertise their products.[18]

This was promotional hard sell; however, Francesco recognized the value of the soft sell too. Thus, from the late 1800s forward, Fratelli Ingegnoli published various gardening manuals under their name, with print runs of thousands of copies. Among these are found titles such as *Dove e come si impianta un orto* (*Where and How to Plant a Garden*), *Le malattie delle piante* (*Diseases of Plants*), and the *Manuale di Praticoltura* (*Manual for Pastureland*). Published in annual editions after 1897 and made available as an insert in trade journals such as the *Gazzetta Agricola*, the *Manuale* proved instrumental in changing farming practices in Italy.

While these titles were probably of greater interest to male readers, in 1895, the lady of the house was offered the cookbook on which I'd like to focus in more detail. It is likely that in this venture the Fratelli Ingegnoli counted on two social phenomena to guarantee the success of their cookbook. First, cookbooks intended for the quickly growing Italian bourgeoisie had begun to make their appearance across the peninsula. Pellegrino Artusi's *La scienza in cucina e l'arte di mangiar bene*, published in 1891, sold widely across Italy, despite the fact that Artusi had had to self-finance the publication at first.[19] Its great success pointed to a new desire for cookery guides by non-professional cooks. Secondly, in the last years of the nineteenth century and early years of the twentieth, many schools and institutes had opened with the specific purpose of offering cooking and sewing lessons to attract the middle-class housewife as she engaged in her '*i lavori donneschi*' (housewifely occupations) as the Marucelliana Library referred to the phenomenon.[20]

The Ingegnoli firm also understood that, despite Artusi's success, cookbooks did not sell themselves, and therefore sales would likely depend on laudatory reviews in popular journals. At the time, reviews were a fairly new genre across Europe, with rules that were quite flexible.[21] The numerous magazines and journals that entered the Italian publishing market in the late nineteenth century offered an optimal space for advertising products and services to the middle-class reader, especially to women readers. Thus, the cookbook *Come si cucinano i Legumi* was distributed widely among magazine and journal publishers. As I examined the reviews closely, I was struck by the ingenuity of the promotional intent. For example, in addition to a recognizable review in one German magazine, I also found an advertisement review embedded into a recipe featuring tomatoes.[22] I found mentions in journals, like *Nuova Antologia*, where one would not expect to find cookbooks among the rather staid and sophisticated literary, science, and political titles usually accepted by this journal.

Some unexpected journals offered brief reviews. For example, the *Rassegna Nazionale*, which focused on socio-political issues, announced that

> Dai solerti Fratelli Ingegnoli, orticoltori in Milano, abbiamo ricevuto un elegante volumetto intitolato: *Come si cucinano i legumi*, col qual si apprende il modo di fare coi **vegetali i più svariati ed appetibili piatti e manicaretti atti ad un'alimentazione nutritiva ed aggradevole** – In 200 e più pagine vengono passati in rivista tutti gli erbaggi commestibili con **un'infinità di ricette e formole per la loro cucinatura** e basterà citare **53 modi per apprestare le patate, 20 per i cavoli, 18 per i piselli, 12 per gli asparagi e via di seguito** – È questa per certo una pubblicazione molto interessante e utile anche alle famiglie ed il tenuissimo costo di una lira dice chiaro non essere edito a scopo direttto di lucro, bensì per spronare alla coltura degli ortaggi.[23]

The *Civiltà cattolica* offered the following brief review:

> In servigio di que' nostri lettori, che amano un cibo leggero per lo stomaco e per la

bocca, non sarà male che almeno una volta ci rivolgiamo ai cuochi e alle cuciniere e diciamo loro: Volete fare, con semplici **vegetali, i piatti più svariati, i più appetitosi manicaretti**, acconci ad un'alimentazione nutritiva ed aggradevole? Il segreto, o meglio, i segreti li troverete in questo libro, il quale v'insegnerà **moltissime formole per la loro cucinatura: dodici per asparagi, diciotto per piselli, cinquantatrè per le patate, eccetera**. E tutta questa scuola gastronomica non vi costerà che una lira [...].[24]

As my added emphasis shows even without translation, the obvious similarity between the two reviews cannot be considered a coincidence, especially since *Gartenflora*, the German magazine mentioned above, and the French magazine *L'Illustration horticole* also carried the same brief review, albeit in German and French respectively.[25] It would appear that not only did the Fratelli Ingegnoli send the cookery volume for review, knowing that its reasonable price of one lira would be attractive to middle-class cooks, but they even included their own pre-written laudatory commentary for neat insertion into magazines and journals. In addition to this self-promotion, they received a personal recommendation from one of the best-selling women authors of the day, Contessa Lara (definitely not a housewife), who recommended the volume without reserve in a literary journal. It is difficult to say whether she was a paid celebrity endorser, but to discover that her review was solicited would not be a surprise.[26]

Did the soft sell strategy work? Most certainly: my research revealed that the cookbook was published twice in 1895 and then was followed by a similar volume, *600 modi di cucinare gli ortaggi* (*Six Hundred ways to cook vegetables*) published in 1902, with subsequent editions in 1909 and 1925.[27] More importantly, though, *Come si cucinano i Legumi* offers ample proof that the Fratelli Ingegnoli were horticultural trailblazers in Italy.

The book approaches vegetables in a simple and practical way, offering a broad range of recipes and preparation methods. *Come si cucinano i Legumi* presents over 450 recipes in alphabetical order, generally using the main vegetable of each dish as the first word of the title. For each vegetable type, the first recipe also carries the botanical name in Latin, and a French translation in bracketed italics. Some of the recipe titles indicate a cooking style (*in istufato, al vapore*); others pay homage to the supposed origin of the recipe (*alla francese, alla siciliana*). The vegetables can go from A all the way to Z because of a new variety of squash, the *zucchetta nana di Milano*; zucchini had first been presented in the Ingegnoli seed catalogue only four years previously, in 1891.[28]

The Fratelli Ingegnoli provided cooking instructions using the impersonal third person *si*. There is no list of ingredients or amounts required; instead the immediate focus is on the practical, on preparation and cooking. As had Pellegrino Artusi before them, the Fratelli Ingegnoli often add interesting tidbits about each vegetable, including information about planting, growing, and harvesting; however, they offer none of the personal anecdotes and folkloristic notes that made Artusi's volume appealing as a story as well as a cookbook. (Artusi's famous recipe book seems conspicuously absent in the Fratelli Ingegnoli cookbook.)

Unexpected inclusions in a book promoting vegetables are recipes for *Aragosta in insalata* (Lobster salad), *erbe vitellate* (veal with herbs), *erbe fini piccionate* (pigeon with herbs), *costolette alla cuciniera* (stuffed with minced chicken and truffles), two *frittata* dishes, and two rice dishes. In addition, there is a recipe for cherry soup. Towards the end of the volume there is an unusual kind of epilogue: the last twelve pages of the cookbook advertise packaged seeds, including prices, to be used to growing the vegetables used in the cookbook recipes. These are not ads for farm use; the seeds come in small *cartocci* or packets, indicating that they are intended for a small family *orto* (urban garden). The section also promotes seed packets for ornamental flowers. While today we are quite accustomed to seeing proprietary cookbooks that offer recipes using ingredients specifically from the book's commercial sponsor, such as the *Pillsbury Cookbook*, I have not found a similar book so early in Italian cookbook history. The doubled discourse of this volume, as purveyor of Ingegnoli brand seeds and simultaneously as authority on cooking the vegetables grown from their products, seems to make the volume a first in its genre.[29]

The Fratelli Ingegnoli's strategy shows in the friendly, conversational prefaces that directly address their readers (there are two such introductions, neither attributed to an author). As its introductory note to '*la nostra gentile lettrice*' (our dear female reader) indicates, *Come si cucinano i Legumi* is directed primarily at women. As intended readers, the cookbook attributes to them some expertise in both cooking and gardening. Another fundamental characteristic attributed to the *gentile lettrice* is her presumed intelligence. The preface addresses a woman who already knows the health benefits of vegetables, and is aware of the economic advantages of growing and preserving them. In an exercise of casual name-dropping, the book reminds her of what Alexandre Dumas (*père*), Jean Anthelme Brillat-Savarin, François Vatel and Paolo Mantegazza (whose often polemical statements and approaches were well known at the time), said of food and eating. The introductory pages also assure their intended reader of her place among the 'the good housewives, dispensers of the joys and of the innocent pleasures of life […] who invest all their care and happiness in making their children smile'.[30] The subsequent pages end with two further assurances for the *gentile lettrice*: 'Let us once more assure our reader that in this treatise on domestic gastronomy especially for vegetables, she will find an abundance of recipes and instructions, all the fruit of family experiences. In all of the recipes there is novelty, ease of preparation, and all that is required to satisfy even the most delicate tastes.'[31] From the outset, then, this book proclaims its authority and its innovative but trusted approach, not to *la cucina* (cuisine) or *il mangiare* (eating) but to a '*gastronomia domestica speciale*' (a special domestic gastronomy). Insisting on such an enhanced status of woman's place in the kitchen, without hint of condescension, helped guarantee that the soft sell of the cookbook worked very well.

A similar kind of soft sell could be inferred from Francesco's other interests: a politician of socialist leaning, member of council in Milan, and later mayor of Lambrate as well as friend of politician Filippo Turati and feminist revolutionary Anna Kuliscioff, in all his efforts, he promoted the Ingegnoli name and company. He helped found various agrarian cooperatives that offered affordable loans to aid struggling farmers in developing their family farms, especially in the south of Italy. Particularly notable was his involvement in re-establishing farming on fertile land in Sardinia that had been abandoned. The project, Surigheddu, has had a difficult history, but is still in existence, although under the supervision of the University of Sassari, and its work in agrobiodiversity is largely supported now by the Regione Sardegna.[32] Among his other community duties, Francesco acted as expert judge at agricultural fairs across the peninsula. He was called upon for his knowledge and expertise in the establishment of numerous parks and gardens, public and private, including the Parco Sempione and the Orto botanico di Brera.[33]

While the Fratelli Ingegnoli enjoyed their greatest successes in the years before 1929 when the enterprise boasted almost 1500 employees and clients such as the Vatican and the Italian royal family, their commitment to horticulture continues today with the same enthusiasm and expertise.[34] Their annual catalogues, now fully online, are stunningly gorgeous; their newest headquarters in via Oreste Salomone in Milan continues to offer excellence and innovation in horticulture and agronomy.[35] They have made themselves experts in the art of bonsai, and are well respected for their work in phyto-pharmacological products as well in innovative planting techniques such as seed tapes and or multisem pills.[36] At the same time, they have not discarded Italy's indigenous horticultural landscapes and traditions. In this contemporary world of fragile ecodiversity, they have recognized the continuing validity of, as Paolo Pejrone notes, 'what the peasant of the past in his basic and traditional simplicity with his total poverty was able to pass on as part of the marvelous and unique flavour of taste of an archaic civilization, composed of wild herbs and humble vegetables'.[37]

The passion of the Fratelli Ingegnoli for their work in agronomy and horticulture is sincere, otherwise they would not have endured in such a competitive business, especially today, at a time of ineluctable changes to landscape and environment. Out of their passion have grown improved plants, seeds, innovations, manuals, cookbooks, and excellent marketing techniques. And a very satisfied clientele.

Notes

1. Janet Ross, *Leaves from our Tuscan Kitchen* (London: J.M. Dent, 1899; 2nd ed., 1900).
2. Pellegrino Artusi, *La Scienza in cucina e l'arte di mangiar bene. Manuale pratico per le famiglie. 104 ristampa*. (Florence: Giunti Marzocco, 1960).
3. Fratelli Ingegnoli, *Come si cucinano I Legumi*, 2nd ed. (Milan: Fratelli Ingegnoli, 1895) <http://www.academiabarilla.it/italian-food-academy/biblioteca-gastronomica-digitale/come-cucinano-legumi.aspx>.
4. Camera di Commercio di Milano, *I locali storici di Milano. La città e il suo sviluppo attraverso l'attività di 99 esercizi con oltre 50 anni di vita* (Milan: Touring Club Italiano, 2004), p. 68.
5. Francesco Ingegnoli, 'La storia dei vivai Ingegnoli, tra viaggi botanici e cataloghi illustrati', *La giornata di studi di Orticola di Lombardia* (18 April 2013) <http://www.orticola.org/convegni/giornata-di-studi/2013/C-01-INGEGNOLI-La-storia-dei-vivai-Ingegnoli.pdf> [accessed 29 April 2017].
6. Ingegnoli, 'La storia dei vivai Ingegnoli'.
7. Camera di Commercio di Milano, p. 69.
8. Francesco Ingegnoli, 'La storia attraverso il vivaio Fratelli Ingegnoli', *Fiori & Forchette*, 2013 <http://www.fiori-forchette.com/products/la-storia-attraverso-il-vivaio-f-lli-ingegnoli/> [accessed 7 May 2017].
9. 'New Garden Plants', *Bulletin of Miscellaneous Information* (Royal Botanic Gardens, Kew) 1890 (1890), 35-58 (pp. 40, 53).
10. *Canadian Horticulturalist*, 16.7 (1893), 235.

11. Camera di Commercio di Milano, p. 69 and Daniel Workman, 'Kiwifruit Exports by Country', *World's Top Exports*, 26 March 2017 <http://www.worldstopexports.com/kiwifruit-exports-by-country/> [accessed 17 May 2017].
12. Camera di Commercio di Milano, p. 68.
13. Camera di Commercio di Milano, p. 68.
14. Camera di Commercio di Milano, p. 69.
15. According to linguist Tullio De Mauro, in 1861 Standard Italian was spoken by only 2.5% of the total population of twenty-five million (*Storia linguistica dell'Italia unita*, 3rd ed. (Roma-Bari: Laterza, 1972), pp. 42-44). While linguistic standardization became a government policy after 1868, Italian food vocabulary continued to be problematic. When, in 1956, Swiss linguist Robert Rüegg asked 124 Italian speakers from 54 provinces across the peninsula to name 242 common concepts, the only food item that all the speakers named in the same way was 'espresso'; the other 241 concepts all had notable variations (*Zur Wortgeographie der italienschen Umgangssprache* (Köln: Romanisches Seminar der Universität, 1956), qtd. in De Mauro, p. 129.
16. I am grateful to food historian Robert W. Brower for pointing out that both front and back covers of the cookbook's first edition were also printed in colour.
17. Ingegnoli, '*La storia dei vivai Ingegnoli*'.
18. Ingegnoli, '*La storia attraverso*'.
19. Pellegrino Artusi, '*Il tempo e le opere*', *Catalogo della mostra bibliografica e documentaria* (Florence: Accademia della Crusca and others, 2011), p. 12.
20. '"*Pranzo di gala e pranzo alla buona*" nella Biblioteca Marucelliana', *Pellegrino Artusi*, Comune di Forlimpopoli, 9 November 2011 <http://www.pellegrinoartusi.it/?s=ingegnoli> [accessed 5 February 2017].
21. Ruggero Bonghi, '*Concetto e ragioni di questa pubblicazione*', *La Cultura*, 1.1 (1882), 1.
22. *Gartenflora: Zeitschrift für Garten und Blumenkunde* 44 (1895), pp. 600-01 for the review and p. 572 for the tomato recipe by G.L.
23. Review of *Come si cucinano I Legumi* by Fratelli Ingegnoli, *Rassegna Nazionale*, 85.17 (1895), 170.
24. Review of *Come si cucinano I Legumi* by Fratelli Ingegnoli, *La civiltà cattolica*, 3.16 (1895), 94-95.
25. *Gartenflora*; Review of *Come si cucinano I Legumi* by Fratelli Ingegnoli, *L'Illustration horticole*, 15 Décembre 1895, 360. In addition, the cookbook was mentioned but not reviewed in *Bulletino della Società toscana di orticultura* (20 (1895), 163) and *La Nuova Antologia* (30.57 (1 June 1895), front matter). Curiously, there was no review in one of the most widely distributed and popular magazines of Italy, *L'Illustrazione italiana*.
26. Contessa Lara (Evelina Cattermole), 'Review of *Come si cucinano i Legumi*', *Roma letteraria* 3 (January/December 1895 [sic]), pp. 260-61.
27. Fratelli Ingegnoli, *600 Modi di cucinare gli Ortaggi* (Milan: Patremolli, 1902).
28. Teresa A. Lust and Harry S. Paris, 'Italian Horticultural and Culinary Records of Summer Squash (*Cucurbita pepo, Cucurbitaceae*) and Emergence of the Zucchini in 19th-Century Milan', *Annals of Botany*, 118.1 (July 2016), 53-69 (p. 66).
29. The Pillsbury Company published its first proprietary book in 1897: entitled *Good Bread and How to Make It/Good Cereals and How to Prepare Them*, it focused on a cereal product named Vitos (Kevin Hunt, 'The Oldest Company Cookbooks We Own', *Taste of General Mills*, 2 March 2016 <http://blog.generalmills.com/2016/03/the-oldest-company-cookbooks-we-own/> [accessed 7 May 2017]).
30. Fratelli Ingegnoli, *Come si cucinano I Legumi*, p. iii (trans. by the author).
31. Ingegnoli, *Come si cucinanoo I Legumi*, p. 2 (trans. by the author).
32. '*Secoli di storia agricola nelle tenute di Surigheddu e Mamuntanas*', *Buongiorno Alghero.it* (10 March 2016) <http://www.buongiornoalghero.it/contenuto/0/11/87685/secoli-di-storia-agricola-nelle-tenute-di-surigheddu-e-mamuntanas> [accessed 7 May 2017].
33. Ingegnoli, '*La storia attraverso*'.
34. Ingegnoli, '*La storia dei vivai Ingegnoli*'.
35. See Fratelli Ingegnoli, '*Catalogo. Anniversario 200 anni, Fratelli Ingegnoli*', 2017 <https://www.ingegnoli.it/ita/> [accessed 5 February 2017].
36. Camera di Commercio di Milano, p. 69.
37. Paolo Pejrone, '*Ecco l'orto dei sogni una pagina alla volta*', *La Stampa* (18 January 2013), 23.

Food in the Context of First-Century Galilee: The Mishnah and the So-Called 'Jesus Diet'

Susan Weingarten

The so-called 'Jesus diet' has become popular recently in the United States.[1] The idea, as I understand it from books with titles like *What Would Jesus Eat?* or *The Maker's Diet*, is that if you truly want to follow Jesus in every area of your life, you cannot ignore your eating habits. Jesus wants you to be thin, and by eating what he ate 'the Holy Spirit works through you and sends your fat to heaven'.[2]

Without entering into the theology of this theory, I should like to take a look at its gastronomy. Some of the suggestions for eating like Jesus are clearly anachronistic. One book stars a tomato on its front cover, but as all symposiasts would know, Jesus would not have eaten tomatoes or indeed potatoes, for these were only brought to Europe and the Middle East from the New World following Columbus' voyage. Other suggestions clearly reflect more of their proposers' world outlooks than that of Jesus: there is no evidence that Jesus was vegetarian or did not drink alcohol. Use is also made of the Hebrew Bible: the proponents of the Jesus diet are quite reasonably unanimous that Jesus would not have eaten ham or pork.

Can we find any further evidence? The New Testament mentions a number of foodstuffs, both in connection with Jesus and in other contexts, but it does not go into very much detail about the foods of the Jewish population of Galilee in the first century CE. But the compilation of Jewish laws that make up the Mishnah, finalized in the third century but drawing on first-century and even earlier sources, has many details of foods and how they were prepared in Roman Palestine.[3] I shall be looking at this textual evidence in this paper, as well as archaeological and geographical evidence, in an attempt to draw a fuller and clearer picture of the food Jesus could have eaten in the landscape of first-century Galilee.

If you google 'Jesus diet,' you come up with about thirty-four million hits. I am afraid I have not looked at all the material. I have taken as my example of the Jesus diet literature one of the early examples, *What Would Jesus Eat? The Ultimate Program for Eating Well, Feeling Great, and Living Longer* by Don Colbert, MD (Nashville: Thomas Nelson, 2002). Note that there are two tomatoes on the cover of this book, and they reappear in some of the recipes.[4]

I am not qualified to discuss Dr Colbert's nutritional recommendations: as far as I can see they seem totally reasonable. What I will take issue with is his picture of what

Food in the Context of First-Century Galilee

Jesus would have eaten as a poor inhabitant of first-century Galilee.

Bread

I will start with bread, 'the food that Jesus ate most often,' according to *What Would Jesus Eat?* This is probably correct. Colbert notes that the breads of Jesus' time were coarse whole-grain breads, which would be likely to become rancid and mouldy if not consumed daily, he writes. He adds: 'Eating a freshly baked loaf of whole-grain bread a day was and is a healthy way to live!'[5]

Stone-Ground – or Ground Stone?

Bread in the first century was certainly whole-grain. It was made by grinding flour in stone mills. There were large bakeries where the flour was ground in mills the height of a man in Roman towns, but in the countryside grain was likely to be ground by women at home. Grinding grain was a backbreaking task carried out by the lowest status women. It was the first in the list of tasks a wife owed to her husband according to the Mishnah: 'These are the works which the wife must perform for her husband: grinding flour and baking bread and washing clothes and cooking food and nursing her child and making his bed and working in wool. If she brought him one maid she need not grind or bake or wash; if two she need not cook or nurse her baby [...].'[6]

The small hand-mills of coarse stone, or the even more primitive saddle querns, were usually made of basalt in Galilee.[7] They left residues of grit in the bread: there are instructions in another part of the Mishnah as to what percentage of impurities was an acceptable amount when buying goods: 'If a man sold grain to his fellow, the buyer must undertake to receive a quarter-*qab* of refuse with every *se'ah*; ten maggoty figs in every hundred figs; ten jars of sour wine in every hundred [...].'[8] It is clear from this ruling permitting a minimum ten per cent of impurities that there were often more. Nowadays we have chemical additives, then they had other impurities. The large amount of grit left its mark on the teeth – skeletons of people from the ancient world show teeth ground down by years of eating gritty bread.[9]

Fresh Bread Every Day?

Would Jesus have had fresh bread every day? I think this is very unlikely. Fuel was expensive to buy, or took many hours to forage. The Tosefta, another Jewish legal collection including early rabbinical sources, writes that most people baked once a week, while professional bakers in villages baked once every three days, and only bakers in cities baked more often.[10] Bread was certainly eaten stale, hard and dry. To stop it going bad, it was dried in the sun or at the side of the fire. For eating, it was dipped into a liquid – water, wine, vinegar, fish-sauce, oil, or stew – or crumbled with a liquid for small children. If in spite of careful drying the bread still went mouldy it was sometimes eaten all the same.[11]

Different Grades of Bread

Colbert notes quite rightly that wheat bread was considered better than barley bread, which was the food of the poor, mentioned in the account of the miracle of the five thousand in John 6.9. Josephus, the Jewish historian of the first century who was the military commander of Galilee, confirms that the poor ate barley while the rich ate wheat.[12] Colbert does not mention the other way of grading bread, according to the fineness of the flour: there was 'clean' bread made with fine flour, and coarse dark bread, *qibar*, from the Latin *cibarius*, with lots of bran. The Mishnah notes the different grades of sieves used to sieve out the bran.[13]

In the early fourth century, a pagan tax collector called Theophanes travelled from Hermopolis in Egypt to Antioch in Syria via Palestine, and back again. The accounts for his journey have been found in Egypt, so we know where he stayed, what he bought there, and even how much he paid for it. He travelled with an entourage of slaves and some other companions, or at least higher-class servants. This is reflected in his accounts (written in Greek): his accountant buys food 'for us' and 'for the boys', that is, for the slaves. The foods where we see this social differential are mainly wine (old for us and new for the boys) and bread: *katharos* (clean bread) for us and *kibarios* (coarse bread) for the slaves. In making this differential, Theophanes is doing just what the rabbis of Roman Palestine objected to, at least in the case of a Jewish slave, who was to be 'with you', in the words of Deuteronomy 15.16. The rabbis explained the biblical phrase 'with you' as meaning 'with you in food and with you in drink': as they explained, 'you should not eat clean bread and he eat coarse bread (*lehem qibar*); you should not drink old wine and he drink new wine; you should not sleep on a feather bed and he sleep on straw [...].'[14]

Fish

The New Testament tells us that Jesus ate fish at the Sea of Galilee, and after the resurrection he even cooked fish and bread over charcoal for himself and his disciples.[15] We have already mentioned the miracle where Jesus is said to have multiplied loaves and fishes for five thousand people.[16] From this Colbert deduces that 'we certainly know that Jesus ate clean, fresh, unpolluted fish almost every day of His life'.[17]

I think this is going too far. Fish was certainly available freshly caught around the Sea of Galilee. We do not know whether the fishermen who caught it normally ate it themselves or simply sold it to provide the rest of the things their families needed. Fishermen were typically some of the poorest people in the Roman world, which is presumably why Jesus sought them out.[18] It is clear they did not always find fish plentiful, for one of Jesus' acts was to send them out to find more fish than they would usually find: a hundred and fifty-three big fish. But would fresh fish have been available daily in Nazareth, a thirty-kilometre uphill climb from the Sea of Galilee? There would certainly have been problems in transporting fish without modern refrigeration – how far could it be brought from the Sea without going bad in the Middle Eastern sun? And would not the cost of transport have added to the cost of the fish? There would probably be no fishing on the Sabbath either. Fresh fish every day

Food in the Context of First-Century Galilee

in the hills of Galilee, as opposed to the shores of its Sea, seems rather unlikely.

Fish Products

Jesus may well, of course, have eaten other fish products rather than fresh fish. Fish could be dried, smoked, or salted, and the first-century Roman author Strabo tells us that there was a salting industry on the shores of the Sea of Galilee at Tarichaeae, (which means salt fish in Greek) or Migdal Nunia (the tower of the fish in Aramaic).[19] In the recent excavations at the first-century site at Migdal some unclear archaeological remains have been interpreted as belonging to the fish-processing industry, but there is as yet no final archaeological report. The Sea of Galilee is a sweet-water lake, but there are saltwater springs in the vicinity, which today are diverted so as not to raise the salinity of the lake. These may have been dried to provide a local source of salt. It is possible that this industry was not large, and served only very local needs, unlike, for example, the salt-fish industries in the Nile delta, where the fish were exported far and wide, even to Palestine.[20] It is clear from the Mishnah that salt-fish was a common food. Before eating, the fish had to be soaked in hot water to remove the excess salt.[21] It is unclear whether it was this salty water from the desalinating process, or whether it was the salty fish-flavoured liquid that was left over from the salting process, that is referred to as *tzir* in the Mishnah; it was often used as a dip for bread.

Fish sauces – *garum, muria,* and *allec* in Latin – were made all over the Roman empire by fermenting whole fish and fish waste with salt so that they would keep longer. These too were used for dips and flavourings for food. The Mishnah mentions *muries* and *hilliq* on many occasions. *Garum*, however, seems to have been a luxury product, out of reach for the poor. A record of this *garum* was found in excavations at Masada, by the Dead Sea, specially imported for King Herod from Spain.[22] Processing fish would have solved problems of the ups and downs of availability, too, so that the large catches would not go bad, but could be saved for times when fish were more scarce.

Freshwater fishes from the Sea of Galilee, including carp, St Peter's fish, and the non-kosher catfish were available in Jesus' day, and have been identified in archaeological excavations in Gamala/

Figure 1. Miracle of the Loaves and Fishes. Basilica di Sant'Apollinare Nuovo. Ravenna, Italy, Sixth century (Wikimedia Commons).

Gamla overlooking the Sea of Galilee and other places in Palestine.[23] Josephus describes the fish in the lake as 'different, both in taste and appearance, from those found elsewhere'.[24] By 'elsewhere', he presumably refers to the Mediterranean and its saltwater fish: there is a rabbinical source that describes the banquet of the righteous in the world to come: they will eat the flesh of the head of the Leviathan, the legendary giant fish.[25] The rabbis disagree about what this will taste like: some think it will be like the head of fish from the Sea of Galilee, while others think it will be like the head of fish from the Mediterranean. The Jewish historian presumably knew the local traditions distinguishing saltwater and freshwater fish.

Cooking Fish

How was fish cooked in first-century Galilee? The simple way of cooking over charcoal used by Jesus himself has already been mentioned, as has desalination of salt-fish in hot water. The Mishnah also talks of cooking fresh fish with leeks, which is said to improve the taste.[26] Colbert is very much against frying fish, on the grounds that this cancels out the benefits of the fish oils. However, Mishnah Beitzah implies that fish was indeed fried, in a discussion of whether 'fish with egg on top of it' is one food or two.[27] Since everyone would agree that fish with slices of hard-boiled eggs on it, for example, could only be counted as two different foods, it seems clear that what the Mishnah means here is fish with an egg batter on it, which was presumably fried. Not as healthy as the proponents of the Jesus diet might wish, but certainly tasty.

Cranes

There are a number of other talmudic passages that confirm that fried fish was served fresh from the Sea of Galilee, although not necessarily always in an egg batter. Paradoxically it is a passage from the Babylonian Talmud that has preserved information here from second- to third-century Palestine, and may perhaps provide the best evidence of the Palestinian setting.[28] This source tells us about an argument that took place in the study-house of Rabbi Yohanan, which he founded at Tiberias, on the shores of the Sea of Galilee. During this argument, Rabbi Yohanan's opponent, his brother-in-law Resh Laqish, was defeated, at which, we are told, he 'screeched like a crane'. I do not know of any other people screeching like cranes in the talmudic literature, so this may be an allusion to the Tiberian sea-scape setting of this episode: millions of migrating birds, including very large numbers of cranes, fly over Tiberias and down the Afro-Syrian rift valley and back twice a year.[29] And cranes are indeed very noisy birds. The Aramaic word for crane used in the Talmud is *kurkhia*, which the dictionary suggests is onomatopoeic, imitating the screech. This word appears in the Aramaic translation of the Bible in a similar context of migratory birds that return to Palestine year after year: 'The stork in the heaven knows her appointed times, and the turtle dove and the swift and the crane observe the time of their coming.'[30]

Digressing for a moment from the cranes in the landscape to cranes as food, we may note that the collection of recipes attributed to the Roman gourmet Apicius has no less than six recipes for cranes, together with even more exotic birds like ostrich and flamingo. One recipe tells us: 'When you cook the crane, its head should not touch the water but should stand clear of the water. When it is cooked, wrap the crane in a hot towel and pull the head off with its sinews: the result will be that the flesh and bones will be left behind: it is impossible to eat it with the sinews left in.'[31]

Cranes were eaten quite commonly in Europe in later centuries, but they would probably not have been eaten by Jews in first-century Tiberias, however, as they are not included in the biblical list of permitted birds in the book of Leviticus.[32]

Returning to the rabbinical argument in the study-house in Tiberias, the report of this row, the Talmud tells us, was news that was so fresh that it was like 'fish straight from the sea to the frying pan'. This expression to indicate the freshness of fish is used a number of times in Palestinian sources, but it is only here that it is associated with Tiberias and the cranes, and can therefore be definitively sited on the Sea of Galilee, rather than the Mediterranean coast. Fried fish is still commonly served in seaside restaurants in Tiberias, although nowadays it tends to be served with potato chips.

It is interesting to note that the verb to fry, *t-g-n*, appears to be derived from the word for a frying pan, *teganon*, which is a Greek word. Serving fried fish 'straight from the sea' was very popular in the Greek world, where tiny fish called *aphye*, fried and eaten whole, were a particular specialty of harbour towns.[33]

Meat

Colbert assumes very reasonably that Jesus would only have eaten kosher meat. He also assumes that Jesus would have eaten meat only rarely – lamb or goat at Passover, to which we might add sacrificial meat from the other two pilgrimages to the Temple at Jerusalem, and at occasional wedding and other feasts. Whether this would have added up to the once a month meat-eating Colbert recommends to his readers is unknown, but is perhaps a little exaggerated.

The rarity and high value of meat as food can perhaps be seen from another mishnaic source, which questions whether it is necessary to publicize food you have found lying in the street:

> What goods belong to the finder and what must be published?
> These goods belong to the finder: scattered fruit, scattered money [...] cakes of figs, bakers' loaves, strings of fish, pieces of meat [...][34]

In other words, poor people were allowed to eat unidentifiable food they picked up off the street, but they had to look for the owner of potentially identifiable food, such as home-made, rather than bakers', loaves etc. By the time all this had happened the food was unlikely to be still fresh, but it was clearly too valuable to be thrown out.

Locusts

Another food Colbert does not discuss at all is locusts.[35] Perhaps they are a little hard to get in modern America. Most creeping things are forbidden to Jews in the biblical book of Leviticus, but an exception is made for certain types of locusts. Once the locusts have eaten all the crops, eating them can make the difference between life and death for the poor. Even if Jesus is not recorded as eating locusts, John the Baptist is.[36] Later Christians, not wanting to think the text really meant what it said, interpreted them away as carobs, still known as *Johannesbrot* in German, but the Greek text of the NT is clear that he ate *akrides* (locusts). The permitted desert locust exists in two forms. One of these, *schistocerca solitaris*, the solitary desert locust, is endemic, i.e. is usually around: although not very common, it could certainly have been eaten by John in the desert. It is only when the climatic conditions are ripe that it changes colour to become *schistocerca gregaris*, the flocking desert locust, and then invasions are not far away. Some present-day Yemenite Jews still consider desert locusts a great delicacy, while Dr David Livingstone, the nineteenth-century African explorer, described their taste as similar to caviar.[37] The Mishnah mentions them frequently, and the laws of eating their flesh are similar to the laws about fish. Locust invasions, as in the biblical plagues of Egypt, could be catastrophic: Rabbi Judah is recorded as saying that one should not say a blessing over them, as they are really a curse.[38]

Eggs

Eggs are not mentioned in the New Testament, as far as I can see, and some apparent references to hens are dubious. The hen with chicks under her wings in Matthew 23.37 is *ornis* in Greek, which can mean a hen, but is also used generally of any bird. But the cock that crowed after Peter disowned Jesus is indubitable, and we may presume this cock was associated with hens and their eggs.[39] Eggs appear frequently, however, in the Mishnah, which even has a section called Egg, *Beitzah*.[40] Perhaps raising hens for their eggs became more common over the years in between the first-century New Testament and the third-century Mishnah. They would have been mostly eggs of domestic birds – hens, geese, and pigeons, as well as foraged eggs of small wild birds. As always, the poor made do with the worst, even addled eggs. The Mishnah tells us of these: only someone with a strong stomach should eat them. We have already mentioned the mishnaic source with egg on fish, which I interpreted as an egg batter.

Vegetables and Pulses

Colbert assumes quite reasonably that Jesus would have eaten a diversity of garlic, onions, vegetables, beans, and lentils. The Mishnah indeed talks very often of vegetables, including garlic, onions, leeks, cabbages, radishes, beetroots (the leaves), gourds, cucumbers, artichokes, mushrooms, lettuce, and parsley.[41] Many kinds of pulses are mentioned, the most important being lentils, beans, peas, chickpeas, and lupins.[42] It is clear that *miqpah* – bean and/or lentil stew – was a common standard food. It sometimes had oil floating on top, and was generally flavoured with garlic.[43] It would be poured out from the cooking pot into various utensils, including broken pots.[44] The root *q-p[h]-y* means to solidify, which is what happens to a liquid mass of cooked lentils poured out and left to cool.[45] Solid masses of food were easier to scoop up with the hands or a piece of bread, for the very poor would not have had many eating utensils. There was also *tavshil*, another more liquid broth, which was apparently less likely to solidify.[46] It did sometimes also include lentils, but also cabbage, peas, leeks, turnips, and sometimes meat.[47] It could be flavoured with a *bouquet garni* or wine.[48]

Herbs

Colbert is not totally exhaustive in his search for herbs in the New Testament. He lists dill, cumin, turmeric, saffron, and mustard as common Middle Eastern spices 'not mentioned in the Bible'.[49] Perhaps he means not mentioned specifically as foods in the Bible, for all readers of the New Testament must be familiar with Jesus' parables of the mustard seed (Mark 4.31, Matthew 13; 31-32). Mustard, *sinapis alba*, grows wild all over Galilee to this day. The Mishnah refers to fields of mustard, and it is clear that it is both a wild and a cultivated plant.[50] Mustard seed has to be 'sweetened' before use by heating it over charcoal.[51]

Dill

Dill (anise in some NT translations) and cumin are both mentioned with mint as herbs that the Pharisees tithe, and they are indeed clearly in common use in the mishnaic sources.[52] Dill is *shevet* in Aramaic, which when written in Hebrew letters as is usual without vowels, *sh-v-t*, is the same as Shabbat, *sh-b/v-t*, the Sabbath, the seventh day. This gave rise to the following midrash:

> *And God blessed the seventh day* (Gen 2.3). [...] He blessed it with tasty dishes. Our teacher [Rabbi Judah haNasi] made a meal for [the Roman emperor] Antoninus on the Sabbath. Cold dishes were set before him. He ate them and found them delicious. [On another occasion] he made a meal for him during the week, when piping hot dishes were set before him. Said he to him 'Those others I enjoyed more.' 'These lack a certain condiment,' he replied. 'Do the royal kitchens lack anything?' he exclaimed. 'They lack the Sabbath,' he retorted, 'Do you indeed possess the Sabbath?'[53]

This story is built on the pun between dill, *sh-v-t*, which gives a taste to food, and the holy Sabbath, *sh-b/v-t*, which God blessed by making it give taste to food. Even cold food on the Sabbath tastes better here than hot food on a weekday. I think that the midrashic pun here is replying to Jesus' criticisms of the Pharisees in the New Testament for insisting on tithing such a minimal food as the herb dill. In response the rabbis of the midrash give the herb great importance: it may be a small herb but it gives a taste which is the essence of the Sabbath, blessed by God himself.

What Would Jesus Drink?

Jesus certainly drank water and red wine and may have drunk various juices and herbal teas as well, writes Colbert but he adds 'we can follow Jesus' example by making sure our water is pure, filtered or distilled'.[54]

Water

Pure water could be difficult to obtain in Palestine of Jesus' days.[55] No rain falls in the country during the summer months, and many streams and pools dry up. Other natural water sources such as perennial rivers, wells, and springs would all be liable to contamination from dead animals, washing, industry, sediment, or sewage. Piped water was supplied to large Roman cities – but through uncovered channels and lead pipes. Water was also often collected in cisterns, but if these were uncovered they would be liable to all sorts of things dropping in and polluting them, while if covered they might grow algae, etc. The size of the Sea of Galilee meant this was a source of relatively pure water for the surrounding towns and villages. Josephus writes that 'its water is sweet to the taste and excellent to drink: clearer than marsh water with its thick sediment, it is perfectly pure'.[56] In Nazareth up on the hill, however, they would have had to rely on local springs and cisterns with all the accompanying problems. Water was so precious that it was often re-used: the Mishnah says on Passover (as opposed to the rest of the year) one must not re-use water that has been used by a baker, since it ferments.[57]

But even before the discovery of bacteria, people were aware that polluted water could kill. One of the solutions was to add wine to the water, relying on its antiseptic qualities to kill many of the lethal germs.

Wine and Vinegar

Colbert rightly rejects the theories of those who want Jesus to be teetotal and suggest he only drank unfermented wine, saying there is no evidence for this. However, he does not bring one of the most convincing arguments against this supposed 'non-alcoholic wine', which is that unfermented grape juice will not keep, particularly in the Galilean setting. Even today, after pasteurization, an opened bottle of grape-juice only keeps a few weeks at most in my fridge. Sometimes the grape juice was boiled down into syrups such as *defrutum* or *passum*, which would have kept longer, but the main process which was used to prolong the shelf-life of grape juice was fermentation. This produced alcohol, which would keep far longer than the raw juice. Even so there was still a risk of the wine going sour – it was this sour wine which was offered to Jesus to drink on the cross – the poor could not afford to be choosy and had to drink even wine which had spoiled and turned to vinegar – presumably also diluted with water to be drinkable.[58] We saw above that the Mishnah allowed ten barrels of sour wine in a hundred when talking of permitted levels of the undesirable in merchandise.[59] Later the Babylonian Talmud will discuss whether this change in state from wine to vinegar means that you no longer say the blessing over wine over the vinegar, but just a more general blessing.[60]

Food in the Context of First-Century Galilee

Conclusion

Leaving aside both the theological and nutritional aspects, we find that gastronomically the modern 'Jesus diet' does not always correspond with what we know about food in its first-century Galilean setting from the Jewish sources or from archaeological data.

Notes

1. A brief preliminary sketch for this paper was published in the *Church Times* 8019 (25 November 2016), 20-21.
2. Johann Hari, *The Independent*, 3 December, 2004; see also R. Merrill, *The Jesus Diet: How the Holy Spirit Coached Me to a 50-Pound Weight Loss* (Royal Oak, MI: New Creations, 2013).
3. For an explanation of the Mishnah, see my paper 'Nuts for the Children: The Evidence of the Talmudic Literature', in *Nurture: Proceedings of the Oxford Symposium on Food and Cookery*, 2003, ed. by R. Hosking (Bristol, 2004), pp. 264-65.
4. The cover also depicts what might be slices of lemon (which did not arrive in the Middle East until early Islamic times), and a potato, from the Americas.
5. Colbert, p. 17, p. 19.
6. MKetubot v, 5.
7. Basalt is a local stone in Galilee, and basalt mills are very commonly found at Roman sites: see D. Glick, 'A Salvage Excavation from Ein ez-Zeitun in Nahal "Iron"', *Atiqot* 51 (2006), 31-69.
8. MBava Batra 6.2.
9. R.J. Forshaw 'Dental Health and Disease in Ancient Egypt', British Dental Journal 206 (2009), 421-34 and bibliography.
10. TPesahim ii,1.
11. Cf TSheviit 6.2.
12. Josephus, *Jewish War* 5.427 (on Jerusalem).
13. MShevi'it v, 9.
14. Sifra Behar 7, quoting a pre-mishnaic source.
15. John 21.9.
16. This miracle appears in all four Gospels (Matthew 14.13-21; Mark 6.31-44; Luke 9.12-17), whereas the miracle of the 4000, which also records the multiplying of loaves and fishes, only appears in Matthew (15.32-39) and Mark (8.1-9).
17. Colbert, p. 35.
18. R.I. Curtis, *Garum and Salsamenta: Production and Commerce in Materia Medica* (Leiden, 1991), p. 131.
19. Strabo, *Geography*, 16.2.45.
20. For a camel caravan carrying fish between Egypt and Palestine, see P.W. Pestman, *A Guide to the Zenon Archive* (Leiden: Brill, 1981). Archaeological remains of the Nile Perch have been found in Palestine: see W. Van Neer and A. Ervynck, 'Remains of Traded Fish in Archaeological Sites: Indicators of Status or Bulk Food?', in *Behaviour Behind Bones: The Zooarchaeology of Ritual, Religion, Status and Identity*, ed. by S. Jones O'Day and others (Oxford: Oxbow, 2004), pp. 203-14.
21. MShabbat xxii 2.
22. *Garum basileos*, garum for the king, was found inscribed on a potsherd at Herod's palace at Masada.
23. O. Lernau and A. Shemesh, 'Fish Remains at Gamla', in *Gamla III The Shmarya Gutman Excavations 1976-1989, Finds and Studies: Part II*, ed. by D. Syon (Jerusalem: Israel Antiquities Authority, 2016), pp. 343-50.
24. Josephus, *Jewish War* iii, p. 508.
25. Pesiqta deRav Kahana, supplement B.
26. MMa'aser Sheni 2.1.

27. MBeitzah 2.1.
28. BT *Qiddushin* 44a. The rabbis named are from the second and third centuries.
29. This year the number of cranes was estimated at 40,000, but there may have been fewer in antiquity. Nebuchadnezzar is said to have chirped like a locust (Midrah Leviticus Rabbah 33 and parallels), but this is a pun on his name and the word for chirping.
30. Jeremiah 8.7.
31. *Apicius*, trans. Christopher Grocock and Sally Grainger (Totnes: Prospect Books, 2006), 6.2.2 (p. 225).
32. See on this the classic article by the late Joop Witteveen, 'On Swans, Cranes and Herons: Part 2: Cranes', *PPC* 25 (1986), 50-59.
33. Andrew Dalby, 'Aphye', in *Food in the Ancient World: From A to Z* (London: Routledge, 2003): pp. 14-15.
34. MBava Metziah 2.1.
35. Although locusts are mentioned by this website which Colbert has teamed up with: 'What Would Jesus Eat? The Science Within the Bible', *The Dr. Oz Show*, 26 March 2013 <http://www.doctoroz.com/article/what-would-jesus-eat-science-within-bible> [accessed 27 April 2017].
36. Matthew 3.1-4.
37. D. and C. Livingstone, *Narrative of an Expedition to the Zambesi and Its Tributaries and of the Discovery of the Lakes Shirwa and Nyassa, 1856-1864* (London: John Murray, 1865), pp. 374-75.
38. On the plague of locusts, see Exodus 10.1-19 ; on locusts as a curse, see Mishnah Berakhot 6.3.
39. Matthew 26.75.
40. See on this my paper 'Eggs in the Talmud', in *Eggs in Cookery: Proceedings of the 2006 Oxford Symposium on Food and Cookery*, ed. by R Hosking (Totnes: Prospect Books, 2007), pp. 270-81.
41. For a convenient summary, see G. Hamel, *Poverty and Charity in Roman Palestine: The First Three Centuries CE* (Berkeley: University of California Press, 1990), pp. 17-20.
42. These last had to be soaked many times to leach out their poisonous alkaloids.
43. On oil on top, see TTevul Yom ii, 2; on garlic, see TNedarim iii 6.
44. TShabbat xiv 6.
45. Hamel, p. 12.
46. *Tavshil* can refer to a broth, but also to any kind of cooked food, including roast, boiled, etc., according to the context.
47. Jerusalem Talmud Shabbat 5d.
48. On *bouquet garni*, see Tosefta Terumot ix, 7; on wine, see MNedarim vi, 7.
49 Colbert, p. 107.
50. See for example MPeah iii, 2 and many other places.
51. Jerusalem Talmud Ketubot 25a.
52. Matthew 23.23 mentions mint, dill and cumin.
53. Midrash Bereshit Rabbah, 11,2.
54. Colbert, p. 143.
55. On the pollution of water sources in later pre-modern periods, see B. Rosen and Z. Greenberg, 'Water Sanitation in Pre-Modern Jerusalem', in *Cura Aquarum in Israel*, ed. by C. Olig, Y. Peleg, and T. Tsuk (Siegeburg: DWhG, 2002), pp. 285-93.
56. Josephus, *Jewish War* iii, pp. 506-07. This description comes just before the account of the battle at Tarichaeae in 67 CE, where so many were slain that, in contrast, 'one could see the whole lake red with blood and covered with corpses' (p. 529).
57. MPesahim 2.8.
58. Matthew 27.48; Mark 15.26; Luke 23.36; John 19.28-9. It is interesting in this context to note that the later Babylonian Talmud, quoting a second to third century Palestinian rabbi, says that 'vinegar restores the soul'.
59. MBava Batra 6.2.
60. Babylonian Talmud Bava Batra 95b.

Feasting is the Finest Prayer: Dreams of the Holy Land in the Pans of Ashkenaz

Michael Yashinsky

A formidably blowing snowstorm pursues the young stand-in for Isaac Bashevis Singer in his short story '*An erev khanike in varshe*' ('A Chanukah Eve in Warsaw'), originally published in the New York newspaper *Forverts* in 1975, three years before Singer won the Nobel Prize for Literature.[1] In the story, set on the first night of the winter festival, the child Isaac loses his way home from Hebrew school. Chanukah commemorates ancient miracles that took place amid the sun and sand of the Land of Israel. But here in the white-blanketed streets of Warsaw in the early twentieth century, Isaac is alienated from the territory of those events. As the letters of the Eastern European dreidel signify, 'A great miracle happened there.'

The boy finally finds his way home. His father presents him with two gifts for the holiday: a dreidel and a *siderl* (a small prayer-book). It is bound in wooden covers, and comes, the father announces, from *Erets Yisroel*, the Land of Israel. Isaac accepts it 'with joy and trembling', thinking of that 'distant and holy country'.[2] The Land of Israel! His narration captures his absolute wonder as he tries to comprehend such a place: '*Mir hot zikh gedakht, az dos siderl shmekt mit faygn, teytlen, bokser...*' ('It seemed to me that the little prayer-book smelled of figs, dates, carobs...').

It is this mental transference – from abstract notions of the hallowed *Erets Yisroel* to the sensory pleasures of food, namely fruits associated with that country – that allows the boy to understand, feel, and even smell the distant land. Once the prayer-book has conjured the fragrances of food, he is able to access spiritual connections to the country:

> I suddenly recalled all the stories from the Torah and its verses. The little prayer-book exhaled, and in its breath were the Dead Sea, Rachel's Tomb, Joseph's dreams, the ladder upon which the angels ascended and descended, King Solomon, the Queen of Sheba, the Temple in Jerusalem.
> [My father] turned to me: 'Everything that comes from the Land of Israel is holy.'[3]

For Eastern Europe's Yiddish-speaking Jews in the generations before the establishment of the State of Israel, foods associated with *Erets Yisroel* carried a similar function as they did for young Isaac. In their self-described 'exile', during the long period when Palestine was governed by the Ottoman and later British Empires, the Yiddish-speaking

Jews of Eastern Europe – from whom Palestine was cut off by language, geography, and seemingly un-bridgeable political distances – maintained a physical connection to the country of their longing with food: agricultural products rare and treasured, and cooking of an exalted kind.[4] This food, vibrant in flavour and colour, realized *Erets Yisroel* for them in a way that the solemn recitation of psalms could not.

Like shtetl Jews' purchasing clods of Israel's earth from returning pilgrims, so that the sacred clay could eventually be sprinkled over their coffins, such food from the Holy Land delivered not just the idea of Israel, but its very landscape, too – the very fruits of its earth. In this way, spiritual longing invested food with religious redolence, which in turn gave to religious feeling an embodied underpinning, a focus reachable to mortal man. Through special foods, the Jews of Ashkenaz – here used to mean the former Yiddish-speaking civilization of Eastern Europe – connected to a special landscape, and, through that landscape, to a special relationship with the Almighty and their national heritage.

*

The focus here is on sources in Yiddish, because it is a diasporic Jewish language, at once both removed from the Land of Israel, and, like the food of the shtetl, containing ties to it both spiritual and tangible. The language of Yiddish builds on its Germanic base with myriad words and expressions – as well as a writing system – derived from Hebrew and Aramaic, known to the Ashkenazim through their prayer and study of the Bible and Talmud. It is a language of fashioning and refashioning, of faithfulness and adaptation, of retelling ancient stories in modern contexts. So, too, this food hearkens back to the oases and orchards of Biblical territories while being prepared in European villages.

Sources from Ladino and other languages of the Sephardic and Mizrachi Jews – coreligionists of the Ashkenazim but, unlike them, originating in the Mediterranean basin and Arabic lands – would likewise be worthy of study for how they document reminiscences of and recipes for this kind of food. But the presence of fruits associated with the Land of Israel has been more appreciated in studies of these cuisines, though perhaps not fully investigated for the spiritual meanings underlying the parallels in flavours.[5]

Gil Marks, in his magisterial *Encyclopedia of Jewish Food*, describes a contrast between Ashkenazic and Sephardic observance of the minor holiday of Tu BiShvat – a date ordained by the Talmud as 'the New Year for the trees'. Marks writes that 'The Sephardim, due to the warm climate […] in their locales, have long manifested a deep devotion' to this holiday, traditionally celebrated by the eating of the Seven Species – seven kinds of fruit and grain Biblically associated with the land of Israel and considered to be especially representative of the agricultural riches of that country. However, the author argues that holiday 'was only marginally celebrated among Ashkenazim, probably because it fell in the dead of winter in northern climates'. But his naming of a number of Ashkenazic food traditions for Tu BiShvat that do recall *Erets Yisroel* belies the underestimation, as do such reminiscences of Old Country customs as one Kadia Molodowsky published in her journal *Svive (Milieu)*.[6]

There, the acclaimed poet, born in the shtetl of Bereze (today in Belarus), rapturously recalls the dried figs and carobs brought home by her father from the study-house, in paper sacks. These were no mere '*frukht*', the author states, using the Germanic word for 'fruit', but rather '*peyres*' the Hebraic word, and they 'made the winter summery'. The play between registers of Yiddish, one workaday and one sacred, is used to elevate certain fruits above others, the figs bringing Land of Israel warmth and succulence to the White Russian winter as the Biblical word '*peyres*' does to the Yiddish language.[7]

This article, then, runs counter to the common conception of a northern cuisine thought to involve 'a diet overwhelmingly consisting of potatoes and dark bread'.[8] As Deuteronomy 8:3 reminds, 'Man doth not live by bread alone.' The more exotic of the Seven Species provided for Yiddish-speaking Ashkenazim a spiritual experience of a tangible kind not readily available in their frozen climes, but all the more prized for its rarity.

*

The burial custom mentioned earlier is worth examining further, being illustrative of the spiritual value gained through Holy Land earth. The procedure involved the sprinkling of earth from the Land of Israel onto the head of the body once it lay in the grave. Historian Yohanan Petrovsky-Shtern provides excellent insight into the custom:

> Diaspora Jews envisioned the land of Israel as a symbol of their distant biblical past, a sign of unification between the chosen people and God, and a reminder of the curses of exile [...]. A place and a physical substance, the land was the dream of many affordable to only a few. Yet East European Jews sought to assure themselves that the distant and unattainable land was in intimate proximity, at least for the deceased.[9]

Petrovsky-Shtern rightly attaches to the Ashkenazim's spirituality a land-based underpinning, but he limits his discussion to soil, and does not consider food connected to that soil. Such food served similar purposes to his sprinklings of dirt – bringing the Land of Israel closer, unifying the Jews to their gloried history in that country and to the close relationship with God they enjoyed there, and building a bridge, material as well as spiritual, away from their beleaguered hometowns. Such transmigrations through earth were not denied to the living.

Still further purposes may be attached to foods recalling *Eretz Yisroel*, namely as: a *sgule*, a Kabbalistic charm, that may bring the Jewish eaters closer to enjoying such food while again dwelling in the land from which it came; a *sgule* against hunger, that the Jews might remember fatter days; a reminder that they must adhere to the Torah, which hallows the Seven Species; and, with the traditional blessing accorded to those fruits, a reminder that this food comes from God, and that it is through Him that the People will be redeemed.

As the Yiddish proverb has it, '*Akhile iz di beste tfile*' ('Feasting is the finest prayer').[10] And as opposed to the burial rite, this prayer could be produced, these purposes enacted, and these pleasures taken, in this world, not only in the paradisiacal afterlife.

Food and Landscape

The bounties of the Galilee could be transported to Poland, and the gold of Jerusalem might glint in Romania.

*

So it did for a girl born in 1934 in Sîrbesti, the site of an agricultural community of around two hundred Jews. In a 2005 Yiddish-language ethnographic interview, Tsipora Yankelevna Furman glowingly describes the Chanukah celebrations of her youth. Chief among her recollections are the festival's unique fare. Amazingly, though they are rarely mentioned in connection to Chanukah in the usual discourse (which names dairy foods and fried treats as the hallmarks of the holiday),[11] she lists some of the very same foods recalled by the young Bashevis as he receives his own Chanukah present. She relates, 'At Chanukah, they would give us a few coins, us children …. And we would play dreidel. It was the greatest joy …. And Father would bring us chocolate, carob pods, and figs for Chanukah.'[12]

In Furman's telling, the carobs and figs are not the stuff of dreams, but treats actually enjoyed on the holiday, and part of the 'great joy' of the celebration. The foods she names, figs and carobs, are associated with the Holy Land, which gives the gift added resonance – these are products of the same territory that witnessed the Chanukah miracles of millennia before, and likely given as a token to remind the children of that place and those events.

This little-recognized food custom of Chanukah may have ancient precedent. A chapter of the Talmud establishes Chanukah, considered the end of the agricultural year, as the last period at which Jews are expected to bring *bikkurim* ('first fruits', the best of the harvest) to Jerusalem's Temple.[13] In the same chapter, the Talmud explains that only the Seven Species may be brought as *bikkurim*; these are listed in Deuteronomy 8:8, which extols the bounty of *Erets Yisroel*:

> 7. For the LORD thy God bringeth thee into a good land, a land of brooks of water, of fountains and depths, springing forth in valleys and hills;
> 8. a land of wheat and barley, and vines and fig-trees and pomegranates; a land of olive-trees and [date] honey;
> 9. a land wherein thou shalt eat bread without scarceness, thou shalt not lack any thing in it […].

The giving of figs on Chanukah and other festivals, in modern times, could be considered a re-contextualization of the sacrament of the *bikkurim*. Without the rites of a Temple offering, the fruits are turned into objects of human enjoyment, though still invested with the lingering magic of having once been used for service to the Divine and imbued with the sacred spirit of the Land of Israel.

Religious tradition translates this connection between land, fruit, and holiness into explicit practice. According to Jewish law, the Seven Species are always blessed before other fruits. But if one has a plate of various Seven Species fruits, which receives the blessing? The Orthodox Yiddish journal *Dos idishe likht* (*The Jewish Light*) specifies that it is the fruit physically closest to its corresponding appearance of the word '*erets*' (land) in Deuteronomy 8:8.[14] Thus, dates, which appear second after their corresponding 'land' in the verse, would take precedence over grapes, which are the third species referenced after their corresponding 'land'. Here is holiness inherent in rootedness: not only to the actual land, but even to the word itself.

Carobs, while not one of the Seven Species, grow wild in the Land of Israel and are intimately linked to it in Jewish tradition. Marks describes how the 'carob's hard, dry texture made it one of the few fruits grown in the land of Israel capable of long-distance shipping without spoilage and, therefore [...] available to Ashkenazim'.[15] It is likely that Furman's carobs were not just reminiscent of the Holy Land, but also would have come from its earth.

Figs, likewise, are native to the Levant but not to Eastern Europe.[16] In Furman's childhood they would probably have been imported from Turkey, though its famous fig harvests were impacted negatively by World War I, or from British Mandate Palestine, which produced an impressive 22,753 tons of figs in 1938, and the same year exported £115,966 worth of products, chiefly agricultural, to Romania.[17]

*

The fruits of *Erets Yisroel*, as seen, were elevated at holiday-time, and became centrepieces of the festive fare: at Chanukah, at other festivals of the *bikkurim* like Sukkos and Shavuos, at Tu BiShvat and the joyous open-air celebration Lag BaOmer, and on Rosh Hashanah, the New Year, when a pomegranate is eaten as a *sgule* that the celebrant might perform as many good deeds in the coming year as there are seeds in that fruit.[18] But these products likely appeared at less exalted times of the year, too, though still carrying the specific aroma of the Holy Land. In modernist poet Yankev Glatshteyn's 1966 elegy for his hometown of Lublin, Poland, '*Kh'tu dermonen*' ('I Do Remember'), he describes the 'singular, smaller destructions' of that civilization now lost to time:

> Jews' Street,
> With which its warm stones
> Musty wood and tombstone bricks,
> Accepted my galloping step.
> The spice vendors,
> The kasha and flour stores,
> The herring stands,
> The kerosene sellers and soapy barbershops,
> The makers of toupées and married women's wigs,
> The almonds, dates, and figs,
> The freshly baked sourdough,
> The rolls of poppyseed and onion,
> The darksome tearooms.[19]

Food and Landscape

Nestled among the workaday items of the Ashkenazic kitchen – those hearty goods characteristic of Eastern Europe – are foods that clearly derive from a different landscape. That Glatshteyn juxtaposes the almonds, dates, and figs, all of Levantine origin, alongside the other foods establishes them as just as much a part of the local Jewish culture as the *zoyer-broyt* and the onion *pletslekh*. But that he groups these three fruits in a single line also sets them apart – these foods are not like the others. These are heralds of *Erets Yisroel*, part of an Eastern European culture he describes later as a '*lebedike tanekhl*' ('a living Bible'), a kind of Israel recalled and re-formed in the Pale of Settlement:

> And He promised you an entire country for an inheritance.
> Then it became dark,
> And you, with weak childish eyes,
> Illuminated the darkness,
> And became the heir apparent
> To your own Canaan.

There in Lublin, with a kingly repast of *mandlen, teytlen un faygn*, Glatshteyn could feel himself part of '*a kiniglekhn hemshekh*' ('a royal continuity'), and, 'in between her scrubbing and cooking', the youth 'crowned' his mother 'as the mother of my entire Jewish Nation'. Here, the food of Israel functions not just as a memento of the glories of the Holy Land, but as a sort of laurel to proclaim the reestablishment of its holy community in the Diaspora, the poet's 'own Canaan' in Poland. His native dominion is '*a land a pitsl*' ('a dinky country') chosen for him by his father, and now destroyed, but where there once blossomed, at least in imagination, '*an eyntsiker faygnboym, / a teytlboym, an eylbert*' ('a single fig tree, a date tree, an olive').

*

Recipes for dishes involving distinctly Levantine ingredients also appear among the more commonplace cutlets, cookies, and compotes of 1938's *Vegetarish-dietisher kokhbukh*. This vegetarian cookbook was authored by Fania Lewando, who ran a popular dairy restaurant in Vilna, the 'Jerusalem of Lithuania'. In its pages are an abundance of dishes involving almonds – an ingredient identified in the pages of the Bible with the Land of Israel's choice earth, and by this time possibly coming from the Jewish pioneers' plentiful almond orchards there.[20] These recipes include a filled almond torte, the nut-studded Jewish biscotti *mandlbroyt*, even a 'Soup of Almonds' involving sweet and bitter varieties, ground, then simmered with onions, celeriac, and sweet cream.[21]

Lewando also gives recipes for eggplant, likewise associated with the Levant. Claudia Roden, in her informative and characteristically colourful account of Israeli cuisine presented at 1981's Oxford Symposium, writes that the culinary practices of Sephardic and Mizrachi Jews living in Palestine were considered closer to those of the Bible, and that '[i]t is not surprising […] that the first Ashkenazi […] immigrants looked up to the Sephardim and emulated their ways. From them they learned how to use the local produce, especially the vegetables which were new to them such as courgettes, aubergines, and artichokes'.²²

And yet, without providing any orientation to the chief ingredient, Lewando gives her readers – Yiddish-speaking Jews in Eastern Europe – recipes such as '*A forshpayz fun bloye baklazhanes*' ('An Appetizer of Eggplants') as well as '*Bloye baklazhanes gefilt mit rayz*' ('Eggplants Stuffed with Rice').²³ The cookbook shows us that Levantine vegetables were not unknown to Europe's Ashkenazim, who might even have enjoyed them at Lewando's restaurant in the centre of bustling Vilna.

The hallowed fig – the first fruit specifically named in the Bible, when Adam and Eve cover themselves with its leaves – is here, too. Lewando provides instructions for '*Vitaminen-tertlekh (tsiastkes) fun faygn*' ('Vitamin-Rich Fig Cakelets'), an un-baked dish consisting of little more than chopped figs, nuts, lemon, and sugar, which remarkably resembles a common method of preparing the fruit in Biblical times.²⁴ Even that iconic dish of the Ashkenazic kitchen, a noodle kugel, is enlivened with fig-morsels.²⁵ Such a dish was perhaps on the bill of fare at Lewando's restaurant, and appears alongside more common recipes like potato and challah kugels. But dishes like it also would have appeared on Ashkenazic tables at Tu BiShvat, when fruit kugels, particularly those involving fruits of the Seven Species, are served at the holiday's seder honouring the plenitude of Israel's fields and orchards.²⁶ Thus the dish is both ingrained in the Ashkenazic cuisine, and tied, by actual ingredients and spiritual associations, with the Jews' orientation toward Zion.

*

441

This orientation, though for generations embedded in Ashkenazic foodways, would become more politically fraught with the establishment of the State of Israel in 1948. The change is apparent in a poem by Rokhl Boymvol, a Soviet-Yiddish writer born in Odessa in 1914. In her '*Pomerantsn*' ('Oranges'), written a year before she immigrated to Israel in 1971, Soviet Jews flock with nervous pride to a marketplace in Moscow.²⁷ There, for the first time, are oranges bearing the label 'Jaffa', announcing their origin in the young State of Israel. The Jews line up before the boxes, beaming. Still, they must play the fool before the vendors; to be openly Zionist in the USSR is criminal. At the climax of the poem, the speaker records the tense transaction between Jewish customer and Gentile seller:

> 'Oranges? From what country?'
> 'I dunno!' the *goy* grunts, grimly.

Soon the customer drops the charade and summons the courage to tell the vendor: 'Don't you see the label here? These oranges come from Israel!'

For millennia, the acrid but fragrant *esreg* – the citron, the Bible's 'fruit of a beautiful tree' blessed by Jews at the harvest festival of Sukkos, then boiled down by Ashkenazim into a sharp jam to be enjoyed at Tu BiShvat – had been the emblematic citrus fruit of Israel.²⁸ The Jaffa orange lacks any such ancient association, but had become the iconic cash crop of the State of Israel and taken the place of the *esreg* as the fruit most aligned with its landscape in the Jewish imagination. More than longing for a spiritual homeland, the oranges at the Moscow marketplace are representative of Israeli agro-industrial and commercial strength, as well as Jewish self-determination. Boymvol's poem heralds a new, predominating flavour in the Diasporic enjoyment of the species of Israel. The Jewish tasting of the Holy Land through the fruits of its earth had taken on resolutely political, even subversive, flavours.

*

Still, today, in homes where the holidays are celebrated with their ancient pomp as filtered through the memory of shtetl custom, the old Holy-Land-by-way-of-Europe food traditions thrive without undue political associations. One such tradition is *esreg* jam. The convection is described by Bella Chagall in her memoir, illustrated by her husband Marc Chagall, of a turn-of-the-century childhood in the White Russian city of Vitebsk. To her, the jam's preparation by the family cook after Sukkos, when the fruit had completed its service as a ritual object, was representative of the holiday itself being '*oysgekokht*', boiled away, together with the citron's flesh.²⁹

The practice endures, still conducted in the Yiddish language. Hasidic Jewish populations, with their greatest concentrations in Brooklyn, New York, still use that mother-tongue as the language of daily life. Its homey rhythms spill over into Hasidic Web forums such as *iVelt* (Y[iddish] World), where, on multiple occasions, the anonymous users have fallen into lively discussions of *esreg* jam or compote: where to find it, how to cook it, whether its consumption by pregnant women is a *sgule* to ensure an easy childbirth or fine, fragrant newborns.³⁰

In one thread, the original poster laments that their *esrogim* have gone bad, and asks in a panic where one can find prepared *esreg* jam in Brooklyn, for they cannot properly celebrate Tu BiShvat without it. The commenters' array of concoctions using this fruit grown in Israeli orchards, then shipped to the New World, is dazzling: one has extra jam the lamenter can snatch, another has made *esreg* ices, still another *esreg* kugel. The most wonderful comment comes later from the original poster: '*Far a noyt ken ekh yoytse zayn mit r' meyer vaynberg's esreg bronfn*' ('In a pinch I can fulfill my obligation with Reb Meyer Vaynberg's *esreg* brandy')!

Deep-reaching spoons stir old jam into new jars there in Brooklyn, bounds away from the shtetl, itself bounds away from the Land of Israel, but still containing all those places – the fragrance of each home and the flavour of each exile. The substance created is a rich compote of Holy Land cultivation, ritual practice, and culinary method, all in service of sacredness, sense-pleasure, and soil, then *gut ayngekokht*, boiled together well.

Notes

1. Isaac Bashevis Singer, '*An erev khanike in varshe*', *Di goldene keyt* 131 (1991), pp. 26-40.
2. All translations in this article are by the author.
3. Singer, p. 36.
4. The Yiddish for 'diaspora' is *goles*, a word of Hebraic origin meaning literally 'exile'.
5. Claudia Roden has presented a terrific kaleidoscope of these cuisines, laden with fruits of the same climate that predominates in the Holy Land (*The Book of Jewish Food: An Odyssey from Samarkand to New York* (New York: Alfred A. Knopf, 2001), pp. 211-34).
6. Gil Marks, 'Tu b'Shevat', in *Encyclopedia of Jewish Food* (Hoboken, NJ: John Wiley & Sons, 2010), p. 593.
7. Kadia Molodowsky, '*Vayehi – un es iz geven amol, amol*', *Svive* 20 (1966), 59.
8. Thus does Marks describe the Ashkenazic cuisine of Poland and the Baltic lands, the home of most Ashkenazic Jews before the Holocaust (*Olive Trees and Honey: A Treasury of Vegetarian Recipes from Jewish Communities Around the World* (Hoboken, NJ: John Wiley & Sons, 2005), p. 9).
9. Yohanan Petrovsky-Shtern, *The Golden Age Shtetl: A New History of Jewish Life in East Europe* (Princeton: Princeton University Press, 2014), pp. 274-75.
10. Nahum Stutchkoff, *Der oytser fun der yidisher shprakh* (New York: YIVO, 1950), p. 238.
11. Marks, 'Chanukah,' *EOJF*, p. 256.
12. Interview with Meyer Khaimovich Furman and Tsipora Yankelevna Furman in Bălți, Moldova, Dov-Ber Kerler and Moisei Lemster, interviewers (Indiana University: AHEYM: The Archive of Historical and Ethnographic Yiddish Memories, Dec. 16, 2005), 45:31-46:28. The Furmans speak in Yiddish in the interview.
13. Mishnah Bikkurim 1:6.
14. '*Farshidene dinim fun brokhes*', *Dos idishe likht* 12:375 (April 1961), pp. 1, 8.
15. Marks, 'Carob,' *EOJF*, p. 90.
16. Colin K. Khoury and others, 'Origins of Food Crops Connect Countries Worldwide', *Proceedings of the Royal Society B* 283:1832 (June 15, 2016), Figure 1.
17. Assistant Trade Commissioner Julian E. Gillespie, Constantinople, 'Cost of Production of Smyrna Figs,' *Commerce Reports* 4:1-17 (Washington, DC: United States Department of Commerce, 1921), p. 350; 'Mandated Territory in Asia: Palestine: Production and Industry; Commerce,' in *The Statesman's Year-Book: Statistical and Historical Annual of the States of the World*, ed. by M. Epstein (London: Macmillan and Co., 1940), pp. 200, 202.
18. Ellen Frankel and Betsy Platkin Deutsch, *The Encyclopedia of Jewish Symbols* (Lanham, Maryland: Rowman & Littlefield, 1992), pp. 123, 140, 182-83.
19. Yankev Glatshteyn, '*Kh'tu dermonen*', in *A yid fun lublin* (1966), republished in *American Yiddish Poetry*, ed. by Benjamin and Barbara Harshav (Berkeley: University of California Press, 1986), pp. 370-85.
20. Yehoash, *The Feet of the Messenger* (Philadelphia: Jewish Publication Society, 1923), pp. 91, 221.
21. Fania Lewando, *Vegetarish-dietisher kokhbukh* (Vilna: G. Kleckina, 1938), pp. 20, 158-59.
22. Claudia Roden, 'Cooking in Israel: A Changing Mosaic', in *National & Regional Styles of Cookery: Proceedings of the Oxford Symposium*, ed. by Alan Davidson (London: Prospect Books, 1981), p. 114.
23. Lewando, pp. 3, 139.
24. Lewando, p. 103; Marks, 'Fig,' *EOJF*, p. 196.
25. Lewando, p. 156.
26. Marks, 'Tu b'Shevat,' *EOJF*, p. 594.
27. Rokhl Boymvol, '*Pomerantsn*', in *Aleyn dos lebn* (Jerusalem: Yidishe kultur-gezelshaft, 1983), p. 55.
28. Leviticus 23:40.
29. Bella Chagall, *Brenendike likht* (New York: Book League of the Jewish People's Fraternal Order, IWO, 1945), p. 98.
30. The titles, translated, include 'What have/are you going to do with your *esreg*?' (January 31, 2007) <http://www.ivelt.com/forum/viewtopic.php?f=3&t=575&start=25> and '*Esreg* jam in honor of Tu BiShvat: where to find?' (February 3, 2015) <http://www.ivelt.com/forum/viewtopic.php?t=25724>.

Contributors

Lecturer in History and Geography at Dublin City University, **Juliana Adelman** writes about the history of Ireland during the nineteenth century.

Volker Bach is a freelance translator, English teacher at a private language school in Hamburg, freelance historical cooking instructor at Hamburg University English Department, and the author of *The Kitchen, Food, and Cooking in Reformation Germany*.

When she's not travelling, **Lucey Bowen** lives near San Francisco, where she's a docent at the Asian Art Museum and writes about culinary and family history.

Catherine Brown, a Scot who lives on West Coast Isle of Arran, writes about the nation's food and drink culture, past and present. She is the author of several books including a fourth edition of *Scottish Cookery*, recently revised and updated.

Voltaire Cang is an academic researcher based in Tokyo. He researches and writes about Japan's 'intangible' heritage, including food and other cultural practices and traditions.

A professor of English and associate dean of McGill University Library's rare and special collections, **Nathalie Cooke** writes about Canadian literature and food history. She is co-editor of *Catharine Parr Traill's Female Emigrant's Guide: Cooking with a Canadian Classic* (2017).

A PhD candidate in Comparative Literature at Brown University, **Edwige Crucifix** explores the intertwining of individual experiences and feminist discourse in nineteenth- and twentieth-century French and Francophone fiction. In her spare time, she travels, cooks and takes care of her orchid collection.

Joshua Evans is a DPhil student at Oxford, researching the microbiogeography of translated fermentation practices. Formerly he was lead researcher at Nordic Food Lab in Copenhagen, where with colleagues he published *On Eating Insects*.

Jessica Fagin is a PhD researcher in Anthropology at Exeter University. Her research focuses on foodways in meat through the intersections of craft, manual and rural labour practices.

Allison Fisher completed an MA at the Courtauld Institute of Art and a PhD at Queen's University (Canada). Now an independent scholar based in Ontario, she explores food, art, and the classical tradition in the Italian Renaissance.

Len Fisher is a scientist, author and broadcaster, whose books range from *How to Dunk a Doughnut* to *Crashes, Crises and Calamities: How We Can Use Science to Read the Early-Warning Signs*. He won a spoof Ig Nobel prize for using physics to work out the best way to dunk a biscuit.

A 2016 Fulbright grantee, **Sara Gardner** writes about Sephardic culinary heritage and cultural identity. She received her BA in International Literary and Visual Studies from Tufts University and currently works for the Hebrew College in Newton, MA.

Christopher Grocock is author of *Apicius* (with Sally Grainger) and of numerous studies of the Roman world and early medieval Europe. He is Head of Classics at Bedales School in England.

Naomi Guttman is the author of three books of poems, most recently, *The Banquet of Donny & Ari: Scenes from the Opera*. She teaches literature and creative writing at Hamilton College, in Clinton, NY.

Hilary Heslop writes about the tensions between food ethics, sustainability, and consumerism. She lives in Melbourne, Australia.

Ben Houge is a composer and digital artist working at the intersection of music, technology, and gastronomy. He is an Associate Professor in the Electronic Production and Design department at Berklee College of Music in Boston, Massachusetts, USA.

Former professor **Sharon Hudgins** has logged more than 40,000 miles on the Trans-Siberian Railroad. She is the author of *The Other Side of Russia: A Slice of Life in Siberia and the Russian Far East*, and a new cookbook, *T-Bone Whacks and Caviar Snacks: Cooking with Two Texans in Siberia and the Russian Far East*.

Tom Hunter raises grassfed Shorthorn beef cattle and Icelandic sheep on his certified organic farm in the Driftless Area of southeast Minnesota.

Fozia Ismail is the founder of *Arawelo Eats*, a platform for exploring East African food from what's being served at her supper club to what it means for our understanding of belonging in a post-Brexit world.

A journalist and author, **Aglaia Kremezi** introduced Greek cooking to the American audience with her Julia Child Award-winning *The Foods of Greece*; her latest book is *Mediterranean Vegetarian Feasts*. She and her husband live on Kea, Cyclades, where they garden, cook, write, and teach cooking to travellers.

Michael Krondl is an artist and author who writes about the history of food, with a special interest in the cultural role of sugar. Among others, his books include *Sweet Invention: A History of Dessert* and *The Donut: History, Recipes, and Lore from Boston to Berlin*.

Jane Levi, a Visiting Research Fellow at King's College London, is currently writing about food and utopias, in particular food for space travel, but her food-related interests are wide and often historical, including a recent project on foundling food from 1740 to 1960.

Don Lindgren is an antiquarian bookseller and co-owner of Rabelais: Fine Books on Food & Drink. He is especially interested in evidence of use and the history and evolution of the cookbook as a physical object.

Contributors

Morna Livingston travels the world with cameras, studying cultural landscapes and the architecture of water. She is Professor Emerita in the School of Architecture and the Built Environment of Jefferson University.

Professor of English at the United States Naval Academy, **Mark McWilliams** writes about food and American culture. He has served as Editor of the Oxford Symposium on Food and Cookery since 2011.

Sandra Mian is a food engineer who works as a consultant for the food industry and home appliance manufacturers. She lives and works in Canada, Brazil, and Mexico.

Giulia Nicolini holds a Masters in Anthropology of Food from SOAS, London, and a Bachelor of Arts in Sociology from the University of Cambridge.

A French art historian currently working at the University of Italian Switzerland, **Guillaume Nicoud** writes about the culinary history of France around 1800.

An Associate Professor of French and Francophone Studies at Vassar College, **Thomas Parker** specializes in early modern literature, philosophy, and cultural studies. His newest project examines foods that have been marginalized and reappropriated by different cultures throughout history.

Olivia Potts is a food writer and cook. She practised as a criminal barrister in London before retraining in patisserie at Le Cordon Bleu.

Charity Robey is feature writer for the *Shelter Island Reporter*, specializing in the food, culture, and history of Eastern Long Island. A programming chair for Culinary Historians of New York, she lives in New York City and Shelter Island, New York.

William Rubel writes about traditional food and foodways. The author of *The Magic of Fire*, about hearth cooking, and an introductory history of bread, *Bread: A Global History*, he is currently writing a history of bread for the University of California Press.

Laura Shapiro is a culinary historian whose books include *Perfection Salad: Women and Cooking at the Turn of the Century* and, most recently, *What She Ate: Six Remarkable Women and the Food That Tells Their Stories*.

Richard Shepro is an international lawyer who teaches at the University of Chicago. A scholar of French food history, he has written for the Symposium about seafood, foie gras, and regulations relating to the threat of mad cow disease.

David Sutton is a literary and archival researcher, Director of Research Projects in the University of Reading Library, member of the governing body of the International Council on Archives, and Treasurer of the Oxford Symposium. His books include *Figs* and *Rich Food, Poor Food*.

Aylin Öney Tan is an architect and conservator, writing food columns for *Hürriyet*

Daily News and *Al-Monitor*. She is a winner of the Sophie Coe Award for Food History, and the author of *A Taste of Sun & Fire: Gaziantep Cookery*.

Molly Taylor-Poleskey is Assistant Professor of Digital History at Middle Tennessee State University. She is working on her first book on food and the rise of Prussia in the seventeenth century.

Emily Tepe researches and teaches about cold climate horticultural crop production at the University of Minnesota. She is the author of *The Edible Landscape*.

Malcolm Thick writes on food history, agricultural history, and also dabbles in the history of science. In 2010 he published *Sir Hugh Plat: The Search for Useful Knowledge in Early Modern London*, and he has also written about market gardening around early modern London.

Amy B. Trubek is the author of *The Taste of Place: A Cultural Journey into Terroir and Making Modern Meals: How Americans Cook Today*. She is the Faculty Director for the Food Systems Graduate Program at the University of Vermont.

Colin Tudge is the author of *Six Steps Back to the Land* and co-founder of the College for Real Farming and Food Culture.

Nicola Twilley is a co-host of *Gastropod*, an award-winning podcast that looks at food through the lens of science and history. A frequent contributor to *The New Yorker* and *The New York Times Magazine*, she is currently working on a book exploring the cold chain and, with co-author Geoff Manaugh, another about the past, present, and future of quarantine.

Anne Urbancic, the Mary Rowell Jackman Professor in the Humanities at Victoria College, University of Toronto, specializes in nineteenth- and twentieth-century Italian literature, which has led her to research the food and foodways of the time.

Susan Weingarten is a food historian and archaeologist living in Jerusalem.

Michael Yashinsky teaches Yiddish language, literature, and culture at the University of Michigan. He is the co-author of *In eynem*, a forthcoming multimedia language textbook, and also writes, directs, and acts in plays and operas.